Who's Who of Jazz

Storyville to Swing Street

John Chilton
Foreword by Johnny Simmen

Da Capo Press · New York · 1985

..., London
... Book Company,
... Life Books,

Fourth edition first published in UK in hardback 1985 by
MACMILLAN LONDON LIMITED
4 Little Essex Street London WC2R 3LF
and Basingstoke

0-333-38478-4

Fourth edition first published in UK in paperback 1985 by
PAPERMAC
a division of Macmillan Publishers Limited
London and Basingstoke

0-333-38479-2

1. Jazz musicians—Biography
I. Title
785.42′092′2 ML3506

Fourth edition first published in the United States
in cloth and paperback by
DA CAPO PRESS INC
233 Spring Street
New York
NY 10013

0-306-76271-4 (cloth)
0-306-80243-0 (paperback)

Bibliography: p.
1. Jazz musicians—United States—Bio-bibliography.
2. Jazz musicians—United States—Biography. I. Title.
ML106.U3C5 1985 785.42′092′2 [B] 84-20062

FOREWORD

Rex Stewart, Bill Coleman, and Buck Clayton were the first to mention the name of John Chilton to me. They all said that he was a fine trumpeter and led a good band. 'That boy is amazing', Rex told me, 'and I mean it', he said, emphasising the point. Later on, when Bill and Buck expressed similarly flattering opinions, I concluded that John Chilton had to be a pretty exceptional musician. I finally managed to hear a few of his solos and realised at once that they had not exaggerated one bit.

Some time later, I received a letter from England, turning the envelope I saw to my surprise that the sender's name was John Chilton. Perhaps he wanted me to investigate the possibilities of an engagement in Switzerland? No, there was no mention of this, but John—he had received my address from Bill Coleman—told me that he was in the process of writing a dictionary of American jazz musicians; from the very beginning up to the inclusion of musicians born before 1920. He asked if I had any information on doubtful points.

From the tenor of this letter, I could tell at once that John is as deeply involved in the history of jazz and the men who play the 'real thing' as he is in his playing and arranging. Having gradually got fed-up with phoney 'jazz journalists' over the years, I was glad to find out that John Chilton is an entirely different proposition. He has the ability, perseverance, and enthusiasm to tackle and finish such a demanding work.

It is my opinion that this is one of the truly valuable books on jazz musicians. It is the work of a musician whose knowledge of jazz and love and devotion to 'the cause' is unsurpassed.

Johnny Simmen, *Zurich, Switzerland*

To

Teresa, Jenny, Martin, and Barnaby

ACKNOWLEDGEMENTS

To Johnny Simmen for his interest, enthusiasm and inspiration;
To Max Jones and Charles Fox who allowed me complete freedom to consult their files;
To Michael Brooks and Jeff Atterton for contacting musicians in New York City;
To Arthur Pilkington for sending me many pertinent news cuttings and for supplying the correct spellings of various place names;
To the late Walter C. Allen for his great kindness in sending me hundreds of items from American newspapers of the 1920s and 1930s.

I am also grateful to the following for their help: Jeff Aldam, Richard B. Allen, Mr. and Mrs. William Alsop, Ernie Anderson, J. P. Battestini, Arthur Bronson, Eric J. Brown, Peter Carr, John Clement, Derek Coller, Ian Crosbie, Karl Dallas, Stanley Dance, John R. T. Davies, Russell Davies, Bertrand Demeusy, Frank Driggs, Bjorn England, John Featherstone, Harold Flakser, Otto Fluckiger, Jim Godbolt, Jim Gordon, Dave Green, David Griffiths, Ralph Gulliver, Lawrence Gushee, Bill Hall, George Hall, Derek Hamilton-Smith, Mrs. Marie Hebert, Karl Gert zur Heide, Mrs. Emma Hill, Dick Holbrook, Norman Jenkinson, Colin A. Johnson, Otto 'Pete' Jones, Wayne Jones, Harold S. Kaye, John Kendall, Carlo Krahmer, Derek Langridge, Paul Larson, Stephen La Vere, John F. Marion, Donald M. Marquis, Mrs. Adele Marsala, Albert McCarthy, Tony Middleton, Alan Newby, Mrs. Alcide Nunez, Bob Osgood, Johnny Otis, Brian Peerless, David Perry, Robin Rathbone, Graham Russell, Howard Rye, Bo Sherman, Phil Speight, Alan Stevens, Mike Sutcliffe, J. R. Taylor, Gianni Tollara, Eric Townley, Sinclair Traill, Peter Vacher, Ralph Venables, Dr. Al Vollmer, C. 'Bozy' White, Bert Whyatt, Tony Williams, John Wood, Laurie Wright, Michael Wyler.

THE AUTHOR

John Chilton, born in London, 1932, is married and has three children. He has spent most of his working life alternating between playing the trumpet and writing on jazz. His books include *Billie's Blues, Stomp Off, Let's Go!, McKinney's Music, Teach Yourself Jazz, A Jazz Nursery*, and *Louis—The Louis Armstrong Story* (which he co-authored with Max Jones). His band has accompanied many jazz greats, including Buck Clayton, Bill Coleman, Roy Eldridge, Charlie Shavers and Ben Webster. For the past ten years, John Chilton's Feetwarmers have worked with singer George Melly. They have made many albums together and have toured throughout Europe, Australia and the United States of America.

INTRODUCTION

This is an anthology of biographies detailing the careers of over 1,000 musicians whose names are part of jazz history.

All the musicians and vocalists given individual entries were born before 1920. Only musicians born or raised in the U.S.A. are included in this volume.

I have refrained from inflicting my assessments of the musicians' skills on the reader; the number of lines allocated to each musician is, in no way, to be taken as a measure of their talent. Thus, career details of the long service 'Ellingtonians' are more concise than those of the more peripatetic musicians. Casual work in 'pick-up' recording groups is not, as a rule, listed.

There must necessarily be omissions. Information obtained on some long-dead jazzmen is at times so contradictory that it seems wiser to omit an entry rather than add to the existing confusion. It has been impossible to trace certain ex-musicians who left the American Federation of Musicians many years ago.

Approximate details of some birth-dates are unavoidable, particularly where the musician himself was never given a birth certificate. One man admitted that, depending on his mood, he was born either in 1913 or 1916, others miraculously got younger as time went by. Over the years, one veteran gave five different birth-dates; less confusing than the musician, who, by his own reckoning, was born in four different places—naturally not on the same date.

Wherever possible, I have ascertained dates by referring to contemporary reviews, news items, and advertisements. This has not always been possible, therefore some entries contain dates which have to remain approximate. Even the most helpful musician cannot always provide an exact date sequence for events that took place in a crowded career.

Naturally, the biographies of many musicians from New Orleans are included, but for detailed listings of men who spent most of their playing lives in Louisiana the reader is advised to consult the following books:

Jazz: New Orleans 1885-1963, by Samuel B. Charters (Revised Edition 1963). Oak Publications, New York.

New Orleans, A Family Album, by Al Rose and Dr. Edmond Souchon. Louisiana State University Press, 1967.

Preservation Hall Portraits, text by Larry Borenstein and Bill Russell. Louisiana State University Press, 1968.

John Chilton, *London*

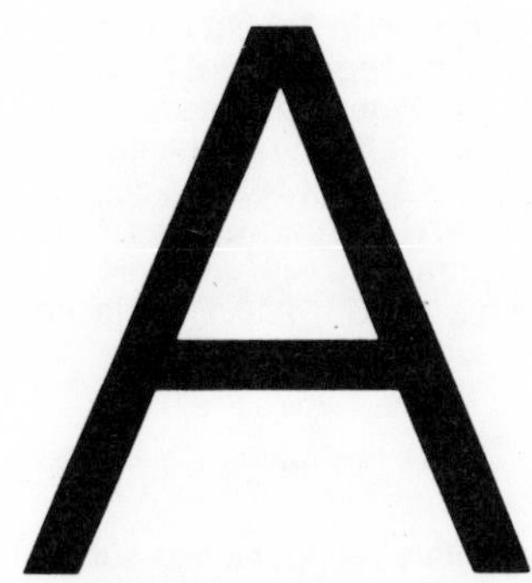

ABBEY, Leon
violin

Born: Minneapolis, Minnesota, 7th May 1900
Died: Chicago, Illinois, 15th September 1975

Led own band in Minneapolis before touring with J. Rosamund Johnson during the early 1920s. Led own band in New York, then worked with Savoy Bearcats. Took own band to South America (1927), and own band to Europe (1928). Played long residencies in France, England, Scandinavia, Switzerland, Holland, etc. Took band to India in 1935 and 1936. Eventually returned to U.S.A. in 1939. Led own big band in New York briefly during 1940. Own trio from 1941, which did extensive touring during the 1940s and 1950s as well as long residencies in Chicago. Retired due to ill health in the 1960s.

ADDISON, Bernard S.
guitar/banjo

Born: Annapolis, Maryland, 15th April 1905

Played violin and mandolin during early childhood, moved to Washington, D.C., in 1920, was soon co-leading a band with Claude Hopkins, worked for a while in Oliver Blackwell's Clowns, then to New York City with Sonny Thompson's Band. Worked in the Seminole Syncopators led by pianist Graham Jackson (1925), whilst with this band accompanied vocaliste Virginia Liston. From 1925 until 1929 worked mainly for Ed Small, first as a sideman, then leading own band. With Claude Hopkins (1927), from 1928 specialised on guitar. With Louis Armstrong at the Cocoanut Grove, New York, then briefly with Bubber Miley's Mileage Makers (September 1930). With Milton Senior's Band in Toledo, Ohio (1931), working with Art Tatum, then with Tatum in group accompanying Adelaide Hall. Joined Russell Wooding's Band at Connie's Inn, worked briefly with Fats Waller and Sam Wooding, then with Fletcher Henderson from early 1933 until summer of 1934. Again worked as accompanist for Adelaide Hall, then led own small band in New York at the Famous Door and Adrian's Tap Room (1935). Accompanist for the vocal group The Mills Brothers from 1936 until 1938 (including tour of Europe 1936), during this period also worked with Mezz Mezzrow's Disciples of Swing (November 1937) and in guitar-duo with Teddy Bunn. With Stuff Smith from 1938 until November 1939, then led own small group, briefly with Sidney Bechet Quartet (March-April 1940), then again led own band until Army service in World War II. After demobilisation toured with Snub Mosley, then free-lanced in Canada for several years. Toured with the Ink Spots in the late 1950s, also took part in the Henderson Re-union Band (July 1957). Worked as accompanist for vocaliste

Juanita Hall and appeared with Eubie Blake at Newport Jazz Festival in 1960. During the 1960s continued free-lancing, but was mainly active as a guitar teacher.

AHOLA, 'Hooley' Sylvester
cornet/trumpet

Born: Gloucester, Massachusetts, 24th May 1902

Of Finnish parentage. Played drums at the age of six, cornet two years later. First professional work with Frank E. Ward's Orchestra in New England (September 1921), stayed with that orchestra for three years, then worked with various bandleaders: Henry Kalis, Franka Bellizia, Lou Calbrese, and Ruby Newman before joining Paul Specht Orchestra in New York. Remained with Specht until February 1927 (including trip to England in 1926), worked briefly with the California Ramblers, Bert Lown, Peter van Steeden, and Adrian Rollini, then sailed to London in December 1927 to join The Savoy Orpheans, left in October 1928 to join Bert Ambrose. Worked with Ambrose until August 1931 (except for brief vacation in the U.S.A. during summer of 1930). Returned to New York, rejoined Peter van Steeden for several years. Worked in N.B.C. staff orchestra, also with Jacques Renard Orchestra, continued studio work until retiring to his home town in 1940. Has played trumpet and percussion in local Cape Ann Symphony Orchestra for many years.

AIKEN, 'Gus' Augustine
trumpet

Born: Charleston, South Carolina, 26th July 1902
Died: New York City, April 1973

Was unable to give exact age; his mother died when he was very young, he was subsequently raised in the Jenkins' Orphanage, Charleston, South Carolina. His elder brother Gene 'Bud' Aiken (trombone/trumpet) died on the 21st August 1927. Both brothers were given extensive musical tuition whilst at the Orphanage and later toured with the Orphanage Bands. Gus left the Orphanage several times during his teens, working with the Tennessee Ten (c.1920), then joined the Green River Minstrel Show. Settled in New York c.1921, joined Willie Gant's Band; from October 1921, toured with Black Swan Masters (directed by Fletcher Henderson). From spring of 1922 until late 1924 was featured with Gonzelle White's touring show (including tour of Cuba—1923). From 1926 until summer of 1929 worked mainly in the Drake and Walker Show, also played in pianist Irving Puggsley's Hot Six (1928) and recorded with Charlie Johnson (May 1929). From 1930 played briefly with various bands including: Charlie Johnson (1930), Mills Blue Rhythm Band (1930), Luis Russell (1931), Elmer Snowden (1932), Ellsworth Reynold's Bostonians (1933), Lucky Millinder (c. 1934). Regularly with Luis Russell from 1934, remained to work under Louis Armstrong's leadership, left in March 1937. In autumn 1937 joined band led by Alberto Socarras and worked in New York and Boston with that band until the early 1940s; with Buddy Johnson Band in 1944, then free-lanced in New York. Played briefly in Jimmy Archey's Band (c. 1951), then formed own band which played residencies at Small's, etc., during the 1960s.

ALBERT, Don
(real name: Albert Dominique)
trumpet/leader

Born: New Orleans, Louisiana, 5th August 1908
Died: San Antonio, Texas, January 1980

Nephew of Natty Dominique; related to Barney Bigard. Did some parade work in New Orleans, then left the city to begin touring with Trent's Number Two Band (1925). Subsequently joined Troy Floyd's Band at the Shadowland Ballroom, San Antonio (1926), worked with that band until September 1929 (also made records accompanying blues singers), then returned to New Orleans to recruit musicians for his own band, which subsequently made its debut at the Dallas State Fair. The band was based in Texas, but toured the Eastern States and worked as far north as Buffalo. From 1932 onwards Don Albert directed the band, and rarely played trumpet. The band did extensive touring in 1937, playing in Mexico and Canada, also played in New York (1937), they temporarily disbanded in San Antonio late in 1937, recommenced regular work before breaking up in Houston in 1939. Don Albert worked for a time as a booking agent, then re-formed for some 18 months before again disbanding in New York (summer 1941). Throughout the

1940s Albert organised bands for specific engagements, including spell at the Broadway Palace Theatre, New York, in May 1949. During the 1950s and 1960s continued to live in San Antonio and resumed part-time playing. Recorded in New Orleans during a 1962 visit, also recorded in Texas with The Alamo City Jazz Band. During a 1966 visit to New York sat in with Buddy Tate's Band; played at the New Orleans Jazz Fest in 1969 and 1971.

ALCORN, Alvin Elmore
trumpet

Born: New Orleans, Louisiana, 7th September 1912

Was originally taught music theory by his sax-playing brother Oliver (1910-81), then studied trumpet with George McCullum, Jr. Played with violinist Clarence Desdune's Band (c.1928), also led own band, then worked with Armand Piron and with the Sunny South Syncopators (1931). Left New Orleans to work from 1932 until 1937 with Don Albert's Band, returned to New Orleans and again worked with Armand Piron. With Paul Barbarin (1940), then from August 1940 with Sidney Desvigne's Orchestra until service in U.S. Army during World War II. Worked briefly in Tab Smith's Band, then worked mainly with Desvigne during the late 1940s. With Richard Alexis, Papa Celestin, and Alphonse Picou in the early 1950s, to California with Octave Crosby in 1954, worked briefly with Kid Ory, then returned to New Orleans, worked with trombonist Bill Matthews, then to California to join Kid Ory, appeared with Ory in the film 'The Benny Goodman Story', and toured Europe with Ory (1956). With George Lewis in 1958, then with Bill Matthews and Paul Barbarin (1959). Continued to play regularly during the 1960s, combining this with his work as an official of the local Musicians' Union. Toured Europe with the New Orleans All Stars early in 1966. Made 'guest' appearances in New York in March 1969. His son Samuel (trumpet) plays regularly in New Orleans. Toured Australia (1973). Continued playing during the 1970s and 1980s.

ALEXANDER, 'Charlie' Charles
piano

Born: Cincinnati, Ohio. c. 1904
Died: California. c. 1970

Studied music in Cincinnati, played in theatre orchestras there. Moved to Chicago and joined J. Rosamund Johnson's company, touring the Keith theatre circuit with them. Returned to Chicago and worked with Johnny Dodds, and Baby Dodds. Played long residency at Bert Kelly's Stables, on Chicago's North Side, joined Louis Armstrong's big band in spring of 1931, remained until they disbanded in New York City in 1932. Moved back to Chicago and worked there before making his home in California. Louis Armstrong jokingly described Charlie as from 'New Orleans' on a 1931 recording.

ALI, Bardu
leader/vocals

Born: New Orleans, Louisiana, 23rd September 1910
Died: Inglewood, California, 29th October 1981

Self-taught guitarist, his brother was a drummer. Moved to New York City in the late 1920s. Had dancing act with brother which was featured with Napoleon Zyas's band at a Chinese restaurant on 116th Street. Was invited to front the band and compare the floor show, this led to many other similar engagements. Fronted Leroy Tibbs' band at Connie's Inn prior to joining Chick Webb's band from 1932-1934. Led own band at Club Florida, New York, prior to visiting London in 1934 with Lew Leslie's 'Blackbirds'. Rejoined Chick Webb in 1935 and continued to front the band until Webb's death in 1939. Led own big band in New York (1940), then moved to California, led own band there during the 1940s before becoming comedian-actor Red Foxx's manager.

ALIX, May
(real name: Liza Mae Alix)
vocals

Born: Chicago, Illinois, 31st August 1904

Worked as a cabaret artiste in Chicago for many years: with Jimmie Noone at the Edelweiss Club (c.1922), with Carroll Dickerson at the Sunset Cafe, and in duo with Ollie

Powers at the Dreamland Cabaret. Whilst working at the Sunset Cafe took part in recording with Louis Armstrong's Hot Five (1926), Connie's Inn Revue (1931-32), at Harlem Opera House, New York (early 1935), then returned to Chicago. Sang at the Panama Club, the It Club, etc. Worked at the Mimo Club, New York, in the early 1940s, then long spell of poor health caused retirement from full-time singing, moved back to Chicago. Toured Europe in late 1920s. Was sometimes billed as 'The Queen of the Splits'.

The name May Alix was also used as a pseudonym by Alberta Hunter.

ALLEN, Charlie
trumpet

Born: Jackson, Mississippi, 25th September 1908
Died: Chicago, Illinois, 19th November 1972

Attended Wendell Phillips High School in Chicago. Worked with trombonist Hugh Swift's Band (1925), Dave Peyton, Doc Cooke (1927), Clifford 'Klarinet' King (1928), then rejoined Doc Cooke. With Earl Hines from summer of 1931 until 1934, briefly with Duke Ellington (1935), with pianist Fletcher Butler's Orchestra in autumn 1935, again with Earl Hines (1937). Since then has worked with many bands, mainly in Chicago, also active as a music teacher. During the 1960s did administrative work for local Chicago Musicians' Union.

ALLEN, 'Ed' Edward Clifton
trumpet

Born: Nashville, Tennessee, 15th December 1897
Died: New York City, 28th January 1974

Family moved to St. Louis in 1904. Piano from age of 10, then specialised on cornet. Joined local military band during his early teens. After working as a truck-driver he did first professional work in 1916. First jobs in a St. Louis roadhouse, then played in Seattle with pianist Ralph Stevenson, returned to St. Louis, then began working on Strekfus Line steamers. Briefly with Charlie Creath, then led own Whispering Gold Band playing aboard the S.S. 'Capitol' (1922), worked for a while in New Orleans until May 1923, then back to St. Louis on the S.S. 'St. Paul'. Played residency at the Chauffeurs' Club, St. Louis, then moved to Chicago (c. late 1924). Joined Earl Hines at the Elite No. 2 Club, left Chicago in July 1925 to go to New York as a member of Joe Jordan's 'Sharps and Flats' accompanying Ed Daily's Black and White Show. Toured with this troupe for over a year, made 'casual' recordings with Clarence Williams in New York, finally left the show in Cleveland and moved to New York. From early 1927 began regular recording work with Clarence Williams, also worked in band led by violinist Allie Ross (1927), remained with this outfit when it became LeRoy Tibbs' Orchestra (1930). Played regularly in Clarence Williams' studio bands, also continued to do outside work including spell with Earle Howard's Band (1932-3). During the late 1930s began playing in New York 'taxi' dance-halls, continued at this work except for brief spell in the mid-1940s when he led his own band at Tony Pastor's Club and Stuyvesant Casino, New York. Permanently with pianist Benton Heath's Band at New York 'taxi' dance-hall from 1945 until 1963, then forced to leave full-time music through ill-health. Was featured on free-lance recording sessions during the 1950s, including one date organised by English trombonist Chris Barber.

ALLEN, Fletcher B.
saxes/clarinet/arranger

Born: LaCrosse, Michigan, 25th July 1905

To New York with Lloyd Scott's Band (1926), subsequently worked with Lloyd and Cecil Scott in New York (1927), then joined Leon Abbey and sailed to Europe with Abbey in January 1928. Worked with Benny Peyton in Budapest in 1929. Worked in Europe during the 1930s, toured with Louis Armstrong (including visit to Britain), also worked in Paris with Freddy Taylor (1935), and in India with Leon Abbey (1936). Led own band for long periods (including residency at Villa d'Este), worked with Benny Carter in Paris (early 1938), later joined Willie Lewis until moving to Egypt with the Harlem Rhythmakers in late 1938. Returned to U.S.A. in 1940, worked as a docker during World War II, later worked on baritone sax with various leaders in New York. Worked with Fred 'Taxi' Mitchell's Big Band (1970-1).

ALLEN, 'Red' Henry James
trumpet/vocals/composer

Born: New Orleans, Louisiana, 7th January 1908
Died: New York City, 17th April 1967

Son of the famous New Orleans Brass Band leader, trumpeter Henry Allen (1877-1952); Red's uncles, George and Sam, were also parade musicians. Began playing violin, took a few lessons from Pete Bocage, played alto horn briefly before specialising on trumpet. Played in his father's band from an early age—received trumpet tuition from his father and from Manuel Manetta. Gigged with the Excelsior Band (1924), also subbed in Sam Morgan's Band; co-led band with clarinettist John Casimir (1925), played regularly in George Lewis' Band and with John Handy at The Entertainers' Club. Played on the S.S. 'Island Queen' with Sidney Desvignes' Band, returned to New Orleans, then joined King Oliver in St. Louis (April 1927), then travelled on to New York with Oliver (May 1927)—during first trip to New York made recording debut with Clarence Williams. Returned to New Orleans (summer 1927), joined Walter Pichon at the Pelican Cafe. Worked on riverboats with Fate Marable (1928-29), was then invited to New York to record under own name for Victor, subsequently joined Luis Russell's Band (summer 1929). Worked mainly with Luis Russell until late 1932, also briefly with Fletcher Henderson in 1932. With Charlie Johnson's Band (late 1932-spring 1933), then joined Fletcher Henderson on a regular basis until November 1934, when he became a member of the Mills Blue Rhythm Band (directed by Lucky Millinder). Remained with Millinder until February 1937—during this period Red subbed in Duke Ellington's Band and worked briefly in the Eddie Condon-Joe Marsala Band. Prolific free-lance recordings during the late 1920s and 1930s with Fats Waller, Victoria Spivey, Wilton Crawley, Putney Dandridge, Billie Holiday, etc. With Louis Armstrong's Orchestra from March 1937 until 28th September 1940. After a vacation in New Orleans, returned to New York, gigged with Benny Goodman (late October 1940), then began year's residency with own newly formed sextet at Famous Door, New York, Red's sextet (featuring J. C. Higginbotham) played residencies in New York, Chicago, and Boston before playing in California (February 1943). Long stint at the Garrick Lounge, Chicago (autumn 1943 to summer 1945), in San Francisco (August 1945), Onyx, New York (November 1945 to February 1946). For the next six years the sextet worked mainly in Chicago and Boston, occasional residencies in California and New York. Red played regularly at the Central Plaza, New York, in 1952 and 1953, appeared occasionally at The Metropole during 1953, then from spring 1954 until May 1965 was regularly featured at The Metropole, also toured with own band—including trip to Bermuda—and toured as a soloist. First visit to Europe in autumn 1959 as a member of Kid Ory's Band, led own sextet/quartet at The Metropole, The Embers, etc., toured Britain as a soloist in 1963, 1964, and 1966. Worked at the Blue Spruce Inn, Long Island (June 1965), L'Intrigue Club, New York (late 1965), Ryan's, New York (1966), etc.; was featured at several U.S. Jazz Festivals in the late 1950s and 1960s. Was taken seriously ill in late 1966, shortly after undergoing an operation Red made his final tour of Britain (February-March 1967). He returned to New York City, and died of cancer six weeks later.

ALLEN, 'Jap' Jasper
string bass/tuba

Born: Kansas City, Missouri, 25th January 1899

Started on the violin during early childhood, then whilst at Lincoln High School took up tuba (taught by Walter Page and Major N. Clark Smith). Left High School and did day work for Kansas City postal authorities, began playing in the local Hod Carriers Band. Played for almost a year in Paul Banks' Band (c.1927), then formed own band. Long residencies in Kansas City, then widespread touring including long contract at Casa Loma Ballroom, Tulsa, in 1930. At this time the band was fronted by O. C. Wynne and was billed as 'Jap Allen and his Cotton Club Orchestra' In the early 1930s the band worked as accompanying unit for vocaliste Victoria Spivey. Circa 1932, Jap disbanded, worked with Tommy Douglas (1934), then settled in St. Louis where he played a long residency at a Chinese restaurant, and gigged with Dewey Jackson and Fate Marable. From 1932 onwards he switched to string bass. In the late 1930s and early 1940s he worked regularly in and around Chicago for various band-leaders including: Artie Starks and Bob Tinsley. He later bought a farm in North Carolina and continued gigging in Durham through the 1950s. Jap's brother, Clifton, was a saxophonist; his son is also a musician.

ALLEN, Moses
string bass/tuba/vocals

Born: Memphis, Tennessee, 1907
Died: New York, 2nd February 1983

High school in Memphis, then studied at Le Moyne College where (with Jimmy Crawford) played in students' band. Joined Jimmie Lunceford in the summer of 1928 and remained with the band until summer of 1942—switched to string bass in 1932. Left to run own shop in New York and has never returned to full-time music. Led own trio during the 1940s and 1950s, continued to play gigs during the 1960s. Was one of the first to experiment with amplified bass.

ALLEN, 'Snags' Napoleon
guitar

Born: Macon, Georgia, 22nd February 1915

Raised in Detroit, played with bands there before moving to New York City. Began free-lance recording career in the 1940s. During the 1950s, 1960s, and 1970s worked as accompanist to many vocalists and vocal groups including Billie Holiday, Dinah Washington, The Supremes, etc.

ALLEN, Sam
piano

Born: Middleport, Ohio, 30th January 1909
Died: California, September 1963

Began playing piano at seven, three years later played accompaniment for silent films in home-town cinema. With Herbert Cowens at Rockland Palace, New York (September 1928), then worked with Alex Jackson in Cincinnati (1929-30). With Dave Nelson's Orchestra, then worked as second pianist in James P. Johnson's Orchestra. With Teddy Hill 1932-37, including European tour. With Stuff Smith from 1938-40, then worked long solo residencies in Washington, D.C., before moving to California. Led own trio for many years, long residencies in Oakland, also worked as regular accompanist for vocaliste Billie Heywood.

ALLEY, Vernon Creede
bass

Born: Winnemucca, Nevada, 26th May 1915

Grandfather was a noted violinist. Studied music at Sacramento College; was also all-city football player. Worked with Wes People's Band (1937), Saunders King (1937-39). Led own band before working with Lionel Hampton from 1940-42 (was featured on electric bass as early as 1940). Played in U.S. Navy Band 1942-46, then led own band in San Francisco area, also accompanied many visiting guest stars and compered radio and television shows.

ALSOP, William M.
alto sax

Born: West Philadelphia, Pennsylvania, 23rd October 1905

Husband of pianiste Olive 'Inez' Alsop (born: Cambridge, Massachusetts, 10th June 1905). To New York with Bobby Neal's Dixieland Ramblers in late 1926, subsequently worked with King Joe and his Jokers, Fess Finlay's Band, Major Bowes' Band, and Fats Waller. Served in Camp Kilmer Service Band during World War II. Has free-lanced in New York for many years.

ALSTON, 'Ovie' Overton
trumpet/vocals

Born: Washington, D.C. c. 1906

With trombonist Bill Brown and his Brownies in New York 1928-30. Joined Claude Hopkins in 1931 and remained until forming his own band which made its debut at the Apollo, New York, in November 1936. Subsequently led own big band at the Plantation (1937), the Ubangi Club (1938), and the Roseland Ballroom (1939-41). For 1941-2 service tours his band was fronted by Noble Sissle and Eubie Blake, then resumed leading big band at the Roseland Ballroom (1942-7). Led at Murraine's Club in 1947, then from 1948-52 regularly at Baby Grand Cafe, New York—working every summer at the Naussau Hotel,

Long Beach. Continued leading own band for private engagements in the 1950s, has since retired from full-time music.

ALVIN, Danny
(real name: Viniello)
drums

Born: New York City, 29th November 1902
Died: Chicago, Illinois, 5th December 1958

Father of the late Teddy Walters (vocals/guitar). First professional work accompanying 'Aunt Jemima' at Central Opera House, New York (1918), during following year began three-year spell accompanying vocaliste Sophie Tucker. Moved to Chicago in 1922, joined Jules Buffano's Band at Midnite Frolics, worked with Frankie Quartell and Charley Straight before joining Midway Gardens Orchestra. Short spell with Joe Kayser's Band, then during 1926 and 1927 worked in Florida with Arnold Johnson's Orchestra. Returned to Chicago, joined Al Morey's Orchestra, then with Wayne King's Band until 1930. Worked with Ted Fio Rito before joining Amos Ostot and his Crimson Serenaders. Led own band in Chicago at 100 Club until 1933, then spent three years working mostly with pianist Art Hodes, usually at the Vanity Fair Cafe. Moved to New York in 1936, extensive gigging before spending two years with Wingy Manone. With Georg Brunis at Nick's from May 1940, then own band at Trocadero, New York. Replaced Dave Tough in Joe Marsala's Band in August 1941. Regularly at Nick's 1942-3 with Georg Brunis, Brad Gowans, etc. Worked in Art Hodes' Trio at Nick's during 1944, following year with Mezz Mezzrow Trio at Ryan's, New York. Worked at Eddie Condon's during late 1946, left in May 1947, returned to Chicago to join Doc Evans' Band at Jazz Ltd from June 1947. With George Zack Trio in Chicago in 1948, later that year joined Johnny Lane Band. Organised own band for residency at Rupneck's late 1949. During the 1950s, led own Kings of Dixieland, ran own club from 1955.

ALVIS, Hayes Julian
string bass/tuba/arranger

Born: Chicago, Illinois, 1st May 1907
Died: New York City, 29th December 1972

Originally a drummer, played in *Chicago Defender* Boys' Band. Drums and tuba with Jelly Roll Morton tour dates 1927 to early 1928. Concentrated on tuba, gigged with many bands in Chicago, then with Earl Hines late 1928-30. To New York with Jimmie Noone in spring 1931, from then on switched to string bass. Worked with the Mills Blue Rhythm Band from 1931 until early 1935 (originally as bassist, spell as band-manager, then reverted to bassist). Joined Duke Ellington in spring 1935 (sharing bass duties with Billy Taylor), left Duke in spring of 1938, formed short-lived band with Freddy Jenkins, then from October 1938 until March 1939 worked in New York with the 'Blackbirds Show'. Joined Benny Carter Big Band at the Savoy in March 1939. With Joe Sullivan from November 1940, during following spring with Bobby Burnet's Band in New York. Joined Louis Armstrong Orchestra until February 1942, then joined N.B.C. Orchestra, also gigged with Joe Sullivan Trio in summer of 1942. Army service from 1943 until 1945, then with Gene Fields Trio and LeRoy Tibbs. During 1946-7 with Dave Martin Trio, also in Harry Dial's Combo, then long spell as house musician at Cafe Society, New York. (From 1940 also active in running own millinery business in New York.) During the 1950s active freelance work in New York, also spell in Boston with Joe Thomas (1952) and took part in Fletcher Henderson reunion sessions in summer of 1957. With Wilbur de Paris on tuba in 1958. Played regularly during the 1960s, including work with vocaliste Dionne Warwick. Was an official of Local 802, A.F. of M. also took active interest in Red Cross work. Toured Europe with Jay McShann (1970).

AMMONS, Albert C.
piano

Born: Chicago, Illinois, 23rd September 1907
Died: Chicago, Illinois, 2nd December 1949

Father of tenor sax Eugene 'Jug' Ammons (1925-74). Piano at 10, worked in Chicago clubs as soloist. With François Moseley's Louisiana Stompers (summer 1929), then played second piano with William Barbee and his Headquarters (1930-1). With drummer Louis P. Banks and his Chesterfield Orchestra from 1930 until 1934, then formed own small group for residencies at various Chicago clubs including: The DeLisa, The It, Club 29, etc. Moved to New York in 1938 and began long association with Pete Johnson—their boogie-woogie duo appearing regularly at the Cafe Society in the late 1930s and early 1940s (they also worked in trio with Meade Lux Lewis). Ammons briefly out of action in spring 1941, when he accidentally cut off the tip of his finger whilst fixing a sandwich. During the early 1940s worked regularly with Pete Johnson, some touring, also residencies in Hollywood, Chicago, etc., then concentrated on solo work. During the mid-1940s suffered temporary paralysis in both hands, but recovered and during last few years of his life played mainly in Chicago: Beehive Club, Tailspin, etc. Severe illness curtailed activity in last year of his life, but played at Mama Yancey's Parlour a few days before his death.

ANDERSON, 'Andy' Edward *Born: Jacksonville, Florida, 1st July 1910*
trumpet

Started on trumpet at the age of 10, first lessons from the bandmaster at Florida State College. At 15 went to St. Emma College in Belmead, Virginia, and was principal trumpet in the College Band. Played with Luckey Roberts at the Everglades Club, Palm Beach, Florida, and travelled to New York with Luckey in the spring of 1926. Luckey Roberts introduced him to Clarence Williams, and for a five-year period played occasionally on recording dates for Williams. During the period 1927-8 worked with drummer George Howe and Luis Russell at The Nest Club, also with Jelly Roll Morton at the Rose Danceland. In 1929 moved into Connie's Inn to work in Louis Armstrong's place whilst Louis was doubling in 'Hot Chocolates' Revue. With Benny Carter at Arcadia Ballroom. Brief spells with Charlie Johnson and Bingie Madison, then joined the Mills Blue Rhythm Band from 1930 until summer of 1934. Joined Charlie Turner's Arcadians and remained when the band was fronted by Fats Waller (1935). With Hazel Scott Big Band early in 1939, in November 1939 joined Joe Sullivan (replacing Murphy Steinberg) remained with Sullivan until January 1941. Played with Frankie Newton 10-piece Band at the Mimo Club, New York, in autumn of 1941, then left full-time music. Ceased playing a number of years ago, but continues to live in New York City.

Not to be confused with the Louisiana trumpeter Andrew 'Andy' Anderson (1905-82)

ANDERSON, 'Buddy' Bernard Hartwell *Born: Oklahoma City, 14th October 1919*
trumpet/piano

Violin at seven, then played trumpet in military band at junior high school, later worked in high school band 'Dud' McCauley's Syncopators. Late 1934 joined band led by bassist Louis 'Ted' Armstrong in Clinton, Oklahoma. Did further studies in Quindario, Kansas, also gigged in and around Kansas City with big band led by Gene Ramey. In summer of 1938 went to Xavier University, New Orleans and played in school orchestra and dance bands. During summer 1939 joined Leslie Sheffield Band in Oklahoma City, then resumed studies before spending three years with Jay McShann (early 1940-3). With Tommy Douglas in Kansas City, brief spells with Winston Williams, Leonard 'Lucky' Enois, etc. To New York with Benny Carter, then during 1944 worked briefly with Sabby Lewis, Roy Eldridge Big Band, and Billy Eckstine Orchestra before breakdown in health which ended his career as a trumpeter. Took up piano, and played regularly in the Oklahoma City area, was also an official of the local musicians' union. Moved to Kansas City in 1971, and continued to play gigs on piano (and organ), occasionally blowing trumpet.

ANDERSON, Kenneth *Born: Pittsburgh, Pennsylvania, 4th August 1904*
piano/trumpet/saxes/arranger

Both parents were musicians. Began playing piano at 10. Moved to Chicago, studied piano, trumpet and saxophone. Worked on trumpet and sax with Clarence Miller's Owl Theater Orchestra in 1923, later with Charles Cook (1924), Walter Duett's Orchestra (1924), then became solo organist at Metropolitan Theater, Chicago, from 1926-28. Piano with Dave Peyton (1929), Sammy Stewart (1930). During the 1930s worked for many bandleaders, mostly in Chicago, including Jimmie Noone, Frankie Jaxon, Jimmy Bell, also arranged for Earl Hines, Chick Webb, etc. Left full-time music to work for state government for 27 years. After retirement he became a music teacher.

ANDERSON, 'Cat' William Alonzo
trumpet

Born: Greenville, South Carolina, 12th September 1916
Died: California, 29th April 1981

Raised in the Jenkins' Orphanage, South Carolina, after being orphaned at the age of four. Played various instruments in the school band from the age of seven, then specialised on trumpet. Did first touring with the Orphanage Band in 1929, three years later (with several of his young colleagues) formed 'The Carolina Cotton Pickers', left this band in late 1935 to join guitarist Hartley Toots in Florida. Left Toots' Band in New York c. September 1936, and gigged with various bands before joining The Sunset Royals Orchestra (later led by 'Doc' (Moran) Wheeler), left the band in spring of 1942. Toured with Special Services Orchestra, then briefly with Lucky Millinder before joining Lionel Hampton c. summer 1942. Brief spell with Erskine Hawkins, then with Sabby Lewis from March 1943, rejoined Lionel Hampton in 1944, then from September 1944 until January 1947 with Duke Ellington. Formed own band for two years, then rejoined Sabby Lewis (1949), brief spell with Jimmy Tyler's Band in Boston (early 1950), then rejoined Duke Ellington. Left Duke in late 1959, again formed own band and free-lanced in Philadelphia in 1961. Again joined Duke Ellington in summer of 1961 and remained (on and off) with Duke through the 1960s. Left Duke early in 1971, prolific session work in California, also plays club dates in Los Angeles, etc. Toured Europe several times during the 1970s.

ANDERSON, Ivie Marie
vocals

Born: Gilroy, California, 10th July 1905
Died: Los Angeles, California, 28th December 1949

From 9 to 13 received vocal training at the local St. Mary's Convent, then two years in Washington, D.C., studying with Sara Ritt. Returned to California and began first professional work at Tait's Club in Los Angeles, later worked at Mike Lyman's Tent Cafe. Toured as a dancer in Fanchon and Marco revue starring Mamie Smith, soon gained feature spot as a vocaliste. Worked at the Cotton Club, New York (1925). After touring with the 'Shuffle Along' revue returned to Los Angeles and was featured with Curtis Mosby's Blue Blowers, Paul Howard's Quality Serenaders, Sonny Clay's Band, and briefly with Anson Weeks' at the Mark Hopkins Hotel, San Francisco. Residency at Frank Sebastian's Cotton Club Culver City; from January 1928 did five months' tour of Australia with Sonny Clay in Fanchon and Marco revue, then toured U.S. heading own show. Featured with Earl Hines in the Grand Terrace Revue in 1930, then from February 1931 until August 1942 with Duke Ellington. Opened own Chicken Shack restaurant in Los Angeles and continued to sing regularly at West Coast night spots. Chronic asthma prevented her from undertaking extensive tours, but she did work in Mexico City (early 1944) and in Chicago (early 1945). Appeared in the Marx Brothers' film 'A Day at the Races'.

ANDRADE, Vernon
bass/violin/leader

Born: Panama, 24th April 1902
Died: New York, 8th February 1966

Began playing violin as a teenager, moved to New York in the early 1920s and played violin in Deacon Johnson's Orchestra (1923) then switched to string-bass and began leading own band at the Renaissance Casino in New York City. His residency there lasted for more than 15 years, during which time he employed many famous jazz musicians. In late life he lead a band that worked in and around New York City.

ARBELLO, Fernando
trombone/arranger

Born: Ponce, Puerto Rico, 30th May 1907
Died: Puerto Rico, 26th July 1970

Trombone from the age of 12, played in High School Band, then worked in local Symphony Orchestra. To New York in mid-1920s, with Earle Howard late 1927, Wilbur De

Paris 1928, June Clark spring 1929-30, briefly with Claude Hopkins, Wilbur De Paris, and Bingie Madison, then regularly with Claude Hopkins 1931-4. Several months with Chick Webb in 1934-5. With Fletcher Henderson 1936-7 (interrupted by a period with Lucky Millinder's Band in late 1936). With Billy Hicks' Sizzling Six in summer of 1937, then rejoined Lucky Millinder. During late 1930s brief spells with Edgar Hayes, Fats Waller, Claude Hopkins, and Benny Carter. With Zutty Singleton Sextet January-March 1940, led own band, then rejoined Fletcher Henderson in early 1941. With Marty Marsala Band from August 1941, then with Jimmie Lunceford from 1942 until 1946 (briefly with Bernie Mann Orchestra in New York early 1945). Led own band throughout the 1950s, also worked with Rex Stewart in Boston (1953) and took part in Fletcher Henderson reunion in 1957. With Machito from 1960. Moved back to Puerto Rico in late 1960s. Led own band at the Hotel San Juan, Puerto Rico in 1969.

ARCHEY, 'Jimmy' James H.
trombone

Born: Norfolk, Virginia, 12th October 1902
Died: Amityville, New York, 16th November 1967

Trombone at 12—first local gig at 13. From 1915-19 studied music at the Hampton Institute, Virginia (during summer vacations worked with band led by pianiste Lilian Jones). Joined Quentin Redd's Band in Atlantic City for a year, then moved to New York in 1923 to join Lionel Howard's Band at the Capitol Palace. Worked in band at Ed Small's (1924), then toured with 'Lucky Sambo Revue' (1925 to mid-1926), 'Tan Town Topics' (late 1926). With Edgar Hayes Orchestra at Alhambra Theatre, New York (1927), also gigged with John C. Smith Orchestra and played residencies with Arthur Gibbs' Orchestra. Played regularly at the Bamboo Inn, New York, first with Ed Campbell (1926), then with banjoist Henri Saparo (1927), later with Joe Steele. With Joe Steele, Bill Benford's Band, and Charlie Skeets' (1929). Toured with King Oliver from April 1930, with Luis Russell (July 1930). Six months with Bingie Madison's Band from early 1931, then rejoined Luis Russell until 1937 (working with Louis Armstrong from 1935-7). With Willie Bryant from c. spring 1937 until 1939, Benny Carter 1939 to early 1940; briefly with Ella Fitzgerald and Coleman Hawkins Big Band, then rejoined Benny Carter early in 1941. Free-lanced in New York, also did dep work in Cab Calloway's Band and subbed for Tricky Sam Nanton and Juan Tizol in Duke Ellington's Orchestra. With Claude Hopkins at the Zanzibar 1944-5 and gigging, then with Noble Sissle at the Diamond Horseshoe occasionally from 1946-8. Featured regularly on Rudi Blesh's 1947 'This is Jazz' radio series. To Europe in February 1948 for appearances at Nice Jazz Festival with Mezz Mezzrow, returned to U.S.A. and began long residency at Savoy Cafe, Boston, with Bob Wilber's Band (from December 1948). In April 1950 Jimmy Archey became leader of the group, after residencies in Boston and New York the sextet toured Europe in 1952. Featured in film 'Jazz Dance' whilst gigging at Central Plaza (1954). Returned to Europe to tour with Mezz Mezzrow from November 1954 until February 1955. From September 1955 until December 1962 was a member of Earl Hines' Sextet (working mainly in San Francisco), during this period also worked for Muggsy Spanier, then regular appearances with all-star pick-up bands in U.S.A. and Canada. Visited Europe with New Orleans All Stars in February 1966, continued playing regularly until shortly before his death.

ARMSTRONG, 'Lil'
(née Lillian Hardin)
piano/arranger/vocals/composer

Born: Memphis, Tennessee, 3rd February 1898
Died: Chicago, 27th August 1971

Studied music for three years at Fisk University, moved with family to Chicago in 1917. Began working as a song demonstrator in Jones' Music Store. Gigged with Curtis Mosby, then joined band led by trumpeter 'Sugar Johnny' Smith. Later worked with Freddie Keppard before leading own band at Dreamland, Chicago (c.1920). Worked on and off with King Oliver from 1921 until 1924. Married Louis Armstrong on 5th February 1924, they separated in 1931 and were divorced in 1938. In 1924 led own band in Chicago (whilst Louis was in New York with Fletcher Henderson), lived briefly in New York, then returned to lead own band, which Louis joined after leaving Henderson in late 1925. Lil was regularly featured on the Louis Armstrong Hot Five and Hot Seven recordings (1925-7). Worked in Hugh Swift's Band (c. 1926) and toured with Freddie Keppard (c. 1928).

Gained Teachers' Diploma at Chicago College of Music in 1928 (after studying with Louis Victor Saar), then studied at New York College of Music (with August Fraemcke) gaining Post Graduate Diploma in 1929. During the early 1930s Lil led her own all-girl band and guested with Ralph Cooper's Orchestra at Harlem Opera House in 1931. Formed own all-male band, broadcasting regularly on N.B.C., W.M.C.A., and W.O.R. Appeared as solo artiste in 'Hot Chocolate' and 'Shuffle Along' revues. Led own all-girl orchestra at Regal Theatre, Chicago (October 1934). In 1935 and 1936 led own all-male big band, playing residencies in Detroit, Buffalo, etc., then settled temporarily in New York, mainly active as house pianiste at Decca recording studios during late 1930s. Left New York in late 1940, began solo residency at the Tin Pan Alley Club, Chicago. Worked mainly as a soloist through the 1940s and early 1950s, long residencies in Chicago: Garrick Stage Bar, Mark Twain Lounge, Nob Hill Club, and at East Town Bar in Milwaukee. To Europe in early 1952, worked mainly in Paris, but made occasional visits to London. During the late 1950s and 1960s played many dates in and around Chicago; tours including dates in Canada. Died whilst taking part in Louis Armstrong Memorial Concert in Chicago.

ARMSTRONG, 'Satchmo' Louis
trumpet/vocals/composer

Born: New Orleans, c. 4th July 1900
Died: Corona, New York, 6th July 1971

Formed vocal quartet whilst in his early teens. Was arrested for firing a pistol in Rampart Street, sent to Coloured Waifs' Home (director 'Captain' Joseph Jones) in January 1913. Some six months later joined the Waifs' Home Band (coached by Peter Davis), first on drums, briefly on alto horn and trombone, then trumpet. After being released in June 1914 Louis worked at various day-jobs including collecting for a scrap-merchant, delivering milk for the Cloverdale Dairy, selling newspapers, unloading banana boats, and delivering coal. For part of this period Louis gave up playing trumpet, but later formed a small band co-leading with drummer Joe Lindsey. Later he played residencies at Matranga's and various other New Orleans 'tonks', and subbed in various bands. In the early months of 1919 replaced his tutor King Oliver in Kid Ory's Band, he also did gigs across the river in Gretna and from November 1918 played evening excursions with Fate Marable on the Streckfus Steamers. In late 1918 Louis married his first wife, Daisy Parker.

In May 1919 Louis left New Orleans by train to join Fate Marable's Band sailing out of St. Louis. Louis played on various boats with Marable and also did gigs ashore until September 1921, when he returned to New Orleans. Worked at Tom Anderson's Cabaret Club, also played for a while with Zutty Singleton's Trio at Fernandez's Club; worked at various clubs and also did street parade work, occasionally with the Silver Leaf Band and Allen's Brass Band, regularly with Papa Celestin's Tuxedo Band. Left New Orleans in the summer of 1922 to join King Oliver in Chicago.

Played residency at Lincoln Gardens with King Oliver, also did some touring. Made record debut with Oliver 31st March 1923. Married pianiste Lil Hardin 5th February 1924. Left King Oliver in June 1924, worked with Ollie Powers' Band before journeying to New York in September 1924, to join Fletcher Henderson. Left Henderson in early November 1925, returned to Chicago to join his wife's band 'Lil Armstrong's Dreamland Syncopators'. On the 12th November 1925 made first recordings under own leadership. During 1926 worked with Lil's Band, also doubled with Erskine Tate's Orchestra at the Vendome Theatre, in April 1926 joined Carroll Dickerson's Orchestra at the Sunset Cafe (and there first met Joe Glaser); continued doubling with Erskine Tate. Continued with Dickerson at the Sunset Cafe until February 1927, then began leading own band 'Louis Armstrong and his Stompers' (directed by Earl Hines) at the same venue. Continued to double with Erskine Tate until April, then began working with Clarence Jones' Orchestra at the Metropolitan Theatre. In late November 1927 Louis, Zutty Singleton, and Earl Hines briefly ran their own club at the Warwick Hall. In late 1927 and again in February 1928 Louis worked with Clarence Jones, in March 1928 rejoined Carroll Dickerson at the Savoy Ballroom, Chicago.

Louis visited New York in February 1929, again worked with Dickerson in Chicago, then guested for a week with Dave Peyton at the Regal Theatre (April 1929). In May 1929 took own band (musical director Carroll Dickerson) to New York. Louis rehearsed with Fletcher Henderson for 'Great Day' Show, then led band at New York ballrooms, later playing residency at Connie's Inn; from September 1929 Louis began doubling in the 'Hot Chocolates' Revue with LeRoy Smith's Orchestra. In January 1930 Louis 'guested' with Luis Russell's Band in Washington, D.C., left Connie's Inn in February and began working at the Cocoanut Grove. Played in Baltimore with the Mills Blue Rhythm Band (then led by drummer Willie Lynch) in April 1930. Moved to California in July 1930 to appear as cabaret soloist at Frank Sebastian's Cotton Club, Culver City. Johnny Collins became Louis' manager. Left California in March 1931, returned to Chicago where a big backing band was organised by Zilner Randolph and Reuben 'Mike' McKendrick. Did touring and residencies in New York, etc., before disbanding in March 1932. Worked as a soloist in California, accompanied by Les Hite and his Orchestra. Left West Coast in June; sailed for first European tour, arrived in England on 14th July 1932. Returned to New York in November 1932, in late December worked with Chick Webb's Band in Philadelphia. In January 1933 Zilner Randolph again organised big band to back Louis for touring. Disbanded in July 1933, returned to play in London, August 1933, subsequently toured Britain, Denmark, Sweden, Norway, and Holland. Moved to Paris in spring 1934, long vacation, then concerts in Paris (November 1934), then toured Belgium, Switzerland, and Italy. Returned to U.S.A. in January 1935, moved back to Chicago where lip trouble enforced a temporary lay-off. Joe Glaser established as Louis' manager. New big band formed (musical director Zilner Randolph) for debut at Indianapolis on 1st July 1935. Toured with band for three months, then began fronting Luis Russell's Band from October 1935 (usually billed as Louis Armstrong and his Orchestra). Played residencies and toured with the Orchestra throughout the late 1930s; was divorced from Lil (they had parted in 1931) and married Alpha Smith in late 1938. Louis began regular filming, also occasionally made solo appearances, including acting in the short-lived musical 'Swingin' the Dream' (November 1939).

In late 1940 Joe Garland was appointed musical director of Louis' big band, Luis Russell remained with the band. In the autumn of 1942 Louis married Lucille Wilson, a marriage that lasted the rest of his life. Continued leading own big band until the summer of 1947. The official debut of the All Stars took place at Billy Berg's Club in Los Angeles on the 13th August 1947, the All Stars played residencies and concerts in the U.S.A. before appearing at the Nice Jazz Festival in France in February 1948. They returned to the U.S.A. and recommenced touring and short residencies. In March 1949 Louis was crowned King of the Zulus at the New Orleans' Mardi Gras. Touring with the All Stars included trip to Europe (September-November 1949).

Despite personnel changes the All Stars went from success to success; in the 1950s, besides working in the U.S.A. and Canada, the group toured Hawaii, Europe, Australia, Japan and the Far East, South America, and Africa. Louis was temporarily out of action following an illness in Spoleto, Italy (June-July 1959), but was playing within weeks and in late 1960 undertook wide-ranging tour of Africa. During the 1960s the All Stars did even more international touring, they appeared in Africa, Australia, New Zealand, Mexico, Iceland, India, Singapore, Korea, Hawaii, Japan, Hong Kong, Formosa, East and West Germany, Czechoslovakia, Rumania, Yugoslavia, Hungary, France, Holland, Scandinavia, and Great Britain. They also continued to make regular appearances in the U.S.A. In June and July 1968 Louis and the All Stars appeared in England, they returned to the U.S.A. in July and recommenced touring, by September Louis was seriously ill in the Beth Israel Hospital, New York. Left hospital in April 1969, recommenced recording in October 1969. Made many television appearances in 1970, also appeared at concerts in Los Angeles and Newport. Recommenced working with the All Stars in Las Vegas (September and December 1970), sang and played at charity concert in England (October 1970). After completing an All Stars engagement in New York (March 1971), suffered heart attack, spent two months in hospital. Died in his sleep at home in Corona, New York. A more detailed account of the great man's career appears in the book 'Louis' (by Max Jones and John Chilton), first published in 1971.

Other books on (or by) Louis Armstrong include: 'Swing That Music', by Louis Armstrong (1936); 'Satchmo, My Life in New Orleans', by Louis Armstrong; 'Horn of Plenty', by Robert Goffin; 'Trumpeter's Tale—The Story of Young Louis Armstrong', by Jeanette Eaton; 'Louis Armstrong', by Albert J. McCarthy; 'Louis Armstrong', by Hugues Panassié.

Louis Armstrong's film appearances include: 'Ex-Flame' (1931), 'Rhapsody in Black and Blue' (1932), 'Copenhagen Kalundborg' (1933), 'Pennies From Heaven' (1936), 'Artists and Models' (1937), 'Cabin In The Sky' (1943), 'Atlantic City' (1944), 'Pillow To Post' (1945), 'New Orleans' (1947), 'A Song is Born' (1948), 'The Strip' (1951), 'The Glenn Miller Story' (1953), 'High Society' (1956), 'Satchmo The Great' (1957), 'Jazz On A Summer's Day' (1958), 'The Five Pennies' (1959), 'Paris Blues' (1961), 'A Man Called Adam' (1966), 'Hello, Dolly' (1969). A more detailed listing of Louis' screen career appears in the book 'Louis' (by Max Jones and John Chilton).

ARODIN, Sidney J.
(real name: Arnondrin)
clarinet/saxes/composer

Born: Westwego, Louisiana, 29th March 1901
Died: New Orleans, Louisiana, 6th February 1948

Took up clarinet at the age of 15, within a year was doing regular gigs. Early work on riverboats including a spell with drummer Johnny Stein, worked with Freddie Newman at The Ringside in the early 1920s; to New York in 1922 with the Original New Orleans Jazz Band, left them in summer of 1925 (during this period it seems that Arodin worked for several months in band led by pianist-comedian Jimmy 'Schnozzle' Durante). Worked in San Antonio, Texas, with New Orleans Rhythm Masters (1926); with New Orleans Harmony Kings (1927), also recorded with Wingy Manone in New York (December 1927). Returned to New Orleans, played with Halfway House Orchestra, Sharkey Bonano, Monk Hazel, Johnny Miller, etc. (1928). Toured with trombonist Sunny Clapp and his Band of Sunshine (summer 1929). Toured (with Chink Martin) in New Orleans Swing Kings (1930)—Arodin recorded with Jones-Collins Astoria Hot Eight, but did not play regularly with either Lee Collins or Davey Jones. Gigged in Kansas City, Missouri, in summer of 1933, then moved to New York with Louis Prima Band in August 1934. Worked with Wingy Manone in 1935, then returned to New Orleans. Led own band, including residency at the Puppy House 1939-40. Seriously ill in 1941, never fully recovered; for the rest of his life underwent long periods of illness in New Orleans and Westwego, made only occasional public appearances. Recovered sufficiently to play for a while on the riverboats, but was taken ill in St. Louis, returned to New Orleans and died shortly afterwards. Composed the melody of 'Lazy River'.

ATKINS, Boyd
saxes/violin

Born: Paducah, Kentucky, c. 1900
Deceased

Raised in St. Louis. With Dewey Jackson and Fate Marable (c.1923), then moved to Chicago. Led own band, worked with Earl Hines at the Elite No. 2 (1925), with Louis Armstrong's Stompers at Sunset Cafe (spring 1927), Clarence Black (late 1927). Led own band at Sunset Cafe (1929-30), toured with own Firecrackers (1930), with Jimmy Bell (late 1930). Worked mainly with Eli Rice from 1931 until 1934, also with Clarence Moore (1932). Led own band in Minneapolis from 1934, with Rook Ganz (1935). Active as bandleader in the late 1930s, long residency at Cotton Club, Minneapolis. With Eddie South (summer 1940), then led own 'Society Swingsters' for several years at the Faust Club, Peoria, Illinois, also led in Chicago. During the early 1950s did arranging, also gigged in Chicago with Big Boy Williams' Combo. Composed 'Heebie Jeebies'.

ATKINS, Ed
trombone

Born: New Orleans, Louisiana. c. 1887
Deceased

Played baritone horn in the Onward Brass Band from c. 1905, later was a regular member of the Olympia Band. Went to Chicago with Manuel Perèz (c. 1915), returned to New Orleans during the following year, played in the Tuxedo Band and with King Oliver and Joe Howard's Band. Service in U.S. Army as a bandsman in the 8th Regiment Brass Band from late 1917. After demobilisation settled in Chicago and played for many bandleaders including: King Oliver, Erskine Tate, Charlie Elgar, Junie Cobb, and Dave Peyton (1928-9). Continued playing in the 1930s; with Art Short Orchestra (1932).

AULD, George (real name: John Altwerger)
saxes/clarinet

Born: Toronto, Canada, 19th May 1919

Began on alto sax during early childhood, studied with Michael Angelo in Toronto. Moved with his family to New York in 1929. Won Rudy Weidoeft Scholarship in 1931 and studied with that alto player for nine months. Gigged on alto, then after hearing Coleman Hawkins' recording of 'Meditation' switched to tenor (1936). Led own small band at Nick's, then worked with Bunny Berigan in 1937 and 1938. Joined Artie Shaw early in 1939 until break-up in November 1939. Briefly led Shaw alumni, then joined Jan Savitt (spring 1940). With Benny Goodman (November 1940 to June 1941), again with Artie Shaw until Shaw disbanded (January 1942). Led own band from February 1942. In 1943 did short stint in U.S. Army, then led own quartet at the Three Deuces, New York, from June 1943 until forming own big band in September 1943. Other than absence through illness in 1945, he continued to lead until mid-1946, then suffered a recurrence of illness, moved to Arizona, then on to California. Soon returned to regular playing, worked with own group at the Three Deuces, New York, from May 1947, then returned to California, led own group and played in Billy Eckstine's Band in 1948. Led own band at Tin Pan Alley Club, New York (spring 1949), then for almost a year acted in the Broadway play 'The Rat Race'. Briefly with Count Basie in spring of 1950, then led own quintet until August 1951, temporarily inactive through illness, then moved to California, opened own Melody Room Club and began free-lance studio work for M.G.M., etc. Did studio work in New York in the late 1950s, then moved to Las Vegas. During the 1960s has continued leading own band (toured Japan during the 1960s), also free-lanced for various leaders including spell in Las Vegas with Benny Goodman (1966). Continued to play regularly during the 1970s and early 1980s, recorded with Les Brown's Band in 1983. Acted in the film 'New York, New York' (1977).

AUSTIN, Cuba
drums

Born: Charleston, West Virginia. c. 1906
Deceased

Originally worked as a tap-dancer. In 1926, when William McKinney quit drumming to concentrate on management, Cuba joined McKinney's Cotton Pickers on drums, having previously sat in with the band on several occasions. Remained as the band's regular drummer through its entire existence; after McKinney left the organisation, Cuba became leader of the Original Cotton-Pickers which did extensive touring (as far south as Freeport, Louisiana), after a 1934 residency at Carlin's Park, Baltimore, the band broke up. Cuba settled in Baltimore and ran his own business, briefly toured with Irving Miller's 'Brown Skin Models' in the mid-1930s, then continued regular part-time playing in Baltimore. Played on and off for over 20 years with orchestras led by pianist Rivers Chambers, also led own trio for various residencies.

AUSTIN, Lovie (née Cora Calhoun)
piano/arranger

Born: Chattanooga, Tennessee, 19th September 1887
Died: Chicago, 10th July 1972

Studied music at Roger Williams' University in Nashville and at Knoxville College. Early marriage to a Detroit movie-house owner, subsequently married a variety artist and accompanied her husband and his partner's act 'Austin and Delaney'. Toured with Irving Miller's 'Blue Babies', then to New York to play for Club Alabam Show. Extensive touring on T.O.B.A. circuit with The Sunflower Girls and leading own Blues Serenaders. Settled in Chicago, and for 20 years was musical director for the Monogram Theatre, later directed at the Gem and Joyland Theatres. During World War II was as a security inspector at a defence plant, then resumed theatre work. Pianiste at Jimmy Payne's Dancing School at Penthouse Studios, Chicago, for many years from the late 1940s. Recorded in 1961.

AUTREY, Herman
trumpet/vocals

Born: Evergreen, Alabama, 4th December 1904
Died: New York, 14th June 1980

Two of his brothers were part-time musicians; their father, Moses Autrey, was a tuba player. Herman started on alto horn at nine, switched to trumpet at 14. Moved to Pittsburgh in 1923, gigged with local bands, then for almost two years did extensive touring with William Benbow's 'Get Happy' Show. Left the show in Florida and became leader of the big band accompanying Billy Wonder's Florida Tip Tops, after touring for several months briefly led own band in Daytona Beach, Florida. Gigged in Boston during 1926, then moved to Washington, D.C. Played in local Deluxe Club and doubled in the pit orchestra at the Howard Theatre, moved to Philadelphia in 1929. From 1929-32 worked mainly at the Standard Theatre, then joined band led by George 'Doc' Hyder. To New York in late 1933, joined Charlie Johnson and whilst with Johnson made recordings with Fats Waller (May 1934). From 1934 until 1939 worked regularly with Fats Waller; whilst Fats was fulfilling solo engagements Herman worked with various bands including Fletcher Henderson (1935), Charlie Turner's Arcadians, and Claude Hopkins (1938). Rejoined Claude Hopkins in 1940, then worked with Stuff Smith (led Stuff's Band in California—1942—whilst the leader was ill). Returned to New York, briefly with Una Mae Carlisle's Band at the Plantation, New York (spring 1943), then formed own small band, which from 1945 played for several years at the Musical Bar, Philadelphia. In 1954 was seriously injured in a car smash, but resumed regular playing in late 1955. During the 1960s played regularly in the 'Saints and Sinners' (also with Tony Parenti in 1965). Toured Europe with the 'Saints and Sinners' in 1968 and 1969, played regularly in and around New York during the 1970s.

B

BACON, Louis
trumpet/vocals

Born: Louisville, Kentucky, 1st November 1904
Died: New York City, 8th December 1967

At the age of three moved with his widowed mother to Chicago. First professional work with Zinky Cohn's Band in Michigan (summer 1926). Moved to New York in 1928 (accompanying dancers Brown and McGraw), worked briefly with Bingie Madison (1928), then joined Lt. J. Tim Brymn's Band (1929). With Chick Webb (1930-4), Duke Ellington (1934), then with Luis Russell. Remained with Luis Russell/Louis Armstrong Band until 1938, when tuberculosis forced temporary retirement from playing. With Benny Carter Big Band at the Savoy Ballroom (March-May 1939), then sailed to Europe to join Willie Lewis (summer 1939). Remained with Willie Lewis until repatriated to the U.S.A. (from Portugal) in September 1941. Joined Cootie Williams' Big Band briefly in spring of 1942, then further bout of serious illness before joining Garvin Bushell Band in August 1944. Did U.S.O. tour of Asia with Jesse Stone Orchestra (1946-7), then persistent lung ailment forced premature retirement from trumpet playing. Played occasionally at Ryan's, New York, in 1959 and again with Garvin Bushell in 1960, but was mainly active as a successful vocal coach. During the 1960s worked as an ambulance driver.

BAILEY, Pearl
vocals

Born: Newport News, Virginia, 29th March 1918

Spent childhood in Washington, D.C. and Philadelphia. Brother Bill a professional entertainer. Won amateur dancing contest at Pearl Theater, Philadelphia (1933), soon afterwards began working in touring shows. Won singing contest at Harlem's Apollo Theater, and was subsequently featured with several big bands, Noble Sissle, Edgar Hayes, etc. Did U.S.O. tours from 1942. Worked with Cootie Williams prior to playing long run at Blue Angel, New York (1944-45), then sang with Cab Calloway. Began working theatres as a solo performer, and as an actress (on stage and in films). Appeared in several movies including 'Carmen Jones', 'That Certain Feeling', 'St. Louis Blues'. Married drummer Louis Bellson in November 1952. During the 1960s starred in Broadway Show 'Hello Dolly'. Despite health problems continued with extensive working schedule during the 1970s and 1980s, including international tours and many television shows. Autobiography 'The Raw Pearl' first published in 1968.

BAILEY, 'Buster' William C.
clarinet/saxes

Born: Memphis, Tennessee, 19th July 1902
Died: Brooklyn, New York, 12th April 1967

Took up clarinet at 13 whilst attending Clay Street School in Memphis. Joined W. C. Handy Orchestra in 1917, and toured with Handy until settling in Chicago in 1919. Worked for Erskine Tate from 1919 until 1923 (including trip to New York in 1921). With King Oliver (late 1923 to October 1924), Fletcher Henderson (October 1924 to July 1927), brief spell with Oscar 'Bernie' Young in Milwaukee, then again with Henderson (late 1927 to late 1928). To Europe with Noble Sissle (May 1929), returned to New York later that year and joined Edgar Hayes at the Alhambra Theatre. With Dave Nelson (late 1930), again with Noble Sissle (1931-3). With Fletcher Henderson (January to September 1934), then with Mills Blue Rhythm Band (October 1934 to November 1935), then rejoined Fletcher Henderson—having previously played broadcasts, etc., with Henderson earlier in 1935. Left the band early in 1937, briefly with Luis Russell/Louis Armstrong and Stuff Smith before joining John Kirby in May 1937. Regularly with Kirby until summer of 1944 (except for brief absence through injured hand in summer 1941). Worked on and off with John Kirby in 1945 and 1946, also led own small band at Spotlite Club, New York (1945). With Wilbur de Paris (September 1947 until April 1949). Led own quartet, and worked with Henry 'Red' Allen in 1950-1, with Big Chief Russell Moore (September 1952 to February 1953). Worked in pit orchestra for 'Porgy and Bess' late 1953-4, regularly with Henry Allen from 1954 (Metropole, New York, Boston, etc.), also did occasional symphony work in New York. Regularly featured at leading jazz festivals during the late 1950s and early

1960s. Briefly with Tyree Glenn in 1959, then resumed with Henry Allen (occasionally doubling bass clarinet). Worked with Wild Bill Davison 1961-3, also with the 'Saints and Sinners' 1963-4. (Appeared in 1962 film 'Splendour in the Grass'.) Joined Louis Armstrong All Stars in July 1965, remained with All Stars until the time of his death. He died in his sleep at his home in Brooklyn.

BAILEY, Mildred
(née Mildred Rinker)
vocals

Born: Tekoa, near Seattle, Washington, 27th February 1907
Died: Poughkeepsie, New York, 12th December 1951

Her brother, Al Rinker, sang in Paul Whiteman's Rhythm Boys. Attended school in Spokane, later worked as a song demonstrator, then joined Fanchon and Marco revue touring West Coast. Worked as solo vocalist on radio station K.M.T.R. and did free-lance work in California before submitting demo-disc to Paul Whiteman. Sang with Paul Whiteman from 1929 until winter 1933 (temporary absence c. September 1932, replaced by Irene Taylor). Married to Red Norvo from 1933 until 1945. In 1934 sang with Ben Bernie, Willard Robison, and did solo theatre tours, temporary retirement, then worked mainly with Red Norvo's Band from 1936-9. In late 1939 did regular radio work with Benny Goodman, then from 1940 concentrated on solo career. Recurrent illness throughout the 1940s, did some touring, and residencies in New York: Cafe Society, Blue Angel, etc., also featured at the Esquire New York Jazz Concert (January 1944). Seriously ill with diabetes and heart trouble in 1949, resumed work in 1950, spell with Joe Marsala at Blue Note, Chicago, in summer of 1950. In 1951 did some touring (accompanied by Ralph Burns), then spent last part of her life in the Poughkeepsie Hospital. Recorded regularly under her own name from 1929.

BAKER, 'Shorty' Harold
trumpet

Born: St. Louis, Missouri, 26th May 1913
Died: New York, 8th November 1966

His brother, Winfield, was a trombonist. Originally a drummer, then switched to trumpet and playing in his brother's band. Lessons from P. G. Lankford in St. Louis. With Fate Marable (c.1930), then with Erskine Tate in Chicago before returning to St. Louis to join Eddie Johnson's Crackerjacks (1932-3), then in band led by his brother. With Don Redman from late 1936 until 1938 (briefly with Duke Ellington in 1938). Joined Teddy Wilson Big Band in April 1939, left early the following year to join Andy Kirk. With Kirk until spring 1942, then co-led sextet with Mary Lou Williams (to whom he was then married). With Duke Ellington from c. September 1942 until Army call-up in spring 1944. Guested with Duke Ellington in 1945, then regularly with Duke from summer 1946 until early 1952. Played with Teddy Wilson Quartet, Ben Webster small band, and free-lanced in New York. Joined Johnny Hodges Band in late 1954. From 1957 until 1963 worked on and off with Duke Ellington, during this period also with Dick Vance, Claude Hopkins, Bud Freeman, George Wein, etc., also led own quartet. Played at the Metropole, New York, in 1964 and had his last dates at The Embers, also in New York, then regular playing was curtailed by illness. He underwent a serious operation late 1965, was temporarily released from the hospital, but was unable to continue trumpet playing. He died of throat cancer in the New York Veterans' Hospital.

BALES, 'Burt' Burton Frank
piano

Born: Stevensville, Montana, 20th March 1916

Began playing piano at 12, later studied arranging and musical theory. Played gigs throughout the 1930s mainly in California. Worked with Lu Watters in 1943 prior to Army service. Led own group 1944-49 then rejoined Watters. With Turk Murphy (1949-50), with Bob Scobey and Marty Marsala during the early 1950s, then concentrated on solo work from 1954-66, playing a long residency at Pier 23, San Francisco. Quit regular playing to work in electronics, but resumed playing solo piano engagements during the mid-1970s.

B

BALLARD, 'Butch' George Edward *Born: Camden, New Jersey, 26th December 1917*
drums

Worked with Bardu Ali, and with Fats Waller before joining Cootie Williams early in 1942. With Louis Armstrong (1946), Eddie 'Lockjaw' Davis (1947-48), with Mercer Ellington (1948), joined Count Basie in spring of 1949. Toured Europe with Duke Ellington (1950) and again worked with Ellington in 1953. Moved to Philadelphia and led own band there for many years, often accompanying visiting guest stars, also worked with Bobby Roberts Band in Philadelphia during the early 1970s.

BALLEW, Smith *Born: Palestine, Texas, 21st January 1902*
vocals/leader *Died: Fort Worth, Texas, 2nd May 1984*

Led own band in Dallas c. 1925, also toured Texas, for a brief spell fronted Dick Voynow's Wolverines. To New York in January 1928 as banjoist with Olsen's Band. From March 1929 led own band at White's Restaurant, New York, from then on specialised as a vocalist. During 1930 briefly returned to Dallas, leading own band. Throughout the early 1930s his band played many residencies in New York, also led an all-star unit (Bunny Berigan, Glenn Miller, etc.) for brief summer season in the early 1930s. Prolific free-lance recording activities, also appeared in many films (usually playing singing-cowboy roles).

BANKS, Billy *Born: Alton, Illinois. c. 1908*
vocals *Died: Tokyo, Japan, 19th October 1967*

Signed by impressario Irving Mills whilst singing in Cleveland, Ohio. Recorded with all-star pick-up groups. Opened at Connie's Inn, New York on 29th June 1932, accompanied by own orchestra, returned to Cleveland during following year and helped run family shoe shop until joining Noble Sissle c. 1934, remained as vocalist-entertainer with Sissle's Band until moving into Billy Rose's Diamond Horseshoe for an unbroken residency of 7,151 performances, from December 1938 until June 1948. Appeared at Diamond Horseshoe in 1949 and 1950. To Europe in March 1952, spent several years in Holland, England, France, etc. (working mainly as a variety artist), then did extensive touring in Asia and Australia before settling in Japan.

BAQUET, George F. *Born: New Orleans, Louisiana, 1883*
clarinet/saxes *Died: Philadelphia, Pennsylvania, 14th January 1949*

Brother of clarinettist Achille Joseph Baquet (1886-1956); another brother, Harold 'Hal' Baquet, died in New York (of stab wounds) in November 1931, Spencer Williams was subsequently acquitted of causing his death. The Baquets' father, Theogene, was a noted clarinettist; George began playing in the Lyre Club Symphony Orchestra (c. 1897). In 1902 he did his first touring with P. T. Wright's Nashville Student Minstrels, then worked for a long spell in the Georgia Minstrels before returning to New Orleans in 1905. Sat in with Buddy Bolden's Band at the Oddfellows' Hall, later did regular gigs with Bolden, doubling with John Robichaux's Orchestra then resident at Antoine's. In 1908 began working regularly with Freddie Keppard, and did parade work in the Onward Brass Band. After completing a long tour, he left New Orleans with Keppard to join Bill Johnson in Los Angeles for the Original Creole Orchestra's first tour in 1914. Left the Original Creoles c. June 1916. Worked for several years in College Inn, Coney Island, then moved to Philadelphia in 1923 to join Sam Gordon's Lafayette Players at the Dunbar Theatre. Became resident of Philadelphia, led own small band there for many years, long stay at Wilson's Cafe leading own 'New Orleans Nighthawks' which became 'George Bakey's Swingsters' in the 1930s. Recorded with Jelly Roll Morton in 1929 and took part in reunion concert with Sidney Bechet in Philadelphia (May 1940).

BARBARIN, Adolphe Paul
drums/leader/composer

Born: New Orleans, Louisiana, 5th May 1899
Died: New Orleans, Louisiana, 10th February 1969

His father, Isadore, was a noted brass player. Three of Paul's brothers were musicians, the most famous being drummer Louis (born: 1902). Paul was Danny Barker's uncle. He began on clarinet, then worked as a freight-lift operator at the Hotel St. Charles in New Orleans, with his earnings he bought his first set of drums. Soon began gigging with the Silver Leaf Orchestra and with Buddie Petit in the Young Olympia Band. Left New Orleans for Chicago in 1917, worked in the Armour & Co. stockyards by day and played with pianist Clarence Parson at the Rinsberg Cafe at night. Later worked with Roi Wolfscale's Trio, then with Eddie Vincent's Band at the Royal Gardens before joining Art Simms' Band. Toured with the Tennessee Ten (c. 1920), including visit to Canada, then led own trio in South Norwalk, Connecticut, for eight months before returning to Chicago. Worked briefly with Freddie Keppard, then with Jimmie Noone (at that time, his brother-in-law) at the Paradise Club. Returned to New Orleans, played at Tom Anderson's Cabaret with Luis Russell, also did parade work with the Onward and Excelsior Bands, and worked briefly with Amos White. In late 1924 returned to Chicago to join King Oliver, eventually began working with Oliver in February 1925. Remained with King Oliver until the summer of 1927, then returned to New Orleans and joined Walter Pichon at the Pelican Cafe, also worked in New Orleans with Armand Piron. In 1928 (c. summer) returned to New York to join Luis Russell at the Nest Club—replacing Lawrence Baltimore. Remained with Russell until January 1932, worked briefly in New York with Walter Pichon, then short spell with Earle Howard at the Rose Danceland (spring 1932). Formed own band which played in New York, then returned to New Orleans to lead own local band, The Jump Rhythm Boys. Rejoined Luis Russell in 1935, remained to work with Louis Armstrong until late 1938, then returned to New Orleans to lead own band. Disbanded in late 1939 and played for a while in Joe Robichaux's New Orleans Rhythm Boys, then led own band at Vinette's Club, New Orleans (1940). Briefly rejoined Louis Armstrong in 1941, then from 1942 until summer of 1943 worked in Henry 'Red' Allen's Sextet. Formed own band which played residency at Club Rio, Springfield, Illinois, from September to December 1943, during following year joined Sidney Bechet and with Bechet played another season at the Club Rio. Returned to New Orleans and formed own band (originally called The Invaders), played with Louis Armstrong and Sidney Bechet at a New Orleans Jazz Foundation Concert (January 1945). Continued to lead own band, also did local parade work. Worked with Art Hodes at Jazz Ltd, Chicago, in 1953, returned to New Orleans in August 1953 and formed own highly successful small band. Played long residencies in New Orleans, but also fulfilled engagements in New York, Los Angeles, Toronto, etc. During the late 1960s also occasionally led the Onward Brass Band in parades. Died whilst taking part in a street parade.

BARBOUR, 'Dave' David Michael
guitar

Born: Long Island, New York, 28th May 1912
Died: Malibu, California, 11th December 1965

Originally played banjo in band at High School in Flushing, New York. First professional work with Wingy Manone (1934). After working with Red Norvo in 1936, played with various studio bands including regular work in Lenny Hayton's Radio Orchestra. Worked with: Hal Kemp, Raymond Scott, Charlie Barnet, Glenn Miller, Herman Chittison, and Lou Holden's Band before joining Benny Goodman from June 1942 until May 1943. From 1943 until 1951 was married to vocaliste Peggy Lee—they worked together regularly during this period. Barbour briefly led his own band in the mid-1940s, also recorded with various leaders including: Charlie Barnet, Teddy Wilson, Boyd Raeburn, Andre Previn, etc. In 1950 made a short-lived attempt at professional acting, appeared in the films 'The Secret Fury' and 'Mr. Music'. For the last 13 years of his life he lived in virtual musical retirement on the West Coast; he occasionally played at charity concerts, and did a recording session in 1962 under Benny Carter's leadership. Suffered for many years with stomach ailments. Wrote several songs that achieved commercial success.

B

BAREFIELD, 'Eddie' Edward Emmanuel *Born: Scandia, Iowa, 12th December 1909*
saxes/clarinet/arranger

His daughter, Dolores, is a professional vocaliste. Played piano at 10, self-taught alto from the age of 13. First professional work in 1926 with Edgar Pillar's Night Owls, then worked with: Isler's Gravy Show, Virginia Raven, Don Phillips, Ethiopian Serenaders, Oscar 'Bernie' Young (spring 1930). With Clarence Johnson Band in North Dakota before playing with Eli Rice's Cottonpickers and with Grant Moore's Band. Led (and co-led) small bands in Minneapolis before joining Bennie Moten—travelled to New York with Moten in 1932, left the band early in 1933, joined Zack Whyte in Columbus, Ohio. Later led own band, then played with the Cottonpickers (sans McKinney) at Carlin's in Baltimore until joining Cab Calloway in autumn of 1933. Remained with Cab until 1936 (including trip to Europe in 1934). Settled in Los Angeles, played with Charlie Echol's Band, then formed own big band in June 1936, led various bands on West Coast, including own trio in 'Bargain with Bullets' Revue in 1937, also worked with Les Hite. Joined Fletcher Henderson in 1938, later that year worked with Don Redman in New York. Rejoined Cab Calloway in 1939, formed own band which played various residencies in New York, including the 'Mimo Club' (summer 1940), also played with Coleman Hawkins, Don Redman, etc. Featured on clarinet in Benny Carter's Sextet in autumn of 1941, brief spell as musical director of Ella Fitzgerald's Band (1942), then staff musician at the A.B.C. studios until March 1946. Worked with Duke Ellington and Wilbur de Paris in 1947, from later that year until 1949 was musical director for the play 'A Streetcar Named Desire'. Did studio work and spell with Sy Oliver, also played in Fletcher Henderson's last band in December 1950. Throughout the 1950s worked regularly as musical director for Cab Calloway, including extensive touring; did theatre and studio work in New York, also toured with Don Redman in 1953 and played briefly in the Dukes of Dixieland in late 1955. Played in Europe with Sam Price (1958). In 1960 was m.d. for the 'Jazz Train' production (including tour of Europe), worked with Paul Lavalle in New York during 1963 and 1965, with Wilbur de Paris in late 1964. Played in 'Jazz Giants' (1967), also took part in filming of 'The Night They Raided Minsky's'. Continues to lead own bands, including tour of Africa (summer of 1969). With 'Saints and Sinners' in Europe (late 1969). Prolific free-lance activities during the 1970s and 1980s, including long spell in the New York production of the show 'One Mo' Time'.

BARKER, 'Danny' Daniel *Born: New Orleans, Louisiana, 13th January 1909*
guitar/banjo/composer

Nephew of Paul Barbarin; husband of vocaliste Blue Lu Barker. Started on clarinet, received tuition from Barney Bigard, then Paul Barbarin taught him to play drums before he specialised on the ukelele. Later switched to tenor banjo and guitar and did first regular work with trumpeter Willie Pajeaud. Played with Lee Collins' Ragtime Band in the late 1920s (including touring), then moved to New York early in 1930. Played with the White Brothers, Billy Fowler, Dave Nelson (1931), Fess Williams, toured with Buddy Harris (1933), Albert Nicholas (1935), James P. Johnson, etc. With Lucky Millinder (1937-8), then joined Benny Carter's Big Band in November 1938, worked regularly with Cab Calloway from 1939 until spring 1946, left to form small group to accompany his wife, Blue Lu Barker. With Lucky Millinder (1947), also gigged with Bunk Johnson in New York (November 1947). Worked mainly with Albert Nicholas in 1948, left in March 1949 to re-form accompanying group for his wife, also free-lanced in New York during early 1950s, including regular stints with actor-trombonist Conrad Janis. Played banjo with Paul Barbarin from 1954 until early 1955, then worked in California with Albert Nicholas. Active free-lance work in the late 1950s and early 1960s: led own small band at Cinderella, 8th Wonder, etc., also appeared as a 'single' at Freedomland. With Eubie Blake at Newport Jazz Festival in 1960, with Cliff Jackson at Ryan's (1963), led own banjo group at New York's World Fair in summer of 1964, etc. Moved back to New Orleans in May 1965 and was appointed Assistant to the Curator of the New Orleans Jazz Museum, continues to play regularly in New Orleans, has also lectured on jazz at several universities. Acted as a Grand Marshal for the New Orleans Jazz Fest (June 1969), in autumn 1969 began residency at The Maison Bourbon in New Orleans. Featured at New Orleans Jazz Fest

(April 1971), also played at first jazz presentation at John F. Kennedy Center in Washington, D.C. (September 1971). Active throughout the 1970s and 1980s, recovered from lung operation (1979).

Throughout his career, Danny Barker has played on many free-lance record dates with: Henry Allen, Chu Berry, Buster Bailey, Sidney Bechet, Lionel Hampton, Jonah Jones, Wingy Manone, Adrian Rollini, Mezz Mezzrow, Teddy Wilson, etc., etc.

BARKSDALE, Everett *Born: Detroit, Michigan, 28th April 1910*
guitar

Husband of pianiste Victoria Raymore. Played alto, violin, bass, piano, and guitar in local bands, then moved to Chicago. With Erskine Tate in the early 1930s, briefly with Clarence Moore at Grand Terrace (early 1932), then joined Eddie South in late 1932 for trip to California. Remained with Eddie South until spring 1939 (excluding trip to Europe in 1937), left briefly, then returned to the group until moving to New York in November 1939. With Benny Carter Big Band for several months from September 1940, worked on and off with Leon Abbey for several years, also worked with Herman Chittison, clarinettist Buster Browne's Quartet (spring 1942), Cliff Jackson Trio (September 1944), Lester Boone Quartet (late 1944), etc. From late 1942 until 1945 also led own quartet for specific engagements. Spent 19 months with C.B.S. studio staff in New York. Worked on and off with Art Tatum's Trio from 1949 until 1955. Worked as musical director for The Ink Spots and toured Europe with them in summer of 1956. Rejoined Art Tatum in September 1956; worked with Tatum until the pianist's last appearance in October 1956. Resumed studio work in New York, also played electric bass with Buddy Tate's Band in the late 1950s. During the 1960s and 1970s worked as a staff musician for television network, playing guitar and bass-guitar. Moved to California and continued to play regularly.

BARNES, 'Polo' Paul D. *Born: New Orleans, Louisiana, 22nd November 1901*
clarinet/saxes/composer *Died: New Orleans, Louisiana, 13th April 1981*

Brother of clarinettist Emile Barnes (1892-1970). Played the toy fife as a child. Studied at St. Paul Lutheran College, started playing alto sax at the age of 18. Did gigs with Kid Rena, then led own Diamond Jazz Band. Played in Young Tuxedo Orchestra (1920), worked with many bands including Maple Leaf Orchestra, Kid Rena, Bebe Ridgley-Celestin's Original Tuxedo Band, during the early 1920s. Regularly with Papa Celestin in 1925-6. Left New Orleans to join King Oliver in St. Louis (April 1927), remained with Oliver until late summer of 1927, then gigged in New York with Chick Webb, Edgar Dowell's Band, and pianist Ginger Young. Toured and recorded with Jelly Roll Morton in 1929, then joined Richard Chetham's Band until rejoining King Oliver from spring 1931 until December 1931. Returned to New Orleans, formed own band, and toured Louisiana, very briefly with Richard M. Jones, then from July 1933 with Vincent Lopresto. Again with King Oliver from February 1934 until June 1935, toured with B. Morris' Orchestra, then returned to New Orleans, gigged with various leaders including Steve Lewis, Chester Zardis, and trumpeter Elmer Talbert, regularly with Kid Howard 1937-9 and in 1941. Service in U.S. Navy 1942-5, then worked mainly with Papa Celestin from 1946-51. Lived on West Coast from 1952, did very little playing for five years, then worked with Alton Purnell's All Stars in 1958. With Paul Barbarin in 1960, worked with Earl Foster and did parade work with the Eureka, then again lived in California, working in the 'Young Men of New Orleans 1961-4. Returned to New Orleans and played at various venues including Preservation Hall. Toured Europe in 1973. Prevented from playing by illness during the last three years of his life.

BARNES, Walter *Born: Vicksburg, Mississippi, 8th July 1905*
clarinet/saxes *Died: Natchez, Mississippi, 23rd April 1940*

Spent childhood in Columbus, Mississippi, then moved to Chicago. Took lessons from

Franz Schoepp, also studied at the Chicago Musical College and the American Conservatory of Music. Led own quartet (1926), worked in Detroit Shannon's Band at The Merry Gardens, was appointed leader of the band, then re-named Royal Creolians. Led for many residencies in Chicago; long spell at Cotton Club, Cicero, until August 1930—the band also played in New York during 1929. During the 1930s the band was a very popular touring attraction throughout the Southern States. By 1938 it was operating as a 16-piece unit, after touring Kentucky, Ohio, Virginia, and Pennsylvania the band moved back to Chicago in July 1938. During the following year Barnes re-formed his band to commence residency at the Savoy Ballroom, Chicago, from October 1939, then recommenced touring. Whilst the band were at the Rhythm Club, Natchez, a disastrous fire occurred; Walter Barnes, eight of his sidemen, and vocaliste Juanita Avery lost their lives in the tragedy.

BARNET, 'Charlie' Charles Daly *Born: New York City, 26th October 1913*
tenor, alto, soprano saxes/vocals

The much-married 'Mad Mab'. Was born into a wealthy family, began playing piano at an early age, saxophone at 12. Studied at Blair Academy in New York, then attended high school in Winnetka, Illinois. At 16 led own band on the S.S. 'Republic', subsequently led bands on Cunard, Red Star, and Panama-Pacific liners; played on many Atlantic crossings (visited England in the early 1930s), also did Mediterranean and South American cruises. Attended Rumsey Academy and played in school band, left to play for almost a year with Frank Winegar's Pennsylvanians, specialising on tenor sax. Left New York with Beasley Smith, then gigged his way across the country, played with 'Flem' Ferguson in Shreveport and with Jack Purvis in Kilgore, Texas. Free-lanced on West Coast, then moved back to New York, formed first big band for three-month residency at Paramount Hotel Grill, New York (spring 1933). During the following year led at Park Central Hotel, New York, Glen Island Casino, Hotel Roosevelt, New Orleans, etc. Formed new band in spring of 1935, disbanded, moved to Hollywood for short-lived acting career, appearing in 'Love and Hisses' (1936) and 'Sally, Irene, and Mary' (1936). Re-formed own band, residencies at Glen Island Casino and touring, disbanded, then re-formed band for residency at Famous Door, New York (1939), Paramount, New York, Playland, Rye, New York, etc., then moved to West Coast, during residency at the Palomar Ballroom, Los Angeles, the band lost all its instruments and orchestrations in a disastrous fire (October 1939). Continued to lead this unit regularly until 1943, during the following 10-year period Barnet formed several excellent big bands. During the 1950s and 1960s he has occasionally organised big bands for specific engagements, the last 'regular' unit played residencies in Las Vegas and New York (late 1966).

Charlie Barnet's film appearances include: 'The Fabulous Dorseys' (solo), 'Music in Manhattan' (band), 'Freddie Steps Out', 'Juke Box Jenny', etc., etc. Early in 1967 his specially-formed band made a short feature film. Throughout his career, Barnet has done as much as anyone in breaking down racial barriers in music. Beginning in the mid-1930s he employed many black musicians including: Benny Carter, Garnett Clark, Roy Eldridge, Dizzy Gillespie, Peanuts Holland, Kansas Fields, Al Killian, Frankie Newton, Roger Ramirez, Paul Webster, Trummy Young, Clark Terry, Oscar Pettiford, etc. Barnet rarely played clarinet, but is heard soloing on his 1939 recording of 'Lament For A Lost Love'. Stanley Dance's book, 'Those Swinging Years' (concerning Barnet's career) was first published in 1984.

BASCOMB, 'Dud' Wilbur Odell *Born: Birmingham, Alabama, 16th May 1916*
trumpet *Died: New York, 25th December 1972*

Brother of Paul and Arthur (a pianist); Dud Jr. plays bass. Began on piano, changed to trumpet whilst at Lincoln Elementary School in Birmingham. After leaving high school played regularly with Bama State Collegians (1932). To New York with that band in 1934, continued with that band (under Erskine Hawkins' leadership) through 1930s—left in 1944. Co-led sextet with brother Paul, then for three years they led a big band. In summer of 1947 began first of two brief spells with Duke Ellington, then led own quintet at Tyler's

Chicken Shack in New Jersey for over three years. Continued to lead own band through the 1960s, also did regular recording studio work. From 1963 made several tours of Japan with tenorist Sam Taylor; toured Europe with Buddy Tate Band in December 1968. Led own band in 1969, including dates in Toronto, Canada. Regularly with Broadway theatre orchestra (1971).

BASCOMB, Paul
tenor sax

Born: Birmingham, Alabama, 12th February 1910

One of the originators of the Bama State Collegians, which subsequently became the Erskine Hawkins Band. Whilst at college did some touring with the C. S. Belton Band out of Florida, then worked regularly with Bama State Band, moved with them to New York in 1934. Remained with Erskine Hawkins until 1944, then co-led band with his brother Dud for several years before branching out with own band. From late 1950s featured in Chicago and Detroit clubs and at Nice Festival (1978). (Recorded with Count Basie 1940 and 1941.)

BASIE, 'Count' William
piano/organ

Born: Red Bank, New Jersey, 21st August 1904
Died: Hollywood, Florida, 26th April 1984

Mother was a pianist. Bill Basie originally played drums in local kids' band. Later concentrated on piano, regular lessons from local teacher, Mrs. Holloway; some tuition from Fats Waller. Worked summers in Asbury Park, played at Leroy's in New York; briefly with June Clark's Band and Elmer Snowden. Then began long spell of touring theatres, accompanying variety acts: Kate Crippen and Her Kids, 'Hippity Hop' Show, with Sonny Thompson Band on Keith Orpheum Circuit. Two years with Gonzelle White Show, left this show in Kansas City (1927); after serious illness, began accompanying Whitman Sisters and working in local theatres. Deputised in Walter Page's Blue Devils in Dallas (July 1928) and shortly afterwards joined the band. Left Walter Page in 1929, briefly with Elmer Payne and his Ten Royal Americans (summer 1929), then joined Bennie Moten's Band. Left Moten early in 1934 to lead own band (under Moten's auspices) in Little Rock, Arkansas. Rejoined Bennie Moten and, after that leader's death in 1935, continued to work for a short time under Buster Moten's leadership. Returned to Kansas City, worked as a single, then with own trio before jointly leading Barons of Rhythm with altoist Buster Smith. Under Basie's leadership the band broadcast over Station W9XBY from their residency at Reno Club, Kansas City—from that time Bill Basie was dubbed 'Count'. John Hammond heard the band and initiated their first national tour. The band left Kansas City, took up a short residency at the Grand Terrace, Chicago, played at Vendome Hotel, Buffalo, then into Roseland, New York, in December 1936. During the following year the band was reshuffled and achieved wide success only after its January 1938 residency at Savoy Ballroom, New York. This success was consolidated during the July 1938 to January 1939 stay at The Famous Door, subsequently the band played in Chicago for six months before returning to New York, they then left for West Coast engagements in fall of 1939. Throughout the 1940s the Basie Band appeared at most of the major ballrooms and theatres throughout the U.S.A. Basie also recorded with Benny Goodman Sextet and made many solo appearances on various radio programmes. During the band's several Hollywood residencies, they were featured in many full-length films. In January 1950 Basie disbanded the big band—he began touring with a small band from April of that year. He re-formed the big band regularly in 1952, in 1954 they toured Scandinavia; again in Europe 1956. First tour of Great Britain in April 1957, they returned later that year, and since then have made regular tours of Europe. During 1963 the band toured Japan. From the mid-1960s the Basie Band did several tours (and many recordings) with various vocalists including Frank Sinatra, Tony Bennett, etc. In the mid-1970s Basie recovered from serious illness and resumed touring. He was, however, forced to play from a wheel-chair during the last years of his life.

Stanley Dance's book 'The World of Count Basie' was first published in 1980.

Films showing the Basie Band include: 'Top Man', 'Choo-Choo Swing', 'Reveille with Beverley', 'Stage Door Canteen', 'Hit Parade of 1943', 'Made in

Paris', 'Cinderfella', 'Sex and the Single Girl', 'Jamboree', 'One More Time?', 'Man of the Family'.

BASSETT, 'Rip' Arthur
banjo/guitar

Born: Chicago, Illinois, 25th October 1903

Began playing banjo in 1922; taught by Joe Ward. Did first gigs at St. Elizabeth Hall, Chicago, first professional work with Al Wynn's Paradise Night Owls in South Bend, Indiana (1924). Worked mainly with Wynn from 1924-6, then with Louis Armstrong's Stompers (co-leader Earl Hines) in 1927. With Clarence Black at the Savoy Ballroom (1929), Boyd Atkins at Sunset Cafe and touring (late 1929-30), Junie Cobb (1931), Ed Carry's Rhythm Aces (1932), Carroll Dickerson (1934-5), also with Erskine Tate, Floyd Campbell, and Tiny Parham. Retired from music and worked in a Chicago machine plant.

BATTLE, 'Puddinghead' Edgar W.
trumpet/trombone/saxes/piano/organ/ arranger/composer

Born: Atlanta, Georgia, 3rd October 1907
Died: New York, 6th February 1977

Father played bass and piano, mother was a guitarist. Began playing trumpet at the age of eight. At 14 played with J. Neal Montgomery and pianist Harvey Quiggs, during following year formed own 'Dixie Serenaders' at Morris Brown University, later worked in band, led by Eddie Heywood Sr., at theatres in Atlanta. Worked in Carnival Bands before widespread touring with Miller Brothers' 101 Ranch Show during spring and summer months, at other times in the year led own band, Dixie Ramblers. Joined Gene Coy's Band in late 1928 as trumpet soloist, then with Andy Kirk before joining Blanche Calloway (1931). Again led own band, worked in Camden, New Jersey, with Ira Coffey (late 1933), then to New York, briefly with Sam Wooding and Benny Carter in 1934. With Alex Hill, before working with Willie Bryant Band on trumpet/trombone/saxes until 1936. In 1936 appeared as a feature act in Broadway Show 'George White's Scandals'—regular broadcasts on N.B.C. Led own band again in 1937, then quit regular playing to concentrate on arranging. Did some gigs, but prolific writing for Cab Calloway, Paul Whiteman, Fats Waller Big Band, Earl Hines, Rudy Vallee, Count Basie, Jack Teagarden, Louis Prima, etc., etc. During World War II began working as an electrician in New York shipyards; later, active in music, organising U.S.O. tours, returned to work in shipyards. During the 1940s (partnered by Shirley Clay) ran own big band which did gigs in New York, in the 1950s organised own 'Cosmopolitan' Record Company which featured the work of several unjustly neglected jazz musicians. Throughout the 1960s continued to lead his own part-time big band comprised of famous veteran musicians. Prolific composer, most famous tune being 'Topsy' (Battle/Ed Durham).

BAUDUC, Ray
drums/composer

Born: New Orleans, Louisiana, 18th June 1906

Ray's brother, Jules, was a well-known New Orleans drummer—their father, Jules Sr., played trumpet. Ray took brother's place in band at Thelma Theatre, New Orleans, whilst still attending school. Later with Six Nola Jazzers, then worked at Old Absinthe House in New Orleans before touring with various bands; during this period first played with Dorsey Brothers in their Wild Canaries Band. Returned to New Orleans to join Johnny Bayersdorffer (September 1924), toured with Bayersdorffer until 1926. Then to New York with Billy Lustig's Scranton Sirens. Played in band directed by Joe Venuti before joining Fred Rich as drummer and featured dancer, toured Britain with Rich in 1927. Returned to New York, played in house band at Post Lodge, Larchmont, then took over drum-chair in Ben Pollack Band whilst the leader conducted (late 1928). With Ben Pollack until 1934, became founder-member of Bob Crosby Band in 1935. Remained with Crosby until disbanding in 1942. Service in U.S. Army Artillery Band until November 1944. Formed own big band for debut early in 1945, co-led with Gil Rodin. Following year led own septet, except for brief spell with Tommy Dorsey, August to October 1946. Rejoined Bob Crosby temporarily in February 1947. With Jimmy Dorsey Big Band from early 1948 until

1950. Free-lanced on West Coast, then with Jack Teagarden from 1952-5. Formed band with former colleague Nappy Lamare, the band enjoyed considerable success: long residencies on West Coast and national tours. Bauduc appeared in the film 'The Fabulous Dorseys'. Worked with Pud Brown (early 1960s). Lived in Bellaire, Texas during the 1970s and early 1980s.

BAUER, 'Billy' William Henry *Born: New York City, 14th November 1915*
guitar

Worked with Jerry Wald's Band in 1939, then spells with Dick Stabile and Abe Lyman. With Woody Herman (1944-46), Benny Goodman (1948), Chubby Jackson, etc. also made many records with Lennie Tristano. Regular television work in the 1950s, including staff work in Bobby Byrne's Orchestra. Played in Europe with Benny Goodman (May 1958), worked with alto saxophonist Lee Konitz often during the late 1950s and 1960s, also led own groups during this period, including long residency at Sherwood Inn, New York. During the 1970s maintained rigorous freelance schedule.

BAUZA, Mario *Born: Havana, Cuba, 28th April 1911*
trumpet/saxes/arranger

Began playing clarinet and oboe at the age of six. Regular musical work from the age of 11, played in Havana with the Romeu Orchestra and the Curbelo Orchestra. Moved to New York, gigged on clarinet and sax with Cass Carr (1931), played with Noble Sissle at Park Central Hotel in 1932, during same year also worked on trumpet and clarinet with Sam Wooding at the Lafayette. Then on trumpet with Chick Webb from 1933 until 1938. Joined Don Redman in late 1938, then with Cab Calloway from December 1939 until 1941. Free-lanced on trumpet, saxes, and clarinet before becoming musical director of Machito Orchestra.

BAYERSDORFFER, Johnny *Born: New Orleans, Louisiana, 1899*
trumpet *Died: New Orleans, Louisiana, 14th November 1969*

Formed first band whilst at Warren Easton High School, gigged with various bands before forming Jazzola Ltd. Band, then with Tony Parenti at The Cave Room, Gruenwald Hotel. In summer of 1923 worked at Arcadia Ballroom, left spring of 1924 to play summer season at Spanish Fort. Left day job with U.S. Civil Service to take own band to Chicago (October 1924), subsequently the band worked in Indianapolis and Los Angeles before returning to New Orleans. The band worked briefly under the leadership of Billy Lustig (violin); Bayersdorffer left in Chicago and free-lanced there for many years, except for spell in New York 1928. Occasionally led own bands at leading hotels, whilst with Lee Shore in 1940 seriously injured in car smash. Returned to professional music, residency at Club Flamingo, then returned to New Orleans in 1950. Played in various night clubs, then returned to government work, occasional club dates (My Oh My Club, 1957, etc.) before retirement.

BEAL, Charlie *Born: Los Angeles, California, 14th September 1908*
piano

Brother of Eddie Beal. Free-lanced in Los Angeles, then joined Les Hite (c. 1930). Moved to Chicago two years later. Did solo spot at Grand Terrace, worked with Jimmie Noone, Erskine Tate, and Frankie Jaxon (late 1932). With Louis Armstrong in spring 1933. With Carroll Dickerson, then toured with Noble Sissle before settling in New York in late 1934. Concentrated on solo work, long residencies at Adrian's Tap Room, The Onyx, Famous Door, etc., before joining Eddie South at the French Casino. Played in Canada for a while, then served in U.S. Army. Played solo residency at the Jococo Room in Los Angeles (1946), during that year also appeared with Louis Armstrong in the film 'New Orleans'. Has worked regularly in Europe from October 1948.

B

BEAL, Eddie *Born: Redlands, California, 13th June 1910*
piano

Originally a drummer, changed to piano in early 1930s. Worked with Earl Dancer, Charlie Echols, Buck Clayton (including long spell in Shanghai 1934-6). Returned to free-lance in California, regular arranging. Served in U.S. Army from 1941 until early 1943, then worked briefly as accompanist for Ivie Anderson. Own trio in Los Angeles for many years—occasionally backed Billie Holiday in California, also worked with Spirits of Rhythm. Did double-piano feature with Earl Hines in film 'The Strip'. Formed own publishing company, also worked as vocal coach. Achieved considerable success as a songwriter.

BEAN, Floyd R. *Born: Grinnell, Iowa, 30th August 1904*
piano/arranger *Died: Cedar Rapids, Iowa, 9th March 1974*

Played drums in school band, but concentrated on piano after high-school days. At 15 led own band, in early 1920s worked with Heinie Greishenback, Bill Hogan, and with Hawkeye Melody Boys at Linwood Inn, Davenport, Iowa. Later played in Cy Mahlberg's Band and Earl Hunt's Band; made his first recordings with Fred Dexter's Pennsylvanians in 1930. Moved back to Davenport in 1932, worked with Jimmy Hick's Band and spell as staffman on radio station WOC. To Chicago in late 1933, year's musical study, then with Eddie Neibauer's Seattle Harmony Kings for two years. Long spell at 3 Deuces, with Jimmy McPartland in late 1930s, then two short spells with Bob Crosby in 1939. At Silhouette Club with Boyce Brown (1940), worked with Wingy Manone later that year, then led own trio at Barrel O'Fun. Ten months with Boyd Raeburn in 1943. In 1944 led own trio at Brass Rail, then worked in Eddie Stone's Big Band until January 1945. Played second piano and arranged for Jess Stacy Band in 1945, extensive free-lancing in Chicago, worked with Paul Mares and Sidney Bechet. Regularly with Isbell Dixielanders in 1949, following year with Miff Mole, then Muggsy Spanier 1951-2, Georg Brunis 1953-7, Bob Scobey 1958, then returned to George Brunis for long spell. At Jazz Ltd. (1960) with Bill Reinhardt Band. During the late 1960s worked mainly in the Cedar Rapids Area.

BEASON, 'Bill' William *Born: Louisville, Kentucky, 1908*
drums

Played drums in Booker T. Washington Centre Band in Louisville, then attended Wilberforce University, Ohio, and there joined Horace Henderson's Collegians in 1924, worked mainly with Horace Henderson through the 1920s. Settled in New York, worked with Bingie Madison's Band 1930-1, Teddy Hill 1935-7 (including trip to Europe), Don Redman 1938 until May 1939. Briefly with Roy Eldridge then replaced Chick Webb during that drummer's last illness; continued working with Ella Fitzgerald Orchestra until the end of 1941, except for a brief period with Horace Henderson in September 1941. Worked on and off with John Kirby in 1943 and 1944, briefly with Eddie Heywood in the summer of 1944. Worked with Ben Webster at the Onyx Club, New York, early in 1945, then worked mainly with John Kirby until 1947, also worked with Sy Oliver and Earl Bostic in 1947. Has been musically inactive for many years, lives in the Bronx, New York.

BEAU 'Heinie' Heinrich John *Born: Calvary, Wisconsin, 8th March 1911*
reeds/arranger

Originally taught by his father, brothers were also musicians. After working with family band played in Milwaukee in Nick Harper's orchestra, worked with Johnny 'Scat' Davis before joining Red Nichols in spring of 1940 with Tommy Dorsey (1940-43), during this time also did brief spell with Benny Goodman in late 1942. Settled in California in 1943, prolific arranging and freelance recordings. Made many recordings with Red Nichols during the 1940s and 1950s. Visited Europe in 1978 and 1981. Continues to play regularly.

BECHET, Sidney Joseph
soprano sax/clarinet

Born: St. Antoine Street, New Orleans, Louisiana, 14th May 1897
Died: Paris, France, 14th May 1959

Youngest of seven children. One of his four brothers, Dr. Leonard V. Bechet (died: 1952), was once a professional trombonist who left music to become a dentist. Another brother, Joseph, played guitar. As a child, Bechet sat in on clarinet with Freddie Keppard and marched with Manuel Perez. Originally self-taught, later received tuition from Lorenzo Tio, Big Eye Louis Nelson, and George Baquet, occasionally subbed for Baquet at 101 Ranch. Played for a while in Silver Bells Band led by his brother, Leonard, then regular engagements with leading New Orleans Bands: Buddie Petit's Young Olympians (1909), John Robichaux's Orchestra, The Olympia (1910), The Eagle (1911-12). Also doubled at Fewclothes Cabaret with Bunk Johnson. During these early years Sidney played cornet regularly for parade work: with Allen's Band c. 1911, also with Jack Carey's Band in 1913. From 1914 until mid-1917 Bechet spent little time in New Orleans (he once estimated it as four months). He left New Orleans in the spring of 1914 with a travelling show (together with pianist Louis Wade and Clarence Williams)—Wade and Bechet cut-out in Galveston, Texas, and joined a touring carnival for two months. During his occasional trips to New Orleans he played mainly at The Claiborne Street Theatre or at St. Catherine's Hall. During 1916 he also worked with Joe Oliver at Big 25 and at Pete Lala's, at this time again did parade work on cornet. Left New Orleans permanently in summer of 1917, acting and playing in The Bruce and Bruce Touring Company through Georgia, Alabama, Ohio, and Indiana. Left in Chicago late in 1917, joined Lawrence Duhé's Band at De Luxe Cafe, later played at Dreamland and at the Monogram Theatre; worked occasionally with King Oliver. Played with Freddie Keppard at The De Luxe, doubling with Tony Jackson at The Pekin Cabaret. At about this time Bechet bought his first soprano saxophone (a curved model), he abandoned his efforts a few weeks later. Auditioned for Jim Europe's Band just prior to the leader's death. Joined Will Marion Cook's Southern Syncopated Orchestra in Chicago and journeyed with them to New York. Played with Lt. Tim Brymn's Orchestra in Coney Island, New York. Then rejoined Will Marion Cook for trip to Europe (June 1919). In London, Bechet bought his first straight-model soprano sax, shortly afterwards he was using it for feature numbers. Bechet remained in London with a breakaway unit from the Southern Syncopated Orchestra; this small band, led by drummer Benny Peyton, played at The Embassy Club and Hammersmith Palais. Moved to Paris in spring of 1920 for engagements with the Southern Syncopated Orchestra at The Apollo, etc., then back to residency at Hammersmith Palais with Benny Peyton's Jazz Kings, also played at Rector's Club in London. Deported from Great Britain, Bechet returned to New York in November 1922. Played with Ford Dabney, then acted and played in Donald Haywood's 'How Come?' Show. After touring, quit the show in New York (spring 1923), worked with Mamie Smith and various bands, then toured with Jimmy Cooper's 'Black and White Revue', then with 'Seven Eleven' Show (spring 1925). Returned to New York, worked with Duke Ellington and with James P. Johnson (temporarily at the Kentucky Club). Led own New Orleans Creole Jazz Band at the Rhythm Club, then opened own Club Basha in New York. In September 1925 left New York with the 'Revue Negre', featuring Josephine Baker (orchestra directed by Claude Hopkins). Left the show, from February until May 1926 toured Russia with band also featuring Benny Peyton and Frank Withers (trombone). After playing Moscow, the band appeared in Kiev, Kharkov, and Odessa. Bechet returned to Berlin, led own small band, then organised 14-piece orchestra for new edition of 'Revue Negre'. After touring Europe (1927), the orchestra disbanded in Munich. Bechet again led own small band, this time in Frankfurt-am-Main. Moved to Paris, joined Noble Sissle at Les Ambassadeurs Club (summer 1928)—doubling E-flat, contra-bass sax. Later that year worked at 'Chez Florence' with The International Five (a nine-piece band). Briefly with Benny Peyton (January 1929), then jailed in Paris for 11 months after being involved in a shooting incident with Gilbert McKendrick. Moved to Berlin, played residency at the Wild West Bar, Haus Vaterland, again toured with the 'Revue Negre', left the show in Amsterdam, sailed back to New York. Rejoined Noble Sissle (early 1931), left Sissle, travelled with Duke Ellington on New England tour (May 1932), then organised New Orleans Feetwarmers with Tommy Ladnier, they played at the Saratoga Club, then in White Plains, Jersey City, before opening at the Savoy, New York, in September 1932. The group disbanded early in 1933. Bechet then worked with Lorenzo Tio at the Nest Club, before joining Willie 'The Lion' Smith at Jerry Preston's Log Cabin Club. Left full-time music temporarily, together with Tommy Ladnier opened own Southern Tailor Shop in New York. Rejoined Noble Sissle in Chicago (1934), and except for short periods, remained in the band until October 1938. Played at Nick's, New York, with Zutty Singleton, fronted Spirits of Rhythm at same venue, and later led own quartet there. From January 1939 played several months at Momart Astoria in trio with Willie 'The Lion' Smith. From July-October spell at Mimo Club, New York, then from February to May 1940 at Nick's. Most of summer in Philadelphia, including concert with George Baquet 26th May 1940. From August 1940, own quintet at Enduro Restaurant, Brooklyn, New York, again at Log Cabin, Fonda (from November 1940 to February 1941), then again at the Mimo. Throughout World War II, Bechet played regularly at Nick's, Ryan's, and various other clubs in New York, also took part in several of Eddie Condon's New York Town Hall concerts. Occasionally led own quartet for residencies outside of New York: Paterson, New Jersey, Philadelphia (1943), Springfield, Illinois (1944). In January 1945 played with Louis Armstrong at a Jazz Foundation concert in New Orleans. From March 1945 led own band at the Savoy, Boston, returned to New York in January 1946, began regular guest-star appearances. Acted in five-day run of the play 'Hear That Trumpet' (October 1946). Did regular teaching in New York, led trio at Ryan's during 1947 (interrupted by an illness in summer of 1947). During 1948 made many appearances at Jazz Ltd., Chicago. Worked at Jimmy Ryan's, New York (spring 1949), to France in May 1949 for jazz festival, returned to Ryan's, Jazz Ltd., etc., returned to Europe in September 1949 (appeared briefly in London in November 1949). Returned to U.S.A. in November 1949 before working again in Europe from June to September 1950. From the summer of 1951, Bechet made his permanent home in France. He returned to the U.S.A. for various tours and guest-star bookings: late 1951, September 1953 (including first trip to San Francisco). Toured Britain in September 1956, Argentina, and Chile in spring 1957. Remained musically active until shortly before succumbing to cancer—led all-star band at the Brussels International Fair in summer of 1958. During the last years of his life he heard his extended works 'Nouvelles Orleans' and 'The Night is a Witch' in public performances. In 1955 he appeared in the French film 'Blues'.

Bechet's autobiography 'Treat It Gentle' was first published in 1960.

BECKETT, 'Fred' Frederic Lee
trombone

Born: Nellerton, Mississippi, 23rd January 1917
Died: St. Louis, Missouri, 30th January 1946

Took up trombone whilst attending high school in Tupelo, Mississippi. Moved to Kansas City, then joined Eddie Johnson's Crackerjacks in St. Louis (c. 1934). Worked with Duke Wright's Band in 1936, Buster Smith, Tommy Douglas, then briefly with Andy Kirk in 1937. With Dee 'Prince' Stewart's Band before joining Nat Towles in Omaha, returned to Kansas City and worked with Buster Smith's Band (spring 1938). With Tommy Douglas Band before joining Harlan Leonard from 1939 until September 1940, then worked with Lionel Hampton's Band until called up for Army service in 1944. Whilst in the Army he contracted tuberculosis which ultimately caused his death.

BEIDERBECKE, Leon Bix
(christened Bix *not* Bismarck)
cornet/piano/composer

Born: Davenport, Iowa, 10th March 1903
Died: Queens, New York, 6th August 1931

Mother was an amateur pianiste, father had own merchant's business in Davenport. Began playing piano at the age of three, cornet at 14—which, for at least the first eight years, he played left-handed. Played in local kids' band, Buckley's Novelty Orchestra, short spell at Terrace Gardens, Davenport. Left Tyler Grade School, Davenport, during 1918. During high-school days (1919-21) began gigging and sitting-in with various bands including: Wilbur Hatch's Quartet at Delavan Lake; Floyd Bean's Band at Linwood Inn, Davenport; Carlisle Evan's Band, and band resident at Tokyo Gardens, South Bend, Indiana. In September 1921 enrolled at Lake Forest Military Academy, near Chicago, whilst at the Academy formed the Cy-Bix Orchestra with drummer Walter 'Cy' Welge, also played in the Ten Foot Band in Chicago. Was expelled from the Academy on 22nd May

1922, returned to Davenport, then moved on to Chicago to join The Cascades Band. Played on Lake Michigan excursion boats and worked in quintet at White Lake, Michigan, during summer of 1922. Gigged in Chicago, returned to Davenport in late November 1922. Worked briefly at the Alhambra Ballroom in Syracuse, then returned to Chicago. Sat in on cornet and piano with Elmer Schoebel's Band, worked occasionally with Vic Bennings' Band at Valentine Inn and played aboard Great Lakes Steamers sailing between Michigan City and Chicago—during this period unsuccessfully auditioned for Art Brown's Novelty Band in Dubuque, Iowa. In October 1923 joined The Wolverines at in on cornet and piano with Elmer Schoebel's Band, worked occasionally with Vic Bennings' Band at Valentine Inn and played aboard Great Lakes Steamers sailing between Michigan City and Chicago—during this period unsuccessfully auditioned for Art Brown's Novelty Band in Dubuque, Iowa. In October 1923 joined The Wolverines at Stockton Club, Hamilton, Ohio, the band moved into Doyle's Dance Hall in Cincinnati, then on to Indianapolis and Chicago before returning to Doyle's. Toured through Indiana and Ohio in Summer of 1924—during this time Bix played briefly with Mezz Mezzrow at the Martinique Inn, Indiana Harbor (whilst The Wolverines were resident at Miller Beach, Gary, Indiana). After that season Bix went to Keuka Lake, Hammondsport, N.Y., for a brief holiday, then to New York City where The Wolverines commenced residency at the Cinderella Ballroom on 12th September 1924. Bix left The Wolverines in November 1924, short try-out with Jean Goldkette, then to Chicago to work for four weeks for Charlie Straight. After being fired by Straight he gigged in Chicago before spending 18 days as a student at the State University of Iowa (2nd-20th February 1925). Worked on piano and cornet before joining Frank Trumbauer in Detroit (September 1925—Trumbauer was then leading a band under the auspices of Jean Goldkette), they did the summer season of 1926 at the Blue Lantern Inn, Hudson Lake, Indiana, then Bix (and Trumbauer) worked in Jean Goldkette's Band until Goldkette temporarily disbanded in September 1927. With short-lived Adrian Rollini Big Band at New York Restaurant from September 1927, joined Paul Whiteman at the Indiana Theatre, Indianapolis (31st October 1927). Worked with Whiteman in Chicago, Toledo, Cleveland, Pittsburgh, Baltimore, New York, etc. Together with Lennie Hayton and Roy Bargy played three-piano version of own composition 'In a Mist' at Carnegie Hall (7th October 1928). Absent from Paul Whiteman through illness (November 1928 until March 1929). To California with Whiteman in May 1929, returned to New York with Whiteman, then suffered another breakdown in health in mid-September 1929. Returned to recuperate in Davenport, back to New York in spring of 1930. Did gigs and free-lance recordings, four-day try-out with the Casa Loma Band in summer of 1930. Free-lanced in New York until November 1930, then again returned to his home town, played occasionally with local bands until returning to New York in January 1931, visited Paul Whiteman in Chicago (February 1931), then to New York. Briefly held a regular job on the 'Camel Hour' radio show (orchestra directed by Charles Previn), then played at various universities, including dates at Campus Club of Princeton (1st and 2nd May 1931), Williams College (10th-11th June), on this engagement Bix took Red Nichols' place in the orchestra, which had previously been billed as a '12-piece Orchestra conducted by Red Nichols'. Sometime during the summer of 1931 Bix moved from his 44th Street Hotel apartment to rent the ground-floor apartment of a block in Queens. He was treated by a doctor during the last few days of his life; he died in the presence of the owner of the apartment, a bass-playing attorney named George Kraslow. Bix was buried at Oakdale Cemetery, Davenport. 25,000 attended the festival that commemorated the 50th anniversary of Beiderbecke's death.

'Bugles for Beiderbecke', by Charles H. Wareing and George Garlick was first published in 1958. 'Bix, Man and Legend' by Richard M. Sudhalter and Philip R. Evans was first published in 1974. A documentary film about Bix, by Canadian producer Brigitte Berman was released in 1981.

BENEKE, 'Tex' Gordon *Born: Fort Worth, Texas, 12th February 1914*
tenor sax/vocals

Began playing soprano at age of nine, worked with several territory bands before joining

Ben Young (1935-37). Featured with Glenn Miller from 1938 until late 1942 (spell as lead alto sax in 1941). Toured with The Modernaires before serving in U.S. Navy Band during World War II. After demobilisation led band billed as 'The Glenn Miller Orchestra led by Tex Beneke', this billing was soon dropped, but Beneke continued to lead a big band that heavily featured Glenn Miller's music for many years. Own band based in California.

BENFORD, 'Tommy' Thomas P. *Born: Charleston, West Virginia, 19th April 1905*
drums

His older brother, Bill, was a noted tuba player. Both received extensive musical tuition whilst at the Jenkins' Orphanage, South Carolina. Began touring with the Orphanage Band at a very early age—including tour of England in 1914. During this visit the band gave several performances in London; the tour was curtailed by the outbreak of World War I. Studied drums with Steve Wright and Herbert Wright; did first professional work in 1920 with the Green River Minstrel Show, later joined the Marie Lucas Orchestra in Washington, D.C. During the 1920s played with many bandleaders in New York including: Elmer Snowden, Charlie Skeet, Jelly Roll Morton, Edgar Hayes, Bill Benford's Orchestra, etc., also subbed for a month with Duke Ellington. During the 1930s worked for several years in Europe with: Eddie South, Freddy Taylor, Garland Wilson, Sy Devereaux, etc., prolific free-lance recordings. With Willie Lewis from 1938, remained in Europe with Lewis until September 1941. With Noble Sissle (in U.S.A.) in 1943, with Snub Mosley (1946-8), Bob Wilbur (late 1948-9), Jimmy Archey (1950-2), etc. During the 1950s played for Rex Stewart (1953), Muggsy Spanier, subbed in George Lewis Band in 1955, also did residencies at Central Plaza and Jimmy Ryan's, New York. Worked with Freddy Johnson in 1959, during the following year went to Europe with the 'Jazz Train Revue' (musical director: Eddie Barefield). From 1956-9 did regular summer seasons with Leroy Parkins and Bob Pilsbury Bands. Worked with trumpeter Joe Thomas (1963), Ed Hall (1963), Danny Barker (1963), the 'Saints and Sinners', etc. Has left full-time music, but continues to play regular week-end gigs, during December 1968 worked in New York with Franz Jackson. Extensive touring with Clyde Bernhardt's Band during the 1970s, also played many free-lance dates. Toured with the Harlem Blues and Jazz Band (1981), worked with Bob Greene's Band in Europe (1982).

BENJAMIN, 'Joe' Joseph Rupert *Born: Atlantic City, New Jersey, 4th November 1919*
bass/arranger/composer *Died: Livingstone, New Jersey, 26th January 1974*

Studied violin and cello before specialising on string bass. Worked as a music-copyist for various arrangers before playing professionally. With Mercer Ellington (1946-47), Billy Taylor Quartet (1950), Fletcher Henderson, (summer 1950), Artie Shaw (1950). In early 1951 worked with Duke Ellington—the first of many occasions that he worked in Duke's Band. With Slim Gaillard (1951), Sarah Vaughan (1953-55). Toured Europe with Gerry Mulligan (1957). Worked with pianist Ellis Larkins (1958), two months with Dave Brubeck in 1958. During the late 1950s, 1960s, and early 1970s undertook strenuous free-lance schedule, playing in several long-running Broadway shows, and took part in many recording sessions. Was in an auto crash after playing an engagement with Duke Ellington at the Rainbow Grill in New York City (January 1974); died a month later from heart failure.

BERIGAN, 'Bunny' Rowland Bernart *Born: Hilbert, Calumet, Wisconsin, 2nd November 1908*
trumpet/vocals *Died: New York City, 2nd June 1942*

Brother Don was a drummer, their mother played piano. Bunny began on violin, then switched to trumpet (continued to double until 1927). At 13 played locally with Merrill Owen and his Pennsy Jazz Band; during the early 1920s sat in with the New Orleans Rhythm Kings in Wisconsin. Though not a student at the University of Wisconsin, he played regularly in the college dance bands throughout his teens. Played in local bands including those led by Jesse Cohen and Cy Mahlberg (1926). Resident at The Chanticleer Ballroom in Madison with local leaders, then played in New York and Philadelphia

(1928). Returned to Wisconsin before making another trip to New York to play with violinist Frank Cornwell's Band at The Hofbrau (early 1929), again returned home before journeying again to New York to join Hal Kemp at the Hotel Taft in the spring of 1930. With Hal Kemp in Europe from May until September 1930. Returned to U.S. and began free-lancing in New York prior to joining Fred Rich Orchestra, during the early 1930s extensive studio work including radio and recording sessions with Benny Krueger, Ben Selvin, etc. Worked in Dorsey Brothers' Band for Broadway Show 'Everybody Welcome' (1931), doubled studio work and free-lance work until spending summer season with Smith Ballew. Joined Paul Whiteman from late 1932 until late 1933, a month with Abe Lyman, then C.B.S. studio work and occasional gigs with the Dorseys, Benny Goodman, etc. Regularly with Benny Goodman from June until September 1935, left Goodman in California, home to Wisconsin, then back to New York to resume at C.B.S. studios. Active as A.R.C. staff man during 1936, combining this with short spells with Red McKenzie, Red Norvo, Ray Noble, and leading own pick-up bands. C.B.S. work in early 1937, recording work with Tommy Dorsey, then from spring 1937 leading own big band, bankruptcy eventually caused disbandment in spring of 1940. With Tommy Dorsey from March until August 1940, then formed own small band for residency at 47 Club, New York. Soon reverted to leading a big band, extensive touring and summer 1941 residency in Columbus, Ohio. To Hollywood in late 1941 to record part of soundtrack for the film 'Syncopation' (sharing trumpet work with George Thow), then returned to big band until contracting pneumonia in April 1942. Left hospital on 8th May 1942, continued one-nighters until 30th May. Suffered a severe haemorrhage and was admitted to the New York Polyclinic Hospital where he died three days later.

BERNARDI, 'Noni' Ernani *Born: Standard, Illinois, 29th October 1911*
alto sax/clarinet/arranger

First musical tuition from his father. First professional work in 1928, with Hank Biagini (1928), Casa Loma Orchestra (1931), Joe Haymes (1934), Tommy Dorsey (1935), Bob Crosby (1936-37). Worked on Detroit radio WWJ then joined Jimmy Dorsey (1937). With Benny Goodman (1938), studio work in New York (1939), then to California with Kay Kyser (1940), was Kyser's musical director until 1945. Briefly led own band at Aragon Ballroom Los Angeles. Left to form own building company, became a Councilman for Los Angeles in 1961, and served for over 20 years.

BERNHARDT, Clyde Edric Barron *Born: Goldhill, North Carolina, 11th July 1905*
trombone/vocals

Family moved to Harrisburg, Pennsylvania, in 1919. Clyde began playing trombone in 1922, soon afterwards did a summer season with Sammy Scott's Band, moved to Columbus, Ohio, then back to Harrisburg in 1924. Worked with local bands and received tuition from Meredith German. Moved to New York in 1928, gigged with several leaders before joining Ray Parker's Band at Shadowland, New York, later worked with Honey Brown's Orchestra at the Bamboo Inn (late 1929). Worked with King Oliver from March until November 1931, then joined Marion Hardy's Alabamians for 18 months. In Camden, New Jersey, with Ira Coffey's Walkathons (autumn 1933). With Vernon Andrade's Orchestra from January 1934 until February 1937; immediately joined Edgar Hayes, and remained with Hayes until August 1941 (including trip to Europe in 1938). Briefly with Horace Henderson in September 1941, then rejoined Edgar Hayes' Band until they disbanded in 1942. Toured with Fats Waller for two months, then worked for a year with Jay McShann from July 1942. With Cecil Scott at the Ubangi Club, New York, before touring with Luis Russell until October 1944. In 1945 with Claude Hopkins at the Zanzibar, New York, then worked with Dud Bascomb's Band. Has made several recordings under the name of Ed Barron. Led own band during the 1950s, continues to free-lance, worked with Joe Garland's Band in the 1960s. Led his own band in U.S.A. and Europe during the 1970s. Featured with The Legends of Jazz during the early 1980s.

B

BERNSTEIN, 'Artie' Arthur
string bass

Born: Brooklyn, New York, 3rd February 1909
Died: Los Angeles, California, 4th January 1964

His brother was a double bassist with the New York Philharmonic. Began playing cello at an early age; did first professional work as a cellist playing in a ship's orchestra on cruise to South America. Qualified as an attorney-at-law at New York University, but after changing to string bass in December 1929 decided to become a professional musician. Freelanced in New York City, and made record debut with Ben Pollack (2nd March 1931). Worked with Red Nichols at Park Central Hotel, New York (summer 1931), then regular studio work with the Dorsey Brothers, Lenny Hayton, Victor Young, etc. (1933-4). Visited Europe for a holiday in 1935, then resumed studio work in New York until joining Benny Goodman from May 1939 until May 1941. Moved to California in 1941 and became staff musician at film studios. Served as a musician in U.S.A.A.F. during World War II, in 1946 resumed work as a studio musician, worked for Universal, then joined Warner Brothers' Studio staff until 1963.

BERRY, 'Chu' Leon
tenor sax

Born: Wheeling, West Virginia, 13th September 1910
Died: Conneaut, Ohio, 30th October 1941

Came from a musical family; his brother, Nelson, is a tenor sax player. Took up sax after hearing Coleman Hawkins playing on a Fletcher Henderson summer tour. Played alto sax at high school, and later, during his three years at West Virginia State College, played alto and tenor with Edwards' Collegians, also worked with Perry Smith and with Fleming Huff in Ohio. Was offered a career as a professional footballer, but decided on music. Whilst with Edwards' Collegians in Bluefield, West Virginia, was sent for by Sammy Stewart. Travelled to join the band in Columbus, Ohio (1929). At the time of his joining he sported a goatee beard and moustache, lead alto Billy Stewart began calling him 'Chu-Chin-Chow', this was later shortened to 'Chu'. (In the late 1930s a photograph was published showing 'Chu' wearing a sweater clearly marked 'Chew'—it is impossible to ascertain whether Leon or the knitter decided on this change of spelling.) 'Chu' travelled to New York with the Sammy Stewart Band for their Savoy Ballroom residency (February-April 1930), he left the band later that year at the Arcadia Ballroom. During the early 1930s worked short spells with several bandleaders including: Cecil Scott, Otto Hardwick (at the Hot Feet Club), Kaiser Marshall, Walter Pichon, and Earl Jackson's Band at the Lennox Club. With Benny Carter in summer of 1932, and again in 1933, also with Charlie Johnson late 1932 to early 1933. Joined Teddy Hill's Band and remained until late 1935. Became a regular member of Fletcher Henderson's Band in late 1935, but had previously worked for Henderson on broadcasts and other dates from the spring of 1934. Left Fletcher Henderson to join Cab Calloway in July 1937. Remained with Calloway until the time of his death (other than absence for a tonsillectomy in June 1939). After playing a one-nighter with Cab in Brookfield, Ohio, 'Chu', Andy Brown, and Lammar Wright set out by car for the next night's venue in Toronto, Ontario. Near Conneaut, Ohio, the car skidded on the road and hit a concrete bridge, Brown and Wright were only slightly hurt, but 'Chu' received severe head injuries. He died four days later without regaining consciousness.

BERRY, Emmett
trumpet

Born: Macon, Georgia, 23rd July 1915

Raised in Cleveland, Ohio; began gigging with local bands, then joined J. Frank Terry's Chicago Nightingales in Toledo, Ohio (1932), left Terry in Albany, New York, in 1933 and gigged mainly in that area during the following three years. Joined Fletcher Henderson in late 1936, and remained until Fletcher disbanded in June 1939. With Horace Henderson until October 1940, briefly with Earl Hines, then with Teddy Wilson's Sextet from May 1941 until July 1942, then joined Raymond Scott at C.B.S. With Lionel Hampton from spring of 1943, week with Teddy Wilson in August 1943, briefly with Don Redman and Benny Carter, then again rejoined Teddy Wilson c. November 1943. With John Kirby Sextet from summer 1944 until January 1945, Eddie Heywood, February until October 1945, then joined Count Basie. Left Basie in 1950, worked with Jimmy Rushing, then with

Johnny Hodges' Band from March 1951 until 1954. In 1955 with Earl Hines and Cootie Williams' Big Band, then from November 1955 until May 1956 toured Europe with Sam Price's Bluesicians. Briefly with Illinois Jacquet, also took part in Henderson Reunion Band in July 1957, toured Europe with Buck Clayton in 1959 and 1961. Worked mainly in Los Angeles 1962-5, then prolific free-lance activities in New York, brief spells with various small bands including Peanuts Hucko (1966), Wilbur de Paris (1967), etc. During the late 1960s has played several times in Toronto, Canada. with Big Chief Russell Moore (1968), Buddy Tate (1969). Moved to Cleveland (1970). Musically inactive during the 1970s.

BERTON 'Vic'
(real name: Victor Cohen)
drums/percussion/vibes

Born: Chicago, Illinois, 6th May 1896
Died: California, 26th December 1951

Brother of jazz writer and drummer Ralph Berton; their father was professional violinist. Vic began on violin and piano, but by the age of seven was playing drums in the pit orchestra at the Alhambra Theatre, Milwaukee. Extensive studies on tympani, and at 16 appeared with Milwaukee and Chicago Symphony Orchestras. Played in Sousa's U.S. Navy Band during World War I, after demobilisation played at Weiss's Cafe in Chicago (c. 1920). Worked with Art Kahn, Paul Beise, and Arnold Johnson, led own band at Merry Gardens, Chicago. In 1924 took over managership of The Wolverines, and occasionally played with the band. With Roger Wolfe Kahn until June 1926, then joined Don Voorhees (occasionally working under Red Nichols' leadership). Prolific free-lance recordings. Briefly with Paul Whiteman in spring of 1927, then free-lanced in New York before moving to California, worked with Abe Lyman. From c. 1930 worked for many years at Paramount Studios, including spell as a musical director during the mid-1930s, also appeared regularly as percussionist with the Los Angeles Philharmonic Orchestra. Studio musician for Twentieth Century-Fox during the 1940s.

BERTRAND, 'Jimmy' James
drums/xylophone/washboard

Born: Biloxi, Mississippi, 24th February 1900
Died: Chicago, Illinois, August 1960

Was a cousin of Andrew Hilaire and of trombonist George Filhe; his uncle, Alphonse Farzan, played string bass for a while with the Original Creole Band. Jimmy moved to Chicago in 1913, studied with Erskine Tate's father, Bill Cussack, Roy Knapp, and Art Layfield. Played in the orchestra at the State Theatre, Chicago, before working with Erskine Tate from 1918 until 1928. Did extensive teaching during 1920s, his pupils included Lionel Hampton and Big Sid Catlett. Led own recording band in the 1920s. Joined Dave Peyton in June 1928 for several months, then worked briefly with Tiny Parham before playing at Harmon's Dreamland with Doc Cooke and J. Pasquall. Led own band, also with Lee Collins, Junie Cobb, Roy Palmer, etc. With Eddie South (including trip to California in late 1932), with Reuben Reeves (late 1934), worked with Walter Barnes, c. 1938. Led own band in 1930s and early 1940s, including residency at the Firehouse Club (1940-1). Left full-time music in 1944 to work in meat-packing plant, continued to gig in the Chicago area until 1945.

BESS, Druie R.
trombone

Born: Montgomery City, Missouri, 24th July 1906

His father, Frank Bess, played trombone and cornet. Started on trombone at the age of nine—lessons from his father and Ed Duncan. From August 1911 played summer shows and picnics (with his father) in Tom Howard's Band. Left home with the Dandy Dixie Minstrel Band in 1921, later that year joined Herbert's Minstrels for two years, then worked in R. M. Harvey's Minstrels (1923-4). In 1925 played in the Newway Jazz Hounds in St. Joseph, Missouri, then with Jesse Stone's Blues Serenaders (1926-7) before joining Chauncey Downs in Kansas City (1927). With Bill Lewis' Dixie Ramblers in Muskogee, Oklahoma (1929), then with Walter Page's Blue Devils from late 1929 until 1931, with Blue Devils until 1933, then with Grant Moore-Pettiford Orchestra in Minneapolis (1933-4).

Moved to St. Louis, with Eddie Randle's Blue Devils 1935-8. During 1939 gigged with Eddie Johnson, Dewey Jackson, and bassist Cecil Scott, then worked on riverboats (and in Pittsburgh) with Fate Marable (1940). With Jeter-Pillars Orchestra 1941-4, then toured with Earl Hines (1944-6). Again with Eddie Johnson (1947), then toured with Ringling Brothers' Circus Band (1948) before returning to St. Louis. Worked with Joe Smith's Dixielanders and with Singleton Palmer during the early 1950s, then free-lanced. Local gigs during 1960s. Played on Streckfus excursion boat 'Admiral' (October 1971).

BEST, 'Johnny' John McClanlan *Born: Shelby, North Carolina, 20th October 1913*
trumpet

Started on trumpet in 1926. Did first gigs in summer of 1928; led own band at high school 1929-30. Following year went to Davidson College, played in College Dance Band, then studied at the University of North Carolina. In May 1932, joined the Duke Blue Devils for six months, then played with the University of N.C. Dance Band until joining Hank Biagnini from autumn 1933 until spring 1934. Returned to N.C. University and joined Les Brown until summer of 1936, then moved to Chicago. Briefly with Charlie Barnet, then joined Artie Shaw in April 1937. Rejoined Shaw in April 1938, left to work with Glenn Miller from September 1939 until September 1942. Served in U.S. Navy, played in Artie Shaw's Naval Band, then played in Europe with Sam Donahue's Navy Band (1944). After demobilisation, with Benny Goodman from November 1945 until November 1946, then became studio musician in Hollywood. With Benny Goodman again 1947 (also in the film 'The Benny Goodman Story'—1955). Did studio work in the late 1940s and 1950s—regular work with Bob Crosby, Billy May, Jerry Gray, etc., and prolific free-lance recordings. Toured with Billy May in 1953. During the late 1950s and 1960s worked five nights a week at the Honeybucket Club in San Diego, combining this with free-lance recording work. In late 1964 toured Japan with re-formed Bob Crosby Bob-Cats. Extensive free-lance playing during the 1970s, including tours of Europe. Suffered a disastrous fall whilst working on own avocado farm (1982), but recovered to play gigs from a wheel-chair in 1983.

BIGARD, 'Barney' Albany Leon *Born: Villere Street, New Orleans, Louisiana, 3rd March 1906*
clarinet/tenor sax *Died: Culver City, California, 27th June 1980*

Brother of drummer Alex (1898-1978); their uncle, Emil, was a noted New Orleans violinist. The Bigard brothers are cousins of Natty Dominique. Started on E-flat clarinet at the age of seven, lessons from Lorenzo Tio Jr. First worked as a photo-engraver, did some parade work on clarinet, but began specialising on tenor sax. In late 1922 joined Albert Nicholas Band at Tom Anderson's Cabaret, in the following year worked with Oke Gaspard's Band at the Moulin Rouge. Left in the summer of 1923, played briefly with Amos White at the Spanish Fort, before returning to work for Albert Nicholas and Luis Russell at Tom Anderson's Cabaret. To Chicago in late 1924 to join King Oliver, after two months with Dave Peyton joined King Oliver for residency at The Plantation, playing tenor until Darnell Howard left the band, from then on specialised on clarinet. Left Chicago with King Oliver in April 1927, played in St. Louis and New York, then after a brief tour left Oliver to join Charlie Elgar at the Eagle Ballroom in Milwaukee (summer 1927). Returned to New York to join Luis Russell for two months, then joined Duke Ellington in December 1927. Remained with Duke until June 1942 (except for brief absence in summer of 1935). Left in California, formed own small band in August 1942, disbanded to join Freddie Slack in November 1942, left in summer of 1943, did some studio work including soundtrack for 'I Dood It' film, then formed own small band for Los Angeles residencies. Led own small band at Onyx in New York, autumn 1944 until early 1945. Returned to Los Angeles, did film-studio work and led own small band in L.A. Played regularly with Kid Ory during 1946, and also took part in filming of 'New Orleans'. Joined Louis Armstrong for debut of the All Stars in August 1947, remained with Louis until the summer of 1952. Returned to West Coast, some free-lancing and leading own small band, then rejoined Louis Armstrong in spring 1953 until August 1955. Led own small band, then spell with Ben Pollack's Band (late 1956), also some studio work including appearance in the film 'St. Louis Blues'. On tour with Cozy Cole's Band from November 1958 until March 1959.

Spell in New Orleans Creole Jazz Band, then led own band at Ben Pollack's Club before playing again with Louis Armstrong's All Stars from April 1960 until September 1961. Joined Johnny St. Cyr's 'Young Men of New Orleans' playing at Disneyland, worked briefly with Muggsy Spanier in San Francisco during the autumn of 1962. Since then has left full-time music, plays mainly in and around Los Angeles, did some gigs with Rex Stewart in 1966 and 1967 and appeared with Art Hodes on Chicago television (February 1968). Recovered from cataract operation (1971) and toured with Hodes, Eddie Condon, Wild Bill Davison (October 1971). Played many festival dates in U.S.A. and in Europe during the 1970s. Toured Europe with Pelican Trio in summer of 1978.

BINYON, Larry — *Born: Cicero, Illinois, 5th July 1908*
tenor sax/clarinet/flute

Played in the University of Illinois Band. First worked with Ben Pollack in Chicago (1927). Regularly with Pollack from July 1928 until June 1930, left to join Red Nichols' Band for the Broadway Show 'Girl Crazy'. Then joined Victor Young studio staff—worked in the Dorsey Brothers' Band for radio and recording work through the early 1930s. Continued to play in New York radio studios until 1946 including long spell as a band organiser. Moved to California, became recording contractor for Local 47; continued to play regularly until 1955 including leading own 20-piece band during the early 1950s for a tour of the Orient playing for U.S. Servicemen.

BIONDI, 'Ray' Remo — *Born: Cicero, Illinois, 5th July 1905*
guitar/violin/trumpet/mandolin — *Died: Chicago, Illinois, 28th January 1981*

Studied violin from childhood, taught by Herbert Butler and Scott Willits of the American Conservatory in Chicago. From the age of 12 began doubling on mandolin, then played guitar and trumpet, worked mainly on violin during early career. High school in Cicero, then studied briefly at the University of Chicago. First professional work with the Blanche Jaros Orchestra in Cicero (c. late 1926). Played mainly in Chicago from 1927 until 1935, worked with Wingy Manone, Danny Alvin, Bud Freeman, Charles Brickner, Don Carter, Danny Altier, Benny Meroff, Henry Busse, Jules Stein, etc. On trumpet and violin with Earl Burtnett's Band (1935) in Chicago, Kansas City, Cincinnati, etc. To New York in 1936 to join Joe Marsala, played trumpet and violin with Marsala and guitar during Eddie Condon's absence. Left in April 1938 to join Gene Krupa on guitar, remained with Krupa until 1945—worked on violin in Gene's 1944 Orchestra. Returned to Chicago in 1945, gigged with small groups and played residency at 606 Club, opened own short-lived club in 1949. Toured with Gene Krupa in 1950-1, then settled in Chicago. Free-lanced on guitar and mandolin, prolific recording activities with Ray Anthony, Louis Armstrong, Woody Herman, Wayne King, vocalist Pat Boone, The Crew Cuts, etc., etc. From 1961 has been active as a teacher of guitar, mandolin, and violin. During the early 1960s did out-of-town gigs with orchestras led by Bobby Christian and Dick Schory; from 1966 week-end gigs in Chicago with Art Hodes, clarinettist Jimmie Granata, etc.

BISHOP, Joe — *Born: Monticello, Arkansas, 27th November 1907*
flugel horn/tuba/arranger/composer — *Died: Houston, Texas, 12th May 1976*

Studied at Hendrix College, Conway, Arkansas. Started on piano in early childhood, then played trumpet and tuba. Worked on tuba with the Louisiana Ramblers in Nuevo Laredo, Mexico, during summer of 1927, then on mellophone with Mart Britt's Band. Tuba with Al Katz and Austin Wylie (1930), then five years with Isham Jones before becoming a founder-member of the Woody Herman Band in 1936. Played flugel horn and arranged for Woody until contracting tuberculosis in September 1940. Returned to work as staff arranger for Woody Herman in 1942, then free-lance arranging. Again seriously ill in 1951, retired from music to run own store in Saranac Lake, New York. Composed: 'Blue Prelude', 'Midnight Blue', etc., also recorded with Cow Cow Davenport and Jimmy Gordon's Vip Vop Band (May 1938).

B

BISHOP, 'Bish' Wallace Henry *Born: Chicago, Illinois, 17th February 1906*
drums

Attended Wendell Phillips High School. Took up drums in early 1920s, became drum-major of the *Chicago Defender's* Boys' Band, later studied with Jimmy Bertrand. First gigs at a small cabaret club in Chicago called the Hunky London. First professional work with Art Simms' Orchestra at Wisconsin Roof Gardens in Milwaukee (1926), subsequently toured with Jelly Roll Morton and worked with Oscar 'Bernie' Young and Hughie Swift before joining Erskine Tate from 1928 until 1930. Briefly with pianist Jerome Carrington, then with Earl Hines from 1931 until August 1937. With Jimmie Noone Quartet (summer 1941), Coleman Hawkins Septet (1943), Don Redman, Walter 'Foots' Thomas in 1944, then with Phil Moore Band in New York (November 1944-5). With John Kirby early in 1946, then Sy Oliver Band (1946-7), with Billy Kyle Sextet in late 1947. Sailed to Europe with Buck Clayton on 24th September 1949, toured with Buck in Europe and has lived in Europe ever since (except for brief return to U.S.A. with pianiste Pia Beck and visits in 1970 and 1978). Has worked with all-star groups in Europe, with Bill Coleman, Don Byas, Ben Webster, etc., in late 1956 replaced ailing Minor Hall in Kid Ory's Band, played dates with Ory in Sweden and Germany. From 1959 until 1963 played residencies in Switzerland and toured Europe with pianist Fritz Tripple's Trio. During the 1960s has lived at Soest, near Amsterdam. Continues to play regularly, toured with Earl Hines and Milt Buckner in 1967 and 1968, also toured with T-Bone Walker in 1968. Regular playing during the 1970s.

'The Wallace Bishop Story' by Kleinhout & Van Eyle first published 1981.

BIVONA, Gus *Born: New London, Connecticut, 25th November 1915*
clarinet/alto sax/flute

Mother was a pianiste, father a guitarist. Started on violin at the age of 10, alto and clarinet at 16. Went to school in Stamford, Connecticut, first jobs with a coloured band led by Spider Johnson. In 1932 toured New England in Leo Scalzi's Brunswick Orchestra, then worked with Frank Dailey in Connecticut. Moved to New York, long spell with Jimmy Monaco Orchestra (1935), then joined Hudson-de Lange Orchestra (1936 to late 1937), several months with Bunny Berigan, then joined Will Hudson in June 1938. With Teddy Powell 1939 to early 1940, led own band in Larchmont, New York, and Westchester Post Lodge. With Benny Goodman from October 1940 until April 1941, then joined Jan Savitt. Briefly with Les Brown, then served in U.S. Navy—led own Naval Air Force Band. After demobilisation played with Tommy Dorsey (1945), Bob Crosby (1946), and again with Tommy Dorsey (1947). Joined M.G.M. studio staff in Hollywood in 1947. Regular studio work and free-lance recordings during the 1950s, worked regularly with actor-pianist Steve Allen, and played residency in New York with him. Continued session work in the 1960s and 1970s, also led own band in California.

BLACK, 'Lou' Louis Thomas *Born: Rock Island, Illinois, 8th June 1901*
banjo *Died: Rock Island, Illinois, 18th November 1965*

Began playing banjo during early childhood. Became professional in 1917, played regularly with local bands. In 1919 joined band led by pianist Carlisle Evans on S.S. 'Capitol', left in 1921 to join the New Orleans Rhythm Kings at Friars' Inn, Chicago. Left the N.O.R.K. in late 1923, worked with the Original Memphis Melody Boys, then made brief return to Carlisle Evans' Band. From 1925 until 1931 was a staff musician on radio WHO in Des Moines, Iowa. Left music in the 1930s, but began playing again in 1961. In 1963 sat in with several bands during a brief stay in New York, then played gigs in Moline, Illinois, from autumn of 1963. Early in November 1965 he was injured in a car crash, whilst recuperating in hospital he suffered a fatal heart attack.

BLAIR, Lee L. *Born: Savannah, Georgia, 10th October 1903*
banjo/guitar *Died: New York, 15th October 1966*

Throughout his life played left-handed. Mostly self-taught, few lessons from Paul Whiteman's banjoist Mike Pingitore. First professional work with Charlie Skeets in New York (c. 1926-8), in 1928 played at Rose Danceland with Jelly Roll Morton. During the next two years recorded and toured with Morton. With band led by trombonist Billy Kato in 1928 and 1930-1. Joined Luis Russell in 1934, remained to work under Louis Armstrong until May of 1940. Long spell of part-time music, then regularly with Wilbur de Paris in the 1950s (including tour of Africa in 1957). Continued to run own chicken farm near New York during the 1960s, but did regular gigs in New York City. Briefly rejoined Wilbur de Paris in summer of 1964, then worked in pianist Jimmy Greene's house-group at Tobin's, New York, and led own small group. In 1964 played at New York World's Fair in banjo trio with Danny Barker, Eddie Gibbs, and pianist Orville Brown.

BLAKE, 'Eubie' James Hubert
piano/composer

Born: Baltimore, Maryland, 7th February 1883
Died: Brooklyn, New York, 12th February 1983

Began playing organ during early childhood, during his teens played in local 'sporting-house' and at 'rent-parties', began composing before the turn of the century. In 1901 toured for a while with a medicine show, then worked as accompanist for Madison Reed. Worked mainly at the Goldfield Hotel, Baltimore, from 1907 until 1915, then whilst playing at River View Park, began long association with Noble Sissle. They moved together to New York and worked as partners for many years: composing, in vocal-piano duo, and as joint orchestra leaders. Together they wrote and produced 'Shuffle Along' (1921), they appeared in Europe; returned to New York (April 1926). Blake remained in U.S.A. when Sissle returned to Europe. During the late 1920s and early 1930s wrote for many shows, revues, etc., ranging from the 'Blackbirds' to Olsen and Johnson's 'Atrocities of 1932'. Resumed partnership with Noble Sissle; in World War II they toured with own show for the U.S.O. Though professionally inactive from 1946, he appeared occasionally on television shows with Noble Sissle and made several concert appearances. Was featured with great success at the New Orleans Jazz Fest in June 1969, and at festivals in Southern California (1971) and Newport (July 1971). Compositions include: 'Memories of You', 'I'm Just Wild About Harry', 'You're Lucky to Me', etc. Was featured at many jazz festivals during the 1970s, both in the U.S.A. and Europe. Honorary Doctorate of Music 1974. Played at President Jimmy Carter's White House Jazz Party (June 1978). 'Eubie', a show based on Blake's music opened in New York in 1978. Blake received the Presidential Medal of Honor in 1981.

BLAKE, Jerry
(real name: Jacinto Chabania)
saxes/clarinet/arranger/vocals

Born: Gary, Indiana, 23rd January 1908
Died: c. 1961

School in Nashville, Tennessee. Started on violin, then alto sax and clarinet, tuition from Lt. Eugene Mikell Sr. Joined Sells-Floto Circus Band in 1924, left in Chicago and joined Al Wynn's Band, subsequently worked for four months with Bobby Lee in Philadelphia, briefly with Charlie Turner's Arcadians, then sailed to Europe with Sam Wooding in June 1928. Left Wooding in Europe c. November 1929 and returned to New York. Spell with Chick Webb, then toured in Zach Whyte's Chocolate Beau Brummels. With Don Redman from late 1933 until late spring 1934, then sailed to Europe to join Willie Lewis. Returned to New York c. May 1935. Worked with Claude Hopkins, then joined Fletcher Henderson in late 1936. Left in April 1938 to join Cab Calloway as musical director. Remained with Cab until June 1942, briefly with Count Basie (June 1942), Earl Hines (September 1942), Lionel Hampton (February 1943), Don Redman (1943). Suffered mental breakdown and spent many years in a sanatorium, where he died c. 1961.

BLAKENEY, Andrew
trumpet

Born: Quitman, Mississippi, 10th June 1898

From the late 1920s worked in California—had previously played in Chicago with King Oliver for two weeks in 1925. With Les Hite (c. 1930), later with Charlie Echols, then worked in Honolulu, Hawaii, for several years—from 1935-9 with drummer Monk McFay and his Five Clouds, later led own band. Returned to the U.S.A. (c. 1941), led own band, then replaced Mutt Carey in Kid Ory's Band during summer of 1947. Led own band at Beverley Cavern (1949), then led for further residencies in California including long spell at the 400 Club, Los Angeles. Played in the 'Young Men of New Orleans' in 1960, then again led own band. Appeared in the Warner Brothers' film 'Hotel' (1966). In the late 1960s played residency at the Roaring Twenties Club in Downey, California. Toured Europe with 'The Legends of Jazz' during the 1970s, continued to play gigs during the early 1980s.

BLAKEY, Art *Born: Pittsburgh, Pennsylvania, 11th October 1919*
(chosen name: Abdullah Ibn Buhaina)
drums

Worked in steel mills as a youth, played piano at night in local clubs. Switched to drums and worked with several bands in and around Pittsburgh before moving to New York, worked with Mary Lou Williams (1942). Joined Fletcher Henderson in early 1943 for a year, then led own band in Boston before joining Billy Eckstine's Big Band in 1944. After leaving Eckstine in 1947 led own group and played on many free-lance recording dates, also stints with Lucky Millinder & Buddy De Franco. Formed Jazz Messengers in 1955, and has led that group ever since, many international tours. In 1971-72 temporarily disbanded for The Giants of Jazz tour with Dizzy Gillespie, Thelonious Monk, etc.

BLAND, Jack *Born: Sedalia, Missouri, 8th May 1899*
guitar/banjo

Played in St. Louis in the early 1920s, then together with Red McKenzie (q.v.) and kazoo-player Dick Slavin founded the 'novelty' jazz trio which was later known as The Mound City Blue Blowers. Their first recording, 'Arkansas Blues' (February 1924), was an instant commercial success, and later that year—with Ed Lang added—they played in England. Bland continued to work with the M.C.B.B. until the early 1930s. Free-lanced in New York for many years, led own trio at Billingsley's Club, New York (1940 to early 1941), also recorded with George Wettling in 1940. Briefly with Marty Marsala (1942). With Art Hodes in Lawrence, Massachusetts and New York (1943-4), then led own group at 51 Club, New York (1944). Retired from full-time music and moved to Los Angeles.

BLANTON, 'Jimmy' James *Born: Chattanooga, Tennessee, October 1918*
string bass *Died: Los Angeles, California, 30th July 1942*

His mother was a pianiste, who led her own band in Tennessee for many years. Jimmy started on violin during early childhood, did first gig at a local store, at the age of eight. Studied theory with an uncle, who specialised in teaching the mathematical aspects of music. Switched to string bass whilst studying at Tennessee State College, played in the State Collegians and gigged with local bands led by 'Bugs' Roberts and drummer Joe Smith. During college summer vacations played with Fate Marable on the riverboats, left college during his third year and moved to St. Louis. Joined Jeter-Pillars Orchestra in late 1937 (playing a three-string bass), continued to work in Fate Marable's Cotton Pickers during summer months. In autumn 1939, whilst playing at the Coronado Hotel Ballroom, St. Louis, was signed by Duke Ellington, bought a four-string bass on hire-purchase (guarantor Gene Porter) and began working with Duke (sharing bass duties with Billy Taylor until Taylor left in January 1940). Whilst working with Duke Ellington in Los Angeles was taken seriously ill (entered Los Angeles Hospital in late 1941, where tuberculosis was diagnosed). In the spring of 1942 was moved from the hospital to the Duarte Sanitarium, near Los Angeles, where he spent the last few months of his life.

BLOOM, 'Mickey' Milton *Born: New York City, 26th August 1906*
trumpet/mellophone *Died: Florida, 11th October 1979*

Brother of pianist-composer Rube Bloom (1902-1976). Started on the bugle, and then switched to trumpet—tuition from Max Schlossberg. Left high school to tour in show featuring comedian George Jessel, then with St. Louis Five until 1923. Subsequently joined the Georgia Melodians. From late 1924 until 1927 was with Irving Aaronson, including two trips to Europe. Did theatre work in New York with Walt Rosner, Vincent Lopez, and George Olson, then worked in Florida and New York with Hal Kemp. Toured Europe with Hal Kemp in 1930. During the early 1930s with Hal Kemp, Andre Kostelanetz, the Dorsey Brothers, then regularly with vocalist Rudy Vallee from 1933 until 1935. Briefly with Ray Noble, then rejoined Hal Kemp late 1935 until 1939. Did studio work in New York, then served in U.S. forces during World War II, after demobilisation resumed studio work. During the 1950s, and 1960s has continued to do session work, also with Paul Lavalle at Freedomland (1960), worked for several years in Hollywood during the 1960s, then moved back to New York.

BLOUNT, 'Sonny' Herman
(chosen name: Sun Ra)
piano/arranger/composer

Born: Birmingham, Alabama. c. May 1914

Toured with John 'Fess' Whatley's Band in the mid-1930s. Then settled in Chicago, played club dates, solo engagements and worked as accompanist. With Fletcher Henderson's Band at Club DeLisa in Chicago (1946-47), worked in Gene Wright's Dukes of Swing (late 1948), also accompanied Stuff Smith, Coleman Hawkins etc. Formed own Arkestra in mid-1950s; several of its early members remained for many years in this widely travelled musical organisation.

BLOWERS, 'Johnny' John
drums/percussion

Born: Spartanburg, South Carolina, 21st April 1911

Father was also a drummer, first gigs were subbing for his father in local theatre orchestra (1927). Gigged with local bands, then finished high school in Fort Myers, Florida, later attended Atlanta College, Georgia, continued working with local bands, then toured Texas and Missouri. Played in Atlanta, Georgia, then moved to New York (with Lou McGarity) in 1937. Started playing at Nick's in December 1937, with Bobby Hackett (early 1938), then several months in Bunny Berigan's Orchestra (1938). From 1940 worked regularly as a studio musician for C.B.S., N.B.C., and A.B.C. Prolific free-lance recordings with: Eddie Condo, Louis Armstrong, Billie Holiday, Yank Lawson, Georg Brunis, etc. During the 1960s continued with studio work, also worked at Eddie Condon's Club (1967) worked often with Johnny Mince (late 1960s). Visited Europe in 1981.

BLYTHE, 'Jimmy' James Louis
piano/composer

Born: Louisville, Kentucky. c. 1901
Died: Chicago, Illinois, 21st June 1931

Moved to Chicago in 1916, where he was taught by Clarence Jones. During the 1920s made countless recordings for Paramount, Gennett, OKeh, and other record companies, as piano soloist accompanying vocalists and leading own studio groups: Washboard Band, Owls, Blue Boys, State Street Ramblers, etc.

I am indebted to Walter C. Allen for sending me details of Blythe's obituary which was published in the Chicago Defender dated 27th June 1931.

BLUE, 'Bill' William Thornton
clarinet/saxes

Born: Cape Girardeau, Missouri, 31st January 1902
Died: c. 1948

Raised in St. Louis, where his father was a part-time music teacher. Worked with many local bands, briefly toured with Wilson Robinson's Bostonians. With Charlie Creath (1924), then in late 1925 went to New Orleans to join up with Dewey Jackson. Returned to St. Louis with Jackson, then to New York, worked in Andrew Preer's Cotton Club Orchestra. To Europe with Noble Sissle (1928), later with bassist John Ricks in Paris (autumn 1928). Returned to New York, joined The Missourians, briefly with Luis Russell, then worked with Cab Calloway briefly until c. early 1931. No trace of musical activities in the late 1930s, it is known that he suffered a breakdown in health and spent the last part of his life in a New York sanatorium. His funeral took place in St. Louis.

Has (understandably) been confused with the trumpet/saxist Thornton Brown.

B

BOCAGE, Peter
trumpet/violin/trombone/banjo/xylophone

Born: Algiers, Louisiana, 31st July 1887
Died: New Orleans, Louisiana, 3rd December 1967

Several relatives were musicians, his brother Harry played bass, Leonard, another brother, played banjo and guitar. Started on violin, from c. 1906 played in Tom Albert's Band, then began working regularly in Billy Marrero's Superior Orchestra and Bab Frank's Peerless Orchestra, began doubling on cornet and baritone horn and worked in the Onward Brass Band from c. 1911. With Papa Celestin at the Tuxedo Dance Hall from 1910-13. Briefly with Fate Marable on S.S. 'Capitol' (on cornet) during 1918, then worked with Armand J. Piron from 1919 until 1928 (including two trips to New York). In 1928, together with several colleagues from Piron's Orchestra, he joined Louis Warneke's Creole Serenaders, regularly with the Creole Serenaders during the 1930s (including broadcasts). Left full-time music in 1939 to become an insurance salesman, but continued to play regularly. Brief spell with Sidney Bechet's Band in Boston, Massachusetts, in April 1945, returned to New Orleans and throughout the 1950s did regular gigs, including work with the Eureka Band. Continued playing in the 1960s, including recording sessions. Collaborated with Armand Piron on several compositions including 'Mama's Gone Goodbye'.

BOLAR, Abe
string base

Born: Oklahoma City, 26th March 1908

Began playing in 1923. First gigs with local band in Guthrie, Oklahoma (December 1924). Became professional musician in August 1926. Played with many bands in and around Oklahoma City, regularly with the Blue Devils from 1932. Moved to New York in 1936, worked with Hot Lips Page, subbed for Walter Page in Count Basie's Band (early 1940), with Lucky Millinder (1940-1), also free-lance recordings. From 1942 until 1963 with pianist Benton Heath, Ed Allen, and Floyd Casey at the New Gardens, New York. Left full-time music to become a taxi-driver, his wife is pianiste Juanita Bolar.

BOLDEN, 'Buddy' Charles Joseph
cornet

Born: New Orleans, Louisiana, 6th September 1877
Died: Jackson, Louisiana, 4th November 1931

Although Bolden has long been regarded as a central figure in the early development of jazz little was known about him factually before the American writer Donald M. Marquis completed the research for his book 'In Search of Buddy Bolden' (first published in 1978). With admirable scholarship Marquis examined the vague John Henry-like stories that had attached themselves to Bolden's music-making and his life style. He established, amongst other things, that Bolden had never been a barber, nor had he ever produced a scandal-sheet. He had, however, led one of the most successful bands in New Orleans during the early years of this century. Bolden began playing cornet regularly during the early 1890s, and by 1895 was playing paid engagements. He formed his own small band which, during the next ten years, played at many local halls, including the Odd Fellows and Masonic, the Providence, the Jackson, and the Funky Butt. From 1902 his band often played in Lincoln Park and in Johnson Park. Bolden worked by day as a plasterer through most of the 1890s, but by 1901 he was a professional musician. His band often played across the river in Algiers, Louisiana, and occasionally played in other towns in Louisiana. Bolden sometimes played in Henry Allen Snr's parade band, and with other marching bands, but there is no record of him ever working in a sporting house or brothel. His health began to fail in March 1906, and alcoholism led to wild bouts of erratic behaviour; he played his last musical date in 1906. His mental condition worsened and he was admitted to the Insane Asylum at Jackson, Louisiana on the 5th June 1907. He remained there for the rest of his life. He was buried in the Holt Cemetery in New Orleans.

BONANO, 'Sharkey' Joseph
trumpet/vocals

Born: Milneburg, Louisiana, 9th April 1904
Died: New Orleans, Louisiana, 27th March 1972

Was nicknamed after boxer Sailor Tom Sharkey. Father was a classical flautist; took up cornet after his brother-in-law had bought him an instrument from Buddie Petit. Played local gigs, then worked briefly in New York with Eddie Edward's Band (1920). Replaced Frank Christian in Chink Martin's Band playing in a Lake Pontchartain dance hall (c. 1921), subsequently with Freddy Newman's Band at The Ringside, New Orleans, and with Norman Brownlee's Band (including first recordings 1925). Auditioned with The Wolverines in late 1924, worked for a while with Jimmy 'Schnozzle' Durante, then led own band on S.S. 'Island Queen'. Briefly with Jean Goldkette in 1927, co-led big band with Leon Prima (1928), then during late 1920s worked in California with Larry Shields' Band. Left full-time music during the early 1930s, but continued to play regularly in New Orleans, including stints with Angelo Gemelli, etc., and long residency at the Hollywood Club. Worked with Ben Pollack 1936, then led own band in New York. From 1936 until 1939 mainly active with own band in New York (sometimes billed as 'Sharkey Bananas'), also worked occasionally in the re-formed Original Dixieland Jazz Band. In late 1939 returned to New Orleans for residency at the Moulin Rouge. Served in U.S. Coastguard during World War II, left the service in early summer of 1945 and subbed for Leon Prima at the Plaza Club, Kenner. Gigged in New Orleans during the late 1940s, then from early 1949 led own band regularly. Led on overseas tours and occasionally played residencies in Chicago (1951), etc., and New York (1955, 1959, etc.,), but was mainly active in New Orleans during the 1960s. Featured at the New Orleans Jazz Fest in June 1969.

BOOKER, Bobby Lee
trumpet

Born: Jacksonville, Florida, 22nd August 1907

Moved to New York in the early 1920s, played local gigs with pianist Gibby Irvis then worked in Atlantic City with pianist Paul Seminole. Toured with T.O.B.A. shows, then co-led The Carolina Stompers (with Tab Smith); to New York with this band where the group disbanded. Did gigs with Dave Nelson then led own band. Toured with Alphonso Trent then worked in New York with Danny Smalls (1932). Brief spells with Jelly Roll Morton, Marion Hardy, Ferman Tapp, Charlie Skeet, Fess Williams, etc. Frequently led own band during the 1930s and 1940s, but also toured South America with the Cotton Club Show in 1938. Worked briefly in Europe as a soloist, 1950. Mostly active as a taxi driver during the 1950s and 1960s, but formed own big band in 1975, which continued into the 1980s, and featured veteran players. Daughter Alyson Williams is a vocaliste.

BOONE, Chester
trumpet/vocals

Born: Houston, Texas, 27th February 1906

First played trumpet in Sunday School Band in Houston, within a year had joined Richardson's Jazz Band playing at the Lincoln Pool. Formed own band in Houston, left in 1929 to tour with Dee Johnson Band, two years later joined Troy Floyd Band, left this band (with Herschel Evans) and joined Grant Moore Band. After a brief stay travelled to Chicago and began rehearsing with Cassino Simpson Big Band—was called back to Houston without playing in public with the band. Formed own band for residency at Harlem Grill, Houston (late 1932), after considerable local success joined the touring 'Brown Skin Models' in October 1936. Travelled with unit to New York, arriving in February 1937. Played with various bands, including spell with Louis Jordan at the Elks' Rendezvous, and recording sessions with Lloyd Phillips and Sammy Price. With Kaiser Marshall's Band (1940). Led own recording band in 1941, later that year played in Horace Henderson Band, then worked regularly in Buddy Johnson Band before spending three years with Luis Russell (1943-6). Toured Pacific area with a U.S.O. Band, when the tour ended in December 1946 quit professional music, but has continued to do trumpet and vocal free-lance work. During 1950s organised own recording company Nu-Tex.

BOONE, Harvey G.
alto sax/clarinet

Born: Newport News, Virginia. c. 1898
Died: 1939

Worked in New York and on tour with Lucille Hegamin and her Blue Flame Syncopators (c. 1921), then studied at New Haven Conservatory of Music. Worked with Duke Ellington in 1926. With Fletcher Henderson (1930-1), Noble Sissle (c. 1933-5), Don Redman (1936-7), then taught music in Atlanta, Georgia.

B

BOONE, Lester
alto sax/clarinet/baritone sax

Born: Tuskegee, Alabama, 12th August 1904

Studied with Professor Tuttle at Illinois College of Music. Played club dates in and around Chicago, then joined trumpeter Alex Calamese at Jeffrey Tavern, Chicago (1927), during same year worked with Charlie Elgar. Later worked with Clarence Black, Carroll Dickerson, Earl Hines (1930), Jerome Carrington, and Louis Armstrong (from March 1931). Left Louis in March 1932, remained in New York, worked with Kaiser Marshall's Band and Billy Maples, then joined the Mills Blue Rhythm Band (1933). During 1934 with Eubie Blake's Orchestra and Willie Bryant, then spell at Savoy, New York, with Hy Clark's Band; with Kaiser Marshall's Band from May 1935. In 1936 worked with Jelly Roll Morton and Jean Calloway, with Cliff Jackson in 1937. With Hot Lips Page, and with Eddie South (in New York and Chicago) during the late 1930s. In 1940 led own band at Hollywood Club, New York, spell with Leon Abbey, then led own quartet at 44 Club, Newark. Later played long residencies at Harvey's and at the Lucky Bar, New York.

BOSE, 'Bozo' Sterling Belmont
trumpet/vocals

Born: Florence, Alabama, 23rd February 1906
Died: St. Petersburg, Florida, June 1958

Sat in with various New Orleans' bands in early 1920s (including Tom Brown's). Then late in 1923 moved to St. Louis, gigged with various bands, then with Crescent City Jazzers and Arcadia Serenaders until 1927. Joined Jean Goldkette in Detroit and during winter 1927-8 played a season for Goldkette at Pla-Mor Ballroom, Kansas City. Then worked for Radio WGN house band in Chicago until autumn 1930. Joined Ben Pollack in November 1930; on and off until May 1933. With Eddie Sheasby in Chicago. Then to New York, extensive studio work with Victor Young, etc., etc. Joined Joe Haymes Band in spring of 1934, remained when Tommy Dorsey assumed leadership in 1935. With Ray Noble in early 1936, occasionally vocals with Noble Band (i.e. 'Big Chief de Sota' recording). With Benny Goodman in August and September 1936, left through illness. Early in 1937 member of Lana Webster Band in New York, then joined Glenn Miller Orchestra until October 1937. With Bob Crosby from August 1938 until early 1939. Played regularly at Nick's, New York; short spell with Bobby Hackett Big Band in spring of 1939. Member of short-lived Bob Zurke Big Band until April 1940, then six months with Jack Teagarden until taking own trio into Muggsy McGraw's Club in Chicago (December 1940). Played with Bud Freeman's Big Band in Chicago (February 1942). Moved back to New York during early 1943, worked with Georg Brunis at Famous Door, then with Bobby Sherwood's Band from July until November 1943. Regularly with Miff Mole Band at Nick's, also with Art Hodes at same venue in June 1944, briefly with Horace Heidt in August 1944, then free-lancing in New York before moving back to Chicago in 1945. Free-lance activities in Chicago, New York, and Mobile before moving to Florida, occasional work with Tiny Hill Band. From March 1948 led own band Municipal Ballroom, St. Petersburg, Florida, then various club residencies before playing at Soreno Lounge, St. Petersburg, from 1950 until 1957. Suffered a long illness before dying of self-inflicted gun-shot wounds.

BOSTIC, Earl
alto sax/arranger

Born: Tulsa, Oklahoma, 25th April 1913
Died: Rochester, New York, 28th October 1965

Started on alto and clarinet whilst at local Booker T. Washington School. Worked with Terrence Holder's Band (1931-2), briefly with Bernie Moten early in 1933, then enrolled at Xavier University in New Orleans, whilst there became proficient on several instruments, worked with Joe Robichaux (c. 1934). Left Louisiana, worked with Ernie Fields' Band before joining Clarence Olden's Band in Columbus, Ohio. Played and arranged for band jointly led by Charlie Creath and Fate Marable 1935-6, then joined Marion Sears' Band in Cleveland, subsequently with Clyde Turpin in Buffalo. To New York in January 1938, joined Don Redman in April 1938. Briefly with Edgar Hayes, then own band at Small's from 1939 (occasionally playing trumpet, guitar, and baritone sax), also worked with Lips Page Band at Mimo's Club, New York, during 1941, later led own band at same venue. Briefly with Lips Page, then joined Lionel Hampton in June 1943, left during following year and formed own band, resident at Small's from August 1944; occasionally worked out of town gigs including residency at Club Bengasi, Washington, during 1947. From early 1950s enjoyed tremendous international success as a popular recording artist. Extensive coast-to-coast touring. Moved to Los Angeles. Suffered serious heart attack in 1956, inactive for three years. Returned to touring in 1959, but work was again curtailed by illness. After a period of semi-retirement, he began a residency at the Midtown Tower Hotel in Rochester, after playing the opening night he suffered another heart attack and died two days later. Prolific arranger during the early 1940s, scored for Artie Shaw, Hot Lips Page, Paul Whiteman, Louis Prima, etc.

BOSWELL, Connee
(originally Connie)
vocals/various instruments

Born: New Orleans, Louisiana, 3rd December 1907
Died: New York, 11th October 1976

The Boswell Sisters were comprised of Connie, Martha, and Helvetia. Connie contracted polio during infancy; throughout her professional career she appeared in a wheel chair. She began playing cello, later played piano, alto sax, and trombone. Martha played the piano, and 'Vet' the violin, all three sisters played in the New Orleans Philharmonic Orchestra. They began to concentrate on close-harmony singing, and were encouraged by the New Orleans cornetist Emmett Hardy. After turning professional they began a series of recordings that won them a world-wide reputation—on many recordings they used all-star accompaniment. The Sisters worked together until 1935, including tours of Europe in 1933 and 1935. From then on, Connie worked as a solo artiste achieving wide popularity on radio, records, and theatre tours. Continued a full-time career until retiring from touring in the 1950s; throughout the 1960s appeared as a guest star on many important television shows. In 1935 Connie married her manager Harold Leedy—she spent the rest of her life with him.

Connee Boswell's many film appearances include: 'Moulin Rouge', 'Artists and Models', 'The Big Broadcast', 'Syncopation', 'Kiss The Boys Goodbye', etc.

BOTHWELL, Johnny
alto sax

Born: Gary, Indiana, 23rd May 1919

During 1940, worked on tenor-sax with Max Miller's Sextet in Chicago, in same year also played alto sax in Bill Fryar's Big Band. Moved to New York, was with Boyd Raeburn's Band from 1944 until summer of 1945, briefly with Gene Krupa, then led own sextet in New York (1946). Own big band 1946-47, then moved to Ohio briefly before playing residency at Tin Pan Alley Club, Chicago (1948). Worked in New England before leading band in New York (billed as Lord John Bothwell) soon afterwards retired from full-time music and moved to Miami in the late 1940s.

BOWMAN, 'Dave' David W.
piano

Born: Buffalo, N.Y., 8th September 1914
Died: Miami, Florida, 28th December 1964

Was raised in Hamilton, Ontario—both parents were Canadians. Began on piano at four, later studied at the Pittsburg Music Institute. Returned to Hamilton and played professionally with Ken Steele (1933-6). In 1936 played for three weeks at the Savoy Hotel, London, with Billy Bissett, then joined Jack Hylton's Orchestra and toured Europe with him for several months. Returned to New York, briefly with Sharkey Bonano, then regularly with Bobby Hackett (1937-9). With Bud Freeman from April 1939, then with Jack Teagarden from July 1940 until joining Joe Marsala in February 1941. With Muggsy Spanier May 1941 until February 1942, then did studio work in New York. Worked with Bud Freeman (1954-5), then moved to Florida, was mainly active as a free-lance. Whilst returning from a gig in a Miami Hotel, his car plunged into a canal and he was drowned.

BOWLES, Russell
trombone

Born: Glasgow, Kentucky, 17th April 1909

His sister, Elizabeth, who was an amateur musician, is the wife of Jonah Jones. Began playing in the Booker T. Washington Community Centre Band, then studied music at high school in Louisville, Kentucky. From 1926 until 1928 worked in Ferman Tapp's Melody Lads, then joined Horace Henderson in December 1928. Left during the following year and worked in a Buffalo theatre orchestra until joining Jimmie Lunceford on 1st January 1931. Remained with Lunceford until that leader's death (1947), then worked for several years under leadership of Eddie Wilcox. Played occasionally with Cab Calloway in the early 1950s. Left full-time playing to work in a New York department store.

BRADFORD, 'Mule' John Henry Perry

Born: Montgomery, Alabama, 14th February 1893
Died: Queens, New York, 20th April 1970

Family moved to Atlanta, Georgia, when Perry was six. By 1906 was working with minstrel shows, joined Allen's New Orleans Minstrels in 1907. Left to work as a solo pianist, played in Chicago (1909), etc. Visited New York in 1910. Toured theatre circuits for several years, as a soloist, in double acts, etc., began prolific composing. Settled in New York, became musical director for Mamie Smith, and was responsible for Mamie's recording debut—generally accepted as the first recording featuring a Negro blues singer. Mamie's 1921 recording of Bradfords' composition 'Crazy Blues' sold over a million copies. He toured with Mamie Smith during the early 1920s, also led own recording bands featuring Louis Armstrong, Buster Bailey, Johnny Dunn, James P. Johnson, etc., etc. Ran own publishing company in New York, also pioneered use of Negro performers on commercial radio. Composed many big-selling numbers including 'You Can't Keep a Good Man Down', 'Evil Blues', 'That Thing Called Love', etc., etc.

For a full account of Perry Bradford's many activities the reader is advised to consult the autobiography 'Born With The Blues', by Perry Bradford. First published in 1965.

BRADLEY, Will
(real name: Wilbur Schwichtenberg)
trombone/composer

Born: Newton, New Jersey, 12th July 1912

Father of drummer 'Bill' Bradley. Raised in Washington, New Jersey, played in local high school band. Moved to New York in 1928, did local gigs before joining Milt Shaw's Detroiters, subsequently with Red Nichols. On C.B.S. studio staff from 1931 until 1934. With Ray Noble 1935-6, then returned to studio work, until forming own band in July 1939 (and adopting new name). This band, which was co-led with Ray McKinley, remained together until June 1942. Since then Will has worked regularly in the New York studios, occasionally organising his own bands for specific engagements. Did brief spell of touring with the Sauter-Finegan Band in 1953. In later years has composed several extended classical works.

BRADSHAW, 'Tiny' Myron
drums/piano/vocals

Born: Youngstown, Ohio, 23rd September 1905
Died: Cincinnati, Ohio, 26th November 1958

Majored in psychology at Wilberforce University, Ohio. Began singing career with Horace Henderson's Collegians. Subsequently worked in New York with Marion Hardy's Alabamians, The Savoy Bearcats, The Mills Blue Rhythm Band (1932), and sang with Luis Russell. Left Russell to form own band which made its debut at the Renaissance Ballroom, New York, in 1934—later that year they recorded for Decca. After residencies in Philadelphia, Chicago, and the Savoy, New York, the band achieved national fame with several big-selling records. Tiny continued to lead throughout the 1940s and early 1950s, including U.S.O. tour of Japan in late 1945. Worked regularly in Chicago, until suffering two strokes which enforced his retirement.

BRADY, 'Stumpy' Floyd Maurice
trombone

Born: South Brownsville, Pennsylvania, 4th August 1910

First learnt to play on his uncle's trombone. Bought his first trombone in 1925, interrupted his medical studies to tour with John Hawkins' Peerless Syncopators (1927). Left to tour with Gordon Emory Band. Then long spell with Zack Whyte's Chocolate Beau Brummels from 1928 until early 1929. With pianist Cliff Barnett's Band in Toledo, Ohio, then played in J. Frank Terry's Band before joining Al Sears' Band in Buffalo. With Sears until early 1930, then joined Andy Kirk at the Savoy Ballroom, New York. Remained with Kirk until 1934 (including recording sessions with Blanche Calloway), then joined McKinney's Cottonpickers replacing Ed Cuffee. With Claude Hopkins from 1936 until 1938, brief return to home-town, then joined Teddy Wilson Big Band (1939). Worked with Lucky Millinder, Al Sears, Count Basie, etc., before touring in Joe Guy's Big Band accompanying Billie Holiday (1945). Left the tour in Mobile, played with Jay McShann in Dallas, then did tour of service bases with Fletcher Henderson. Played briefly in Roy Eldridge and Cat Anderson Bands, then a long spell of illness, causing Stumpy to give up alcohol permanently. Quit playing during the 1950s, but recommenced gigging in the 1960s, playing with Slide Hampton's Band, Lucky Roberts' Orchestra, and with Edgar Battle's Big Band.

BRAUD, Wellman
(originally Breaux)
string bass

Born: St. James Parish, Louisiana, 25th January 1891
Died: Los Angeles, California, 29th October 1966

Began playing violin at the age of seven, later played violin and bass in string trios in New Orleans, including residency at Tom Anderson's Cabaret—also learnt the trombone. Moved to Chicago in 1917, toured with John H. Wickliffe's Band, then joined the Original Creole Orchestra at the Pekin Cafe, Chicago, played with this band at Dreamland and De Luxe Cafe, then joined Charlie Elgar's Orchestra c. 1922. To London with the Plantation Orchestra in March-May 1923—doubling string bass and trombone. Returned to New York, spell with Wilbur Sweatman, then played for various revues including '7-11 Burlesque Company' (1926), Vaughn's 'Lucky Sambo' (1926-7). Joined Duke Ellington in mid-1927 and remained until May 1935 (sharing bass duties with Billy Taylor for last few months). Left to organise band with Jimmy Noone for residency at their own short-lived Vodvil Club on 132nd Street, New York, with Kaiser Marshall Band, then late in 1935 became player-manager of The Spirits of Rhythm. Formed own trio in 1937, which he led for several years, combining this work with many other bands including: Hot Lips Page (1938), Edgar Hayes (1939), Sidney Bechet (1940-1), Al Sears (1943), Garvin Bushell (1944), etc. Subbed in Duke Ellington's Orchestra (summer 1944), then worked regularly in New York with Garvin Bushell's Band (1944). Left full-time music to manage own pool-hall and meat-marketing business, but continued to do regular gigs, including week-end work with Bunk Johnson in New York (November 1947). In early 1956 he returned to full-time music and joined Kid Ory (touring Europe with Ory later that year). During the 1960s he lived in California; worked with Joe Darensbourg (1960). Suffered a mild heart attack in the summer of 1961, celebrated his return to good health by sitting in with Duke Ellington in autumn 1961. Worked regularly accompanying Barbara Dane in San Francisco, brief spells of semi-retirement. In the early autumn of 1966 he toured Oregon with pianist Kenny Woodson, shortly after this he suffered a fatal heart attack at his home in Los Angeles.

BRERETON, Clarence
trumpet

Born: Baltimore, Maryland, 1909
Died: New York, 1954

Nicknamed 'Minnow' because of his diminutive size. With drummer Ike Dixon (1929-30). On the recommendation of Buster Bailey he joined Noble Sissle in 1932, remained with Sissle until summer of 1938, after a brief absence rejoined the band until joining the U.S. Army in 1942. After demobilisation joined John Kirby Sextet from c. January 1946 until September 1946. Then mainly active as a free-lance with drummer Henry 'Chick' Morrison (1950); died of complications following an attack of the mumps. (Whilst with Noble Sissle, Brereton recorded with Sidney Bechet in 1938.)

BRIDGES, Henry
tenor sax

Born: Oklahoma City. c. 1908

Played in local bands with Charlie Christian; then with Christian, toured with Alphonso

Trent (1938) and played in Leslie Sheffield's Band (1939). Featured with Harlan Leonard from September 1939 until being called up for service in the U.S. Army. Led service band in the U.S.A. and Europe, after demobilisation moved to California and left full-time music. Has lived in Los Angeles for many years, works for local postal authorities but continued gigging through the 1950s.

BRIGGS, Arthur *Born: St. Georges, Grenada, 9th April 1899*
trumpet

Raised in Charleston, South Carolina. Was never in the Jenkins' Orphanage Band, but received private tuition from the Orphanage's Brass Teacher, Lt. Eugene Mikell. Later, played in the 369th U.S. Infantry Band, but was too young to sail to Europe and was transferred to the U.S. Home Guard. Sailed to Europe as a member of Will Marion Cook's Southern Syncopated Orchestra in June 1919. Played in England and France, then returned to U.S.A. with Will Marion Cook in 1921. Played in New York with violinist Leslie Howard's Orchestra, then returned to Europe in 1922 and formed own Savoy Syncopated Orchestra in Brussels. The orchestra left Belgium in 1924 to play residencies at the Weinburg Bar, Vienna—and there became the first jazz group to feature arrangements by Spike Hughes. After leaving for long residencies in Germany 1926-8, Arthur Briggs disbanded and joined Noble Sissle in summer 1928. Worked again with Sissle in 1929, with Sissle at Ciro's in London (late 1930), then returned to the U.S.A. (December 1930) and played with Sissle's Band in New York and on southern tour before returning to Europe in 1931. Co-led band with Freddy Johnson; spell with Barretto's Cuban Orchestra in 1934, then formed own band which played many long residencies (mainly in Paris), also played in Egypt in 1937. Worked and recorded with Coleman Hawkins in 1935. Arthur Briggs remained in Europe during the Nazi occupation and was interned in the St. Denis Concentration Camp. Played at the Pavilion d'Armeonville in 1945, then from 1946-51 led own band at 'Chez Florence' in Paris. Throughout the 1950s and early 1960s continued to play successful residencies in France, including regular seasons at Aix-les-Bains Casino (1958-63). Since 1964 has been a Professor at the Cultural Centres in Saint Gratien, Chantilly, Saint Ouen, and Liseux, teaching brass and saxes.

BRIGGS, Pete *Born: Charleston, South Carolina. c. 1904*
tuba/string bass

Distant relative of Arthur Briggs. Toured with the Jim Jam Jazzers in the early 1920s, then worked with the Lucky Boy Minstrels (late 1923). Worked in Chicago with Carroll Dickerson (c. 1926), with Louis Armstrong's Stompers at the Sunset Cafe (1927), also doubled with Jimmie Noone at the Apex Club (1927). Took part in Louis Armstrong's Hot Seven recordings (1927). With Carroll Dickerson (1928), to New York with Dickerson and Louis Armstrong (1929). Soon joined Edgar Hayes' Orchestra at the Alhambra, New York (1929-30). During the 1930s worked for several years in New York in Vernon Andrade's Orchestra. With Herman Autrey's Band in Philadelphia (1943-4). Left music to run own farm.

BRIGHT, Delbert *Born: Leavenworth, Kansas, 17th June 1913*
alto sax/clarinet

Lived in Chicago from late childhood. Worked with Tiny Parham (1932), Frankie Jaxon (1932), Erskine Tate (1933), Carroll Dickerson (1934), Zutty Singleton (summer 1935), then with Albert Ammons' Rhythm Kings at Club De Lisa (1935-6). With Horace Henderson (summer 1937), then formed own band which played residencies in Chicago (including Swingland 1938), again with Horace Henderson (1939-40). Re-formed and led own band throughout the 1940s. Left full-time music but continued to gig during the 1950s.

BRINSON, 'Ted' Theodore *Born: Albuquerque, New Mexico, 28th November 1910*
guitar/composer

Was taught violin by his father, and piano by his mother. Played in duo 'Ed and Ted' with

Eddie Carson on local radio station (1926). Joined band led by Lester Young's father, Billy Young in 1926. Resumed work with Eddie Carson, this time in Hot-Ten-Tots Band then joined Art Bronson's Bostonians (1930), later that year worked with King Oliver. With George E. Lee (1931) then joined Oklahoma Blue Devils. With Andy Kirk from 1933 until 1939. Settled in California, worked with Paul Howard during the 1940s, and various other leaders during the 1950s, including Sammy Franklin (1954). Opened own recording studio in Los Angeles during the early 1970s and achieved considerable success.

BRITTON, 'Joe' Joseph E.
trombone

Born: Birmingham, Alabama, 28th November 1903
Died: New York, 12th August 1972

Taught by 'Fess' Whatley. Did regular tours with Bessie Smith from 1924 until 1926, first with Fred Longshaw's Orchestra, then with Bill Woods' Orchestra. With Frank Bunch and his Fuzzie-Wuzzies (1927). Lived in New York from the early 1930s, worked with Ellsworth Reynolds' Bostonians (c. 1933), Teddy Hill at the Lafayette Theatre (1934), Kaiser Marshall's Band (1935), Charlie Johnson (1936), Edgar Hayes (1937), Vernon Andrade's Orchestra (1938-9). Recorded with Jelly Roll Morton in 1940; with Benny Carter (1941), Lucky Millinder (1942-4), Jay McShann (1946). Retired from full-time music, but continued to gig in the 1960s, including regular work with band led by saxist Wesley Fagan.

BROOKS, Harvey Oliver
piano/composer

Born: Philadelphia, Pennsylvania, 17th February 1899
Died: Los Angeles, California, 17th June 1968

Not related to pianist Harry Brooks (born: 1900). On tour with Mamie Smith during the early 1920s, left to settle in California. Co-led 'Quality Four' with Paul Howard from 1923, later worked in Paul Howard's Quality Serenaders until 1930. From 1931 until 1935 worked mainly in Les Hite's Orchestra, later led own band and worked as musical director for films. In early 1952 joined Kid Ory's Band, subsequently worked with Teddy Buckner, then with Joe Darensbourg (1957-60). From 1961 played in the Young Men of New Orleans, led that group during the last year of his life. Prolific composer.

BROWN, Ada
(née Scott)
vocals

Born: Junction City, Kansas, 1st May 1889
Died: Kansas City, Missouri, 31st March 1950

Sang with George E. Lee and Bennie Moten during the early 1920s (recorded with Moten in 1926), later starred in many Broadway shows, and did widespread theatre tours throughout U.S. and Canada, featured at London Palladium in late 1930s. Sang in the film 'Stormy Weather' (1943), during that year worked in 'Harlem to Hollywood'. Her long-time accompanist was pianist Harry Swannagan. Retired to K.C. in the late 1940s.

BROWN, Andrew
bass sax/saxes/clarinet

Born: 2nd February 1900
Died: New York City, August 1960

From 1925 worked in The Cotton Club Orchestra (led by Andrew Preer until 1927), continued working with the band as 'The Missourians', and subsequently with Cab Calloway from 1930 until 1945 (including trip to Europe 1934). From 1945 ran own teaching studio in New York City.

BROWN, Boyce
alto sax/clarinet

Born: Chicago, Illinois, 16th April 1910
Died: Hillsdale, Illinois, 30th January 1959

His brother, Harvey, was a guitarist. At 17 did first professional work with drummer Don Carter's Band in Chicago. During the early 1930s worked with Benny Meroff, including bookings at Palace Theatre, New York (1931). With Wingy Manone at Fort Tavern, Chicago (1933), Paul Mares (late 1934-5), Johnny's Original Playboys (1936), then long spell leading own small group at Liberty Inn, Chicago, in the late 1930s and 1940s, recorded with Jimmy McPartland (1939), Wild Bill Davison (1940). Worked in trio led by pianist Chet Roble, in Chicago (1947-8), also in Ventura, California (summer 1948). With Danny Alvin (1949), then again worked at Liberty Inn during the early 1950s. In the autumn of 1953 adopted the name 'Brother Matthew' and entered a monastery, after taking his vows in February 1956, he emerged briefly to record an L.P. with Eddie Condon (April 1956) and to make television appearance (May 1956). He died of a heart attack at the R.C. Servite Seminary in Hillsdale, Illinois.

BROWN, Cleo *Born: Meridian, Mississippi, 8th December 1909*
piano/vocals

Her brother, Everett, was a pianist; their father was the pastor of the Pilgrim Baptist Church in Meridan. In 1919 the family moved to Chicago, Cleo studied music and began playing piano for a touring show. During the late 1920s played several residencies in and around Chicago including the Kelshore Rooms, Lake Villa, etc., also gigged with various bands. In 1932, whilst playing and singing in a local rhumba band, was signed by Texas Guinan and began appearing regularly on Chicago radio programmes. Then had own series on WABC. Led own group at Three Deuces, Chicago, extensive recordings, and regular work in New York, Hollywood, etc., during the late 1930s. After working as a piano teacher, was taken seriously ill and was in a California sanatorium from late 1940 until 1942. Resumed regular engagements, did long spells in Chicago at the Three Deuces, Silver Frolics, etc., then moved to California.

BROWN, Henry *Born: Troy, Tennessee, 1906*
piano/vocals

Moved with family to St. Louis (c. 1918). Played piano whilst still at school, and from the age of 16 began gigging in local bars. During the late 1920s and 1930s teamed with trombonist Ikey Rodgers (died: c. 1941) for regular work and recording sessions. Also played in recording sessions accompanying various vocalists. During the 1930s did a variety of day jobs but continued gigging. Army service during World War II, then returned to St. Louis. Continued part-time playing through to the 1960s, recorded in 1960.

BROWN, Hillard L. *Born: Birmingham, Alabama, 12th May 1913*
drums

Began playing drums in 1926, taught by Richard Barnett, Oliver Coleman and others. First gigs in Chicago (December 1933). First professional work in band led by pianist Ruth Oldham at Monogram Theater, Chicago (July 1934). With Johnny Long, Tony Fambro, Les Wilcox (1935), Eddie McLaughlin (1936), Erskine Tate (1937), Les Wilcox (1937-38), Sonny Thompson (1939), Bobby Tinsley (1939), Tiny Parham (1940-41), Walter Fuller (1942), Carroll Dickerson, Jay McShann (1943), Jesse Miller (1944). Brief tour with Duke Ellington (October 1944). With Billy Eckstine (1944), Ben Webster at Onyx Club, New York (1945) and Dallas Bartley (1945). Own band in Chicago from 1946 until 1954, then became Business Agent for musicians' union until the mid-1960s. Resumed free-lance playing during the 1970s, often worked with Art Hodes, combining this with work in real estate.

BROWN, John Benjamin Peabody *Born: Dayton, Ohio, 13th March 1906*
string bass

Began on violin at the age of 10, subsequently worked with his father's band and other local bands. Moved to New York in 1928, played violin and banjo in Herbert Cowens' Royal Garden Orchestra at Rockland Palace (September 1928). Worked with Sam Wooding from 1932, switched to string bass in 1935. With Snub Mosley from 1936, with Stuff Smith 1938-41, again with Snub Mosley, then with Wilbur de Paris and Herbert Cowens in Lunt-Fontaine New York show 'The Pirate' 1941-2. Mainly with Claude Hopkins from 1945 until 1950, first in big band at the Zanzibar, New York, later in quartet. Worked with Fletcher Henderson for that leader's last job (December 1950). To Europe on U.S.O. tour with Snub Mosley (1952). Rejoined Claude Hopkins in 1953, also worked with Herman Chittison in 1954. In 1955 joined Jonah Jones, and throughout the 1960s continued to work with Jonah.

BROWN, Lawrence *Born: Lawrence, Kansas, 3rd August 1907*
trombone

His brother, Harold, is a professional pianist; their father was a minister. Lawrence started on piano, violin, and tuba, then specialised on trombone. Whilst studying medicine at Pasadena Junior College played in school orchestra. Professional at 19 with Charlie Echols' Band, left after six months to join Paul Howard. Worked with Leon Herriford and Curtis Mosby's Blue Blowers before rejoining Paul Howard. Worked as a 'house-man' at Sebastian's Cotton Club in Culver City, played with various leaders including Les Hite. In the spring of 1932 was signed by impresario Irving Mills and joined Duke Ellington. Remained with Duke until March 1951 (except for brief absence in summer of 1943). With Johnny Hodges' Small Band until spring of 1955, did studio work in New York (including spell at C.B.S.), then rejoined Duke Ellington in May 1960. Other than brief absences worked regularly with Duke throughout the 1960s, also led own recording bands. Left Duke early in 1970. Worked for U.S. Government (1971). Retired from Government service in 1974 and moved to California.

BROWN, 'Pud' Albert *Born: Wilmington, Delaware, 22nd January 1917*
reeds/trumpet

Both parents (and brothers and sisters) were musical. First toured in Brown Family Band in 1927, billed as 'World's Youngest Saxophone Player'. Worked in theatre orchestras during the early 1930s, then spells with Count Balooki, Marshall Van Poole, Lou Clancy and Phil Levant. Moved to Chicago worked with Bud Freeman, Jimmy Dorsey, Bud Jacobson and Pete Daily. Gigged in Shreveport, Louisiana, from 1945 until 1949 then moved to Los Angeles. Lived in California from 1949-73, worked there with Nappy Lamare, Jack Teagarden, Teddy Buckner and Kid Ory, also led own band. Began doubling on cornet and trumpet in the early 1960s. Moved back to Shreveport in 1973, worked a great deal in New Orleans, often with Les Muscutt at the Blue Angel on Bourbon Street. Recorded with own all-star band in 1977. During career occasionally played string-bass. Worked regularly in New Orleans during early 1980s, including residency in New Orleans production of 'One Mo' Time'.

BROWN, 'Pete' James Ostend *Born: Baltimore, Maryland, 9th November 1906*
alto/tenor sax/trumpet/violin *Died: New York City, 20th September 1963*

Father (originally from Barbados) played trombone; mother was a pianist. Pete's cousin, Estelle Carroll, was a vocaliste. Played piano from the age of eight, spell on ukelele, then specialised on violin. Played in local movie-house from the age of 12, was featured as soloist at high school concerts. Began working in a Baltimore theatre orchestra, changed to alto and tenor in 1924, continued theatre work, then played with The Southern Star Jazz Band, The Baltimore Melody Boys (1926), and Johnny Jones' Orchestra. Joined Banjo Bernie Robinson in Atlantic City (early 1927), moved to New York with that band in June 1927, played residency at the Capitol, then at the Sugar Cane Club (where Pete began doubling trumpet—1928). From c. 1930 until 1935 worked on and off with Charlie Skeets (worked with this band for Clarence Williams' recording in March 1935). From c. 1933 until 1936 worked in Fred Moore's Trio (with Don Frye) at the Victoria Cafe, New York, from January 1937 played with the Trio at Brittwood Club, then became an original member of the John Kirby Band in May 1937. Left Kirby in May 1938, formed own band which played many residencies in New York including: Kelly's, The Onyx, etc. During this period played on several recordings organised by jazz-writer Leonard Feather, also recorded with Willie 'The Lion' Smith (1937), Frankie Newton, etc. Co-led band with Frankie Newton at Kelly's Stables (early 1940), then led own band at Martin's, Jimmy Ryan's, Keely's, etc., 1941-3. With Frankie Newton in Boston (spring 1943), briefly fronted Louis Jordan's group whilst the leader did solo tour (1943). Led own small groups from 1944: Garrick, Silhouette (Chicago), Three Deuces, Kelly's, Club Cobra, etc. (New York). Continued to lead own small groups during the 1950s, but persistent ill health curtailed regular playing in the later years of his life. Featured at the Newport Jazz Festival in 1957, continued playing in the early 1960s, played long residencies at the Club Arlington in Brooklyn, New York, and also appeared at the Village Gate. From the late 1950s doubled on tenor sax. Regularly gave sax tuition from the 1930s, pupils include baritone saxist Cecil Payne and Flip Phillips.

BROWN, 'Steve' Theodore
string bass

Born: New Orleans, Louisiana, 1890
Died: Detroit, Michigan, 15th September 1965

Brother of Tom Brown. Originally played tuba in his brother's band, then string bass, went to Chicago with the band (May 1915). Joined New Orleans Rhythm Kings in Chicago replacing Arnold Loyacano (1923), also doubled with Murphy Steinberg's Band at the Midway Gardens. With Jean Goldkette from 1924 until 1927, joined Paul Whiteman on 31st October 1927, left in February 1928. Rejoined Jean Goldkette in 1928, played season in Kansas City, then settled in Detroit. Free-lanced with many local bands, also occasionally led own band in the 1930s and 1940s, gigged with local jazz groups in 1940s; with Gordon Sullivan's Dixieland Band (1945), Frank Gillis Dixie Five (1950), etc.

BROWN, Tom
trombone/string bass

Born: New Orleans, Louisiana, 3rd June 1888
Died: New Orleans, Louisiana, 25th March 1958

Brother of Steve Brown. Early nickname was 'Red'. Began on violin at nine, later played trombone in Papa Jack Laine's Reliance Bands, led own band from c. 1910. Took own Brown's Ragtime Band to open at Lamb's Cafe, Chicago, on 15th May 1915. During September 1915 the band, billed as The Five Rubes began playing dates in New York. The group soon disbanded, but Brown reorganised and opened at the North Star Inn, Chicago in April 1916, a few months later he again disbanded and began working in Clint Brush's Orchestra. Later worked in Chicago with Ray Miller, Vincent Lopez, Harry Yerkes, Sol Wagner, Husk O'Hare, etc. before moving back to New Orleans in the late 1920s where he opened a music shop, but also did gigs with Johnny Bayersdorffer, Norman Brownlee, etc. Worked regularly on string bass during the 1930s including long spell in Val Barbara's Orchestra. Followed the trade of radio-electrician and owned own radio and music shop. Continued to gig on trombone and string bass in New Orleans and Eunice, Louisiana, during the 1940s, recorded with Johnny Wiggs in 1951.

BROWN, Vernon
trombone

Born; Venice, Illinois, 6th January 1907
Died: Los Angeles, California, 18th May 1979

Husband of vocaliste Edythe Harper. With Frank Trumbauer in St. Louis (1925-6), worked with Ambassador Bell Hops, then gigged in Chicago. Worked with Jean Goldkette in 1928. During the early 1930s worked with Benny Meroff and Joe Gill. Moved to New York, with Mezz Mezzrow's Disciples of Swing (November 1937), with Benny Goodman from December 1937 until July 1940. With Artie Shaw (July 1940) until briefly joining Jan Savitt in March 1941. With Muggsy Spanier Big Band spring 1941 until early summer of 1942, then joined the Casa Loma Band. Regular studio work in New York from the mid-1940s, has also worked briefly on several occasions with Benny Goodman including trip to Europe in 1958. Extensive free-lance recordings, including several sessions with Eddie Condon alumni. Led own band in Seattle during 1950, then resumed studio work in New York, was on A.B.C. staff in late 1960s; played in Toronto with Tony Parenti in 1963.

BROWN, Willard S.
saxes/clarinet

Born: Birmingham, Alabama, 1909
Died: New York City, 5th July 1967

Worked in Chicago with Tiny Parham, Erskine Tate, etc.; recorded with Jabbo Smith (1929). With Grant Moore's Band (1930-1), toured briefly with Louis Armstrong. During the late 1930s worked in New York with Snub Mosley and Eddie Durham (1940), then in Chicago with Walter Fuller and bassist Dallas Bartley. In California with Benny Carter (1943), with Louis Armstrong Big Band (1944), occasionally with Duke Ellington from October 1944 until spring 1945. With Sy Oliver in late 1946-7, regularly with Snub Mosley from 1948 (including U.S.O. tour of Britain in 1952). Worked on and off with Lucky Millinder in the 1950s, with Cab Calloway in 1959. With Milton Larkin in the 1960s.

BROWNE, 'Toby' Scoville
clarinet/saxes

Born: Atlanta, Georgia, 13th October 1915

First professional work with Junie Cobb's Band in Chicago (c. 1929). With the 'Midnight Ramblers' in Chicago (1930); with band led by drummer Fred Avendorph (1931-2), Louis Armstrong (1933 and summer 1935), Jesse Stone (1934), Jack Butler, Claude Hopkins (1936), Blanche Calloway (1937), studied at Chicago College of Music (1938-9). With Don Redman, Slim Gaillard, Fats Waller, Buddy Johnson, Hot Lips Page (1939-41), Lucky Millinder (spring 1942), left to lead own quartet. With Hot Lips Page, then spell in Eddie Heywood's Trio until service in U.S. Army from May 1943. After demobilisation with Claude Hopkins (late 1945), then with Teddy Wilson at C.B.S.; Buck Clayton Sextet (spring 1947), again with Claude Hopkins (late 1947)—extensive studies of classical music. With Claude Hopkins' Small Band (1949). Through the 1950s and 1960s has regularly led own small groups. With Lionel Hampton as featured clarinettist (1956-7), including overseas tours, with Muggsy Spanier (1959-60). Occasionally worked with Claude Hopkins during the 1960s, continues to play regularly.

BRUNIS, Georg
(originally George Clarence Brunies)
trombone/vocals

Born: New Orleans, Louisiana, 6th February 1902
Died: Chicago, Illinois, 19th November 1974

One of famous musical family, brother of Albert (d. 1978), Henry, Merritt, and Richard. At the age of eight was playing alto horn in Papa Jack Laine's Band, also worked with family band. First played trombone in band led by Laine's son, Alfred: 'Pantsy' Laine and his Wampas Cats. During his teens played at Brunnin's Hall and at Martin's, near Lake Pontchartrain, with Leon Roppolo. Moved to Chicago c. 1919, worked in band led by New Orleans drummer Joe 'Ragababy' Stevens, then spell with Elmer Schoebel at Blatz Palm Gardens before playing on S.S. 'Capitol'. Returned to Chicago c. 1921, joined Friar's Society Orchestra and thus became founder-member of the New Orleans Rhythm Kings. Left the N.O.R.K. in 1924, worked with Eddie Tancil's Band in Chicago, then joined Ted Lewis (1924). Remained with Ted Lewis until 1934 (including trip to Europe), worked with Louis Prima (1934), then toured as leader of the Mills Cavalcade Orchestra (early 1935). Brief spells with Ted Lewis, but from 1936 was virtually a 'house-musician' at Nick's, New York. Worked with Sharkey Bonano, Louis Prima, Chauncey Morehouse, Bobby Hackett, etc. Left Bobby Hackett in spring of 1938, free-lanced, then returned briefly to New Orleans before joining Muggsy Spanier Ragtimers from April 1939 until they disbanded in December of that year. Led own band at Nick's (1940), then worked with Art Hodes (late 1940 to early 1941), again worked at Nick's (1941-2), brief spell working in Mobile shipyards, led at Famous Door (early 1943), then again with Art Hodes. Rejoined Ted Lewis from August 1943 until January 1946, again at Nick's (1946). Mainly with Eddie Condon January 1947 to June 1949, moved back to Chicago, led own band at Sky Club, briefly with Johnny Lane Band (September 1949), led at Blue Note (late 1949). With Art Hodes (1950), then led own band at Club 1111 (1951-9). During the late 1950s and early 1960s also led in Madison, Wisconsin, and in Cincinnati. Briefly with Muggsy Spanier (late 1961), with Brian Shandley's Band (early 1962). Lived in Biloxi, Mississippi, for six months from late 1965, then returned to Chicago. Played at 1968 New Orleans Jazz Festival with Art Hodes. Was seriously ill in the late 1960s but recommenced blowing and began working with Smokey Stover's Band in September 1969. Played Manassas Festival (1970). Continued to play regularly, some dates with Gene Mayl's Dixieland Rhythm Kings and with Smokey Stover (1971).

BRYAN, 'Mike' Michael Neely — *Born: Byhalia, Mississippi, 1916*
guitar — *Died: Los Angeles, California, 20th August 1972*

Went to school in Germantown, Tennessee, later taught himself to play guitar. Gigged around Memphis, then played in Chicago with Red Nichols, later had own band in Greenwood, Mississippi, 1938-9. With Benny Goodman from November 1940 until May 1941, short spells with Bob Chester and Jan Savitt, then with Artie Shaw until service in U.S. Army from March 1942 until November 1944. Briefly with Slam Steward Trio at Three Deuces, New York, then with Benny Goodman from January 1945 until September 1946. Did studio work in California for several years. Visited England in late 1962, after touring Europe with the Goodyear Band, as musical director. During the 1960s ran own car agency in Los Angeles, later ran own music shop.

BRYANT, 'Willie' William Steven — *Born: New Orleans, Louisiana, 30th August 1908*
vocals/leader/compere — *Died: Los Angeles, California, 9th February 1964*

Family moved to Chicago in 1912. Short-lived attempt to play trumpet, then worked as a candy-seller at the Grand Theatre, Chicago. In 1926 began working as a soft-shoe dancer in the Whitman Sisters' Show, did extensive touring throughout the 1920s, also partnered Leonard Reed in a vaudeville dance act. Continued touring until 1933. Solo spot in 'Chocolate Revue' (1934), also partnered Bessie Smith in 'Big Fat Ma and Skinny Pa' stage feature. Brief spell as vocalist with Buck and Bubbles' Band, then began fronting own big band (late 1934). Continued leading big band until late 1938. From January 1939 worked as an actor, master of ceremonies, and disc-jockey. Did U.S.O. tours during World War II, re-formed band 1946-8, then resumed compere work, had own series on C.B.S. television in 1949. Moved to California in the 1950s, dee-jayed programmes in San Francisco and Los Angeles. Died of a heart attack.

BUCKNER, 'Milt' Milton — *Born: St. Louis, Missouri, 10th July 1915*
piano/organ/vibes/arranger — *Died: Chicago, 27th July 1977*

Brother of altoist Ted Buckner; another brother, George, who died in 1969, was a trumpeter. Orphaned at the age of nine and raised in Detroit. Received musical education from his uncle, trombonist John Tobias. In 1930 did first arrangements for Earl Walton's Band. Studied at the Detroit Institute of Arts for two years, during this time gigged with The Harlem Aristocrats, Mose Burke and The Dixie Whangdoodles, later played and arranged for McKinney's Cotton Pickers. Worked mainly in Detroit throughout the 1930s with: Lanky Bowman, Howard Bunts, Don Cox, and Jimmy Raschelle. Joined Lionel Hampton in November 1941 as assistant director and staff arranger, remained with Hampton until September 1948. Left to form own sextet, later led own big band, rejoined Lionel Hampton from July 1950 until August 1952. Later specialised in playing Hammond organ, featuring this with his own highly successful trio. Annual tours of Europe during the late 1960s; during 1969 spent several months in Europe in duo with drummer Jo Jones. Toured Europe during the early 1970s. The last part of his life was spent working in Illinois Jacquet's Trio.

BUCKNER, 'Ted' Theodore Guy — *Born: St. Louis, Missouri, 14th December 1913*
alto sax — *Died: Detroit, Michigan, 12th April 1976*

Brother of Milt and George (trumpet). Played regularly in Detroit during the 1930s, with Jimmie Lunceford from 1937 until 1943, then led own groups in and around Detroit, also toured in band led by Todd Rhodes. Continued to play regularly, during the 1960s co-led big band in Detroit with trombonist Jimmy Wilkins (brother of sax-player Ernie Wilkins). Toured France with Sam Price (1975).

BUCKNER, 'Teddy' John Edward
trumpet/flugel horn/vocals

Born: Sherman, Texas, 16th July 1909

Five years of childhood spent in Silver City, New Mexico. Learned drums and ukelele from an uncle, then took trumpet lessons from Harold Scott. At 15 worked with Buddy Garcia's Band in Los Angeles, with 'Big Six' Reeves before joining Speed Webb in California. Worked with various West Coast bandleaders including: Sylvester Scott, Sonny Clay, Edyth Turnham, Curtis Mosby, etc. In 1934 went to Shanghai for almost a year as a member of Buck Clayton's Big Band. Returned to California, worked with Lorenzo Flennoy, the 'Brownskin Models Revue', and Cee Pee Johnson's Band. In the summer of 1936 joined Lionel Hampton's Band at the Paradise Club, Los Angeles, in November 1936; when Hampton joined Benny Goodman, Teddy was appointed leader. Through the 1930s and 1940s did regular film work, appearing in many films, also worked as Louis Armstrong's 'stand-in' in 'Pennies from Heaven' (1936). From 1943 regular stints with Benny Carter, with Cee Pee Johnson's Band (1944-5), briefly with Johnny Otis (1947). Worked with the Solid Blenders Sextet, briefly with Lionel Hampton before returning to Benny Carter (autumn 1948). Joined Kid Ory in July 1949, worked mainly with Ory until 1954, then formed own small band. Featured in the film 'Pete Kelly's Blues'; worked in Europe (summer 1958) mainly with Sidney Bechet. From the mid-1950s through the 1970s has led own band in long residencies in California: 400 Club, Beverley Cavern, Los Angeles; The Huddle, West Corvina, etc. Appeared in films during the 1960s.

BULLOCK, 'Chuck' Charles
vocals

Born: Butte, Montana, 16th September 1908
Died: California, 15th September 1981

Although this vocalist recorded over 500 titles during the 1930s, he seemingly shunned all personal publicity. He moved to the West Coast c. 1945 and was engaged in real estate transactions; he appeared on a 'Tribute to Bunny Berigan' radio programme in the mid-1950s.

BUNN, 'Teddy' Theodore Leroy
guitar/vocals

Born: Freeport, Long Island, 1909
Died: Lancaster, California, 20th July 1978

His brother, Kenneth, was a violinist; their mother played the organ, their father was an accordionist. First professional work accompanying a calypso singer, first recordings with Spencer Williams. Recorded with Duke Ellington in 1929, was later to deputise for Fred Guy on a tour of New England with Duke Ellington. Worked in the Washboard Serenaders during the early 1930s, then joined group known as Ben Bernie's Nephews, this unit moved to New York to play a long residency at Chick Groman's Stables and changed their name to The Spirits of Rhythm. The group played long engagements at The Onyx, Nick's, etc., also worked in Philadelphia and Chicago as well as touring. Bunn left in 1937, worked briefly in the original John Kirby Band (May 1937), then led own trio and duo at various New York clubs before rejoining The Spirits of Rhythm in April 1939. Prolific free-lance recordings in the 1930s. After residency at New York's World Fair the group moved to California in 1940, and for a period of 10 years disbanded and re-formed with great regularity. Bunn was briefly absent from the music scene in 1942, led own Waves of Rhythm (1944), later led own small groups in Los Angeles, Sacramento, etc. During the 1940s and 1950s worked on several occasions with Edgar Hayes. In 1954 worked for several months in Honolulu with Jack McVea's Band. Returned to Los Angeles and again led own group, also worked with Edgar Hayes, Hadda Brooks, Bill Moore, Jack McVea, etc. Briefly with Louis Jordan in 1959. In the late 1950s toured with a 'rock-and-roll' show. During the 1960s played less regularly through recurring illness, worked in Hawaii (1969). Although Teddy specialised on guitar, he did work briefly on banjo with Cecil Scott in New York (January 1929). Retired from music during the 1970s.

B

BURBANK, Albert
clarinet

Born: New Orleans, Louisiana, 25th March 1902
Died: New Orleans, Louisiana, 15th August 1976

A pupil of Lorenzo Tio Jr. Gigged with various bands in the 1920s, regularly with drummer Kid Milton in the early 1930s. After U.S. Navy service in World War II worked with drummer Albert Jiles and trumpeter Dee Dee Pierce (1947), then long spell with Herb Morand. During the early 1950s worked regularly with Paul Barbarin, then played in Los Angeles in 1954 (with Kid Ory summer 1954), returned to New Orleans and worked regularly with various leaders: Bill Matthews, Octave Crosby, Ernie Cagnoletti, also engagements with marching bands. Regular dates with Papa French's Band in the 1960s. Played in Australia with the Preservation Hall Band September 1971). In 1975 a stroke ended his clarinet playing, but he continued to sing occasionally at Preservation Hall.

BURKE, 'Ed' Edward
trombone

Born: Fulton, Missouri, 13th January 1909

Was originally a violinist; doubled trombone and violin with Walter Barnes from 1928 until 1930. Worked with Cassino Simpson (1931), Ed Carry's Orchestra (late 1932-3), with Kenneth Anderson (summer 1934), Erskine Tate (late 1934-5). With Horace Henderson from summer of 1937, then with Earl Hines from 1938 until 1940, Walter Fuller (September 1940), with Coleman Hawkins in Chicago (spring 1941). Moved to New York, long spells with Cootie Williams' Big Band from 1942. Toured with Cab Calloway (1950-1), worked with Buddy Johnson in the mid-1950s. Has left full-time music but continued to do regular gigs in the 1960s, mainly with Lem Johnson, also with Wally Edwards' rehearsal band. Appeared with Bobby Booker's Big Band in the early 1980s.

BURKE, Raymond N.
(real name: Barrois)
clarinet/saxes

Born: New Orleans, Louisiana, 6th June 1904

Entirely self-taught, though three of his uncles were musicians. First regular work with Blind Gilbert's Band in the mid-1920s. Played in New Orleans throughout the 1930s, long spell with Henry Walde's Melon Pickers at the Plantation Club. Worked briefly in Kansas City in the late 1930s. During the 1940s led own bands at various venues: Vanity Club, Stork Club, La Louisiane, etc., also played dates with Sharkey Bonano, Johnny Wiggs, trumpeter George Hartman (died: 1966), etc. Worked in the New Orleans All Stars in the early 1960s, has continued to play regularly including appearances at the New Orleans Jazz Fest (1969). For many years has kept a curio shop on Bourbon Street. Visited London in January 1973. Regularly with the Preservation Hall Band in 1970s and early 1980s.

BURNESS, 'Les' Lester
piano

Born: Jersey City, 1913

Did a great deal of touring with Mal Hallett's Orchestra before joining Bunny Berigan early in 1937. Joined Artie Shaw in April 1937 and remained until late 1938. Worked with Tony Pastor for several years beginning in late 1940. Still active, lives in Jersey City.

BURNET, 'Bob' Robert W.
trumpet/arranger

Born: Chicago, Illinois, 1912
Died: Guadalajara, Mexico, 3rd August 1984

Mother was a singer. Started on drums at five, then took piano lessons until the age of 14, played banjo in school orchestra at 15. After preparatory school in Lausanne, Switzerland, he attended Berkshire School and whilst there swapped a watch for a trumpet, subsequently became leader of the school orchestra. Later studied at Yale University and played in student bands there. Played for a while with hotel bands in Bermuda before returning to Chicago. Joined Eddie Neibauer's Orchestra, then moved to gig in New York. With Charlie Barnet from 1938 until 1940, then led own sextet (featuring five black musicians) at Cafe Society (Uptown) in February 1941, the sextet worked briefly at Nick's before disbanding, Bob then rejoined Charlie Barnet. During World War II he served as a radio engineer in the U.S. Army including postings in Africa, Italy, and Austria. After demobilisation returned to Chicago, gigged for Ray O'Hara, worked in electronics, then studied briefly at Northwestern University. Recorded with Freddie Wacker's Windy City Six for the Dolphin label. Moved to Guadalajara, Mexico, in 1958. During the 1960s occasionally played flute in the local symphony orchestra.

BURNS, 'Billy' Henry William
trombone

Born: Cleveland, Ohio. c. 1904
Died: New York City, December 1963

With Paul Craig's Band at Silver Slipper Club in Buffalo, from 1927 until April 1928, then joined Sam Wooding at the Great Lakes Theatre, Buffalo. To Europe with Wooding in 1929. With Noble Sissle in Europe (1930). Long spells with Willie Lewis in Europe, also worked with Fud Candrix in Belgium, and with Freddy Johnson and Romeo Silva's Orchestra. Left Lewis in December 1938 to play in Egypt with The Harlem Rhythmakers (Bill Coleman, etc.), returned to Europe to rejoin Willie Lewis in Holland. Returned to the U.S.A. in 1941, after working with Lewis in Switzerland and Portugal. Did occasional gigs but was employed for 20 years as a bartender in New York. Was hospitalised with arthritis during the 1950s, died of cancer.

BURROUGHS, 'Mouse' Alvin
drums

Born: Mobile, Alabama, 21st November 1911
Died: Chicago, Illinois, 1st August 1950

Raised in Pittsburgh. At 16 made debut (with Roy Eldridge) in a kids' band at Sharon, Pennsylvania—swift return to Pittsburgh. Worked with Walter Page's Blue Devils 1928-9, with Alphonso Trent (1930). Settled in Chicago, played with various leaders including spell with pianist Hal Draper's Arcadians in 1935. With Horace Henderson from July 1937 until 1938. With Earl Hines from September 1938 until late 1940. With Milton Larkin's Band at Rhumboogie, Chicago (1941), with Benny Carter in late 1942. Led own band, then worked with Henry 'Red' Allen from 1945 until April 1946. Led own band for a while, then joined George Dixon's Quartet, was a member of this group at the time he suffered a fatal heart attack.

BUSHELL, Garvin Payne
clarinet/saxes/flute/bassoon/oboe

Born: Springfield, Ohio, 25th September 1902

Both parents taught singing; his uncle was a clarinettist. Started on piano at six, clarinet at 13. Studied at Wilberforce University, during summer vacations played for travelling tent shows. Moved to New York in 1919, accompanied variety artistes, toured with Mamie Smith's Jazz Hounds, then played in house band at LeRoy's, New York. Toured with Ethel Waters' Black Swan Jazz Masters—directed by Fletcher Henderson (1921-2). Returned to LeRoy's (1923), then toured with variety acts before joining Sam Wooding at the Club Alabam (early 1925), sailed to Europe with Wooding in May 1925. Returned to U.S.A. with Wooding in 1927, continued working with the band in early 1928, then worked with Keep Shufflin' revue, extensive free-lance recordings, also worked with Johnny Dunn. In Otto Hardwick's Band in New York (1931), briefly with Fess Williams in 1933. With Fletcher Henderson from summer of 1935 until joining Cab Calloway in February 1936, left Cab in November 1937 and began working for Chick Webb. Remained after that leader's death (1939), worked briefly under Ella Fitzgerald's leadership, then worked with Eddie Mallory and Edgar Hayes before leading own sextet in Philadelphia (late 1941). Led own band at Tony Pastor's Club in New York (1943-4), took own band to California in October 1944. Continued to lead own band during the 1940s, also gigged and recorded with Bunk Johnson in November and December 1947. Played bassoon with the Chicago Civic Orchestra in 1950; led own band in New York and New Jersey during the 1950s. Played in Fletcher Henderson Reunion Band at Great Bay Festival in summer of 1958. Worked with Wilbur de Paris Band from September 1959 until summer of 1964 (including overseas tours); toured Africa with Paul Taubman's Concert Orchestra in September 1964. With

Cab Calloway (1966). Moved to Puerto Rico in spring of 1967, is now mainly active as a music teacher. Lived in Las Vegas during the late 1970s, visited New York in 1980.

BUSHKIN, 'Joe' Joseph
piano/composer/trumpet

Born: New York City, 7th November 1916

His father, who ran a barber-shop in New York, arrived from Kiev, Russia, in 1909. First gigs were college dates on Long Island with band led by Benny Goodman's brother, Irving Goodman. In 1932 began working at the Roseland Ballroom, New York, with Frank LaMarr's Band. Became intermission pianist at The Famous Door in 1935, then worked with Bunny Berigan's Boys (and Red McKenzie) at The Famous Door. Played with Eddie Condon-Joe Marsala Band at Brighton Beach, Coney Island, in summer of 1936, in December of that year worked with Eddie Condon for a cruise on the 'Empress of Britain'. Free-lanced in New York, then joined Joe Marsala in December 1937 (doubling trumpet). With Bunny Berigan from April 1938 until August 1939, then joined Muggsy Spanier's Ragtimers until December 1939. Brief return to Joe Marsala, then joined Tommy Dorsey on 20th January 1940. Joined U.S. Army Air Force in January 1942, played trumpet in service band, then led 410 A.A.F. Orchestra in Douglas, Arizona, later toured with 'Winged Victory' Show, then became musical director, toured Pacific area with Winged Pigeons, also did shows on Radio Tokyo (late 1945). Was demobilised in February 1946, did studio work, then with Benny Goodman from spring until November 1946, also led own band for two short advertising films. In February 1947 went to Rio de Janeiro in Bud Freeman's Trio, returned to New York in summer of 1947, brief spell of inactivity through dislocated shoulder, then resumed studio work. Acted and played in Broadway play 'The Rat Race' (October 1949 until May 1950). Played residency at The Little Club, New York, then in November 1950 began long residency with own quartet at The Embers, New York. In 1951 briefly led own big band at Paramount Theater, New York. Visited Europe early in 1953, returned to U.S. to tour with Louis Armstrong's All Stars (April-June 1953). Continued to lead own small groups throughout the 1950s and 1960s: The Embers, Sands, Las Vegas, etc., also regularly featured on television shows, 'Johnny Midnight', etc. Appeared in film version of 'The Rat Race' (1960), did concert at New York Town Hall in March 1964 (playing piano and trumpet), lived in Marin County, San Francisco, in the 1960s, moved to Hawaii in summer of 1965 for two and a half years, played residency at the Gauguin Club, also toured Hawaiian Islands for U.S. State Department. Moved to Santa Barbara, California; played residency at Hotel Plaza (July 1969), then played Theatrical Club, Cleveland, before living for a while in London (late 1969). Worked in Las Vegas (1970), residing in Santa Barbara (1971). Worked in London as Bing Crosby's accompanist (1977). Was active in raising thoroughbreed horses during the late 1970s and 1980s, but also played musical dates including residencies at Cafe Carlyle, New York in 1982 and 1983.

BUTLER, 'Jack' Jacques
trumpet/vocals

Born: 29th April 1909

Raised in Washington, D.C., studied dentistry at Howard University, began playing trumpet at the age of 17. Moved to New York City, worked with Cliff Jackson in the late 1920s, with Horace Henderson (1930-1). Led own band (in New York and on tour) 1934-5, worked with Willie Bryant, then to Europe. Joined Willie Lewis Band (late 1936), worked mainly with Willie Lewis until 1939, then toured Scandinavia from June 1939. Was in Norway at the commencement of World War II, returned to the U.S.A. in April 1940. Led own band, worked with Mezz Mezzrow (spring 1943), with Art Hodes (summer 1943-4), with Bingie Madison (1945), with bassist Cass Carr (summer 1947). Worked in Toronto, Canada (1948). Returned to Europe in late 1950, led own band on various tours, then played long residency at La Cigale, Paris, from 1953 until returning to the U.S.A. in 1968. Still plays regularly in New York.

Appeared in the Film 'Paris Blues' (1961).

BUTLER, **Roy**
reeds

Born: Richmond, Indiana. c. 1902

Toured with carnival bands before joining Sammy Stewart, worked with Jimmy Wade (1925). With banjoist Henri Saparo in New York (1927). To Europe with pianist Anthony Spaulding in July 1928. Worked with Harry Fleming in Europe during the late 1920s, also worked with Herb Flemming, both in Europe and in South America (1933). To India (December 1933), worked there with Crickett Smith, Leon Abbey, Teddy Weatherford, etc. Returned to U.S.A. in October 1944, left full-time music, but continued to play engagements, and often played oboe in local orchestras in Chicago.

BUTTERFIELD, **'Billy' Charles William**
trumpet

Born: Middleton, Ohio, 14th January 1917

Husband of vocaliste Dotty Dare Smith. Started on violin, then bass and trombone before specialising on trumpet. Attended high school in Wyoming, then studied medicine at Transylvania College; played in college dance bands. With Dick Raymond, Andy Anderson before joining Austin Wylie in Pittsburgh (c. January 1937). With Bob Crosby from September 1937 until June 1940; recorded sound-track for 'Second Chorus' film, then worked with Bob Strong Band in Chicago (August 1940), then joined Artie Shaw from September 1940 until February 1941. With Benny Goodman from March 1941 until early 1942, then joined Les Brown's Band before becoming studio musician at C.B.S. and N.B.C. until Army call-up. After being demobilised in late 1945 formed own band, continued to lead own band in 1946 and 1947 (including residencies on West Coast, etc.). Played at Nick's, New York, from late 1947, then resumed studio work in New York. Throughout the late 1940s and 1950s continued to play at Nick's, Condon's, etc., also occasionally led own small band on college tours, etc. Prolific free-lance recordings and several brief stints with Benny Goodman (including Newport Jazz Festival in 1958). Moved to Smithfield, Virginia, early in 1959, active as a teacher, also led own band. From 1968 worked regularly in The World's Greatest Jazzband, left in early 1973, and undertook widespread free-lance activities. Often featured at festivals in U.S.A. and Europe during the early 1980s.

Not related to trombonist Charles F. Butterfield (died 1979).

BUTTERFIELD, **Erskine**
piano/composer

Born: Syracuse, New York, 9th February 1913
Died: New York City, July 1961

Began on piano at the age of nine, attended school in Newark, New Jersey, then became full-time music student. Worked with Noble Sissle, briefly with the Savoy Sultans, then led own band before joining N.B.C. studio staff in 1938. After service in U.S. Army during World War II, led own trio in Minneapolis, then resumed studio work in New York.

BUTTS, **'Jimmy' James H.**
string bass/vocals

Born: New York City, 24th September 1917

In the late 1930s worked with Dr. Sausage and his Five Pork Chops (led by drummer Frank Tyson), also played in Daisy Mae's Hepcats. With Les Hite (spring 1941), then with Chris Columbus Band (1942), Don Redman (1943), Art Hodes, Lem Johnson, Tiny Grimes (1944), Noble Sissle (1945), then did U.S.O. tour of the Pacific with vocaliste Frances Brock. Led own small groups in the late 1940s and 1950s, also worked in duo with Doles Dickens. Led in Canada and U.S. during the 1960s, worked with pianiste Juanita Smith in the late 1960s. Continues to work regularly mostly in the New York area.

BYAS, **'Don' Carlos Wesley**
tenor sax

Born: Muskogee, Oklahoma, 21st October 1912
Died: Amsterdam, Holland, 24th August 1972

Began on violin, then switched to alto sax. As a teenager worked with Benny Moten and Terrence Holder, also played in Oklahoma City with Walter Page's Blue Devils (c. 1929).

In 1931-2 led own band Don Carlos and his Collegiate Ramblers (based at Langston College, Oklahoma). In 1933 left Oklahoma with Bert Johnson and his Sharps and Flats, changed to tenor sax with this band, worked in California and then remained in Los Angeles. In July 1935 played in Lionel Hampton's Big Band, then joined big band led by Eddie Barefield. With Buck Clayton's 14 Gentlemen of Harlem in spring of 1936, briefly with Lorenzo Flennoy, subsequently worked under Charlie Echols' leadership from August 1936. To New York with Eddie Mallory's Band (March 1937) accompanying Ethel Waters, remained with this band for about 18 months, then worked briefly with Don Redman and Lucky Millinder before joining Andy Kirk in February 1939. Left Kirk in July 1940, worked with Edgar Hayes' Band and also toured with Benny Carter (September 1940). Joined Count Basie from January 1941 until November 1943, then worked in New York with Dizzy Gillespie. During 1944 gigged with many all-star bands on 52nd Street, in 1945 led own band at Three Deuces, etc. In September 1946 came to Europe as a member of Don Redman's Band and lived in Europe until his death. In 1950 played in Europe with Duke Ellington, also toured with Norman Granz's 'Jazz at the Philharmonic' and visited Britain as a soloist in 1965. Was regularly featured at jazz festivals throughout Europe and continued his prolific recording career. Lived in Holland for several years. Usually toured as a soloist, working with local rhythm sections. Temporary return to U.S. (1970), featured at Newport Jazz Festival (July 1970), also played club dates before returning to Europe.

C

CACERES, 'Ernie' Ernesto
clarinet/baritone and alto sax

Born: Rockport, Texas, 22nd November 1911
Died: Texas, 10th January 1971

Brother of Emilio (violin) and Pinero, who died in 1960 (trumpet and piano). Clarinet from an early age, also studied guitar and saxophone. Worked with local bands from 1928, then worked with family trio. Long spell with brother Emilio's small band including residencies in Detroit and New York. Joined Bobby Hackett in summer of 1938, played tenor sax in Jack Teagarden's Band from February 1939. Briefly in big band led by Bob Zurke, then with Glenn Miller from February 1940 until summer of 1942. With Johnny Long's Band from March 1943, with Benny Goodman in October 1943. Joined Tommy Dorsey in December 1943. Worked with Benny Goodman and Woody Herman in 1944, U.S. Army service from spring 1945. Played at Nick's, New York, in 1946, with Billy Butterfield in 1947. Took part in many recordings with Eddie Condon alumni during the 1940s and 1950s. Own quartet at the Hickory Log, New York, in 1949. Regular television work with Garry Moore Orchestra from 1950 until 1956. With Bobby Hackett Band at Henry Hudson Hotel, New York, for a year from November 1956, free-lance session work, recordings, etc. During the early 1960s worked regularly with Billy Butterfield, featured at several jazz festivals, then settled in San Antonio, Texas, continued to work with local bands. Died of throat cancer in a San Antonio hospital.

CAIAZZA, Nick
tenor sax/clarinet

Born: New Castle, Pennsylvania, 20th March 1914

First musical tuition from Ralph Gaspare. Left home in 1932, toured the Middle West with the Keystone Serenaders. Toured with Joe Haymes in 1936-7. Worked with Muggsy Spanier Ragtimers (November-December 1939), then with Woody Herman (early 1940) before joining Will Bradley-Ray McKinley Band. Worked at Nick's with Bobby Hackett (late 1940), then stint with Dick Roger's Band before joining Muggsy Spanier Big Band from April 1941, left during spring of 1942, briefly with Teddy Powell, then with Alvino Rey until touring with Chico Marx Band in the summer of 1943. During 1944 and 1945 made many 'V' Disc recordings with Louis Armstrong, Jack Teagarden, Hot Lips Page, etc. Worked as C.B.S. and N.B.C. staff musician from the mid-1940s. From 1950 until 1959 was on Paul Whiteman's A.B.C. studio staff, during this period also worked with Tommy Dorsey, Ray McKinley, Benny Goodman, and Billy Butterfield; recorded with the New York Philharmonic Orchestra. Studied composition with Paul Creston in New York, in 1960 moved to Boston. Several of his extended compositions have been publicly performed. During the late 1960s taught at the Berklee School of Music.

CALDWELL, 'Happy' Albert W.
tenor sax/clarinet

Born: Chicago, Illinois, 25th July 1903
Died: New York, 29th December 1978

Attended Wendell Phillips High School in Chicago, studied pharmacy. Took up clarinet in 1919. Played clarinet in 8th Illinois Regimental Band, after Army service took lessons from his cousin, Buster Bailey. Returned to studies until 1922, then joined Bernie Young's Band at Columbia Tavern, Chicago, made first records with Young in 1923 ('Dearborn Street Blues'), began doubling tenor c. 1923. Toured in Mamie Smith's Jazz Hounds, remained in New York (1924). Did summer season at Asbury Park, then joined Bobby Brown's Syncopators (1924). Worked with Elmer Snowden (1925), also with Billy Fowler, Thomas Morris, etc. With Willie Gant's Ramblers (summer 1926), worked with Cliff Jackson, also toured with Keep Shufflin' revue (early 1927). With Arthur Gibbs' Orchestra (summer 1927 to summer 1928), recorded with Louis Armstrong (1929), also worked with Elmer Snowden again, Charlie Johnson, Fletcher Henderson, etc. Regularly with Vernon Andrade's Orchestra from 1929 until 1933. With Tiny Bradshaw (1934), Louis Metcalfe (1935), then led own band, mainly in New York. Recorded with Jelly Roll Morton (1939), with Willie Gant (1940). After leading his Happy Pals at Minton's in early 1941, he moved to Philadelphia for three years, occasionally led own band, also worked with Eugene 'Lonnie' Slappy and his Swingsters and Charlie Gaines. Returned to New York in January 1945. Active with own band throughout the 1950s and 1960s, many private engagements and residencies at Small's (1950-3), Rockland Palace (1957), etc., also gigged with Louis Metcalf and Jimmy Rushing. Toured Scandinavia in 1975.

C

CALLENDER, 'Red' George Sylvester — *Born: Richmond, Virginia, 6th March 1918*
string bass/tuba

Learnt to play several instruments whilst a student at the Industrial School in Bordentown, New Jersey. At 15 worked with Banjo Bernie's Band. Moved to California in the mid-1930s. With Louis Armstrong in Los Angeles (November 1937), subsequently with Nat 'King' Cole and various bands in California. Long spells of studio work, also led own trio at Suzi-Q Club in Hollywood. With Errol Garner's Trio (late 1946), with Johnny Otis (1947), then led own band in Hawaii until 1950. Returned to Hollywood, two years with Jerry Fielding, then extensive free-lance work in film, television, and recording studios, occasionally leads own small groups. Has appeared in many films including 'I Dood It' (with Hazel Scott), 'New Orleans' (with Louis Armstrong), and 'St. Louis Blues' (with Barney Bigard).

CALLOWAY, Blanche — *Born: Baltimore, Maryland, 1902*
vocals — *Died: Baltimore, Maryland, 16th December 1978*

Sister of Cab Calloway and Elmer Calloway. Featured at New York's Ciro Club during the mid-1920s, then did extensive touring with travelling revues and played residencies in Chicago. Fronted Andy Kirk's Band for residency at Pearl Theatre, Philadelphia (1931), from then on led own touring band until September 1938, when bankruptcy (filed under married name of Blanche Calloway Pinder) forced her to disband. Worked as a solo artiste for several years. During the early 1960s took up appointment as director of a Florida radio station, later founded Afram cosmetic company.

CALLOWAY, 'Cab' Cabell — *Born: Rochester, New York, 25th December 1907*
vocals

Brother of Blanche and bandleader Elmer; Cab's daughter, Chris, is a vocaliste. Raised in Baltimore, attended Douglass High School, occasionally sang with the Baltimore Melody Boys. Moved with family to Chicago, studied at Crane College, then appeared in 'Plantation Days' show at Loop Theatre (together with his sister, Blanche). Worked as relief drummer and master of ceremonies at the Sunset Cafe, toured M.C.A. circuit, also worked in 'tabloid' show with Blanche, left in Dayton, Ohio, and returned to work in Chicago. Worked with The Missourians in New York (autumn 1928), then returned to Chicago, acted as master of ceremonies with The Alabamians at the Merry Gardens, Chicago (April 1929)—specialising in personality vocals. Featured in 'Hot Chocolates' Revue, New York, then fronted The Alabamians at the Savoy, New York (October 1929). Began working regularly with The Missourians and began fronting the band—the billing being changed to Cab Calloway and his Orchestra. In February 1931, the 'new' band began its first important residency at the Cotton Club, New York, featured on and off at that venue until January 1932, by which time Cab had gained a national reputation. The band visited Europe in 1934, appearing in England in March and April 1934. Cab made 'Hi-De-Ho' a national catch phrase; during the mid-1930s he occasionally played alto saxophone. During the late 1930s and early 1940s Cab's Band was consistently in the top ten highest earning bands in the U.S.A., undertaking widespread touring in U.S.A. and Canada. Cab disbanded in April 1948 and began working with a sextet, he re-formed big bands for specific engagements in Miami (early 1949), South America, and Canada, etc. Cab made a solo visit to England in the summer of 1948. From June 1952 until August 1954 he played the role of 'Sportin' Life' in Gershwin's 'Porgy and Bess' (including London run in 1952). He did a solo tour of Britain in 1955; during the late 1950s he occasionally toured with 'Porgy and Bess', also formed up big bands for short residencies in New York, Las Vegas, etc. He was featured with the touring 'Harlem Globetrotters' Show during the mid-1960s, during the late 1960s he reverted to full-time stage work, starring in 'Hello, Dolly' alongside Pearl Bailey. Cab's autobiography 'Of Minnie The Moocher and Me' was published in 1976. Continued to work regularly through the 1970s and 1980s, featured in various shows including 'Bubbling Brown Sugar'.

Film appearances include: 'The Big Broadcast' (1933), 'International House', 'The Singing Kid', 'Stormy Weather', 'Sensations of 1945', 'St. Louis Blues', etc.

CAMPBELL, Floyd
drums/vocals

Born: Helena, Arkansas, 17th September 1901

Father, Wilson Campbell, was a pianist, brother Bill Campbell a pianist and song-writer. Took up drums in 1922 and played gigs around Helena area. With Charlie Creath (mainly in St. Louis) from 1924-25. On riverboats with Fate Marable, Dewey Jackson, 1925-27. Led own band for more than 40 years starting in 1927—first in St. Louis, then in Cincinnati, on tour before making Chicago his home.

CAREY, 'Mutt' Thomas
trumpet

Born: Hahnville, Louisiana, 1891
Died: Elsinore, California, 3rd September 1948

Also known as 'Papa Mutt'. Brother of Jack (trombone/leader) and Peter (alto horn); several other brothers were also musicians. Started on drums and guitar, then played alto horn before changing to cornet c. 1912. Played cornet in the Crescent Orchestra (led by his brother, Jack) from 1913, also regular parade work with other bands before joining Kid Ory in 1914 (replacing Lewis Matthews). In 1917 toured with the 'Mack and Mack' show (along with Johnny Dodds and Steve Lewis), played briefly in Chicago with Lawrence Duhé's Band, then returned to New Orleans (1918). Worked with Chris Kelly (on second trumpet) at the Bulls' Club, then joined Wade Whaley's Band in Bucktown. Went to California in November 1919 to join Kid Ory. In 1925, when Ory left for Chicago, he handed the leadership to Carey who subsequently led own big band The Jeffersonians during the late 1920s and 1930s. The band did regular work at Hollywood film studios, including providing atmosphere music on silent-filmsets. During the early 1940s Carey worked as a Pullman-porter but continued gigging. He rejoined Kid Ory in 1944, continued day work for a while, then resumed full-time music and played regularly for Kid Ory until the summer of 1947. Led own recording band in New York in late 1947, then returned to California and gigged with his own band. He was organising a new band at the time of his death. He appeared briefly in the film 'New Orleans'.

CARHART, George
guitar/banjo

Born: 21st July 1905

Taught by Elmer Snowden. Played in school band at George Washington High in New York City. Played various summer seasons, then organised own all-star band which played regularly in Europe during the late 1920s (some of the musicians employed were Bud Freeman, Danny Polo, Jack Purvis, Dave Tough, etc. Continued to lead bands during the 1930s, and played on several liner cruises. Retired, lives in New Jersey.

CARLISLE, Una Mae
piano/vocals/composer

Born: Xenia, Ohio, 26th December 1915
Died: New York City, 7th November 1956

A protegée of Fats Waller, was discovered by Fats whilst he was working in Cincinnati in late 1932. Worked with Waller for a while, was then featured as a solo act. Worked (and recorded) in Europe 1937-9, appeared in England, France (including long residency at Boeuf sur le Toit), Germany, etc. Returned to U.S.A., solo work at Village Vanguard (late 1940), spell in hospital (1941), then played at Kelly's Stables, Plantation Club, Hotel Dixie, etc. Enjoyed considerable success with compositions 'Walkin' By the River' and 'I See A Million People'. Own radio and television series in the late 1940s. Suffered for many years with mastoid trouble which forced her to retire in 1954.

CARLSON, Frank L.
drums

Born: New York City, 5th May 1914

Brother Anthony G. Carlson is a string-bassist. With Gene Kardos and Clyde McCoy prior to working with Woody Herman from 1937 until 1942. Moved to California where he took part in many free-lance recordings, ranging from jazz dates to work with Los Angeles Philharmonic. Now lives in Hawaii.

C

CARNEY, Harry Howell
baritone sax/clarinet/bass clarinet

Born: Boston, Massachusetts, 1st April 1910
Died: New York City, 8th October 1974

Brother, Ray, was a pianist. Harry began on piano, then specialised on clarinet before taking up alto saxophone. Joined a 'Knights of Pythias' student band at 13. Worked in Boston with Bobby Sawyer and pianist Walter Johnson. Journeyed to New York (with boyhood friend Charlie Holmes) early in 1927, gigged with Fess Williams at the Savoy Ballroom, then worked at the Bamboo Inn with banjo-guitarist Henri Saparo, briefly with pianist Joe Steele. Joined Duke Ellington during the last week of June 1927, playing first date at a one-nighter at Nuttings-on-the-Charles, near Boston. Other than brief absences worked regularly with Duke Ellington. Originally played alto with the band, but soon began specialising on baritone sax.

CARPENTER, 'Wingie' Theodore
trumpet/vocals

Born: St. Louis, Missouri, 15th April 1898
Died: New York, 21st July 1975

Had left arm amputated after being involved in an accident during his early teens—the operation was performed by Doc Cheatham's uncle, a noted surgeon. Took up trumpet some time later, by 1920 was working in travelling carnival shows, toured with Herbert's Minstrel Band in 1921. Settled in Cincinnati for a while, worked with Wes Helvey, Clarence Paige, Zack Whyte, etc., worked with Speed Webb (1926), later played residency in Buffalo with Eugene Primus (1927). From late 1926 until 1928 worked on and off with the Whitman Sisters' Show (usually with pianist Troy Snapp's Band). During the early 1930s was featured with Smiling Billy Steward's Celery City Serenaders, also worked with another Florida band, led by Bill Lacey. In the mid-1930s did regular touring with various bandleaders including: Jack Ellis, Dick Bunch, and Jesse Stone. Settled in New York, worked with Campbell 'Skeets' Tolbert and Fitz Weston, mainly active as leader of own small band from 1939. Long residencies at The Black Cat, New Capitol, Tony Pastor's, The Yeah Man, etc. Continued to lead own band during the 1960s, playing occasional dance dates.

CARR, 'Peck' Mancy
banjo/guitar

Born: Charleston, West Virginia. c. 1900
Believed deceased

Chiefly remembered for his recorded work with Louis Armstrong in 1928 and 1929. Worked with Carroll Dickerson in 1924, then played in Lottie Hightower's Night Hawks (1925) before rejoining Carroll Dickerson, worked with that leader for several years and went with him (and Louis Armstrong) to New York in 1929. Returned to Chicago, then moved back to West Virginia and worked there with his brother. Is thought to have died many years ago. Has mistakenly been referred to as a white musician; his name has been misprinted as 'Cara' on countless occasions.

CARROLL, 'Bob' Robert
tenor sax

Born: Louisville, Kentucky. c. 1905
Died: New York City, 1952

Worked with local bands including the Kentucky Derbies, left Louisville as a member of Benny Carter's Band. With Horace Henderson (1930), subsequently with Don Redman from 1931 until late 1936. Joined Teddy Hill in spring of 1937 (replacing Cecil Scott). Rejoined Don Redman in the late 1930s, with Teddy Wilson Big Band from January 1940, briefly with Edgar Hayes until July 1940. With Horace Henderson (autumn 1941), with Fats Waller in 1941-2. After serving in the U.S. Army he did less and less playing, and led a vagrant existence in New York City; he died of a combination of malnutrition and alcoholism.

CARRUTHERS, 'Jock' Earl Malcolm
baritone and alto saxes/clarinet/vocals

Born: West Point, Missouri, 27th May 1910
Died: Kansas City, 5th April 1971

Attended school in Kansas City, Kansas, then studied at Fisk University. Worked with Benny Moten in 1928, then spent three years in and around St. Louis, working with Dewey

Jackson and Fate Marable. Joined Jimmie Lunceford in 1932, and remained after that leader's death (1947) to work first in Joe Thomas-Ed Wilcox Band, then with Ed Wilcox. After the band broke up he moved back to Kansas City, Kansas, where he continued to work as a musician throughout the 1960s.

CARRY, 'Scoops' George Dorman
alto sax/clarinet

Born: Little Rock, Arkansas, 23rd January 1915
Died: Chicago, August 1970

His brother Ed (guitar) was a bandleader in Chicago, their mother was a music teacher. Studied music from the age of eight, spent several years at the Chicago Music College. During the 1930s attended Iowa University. Worked with Cassino Simpson at the Garrick Theatre, Chicago, with the Midnight Revellers (May 1930), on tour with Boyd Atkins' Firecrackers (summer 1930), toured R.K.O. circuit with Lucky Millinder (autumn 1931), then worked with brother Ed's Orchestra from 1932. With Zutty Singleton in 1936 (briefly with Fletcher Henderson), then joined Roy Eldridge in Chicago (1937), brief spell with Art Tatum Quartet in 1938. With Horace Henderson in early 1939, later that year in Darnell Howard's Quartet. Briefly with Bob Shoffner early in 1940, then several months with drummer Floyd Campbell's Gangbusters before joining Earl Hines in October 1940. Remained with Earl until 1947, featured on clarinet in 1946 small-band recordings. Left full-time music in 1947, studied law and later established his own practice in Chicago, subsequently he became a state attorney in Chicago.

CARTER, 'Benny' Bennett Lester
alto sax/trumpet/arranger/composer— has also recorded on tenor sax/clarinet/ trombone/piano

Born: New York City, 8th August 1907

His cousin, Theodore 'Cuban' Bennett (1902-65), was a distinguished trumpet player; Darnell Howard was also Benny's cousin. Benny's father was a self-taught guitarist, his mother played organ and piano. Began on piano at an early age, did odd jobs as a milkman's assistant, laundry deliverer, and upholsterer in order to save up for an instrument. Inspired by Bubber Miley, a local San Juan resident, he bought a second-hand trumpet; after several hours abortive blowing he returned to the shop and swapped it for a 'C' melody sax. Subbed for Ben Whittet at John O'Connors' Club, then in August 1924 joined June Clark's Band and switched to alto sax. Soon afterwards he joined Billy Paige's Broadway Syncopators at the Capitol, New York, went to Pittsburgh with them in October 1924. They soon disbanded and Benny (with 'Cuban' Bennett) worked with Lois Deppe's Serenaders, then on baritone with Earl Hines at the Grape Arbor in Pittsburgh (late 1924). In May 1925 he went to Wilberforce College, Ohio, intending to study theology, but joined Horace Henderson's Collegians instead. Left Horace Henderson in 1926, during that summer worked with Billy Fowler's Band in Baltimore and New York. Briefly with James P. Johnson, also spent two weeks in Duke Ellington's Band (deputising for Harvey Boone). Short spell with Fletcher Henderson, then spent over a year with Charlie Johnson. Rejoined Horace Henderson in Detroit, briefly with Fletcher Henderson (autumn 1928), then formed own band for Arcadia Ballroom, New York (late 1928). Led own band in New York and on tour, then again with Fletcher Henderson from January 1930. Joined Chick Webb c. March 1931, left during the summer of 1931 to become musical director of McKinney's Cotton Pickers. From this period onwards regularly doubled on trumpet. Worked with McKinney's for almost a year, during this period also played dates with Don Redman and Fletcher Henderson. Led own band again from c. September 1932 (briefly fronted by Fletcher Henderson in Pennsylvania, December 1932). Mainly active leading own band 1933-4, some touring, also residencies at Lafayette Theatre, Savoy Ballroom, New York, etc. Rejoined Fletcher Henderson briefly in September 1934. Carter had been arranging regularly since the time he joined Charlie Johnson's Band, he arranged for Duke Ellington, Teddy Hill, McKinney's, Mills Blue Rhythm Band, Fletcher Henderson, etc.; in 1934 he began arranging for Benny Goodman. Worked on trumpet with Willie Bryant in spring 1935, subsequently worked occasionally for Charlie Barnet before settling in Europe. After emigration delays, Carter joined Willie Lewis's Band in Paris in the summer of 1935. On the 18th March 1936 he took up appointment as staff arranger for Henry Hall and his Orchestra in London, after touring Scandinavia (autumn 1936) he returned to London. Moved on to the Continent, played with Freddy Johnson in Amsterdam from March 1937, also appeared in France before leading International Band at Scheveningen, Holland, during summer 1937. Led band at Boeuf sur le Toit in Paris before returning to U.S.A. in May 1938. After a long vacation, he organised own big band which made its official debut at The Savoy Ballroom, New York. Led own big band 1940 to summer 1941, then cut down to a sextet in autumn 1941. Moved to West Coast early in 1943, led own band at Billy Berg's Club, Los Angeles, followed by residencies at The Hollywood, Casa Manana, etc. Started 1944 with a residency at The Apollo in New York, continued to lead own band through 1944. In 1945 made the permanent move to Los Angeles, residencies at The Trocadero, Hollywood, Plantation Club, etc. Reorganised new seven-piece band in summer of 1947, residency at Billy Berg's Club from July. Continued to do occasional tours, but from the late 1940s worked mainly as a composer-arranger for the film industry. Led own bands in and around Hollywood during the 1950s, regular big band residency in Los Angeles (1955). In the 1950s and 1960s did brief overseas tours with Norman Granz's Jazz at the Philharmonic. Played solo engagements in Cologne, Germany (late 1961). In the late 1950s and 1960s scored for several national television series including M Squad, Alfred Hitchcock's series, the Chrysler Theatre programmes, etc., also acted as musical director for various vocal stars. Restricted his playing to the alto sax during the 1960s. Brief spell with Duke Ellington early in 1968, later that year played solo dates in Britain. During the past 25 years Benny Carter has arranged and composed music for dozens of important films; films in which he played include: 'Stormy Weather', 'The Snows of Kilimanjaro', 'The View from Pompey's Head', 'As Thousands Cheer', 'Clash By Night', etc. Played briefly in Copenhagen (June 1971), doubled trumpet during this engagement. Did regular tours during the 1970s and early 1980s, including Europe and Japan. A two volume work 'Benny Carter' by Berger, Berger and Patrick was first published in 1982.

CARVER, Wayman Alexander
flute/saxes/clarinet

Born: Portsmouth, Virginia, 25th December 1905
Died: Atlanta, Georgia, 6th May 1967

Father was a clarinettist. Uncle, D. D. Copeland, a flautist, led municipal band. Wayman played flute from an early age. Toured for several years with J. Neal Montgomery's Collegiate Ramblers, then formed own band. Moved to New York, played with Elmer Snowden 1931-2, then led own band before joining Benny Carter 1933. With Chick Webb from 1934—remained when Ella Fitzgerald became leader, left in February 1940, spell out of professional music, then returned to Ella in 1941. Left full-time music, active as a teacher and arranger, then appointed associate Professor of Music at Clark College, Atlanta, Georgia, and held that post until his death.

CARY, 'Dick' Richard Durant
piano/alto horn/trumpet/arranger

Born: Hartford, Connecticut, 10th July 1916

Played violin from early childhood, appeared with the Hartford Symphony Orchestra whilst at high school. Later, specialised on piano, played solo residency at Nick's in New York in 1942. Arranged for Benny Goodman in 1943, played for a month in the Casa Loma Band (August 1943), then worked with Brad Gowans before serving in the U.S. Army. After demobilisation, played in Billy Butterfield's Band, then led own band in Meridan, Connecticut (late 1946). Was the original pianist in Louis Armstrong's All Stars (August 1947 until January 1948), during 1949 worked at Nick's and with Jimmy Dorsey; played trumpet with Tony Parenti (late 1949). Briefly on piano with Jimmy Dorsey (spring 1950), did studio work during the early 1950s (including a stint in Jerry Jerome's T.V. Band), continued to play jazz dates with Muggsy Spanier (late 1952), worked and recorded with Eddie Condon during the 1950s, including spell on trumpet in 1954. With Bobby Hackett Band (alto horn and arranger) from November 1956. Worked with Max Kaminsky during 1958, also active as arranger and composer. Moved to West Coast in 1959, prolific composing and free-lance arranging, also worked with Bob Crosby, Red Nichols, Ben Pollack, etc. Toured Far East with Eddie Condon in spring 1964, then worked for a while in Los Angeles with Matty Matlock. Temporarily ceased doubling on brass in the early 1960s, but continued to work regularly on piano, was featured at several U.S. jazz festivals in the late 1960s. Occasionally led own band (1970-1), playing trumpet, alto horn and piano. Toured Europe (1977). Continued widespread touring during the 1970s and early 1980s, including Europe, and Australia.

CASEY, 'Al' Albert Aloysius *Born: Louisville, Kentucky, 15th September 1915*
guitar

Father was a drummer. Started on violin at the age of eight, then played ukelele. Moved to New York in 1930, studied guitar whilst at the DeWitt Clinton High School, received some tuition from James Smith. First professional work with Fats Waller in 1934, worked regularly with Fats throughout the 1930s. With Teddy Wilson Big Band 1939-40, then with Buster Harding's Quartet at Nick's, New York, in May 1940. Worked with Fats Waller again from October 1940 until 1942. Led own trio from 1943, various residencies including: Onyx, New York, Garrick, Chicago, Randini's, Los Angeles, etc., etc. Featured at Metropolitan Opera House concert in January 1944, played briefly in Clarence Profit's Trio (early 1944), with Billy Kyle Trio (1949), etc. Extensive free-lance work in the 1950s, then worked regularly in tenorist King Curtis All Stars until 1961, then played long residency with Curley Hammer's Sextet in New York. Resident at Baby Grand, Harlem (1971). Worked for two years as a Xerox operator, continued gigging at weekends, then resumed touring including dates in Europe. A broken leg hampered activities from the mid-1970s, but by the early 1980s was working regularly including annual tours of Europe.

CASEY, Floyd *Born: Poplar Bluff, Missouri, 1900*
drums/washboard *Died: New York, 7th September 1967*

Worked regularly on the riverboats during the early 1920s; with Ed Allen's Whispering Gold Band in 1922. Played in St. Louis with Dewey Jackson (c. 1921), with saxist Jimmy Powell's Jazz Monarchs (c. 1925-6), moved to New York and from 1927 was featured on many recordings with Clarence Williams, worked with trombonist George Wilson at Capitol Palace, New York in 1927. During the 1930s played many 'taxi'-dance-hall jobs in New York. With Jimmy Reynold's Band in 1941, worked in Ed Allen's Band, then (with Ed Allen) played in band led by pianist Benton Heath at the New Gardens, New York for many years.

CASEY, 'Bob' Robert Hanley *Born: Johnson County, Illinois, 11th February 1909*
string bass/guitar

Began on tenor-banjo at 14, self-taught. Played week-end dances in Southern Illinois; with Egyptian Transportation System Orch. (1926-7). Moved to St. Louis in December 1927, with Joe Gill (1929-31), Joe Reichman (1932). Began playing bass in 1929, doubled guitar for several years. Moved to Chicago, with Wingy Manone (1933), Russ Kettler, The King's Jesters, etc., also staff musician at N.B.C. Chicago. With Muggsy Spanier from July 1939. After Muggsy disbanded, returned to Chicago, briefly with Pete Daily, then with Gus Arnheim and Charlie Spivak. Joined Brad Gowans at Nick's, New York in October 1943, several years at Nick's and at Condon's Club, also worked with Art Hodes, Bobby Hackett, etc. Moved to Florida in 1957, played with Dukes of Dixieland (1962). Emerged from semi-retirement to play dates in New York (1971).

CASTLE, Lee *Born: New York City, 28th February 1915*
(real name: Castaldo)
trumpet

His brother, Charles, is a trombonist. Played in junior bands on drums, began on trumpet at 15, became professional at 18. Worked with Joe Haymes, Dick Stabile, and Artie Shaw before joining Red Norvo in July 1937. Joined Tommy Dorsey in September 1937, left the band when Tommy sent him to study with the Dorseys' father in Lansford, Pennsylvania, rejoined in late 1938. Briefly with Glenn Miller, then with Jack Teagarden from April until

December 1939. Led own band in 1940, briefly with Will Bradley, then joined Artie Shaw in early 1941. Led own band from March 1942—adopted new name—signed the band over to Richard Himber in late 1942, then joined Benny Goodman until late 1943 (appeared in the films 'Stage Door Canteen' and 'The Girls They Left Behind'). Led own big bands in the 1940s, formed Dixieland outfit in 1949. With Artie Shaw (1950), with the Dorsey Brothers from 1953, fronted Jimmy Dorsey's Band during that leader's last illness, subsequently became leader and part owner of the Dorsey Brothers' Orchestra. In 1978, continues to lead The Jimmy Dorsey Orchestra.

Authored excellent book containing transcriptions of Louis Armstrong's recorded solos.

CATLETT, 'Big Sid' Sidney
drums/composer

Born: Evansville, Indiana, 17th January 1910
Died: Chicago, Illinois, 25th March 1951

Brief spell on piano, then played drums in school band. Family moved to Chicago where he attended the Tilden High School, received drum tuition from Joe Russek. Replaced Dick Curry in Darnell Howard's Band at Club Arlington, Chicago (c. 1928). Joined Sammy Stewart at Michigan Theatre, Chicago (1929), toured with Stewart and played residencies in New York (spring 1930). Worked with Elmer Snowden in New York (1931-2), then from June 1932 until late 1933 worked on and off with Benny Carter; played (and sang) with Rex Stewart's Band at Empire Ballroom from June 1933. Took part in several freelance recording sessions, with Spike Hughes, Eddie Condon, etc. Also worked with Sam Wooding briefly and regularly with McKinney's Cotton Pickers. With Eddie King's Band at Dave's Tavern, Chicago (summer 1934), then with bassist William Lyle's Band for several months from September 1934. Briefly led own band in Chicago, then joined Jeter-Pillars Band in St. Louis (1935). With Fletcher Henderson from February 1936, left c. September 1936 and joined Don Redman until late 1938. With Louis Armstrong from late 1938 until early 1941, briefly with Roy Eldridge, then worked on and off with Benny Goodman from June until October 1941. Rejoined Louis Armstrong from late 1941 until summer 1942, then with Teddy Wilson from c. August 1942 until early 1944 Led own quartet from spring 1944 until 1947, residencies in New York (Three Deuces, Spotlite, Downbeat, etc.), Los Angeles, Chicago, Detroit, etc., also toured with 'Concert Varieties' and subbed for Sonny Greer with Duke Ellington (1945). Briefly led own big band in late 1946. With Louis Armstrong All Stars from August 1947, was forced to quit touring through illness (spring 1949). Became resident drummer at Jazz Ltd, Chicago, from spring 1949, worked with Muggsy Spanier, Sidney Bechet, etc. Also worked in New York with Eddie Condon in 1949 and took part in Carnegie Hall concert with John Kirby (December 1950). Was ill with pneumonia early in 1951, returned to play at Jazz Ltd. He attended an Easter week-end jazz concert at the Chicago Opera House, whilst talking to Slam Stewart in the wings he suffered a fatal heart attack.

CELESTIN, 'Papa' Oscar Phillip
trumpet/vocals

Born: La Fourche Parish, Napoleonville, Louisiana, 1st January 1884
Died: New Orleans, 15th December 1954

Original nickname was 'Sonny'. Early efforts on the guitar and mandolin, then worked for a few years as a cook on the Texas and Pacific Railroad. Settled in St. Charles, Louisiana, and began playing trombone and trumpet in local brass band. Moved to New Orleans in 1906 and joined the Indiana Brass Band on cornet. Later worked in Allen's Brass Band and with Jack Carey, The Olympia Band, etc., before leading own band at Tuxedo Hall, New Orleans, from 1910 until the hall closed in 1913. Led own band at Villa Cafe, then co-led band with trumpeter/bassist Ricard Alexis, later billed as the Original Tuxedo Brass Band. In about 1917 he helped trombonist William Ridgely organise the Original Tuxedo Orchestra, the two men co-led on and off until split up in 1925, then Celestin led his own Tuxedo Jazz Orchestra. The Orchestra did several recording sessions in the late 1920s, played regularly in New Orleans and also toured throughout the Gulf Coast States until the early 1930s. Celestin then left full-time music but continued to lead own band in New Orleans, including residency at the Pelican Roof in 1939. He worked in the local shipyards during World War II, until being seriously injured by a hit-and-run motorist in 1944. Began playing more regularly from 1946, recommenced recording in 1947. During the late 1940s led at The Paddock, New Orleans, also made regular radio and television appearances and occasional tours. In May 1953 went to Washington to play for President Eisenhower, later that year the band appeared in the film 'Cinerama Holiday'.

CHALLIS, 'Bill' William H.
arranger/originally sax/clarinet

Born: Wilkes Barre, Pennsylvania, 8th July 1904

Self-taught pianist, played 'C' melody sax at high school (1921), later studied Economics and Philosophy at Bucknell University and led own student band. Graduated in June 1925 and joined Dave Harmon's Band as saxist/arranger. Submitted arrangements to Jean Goldkette and was asked to join Goldkette's organisation as staff arranger (autumn 1926). Worked for a year with Goldkette, then joined Paul Whiteman until the spring of 1930. Occasionally led own radio orchestra in the 1930s, but was mainly active as a free-lance arranger for: Fletcher Henderson, Frank Trumbauer, the Dorsey Brothers, Lennie Hayton, The Casa Loma Band, Nat Shilkret, etc., etc. Has continued to work as a highly successful arranger until the present time, lives in Massapequa, New York.

CHAMBERS, 'Elmer' Dallas Elmer
trumpet

Born: Bayonne, Jersey City, 1897
Died: Jersey City. c. 1952

Also known as 'Frog' and 'Muffle Jaws'. Met Sam Wooding in U.S. Army Band during World War I. After demobilisation played with Wooding at Scott's, Atlantic City, subsequently in Detroit and New York. Left Wooding in 1923, began working with Fletcher Henderson, joined Henderson regularly from 1924 until 1926. With Billy Fowler's Strand Roof Orchestra c. 1926-7, then toured with travelling revues. Left full-time music to work in Jersey City.

CHAMBERS, Henderson Charles
trombone

Born: Alexandria, Louisiana, 1st May 1908
Died: New York City, 19th October 1967

Attended local school, then studied at Leland College, Baker, Louisiana. Began playing trombone with student band at Morehouse College, Atlanta, Georgia, first professional work with Neil Montgomery in 1931. With Doc Banks in Nashville (1932), then worked in saxist Jack Jackson's Pullman Porters, later fronted by Speed Webb (1933). With Zack Whyte (1934), then played in Kentucky with Al Sears' Band (1935-6). With Tiny Bradshaw (1937-8). To New York in 1939, worked with Chris Columbus Band at Savoy Ballroom until late 1940, then with Louis Armstrong from January 1941 until 1943. With Don Redman in 1943, joined Ed Hall Sextet in summer of 1944, worked on and off with Ed Hall for four years, also played with Don Redman, Sy Oliver, etc. With Lucky Millinder (1950-3), Count Basie, Jerry Fielding (1954), did occasional tours with Cab Calloway, also worked with Doc Cheatham in Boston (late 1955). Occasionally with Duke Ellington in 1957, regular free-lance studio work, spell with band led by Mercer Ellington (1959). Toured with Ray Charles (1961 to late 1963), then with Count Basie from January 1964 until 1966. During last years of his life assisted Edgar Battle in running big rehearsal band. Died of a heart attack.

CHEATHAM, 'Doc' Adolphus Anthony
trumpet

Born: Nashville, Tennessee, 13th June 1905

Gained nickname through having several relatives in the medical profession. Was originally taught by Professor N. C. Davis in Nashville. First professional work with Marion Hardy's Band for the 'Sunshine Sammy' Show, then toured with John 'Bearcat' Williams' Synco Jazzers (c. 1924). Moved to Chicago, played cornet, soprano and tenor saxes in

Albert Wynn's Band, then led own band (1926). Recorded on soprano with Ma Rainey. Joined Bobby Lee in Philadelphia (on trumpet), then worked in Philadelphia with Wilbur de Paris (1927 to early 1928). Brief spell with Chick Webb, then joined Sam Wooding in New York and sailed with him to Europe in June 1928. Left Wooding and returned to U.S. early in 1930, with Marion Hardy's Alabamians 1930-2, except for spell in McKinney's Cotton Pickers from summer of 1931 until 1932. With Cab Calloway from 1933 until 1939 (including 1934 trip to Europe). Went to Europe for a vacation (August-October 1939), returned to New York and joined Teddy Wilson Big Band in October 1939. Briefly with Benny Carter in 1940, then worked for a while with Fletcher Henderson (1941) and Teddy Hill. With Eddie Heywood Sextet from September 1943 until 1945, then taught regularly at own New York studio, also played with Claude Hopkins in 1946. From spring of 1948 began playing regularly in Marcelino Guerra's Band, continued with Guerra until 1950, took vacation in Europe and played concerts for the Hot Club of France. Throughout the 1950s and 1960s, Doc has done a considerable amount of work with Latin-American bands, Perez Prado (1951-2), Machito, etc. Toured with Cab Calloway (summer 1951), worked mainly in Boston (1952-5) with Vic Dickenson, etc., also spell leading Wilbur de Paris' 'second' band. Did regular recordings and tours with Wilbur de Paris (including Africa in 1957 and Europe in 1960), also toured Europe with Sam Price in 1958 and Africa with Herbie Mann in 1960. Led own band at the International on Broadway, New York, for five years (1960-5). Regularly with Benny Goodman from May 1966 until January 1967 (including trip to Belgium), also toured Europe with the 'Top Brass' package in 1967. Doc continues to free-lance in many varied musical aggregations, including regular appearances as soloist with Ricardo Ray's Latin-American Band. Frequent playing trips to Puerto Rico. Is the author of a booklet on improvisation. Throughout his career Doc has taken part in many free-lance recording sessions: with Count Basie, Max Kaminsky, Pee Wee Russell, John Handy, Leonard Gaskin, Juanita Hall, etc., etc. Played at President Jimmy Carter's White House Jazz Party (June 1978). Maintained rigorous international touring schedule during the late 1970s and early 1980s.

CHITTISON, Herman
piano

Born: Flemingsburg, Kentucky, 1909
Died: Cleveland, Ohio, 8th March 1967

Began playing piano at the age of eight, later studied at the Waldron Boys' School in Nashville, Tennessee, brief spell at the Kentucky State College (1927), left to play with the Kentucky Derbies at the Lexington State Fair. Worked with Zack Whyte from 1928 until 1931, then toured as accompanist for comedian Stepin Fetchit, later toured with Adelaide Hall and Ethel Waters, also did free-lance recordings with Clarence Williams. Joined Willie Lewis in New York (spring 1934) and then sailed to Europe with Lewis. Worked on and off with Lewis in Europe from 1934 until 1938, also toured with Louis Armstrong (1934), led own band and worked in Egypt accompanying vocaliste Arita Day (Dao) early in 1935. Left Lewis late in 1938 and worked with several ex-Lewis sidemen (Bill Coleman, Joe Hayman, etc.) in Egypt as The Harlem Rhythmakers. Returned to New York in spring 1940, formed own trio, also toured again with Stepin Fetchit in the autumn of 1940. Throughout the 1940s and 1950s led own trio for many New York residencies: The Blue Angel, Le Ruban Bleu, Bobili Club, etc., etc., also did regular weekly broadcasts for seven years in the C.B.S. radio series 'Casey—Crime Photographer'. Continued playing regularly in the early 1960s, residencies in Boston, New York, etc., also recorded L.P.s in 1962 and 1964. Worked mainly in Cleveland during the last two years of his life; he died of lung cancer.

CHRISTIAN, 'Buddy' Narcisse J.
banjo/guitar/piano

Born: New Orleans, Louisiana. c. 1895
Died: c. 1958

Played in New Orleans from c. 1910, with various leaders at the Tuxedo c. 1912-13, then on piano with King Oliver at Lala's Cafe c. 1915-16. Moved to New York c. 1919, worked regularly on banjo and piano; with Lucille Hegamin c. 1921, June Clark c. 1923, took part in many of Clarence Williams' recording sessions during the 1920s. With Charles Matson

Band in New York (1927), early in 1929 formed banjo-duo with Fred Jennings. No details of musical activity during the 1940s and 1950s, was a member of New York Local 802 until his death.

CHRISTIAN, 'Charlie' Charles
guitar

Born: Dallas, Texas, 29th July 1916
Died: New York, 2nd March 1942

All four of his brothers were musicians, two (at least) worked professionally: Edward (piano/bass) and Clarence; their father, a blind musician, played guitar and sang. The family moved to Oklahoma City in 1921. Charlie started on trumpet, then specialised on guitar from the age of 12, he also worked on string bass and piano during the 1930s. Played in the family band from early teens, did local club work at 15 and there met Lester Young for the first time. Played in his brother's band, The Jolly Jugglers, during the early 1930s, and is also reported to have worked as a tap-dancer, singer, baseball pitcher, and prize-fighter. Played in Anna Mae Winburn's Band, led own band, worked with trumpeter James Simpson in Oklahoma City and toured (playing bass and guitar) with Alphonso Trent c. 1938. With Leslie Sheffield Band in 1939 (by this time, Charlie's musical skill had been noticed by Teddy Wilson, Norma Teagarden, and Mary Lou Williams). On the recommendation of John Hammond he joined Benny Goodman in Los Angeles in August 1939, subsequently made New York debut with Benny Goodman in September 1939. Was featured mainly with the sextet, but occasionally played with the full band. Whilst on a Middle West tour with Goodman he was taken ill and was subsequently admitted to Bellevue Hospital, New York, in June 1941, where tuberculosis was diagnosed. He was transferred to the Seaview Sanitarium, Staten Island, and spent the rest of his brief life there.

CHRISTIAN, Emile Joseph
trombone/string bass

Born: New Orleans, Louisiana, 20th April 1895
Died: New Orleans, Louisiana, 3rd December 1973

Brother of Frank Christian (trumpet) and Charles Christian (trombone). Emile's early nickname was 'Boot-mouth', he began on cornet (taught by Frank) and by 1912 was playing in Ernest Giardina's Band. In 1916 was offered the job as cornetist with Johnny Stein's Band for a residency in Chicago, he preferred to continue parade work and Nick LaRocca took the job. Went to Chicago in following year to join Bert Kelly's Band at the Greene Goose Club, began doubling trombone at this venue and joined the Original Dixieland Jazz Band in New York in 1918 (Eddie Edwards having joined the U.S. Army). Played in England with the O.D.J.B. 1919-21, returned to New York, did three weeks with Phil Napoleon in the Original Memphis Five, then returned to England with the American (and Broadway) Sextets (1922-3). From 1924 doubled on trombone and string bass with various bands in Europe: with Eric Borchard in Berlin (1924), with Tommy Waltham's Ad Libs, Al Wynn's Band in Berlin and Hanover (c. 1928), Leslie Sterling in Paris, etc. (c. 1928-30). Mainly with Lud Gliskin's Band (1930-4), then in Switzerland with Benton Peyton's Jazz Kings (spring 1935). With Benny French in Paris (1936), then to Taj Mahal Hotel, Bombay, India, with Leon Abbey (November 1936). With Leon Abbey in France, Denmark, etc. (1937-9), returned to U.S.A. in October 1939. Played trombone and bass at Monte Carlo Club, New York, in 1940, then worked in a defence plant during World War II. Moved back to New Orleans and was active on string bass and trombone during the 1950s and 1960s: with Armand Hug, late George Girard, Leon Prima, Sharkey Bonano, etc., toured with Louis Prima in 1957. Was featured at Disneyland Jazz Festival (1967), New Orleans Jazz Festivals in 1968 and 1969.

CHRISTIAN, 'Buddy' Howard Seton
drums

Born: Nyack, New York, 26th October 1917

Played first dance gig at age of 8; worked with various bands around Nyack from 1931. Summer season with Bob Sylvester's Band in Virginia (1936). Joined Red Norvo in 1939. During the 1940s worked for Bobby Parks, Charlie Spivak, Teddy Powell, Ina Ray Hutton, Joe Marsala, George Auld, Buddy Morrow and Ray McKinley. From 1947 worked mainly in and around New York as a free-lance. Continued to play jazz gigs during the 1970s, including work with Pee Wee Erwin.

CLARK, Garnett
piano

Born: Washington, D.C. c. 1914
Died: L'Hopital Sainte Anne, France. c. late 1938

Played piano for drummer Tommy Myles' Band in Washington from c. 1930. Moved to New York (c. 1934), played at Pod's and Jerry's, recorded with Alex Hill and together with Benny Carter worked for Charlie Barnet. Went to Europe with Benny Carter in 1935 and together they joined Willie Lewis' Band in Paris for a short while. Did solo work in 1936, also toured Switzerland as accompanist for Adelaide Hall. In autumn 1937 he suffered a mental breakdown and spent the rest of his life in a hospital.

CLARK, 'June' Algeria Junius
trumpet

Born: Long Beach, New Jersey, 24th March 1900
Died: New York, 23rd February 1963

Family moved to Philadelphia in 1908. Was taught piano by his mother, then played bugle before graduating to baritone horn and cornet. Worked as a Pullman porter before becoming a professional musician with S. H. Dudley's 'Black Sensations'. June and James P. Johnson left the show and worked together in Toledo, Ohio, where they first met Jimmy Harrison. In late 1920 June returned to gig in Philadelphia, then joined band accompanying Josephine Stevens for a year. Did theatre tours with Willie 'The Lion' Smith and with 'Holiday in Dixie' show, show folded in Detroit, June worked in the Buick factory for a while, then rejoined Jimmy Harrison and played in Fess Williams' Band. Settled in New York, led own bands at various venues: Ed Small's, Palace Gardens, Tango Gardens, Monterey Club, etc., etc. (1924-30). Also took band to Saratoga for summer of 1925 and worked for brief spells with various other leaders. Occasionally led own band during the early 1930s, also worked with banjoist Ferman Tapp, Wen Talbot, Jimmy Reynolds in New York (1933-5) and with Harry Marsh, George Baquet, etc., in Philadelphia (1934-5). Led band at Red Pirate Club, New York (late 1935 to early 1936), with Vance Dixon at the Quogue Inn, London Island, until September 1936, then six months with Charlie Skeets in New York. Quit regular playing owing to failing health, worked for a while as Louis Armstrong's road manager, then entered Otisville Sanitarium in August 1939 suffering from tuberculosis. Left Otisville in October 1941, worked as musical adviser to various bands, with Earl Hines as a musical assistant (1944), then became road manager for the famous boxer Sugar Ray Robinson, remained with Sugar Ray until forced to quit through illness shortly before his death.

CLARK, Spencer W.
bass sax/cornet/multi-instrumentalist

Born: Baltimore, Maryland, 15th March 1908

Family moved to New York in 1909. Played mandolin, marimba, and clarinet before doing first gigs on 'C' melody sax in New Rochelle, New York (c. 1923). Specialised on bass sax after hearing Adrian Rollini, worked in local movie-house orchestra from late 1924. Subbed for Rollini during 1925 and 1926—on record and with the California Ramblers at the Ramblers' Inn. During this period worked briefly with Joe Tenner's Stage Band and played on Atlantic liners with George Carhart (1926). In autumn 1926 led 'Little Ramblers' (Lenny Hayton, Carl Kress, etc.) at Ramblers' Inn. With various bands until sailing to Europe with George Carhart in July 1928, with Bud Freeman, Jack Purvis, Babe Russin, etc. Worked in France with George Carhart and Danny Polo, then joined Julian Fuhs in Berlin. With Lud Gluskin in Europe (on bass sax, trumpet, and guitar) from March 1929 until returning to the U.S.A. in January 1931. With Bert Lown in New York for most of 1931, briefly with Will Osborne, then with Fred Waring (1932). On trumpet with Ozzie Nelson (late 1932 to early 1933), sax with Irving Conn (1933-6) and with Dick Stabile (1936-8), also worked on string bass during this period. Left full-time music, worked for a newspaper, continued gigging until August 1939, then entered aviation. Worked for commercial and private airlines until moving to Illinois in 1954. Became Purchasing Agent for City of Highland Park, later began playing bass sax again; worked (and recorded L.P.) with

Freddie Wacker's Windy City Seven (1957). Continued to play occasional gigs in the 1960s. Moved to North Carolina in 1971. Made guest appearances at many jazz festivals during the 1970s and early 1980s. Visited Europe 1980.

CLARKE, George F. *Born: Memphis, Tennessee, 28th August 1911*
tenor sax

Became Jimmie Lunceford's pupil whilst attending Manassas High School in Memphis, thus became a member of Lunceford's first band and remained with him until 1933. Settled in Buffalo and played for various leaders: Guy Jackson, Stuff Smith, Lil Armstrong, etc. Worked again with Stuff Smith in 1939, then led own band which played a long residency at The Anchor Bar, Buffalo, throughout the 1940s. Moved to New York in 1954, played regularly with Cootie Williams (including tour of Europe in early 1959); toured Africa with Cozy Cole in late 1962. Free-lances and occasionally leads own band.

CLARKE, 'Pete' Frank *Born: Birmingham, Alabama, 10th March 1911*
alto/baritone/clarinet *Died: New York City, 27th March 1975*

Brother of Dick (trumpet) and Arthur 'Babe' (saxes). Studied music with 'Fess' Whatley at the Industrial High School in Birmingham. Toured with Montgomery's Collegiate Ramblers (1927), then worked with Wayman Carver's Ramblers (1929). With Chick Webb from 1930 until 1936 (recorded with Duke Ellington in 1936). Joined Louis Armstrong (spring 1937 until 1938), then with Teddy Wilson Big Band (April 1939 until 1940). With Rex Stewart (early 1946), to Europe with Don Redman in September 1946, briefly with John Kirby (on clarinet) in 1947. With Happy Caldwell at Small's in the early 1950s, continued to work regularly during the 1960s. On baritone sax with Reuben Phillips at The Apollo, also played clarinet with Danny Barker's Band (1962) and worked in Jimmy Jones' Orchestra (1963). Played occasionally at Jimmy Ryan's, New York (1970-1).

CLARKE 'Klook' Kenneth Spearman *Born: Pittsburgh, Pennsylvania, 9th January 1914*
drums

Brother and father were musicians. Worked with Leroy Bradley's Band in the early 1930s, brief spell with Roy Eldridge then worked in St. Louis with Jeter-Pillars Band. Joined Edgar Hayes, and toured Europe with Hayes in spring of 1938. With Teddy Hill's Band (1940-41), then became house-musician at Minton's Club in New York City. Worked briefly with Louis Armstrong and with Ella Fitzgerald before year with Benny Carter 1941-42. With Henry Allen Sextet in Chicago, then led own band in New York before service in U.S. Army. With Dizzy Gillespie 1946, and again in 1948, after European tour remained for some months in France. Toured United States with Billy Eckstine. Founder member of The Modern Jazz Quartet in 1952, remained with them until 1955 then extensive free-lance work before moving to Europe in summer of 1956. Since then has worked all over Europe. Co-led big band with pianist François 'Francy' Boland from 1960 until 1973. Revisited U.S.A. in 1972.

CLARK-SMITH, Major N. *Born: Kansas, 31st July 1877*
multi-instrumentalist *Died: Kansas City, Missouri, 7th October 1935*

One of the most brilliant music teachers that America has ever produced. Dozens of black musicians listed in this book cite Clark-Smith as their most important teacher—he enjoyed great success at Tuskegee, in Kansas City and in Chicago.

CLAXTON, Rozelle *Born: Memphis, Tennessee, 5th February 1913*
piano/organ/arranger

Member of a large musical family. Originally, his sister taught him to read music, played piano from the age of 11. From c. 1930 played in trumpeter Clarence Davis' Rhythm Aces, worked with this band when they toured with W. C. Handy (1932). Played and arranged for

Harlan Leonard from c. 1934, played many solo residencies in Chicago during the late 1930s, also worked with Ernie Fields (1939), Eddie South (1940)—briefly subbed for Count Basie in summer 1939. Played solo residency at Elmer's, Chicago (1940), then with Walter Fuller from September 1940. Worked with George Dixon's Quartet from September 1946. Prolific free-lance arranger, has scored for: Count Basie, Earl Hines, Red Norvo, Jimmie Lunceford, Andy Kirk, etc., has also worked as accompanist for various singers, including spell with Pearl Bailey in 1958. From 1959 has worked on and off with Franz Jackson, also plays solo piano and organ residencies.

Has sometimes been confused with the Chicago pianist, Rozelle I. Gayle, who has worked for many years in California.

CLAY, Shirley
trumpet

Born: Charleston, Missouri, 1902
Died: New York City, 7th February 1951

Worked with bands in and around St. Louis from 1920, toured with John 'Bearcat' Williams' Synco Jazzers (c. 1923-4), then settled in Chicago. Regularly with Detroit Shannon's Band (c. 1925-6), Carroll Dickerson (1927), briefly with Louis Armstrong (and Earl Hines) Stompers (1927), then with Clifford 'Klarinet' King Big Band (1928), also took part in many free-lance recording sessions. With Earl Hines (1929-31), Marion Hardy (1931), then with Don Redman from late 1931 until late 1936. During this period Shirley Clay recorded with other leaders: Benny Goodman (1933), Putney Dandridge (October 1935), and with Ben Pollack (1933). With Claude Hopkins (1937-9), brief return to Earl Hines in 1940, then played in Leon Abbey's Band. With Horace Henderson (autumn 1941), Cootie Williams' Big Band (1942); from June 1943 did six months' U.S.O. tour in band led by Herbie Cowens. Led own band at Cinderella Club, New York (1944), with George James' Band (June 1944), then rejoined Claude Hopkins (October 1944). Again led own band, then played in Harry Dial's Quartet until spring of 1946. Led own band before working at Camp Unity, Wingdale, N.Y., in Manzie Johnson's Band (from September 1949), during last years of his life often co-led bands with Edgar Battle.

CLAY, 'Sonny' William Rogers Campbell
drums/multi-instrumentalist

Born: Chapel Hill, Texas, 15th May 1899

Did first gigs in Phoenix c. 1911, began doubling saxophone/trumpet/trombone. Did season at Riverside Park, Arizona, moved to West Coast c. 1916. Played drums with Jelly Roll Morton, drums and xylophone with Johnny Spikes, also worked with George Morrison's Band. Played with Kid Ory during the early 1920s, then played piano, sax, and drums in own Eccentric Harmony Six (late 1922). Led own bands in Los Angeles area from then until the early 1940s, played for many theatre shows, also did extensive touring including trip to Australia (from January 1928). Retired from full-time music in the 1940s, did occasional gigs and worked as a piano-tuner.

CLAYTON, 'Buck' Wilbur Dorsey
trumpet/arranger/composer

Born: Parsons, Kansas, 12th November 1911

Father played tuba and trumpet in local church orchestras. Buck began playing piano at the age of six, switched to trumpet in his early teens, took lessons from his father. At 19 went to California for four months, after a succession of non-musical jobs he returned to Kansas, completed high school studies, then returned to West Coast. Worked with various bandleaders in Los Angeles including: Irwing Brothers, Duke Ellighew, Lavern Floyd, Charlie Echols, and Earl Dancer. Received musical advice from Mutt Carey but never took lessons from him. In 1934 Buck was appointed leader of Earl Dancer's Band, this 14-piece unit was heard by Teddy Weatherford who booked the full band for a residency at the Canidrome Ballroom, Shanghai. Weatherford occasionally played concerts with the band in Shanghai but was not a regular member of the group. Later, Buck led a smaller band at the Casanova Club, Shanghai. Returned to Los Angeles in 1936 and again led own big band, The 14 Gentlemen from Harlem, also gigged with various bandleaders including Charlie Echols. Led own band at Sebastian's Cotton Club, Culver

City, during this residency Lionel Hampton guested with the band. In autumn 1936, whilst on his way to New York to join Willie Bryant's Band, Buck stopped off in Kansas City where Count Basie persuaded him to take the trumpet place recently vacated by Hot Lips Page. Remained with Count Basie until Army call-up in November 1943 (except for temporary absence in mid-1942 for a tonsillectomy). Was stationed for most of the time at Camp Kilmer, New Jersey, and played regularly with all-star service bands. Honourable discharge early in 1946. Did arrangements for Count Basie, Benny Goodman, Harry James, etc. In October 1946 took part in first national Jazz at the Philharmonic tour and subsequently played on several of Norman Granz's tours. From 1947 led own sextet at Cafe Society (Downtown), New York. On 24th September 1949 sailed for first tour of Europe, led own band in France, returned to U.S.A. in June 1950. Long spells with Joe Bushkin Quartet, also worked with Tony Parenti, and led band on tours with Jimmy Rushing. Returned to Europe in 1953, worked mainly with Mezz Mezzrow. Throughout the 1950s achieved considerable success with own specially formed recording groups. Appeared with Benny Goodman in 'The Benny Goodman Story', also played with Goodman in New York in 1957. To Brussels in summer 1958 to work with Sidney Bechet at the World's Fair Concerts. Toured Europe early in 1959, in late 1959 joined Eddie Condon's Band; during the 1960s played for Condon on several occasions, including tour of Japan, Australia, etc., in the spring of 1964. Toured with Jimmy Rushing in summer of 1962, worked with Peanuts Hucko early in 1964. During the 1960s Buck made annual tours of Europe and was featured at major jazz festivals throughout the U.S.A. After appearing at the New Orleans Jazz Fest in June 1969, Buck was temporarily absent from music whilst he underwent lip surgery. Played dates in New York, Washington and Cleveland (spring 1970), then had hernia operations. Recommenced practising in the late summer of 1971. State Department tour of Middle East (1977). Toured France (spring 1978). Taught at Hunter College during the early 1980s, also led The Countsmen on tour of Europe in 1983.

CLESS, 'Rod' George Roderick
clarinet/saxes

Born: Lennox, Iowa, 20th May 1907
Died: New York City, 8th December 1944

Was a brother-in-law of Bud Freeman. Played in first band whilst attending Drake University, later played in Varsity Five at Iowa State University. Left in 1925, moved to Des Moines, Iowa, first met Frank Teschemacher there. Two years later moved to Chicago and played with 'Tesch' in Charlie Pierce's Orchestra and various other bands. In late 1928, toured the South (including New Orleans) with Frank Quartell's Band. Returned to Chicago, played residency at the Wig-Wam Club, then joined Louis Panico Band (1929). Briefly with Jess Stacy's quartet, then commercial work (mostly on saxophone) at various clubs in Chicago including long stay at The High Hat. Played in Frank Snyder's Rhythm Kings in 1936, next three years worked mainly at Silhouette Club, Winosa Gardens, also taught clarinet. In April 1939 joined Muggsy Spanier's Ragtimers in Chicago, remained until they disbanded in New York in December 1939. With Art Hodes (1940-1), Marty Marsala (1941), also toured Canada with Ed Farley's Band in Late 1941. With Art Hodes, Georg Brunis, and Bobby Hackett in 1942, briefly with 'Wild Bill' Davison early in 1943, then again worked with Art Hodes. Worked in Canada (early 1944). From mid-1944 played at the Pied Piper Club in New York with Max Kaminsky. On 4th December 1944, after leaving that club, he suffered grave injuries as a result of falling over apartment railings—he died four days later in St. Vincent's Hospital, New York.

CLINTON, Larry
trumpet/arranger

Born: Brooklyn, New York, 17th August 1909

Principally remembered for the big swing band that he led from 1937 until 1941. From summer of 1942 until 1946, served in the Army Air Force including long posting in the Orient. Temporarily reorganised own band from 1948 until 1950. Prolific free-lance arranger from the early 1930s, scored for Ferde Grofé, Isham Jones, Casa Loma, Dorsey Brothers, Tommy Dorsey, etc., etc., in recent years has been active as an 'a-and-r' man for New York record companies.

COBB, **Arnett Cleophus**
(real name: Arnette Cobbs)
tenor sax

Born: Houston, Texas, 10th August 1918

Played piano and violin before specialising on tenor sax. First professional work with drummer Frank Davis in 1933, subsequently with Chester Boone (1934-6) and Milton Larkin (1936-42). With Lionel Hampton from November 1942 until early 1947, then formed own band. Was forced by illness to disband in 1948, resumed leading from 1951 until 1956, then seriously injured in a car crash. Resumed touring in 1957 and 1958, then returned to Houston, led own big band there during the late 1950s. In 1960 managed the El Dorado Club in Houston, continued leading own band, but long spells in hospital eliminated touring. Featured at Club Magnavox, Houston (summer 1970). Toured Europe several times during the 1970s and early 1980s.

COBB, **'Junie' Junius C.**
piano/banjo/clarinet/saxes/composer

Born: Hot Springs, Arkansas. c. 1896
Died: c. 1970

Brother of the late Jimmy Cobb (trumpet). First piano lessons from his mother at the age of nine. During his teens worked in small band with Johnny Dunn. Moved to New Orleans to study house-building, and there bought first clarinet. Left University to live in Chicago, gigged on piano, then formed own band for residency at the Club Alvadere (1920-1), worked on clarinet with Everett Robbins and his Jazz Screamers (1921), later played in Mae Brady's Orchestra in Chicago and firmly established himself as a multi-instrumentalist. With King Oliver (mainly on banjo) from late 1924 until spring 1925—later worked with King Oliver from late 1926 until spring 1927. With Jimmie Noone late 1928 to spring 1929, then led own band in Chicago. Left to Europe in early 1930, played saxophone and fronted band at Jose Alley's Royal Box Club in Paris, returned to Chicago (c. August 1930). Led own band in Chicago during the early 1930s, residencies at Club Metropole, Club DeLisa, etc. Disbanded in the depression period and formed double act with vocaliste Annabelle Calhoun, they worked together until c. 1946, then Junie did long residencies as a solo pianist. He retired from full-time music in 1955, but continued to play regularly—usually on piano, sometimes on banjo and clarinet. During the 1960s played with: Jasper Taylor's Creole Jazz Band (1962), solo piano at 'The Old Place' (1964), with Walbridge's Hot Four—on banjo (1967), and gigs with drummer Wayne Jones. A prolific composer, his works range from 'Once or Twice' to the World War II song 'Put the Axe to the Axis'.

COHN, **Zinky Augustus**
piano

Born: Oakland, California, 18th August 1908
Died: Chicago, Illinois, 26th April 1952

Lived in Chicago from 1917—studied at the Chicago Music College. Led own band for summer season at Harbor Springs, Michigan, in 1926. Played in band led by Roy Palmer (c. 1928), then with clarinettist Angelo Fernandez at Club de Athens, Chicago, in late 1928. Briefly with Jerome Pasquall, then worked with Jimmie Noone from June 1929 until 1931. To Europe as accompanist for Arlene and Norman Selby; back to Chicago, briefly with Walter Barnes (late 1931), Ralph Cooper, Erskine Tate and Alex Calamese's Virginia Ramblers (1932). From 1933 played many dates with Eddie South in Chicago (and in New York—1934 and 1936), with Carroll Dickerson in 1934-5, then briefly joined Jimmie Noone. With Eddie South 1936-7—left the band before their European tour and led own group at The Annex, Chicago (1937). During following year became business manager of local musicians' union, continued to play whenever possible, also taught piano. Travelled with Ethel Waters as her accompanist in 1944. From 1950 until time of his death, he regularly organised Monday night sessions at Jazz Ltd., Chicago.

COKER, **Henry L.**
trombone

Born: Dallas, Texas, 24th December 1919
Died: Los Angeles, California, 23rd November 1979

Raised in Omaha, Nebraska. Played piano from an early age—studied music at Wiley College, Texas. First regular work with trumpeter John White's Band (1935), with Nat

Towles' Band from 1937-9, then worked in Honolulu, Hawaii, with drummer Monk McFay and others until 1941, in Pearl Harbour Hospital with broken ankle in 1942 before being repatriated to U.S.A. With Benny Carter from c. 1944 until 1946, also did studio work, with Eddie Heywood (1946-7), Benny Carter (1948). Regularly with Illinois Jacquet in late 1940s and early 1950s, three months serious illness in late 1951. With Count Basie from February 1952 until 1963, then did extensive studio work in New York, Regularly with Ray Charles' Orchestra from 1966, also freelanced in California.

COLE, 'Cozy' William Randolph
drums

Born: East Orange, New Jersey, 17th October 1909
Died: Columbus, Ohio, 29th January 1981

Two of his brothers became professional pianists: 'Teddy' and Donald Reuben June. Family moved to New York in 1926. Played drums from an early age, became professional in 1928. With Wilbur Sweatman (c. 1928), own band in late 1920s, recorded with Jelly Roll Morton in 1930. With Blanche Calloway (1931-3), mainly with Benny Carter (late 1933-4), Willie Bryant (1935-6), Stuff Smith (early 1936-8), with Cab Calloway from November 1938 until August 1942. Briefly with Raymond Scott from September 1942, remained on C.B.S. staff until August 1943—during this period also led own trio at The Onyx Club, New York. Brief trip to Canada with Miff Mole's Band August 1943, then theatre orchestra work for 'Carmen Jones' New York production. Worked with Benny Goodman for 'Make Mine Music' film (June 1944), also led at The Onyx until August 1944. For a brief period doubled in 'Carmen Jones' and in the 'Seven Lively Arts' production, briefly with Benny Goodman February to March 1946. During the 1940s did extensive studies at Juilliard. Regular studio work 1946-8, led own quintet in 1948, septet in early 1949. With Louis Armstrong All Stars from spring of 1949 until October 1953. Played regularly at The Metropole, New York, during the 1950s, also did free-lance studio work; in 1954 started drum-tuition school in partnership with Gene Krupa. In autumn of 1957 toured Europe with 'All Stars' led by Jack Teagarden and Earl Hines. In 1958 Cozy gained a 'hit-parade' success with his single 'Topsy' and subsequently led own band on national tours, he reverted to studio work and free-lancing. Led own group at The Metropole during early 1960s, toured Africa with own quintet (autumn 1962 to early 1963), regularly featured on television shows. Joined Jonah Jones Quintet in 1969.

Cozy Cole appeared in several films including: 'Make Mine Music', 'The Glenn Miller Story', etc., also did soundtrack for 'The Strip'.

COLE, June Lawrence
string bass/tuba/vocals

Born: Springfield, Ohio, 1903
Died: New York, 10th October 1960

In 1923 played in the Synco Jazz Band in Springfield and thus became an original member of McKinney's Cotton Pickers. Left the band in late 1926 to join Fletcher Henderson, with Henderson until late 1928, then sailed to Europe to join Benton Peyton. Toured Europe with Peyton until late 1929, then joined Sam Wooding. Remained in Europe with Willie Lewis after Wooding had disbanded in November 1931. From early 1936 was forced by serious illness to quit playing for almost three years—long spell in the American Hospital in Paris. Returned to Willie Lewis in January 1939 and remained with the band until return to U.S.A. in September 1941. Led own small group during the 1940s, also played in Willie 'The Lion' Smith's Quartet in 1947, later ran own record shop on 116th Street in Harlem but continued to gig in New York. Led own band at Club 845, New York, for two years during the early 1950s, in the late 1950s gigged at Small's and Wells' Bar in New York.

COLE, Nat 'King'
real name: Nathaniel Adams Coles
piano/vocals

Born: Birmingham, Alabama, 17th March 1917
Died: Santa Monica, California, 15th February 1965

Three of his brothers, Isaac, Fred, and Eddie, became professional musicians. The family was raised in Chicago. By 1934 Nat was leading own Royal Dukes in Chicago; in 1936 he made his first recordings in band led by his brother Eddie (who was then playing string bass). Soon afterwards toured with a 'Shuffle Along' revue company, left the show and settled in Los Angeles, did local gigs before forming own trio (1937). From 1944 onwards achieved international fame with a series of best-selling records. During the 1940s also continued to record with all-star jazz groups, but during the latter part of his life was known principally as a vocalist. A cancer victim, he played his last engagements in 1964.

'Nat King Cole', a biography by Maria Cole and Louie Robinson first published in 1971.

COLE, Rupert — *Born: Trinidad, British West Indies, 8th August 1909*
alto sax/clarinet

Father of drummer/vibes player Ronnie Cole. Educated in Barbados, first studied clarinet there. Moved to New York in 1924, taught himself to play alto sax and began gigging. With Bill Brown and his Brownies in 1929, toured with Horace Henderson before working with Don Redman from 1932 until 1938. In Louis Armstrong's Big Band from 1938 until 1944, brief return to Don Redman, then with Cootie Williams' Big Band 1945-6. Worked with Lucky Millinder in the 1950s, occasionally with Wilbur de Paris. Left full-time music but continues to free-lance, worked regularly in George Wettling's Trio in New York (1964).

COLEMAN, Oliver Steward — *Born: Beaumont, Texas, 1914*
drums/arranger — *Died: Chicago, 6th November, 1965*

Was for many years one of Chicago's leading drummers, and one of its successful percussion teachers. During the 1930s worked with Ray Nance, Earl Hines, Erskine Tate and Horace Henderson.

COLEMAN, 'Bill' William Johnson — *Born: Centerville, near Paris, Kentucky, 4th August 1904*
trumpet/fluegel horn/vocals — *Died: Toulouse, France, 24th August 1981*

Moved with family to Cincinnati in 1909. Early efforts on clarinet and 'C' melody sax, then specialised on trumpet. Worked for Western Union as a messenger boy, took trumpet lessons from Wingie Carpenter. Debut in amateur band led by J. C. Higginbotham, also played in a roadhouse quintet with Edgar Hayes. First professional work with Clarence Paige, also worked with Wesley Helvey in Cincinnati, then joined band led by Lloyd and Cecil Scott, moved with them to New York in December 1927. Worked in Lloyd W. Scott's Band until joining Luis Russell in 1929, then rejoined his colleagues in Cecil Scott's Bright Boys (late 1929 to spring 1930). Worked with Charlie Johnson (1930), then spells with Bobby Neal and Johnny Monnegue before rejoining Luis Russell twice (1931-2). Toured with Ralph Cooper's Kongo Knights, then went to Europe with Lucky Millinder (June until October 1933), joined Benny Carter in New York (late 1933). With Teddy Hill (late 1934 to spring 1935)—during this period recorded with Fats Waller. Returned home to play briefly with Clarence Paige again (July and August 1935), then sailed to Europe to work in Freddy Taylor's Band (September 1935). Left Paris for residency in Bombay, India, with Leon Abbey's Orchestra (November 1936 to April 1937). Returned to Paris, where he joined Willie Lewis from June 1937 until December 1938, then co-led Harlem Rhythmakers/Swing Stars in Cairo and Alexandria. Left Egypt to return to U.S.A. in March 1940, joined Benny Carter's Orchestra in May 1940. Worked with Fats Waller before joining Teddy Wilson Sextet from July 1940 until May 1941. With Andy Kirk's Band from September 1941 until February 1942, did radio work with Roger Kay's Band and toured with Noble Sissle. Led own trio at Cafe Society, New York (late 1942 to early 1943), then spent 10 months in pianist Ellis Larkin's Trio (including Carnegie Hall Concert on 10th April 1943). With Mary Lou Williams' Trio (1944), then on West Coast with John Kirby Sextet (early 1945, returned to New York, then co-led band with George Johnson at Savoy, Boston (June 1945), later that year did U.S.O. overseas tour with Herbie Cowens, played a month in Japan. Worked with Sy Oliver (late 1946-7), worked in Billy Kyle's Sextet (late 1947-8). Moved to France in December 1948. Other than vacations in the U.S.A. in 1954 and 1958, Bill has lived in France ever since. Has led own bands in France, Belgium, Switzerland, Holland, Sweden, Italy, Spain, and Germany, has made many appearances at European Jazz Festivals, including guest spot with Count Basie at Antibes in 1961. Toured Britain as a soloist in 1966 and 1967, was featured at 'Jazz Expo' in London (October 1969). Toured extensively during the mid 1970s.

'Trumpet Story' by Bill Coleman, was first published in 1981.

COLLINS, Booker *Born: Roswell, New Mexico, 21st June 1914*
string bass/tuba

Studied music at the New Mexico Military Institute. First professional work with Bat Brown's Band, then with Bert Johnson before joining Andy Kirk in 1934. Remained with Kirk until the early 1940s; from 1946 until the early 1950s regular member of Floyd Smith's Trio. Retired from full-time music.

COLLINS, John Elbert *Born: Montgomery, Alabama, 20th September 1913*
guitar

Mother was pianiste-bandleader Georgia Gorham. Originally played clarinet, then switched to guitar, moved to Chicago and studied with Frank Langham. Worked (with his mother) in trumpeter Elbert B. Topp's Orchestra at Radio Inn, Chicago, in 1932, then regularly in his mother's band until early 1935. With Jimmy Bell and his Tampa Tunesters in spring 1935, then worked at Three Deuces, Chicago, with Art Tatum and Zutty Singleton before joining Roy Eldridge in September 1936. With Roy Eldridge in Chicago, New York, etc., until 1940. In 1941-2 worked for various leaders including Lester Young (early 1941), Fletcher Henderson, and Benny Carter (1942). Served in U.S. Army until 1946, then with Slam Stewart Trio (spring 1946-8). To Paris in Errol Garner Trio (May 1948), then worked mainly with pianist Billy Taylor until early 1951 (brief spells with Coleman Hawkins, 1949 and Artie Shaw, late 1950). With Art Tatum Trio (May-August 1951). Joined Nat 'King' Cole Trio on 5th September 1951 and remained until that leader's death. During the late 1960s has continued playing regularly, long spell with vocalist Bobby Troup's Trio. Worked with Cat Anderson in California (spring 1971). Led own quartet during the 1970s. Guested with various bands during the early 1980s, also led own trio in Europe (1982).

COLLINS, Lee *Born: Robinson Street, New Orleans, Louisiana, 17th October 1901*
trumpet/vocals *Died: Chicago, Illinois, 3rd July 1960*

His father, John Collins, was a trumpeter; his uncle was a trombonist. Started on trumpet at 12, tuition from his father and 'Professor' Jim Humphrey. At 15 did first regular playing at the Zulu's Club, then with Pops Foster organised the Young Eagles. In 1917-18 worked with the Columbia Band and the Young Tuxedo Orchestra, continued playing with the Young Eagles. Played with Bud Roussel's Band, Papa Celestin, Jessie Jackson's Golden Leaf Orchestra, and Zutty Singleton (1919-22). Residency at the Cadillac Club, then toured Florida with own band (1923). In 1924 moved to Chicago to join King Oliver, recorded with Jelly Roll Morton, returned to New Orleans when the Lincoln Gardens burnt down. Joined Jack Carey at 101 Ranch, then led quartet at the Entertainers. Toured with 'Professor' Sherman Cook's Revue, worked with Clarence Desdune, settled for a while in Dallas. Moved back to New Orleans, led at Club Lavida, later featured with Davey Jones at the Astoria Gardens then led own Ragtime Band: again toured Florida with own band. Co-led band for Jones-Collins Astoria Hot Eight recordings (1929). In 1930 moved briefly to New York, worked with Luis Russell Band (no recordings) at the Saratoga Club whilst Henry 'Red' Allen went on a vacation to New Orleans. Moved to Chicago, joined Dave Peyton (1931), worked mostly at the Regal Theatre, but also one visit to New York for Lafayette Theatre booking. From 1932 worked for various bandleaders in Chicago including: W. McDonald and his Chicago Ramblers (1932), the Dodds Brothers, Zutty Singleton, Sherman Cooke, etc., then formed own band for touring. During the late 1930s played long residency at the Derby Club, Calumet City. Moved back to Chicago in November 1939, led own band at various clubs including: the 600, The Ship, Royale Cafe, Marathon, etc. Brief spell with Jimmy Bertrand at The Firehouse (late 1940). Own trio at the Victory Club on Clark Street from mid-1945, played at the Casablanca Club (late 1946) and in 1948 did brief concert tour with Kid Ory, led on and off at the Victory Club throughout the late 1940s, also worked with Johnny Lane Band (August to October

1949) and with Art Hodes' Band (1950 and 1951). To Europe to join Mezz Mezzrow Band for tour commencing November 1951, left through illness and returned to Chicago, again took up residency at the Victory Club. In summer of 1953 played with Joe Sullivan's Band in San Francisco, during the following year played in New Orleans, then toured Europe again with Mezz Mezzrow (from November 1954), was taken ill on tour and returned to Chicago, then suffered a stroke and for last years of his life was musically inactive through chronic emphysema.

'Oh, Didn't He Ramble' (the life story of Lee Collins) by Gillis and Miner, first published in 1974.

COLLINS, 'Shad' Lester Rallingston
trumpet

Born: Elizabeth, New Jersey, 27th June 1910
Died: New York City, June 1978

Raised in Lockport, New York. First professional work in band led by Charlie Dixon (fronted by vocaliste Cora LaRedd), then from late 1929 until 1930 in band led by pianist Eddie White. With Chick Webb (1931), Benny Carter (1933), Tiny Bradshaw (1934), Teddy Hill (1936-7), short stay with Don Redman, then with Count Basie from December 1938 until January 1940. In February 1940 joined Benny Carter's Band, then from October 1940 worked in Freddy Moore's Band. With Lester Young Sextet in New York (February 1941), then worked with Buddy Johnson until replacing Dizzy Gillespie in Cab Calloway's Band in September 1941. With Cab until June 1943 and again 1944 to 1946. With Buster Harding's Band (1948), Al Sears (1950), toured with Jimmy Rushing in the early 1950s, then worked in New York for various leaders including long spell with tenorist Sam 'The Man' Taylor. Left full-time music, but continued to gig in the 1960s.

COLUMBUS, 'Chris'
(real name: Joseph Christopher Columbus Morris)
drums/leader

Born: Greenville, North Carolina, 17th June 1902

Drummer Percival 'Sonny' Payne (1926-79) was his son. Led own band through the 1930s, 1940s, and 1950s; played regularly with Louis Jordan in 1949. Worked mainly in Wild Bill Davis Trio (late 1950s to early 1960s), then accompanied vocaliste Damita Jo. Led own band during the 1970s, also toured Europe with Wild Bill Davis (1972).

COMEGYS, James Leon
trombone

Born: Maryland, 7th June 1917

With Theodore 'Cuban' Bennet, Lucky Millinder, Bobby Johnson, and the Hardy Brothers during the late 1930s. During the 1940s worked with Les Hite, Fletcher Henderson, Hot Lips Page, before serving in U.S. Army Band. Later worked with Tiny Bradshaw, Chris Columbus, Erskine Hawkins, Dizzy Gillespie, etc. With Count Basie in 1951. Toured Europe with Freddie Mitchell in 1953. Spent some years touring with Ray Charles and his Orchestra before leaving full-time music.

COMPTON, J. Glover
piano

Born: Harrodsburg, Kentucky, 1884
Died: Chicago, Illinois, 11th June 1964

Husband of vocaliste Nettie Lewis. Played at Cosmopolitan Theatre in Louisville, then formed double piano act with Tony Jackson. Later played in Wyoming and St. Louis, then moved to Chicago in 1910. Solo pianist at the Elite No. 1 Club until 1912, then moved to West Coast. Played long residencies in San Francisco and Seattle before returning to Chicago in 1921. From autumn 1921 with Jimmie Noone at the Edelweiss Gardens. With Noone and with Ollie Powers at various venues including: Paradise Gardens, The Panama, Dreamland, The Oriental, etc. To Paris in May 1926 for residency at Bricktop's Club, remained in France until 1939, long contract at Harry's New York Bar, also played at Zelli's Royal Box. Returned to Chicago, played briefly with Jimmie Noone, then long solo residency at the B. and M. Tap Bar. In later years owned own bar on Chicago South Side, continued to play piano until suffering a stroke in 1957.

CONAWAY, Sterling Bruce
banjo/mandolin/guitar

Born: Washington, D.C., 1898

Brother of banjo-guitarist Lincoln Conaway (died: October 1968). Worked on banjo and mandolin with Duke Ellington in Washington (c. 1920), moved to Chicago, with Carroll Dickerson (c. 1923). Worked mainly in Europe in the late 1920s and 1930s, with Noble Sissle (1931), Freddy Johnson (1933-4), Freddy Taylor (1935), Leon Abbey (1937), etc., also led own band. Lives in New York, has retired from full-time music.

CONDON, 'Eddie' Albert Edwin
guitar/banjo/vocals

Born: Goodland, Indiana, 16th November 1905
Died: New York City, 4th August 1973

Started on ukelele, then switched to banjo. Did local gigs with Bill Engleman's Band in Cedar Rapids (September 1921), later worked in Hollis Peavey's Jazz Bandits (1922). Played in Chicago and Syracuse with Bix Beiderbecke, then rejoined Peavey's Jazz Bandits. Returned to Chicago in 1924, gigged with the Austin High Gang, also did residencies and summer seasons with: Bob Pacelli, Charlie Pearce, Charles 'Murph' Podolsky, Irving Rothschild, Roy Peach, Louis Panico, Jack Gardner, etc. Co-led recording group with Red McKenzie in 1928. To New York in 1928, led own recording group and gigged, free-lance recording sessions with Louis Armstrong and Fats Waller. Toured with Red Nichols (1929), then worked in New York and Florida with Red McKenzie and the Mound City Blue Blowers (1930-1) and again in 1933. Played piano with George Carhart's Band on cruise to South America. Worked with Mike Reilly and Eddie Farley (1935), then with Red McKenzie in New York. Critically ill with pancreatitis in April 1936, from summer of 1936 co-led band with Joe Marsala, played on liner cruise with Marsala (December 1936). Left early in 1937, worked regularly at Nick's; with Bobby Hackett from summer of 1938, Bud Freeman's Summa Cum Laude Band (1939-40). Regularly led own recording band through the 1930s. With Bobby Hackett (1940), Joe Marsala (1941). In 1942 organised first televised jam session and began running own jazz concerts at New York Town Hall. Worked at Nick's with Brad Gowans (1943), spell with Joe Marsala Big Band, then with Miff Mole (1944). In December 1945 opened own club in New York, the club changed premises in February 1958 and finally closed in July 1967. From the 1950s Condon only played occasionally at the club, he did brief tours and occasional residencies in Chicago, California, Canada, etc. Led group for tour of Britain (early 1957) and Japan, Australia, and New Zealand (spring 1964). Underwent serious operations in 1964 and 1965. Early in 1970 worked with Roy Eldridge-Kai Winding group in New York, sharing guitar duties with Jim Hall. During the late 1960s and 1970s appeared at many U.S. jazz festivals. Led group in Raleigh, North Carolina for part of 1970. Toured with Barney Bigard, Wild Bill Davison and Art Hodes (October 1971). His autobiography 'We Called It Music' first published in 1948.

CONNIFF, Ray
trombone/arranger

Born: Attleboro, Massachusetts, 6th November 1916

Originally took trombone lessons from his father. Worked with local bands from the age of 16. With Dan Murphy (1936), Hank Biagini (1936), Bunny Berigan (1937-9). With Bob Crosby from June 1939, until December 1940. Worked for Artie Shaw, then formed own eight-piece band in spring 1941. With Harry James, Dave Matthews, Artie Shaw, etc., then free-lance studio work, prolific recordings. Was on A.B.C. staff in New York in 1954, following year ceased playing trombone to concentrate on leading own band which has achieved widespread commercial success.

COOKE, 'Doc' Charles L.
piano/arranger

Born: Louisville, Kentucky, 3rd September 1891
Died: 25th December 1958

In 1909 was working as a composer-arranger in Detroit, subsequently moved to Chicago where he led his own bands at several venues, also acted as musical director for Riverview Park. From 1922 led own 16-piece band at Harmon's Dreamland, Chicago, played there regularly for almost six years, then worked at 20th Century Theatre, White City

Ballroom, etc., until moving to New York in 1930. During the 1930s was staff arranger at R.K.O. and at Radio City Music Hall, occupied similar positions during the early 1940s, then left full-time music and retired to New Jersey. Was a Doctor of Music, having gained this honour at the Chicago College of Music in 1926, previously became Bachelor of Music at Chicago Musical College. Was usually billed as 'Doc' Cook.

COOPER, Harry R.
trumpet

Born: Lake Charles, Louisiana, 1903
Died: Paris, France, 1961

Left Louisiana as a child and moved with family to Kansas City, Missouri. Attended Lincoln High School and took up trumpet in Reserve Officers' Training Corps Band. Whilst at high school gigged with Bennie Moten, George E. Lee, and bassist James Smith. Left Kansas City in 1922; whilst studying architecture at Hampton Institute, Virginia, gigged with local bands, then moved on to Baltimore, Maryland. Joined band accompanying singer Virginia Liston and went with this group to New York for first recordings (OKeh). With augmented personnel this band became the Seminole Syncopators (led by pianist Graham Jackson), they played a three-month residency at the 81 Theatre in Atlanta, Georgia, then Cooper returned to New York and joined Billy Fowler (late 1924). Gigged with Elmer Snowden, also led own band at the Blackbottom Club and worked with violinist Andrew Preer's Cotton Club Orchestra (1925). With Billy Fowler (1926), worked on and off with Duke Ellington in 1926, led own band before joining Leon Abbey. Worked in Europe with Leon Abbey from early 1928, joined Sam Wooding in late 1929. Remained in Europe for the rest of his life, occasionally worked for other leaders but usually led own bands. Recorded in Paris during the Nazi occupation.

CORLEY, George
trombone/arranger

Born: Austin, Texas, 7th September 1912

Brothers Wilford a tenor-saxist, John a trumpeter. Piano at 8, trombone at 16. Played in high school band, later organised own Royal Aces. Joined Terrence Holder in 1930, left to join Troy Floyd in 1932. Long spell working mainly in Texas with Tommy Brooks, Sammy Holmes, Clifford 'Boots' Douglas, and Howard Brown. Toured with Henry 'Rabbit' Thompson, left that band in California and joined Ben Watkins from 1943 until 1950. Worked mainly in Texas from 1955-1962 then worked for several years in California with vocalist Jimmy McCraklin.

CORNELIUS, 'Corky' Edward
trumpet

Born: Indiana, 3rd December 1914
Died: New York, 3rd August 1943

Was the husband of vocaliste Irene Daye. Originally taught music by his father, was raised in Binghampton, N.Y. Worked with Les Brown, Frank Dailey, and Buddy Rogers before joining Benny Goodman (April until August 1939). With Gene Krupa from September 1939 until late 1940. With Glen Gray and the Casa Loma Band from summer of 1942. Died of a kidney ailment.

COTTRELL, Louis
clarinet/saxes

Born: New Orleans, Louisiana, 7th March 1911
Died: New Orleans, Louisiana, 21st March 1978

Son of the famous drummer Louis Sr. (died: 1927). Worked regularly with the Young Tuxedo Orchestra from the mid-1920s, also played for the Golden Rule Band, Sidney Desvigne, William Ridgely, etc. Left New Orleans to join band led by Don Albert, worked throughout the 1930s with Don Albert, then returned to New Orleans. Worked again with Sidney Desvigne in the 1940s, became president of the A.F.M. Local 496. Occasional parades with Kid Howard's Brass Band in the 1950s. Did regular work and recordings with Paul Barbarin during the 1950s, worked in Pete Bocage's Creole Serenaders in the early 1960s. Worked mainly on clarinet, and was featured with own trio at the New Orleans Jazz Fest in late 1960s and early 1970s. Worked regularly until the night before his death.

COURANCE, 'Spider' Edgar — *Born: Cincinnati, Ohio, 1903*
tenor sax/clarinet — *Died: New York City, 12th October 1969*

Worked in Wesley Helvey's Band in Cincinnati (1926), also played briefly in J. C. Higginbotham's Band. Gigged in New York during the early 1930s, then worked regularly with Tiny Bradshaw (1934). Worked in France with Freddy Taylor from September 1935, with guitarist Oscar Aleman in Paris (early 1937), then rejoined Freddy Taylor (c. June 1937), with Fletcher Allen's Band in Paris (April 1938). Recorded in France with Bill Coleman; to Egypt with Coleman (late 1938). Returned to New York in 1940, did overseas U.S.O. tours with Herbie Cowens' Band in 1945 and 1947. Regular gigs with Wingie Carpenter during the 1950s, but was forced to quit playing after suffering a heart attack in 1966.

COWENS, 'Kat' Herbert — *Born: Dallas, Texas, 24th May 1904*
drums/leader

From a musical family, two brothers played drums, one sister was a dancer, another was a singer. Started work as a shoe-shine boy, with money earnt from street-dancing he bought his first set of drums. Joined The Satisfied Five in Dallas (led by Karl and Fred Murphy), then moved to Wichita Falls, Texas, to join Frenchy's New Orleans Jazz Band—led by Lux Alexander, subsequently worked with Charlie Dixon (tuba) and his Jazzlanders, left this band to finish high school. Left school in June 1922, did a short theatre tour, then rejoined the Murphy Brothers in Dallas. Left to tour with Cleo Mitchell's 'Shake Your Feet' company, made first visit to New York in December 1926. Left that show in 1927 and joined the Kansas City Blackbirds Band of Eddie Heywood Sr., then playing for Jimmie Cooper's Black and White Revue. Returned to New York after a long tour, led own band at the Rockland Palace, New York (September 1928), then worked for several bandleaders including: 'Doc' Crawford, Billy Fowler, Dave Nelson, Lucky Millinder, Eubie Blake, Ferman Tapp, Charlie Johnson, and Charlie Turner—toured briefly with Fats Waller (replaced by Arnold 'Scrippy' Boling). With Stuff Smith from November 1938 until January 1941, then briefly with Fletcher Henderson in New York (1941). With Garvin Bushell in Philadelphia (1942), then long spell playing for the Broadway show 'The Pirate'. Regularly led own bands on U.S.O. tours from June of 1943, did annual overseas' tours to: the Far East, Japan, Europe, the Mediterranean area, etc., etc. When not touring leads own small bands in New York and New Jersey, played regularly with Louis Metcalfe in 1963-4. Extensive tour of Far East and Alaska during winter of 1968-9. Led own band for tour of the Orient (late 1970). Moved back to Dallas, continued to play there during 1980s.

COX, Ida — *Born: Cedartown, Georgia, 1889*
vocals — *Died: Knoxville, Tennessee, 10th November 1967*

Wife of Texas pianist-organist Jesse 'Tiny' Crump. Sang in local African Methodist Choir during childhood, ran away from home to tour with White and Clark's Minstrels on the T.O.B.A. circuit. Became solo artiste, commenced recording in 1923. During the 1920s and early 1930s toured with own 'Raisin' Cain' show, then headed the 'Darktown Scandals' company. Played solo residencies in New York in 1939 (at this time managed by the famous blues singer Big Bill Broonzy), also appeared at Spirituals to Swing concert at Carnegie Hall. Continued to work regularly until suffering a stroke in Buffalo, N.Y. (1945), eventually retired to Knoxville in 1949. Resumed recording in 1961, recorded an L.P. with all-star jazz accompaniment. Died of cancer.

CRAWFORD, 'Jimmy' James Strickland — *Born: Memphis, Tennessee, 14th January 1910*
drums — *Died: New York, 28th January 1980*

First instrument was the alto horn, then switched to drums. To LeMoyne College, then met Jimmie Lunceford whilst studying at Manassas High School. Began doing local work with Lunceford, made professional debut with the band in Lakeside, Ohio (summer 1928). Remained with Lunceford until early 1943. Short spell with Ben Webster, then led own group at the Three Deuces, New York, until service in U.S. Army from summer of 1943 until August 1945—was stationed at Camp Kilmer, New Jersey, played in all-star services band with Sy Oliver, Buck Clayton, etc., also with Walter Gross Service Band (1945). Mainly with Edmond Hall's Sextet from late 1945 until 1949, briefly with Harry James in mid-1946, with Ed Hall in New York and Boston. Played in Fletcher Henderson's last group in December 1950. Did long spell with the Broadway show 'Pal Joey' during the early 1950s, and since then has played for many Broadway shows. Took part in Henderson Reunion Band in summer of 1957, toured with Lena Horne's show 'Jamaica' in 1958. Prolific free-lance recording work; continues to play for Broadway shows, worked with Tyree Glenn at The Roundtable, New York, in 1969. Ill health restricted activities during the late 1970s.

CRAWFORD, Forrest
tenor sax/clarinet

Born: St. Louis, Missouri. c. 1908

First professional work with Joe Gill's Band in 1934. Moved to New York early in 1936, gigged with various bands and took part in recording sessions including dates with Bunny Berigan. In autumn of 1937 was forced to quit playing through tuberculosis, returned to St. Louis, by early 1939 had sufficiently recovered to lead own band at the 'Showboat Ballroom'. Subsequently left full-time music, no trace of his activities.

CRAWLEY, Wilton
clarinet/vocals/contortionist

Born: Smithfield, Virginia. c. 1900.
Deceased.

Brother of clarinet/sax player Jimmy Crawley. Family moved to Philadelphia where the brothers formed their own band. During the 1920s and 1930s Wilton Crawley enjoyed wide success with his own variety act, he is now chiefly remembered for the recording sessions that he made with Jelly Roll Morton. Performed in England, early 1930.

CREATH, 'Charlie' Charles Cyril
trumpet/sax/accordion

Born: Ironton, Missouri, 30th December 1890
Died: Chicago, Illinois, 23rd October 1951

Brother of pianiste Marge (who for over forty years was Mrs. Zutty Singleton). Another sister, Pauline, also played piano. Started on alto saxophone, then switched to trumpet in early teens. At 16 worked in Pop Adams' Circus Band, then toured with P. G. Lowry's troupe. Later toured with Drake and Walker's Musical Comedy Show and the Hagen Beck-Wallace Circus Band. Did theatre work, then led own band in Seattle, returned to St. Louis c. 1918. Took over band led by girl pianiste Marcella Kyle c. 1921 and led that band at Alamac Hall. Several bands worked under Creath's name in and around St. Louis during the early 1920s. Creath himself played many residencies including long stay at Jazzland. Joined Fate Marable on S. S. 'Capitol' in late 1926, inactive through illness from 1928 until 1930, from that date doubled sax and accordion. Worked with Harvey Lankford's Synco High-Hatters (1933), then co-led band with Fate Marable during the mid-1930s. Subsequently moved to Chicago, ran own night club for a while, then worked as an inspector in an aircraft factory (1944). Was ill for several years before dying of natural causes.

CROSBY, 'Bob' George Robert
vocals/leader

Born: Spokane, Washington, 25th August 1913

Brother of 'Bing' (1903-77). Attended Gonzaga College, first professional work with Anson Weeks in San Francisco, also toured with Weeks. Joined Dorsey Brothers' Orchestra (1934). During the spring of 1935, Gil Rodin (then rehearsing a new band mainly comprised of ex-Ben Pollack musicians), was advised by agent Frank 'Cork' O'Keefe to find someone to front the band, he suggested three candidates and the band chose Bob Crosby, thus the Bob Crosby Orchestra came into being. It made its official debut in June 1935. For the next seven years the Bob Crosby Orchestra (and the smaller band-within-a-band The Bob Cats) achieved great success in person and on record. The original band broke up in December 1942. Crosby subsequently appeared in various films, including 'The Singing Sheriff', and occasionally fronted a big band before joining the U.S. Marines in 1944. He led his own service band for part of his service career, and served in the Pacific war zone. In late 1945, after demobilisation, Bob Crosby often formed various big bands, for tours or for radio series. During the 1950s, and 1960s was mainly active as a solo radio and television performer (appeared at the London Palladium in May 1958, also had own television series in Australia during the 1960s). Throughout this period Bob occasionally resumed leading a big band, and sometimes organised reunions of the Bob Cats. During the 1970s and 1980s Bob devoted most of his time to leading his own big band, and did frequent tours and residencies, he also continued to re-assemble the Bob Cats and was featured with them at the Nice Festival in 1981.

Bob Crosby appeared in over 20 movies, his band was featured in several of them, including 'Let's Make Music', 'Reveille With Beverly', 'Presenting Lily Mars', etc. 'Stomp Off, Let's Go' (the story of Bob Crosby's Bob Cats & Big Band) by John Chilton was first published in 1983.

CROSBY, Israel
string bass

Born: Chicago, Illinois, 19th January 1919
Died: Chicago, Illinois, 11th August 1962

Played trumpet from the age of five, changed to trombone and tuba, at 13 was gigging regularly on these instruments. Changed to string bass in 1934, with Johnny Long, Anthony Frambro, then with Albert Ammons in the Club DeLisa in Chicago. After making record debut with Gene Krupa spent two years with Fletcher Henderson (1936-8). Left in 1939 to spend a year working with Three Sharps and a Flat. Joined Horace Henderson in September 1940, left in following May to spend two years in Teddy Wilson Band. In the summer of 1944 joined Raymond Scott at C.B.S.—spent several years as a free-lance studio musician, also with James P. Johnson (1945). From 1951-3 was with pianist Ahmad Jamal, briefly with Teddy Wilson Trio, then worked with Benny Goodman (late 1956 to early 1957 tour of Asia). Returned to work with Ahmad Jamal Trio until the trio disbanded in the spring of 1962, then joined pianist George Shearing—last recordings were made with Shearing in June 1962. During the following month returned to Chicago for a medical check-up—died of a blood clot on the heart in the West Side Veterans' Administration Hospital, Chicago.

CRUMBLEY, Elmer E.
trombone/vocals

Born: Kingfisher, Oklahoma, 1st August 1908

Brother George is a trumpeter. Family moved to Denver, Colorado, in 1910, then to Omaha, Nebraska, in 1915. First regular band work with Lloyd Hunter in 1923, with Hunter until 1926, then six months in Dandie Dixie Minstrels before rejoining Lloyd Hunter's Seranaders until 1929. To Kansas City with George E. Lee Band until the autumn of 1930, briefly with Bill Owens in Omaha, and Tommy Douglas in Lincoln, Nebraska. Worked with saxophonist Grant Moore's Band before rejoining Lloyd Hunter from late 1931 until September 1932—during this period also worked with Thamon Hayes; briefly with Zack Whyte, Grant Moore, Jabbo Smith. With Doll Vine and Erskine Tate in Chicago before leading own band in Omaha during 1934. Joined Jimmie Lunceford in December 1934 and, other than short periods of absence, remained until the leader's death in 1947; subsequently worked with Eddie Wilcox Band. With Lucky Millinder during the early 1950s, then played in Erskine Hawkins' Band. To Europe in October 1958 with Sammy Price. Worked with Reuben Phillips Band at Apollo during late 1950s and early 1960s. Continues to play regularly, during mid-1960s played with big bands specially re-formed by Cab Calloway and Earl Hines.

CROWDER, 'Bob' Robert Henry
tenor sax/clarinet/violin

Born: 1912

Known as 'Little Sax'. Worked in Milwaukee during the early 1930s, then with Francois Mosely's Louisianians (1932), with Punch Miller at the Harlem Club, Chicago (1933). With pianist Leo Montgomery and his Creole Playboys (summer 1934), then toured with François Mosely. Joined Horace Henderson in July 1937, then with Earl Hines (1938-40), with

Walter Fuller (September 1940), with pianist Fletcher Butler (early 1941), Coleman Hawkins in Chicago (April 1941), then again with Earl Hines. Quit touring and settled in Chicago, continued to play regularly through the 1960s. His wife, Lorraine, usually plays piano in her husband's band.

CUFFEE, 'Ed' Edward Emerson
trombone

Born: Norfolk, Virginia, 7th June 1902
Died: New York City, 3rd January 1959

Boyhood friend of Jimmy Archey. Moved to New York in the mid-1920s, shortly afterwards became a regular on Clarence Williams' recording sessions. Worked with pianist LeRoy Tibbs at Connie's Inn in 1929, then worked with Bingie Madison before working with McKinney's Cotton Pickers (1930-4), during this period worked briefly in Ellsworth Reynolds-Kaiser Marshall Bostonians. With Fletcher Henderson (1936-9), gigged in New York before joining Leon Abbey (1940). Joined Count Basie in January 1941, left seven months later, worked occasionally with Leon Abbey, regularly in Chris Columbus Band in 1944. Gigged and recorded with Bunk Johnson in late 1947. Left full-time music to work as an electrician, but continued gigging in the 1950s.

Ed Cuffee's name was once printed as Cuffee Davidson, the error snowballed and for over 30 years he has been mistakenly referred to by this name.

CULLEY, Wendell Philips
trumpet

Born: Worcester, Massachusetts, 8th January 1906

Brother Ray was a drummer. Played with local bands, then moved to New York in 1930. Played with Bill Brown, Horace Henderson, then joined Cab Calloway, left in the summer of 1931. Joined Noble Sissle Orchestra and remained with that outfit for 11 years. Played for Lionel Hampton from 1944 until 1949. Long-time member of Count Basie Band from late 1951 until late 1959. Left music, moved to West Coast where he has achieved considerable success in the insurance business.

CURL, Langston W.
trumpet

Born: Charles City, Virginia, 18th March 1899

Began playing trumpet at the age of six, taught by a cousin. Gigged with bands in and around Norfolk, Virginia, then turned professional by joining McKinney's Cotton Pickers in Detroit (1927). Remained until 1931, then spent over three years with Don Redman. After touring with band fronted by Jessie Owens, quit full-time music in 1937. Worked for a Bridgeport brass company from 1937 until 1964. Now lives in retirement at his home in Bridgeport, Connecticut.

CUTSHALL, 'Cutty' Robert Dewees
trombone

Born: Huntington County, Pennsylvania, 29th December 1911
Died: Toronto, Canada, 16th August 1968

Worked with bands in Pittsburgh, including Harry Baker's Band (1936-37), also toured with Charley Dornberger. Spent two years with Jan Savitt (1938-40), then joined Benny Goodman until U.S. Army service from May 1942. Returned to Benny Goodman from May until December 1946. Free-lanced in New York, regularly with Billy Butterfield in 1948. From 1949 worked regularly for Eddie Condon (including tour of Great Britain in 1957), also played for Peanuts Hucko, Billy Butterfield, etc., and did studio work. During the 1960s worked on several residencies and tours with Yank Lawson, Max Kaminsky, and Peanuts Hucko, also with Bob Crosby in New York in summer of 1968. Whilst playing residency at the Colonial Tavern, Toronto (with Eddie Condon) he suffered a fatal heart attack and died in his hotel room.

DAILY, 'Pete' Thaman Pierce
cornet

Born: Portland, Indiana, 5th May 1911

Played baritone horn whilst in early teens, then variety of instruments before working on tuba, bass saxophone and cornet (first recordings with Jack Davies and his Kentuckians, 1930). From 1932 began working exclusively on cornet. Worked regularly with pianist Frank Melrose in Calumet City and Chicago during 1930s, but also played with Bud Freeman, Boyce Brown, etc. Worked with Frank Melrose Band in Ship Club, Gary, Indiana in 1939, during 1940 worked briefly in The Schnicklefritzers, then led own band in Chicago. To California in 1942 with Mike Riley's Band, briefly with Ozzie Nelson, then joined U.S. merchant marine—sailed to India and sat in with Teddy Weatherford's Band. Again with Ozzie Nelson in 1945, then organised own band on West Coast. Played many residencies: Hangover, Sardi's, etc., regular appearances at 'Dixieland Jubilees'. Led own band throughout the 1950s, switched to valve trombone, moved to Gary, Indiana, in 1962, worked in Chicago with Smokey Stover's Band (early 1964). During the late 1960s lived in San Antonio for two years, then moved back to Los Angeles. His son Dennis plays cornet and trombone. Recovered from serious accident and played Sacramento Festivals in 1976 and 1977. During the early 1980s activities restricted as the result of a stroke.

DAMERON, 'Tadd' Tadley Ewing
piano/arranger/composer

Born: Cleveland, Ohio, 21st February 1917
Died: New York City, 8th March 1965

First important work with Freddie Webster's Band in Cleveland, then worked with Zach Whyte and Blanche Calloway. Highly active as an arranger during the 1940s, writing for many bands including Harland Leonard's, Dizzy Gillespie's, Jimmie Lunceford's, George Auld's, etc. Also continued to play piano regularly, often with own small band. In May 1949 went to play in Paris with Miles Davis, remained in Europe and briefly worked as staff arranger for English bandleader Ted Heath. Returned to U.S.A., worked with Benjamin 'Bull Moose' Jackson during the early 1950s, again led own band in the 1950s. Went to jail in 1958 for narcotics offences. Returned to full-time music in the early 1960s, doing arrangements for many famous bands until activity curtailed by the onset of cancer.

D'AMICO, 'Hank' Henry
clarinet/saxes

Born: Rochester, N.Y., 21st March 1915
Died: Queens, New York, 3rd December 1965

Originally played violin, then clarinet in high school band in Buffalo. Worked on lake steamers sailing to and from Chicago. After playing with Paul Specht in 1936 joined Red Norvo early in 1937. Led own Radio Octet in November 1938, then brief return to Red Norvo before joining Richard Himber in 1939—left Himber in April 1940, with Bob Crosby from May 1940 until summer 1941. Led own big band (1941-2), with Les Brown (summer 1942), then worked with Red Norvo before brief spell with Benny Goodman from November 1942. Staff musician at C.B.S. from early 1943 (for a while also doubled in Cozy Cole's Trio at The Onyx). Spent August 1943 in Toronto with Miff Mole's Sextet, briefly with Tommy Dorsey late in 1943, then from 1944-54 at A.B.C. studios; regular jazz gigs. Briefly with Jack Teagarden (1954). During the late 1950s and early 1960s worked mainly with small groups, occasionally led own band. Worked in Morey Feld's Trio in 1964. Died of cancer.

DANDRIDGE, 'Putney' Louis
vocals/piano

Born: Richmond, Virginia, 13th January 1902
Died: Wall Township, New Jersey, 15th February 1946

From 1918 until 1926 did regular tours with the Drake and Walker Show. Played in Buffalo for many years; then, during early 1930s, was regular accompanist to tap-dancer Bill 'Bojangles' Robinson. Led own band in Cleveland 1932-4. Solo piano spot at Adrian's Taproom from March 1935, then worked regularly in New York—various residencies including long spell at The Hickory House. In 1935 and 1936 he recorded many vocal sides with all-star accompaniment.

D

DARENSBOURG, **'Joe' Joseph Wilmer** *Born: Baton Rouge, Louisiana, 9th July 1906*
clarinet/saxes

Father was an amateur cornetist; Joe's cousin is Sayou Darensbourg. First played violin and piano, then received clarinet lessons from Manuel Roque in Baton Rouge and Alphonse Picou in New Orleans. First played in band co-led with his brother Frank (a violinist), also sat in with Buddie Petit in Baton Rouge. First professional work (1923) with Martel Family Band in Opelousas, then toured with a medicine show. Gigged in St. Louis with Fate Marable and Charlie Creath, then played for a year in Harrisburg, Illinois, where he was gunned down by gangsters. After his recovery he played for a brief spell with Jelly Roll Morton in Cairo, Illinois, then travelled across country in Al G. Barnes' Circus Band, left this outfit in Los Angeles and worked in Mutt Carey's Jeffersonians. After a brief return to New Orleans rejoined Mutt Carey. During the late 1920s played aboard various passenger liners, then led own bands in Seattle and Vancouver. In early 1930s toured with Vic Sewell Band, then after being injured in a car crash, returned to work on passenger boats, mostly on the Alaska run, left to work on West Coast. In early 1940s played regularly with pianist Johnny Wittwer and Doc Exner in Seattle, then joined Kid Ory in 1944, left in August 1945, brief return from October 1945. Played with the Red Foxx Hungry Hounds, Joe Liggins and his Honey-Drippers and Wingy Manone before joining Kid Ory in September 1949. During 1950s played with Gene Mayl's Dixie Rhythm Kings in Ohio, with Teddy Buckner, then led own band which achieved great popular success with their recording of 'Yellow Dog Blues'. In 1961 worked in John St. Cyr's Young Men of New Orleans (at Disneyland, Hollywood), then joined the Louis Armstrong All Stars in September 1961. Left Louis in June 1964, again led own band, then long spell with Young Men of New Orleans. Own group in Del Mar (1969), own quartet at Calabassas Inn (1971). Visited Europe during the 1970s. Appeared at festivals, and continued playing regularly during the early 1980s.

DARR, **Jerome** *Born: Baltimore, Maryland, 21st December 1910*
guitar

Worked with the Washboard Serenaders from 1933 until 1936 (including trip to Europe). With Buddy Johnson in the early 1950s, then worked with tenorist Paul Quinichette, Rex Stewart, Cootie Williams, etc. Joined Jonah Jones in July 1968.

DASH, **St. Julian Bennett** *Born: Charleston, South Carolina, 9th April 1916*
tenor sax *Died: New York City, 25th February 1974*

Played in high school bands then moved to New York to study embalming. Led own band at Monroe's Uptown House (c. 1936). Joined Erskine Hawkins in 1938, featured with this band for many years, later, led own band then left full-time music. Was head of receptionists at a New York company. Own quintet (1970-1), they recorded an L.P. in 1970; in May 1971 Julian took part in Erskine Hawkins' reunion recording session.

DAVENPORT, **'Cow Cow' Charles** *Born: Anniston, Alabama, 26th April 1895*
piano/vocals *Died: Cleveland, Ohio, 2nd December 1955*

One of eight children, he began studying at a theological school, but was expelled for playing ragtime piano. On his way back to Anniston he began working in Birmingham. Then joined Barkoot's travelling carnival troupe, later leaving to work as a solo act. He then teamed with singer Dora Carr and they appeared in vaudeville as 'Davenport & Co.' The partnership ended when Dora Carr married, 'Cow Cow' worked as a single in Chicago, then temporarily teamed up with Ivy Smith. During the mid-1920s he acted as talent scout for Vocalion Record Company, he left to return to vaudeville. After a disastrous tour he spent six months in prison in Montgomery, Alabama. Moved to Cleveland where he made unsuccessful attempt to run a music and record shop. He returned to theatre work until 1935 when he opened own cafe in Cleveland. He suffered a stroke in 1938 which temporarily affected his right hand—during that year he was featured as a vocalist with a pick-up recording unit. After his health returned he moved to New York, he worked for a time as the washroom attendant at The Onyx Club, but was helped by Art Hodes who featured him on WNYC broadcasts. He left New York and worked for a time at the Plantation Club in Nashville, then returned to Cleveland to play at the Starlite Grill. Late in his life (with Art Hodes' help) he gained ASCAP ratings for his part in the compositions 'Mama Don't Allow' and 'I'll Be Glad When You're Dead You Rascal You'. During the last year of his life he played at the Pin Wheel Club in Cleveland.

DAVIDSON, Leonard — *Born: Jonesboro, Arkansas, 13th July 1896*
saxes/clarinet

First regular work with violinist Roland Bruce's Band in Kansas City (1918), then worked in Nebraska, Oklahoma, and Texas before moving to Hollywood in 1924. Briefly with Reb Spikes before long stay with Sonny Clay's Orchestra (1924-33). With drummer Alton Redd's Band (1933-34), the Atwell Rose Band (1935-36), then worked with Sammy Franklin's Orchestra from 1936 until retiring from music in the mid-1950s.

DAVIS, 'Ham' Leonard — *Born: St. Louis, Missouri, 4th July 1905*
trumpet — *Died: New York City, 1957*

First played trumpet in the Odd Fellows Boys' Band in St. Louis. Worked in Charlie Creath's Bands in 1924 and 1925, then moved to New York; with Charlie Skeets in 1926, with Edgar Hayes at the Alhambra Theatre in 1927, also worked with pianist Arthur Gibbs' Band in New York 1927-8. Recorded with Eddie Condon (1929). With Charlie Johnson (1928-9), Elmer Snowden (1930-1), Don Redman (1931), Russell Wooding (1932), Benny Carter (1933), Luis Russell (1934-5). With Louis Armstrong's Orchestra from October 1935 until spring 1937, then rejoined Edgar Hayes until autumn 1938 (including trip to Europe). Worked with the 'Blackbirds' show in New York, October 1938 until spring 1939. Free-lanced in New York, then worked with Sidney Bechet nine-piece band at Mimo's in March 1940, again worked with Edgar Hayes before joining Maurice Hubbard's Band in September 1940. During the 1940s worked on and off for several years in band led by Alberto Socarras, also with George James in 1943. Left full-time music, but continued gigging.

DAVIS, 'Lem' Lemuel Arthur — *Born: Tampa, Florida, 22nd June 1914*
alto sax — *Died: New York City, 16th January 1970*

Worked regularly with pianist Nat Jaffe during the early 1940s, with Roger Kay (late 1942), toured in Coleman Hawkins' Septet (1943). Joined Eddie Heywood (early 1944), briefly with Rex Stewart (1946), and with John Kirby (1946), then rejoined Eddie Heywood's Sextet. During the 1950s and early 1960s worked in New York in pianist Teacho Wiltshire's combo, took part in the first of the Buck Clayton jam-session recordings.

DAVIS, 'Pike' Clifton — *Born: Baltimore, Maryland, 1896*
trumpet — *Died: Baltimore, Maryland, 13th September 1976*

Worked in Baltimore with Eubie Blake in 1915, then joined pianist Joe Rochester. In 1921 and 1922 worked in band led by violinist LeRoy Smith, then joined the Plantation Revue and visited London (1923). Worked for Ford Dabney, and played on various vaudeville tours, again with LeRoy Smith before rejoining the Plantation Revue, visited London with this company in 1926. Worked in U.S.A. with the Plantation Revue, returned to Europe with Noble Sissle in May 1929. Returned to New York, worked with Joe Jordan (summer 1930). From 1931 until 1934 worked in the 'Rhapsody in Black' show, then joined Lew Leslie's 'Blackbirds' and again returned to Europe in August 1934. Continued show work for many years, then returned to Baltimore. During the early 1960s continued to play, working mainly in Rivers Chambers' Orchestra.

DAVIS, Thomas Maxwell
tenor sax

Born: Independence, Kansas, 14th January 1916
Died: Los Angeles, 18th September 1970

Began on violin, then changed to alto sax, led own band in Kansas before joining Eugene Coy's Band on tenor sax. Worked mainly in Seattle with Coy from 1939-41. Led own band in California on and off during the 1940s and 1950s, but also played with Happy Johnson, Jake Porter, Benny Carter, Jesse Price, etc. Was featured on many free-lance recordings in the 1950s and 1960s, was also active as an arranger.

DAVIS, 'Wild Bill' William Strethen
organ/piano/arranger/composer

Born: Glasgow, Missouri, 24th November 1918

Raised in Parsons, Kansas. Learnt piano and guitar. Left high school in 1937 after winning musical scholarship to study at Tuskegee, remained there for two years, then attended Wiley College in Texas—arranged and played guitar for Milt Larkin's Band (c. 1940). Moved to Chicago, did some arranging for Earl Hines, also scored for several floor shows. Joined Louis Jordan (on piano) 1945-7. Switched to organ in 1948, worked in Chicago (1948), New York (1949). Formed own trio in 1951, long residencies in New York, Los Angeles, Atlantic City, etc. Has arranged for many bands including Duke Ellington, Count Basie ('April in Paris'), etc. Joined Duke Ellington in September 1969, toured Europe with Duke in November 1969. Toured widely as a soloist during the 1970s. Worked with Lionel Hampton (1979). Was featured at many festivals during early 1980s, also led own group in Europe.

DAVISON, 'Wild Bill' William Edward
cornet

Born: Defiance, Ohio, 5th January 1906

Began on mandolin, banjo, and guitar—switched to mellophone and cornet. First in local bands The Ohio Lucky Seven and James Jackson's Band, then with Roland Potter's Peerless Players in Cincinnati. Joined Chubb-Steinberg Orchestra and made recording debut in April 1924—this band was subsequently jointly led by Art Hicks and Paul Omer—as the Omer-Hicks Orchestra it played in New York in early 1926. Wild Bill left the band, returned to his home town, then joined Seattle Harmony Kings (then led by trombonist Neibauer, died 1963) and with this band travelled to Chicago. Worked mostly in and around Chicago during five-year period 1927-32, long spell with Benny Meroff, also worked with Charles Dornberger and Ray Miller, etc. In late 1931 began organising own big band—after intensive rehearsals the band worked briefly at Guyon's—after the accidental death of Frank Teschemacher, Wild Bill moved to Milwaukee and worked there for most of the time between 1933 and 1941. He led his own small groups at various clubs including East Side Spa and Schmitz's—also worked for other leaders including Charles 'Murph' Podolsky. During these eight years Wild Bill occasionally doubled on valve trombone. Moved to New York in the spring of 1941, led own band at Nick's, also own band in Boston (1943). Took part in Katherine Dunham Revue during 1943, and worked at Ryan's with Brad Gowans, the year closed with Wild Bill joining the U.S. Army. After demobilisation worked with Art Hodes, then led own band in St. Louis before becoming a regular at Eddie Condon's Club from December 1945—toured Britain with Eddie Condon in February 1957. Moved to West Coast in 1960, played at 400 Club, Los Angeles, worked with clarinettist Johnny Lane in summer of 1961, toured with own band (1962), with Salt Lake City Six in 1963, also spell with Surf Side Six. Led own band at The Metropole in spring 1964, continued touring with own band. Has made several solo tours of Europe, most recently in November 1967. Led Jazz Giants (1968), own band (1969-70), guested with many bands (1970-1). Toured with Bigard, Condon, Hodes (October 1971). Often worked in Europe during the 1970s. Played at Newport Jazz Festival 1978. Continued widespread international touring during early 1980s, including Europe and South America.

D

DEAN, **Demas**
trumpet

Born: Sag Harbor, Long Island, New York, 6th October 1903

Began on cornet at 10, later studied violin. A brother and six sisters all played part-time music. Whilst still at high school gigged with Mazzeo's Brass Band, and did summer work with Beatrice Van Houten. Studied at Howard University 1922-3 and gigged with many leaders including: 'Doc' Perry, Elmer Snowden, Russell Wooding, Roscoe Lee, etc. Toured and recorded with Lucille Hegamin and her Dixie Daisies (1923-4). Worked with Billy Butler, Ed Campbell, and Leon Abbey in New York, and with Ford Dabney's Orchestra in Florida, then joined Allie Ross's Orchestra. In May 1927 went to South America with Leon Abbey and his Orchestra. Returned to New York, rejoined Allie Ross for 'Blackbirds of 1928' show—recorded with Bessie Smith (February 1928). Sailed to Europe with Noble Sissle in May 1929, returned to U.S.A., with Joe Jordan (summer 1930), then worked with Pike Davis Orchestra for 'Rhapsody in Black', etc. (1931-4). Rejoined Noble Sissle in 1934 and remained with Sissle until leaving full-time music in 1944. Moved to California and did day work for the Los Angeles Post Office until retiring in 1965. Lives in Los Angeles.

DE CAILLAUX, **Pierre**
(real name: Lionel Jones)
piano/composer

Born: Columbus, Ohio, 1897
Died: U.S.A., 16th March 1956

Travelled to Europe as a member of the Southern Syncopated Orchestra (1919). After break-up of S.S.O. joined Benny Peyton's Jazz Kings and worked with them in London (1920-21). Left and led own band in Britain, also taught at the Royal Academy in London. Led own orchestra in Scandinavia during the 1920s, conducted various orchestras in Britain during the 1930s, and worked briefly as leader of visiting Blackbirds Show (1935). Was a musical director in Germany during the late 1930s, returned to the USA and became a music-therapist at New York's Belle Vue Hospital.

DEDRICK, **'Rusty' Lyle F.**
trumpet/composer

Born: Delevan, New York, 12th July 1918

With Dick Stabile (1938-39), Red Norvo (1939-41). With Claude Thornhill from 1941 until joining Army Air Corps Band at Fort Dix early in 1942. After demobilisation in 1945 worked briefly with Ray McKinley then rejoined Claude Thornhill for a year prior to becoming a studio musician, working mainly in New York. During the late 1960s and early 1970s worked with trombonist Urbie Green and with Lionel Hampton and took part in jazz festivals. Worked at Manhattan College of Music from 1971, and later became Director of Jazz Studies there.

DEEMS, **Barrett**
drums

Born: Springfield, Illinois, 1st March 1914

Started on drums at 10, joined union at 14. With Paul Ash in 1929, later led own band, then worked mainly with Joe Venuti from 1937 until 1944. Led own quartet at Hotel Sherman, Chicago (1945), then joined Jimmy Dorsey. With Red Norvo (1948), later that year worked with Eddie Wiggins' Band in Chicago. In 1949 again led at Hotel Sherman, etc. Briefly with Wingy Manone and Charlie Barnet, then with Muggsy Spanier from June 1951 until January 1954. With Louis Armstrong All Stars (May 1954 until February 1958). Briefly with 'Saints and Sinners' in 1960, then with Jack Teagarden until that leader's death (January 1964), then from February 1964 began long association with The Dukes of Dixieland, later became house drummer at Jazz Ltd., Chicago. Continues to play in Chicago, worked with Georg Brunis (spring 1970). Occasional touring during the 1970s, but regularly with Joe Kelly's Gaslight Band. Resumed widespread touring during the early 1980s, including work in South America with Wild Bill Davison and tours of Europe with Keith Smith.

D

DE FAUT, 'Volly' Voltaire
saxes/clarinet/violin

Born: Little Rock, Arkansas, 14th March 1904
Died: S. Chicago, Illinois, 29th May 1973

Raised in Chicago, studied at Englewood High School. Began on violin at six, sax and clarinet at 14. With Sig Meyers (c. 1922), with New Orleans Rhythm Kings (1923), later that year joined the Midway Gardens Orchestra, subsequently with Art Kassel. Recorded with Muggsy Spanier in 1924 (Stomp Six/Bucktown Five) and with Jelly Roll Morton in 1925. Worked with Merritt Brunies at the Friars Inn, Chicago, until 1926, then joined Ray Miller in Detroit, briefly with Isham Jones in Detroit, then moved back to Chicago and worked in local theatres. With Jean Goldkette (1928-9), then worked for almost 10 years as a studio musician for WGN radio station, then organised own dog-breeding business, served in U.S. Army as a musician. After demobilisation again ran own business, began gigging again from the mid-1940s, played with Bud Jacobson's Jungle Kings (1945), and took part in many Chicago jam sessions. Lived for five years in Davenport, Iowa, then moved back to Chicago in late 1965. Often worked with Art Hodes in late 1960s. Visited New Orleans in 1971.

DE PARIS, Sidney
trumpet/tuba/vocals

Born: Crawfordsville, Indiana, 30th May 1905
Died: New York City, 13th September 1967

Brother of Wilbur; their father was a bandmaster and music teacher. Played in Washington, D.C., in band led by pianist Sam Taylor (1924), during following year worked in New York in Andrew Preer's Cotton Club Orchestra. With Charlie Johnson (1926-7), played at Pearl Theatre, Philadelphia, in band managed by brother Wilbur (1927-8), again with Charlie Johnson (1928-31), also led own band in 1931, briefly with Benny Carter, also recorded with McKinney's Cotton Pickers (1929). With Don Redman from 1932-6, briefly with Noble Sissle in Cleveland, then during 1937-8 worked with Willie Bryant, Charlie Johnson, and the brief-lived Mezz Mezzrow Disciples of Swing (November 1937), played in New York with the 'Blackbirds' show from October 1938 until early 1939. Rejoined Don Redman for a few months early in 1939, then led own eight-piece band in Baltimore before joining Zutty Singleton's Band in New York late 1939 to spring 1940. Recorded with Jelly Roll Morton (1939), worked and recorded with Sidney Bechet (1940). Joined Maurice Hubbard's Band (August 1940), then from November 1940 until September 1941 in Benny Carter's Big Band. Rejoined Zutty Singleton in September 1941, also worked for a few weeks with Charlie Barnet. Gigged and recorded with Art Hodes (1942), in spring 1943 began working in small band led by Wilbur, toured with Roy Eldridge Big Band in summer of 1944, worked with Dick Ward's Band (spring 1945), Claude Hopkins (1946). Occasionally led own band, but from 1947 worked regularly with Wilbur, they played for many years at Jimmy Ryan's in New York. Sidney remained at Ryan's whilst Wilbur and the rest of the band toured Africa (spring 1957); he regularly doubled on tuba, also recorded with Wingy Manone on tuba (1958). Frequent spells of ill health during the early 1960s, worked on and off with Wilbur from the autumn of 1964, doubling trumpet and flugel horn.

DE PARIS, Wilbur
trombone/leader/occasionally drums

Born: Crawfordsville, Indiana, 11th January 1900
Died: New York City, 3rd January 1973

Brother of Sidney; their father was a bandmaster and music teacher. Began on alto horn at the age of seven, and was soon working with his father's carnival band. Later played tent shows and toured T.O.B.A. circuit. Travelled to New Orleans (c. 1922) with Mack's Merry-makers, sat in (on 'C' melody sax) with Louis Armstrong, then at Tom Anderson's also gigged with Armand Piron. From 1925 regularly led own band in Philadelphia, also worked with LeRoy Smith, etc , and with Bobby Lee in Atlantic City. In 1927-8 managed big band resident at the Pearl Theatre, Philadelphia. During the 1930s worked with LeRoy Smith, Dave Nelson, Noble Sissle, Mills Blue Rhythm Band, Edgar Hayes, etc. With Teddy Hill from late 1936-7, including trip to Europe, then with Louis Armstrong (November 1937 until September 1940). Briefly with Ella Fitzgerald Orchestra, then worked in theatre for 'The Pirate' show (1942), later toured with Roy Eldridge Big Band, from spring of 1943 began leading own small band, disbanded to join Duke Ellington from late 1945 until c. May 1947. Re-formed own highly successful small band, mainly resident at Jimmy Ryan's in New York from 1951 until early 1962 (toured Africa in spring of 1957). Continued to lead at 'Room at the Bottom' (1962), 'Broken Drum' (1964), 'Mardi Gras Show' at Jones Beach (1965), etc. Own rehearsal studio in New York (1971). Led own Zeba Band (1971).

DESVIGNES, Sidney
trumpet

Born: New Orleans, Louisiana, 11th September 1893
Died: Pacoima, California, 2nd December 1959

Whilst in his teens played in Leonard Bechet's Silver Bell Band. Worked with Excelsior Brass Band from c. 1919, later in the Maple Leaf Orchestra. With Fate Marable from 1921, then worked in Ed Allen's Whispering Gold Band, returned to work on riverboats with Fate Marable. In summer of 1926 led own band at St. Bernard's Country Club in New Orleans, then long spell as leader, mainly on the S.S. 'Island Queen'. From the early 1930s led own big band in New Orleans. Left New Orleans and opened own night club in Los Angeles during the 1950s.

DIAL, Harry
drums/vocals

Born: Birmingham, Alabama, 17th February 1907

Brother, Harvey, was a trumpeter. Raised in St. Louis from 1909, began playing drums in local Odd Fellows' Band. First professional work in August 1921, led own band in 1922, also gigged with other leaders including clarinettist Sidney Costella and Dewey Jackson. Joined Fate Marable on Steamer 'J.S.' in 1923, and for next three years worked mainly with Marable, took brief leave of absence to work in Chicago (c. 1924), also played with: Norman Mason's Carolina Melodists, with Dewey Jackson on S.S. 'Capitol', and in Jimmy Powell's Jazz Monarchs at the Chauffeurs' Club, St. Louis. Left Jimmy Powell, briefly visited Chicago in late 1927; moved to Chicago in February 1928, joined band led by violinist Wilson Robinson, then played for over a year with Clifford 'Klarinet' King's Big Band (1928-9). With Jerome Don Pasquall's Band in 1930, also led own recording band. Played with Oscar 'Bernie' Young, pianist Ira Coffey, and Ida Mae Marples before joining Louis Armstrong Big Band in March 1933 (replacing 'Yank' Porter). After Louis Armstrong disbanded rejoined Ida Mae Marples for three months, worked in Camden, New Jersey, with Ira Coffey's Walkathons (late 1933), then moved to New York (January 1934). With Emperor Jones' Band at Small's Paradise, then worked for Sam Wooding, banjoist Ferman Tapps, and Wen Talbot before becoming house drummer at Jerry Preston's Log Cabin. Brief spell with Fats Waller in spring of 1935, then with Chin Lee's Band. Played in Ed Allen's Band from 1937-40, also did regular work as music copyist during late 1930s and 1940s. Did defence plant work during World War II, continued gigging, played occasionally with Ed Allen, and in Sammy Stewart's small group. Led own band from 1946, residencies at The Palace, Swing Rendezvous, etc., then long residency at Small's Paradise from 1947 until 1955. Has continued leading own small band in New York during the 1960s, recorded L.P.s in 1961 and 1965

DICKENSON, 'Vic' Victor
trombone/vocals

Born: Xenia, Ohio, 6th August 1906

After early efforts at the organ, was given a trombone by his elder brother, gigged with The Elite Serenaders (1921). Left school to work for his father, who was a plastering contractor, c. 1922 the family moved to Columbus, Ohio. Played local gigs with Roy Brown's Band, also worked in The Night Owls, and in band co-led with his brother, saxist Carlos. First professional work with Don Phillips' Band in Madison, Wisconsin (c. 1925), returned to Columbus for a while, then in spring 1927 worked at Palais Royale, South Bend, Indiana, with drummer Willie Jones and his Orchestra (directed by saxist Leonard Gay). With Bill Broadhus Band in Lexington, and Wesley Helvey, subsequently worked in Leonard Gay's Orchestra, including residency in Madison, Wisconsin (summer 1929). With Speed Webb's Band for a year from autumn 1929, then joined Zack Whyte's Chocolate Beau Brummels; whilst in New York in December 1930, made first recording (vocal on Luis Russell's 'Honey That Reminds Me'). Left Zack Whyte early in 1932 and moved to Kansas City, Missouri, joined Thamon Hayes' Kansas City Skyrockets, left, played briefly with Clarence Paige's Royal Syncopators, then toured with Thamon Hayes. With Blanche Calloway from summer 1933 until 1936, then with Claude Hopkins (1936-9). Joined Benny Carter Big Band in late 1939, then with Count Basie for a year from January 1940. Rejoined Benny Carter February 1941, during summer of 1941 did a season with Sidney Bechet, with Frankie Newton in autumn 1941, then worked with Hot Lips Page in Chicago and New York before working summer season with Frankie Newton in 1942. Returned to New York with Newton, played residency at Cafe Society (Downtown), then joined Eddie Heywood from September 1943. Worked with Heywood in New York and California until October 1946—but was absent through illness for part of 1945 and 1946. Free-lanced in California in 1947-8, led own band at Billy Berg's Club in Los Angeles and Boston, etc. (1948). Worked mainly in Boston from 1949 until the mid-1950s, led own band, also with Ed Hall, Frankie Newton, etc. Regularly with Bobby Hackett in 1951 and 1956. Moved to New York, played with Henry 'Red' Allen at the Metropole (early 1958), to Europe for appearances at the Cannes Festival in July 1958, worked with Sam Price in Belgium. Led own group at Arpeggio Club, New York, for part of 1959. During the 1960s did several tours and jazz festival appearances with pianist George Wein's All Stars including European tour in spring 1961, played in Wild Bill Davison's Band 1961-2, also worked regularly in the Saints and Sinners Band (co-leading with Charles 'Red' Richards). Worked occasionally at Eddie Condon's Club; toured Asia and Australia with Condon in spring 1964. Toured Europe as a soloist in 1965, then regularly with the Saints and Sinners until co-leading successful quintet with Bobby Hackett (late 1968-70). Worked with The World's Greatest Jazz Band (spring 1970). Extensive free-lancing during the 1970s. Played regularly during the early 1980s, and worked at Nice Festival in 1982.

DICKERSON, Carroll *Born: 1895*
violin/leader *Died: October 1957*

Led own band in Chicago from 1920, at Entertainers' Cafe (1921), residency at Sunset Cafe (1922-4); in late 1924 formed new band for 48-week tour on Pantages Circuit (most of the band personnel then worked as Lottie Hightower's Nighthawks). Dickerson returned to Chicago; in spring of 1926 re-formed own band for Sunset Cafe residency (featuring Louis Armstrong). Subsequently led at the Savoy Dance Hall (1927-9). The band left Chicago in spring of 1929 (together with Louis Armstrong). After gigging in New York under Louis Armstrong's name, the band began residency at Connie's Inn until spring of 1930. They then disbanded, Dickerson remained in New York and worked briefly with the Mills Blue Rhythm Band, then toured with King Oliver. Returned to Chicago in the early 1930s and resumed leading own band, after residency at 'Swingland', Chicago in 1937, he temporarily left full-time music, but made 'come-back' early in 1939 and continued leading own bands during the 1940s. Long residency at Rhumboogie, Chicago.

DICKERSON, Roger Quincey *Born: Paducah, Kentucky c. 1898*
trumpet *Died: Glen Falls, New York, 21st January 1951*

Raised in St. Louis, Missouri. Played in local theatres from 1918-20. Left St. Louis with Wilson Robinson's Bostonians (1923), after extensive touring, the band gained residency at New York's Cotton Club—by then violinist Andrew Preer was fronting the band. After Preer's death in May 1927, the band worked for a time as The Cotton Club Orchestra, then became known as The Missourians. From 1930 they became Cab Calloway's Orchestra—Dickerson left the band in 1931. Left full-time music and worked for many years as a taxi-driver, he suffered a long illness before dying of a throat ailment.

DILLARD, 'Bill' William *Born: Philadelphia, Pennsylvania, 20th July 1911*
trumpet/vocals

In the early 1920s was given a bugle by one of the musicians accompanying politician

Marcus Garvey's tour, learnt to play the bugle without a mouthpiece! On 12th birthday was given a cornet by his father. Received tuition from Clarence Smith, played in local high school orchestras, then worked with Linwood Johnson and Josh Saddler in Philadelphia. Moved to New York City in 1929, played at dancing schools with Bobby Neal, Howard Hill, etc., then toured Pennsylvania with Jelly Roll Morton (also recorded with Morton). Played in Bingie Madison's Band (c. 1930), then with Luis Russell (1931-2), also recorded with King Oliver. With Benny Carter in 1933 (including recordings with Spike Hughes), with Ralph Cooper's Kongo Knights, then to Europe with Lucky Millinder until autumn 1933, then rejoined Benny Carter. Left in spring 1934 to work for LeRoy Smith, then joined Teddy Hill in September 1934. Remained with Teddy Hill until 1938 (including tour of Europe in 1937). In 1938 and 1939 worked in pianist Dave Martin's Band at the St. George Hotel, Brooklyn. Briefly with Coleman Hawkins' Big Band in late 1939, then in Louis Armstrong's Orchestra from January-November 1940. With Red Norvo at Kelly's Stables late 1942 to spring 1943, then embarked on highly successful stage career as singer-actor (occasionally playing trumpet). Broadway shows include: 'Carmen Jones' (1943), 'Anna Lucasta' (1945), 'Memphis Bound', 'Beggars' Holiday' (1946), etc. Played in France in spring of 1949 accompanying blues singer Huddie Ledbetter. Returned to Broadway, played trumpet and acted in 'Regina' show, then in 'Lost in the Stars' (1950), 'Green Pastures' (1951), 'My Darlin' Aida' (1952), etc. Has appeared on numerous television shows and was also regularly featured in the radio series 'Love of Life'. From the late 1950s through to the 1970s played and sang at many private engagements, also led own big band for specific bookings. During the early 1980s was featured in the touring 'One Mo' Time' show, and worked in Europe and in Australia with that production.

DIXON, 'Charlie' Charles Edward — *Born: Jersey City. c. 1898*
banjo/arranger — *Died: New York City, 6th December 1940*

Gigged in New York and Boston before joining Sam Wooding at The Nest Club (1922), subsequently with 'Shrimp' Jones' Band in New York, and became regular member of Fletcher Henderson's Band from January 1924 (having previously recorded with Henderson). Left Henderson (c. 1928), but continued arranging for the band. Led band accompanying Cora LaRedd, then mainly active as arranger-composer during the 1930s, including spell as staff arranger for Chick Webb, also scored for Club Plantation revues.

DIXON, George — *Born: New Orleans, Louisiana, 8th April 1909*
trumpet/saxes/arranger

Spent the first few years of his life in New Orleans, where his father, a minister, was then preaching. Subsequently the family moved to Mississippi, then to Arkansas. In 1922, whilst living in Natchez, Mississippi, George started on violin, then studied at Arkansas State College in 1925-6, led school band from 1926 and began doubling on alto sax. Left college in 1926 and moved to Chicago, gigged in Chicago and Gary, Indiana, 1926 and 1927. In late 1928 joined Sammy Stewart in Columbus, Ohio (featured on trumpet, sax, and violin). Remained with Sammy Stewart until May 1930, left the band in New York and travelled to Chicago to join Earl Hines in mid-May 1930. Remained with Earl Hines until joining U.S. Navy in September 1942. Led band at Naval Air Station in Memphis, Tennessee, until honourable discharge in August 1945. Returned to free-lance in Chicago, played with: Floyd Campbell, Ted Eggleston, Eddie King, etc. Then formed own band which, from April 1946, played long residency at Circle Inn, Chicago. Left full-time music in 1951, but has continued to lead own band in Chicago until the present time.

DIXON, 'Joe' Joseph — *Born: Lynn, Massachusetts, 21st April 1917*
clarinet/saxes

Brother of trombonist 'Gus' Dixon. Began clarinet at eight, local tuition, then studied in Boston. Led own high school dance band, then to New York in 1934, joined Billy Staffon. With Tommy Dorsey (summer 1936 to early 1937), briefly with Gus Arnheim, then a year with Bunny Berigan from May 1937. Served in U.S. Navy during World War II, then played for several months with Eddie Condon in 1946 before joining Miff Mole at Nick's. Active as a free-lance musician in late 1940s and 1950s, then led own quintet which played residencies on Long Island during late 1950s. Out of music for a while in the early 1960s due to injuries sustained in a car crash, worked as a disc-jockey, then re-formed own small group. Worked with own group in the 1970s, also active as a music teacher.

DIXON, Lawrence
guitar/banjo/cello

Born: Chillicothe, Ohio. c. 1895
Died: Chicago, Illinois, January 1970

Father was also a musician. Joined Sammy Stewart in Ohio, and originally went to Chicago with him in 1923. Left Sammy Stewart in 1928, joined Dave Peyton at the Regal Theatre, Chicago (playing cello), doubled for a while in Paul Jordan's Orchestra. With Clarence Moore (early 1929), then (c. 1930) joined pianist Grant Williams at the Algiers Club, Chicago. With Earl Hines' Orchestra from 1931 until 1937, then free-lanced in Chicago. During the 1950s and early 1960s played regularly in Franz Jackson's Original Jass All Stars, but ill health forced him to give up regular playing in the summer of 1963.

DIXON, Vance
saxes/clarinet/vocals

Born: Parkersburg, Virginia. c. 1895
Deceased

Was for many years musical director of Lois Deppe's Serenaders, left Deppe in late 1925, worked in Chicago with Sammy Stewart (early 1926), later with Clarence Jones (1928), and Erskine Tate (1930), also led own group Vance Dixon and his Pencils. Worked in New York with banjoist Ikey Robinson's Quartet at Casa Mia Club, Brooklyn (1933-4), and with trumpeter June Clark at the Quogue Inn, Long Island (1936).

DODDS, 'Baby' Warren
drums

Born: Robson Street, New Orleans, Louisiana, 24th December 1898
Died: Chicago, Illinois, 14th February 1959

Gained his nickname through being the youngest of six children—brother of Johnny Dodds. Whilst doing day work in a sack-making factory (c. 1912), took first drum lessons from Dave Perkins, later studied with Walter Brundy and Louis Cottrell Sr. Occasional parade work with Bunk Johnson, but first regular gigs with Willie Hightower's American Stars. Played for a while at Fewclothes Cabaret, then spell with Manuel Manetta at The Casino before returning to Fewclothes Cabaret. Worked with Frankie Dusen's Eagle Band, then with Papa Celestin before joining Fate Marable on the S.S. 'Sydney' in autumn 1918. Remained with Marable until September 1921, returned to New Orleans, then was sent for by King Oliver. Joined Oliver in San Francisco, moved to Chicago with Oliver in 1922, left the band c. late 1923. Early in 1924 worked in Honore Dutrey's Band at Dreamland, then played at Kelly's Stables with Freddie Keppard and Johnny Dodds. During the period 1925-30 played for various leaders in Chicago including: Willie Hightower, Lil Armstrong, Ralph Brown, Charlie Elgar, Hugh Swift, etc. Worked regularly at Kelly's Stables with Johnny Dodds from 1927-9, also did extensive free-lance recordings including sessions with Louis Armstrong, Jelly Roll Morton, etc. Briefly with Dave Peyton at Club Baghdad (December 1927 to January 1928). Throughout the 1930s played many residencies in Chicago with small groups led by Johnny Dodds, also helped his brother Bill run a taxi service. From 1936 to 1939 worked on and off as house drummer at The Three Deuces, Chicago. In January 1940 played at 9750 Club with brother Johnny's Band, teeth trouble forced Johnny to leave, and Baby became leader until the end of the residency in March 1940. Gigged in Chicago, then spell with Jimmie Noone at The Coach Club, Chicago, late 1940 to spring 1941. Recorded with Bunk Johnson (1944), worked with Bunk (1945) including first visit to New York in September 1945, returned to gig in Chicago, then back to New York. With Art Hodes in 1946 and 1947, regularly featured on Rudi Blesh's 'This is Jazz' radio series. To Europe in February 1948 to play at Nice Festival with Mezz Mezzrow, did brief tour, then returned to U.S.A. With Art Hodes in New York (April-September 1948), returned to Chicago, worked at Beehive Club with Miff Mole (late 1948 to March 1949). Whilst visiting New York in spring 1949 suffered a stroke, whilst recuperating played occasionally with band led by trombonist Conrad Janis. Had second stroke in spring 1950, but resumed playing the following year. Worked with Natty Dominique in 1951 and 1952 (sharing drum duties with Jasper Taylor), also visited New

York in 1951 and 1952. Played at Ryan's, New York, in December 1952, was again taken ill and returned to Chicago to convalesce. In late 1954 played again in New York with Don Frye Trio at Ryan's, then returned to Chicago. By this time Baby was suffering from partial paralysis, he played occasionally until 1957, but was then forced to quit.

'The Baby Dodds Story', as told to Larry Gara, was first published in 1959.

DODDS, 'Johnny' John M.
clarinet/occasionally alto sax

Born: Waverley, Louisiana, 12th April 1892
Died: Chicago, Illinois, 8th August 1940

One of six children—brother of Baby Dodds. Started on clarinet at 17, took lessons from Lorenzo Tio Jr. and Charlie McCurdy. Did day work until joining Kid Ory at the Come Clean in Gretna (c. 1911). Occasional parade work with Jack Carey and various other marching bands, worked on and off with Kid Ory until 1917. Short spell with Fate Marable on S.S. 'Capitol', then left New Orleans to tour with Billy and Mary Mack's Merrymakers Show (1917-18). Returned to New Orleans and briefly rejoined Kid Ory (1919), then went to Chicago to join King Oliver. With King Oliver in California and Chicago, then worked with Honore Dutrey at Dreamland, Chicago (early 1924). Joined Freddie Keppard at Bert Kelly's Stables, Chicago (c. spring 1924), was later appointed leader at this venue, and played residency there for almost six years—Keppard frequently returned to front the band. Prolific free-lance recordings from 1924 including Louis Armstrong's Hot Fives and Hot Sevens, King Oliver, Jelly Roll Morton, etc., etc. Led own small band at Chicago clubs throughout the 1930s: Three Deuces, New Plantation, Calahan's, Lamb's Cafe, The 29, 47th and State, etc. In January 1938 Dodds made his only trip to New York, to take part in a recording session, returned to Chicago to play residencies at Three Deuces, Club 29 (1938), and Hayes Hotel. Suffered a severe heart attack in May 1939, and was inactive until starting residency with own quartet at the 9750 Club on 20th January 1940, soon afterwards he was again forced to quit playing through teeth trouble. Within a few weeks he was equipped with new teeth and returned to play week-end dates at the same venue with Baby Dodds' Quartet until the residency ended on 18th March 1940. From then until his death he did occasional gigs and one recording session; but concentrated his energies on supervising the apartment block that he owned at 39th and Michigan, Chicago.

DOGGETT, 'Bill' William Ballard
organ/piano/arranger

Born: Philadelphia, Pennsylvania, 16th February 1916

Played with Jimmy Gorham Band from the mid-1930s, formed own band with several of his colleagues in 1938; band fronted by Lucky Millinder for 1938 tour. With Lucky Millinder until joining Jimmy Mundy (late 1939), with Lucky Millinder (1940-2). From summer of 1942 spent two years as pianist-arranger with The Ink Spots, also arranged for Lionel Hampton, Count Basie, and Louis Armstrong Big Band, etc. With Willie Bryant (1946), with Louis Jordan from 1948. From 1951 has specialised on organ; has led own small combo with great success throughout the 1950s and 1960s. Toured France in 1963. Widespread touring during the 1970s and early 1980s, including regular appearances in Europe.

DOMINIQUE, 'Natty' Anatie
trumpet

Born: New Orleans, Louisiana, 2nd August 1896
Died: Chicago, Illinois, 30th August 1982

Uncle of Don Albert; cousin of Barney Bigard. Received tuition from Manuel Perez, did occasional parade work in New Orleans before leaving for Chicago in June 1913 to play in Artie Steur's Brass Band. Subsequently played in Detroit and Michigan with Bob Crucett's Band. Returned to Chicago in the early 1920s, joined Carroll Dickerson's Orchestra at Entertainer's Cafe, and gigged with Al Simeon's Hot Six. Worked in Jimmie Noone's Small Band, then toured Pantages Circuit for almost a year with Carroll Dickerson, returned to Chicago and played with the same leader at the Sunset Cafe, briefly in Louis Armstrong's Stompers at the Sunset (1927). Joined Johnny Dodds' Band at Bert Kelly's Stables early in 1928, and continued to work regularly with Dodds through the 1930s. Left full-time music in the early 1940s and worked as a redcap at the Chicago airport. After appearing at a Chicago jazz concert in March 1949, began regular part-time playing. Led own band during the 1950s.

D

DONAHUE, 'Sam' Samuel Koontz
tenor sax/trumpet/arranger

Born: Detroit, Michigan, 18th March 1918
Died: Reno, Nevada, 22nd March 1974

Began on clarinet at age of 9, later played in Redford High School Band. Played local jobs in Michigan before leading own band. With Gene Krupa (1938-40), briefly with Harry James and Benny Goodman (October 1940), then led own band prior to joining U.S. Navy in 1942. Led big service band which played in Europe during World War II. Own band again from 1946, combined this with teaching until re-entering U.S. Navy for some months in 1952, worked with Tommy Dorsey, then fronted Billy May's Band on tour in 1956. Led own band in late 1950s, then fronted Tommy Dorsey 'Memorial' Band 1961-65 after working with Stan Kenton. Led own band in the late 1960s, became musical director for New York 'Playboy' Club, prior to leading own band in Nevada from 1969.

DONNELLY, 'Muttonleg' Theodore
trombone

Born: Oklahoma City, 13th November 1912
Died: New York City, 8th May 1958

Violin from the age of eight, switched to trombone 12 years later. Played with George E. Lee's Band; with Tommy Douglas from 1934. With Andy Kirk from 1936 until early 1943. Did U.S.O. tour with Al Sears in summer of 1943, then joined Count Basie from December 1943 until 1950. Worked mainly with Erskine Hawkins from early 1951 until 1957. Briefly with Illinois Jacquet (March 1950).

DORSEY, 'Bob' Robert
saxes/clarinet

Born: Lincoln, Nebraska, 10th September 1915
Died: 19th February 1965

First professional work with Nat Towles in the late 1930s, then with Horace Henderson before joining Cootie Williams' Big Band in 1942. Subsequently with Cab Calloway (1945-6). Specialised on tenor sax during the 1950s and early 1960s.

DORSEY, 'Jimmy' James
clarinet/alto sax/occasionally trumpet

Born: Shenandoah, Pennsylvania, 29th February 1904
Died: New York City, 12th June 1957

Brother of Tommy Dorsey; their father, Thomas F. Dorsey, was originally a coal-miner who later became a music teacher and director of the Elmore Band in Shenandoah. Jimmy began on slide trumpet and cornet during early infancy. In September 1913 he played in New York (for two days) in a variety act: J. Carson McGee's King Trumpeters. Played cornet in his father's band from the age of seven, switched to sax in 1915. Worked for a week in local coal mine (c. 1917), left to concentrate on music. With Tommy, formed Dorseys' Novelty Six which later became Dorseys' Wild Canaries; they played long residency in Baltimore and became one of the first jazz groups to broadcast. Disbanded to join Billy Lustig's Scranton Sirens and with that group made first (private) recordings: 'Three O'Clock in the Morning/Fate'. Joined California Ramblers (c. September 1924). From 1925 did prolific free-lance radio and recording work, also regularly with Jean Goldkette, Henry Thies, Ray Miller, Vincent Lopez, Paul Whiteman, Red Nichols, etc., during the 1920s. With Ted Lewis in 1930 (including tour of Europe), left in August 1930, returned to the U.S.A. and recommenced studio work with: Fred Rich, Jacques Renard, Victor Young, Andre Kostelanetz, Rudy Vallee, Lennie Hayton, Rubinoff Orchestra, etc., etc. During the late 1920s and early 1930s the Dorsey Brothers also led their own studio groups and occasionally organised bands for specific engagements: 'Everybody's Welcome' Broadway show, etc. From the spring of 1934 they organised a band on a full-time basis, after playing dates outside of New York the band made its official debut at the Sands Point Beach Club, Long Island, in July 1934. After dates at the Riviera, Palisades, and Palais Royale, they began residency at the Glen Island Casino in May 1935. Whilst playing at this venue Jimmy and Tommy had a violent disagreement which resulted in Tommy's leaving to form his own band. Jimmy continued to lead the band for many years, and achieved widespread success with several best-selling records. The Dorsey Brothers appeared together in the biographical film 'The Fabulous Dorseys' (1947). During the late 1940s and early 1950s Jimmy formed and re-formed his own big bands, but from spring of 1953 was featured with Tommy Dorsey's Orchestra (usually billed as 'The

Fabulous Dorseys'), he became sole leader after Tommy's death. In the last year of his life ill health forced him to hand over the leadership to Lee Castle. He died of cancer. Films include: 'That Girl From Paris', 'Shall We Dance?', 'The Fleet's In', 'I Dood It', 'Lost in a Harem', '4 Jacks and a Jeep', 'The Fabulous Dorseys', etc.

Throughout the 1920s and 1930s Jimmy Dorsey occasionally played trumpet and cornet.

DORSEY, 'Tommy' Thomas — *Born: Shenandoah, Pennsylvania, 19th November 1905*
trombone/trumpet — *Died: Greenwich, Connecticut, 26th November 1956*

Brother of Jimmy (q.v.). Taught trumpet by his father, later concentrated on trombone, but throughout his career occasionally played trumpet, including recorded work; he very occasionally played clarinet whilst on tour with his own big band. Together with Jimmy, played in Dorseys' Novelty Six/Wild Canaries, Billy Lustig's Scranton Sirens, Jean Goldkette's Orchestra, Henry Thies Orchestra, etc. Prolific free-lance radio and recording work from 1925, regularly with Paul Whiteman (1927-8), also worked for Vincent Lopez, Roger Wolfe Kahn, Nat Shilkret, Rubinoff Orchestra, Rudy Vallee, Victor Young, Walt Rosner, Fred Rich, etc., etc. In the late 1920s and early 1930s co-led recording bands with Jimmy; they also played outside dates together. During the early 1930s Tommy continued with studio work, except for temporary absence for an appendectomy in spring of 1932. The jointly led band became a full-time prospect from the spring of 1934, some 15 months later Tommy split from the band whilst they were playing a residency at the Glen Island Casino, he rejoined the band for a few days later in June 1935, then left permanently and was eventually replaced by Bobby Byrne. Tommy soon formed his own band from members of Joe Haymes' Band, they played at the French Casino and did a road tour, then with more personnel changes made their official debut at the Hotel Lincoln in New York. Continued to lead own successful big band for many years which always had an impressive array of jazz soloists and also featured vocals by Frank Sinatra, Bob Eberly, Dick Haymes, Jo Stafford, etc., etc. During the early 1940s Tommy Dorsey (like several other big band leaders) temporarily added a string section—his 1942 tours featured a 31-piece ensemble. Continued to lead through the 1940s and early 1950s (reorganisation in 1947). Featured with Jimmy in the 1947 film 'The Fabulous Dorseys'. Though Tommy Dorsey never toured Europe he sat in with Mezz Mezzrow and Bill Coleman during a holiday in Paris (October 1951). From May 1953 the Dorsey brothers began working together again, Jimmy Dorsey being featured with Tommy Dorsey's Orchestra. This arrangement continued until Tommy's untimely end; he choked to death after inhaling undigested food particles. Films include: 'Las Vegas Nights', 'Girl Crazy', 'Dubarry was a Lady', 'Presenting Lily Mars', 'Ship Ahoy', 'Broadway Rhythm', 'I Dood It', 'A Song is Born', 'The Fabulous Dorseys', etc.

'Tommy and Jimmy—The Dorsey Years' by Herb Sanford, first published in 1972.

DOUGHERTY, 'Eddie' Edward — *Born: Brooklyn, New York, 17th July 1915*
drums

Began playing drums at the age of 13—tuition from Billy Gussak. Gigged around New York, then did first professional work with Kenny Watts and his Kilowatts at Dicky Wells' Club in Harlem. Remained with Kenny Watts for several years until 1940, also did extensive recording work with Mildred Bailey, Frank Froeba, Billie Holiday, Cliff Jackson, Harry James, James P. Johnson, Pete Johnson, Taft Jordan, Art Tatum, Mary Lou Williams, etc. Subbed for Dave Tough in Bud Freeman's Summa Cum Laude Band in 1940. Subsequently worked with Frankie Newton, Joe Sullivan, Benny Carter (1941), Benny Morton (1944-5), Wilbur de Paris, Teddy Wilson, Albert Nicholas, Leslie Millington, and band led by tenor saxist 'Skinny' Brown. Left full-time music many years ago, but continues to free-lance.

D

DOUGLAS, Billy
trumpet/vocals

Born: New Haven, Connecticut. c. 1908
Deceased

Received first musical tuition from saxist Larry Ringold, at the time they were both living in a local Boys' Institution. Worked with local bands in Connecticut, then in New York with Earle Howard's Band from spring 1932 until spring 1933, later worked with Earle Howard in Boston, then played in Hartford, Connecticut, in Percy Nelson's Band from October 1933 until May 1934. During the following year, whilst touring the Carolina States with Jimmy Gunn's Band, was signed as featured soloist with Don Albert's Band. Remained with Don Albert until late 1937. Long spell of free-lancing. Played on Earl Hines' recording session (1945). Lived for many years in his home state.

DOUGLAS, 'Boots' Clifford
drums

Born: Temple, Texas, 7th September 1908

Began playing drums at 15; played first gigs in Turner's Park, San Antonio (1926). Worked with Millard McNeal's Southern Melody Boys in the 1920s, then formed own band, Boots and his Buddies, who worked mainly in Texas during the 1930s and early 1940s (recording for Bluebird regularly between 1935 and 1938). Moved to Los Angeles in 1950, left full-time music and worked for the County Authorities until retiring in 1974.

DOUGLAS, 'Tommy' Thomas
saxes/clarinet

Born: Eskridge, Kansas, 9th November 1911

Several brothers were musicians including tenor saxist Roy Douglas. Attended school in Topeka, then studied at the Boston Conservatory (1924-8), also did summer touring with Captain Woolmack's Band. Moved to Kansas City in late 1920s, worked with Paul Banks, stints with George Lee (1931-4), led own band, also toured with Jelly Roll Morton and Jap Allen (c. 1931) before joining Clarence Love's Orchestra (1932-3). Briefly with Bennie Moten in 1934, then again formed own band, touring throughout Middle West from the mid-1930s, also various residencies in Kansas City including Antlers' Club (1938). Worked as musical director for George E. Lee in 1939, then again formed own band. Briefly with Duke Ellington in 1951 (2nd March until 24th March), then resumed leading own band. Has continued leading (mainly in Missouri) during the 1950s and 1960s.

DOWELL, 'Saxie' Horace Kirby
alto, tenor sax/clarinet

Born: North Carolina, 29th May 1904
Died: Scottsdale, Arizona, 22nd July 1974

Attended University of North Carolina and there joined band led by Hal Kemp. Worked with Hal Kemp from 1924 until April 1939 (including European tours). Formed own band in 1939 and continued to lead until joining U.S. Navy in 1942. Led own U.S. Naval Band which gained considerable fame by remaining on duty whilst the aircraft carrier U.S.S. 'Franklin' was sinking. After demobilisation he formed his own commercial band (from April 1946), was later active as a song publisher.

DRELINGER, Art
tenor sax/bass sax/clarinet

Born: Gloucester, Massachusetts, 20th August 1916

Played with local bands before moving to New York in 1935. With Adrian Rollini at Adrian's Tap Room (1936), also worked with Red McKenzie, and Wingy Manone at The Famous Door. With Bunny Berigan in spring 1937, brief trip to Europe, then with Jack Jenney's Studio Band and Artie Shaw before working for Paul Whiteman from spring 1938 (regularly featured with Whiteman's Swing Wing). Studio musician from the early 1940s, 25 years with C.B.S. radio and television. Prolific recording career including sessions with Louis Armstrong, Billie Holiday, etc., etc.

DuCONGE, Peter
saxes/clarinet/cello

Born: New Orleans, Louisiana. c. 1903
Died: Michigan. c. 1965

Three of his brothers were professional musicians: Adolphus (piano), Albert (trumpet), and Earl (tenor sax)—their father, Oscar, was a noted bandleader in New Orleans around the turn of the century. Peter's first paid work was with Edmond Faure at the Elite Club, he left New Orleans as a musician working aboard the S.S. 'Capitol'. After a spell on the riverboats settled in New York, toured with J. Vaughn's Lucky Sambo Orchestra (early 1927), then played with Bill Brown and his Brownies (1927), left in January 1928 to sail to Europe with Leon Abbey. Whilst working in Paris (1929) he married the famous Ada 'Bricktop' Smith—they were subsequently divorced. Remained in Europe throughout the 1930s, working for various leaders including: Leon Abbey, Louis Armstrong (on 1932 and 1934 tours), Coleman Hawkins (1935), Benny Peyton, Freddy Johnson-Arthur Briggs. At the outbreak of World War II he returned to the U.S.A., he lived in New York for a while, then moved back to his home city.

DUDLEY, 'Jimmy' James
all saxes/clarinet

Born: Hattiesburg, Mississippi, 11th June 1903
Died: Milwaukee, 1972

Raised in St. Louis. Began on violin in 1913, studied with Jimmie Harris and Frank Wirth, encouraged to play sax by Bert Bailey. With Charlie Creath in Milwaukee, then with Everett Robbins, Charlie Elgar and Eli Rice. Club work in Detroit, then, after audition arranged by Billy Minor, with McKinney's Cotton Pickers for several years. Led own band (1934-42), long stay at the Moonglow in Milwaukee, also played in Chicago; regular broadcasts. Briefly with Bernie Young (1942), then own band in Milwaukee, long residencies at The Elbow Room, Thelma's Back Door, etc. Seriously ill in Milwaukee (1971).

DUNCAN, 'Hank' Henry James
piano

Born: Bowling Green, Kentucky, 26th October 1894
Died: Long Island, N.Y., 7th June 1968

Student at Fisk University, Nashville. Own band in Louisville (1918), then own Kentucky Jazz Band in Detroit (1919). Lived in Buffalo (1921-5), then moved to New York, joined Fess Williams (c. 1925) and stayed in the band for five years—brief spell as director whilst Fess Williams was in Chicago in 1928. Toured with King Oliver (1931), then with Bechet-Ladnier before joining Charlie Turner's Arcadians, remained as second pianist when Fats Waller toured with the band. Played solo spots at various New York clubs, then with Zutty Singleton Trio at Nick's, New York (1939). During the early 1940s worked in small groups led by Bingie Madison, Goldie Lucas, Mezz Mezzrow, Sidney Bechet, etc., etc. From March 1947 until May 1963 was resident pianist at Nick's—except for a stint at The Metropole (May 1955 until August 1956). After leaving Nick's continued doing club dates, and brief spell with Lee Blair (autumn 1964).

DUNHAM, 'Sonny' Elmer Lewis
trumpet/trombone

Born: Brockton, Massachusetts, 16th November 1914

Started on trombone, valve at seven, slide at 11. Worked in local bands from the age of 13. To New York in the late 1920s, six months with Ben Bernie, then two years with Eric 'Paul' Tremaine's Orchestra—during this time Sonny switched to trumpet, occasionally doubling trombone. Led own band for three months, then joined the Casa Loma Orchestra (directed by Glen Gray) in early 1932. Left in 1936 to form own band, disbanded early in 1937 and lived for three months in Europe. Returned to U.S.A. in June 1937, rejoined Casa Loma in November 1937. Formed own band in January 1940 and continued to lead through the 1940s. Briefly with Bernie Mann in 1951, then short spell with Tommy Dorsey from September 1951. Resumed leading own band, working mainly in Florida during the 1960s (on trombone). Sonny's sister Louise (1906-40) was a professional saxophoniste.

Sonny Dunham's Band was seen in the 1942 film 'Off the Beaten Track'.

D

DUNN, Johnny
trumpet

Born: Memphis, Tennessee, 19th February 1897
Died: Paris, France, 20th August 1937

Brother-in-law of drummer Floyd Campbell. Attended Fisk University in Nashville. Began working as a solo act at the Metropolitan Theatre, Memphis (c. 1916), was signed by W. C. Handy and worked with Handy until c. 1920. Featured in 'Dixie to Broadway' revue, left to work in Mamie Smith's Jazz Hounds, then formed own Jazz Hounds accompanying Edith Wilson (appeared in 'Put & Take' show, 1921). Regular recording work with Perry Bradford during the early 1920s. Joined Will Vodery's Plantation Orchestra in February 1922, worked in Europe with the Plantation Orchestra (1923). Work in U.S. with Plantation Orchestra, also worked as a solo act and led own band. Sailed to Europe with 'Blackbirds of 1926' (1926). Returned to U.S.A., toured as a solo act, led own big band in New York (November 1927). Variety tour and residency in Chicago (March 1928), then led own Breakdown Band in New York (April 1928). Rejoined Lew Leslie's Blackbird company, left to work in Paris with Noble Sissle (1928), also featured with bassist John Ricks' Band in Paris (September 1928). Formed own New Yorkers Band for work in Europe, during the early 1930s also worked with Joe Baker's Orchestra at the Casino de Paris. For the last few years of his life he worked mainly in Holland, also in Denmark (1935). Returned to Paris in 1937, died in the American Hospital.

DURANT, 'Ray' Horatio
piano

Born: Panama, 1910

Originally played piano and trombone. Moved to U.S.A. in 1929. Did first work in New York on trombone with Bob Sylvester's Band at the Savoy Annex; whilst with this band switched exclusively to piano. Later worked with Napoleon's Savoy Ramblers, then joined Claude Hopkins at the Cotton Club, New York—playing piano whilst Hopkins conducted. Led own band for several years, then from 1939 until 1944 was accompanist for The Deep River Boys. After service in U.S. Army resumed vocal accompaniment work, later led band for two years for 'A Streetcar Named Desire' tour. Resumed as staff accompanist for The Deep River Boys in January 1955, held that position for many years, taking part in the group's overseas tours.

DURHAM, Eddie
trombone/guitar/arranger

Born: San Marcos, Texas, 19th August 1906

Brother of: Joe (bass), Allen (trombone), Roosevelt (violin/piano/guitar), Earl (piano), Clyde (bass), and Sylvester (piano/organ). First played guitar in co-led Durham Brothers' Orchestra, then began doubling on trombone. Toured (on trombone) with the 101 Ranch Circus Band until 1926, then worked with Edgar Battle's Dixie Ramblers. During the late 1920s played in the Middle West with Eugene Coy, Jesse Stone, Terrence Holder, and Walter Page's Blue Devils. Briefly with Elmer Payne's Ten Royal Americans (summer 1929), then joined Bennie Moten (1929). Remained with Moten until 1933, worked for a week with Cab Calloway, briefly with Andy Kirk. Worked as a staff arranger for Willie Bryant, then joined Jimmie Lunceford (early in 1935) as trombonist-arranger, was also featured as solo guitarist, was one of the pioneers of amplified guitar work. Joined Count Basie in 1937, principally as arranger, but also featured on trombone and guitar. Left (c. July 1938) to concentrate on full-time arranging; scored regularly for Ina Ray Hutton, Glenn Miller, Jan Savitt, Artie Shaw, etc. Formed own big band in June 1940, later that year was musical director for Bon Bon (Tunnell) and his Buddies. In 1941-3 toured as musical director for all-girl International Sweethearts of Rhythm, later he directed his own all-girl band. During 1947 he toured with the Cavalcade of Jazz, and in 1952-3 led small touring band accompanying vocalists Wynonie Harris and Larry Darnell. Continued regular arranging throughout the 1950s and 1960s, including scoring for and playing with Swingers Inc. From 1957 through the 1960s has led own small band for residencies on Long Island. A prolific composer; his joint composition (with Edgar Battle) of 'Topsy' was made into an international hit by Cozy Cole's Band, he was also part-composer of 'I Don't Want to Set the World on Fire'. In October 1969 joined Buddy Tate on trombone (doubling guitar). Was featured with the Harlem Blues and Jazz Band during the early 1980s.

DUTREY, Honore
trombone

Born: New Orleans, Louisiana, 1894
Died: Chicago, Illinois, 21st July 1935

Had two older brothers, Pete (violin) and Sam (alto/tenor/clarinet). Worked in Melrose Brass Band (c. 1910), then with various bands including Buddie Petit-Jimmie Noone Band, John Robichaux's Orchestra. Regularly with the Silver Leaf Orchestra from c. 1913 until joining U.S. Navy in 1917. During his service career he was involved in an accident that permanently damaged his lungs—it is reported that he suffered carbide poisoning whilst working in the torpedo room of his ship. After his release he moved to Chicago, worked with King Oliver from January 1920 until 1921, and again from mid-1922 until early 1924, then led own band at the Lincoln Gardens, Chicago, until June 1924. Toured with Carroll Dickerson and later worked with Dickerson at the Sunset Cafe, Chicago. Played in Johnny Dodds' Band at Kelly's and also worked in Louis Armstrong's Stompers at the Sunset Cafe. Retired from music c. 1930.

E

EASON, 'Leon' Thomas Leon
trumpet/vocals

Born: Rich Square, North Carolina, 12th November 1910

Began on violin and clarinet (1927), then worked in vaudeville as a professional dancer partnered by Herbert Harper. Inspired by Louis Armstrong began practising the trumpet, and did first professional playing with Hubert Raveneau's Band (1930). From 1931-6 worked mainly in New Jersey with The Alabams, accompanied Buck and Bubbles, Ada Brown, Adelaide Hall, etc., with this group, also worked with Jean Calloway in 1932. Formed own band in 1936, played residencies in Newark at Park Rest, Miami Club, Alcazar, etc. Led in Albany during the early 1940s, then service in U.S. Army 1943-4. Toured with Gene Phipps' Band (1944), with Tommy Gill's Band in Atlantic City (1945), with Grachan Moncur's Strollers (1947), then with Red Lincoln's Band (1948-51) including recordings. Spell with Jack Alberson's Band, then from 1952 worked as a soloist. From 1956-67 led own trio at Pitt's Place in Newark, recorded for Blue Note in 1958.

ECKSTINE, Billy
(real name: William Clarence Eckstein)
vocals/trumpet/ valve trombone

Born: Pittsburgh, Pennsylvania, 8th July 1914

Attended high school in Washington, D.C. Whilst there sang with band led by drummer Tommy Myles, returned to Pittsburgh until 1936. Sang in Buffalo, and Detroit (1937) before moving to Chicago in 1938 for residency at De Lisa Club. Joined Earl Hines as vocalist in late 1939, also occasionally played in trumpet section. Solo act (1943), sometimes billed as Billy Xtine. Formed own big band in June 1944 which featured many great players including Dizzy Gillespie, Charlie Parker, Miles Davis, Fats Navarro, etc., the big band lasted until 1947, led short-lived small group then became solo-act gaining international reputation. Widespread international touring during 1950s, 1960s and 1970s.

EDISON, 'Sweets' Harry
trumpet

Born: Columbus, Ohio, 10th October 1915

Began on trumpet at 12. Gigged with local bands, then toured with Alphonso Trent's Band (at that time temporarily led by guitarist Anderson Lacy), also worked with Eddie Johnson's Crackerjacks. Joined Jeter-Pillars' Band in Cleveland (summer 1933) and for next three years worked in St. Louis, etc., with this band. Joined Lucky Millinder in February 1937, then from June 1938 until February 1950 worked with Count Basie. Played in small group led by Jimmy Rushing before regular tours with J.A.T.P. from September 1950. Joined Buddy Rich Band early in 1951 and for next two years worked on and off with Rich including work in California accompanying Josephine Baker Revue (1953). Remained on West Coast, did studio work including many sessions with the Nelson Riddle Orchestra, starting with Frank Sinatra's 'Wee Hours' album. Led own small group in Los Angeles, Las Vegas, etc., then moved back to New York in September 1958. Led own group mainly in New York during late 1950s and early 1960s (Arpeggio, Roundtable, etc.) and continued free-lance session work. Worked with George Auld Band in spring 1964, later that year toured Europe with J.A.T.P. package (partnering Coleman Hawkins). From the mid-1960s has been featured on several occasions with Count Basie, occasionally rejoining the band for brief spells. During the late 1960s worked regularly in California, mainly leading own small group at Memory Lane, Los Angeles, 1966-70, also continued to free-lance with various big bands, etc. Featured in the film 'Jammin' The Blues'. Visited Europe with Count Basie (1970). Active in California, often with Louis Bellson Band (1971). Undertook several tours of Europe during the late 1970s and early 1980s, some with Eddie 'Lockjaw' Davis. Toured Europe with 'The Countsmen' (1983).

EDWARDS, 'Bass' Henry
tuba/string bass

Born: Atlanta, Georgia, 22nd February 1898
Died: New York, 22nd August 1965

At 14 began playing in local Odd Fellows' Band, subsequently studied music at Morris Brown and Morehouse Colleges in Atlanta. During World War I played in U.S. Army Bands, including spell with Lt. J. Tim Brymn's 350th F.A. Band. From 1919 played in Philadelphia with various concert orchestras and with Madam I. O. Keene Dance Orchestra (1919-20). With Charlie Taylor Orchestra in Philadelphia and Atlantic City (1921-3), then joined Sam Wooding (1923). With Charlie Johnson (1923-5), then during 1925 joined Duke Ellington, left Duke c. spring 1926. Worked with Leon Abbey in New York and on tour of South America (spring 1927), returned to New York and joined Allie Ross Orchestra. Played for 'Blackbirds' show, then joined Noble Sissle, and sailed to Europe with Sissle in May 1929 (featured on brass bass). Returned to New York, worked with Fats Waller, James P. Johnson, and Eubie Blake, then rejoined Allie Ross for 'Rhapsody in Black' show. With Charlie Matson Orchestra (c. 1933), then worked mainly on string bass with various light and classical orchestras. From the late 1930s played with many orchestras including: New York Symphonic Band, W.N.Y.C. Symphony Orchestra, etc., etc.

'Bass' Edwards has often been confused with the New York string bass/tuba player Sumner Leslie 'King' Edwards (died: c. 1950). 'King', who worked in Europe with Louis Mitchell, Sam Wooding, etc., was the brother of trumpeter Maceo Edwards.

EDWARDS, 'Eddie' Edwin Branford
trombone/violin

Born: New Orleans, Louisiana, 22nd May 1891
Died: New York City, 9th April 1963

Began on violin at 10, took up trombone at 15, but did first gigs on violin in local theatre orchestra c. 1910. Played trombone with Papa Laine's Reliance bands c. 1912, worked regularly with Ernest Giardina's Orchestra from 1914. Played semi-professional baseball in and around New Orleans. Went to Chicago (1st March 1916) with band led by drummer Johnny Stein (real name: Hountha), played at Schiller's in Stein's Dixie Jazz Band. Left Stein in late May 1916 and (with Nick LaRocca) became founder-member of The Original Dixieland Jazz Band. Played with the band in New York until serving briefly in the U.S. Army (July 1918 to March 1919). Formed own band and played in band led by comedian-pianist Jimmy 'Schnozzle' Durante, then rejoined O.D.J.B. and remained until the group broke up early in 1925. Led own band at Rosemont, Silver Slipper, New York, etc., during the late 1920s. Left full-time music, had own newspaper stand, and also worked for several years as a part-time sports coach. Returned to regular playing to join the re-formed O.D.J.B. in autumn 1936, worked with LaRocca until February 1938, then continued gigging with Larry Shields, Tony Spargo, etc., until 1940. Did part-time playing in New York during the early 1940s, then in 1943-4 toured with the Katherine Dunham Revue. Continued occasional playing in and around New York until shortly before his death.

EFFROS, 'Bob' Robert
trumpet

Born: London, England, 6th December 1900
Died: New York City, 12th September 1983

Family moved to the U.S.A. when Bob was three years old. Lived in Memphis, Tennessee, started on drums, then took up trumpet. Regimental bugler in U.S. Army (1917-19), after demobilisation joined band accompanying Bea Palmer (Baltimore, 1919). Long stay in Vincent Lopez Orchestra from 1921 until February 1927 (including tour of Europe). Became a house musician for the Vitaphone Company, later in the 1930s was a free-lance studio musician playing with Nat Shilkret, Harry Reser, etc., etc. Regularly with D'Artega Orchestra in the early 1940s, continued studio work for many years.

ELDRIDGE, 'Joe' Joseph
alto sax/violin

Born: Pittsburgh, Pennsylvania, 1908
Died: 5th March 1952

Was the brother of Roy Eldridge. With Henri Saparo's Band in New York (1927), later led 'Elite Serenaders' at Renaissance Ballroom, and in Pittsburgh. During the early 1930s worked with Speed Webb, Cecil Scott, Ken Murray, etc., then co-led band with Roy in Pittsburgh (1933). With the Cotton Pickers in Baltimore, then with Blanche Calloway from late 1935 until autumn 1936. Joined Roy's band in Chicago c. November 1936, moved to New York with the band (1938-40). Spell with Buddy Johnson, then with Zutty Singleton's Quartet in New York (1941-3), briefly led at Ryan's, then moved to Los Angeles to rejoin Zutty (April 1943). In 1944 worked (on tenor) in Roy's Band, with Hot Lips Page (1945).

Lived in Canada during the late 1940s, worked with Raymond Vin's Band in Quebec (1949). Moved back to New York in 1950 and did some teaching in last year of his life.

ELDRIDGE, 'Roy' David
trumpet/fluegel horn/vocals/ drums/piano/composer

Born: Pittsburgh, Pennsylvania, 30th January 1911

Brother of Joe Eldridge, cousin of Reunald Jones. Nicknamed 'Little Jazz' by Otto Hardwick. Played drums at the age of six, then spell on bugle before graduating to trumpet—taught by P. M. Williams and by his brother Joe. Led own juvenile band (which included Alvin Burroughs) for 'Rock Dinah' touring show (late 1927), after being stranded in Sharon, Pennsylvania, joined the Greater Sheesley Carnival Band, playing trumpet, tuba, and drums. After being stranded again, this time in Little Rock, Arkansas, worked with Oliver Muldoon, then returned to Pittsburgh and led own band for several months—Roy Elliott and his Palais Royal Orchestra, worked in St. Louis before joining Horace Henderson's Dixie Stompers for eight months in 1928. Returned to Pittsburgh, then worked with The Nighthawks in Detroit, very brief spell with Zach Whyte, then joined Speed Webb (1929-30), also worked in Milwaukee with Johnny Neal's Midnite Ramblers. Moved to New York in November 1930, worked with Cecil Scott, then joined Elmer Snowden's Band. Subsequently worked with Charlie Johnson at Small's, then in Teddy Hill's Orchestra before touring with the 'Hot Chocolates Show'. Co-led band (with Joe) in Pittsburgh during 1933; at the Pythian Temple, Mapleview Park, etc., then worked with McKinney's Band in Baltimore. Returned to New York, rejoined Teddy Hill at the Savoy Ballroom (1935), led own small band at Famous Door (October 1935), subsequently joined Fletcher Henderson. Left in September 1936 to form own band for long residency at Sam Beer's Three Deuces Club in Chicago (brief absence through pneumonia in autumn 1937). Toured with own band in 1938, made New York debut at Savoy Ballroom in August 1938, briefly left full-time music to study radio engineering, guested with Mal Hallett's Band at Loew's, New York, in October 1938. Re-formed own band for Famous Door (November 1938), led at the Arcadia Ballroom from January 1939, also played dates at the Apollo Theatre. After leading at the Golden Gate Ballroom played residency at Kelly's Stables, New York, from April until October 1940, then returned to Chicago, led own small group for residency at Capitol Lounge. Joined Gene Krupa as featured soloist in April 1941, remained until the band broke up in spring of 1943 (whilst with Krupa, Roy occasionally played drums whilst Gene fronted the band). From June 1943 again led own band, residency at Folies Bergeres Club in New York (August-September 1943), played for a month in Toronto, then residency at Review Club, Chicago, until early 1944. Returned to New York, worked with Paul Baron's Band on C.B.S., also led own band, solo stint on West Coast before joining Artie Shaw in October 1944. Left Shaw in September 1945, led own big band from February 1946, residencies in Chicago, New York, California, etc. Later cut down to a small group. In February 1949 rejoined Gene Krupa, left in September 1949 to feature in first national J.A.T.P. tour. To Europe with Benny Goodman in April 1950, when Goodman returned home in June, Roy toured Europe as a single. After a long stay in Paris returned to New York in April 1951. Within a week was leading own quintet at Birdland, New York, from then on, through the 1950s, Roy continued to lead own small groups, made many guest star appearances and was regularly featured with Norman Granz's J.A.T.P. tours (including many trips to Europe). Beginning in 1952 did regular club and concert dates in quintet co-led with Coleman Hawkins, together they did several overseas tours for Norman Granz and also appeared at many jazz festivals in the U.S.A. Roy also did solo appearances at festivals—in July 1957 he played drums at the Great South Bay Festival. During the 1950s he also recorded on drums and piano. In the late 1950s and early 1960s played many dates with clarinettist Sol Yaged, also led own small groups in New York at the Village Vanguard, The Embers, etc. Worked mainly in small group accompanying Ella Fitzgerald from late 1963 until March 1965, later led small group (with tenorist Richie Kamuca). Worked with Count Basie from 1st July until 17th September 1966, then re-formed own small group. Toured Europe with 'Jazz From a Swinging Era' package in spring of 1967, then continued to lead own small groups and work as a single. Featured at many U.S. jazz festivals in the late 1960s including the New Orleans Jazz Fest (1969).

Led quartet at Half Note, N.Y. (1969 and spring 1970). Regularly at Jimmy Ryan's from September 1970, featured at London House, Chicago (1971), Monterey Festival (1971), also did international touring, featured at President Jimmy Carter's White House Jazz Party (June 1978). Worked regularly at Jimmy Ryan's Club until suffering a heart attack in October 1980. Made occasional guest appearances as a vocalist during the early 1980s.

ELGAR, 'Charlie' Charles A. *Born: New Orleans, Louisiana, 13th June 1885*
violin/saxes/clarinet/leader *Died: Chicago, August 1973*

Began studying violin at the age of 12, later studied at the Medard Academy, Marquette University, and Coleridge Taylor School of Music, Chicago. Played in New Orleans with various string ensembles, and played in the Bloom Philharmonic Orchestra in 1903. Finally left New Orleans c. 1913, moved to Chicago, led own quintet at the Fountain Inn, then organised 15-piece band for residencies in Chicago including long stays at Dreamland. Worked in Europe with Will Marion Cook's Southern Syncopated Orchestra, returned to Chicago and led own big band at various venues including Arcadia Ballroom (1927-8), Savoy Ballroom (1928-9), Sunset Cafe (1929-30), also led in Milwaukee at the Wisconsin Roof Gardens (1925-7) and at the Eagles Ballroom (1928). During the 1930s did extensive teaching, having been a part-time teacher throughout his career. Served as President of the Local 208 American Federation of Musicians for many years.

ELLINGTON, 'Duke' Edward Kennedy *Born: Washington, D.C., 29th April 1899*
piano/composer/arranger *Died: New York City, 24th May 1974*

Father of trumpeter-composer Mercer Ellington (born: 1919). During early childhood was nicknamed Duke by a neighbour. Attended Armstrong High School in Washington from February 1914 until June 1917; won a poster design contest (organised by the N.A.A.C.P.), left high school before graduation and started own sign-painting business. Whilst still in high school, Duke had begun gigging at the Washington True Reformers' Hall, soon afterwards he began subbing for pianist Lester Dishman at the Poodle Dog Cafe, whilst working there wrote first composition 'Soda Foutain Rag'—soon followed by his first tune with lyrics: 'What Are You Going To Do When The Bed Breaks Down?'. Studied harmony with Henry Grant. Did regular work as relief pianist at Abbott House, also played at the Oriental Theatre and gigged with various band leaders: Louis Thomas, Daniel Doyle, Oliver 'Doc' Perry, Elmer Snowden, etc., and was one of the five pianists in Russell Wooding's 34-piece orchestra. Together with Otto Hardwick and Arthur Whetsol did brief season in Wisconsin before forming regular band, The Duke's Seranaders. To New York for a week with Wilbur Sweatman (5th-11th March 1923), returned to Washington, then worked in Atlantic City with Elmer Snowden. Worked at Barron Wilkins' Club, New York, with The Washingtonians, in September 1923 they began a residency at the Hollywood Club, New York (then led by Elmer Snowden). Early in 1924 Duke became the leader of The Washingtonians, during the following year he and lyricist Joe Trent wrote the score for the 'Chocolate Kiddies' revue. From 1925 until 1927 the band did regular tours through New England, including residencies at the Charleshurst Ballroom in Salem, Massachusetts. The band played long residencies at the Kentucky Club (the renamed Hollywood) from spring 1924 until 1927, during this period also worked at other New York clubs including: The Flamingo, Harry Richman's, Ciro's, etc., also appeared in the 'Messin' Around' revue at the Plantation Cafe, and played many dates at New York theatres. The band left New York for New England tour on the 20th June 1927, returned to the Kentucky Club, then appeared at the Lafayette, New York, and Standard Theatre in Philadelphia before commencing residency at the Cotton Club, New York, on the 4th December 1927. The orchestra finally left the Cotton Club during February 1931. The residency was not continuous, the orchestra did regular tours and dates at many New York theatres including: The Palace, The Paramount, The Fulton, The Savoy, etc., and travelled to California (in August 1930) for local engagements and filming. The orchestra did extensive touring in 1931 (Paramount-Publix Theatres, etc.), then again played residencies in Boston and California before returning to The Paramount, New York, in February 1932, later returning to California (Golden Gate Theatre, Paramount, Los Angeles, etc.). They arrived in England on 9th June 1933; residency at the London Palladium, then toured Bolton, Liverpool, Glasgow, Blackpool, etc., before playing concerts in Paris. Sailed back to New York (2nd August 1933), later that year did first Southern tour, then played residency at Cotton Club, Culver City. Toured Texas, Louisiana, Canada, etc. (summer 1935), played residency at Congress Hotel, Chicago (May-June 1936), etc. Residency at The Cotton Club, New York (from 20th March 1937), then resumed widespread touring. From 1st July until 10th August 1938 Duke was away from the scene whilst undergoing surgery for hernia, during this period wrote the music for the ballet 'City Woman'. In March and April 1939 the orchestra toured France, Belgium, Holland, Denmark, and Sweden. By 1940 Billy Strayhorn (q.v.) had joined Duke as staff arranger and collaborator, the orchestra continued touring and residencies, then appeared in 'Jump for Joy' revue in Los Angeles from August 1941. In 1943 did first of the Carnegie Hall Concerts, during that year also played residency at The Hurricane Club, New York (April-September). In 1944 and 1945 continued touring, also residencies in Hollywood, Chicago, and at the Zanzibar, New York (September-October 1945). After a brief spell in hospital (spring 1948) Duke, Ray Nance, and vocaliste Kay Davis toured variety halls in Great Britain (June-July 1948). Through the 1940s, 1950s, and 1960s Duke continued to lead (and compose) with undiminished success. In the autumn of 1958 the orchestra made a triumphant return to Britain, they subsequently made several tours of Britain in the 1960s. During the 1960s they also toured Europe, the Far East, the Middle East, India, Japan, South America, Senegal, etc. Early in 1970 they toured Japan, Australia and New Zealand. Toured Russia, France and Britain (autumn 1971). Died of cancer in the Harkness Pavilion of the Columbia Presbyterian Medical Center, New York.

Duke Ellington's compositions (and part-compositions) include: 'Mood Indigo', 'Solitude', 'Sophisticated Lady', 'Harlem Airshaft', 'I Got It Bad and That Ain't Good', 'In a Sentimental Mood', 'Black and Tan Fantasy', 'It Don't Mean a Thing if it Ain't Got that Swing', 'Daybreak Express', etc., etc. His extended works include: 'Black, Brown, and Beige', 'Liberian Suite', 'The Tattooed Bride', 'Such Sweet Thunder', 'Harlem', 'Suite Thursday', 'Night Creature', 'Impressions of the Far East', 'Virgin Islands Suite', 'In The Beginning God', etc. Duke also scored for the films: 'Anatomy of a Murder', 'Paris Blues', 'Assault on a Queen', and wrote for the stage productions of: 'Beggar's Holiday', 'Jump For Joy', 'Pousse Cafe', 'Tu Caret', 'My People', etc. Film appearances include: 'Black and Tan Fantasy', 'Check and Double Check', 'Murder at the Vanities', 'Many Happy Returns', 'Belle of the 90s', 'Symphony in Black', 'Hit Parade of 1938', 'Cabin in the Sky', 'Reveille with Beverly', 'Anatomy of a Murder', 'Paris Blues', etc. In 1967 Togo issued a Duke Ellington commemorative postage stamp. Duke received N.A.A.C.P.'s Spingairn Medal in 1959. In 1970 was made member of Swedish Royal Academy of Music, and U.S. National Institute of Arts and Letters. Hon. Doctorate of Music, St. John's University, Queens (1971). Books on Duke Ellington include: 'Duke Ellington', by Barry Ulanov; 'Duke Ellington', an anthology edited by Peter Gammond; 'Duke Ellington', by G. E. Lambert; 'The World of Duke Ellington', by Stanley Dance, 'Music is My Mistress', by Duke Ellington; 'Duke Ellington in Person: An Intimate Memoir', by Mercer Ellington with Stanley Dance.

ELLINGTON, Mercer Kennedy
trumpet/composer

Born: Washington, D.C., 11th March 1919

Son of Duke Ellington. Moved to New York, studied composing and arranging. First led own band in 1939. Served in U.S. Army from 1943-45, played in service bands. Led own band in the late 1940s, then began first of many occasions on which he played in his father's band, previously had written several numbers for Duke's Band, and also for small bands led by Duke's sidemen. Led own band again in late 1950s, ran own music company and worked as a disc-jockey in the 1960s before joining Duke more or less permanently until Duke's death in May 1974, whereupon Mercer took over leadership of the band, retaining some of the previous sidemen, but also adding young musicians including his son Edward Ellington II (born: 1944) on guitar. The band undertook several widespread tours during the 1970s. In 1978, co-authored (with Stanley Dance) a book on his father's career. Conducted orchestra for the 'Sophisticated Ladies' musical during the early 1980s.

ELLIOTT, 'Sticky' Ernest
saxes/clarinet

Born: Booneville, Missouri, February 1893

Worked with Hank Duncan's Band in Detroit (1919), moved to New York, worked with Johnny Dunn (1921), Mamie Smith (1922), etc. Various recordings in the 1920s, including two sessions with Bessie Smith. With Cliff Jackson's Trio at the Cabin Club, Astoria, New York (1940), with Sammy Stewart's Band at Joyce's Manor, New York (1944), in Willie 'The Lion' Smith's Band (1947). Has retired from music, but continues to live in New York.

ELLIS, Seger Pillot
piano/vocals/composer

Born: Houston, Texas, 4th July 1906

Husband of vocaliste Irene Taylor. Piano from an early age. First professional work on Radio KPRC, was heard by a Victor talent scout and made first records, later went to New York, recorded as a vocalist and achieved enormous popular success. Visited Great Britain in 1928. Whilst on tour in Cincinnati he discovered the Mills Brothers vocal group and assisted in their management for several years. Worked mainly as a solo artiste in the early 1930s, guest appearances with Paul Whiteman, etc., also appeared with Ida Lupino in the 1934 film 'One Rainy Afternoon'. From autumn 1936 until summer of 1937 led own unusual line-up 'The Brass Choir', later led own orthodox big band. Joined U.S. Army in September 1942, released in 1943, did defence plant work, then settled again in Texas, did some solo work, but mainly active as a composer and arranger.

ELMAN, 'Ziggy'
(real name: Harry Finkelman)
trumpet/multi-instrumentalist

Born: Philadelphia, Pennsylvania, 26th May 1914
Died: Van Nuys, California, 26th June 1968

Lived in Atlantic City from early childhood. Local gigs on many instruments from early teens. Became resident musician at Steel Pier, Atlantic City, during the early 1930s, originally working on trombone. Left Alex Bartha's Band at that venue to join Benny Goodman (September 1936), left Goodman in July 1940, played for a month in Joe Venuti's Band, then joined Tommy Dorsey in August 1940. Left in 1943 for service in U.S. Army. Rejoined Tommy Dorsey in February 1946, brief spell on baritone sax, then rejoined trumpet section (whilst with Dorsey occasionally doubled trombone whilst Tommy Dorsey played trumpet). Formed own band in January 1947, rejoined Tommy Dorsey in May 1947. Formed new band in Los Angeles in July 1948, began specialising in studio work during the following year. Worked in Van Alexander's Orchestra (1950), also extensive film and television work. Appeared in the film 'The Benny Goodman Story', but through illness was unable to play (the version of his feature 'And The Angels Sing' was soundtracked by Manny Klein). Continued to work in the studios until the early 1960s, also ran own music store. Died of a liver ailment.

Throughout his career, Ziggy occasionally did section work on instruments other than trumpet, i.e. clarinet, baritone sax, and trombone.

ENNIS, 'Skinnay' Robert
drums/vocals

Born: Salisbury, North Carolina, 13th August 1909
Died: Los Angeles, California, 3rd June 1963

Became a drummer whilst studying at the University of North Carolina. In 1925 became founder-member of Hal Kemp's Band, remained with Kemp until 1938 (including European tours). Formed own commercial band in 1938, mainly active in Hollywood, with the leader taking comedy roles on various radio shows, including long residency on Bob Hope's programme. The band appeared in many films; during the early 1940s the bands' staff arranger was Gil Evans. Led own service band during World War II, then resumed work in Hollywood. From 1958 led for residency at the Statler-Hilton in Los Angeles. Suffered an accidental death; choked on a bone whilst dining in a Beverly Hill restaurant.

ERWIN, 'Pee Wee' George
trumpet

Born: Falls City, Nebraska, 30th May 1913
Died: Teaneck, New Jersey, 20th June 1981

Raised in Kansas City, his father, James O. Erwin (died: 1938), was a professional trumpeter. Played in many local bands, then went to New York in 1932 with Joe Haymes. Spent almost two years with Isham Jones, then joined tenorist Freddie Martin (1934). Worked with Benny Goodman (November 1934 to May 1935), then joined Ray Noble. Rejoined Benny Goodman (February 1936 until September 1936), left Goodman in California, worked again with Ray Noble, then joined Tommy Dorsey from February-July 1939. Worked in Florida for a while, then joined Johnny Green's Orchestra in January 1940, later that year formed own big band. Disbanded early in 1942 and joined Bob Allen's Band in New York. Very brief return to Benny Goodman (late 1942), then mainly active as studio musician until 1949, commenced leading own Dixieland unit at Nick's, New York. Was practically resident at the club until the late 1950s, also worked with Tony Parenti in 1957, and continued studio work. During the 1960s active as a studio musician, also ran a trumpet school with Chris Griffin. Active free-lance during the 1970s, regularly with the New York Jazz Repertory Company.

ESCUDERO, 'Ralph' Rafael
string bass/tuba

Born: Manati, Puerto Rico, 16th July 1898
Died: Puerto Rico, 10th April 1970

Began playing bass at the age of 12 in school band, taught by Fernando Cellejo and Fermin Ramirez. Moved to New York City and commenced professional career in the New Amsterdam Musical Association, working for the Clef Club of New York and the Manhattan Elks' Band, and Lucille Hegamin (1921), subsequently toured with the 'Shuffle Along' revue. Whilst working with Wilbur Sweatman at the Howard Theatre, Washington, D.C., was heard and signed by Fletcher Henderson. Remained with Henderson until late 1926, then worked with McKinney's Cotton Pickers from 1927 until summer of 1931. Briefly with Ellsworth Reynolds and Kaiser Marshall's Bostonians and The Savoy Bearcats, also toured with W. C. Handy. Worked in New York and California before returning to Puerto Rico, where he continued to work regularly with bands and orchestra. In 1969 was a member of the Arturo Somohano Philharmonic Orchestra.

ETRI, 'Bus' Anthony
guitar

Born: New York City, 1917
Died: Culver City, California, 21st August 1941

His brother Ben is a saxophonist, a cousin, Tony Mottola plays guitar. Worked with Hudson-de Lange Band in 1935, prior to becoming member of Will Hudson's own band. Joined Charlie Barnet's Band in 1938 and remained with Barnet until being involved in a fatal auto crash whilst playing dates in California.

EUBANKS, Horace
clarinet/saxes

Born: East St. Louis, Illinois. c. 1900
Died: Missouri

Worked with Jelly Roll Morton in Vancouver, Canada (c. 1920), subsequently moved on to Chicago. Worked with Doc Watson's Band, then returned to St. Louis, worked with Charlie Creath (1925). Led own 'Dixie Strutters' in Chicago (1927), joined violinist Wilson Robinson (1928). With Benny Peyton in Europe (1929), G. Compton (1931), Willie Lewis (late 1931). To U.S. (1934), joined Carroll Dickerson in Chicago (autumn 1934), then with Zutty Singleton's Band (early 1935 until August 1935). Moved back to St. Louis, worked for Fate Marable and Charlie Creath from 1936. Suffered severe illness and spent some years in the Missouri State Mental Hospital during the 1950s.

EUROPE, James Reese
piano/violin

Born: Mobile, Alabama, 22nd February 1881
Died: Boston, Massachusetts, 9th May 1919

Family moved to Washington, D.C., when he was 10. Studied music there, and first went to New York in 1904. Toured as musical director for travelling shows, then organised New Amsterdam Musical Association in New York (1906), subsequently formed the Clef Club Orchestra. Through the 1910s led own 'Society Orchestra' which accompanied dancers Vernon and Irene Castle in 'Watch Your Step' (1912). Then, as Lieutenant in U.S. Army directed 369th Infantry Regiment Band, known as The Hell-Fighters, which toured Europe during World War I. The band returned to the U.S.A. in February 1919 and began a triumphant tour of American cities. During a performance in Boston, Europe was stabbed whilst in his dressing-room by a snare-drummer in the band, Private Herbert Wright, he died shortly afterwards.

EVANS, 'Doc' Paul Wesley
cornet

Born: Spring Valley, Minnesota, 20th June 1907
Died: Minneapolis, 10th January 1977

Played saxophone, violin, and piano whilst at West Concord High School; graduated from Carleton College in 1929, during the late 1920s worked on cornet and sax in Dave Wing's Band. Specialised on cornet from 1931, played mainly in and around Minneapolis, also active as an arranger. Worked for a time as a teacher, was also a professional dog-breeder. During the late 1930s joined Red Dougherty's Dixieland Band, then led own band. Occasional playing trips to New York in the 1940s, also led own band for several residencies in Chicago: Jazz Ltd., The Tailspin, The Blue Note, etc. Worked in Miff Mole's Band (1949), then led own band at the Bar of Music and other Chicago venues. During the 1950s and 1960s led own band in Minneapolis, Syracuse, etc. During the 1960s ran own Rampart Street Club in Mendota, Minnesota, also directed local symphony orchestra.

EVANS, 'Gil'
(real name: Ian Ernest Gilmore Green)
piano/arranger/composer

Born: Toronto, Canada, 13th May 1913

Lived in British Columbia, and Spokane, Washington before settling in California. Played in high school bands, and co-led Briggs-Evans Orchestra in 1933, this band formed the nucleus of band that Evans led at Balboa Beach from 1936 until 1939, vocalist Skinnay Ennis took the band over, and Evans remained as staff-arranger for almost two years before moving to New York in 1941 where he joined Claude Thornhill as staff-arranger until U.S. Army service in 1942. After release re-joined Claude Thornhill. This led to a series of recordings with Miles Davis that won international acclaim. Later led own band, and did widespread free-lance writing during the 1960s. After a period of lesser activity as a bandleader Evans again led own big band in U.S.A. and Europe during the 1970s and 1980s, including tours of Europe in 1981 and 1983.

EVANS, Herschel
tenor sax/clarinet

Born: Denton, Texas, 1909
Died: New York, 9th February 1939

Did early work in 'T.N.T.' (Trent's Number Two) Band in Texas (c. 1926), then worked in The St. Louis Merrymakers (a Texas band). Brief spells with Edgar Battle, Terrence Holder, and with Sammy Holmes in Texas before joining Troy Floyd's Band in Texas (1929). Left Troy Floyd in 1931, stints with Grant Moore's Band, then worked with Benny Moten (February 1933-5), worked in Kansas City with Hot Lips Page's Band, moved on to Chicago, played briefly in Dave Peyton's Band (autumn 1935), then settled in Los Angeles. With Charlie Echols' Band in Los Angeles, also worked with Lionel Hampton's Band at the Paradise Cafe and with Buck Clayton's Band in the 'Brownskin Revue'. Joined Count Basie (with Buck Clayton) in autumn 1936 and remained with Basie until fatal illness. He had been unwell for some months and collapsed whilst working with Count Basie at the Crystal Ballroom, Hartford, Connecticut. He was admitted to the Wadsworth Hospital in New York where he succumbed to a cardiac condition. His burial took place in Los Angeles.

E

EVANS, 'Slim' Ray
(real name: Otis Nelrouter)
reeds

Born: Cincinnati, Ohio, 7th June 1902
Deceased

Played drums in U.S. Army Band (1921), switched to alto sax before leaving the Army in 1924. Joined the O.S. Orchestra prior to working with Red Kauffman on the 'Island Queen' riverboat. With Wild Bill Davison in 1927, then stints with Jack Crawford and Joseph Chernearski before joining Wild Bill Davison's Big Band in 1932. Led own sextet until 1939 then rejoined Army. Led own service band in Hawaii. Spent last 15 years of his life in a Los Angeles hospital but played ocassional weekend gigs during that period.

EVANS, 'Stump' Paul Anderson
saxes

Born: Lawrence, Kansas, 18th October 1904
Died: Douglas, Kansas, 29th August 1928

Was taught music by his father, Clarence E. Evans, who played alto horn. 'Stump', so called because of his tiny stature, started on alto horn then changed to trombone and began playing in the Lawrence High School Band. He soon changed to alto sax before specialising on baritone sax during the early 1920s. Moved to Chicago and worked with Oscar 'Bernie' Young, King Oliver, Jimmy Wade, and with Erskine Tate. Was forced to leave Erskine Tate's Band after contracting pulmonary tuberculosis. Moved back to his home town and died there, is buried in Maple Grove Cemetery in North Lawrence, Kansas.

EWELL, 'Don' Donald Tyson
piano

Born: Baltimore, Maryland, 14th November 1916
Died: Deerfield, Florida, 9th August 1983

After leaving high school in 1934, majored in composition at Peabody Conservatory. Played local gigs then led own trio in Baltimore before joining The Townsmen for almost four years until he led own trio in 1941. Army service for four years then to New York, sat in with Bunk Johnson, later worked with him in 1945-46 and 1947. During the late 1940s worked with Sidney Bechet, Muggsy Spanier, Miff Mole, etc. Played residencies in Chicago with own group in early 1950s, also played with Georg Brunis, Lee Collins, etc. Moved to California, worked with Kid Ory, and led at Hangover Club in San Francisco prior to working with Jack Teagarden for several years. Lived in New Orleans during the 1960s, led own group also worked with many leaders and did solo tours, including Europe in 1971. Played residency at the Royal Orleans Hotel in New Orleans in 1978. Toured Europe during the early 1980s.

EWING, 'Streamline' John
trombone

Born: Topeka, Kansas, 19th January 1917

First professional work at 17 in local orchestra led by Richard Harrison. With Horace Henderson (1938), with Earl Hines (c. 1939), and again from April 1941 and 1942. Week in Louis Armstrong Big Band, then with Lionel Hampton until joining Jimmie Lunceford in 1943. With Lunceford until 1945, then with Cab Calloway (1946), Jay McShann (1948). In 1950 worked in Cootie Williams' Big Band; with Louis Jordan and Earl Bostic, then moved to California. Played regularly in band led by George Jenkins during the early 1950s, also took part in free-lance recording sessions. With Teddy Buckner from 1956, toured with Horace Henderson early in 1962 and played gigs with Rex Stewart in 1967. Played in Young Men of New Orleans in the late 1960s. Continued to play regularly during 1970s and early 1980s, many dates with Teddy Buckner.

FARLEY, 'Eddie' Edward J.
trumpet/vocals/composer

Born: Newark, New Jersey, 16th July 1904

With Bert Lown and his Hotel Biltmore Orchestra (1929-30). Worked in orchestra led by drummer Will Osborne during the early 1930s, then formed band with Mike Riley as co-leader. They achieved popular success in New York in 1935, aided by their hit record 'The Music Goes 'Round and Around'. This band broke up in 1936, and both co-leaders formed their own bands. Farley continued to lead during the late 1930s and 1940s, playing residencies in New York, Midnight Club, Philadelphia, Toronto, and at Meadowbrooks, etc. During the 1950s he played long residency at the Ivanhoe Club, Irvington, near his home in New Jersey.

FATOOL, 'Nick' Nicholas
drums

Born: Milbury, Massachusetts, 2nd January 1915

Attended high school in Providence, Rhode Island. Professional with Joe Haymes in 1937, worked at Taft Hotel with George Hall (1938), then spell in Dallas, Texas, with Don Bestor's Band (summer 1938). With Benny Goodman from May 1939 until July 1940, then joined Artie Shaw until 1941. Briefly with Claude Thornhill and Les Brown (early 1942), then with Jan Savitt before working with Alvino Rey (1942 to early 1943). With Eddie Miller Band in California (spring 1943), then began many years of studio work. Was featured regularly at annual Dixieland Jubilees during the 1940s and 1950s, worked occasionally with Harry James, also led own band. With Matty Matlock, etc., in the various 'Pete Kelly's Blues' presentations. During the late 1950s and 1960s worked several times with Bob Crosby including tour of Orient in late 1964, subsequently with Phil Harris, Pete Fountain, etc. Active throughout the 1970s and early 1980s, including tour of Europe with Bob Crosby (1981).

FAZOLA, Irving Henry
(real name: Prestopnik)

Born: New Orleans, Louisiana, 10th December 1912
Died: New Orleans, Louisiana, 20th March 1949

clarinet/saxes

His brother Louis was also a musician; brother-in-law was trombonist Joe Rotis, (1917-65). Attended Warren Easton High School in New Orleans. Began on piano, switched to clarinet at 13. At 15, did first paid work with Candy Candido's Little Collegians. Gained professional name from three notes of the tonic-sol-fa: Fa-soh-la. Regular jobs with Louis Prima, also worked with Sharkey Bonano, Armand Hug, Ellis Stratakos, Roy Teal, etc. Joined Ben Pollack in New Orleans (late 1935), with Pollack in Chicago, New York, etc., left in California, returned to New Orleans to work in band led by drummer Augie Schellang (spring 1937). Few months with Gus Arnheim from May 1937; joined Glenn Miller c. September 1937. Returned to New Orleans, rejoined Ben Pollack there (January 1938); left to work with Bob Crosby from spring 1938 until May 1940. With Jimmy McPartland in Chicago (July 1940), returned to New Orleans in October 1940, joined Tony Almerico's Band. With Claude Thornhill (1941)—occasionally playing bassoon—joined Muggsy Spanier on 31st December (1941). With Teddy Powell for a year from spring 1942, dates with Georg Brunis at The Famous Door, New York, then with Horace Heidt from May 1943 until returning to New Orleans in October 1943. Led own band on radio WWL (1943-7), and at local clubs, also worked with Tony Almerico on S.S. 'President' (summer 1944), with Louis Prima (late 1944), and Leon Prima (1945). Regular broadcasts with Ogden Lafaye's Trio in 1948, left in November 1948, and was replaced by trumpeter Alois 'Al' Hirt. Despite blood-pressure problems, Fazola continued to work regularly until the time of his death; he died in his sleep.

FELD, 'Morey
drums

Born: Cleveland, Ohio, 15th August 1915
Died: Colorado, 28th March 1971

With Ben Pollack (1936), Joe Haymes (1938), briefly with Summa Cum Laude Band in 1940. With Benny Goodman from December 1943 until March 1944 and from September 1944 until November 1945. With Eddie Condon in 1946, briefly with Buddy Morrow's Band (spring 1946), then resumed at Condon's. Prolific free-lance recordings from 1940.

Worked with Benny Goodman again on several occasions during the 1950s, also with Billy Butterfield, Joe Bushkin, Bobby Hackett, Peanuts Hucko, etc. Worked as A.B.C. staff musician from 1955. Led own trio at New York's World Fair (1964), worked at Eddie Condon's in 1965, several months with Benny Goodman in 1966—during that year opened own drum school. Did overseas touring with George Wein's Newport All Stars, moved to California in 1968, then moved to Denver, Colorado, worked regularly there in Peanuts Hucko's Band (1969). In 1968 also played briefly in The World's Greatest Jazz Band. Died in a fire that destroyed his home in Bow Mar, near Denver.

FIELDS, 'Kansas' Carl Donnell *Born: Chapman, Kansas, 5th December 1915*
drums

Moved to Chicago in 1928. Did club gigs in Chicago from the mid-1930s, later worked with Jimmie Noone, trumpeter 'King Kolax', Walter Fuller, and Johnny Long before joining Roy Eldridge in December 1940; remained until Roy joined Gene Krupa (1941), brief return to Johnny Long Band, then formed own combo. In 1941-2 worked with Ella Fitzgerald, Benny Carter, Edgar Hayes, Charlie Barnet, Roger Kay Jumptet, etc., then served in U.S. Marines until 1945. Joined Cab Calloway, then briefly with Claude Hopkins (1946). With Sidney Bechet in 1947 and again in 1949, also worked with Dizzy Gillespie, Eddie Condon, Roy Eldridge, etc., and led own band at Cafe Society Downtown, New York. To Europe in January 1953, toured with Mezz Mezzrow, then settled in France; featured with many bands on the Continent, regular appearances at European jazz festivals. Moved back to Chicago in 1965, free-lance studio work, recorded with Dizzy Gillespie, etc.

FIELDS, 'Ted' Edward *Born: Cleveland, Ohio. c. 1905*
drums *Died: March 1959*

With Paul Craig's Band at Silver Slipper Club in Buffalo (1927), then joined Sam Wooding and sailed to Europe with Wooding in May 1928. With Wooding until November 1931, then joined Willie Lewis until returning to New York, in autumn of 1938. Joined Benny Carter Big Band at the Savoy, New York, in spring of 1939. Left full-time music in the 1940s, but continued to play gigs—regularly with Sammy Stewart's Sextet in New York in 1944.

FIELDS, 'Geechie' Julius *Born: Georgia. c. 1903*
trombone

Was raised in the Jenkins' Orphanage, South Carolina, taught trombone by Gene 'Buddy' Aiken and Jake Frazier, did regular tours with the Orphanage Band. Settled in New York and worked for various leaders at John O'Connor's Club (c. 1924). With Earle Howard's Band at Strand Danceland (late 1926), rejoined Howard briefly in 1927. With Charlie Skeete (1929), Bill Benford's Band (late 1929-30). Recorded with Jelly Roll Morton in 1928 and 1930; was once married to vocaliste Myra Johnson. Left full-time music in the 1930s, later became a boxing coach and trainer for an athletics club in New York.

FIELDS, 'Herbie' Herbert *Born: Elizabeth, New Jersey, 24th May 1919*
saxes/clarinet *Died: Miami, Florida, 17th September 1958*

First regular work with Fred Allen's Band (c. 1936), full-time studies at Julliard (1936-8), then co-led band with pianist-arranger George Handy (1939). Briefly with Woody Herman, then with Leonard Ware Band in New York (1940) until joining Raymond Scott in 1941. U.S. Army Service (1942-3), led band at Fort Dix. Formed own band, then with Lionel Hampton from December 1944 until February 1946. Led own small band in 1946, following year formed big band. Reverted to small band, played residencies in Chicago, Blue Note, New York, etc., through the 1940s. Moved to Florida in the 1950s, did a variety of commercial work, but played infrequently during last year of his life. He committed suicide by taking a large overdose of sleeping pills.

FITZGERALD, Ella
vocals/composer

Born: Newport News, Virginia 25th April 1918

Raised in Yonkers, New York. Won prize for singing at Apollo Theater amateur night contest, also won audition at Harlem Opera House and soon afterwards made professional debut (week of 16th February 1935) singing with Tiny Bradshaw's Band at Harlem Opera House. Soon afterwards joined Chick Webb's Band, and became featured singer often working with Webb's Band at the Savoy Ballroom, New York City. After Webb's death in 1939, Ella led the band until 1941, then began working as a solo artist. From 1948 onwards appeared regularly at shows promoted by impressario Norman Granz who later became Ella's manager. By the 1950s Ella had gained an international reputation, further consolidated by many international tours during the 1960s, 1970s and 1980s.

FLEAGLE, 'Brick' Jacob Roger
guitar/arranger

Born: Hanover, Pennsylvania, 22nd August 1906

Began on banjo at 17, worked with bands in Florida, then toured with Sam Robbins and his Baltimoreans (1926). Switched to guitar, worked with Orville Knapp, Roy Ingram, Hal Kemp, etc., during the late 1920s and early 1930s. Led own band at Arcadia Ballroom, New York (1934-5), with Joe Haymes (1936); was a life-long friend of Rex Stewart and frequently appeared on record with Rex. From the 1930s did arrangements for many bands including: Chick Webb, Jimmie Lunceford, Fletcher Henderson, Rex Stewart small groups, Duke Ellington (also worked as copyist for Duke). Radio and recording studio work in late 1930s and 1940s, worked regularly in D'Artega Orchestra in early 1940s. In June 1943 (together with Rex Stewart) played briefly in New Mexico with Dick Ballou's Band. For the past 25 years has run own arranging and copying business.

FLEMMING, Herb (Niccolaiih El-Michelle)
trombone/vocals

Born: Georgia (?) 5th April 1898
Died: New York, 3rd October 1976

From 1910 until 1913 studied music at Dobbs Chauncey School in New York—played mellophone and euphonium. Joined 15th New York National Guard Band led by Jim Europe and Lt. Eugene Mikell (1917), sailed to France in Jim Europe's 369th U.S. Infantry Band in winter of 1917. Was demobilised in New York in 1919. Studied trombone, cello, and musical theory at Frank Damrosch's Conservatory in New York. Worked at the Shuffle Inn, New York, in late 1921 with pianist Fred Tunstall and others, joined Lafayette Theatre Orchestra in 1922—in late 1921 made record debut with Johnny Dunn. In 1924 co-led in Philadelphia with Bobby Lee, joined Sam Wooding in 1925 and sailed to Europe in May 1925. Toured throughout Europe with Wooding, the band also played in South America (1927) before returning to U.S.A. in August 1927. Brief tour of Loew's Theatre Circuit with Sam Wooding, then joined Lew Leslie's 'Blackbirds' revue. Played in New York, London, and Paris with the Blackbirds (1929), then led own International Rhythm Aces in Europe before joining Sam Wooding in Berlin (June 1930). Left Wooding in Europe, led group for Josephine Baker's 'Joie de Paris' revue, then took own revue to Buenos Aires. Returned to Paris (summer 1933), then went to India: played six months' residency at Grand Hotel, Calcutta, then worked in Ceylon and Shanghai. In 1935 worked with Sestto Carlin's Society Orchestra in San Remo, Italy, then long residency as vocalist at The Sherbini Club, Berlin (1935-7)—during this period worked for the U.S. Olympic Team, mainly as an interpreter. Returned to U.S.A. in 1937, union regulations prevented him fulfilling contract to join Earl Hines at Grand Terrace, worked as a vocalist at The Town Club, Cicero, Illinois. Joined Fats Waller at Hotel Sherman, Chicago, on 31st December 1940, worked on and off with Fats until 1942; featured on trombone and vocals. Toured with Noble Sissle, then settled in California, worked as an Internal Revenue Inspector from 1942 until 1948, but continued to play whenever possible including appearances in the films 'Pillow to Post' and 'No Time for Romance'. Returned to New York in 1949, trip originally planned as a vacation, then Herb resumed full-time playing and singing. Extensive free-lance work, then residency at The Metropole, New York, with Henry 'Red' Allen (1953-8), also toured with Henry. In 1964 moved to Spain, played 16-month residency in Madrid, then worked in Torremolinos before moving to Malaga. Recorded in Germany with Albert Nicholas, Wallace Bishop, Benny Waters etc., in February 1969. Spent the last years of his life in the New York City area.

A book about Flemming, 'A Jazz Pioneer Around the World', by Egino Biagoni, was first published in 1978.

FLOOD, Bernard — *Born: Montgomery, Alabama, 16th December 1907*
trumpet

Studied music at Tuskegee Institute, Atlanta. First professional work in New York with Bobby Neal (1930-1), then with Fess Williams (1931-2), Teddy Hill (1933-5). Brief spells with Chick Webb and Luis Russell, with Charlie Johnson (1936-7), Edgar Hayes (1937-8) including tour of Europe, briefly with Hazel Scott Big Band early in 1939, then with Louis Armstrong from summer of 1939 until 1940. With Jimmy Reynold's Band in New York (spring 1941), rejoined Louis Armstrong (1942-3). Served in U.S. Army (1943-5), with Luis Russell (1946-7), also worked with Duke Ellington during this period. Led own band for several years, also worked regularly with Happy Caldwell (1949-53). Has now retired from full-time playing, but continues to gig.

FOSDICK, Dudley — *Born: Liberty, Indiana, 1902*
mellophone — *Died: 27th June 1957*

Brother of Gene (sax/clarinet). After attending Northwestern University and Columbia University began playing in band led by his brother, The Hoosiers (1922-3). With Red Nichols at Pelham Heath (1924), then joined Ted Weems, rejoined brother's band, then called The Melody Artists (1926). With trumpeter Tommy Gott's Band in New York (1927), Don Voorhees (1928), then worked for several years for Roger Wolfe Kahn. Regular free-lance recordings in the late 1920s. Studio musician during the early 1930s (with Henry King Orchestra, Willard Robison, etc.). Joined Guy Lombardo on 1st September 1936 and remained with that orchestra for almost 10 years. Did studio work in the early 1950s; at the time of suffering a fatal heart attack was Director of the Department of Modern Music at Roerich Academy of Arts.

FOSTER, George — *Born: New York City, 14th July 1915*
drums — *Died: New York, 20th October 1979*

Began playing drums whilst at junior high school. Did first gigs in 1931, with Beverly Peer (then playing piano), continued gigging in and around New York; joined Ray Parker's Band at Harlem Opera House for a brief spell (1935). With Fess Williams (1936), toured and recorded with Lil Armstrong (spring 1937), with Ovie Alston Band (1938-40), but did not play in Claude Hopkins Band. Played in the 369th National Guard Regimental Band during World War II. With Wilbur de Paris (1954-5), Jonah Jones (August 1958 until January 1961). Freelanced in New York during the 1970s.

FOSTER, 'Pops' George Murphy — *Born: On a plantation in McCall, Louisiana, 18th May c. 1892*
string bass/tuba — *Died: San Francisco, 30th October 1969*

Younger brother of banjo-guitarist Willard Foster. Family moved to New Orleans when 'Pops' was 10; he played cello for three years, then switched to string bass. Began working in Rosseals Orchestra (c. 1906), then with Jack Carey at 101 Ranch; with Magnolia Orchestra (1908). Began working with Kid Ory (c. 1908), also worked in New Orleans with The Tuxedo, The Eagle, Armand Piron, King Oliver, etc. Worked briefly with Fate Marable in 1917, joined him regularly on riverboats in summer 1918. Remained with Marable (doubling tuba) until 1921, worked in St. Louis with Charlie Creath and Dewey Jackson, then played in Ed Allen's Whispering Gold Band before moving to Los Angeles to join Kid Ory (c. 1923). Worked with Kid Ory and later with Mutt Carey, also played at various taxi-dance-halls in Los Angeles for two years until 1925. Moved back to St. Louis and again worked with Charlie Creath and Dewey Jackson. Joined Luis Russell in 1929, worked with Luis Russell and Louis Armstrong throughout the 1930s (brief absence from band in late 1937). Left Louis Armstrong in spring 1940, spell in hospital until September 1940. Briefly with Teddy Wilson, then joined Happy Caldwell's Happy Pals in New York (late 1940 to early 1941) before forming duo with guitarist Norman 'Isadore' Langlois. Employed as a New York subway worker from 1942-5, but continued to do regular gigs. With Sidney Bechet (1945), with Art Hodes (1945-6), played regularly on Rudi Blesh's 'This is Jazz' radio series. To Europe in February 1948, played at Nice Jazz Festival with Mezz Mezzrow's Band and did brief tour of France with Mezzrow, then returned to play in Bob Wilber's Band in Boston, subsequently it became Jimmy Archey's Band (1950), toured Europe with Archey in late 1952. Played regularly at Central Plaza, New York—appeared in 'Jazz Dance' film (1954). Played briefly in New Orleans with Papa Celestin (1954). To Europe with Sam Price's Bluesicians (December 1955 to May 1956), then moved to San Francisco. With Earl Hines' Small Band during the late 1950s and early 1960s, free-lanced from 1962, with Eddie Smith Band (1963), Elmer Snowden Trio (1963-4). Toured Europe in New Orleans All Stars (early 1966). Remained based in California, but did widespread touring in U.S.A., Canada. Recovered from serious illness in 1968 and briefly resumed playing.

'The autobiography of Pops Foster' as told to Tom Stoddard, was first published in 1971.

FOWLKES, 'Charlie' Charles Baker
baritone sax

Born: New York, 16th February 1916
Died: Dallas, Texas, 9th February 1980

Noted for his long stay with Count Basie's Orchestra, first joined Basie in 1953, and worked mainly with Basie for the rest of his life, he died whilst touring with the band. Prior to 1953 worked with Tiny Bradshaw (for six years), with Lionel Hampton (four years) and with saxist Arnett Cobb.

FRANCIS, 'Panama' David Albert
drums

Born: Miami, Florida, 21st December 1918

Worked in Florida with George Kelly's Cavaliers from 1934, later joined the Florida Collegians. Moved to New York in summer of 1938, joined Tab Smith. Brief spell with Billy Hicks' Sizzling Six, then joined Roy Eldridge in mid-1939. With Lucky Millinder (1940-6); Cab Calloway (early 1947 until late 1952). Free-lanced in New York, prolific recordings, played regularly at Central Plaza sessions, and also led own band in Montevideo (1954). Regular studio work in California (1971), also with Teddy Wilson Trio (spring 1971), toured Japan with Sam 'The Man' Taylor (1970-1). Moved back to New York City (1973), toured Europe with Warren Covington (1974), featured at many international jazz festivals during the 1970s. Led own Savoy Sultans during the 1970s and early 1980s, also guested occasionally with other leaders.

FRANZELLA, Sal
clarinet/bass clarinet/saxes

Born: Rampart Street, New Orleans, Louisiana, 25th April 1915
Died: New Orleans, Louisiana, 8th November 1968

Father played clarinet in French Opera House in New Orleans. Sal Jr. began on piano at the age of nine, briefly played 'C' melody sax, then alto sax and clarinet at the age of 12. Studied in New Orleans with Belgian tutor Jean Paquay. Joined union at 13, at 14 did professional work in Saenger Theatre Orchestra. Toured with Louis Prima, then returned to New Orleans. In January 1937 began touring with Benny Meroff, left in New York and began doing C.B.S. studio work; worked in re-formed Isham Jones Band at Lincoln Hotel, also worked in Chicago again with Louis Prima. With Paul Whiteman from spring 1938 until joining N.B.C. staff in 1941. Mainly active as studio musician until 1947—brief spell with Paul Whiteman in spring 1943, also worked with Phil Napoleon (late 1946). Moved to California and did studio work there during the 1950s and 1960s. Played briefly in New Orleans during visit in early 1950. Made regular appearances with symphony orchestras from 1955. Moved back to New Orleans in last years of his life. Worked with the Pops Orchestra and did jazz gigs.

F

FREEMAN, 'Bud' Lawrence — *Born: Chicago, Illinois, 13th April 1906*
tenor sax/clarinet/composer

Started on 'C' melody sax in 1923, few lessons from Jimmy McPartland's father, then studied for six months with Duke Real. Early cohort of the Austin High Gang, played regularly with the McPartland's, Teschmacher, etc., in The Blue Friars. Tenor sax from April 1925. The Blue Friars worked under Husk O'Hare's management as The Red Dragons and began broadcasting on station WHT; when the original Wolverines disbanded the group worked as Husk O'Hare's Wolverines, played at White City Ballroom, Chicago, etc. (1926). Later that year Bud joined Herb Carlin, then toured with Art Kassel. Returned to Chicago and played for various leaders including: Spike Hamilton, Charles Pearce, Thelma Terry, Jack Gardner (at the Commercial Theatre), etc., and recorded with McKenzie and Condon Chicagoans, led own recording band, etc. Joined Ben Pollack in Chicago (late 1927), moved with the band to New York in February 1928. Left in summer of 1928, briefly accompanied Bea Palmer (left after a week) and sailed to Europe playing aboard the 'Ile de France'. Played for a fortnight in France, then returned to New York, toured with Red Nichols, then worked for: Meyer Davis, Zez Confrey, Roger Wolfe Kahn, Gene Kardos (1933) before returning to Chicago. With Joe Haymes from spring 1934 until joining Ray Noble's Orchestra opening at Rainbow Room, Radio City, New York (1935). With Tommy Dorsey from April 1936 until joining Benny Goodman in March 1938, left Goodman in November 1938. In April 1939 took own Summa Cum Laude Band into Kelly's, New York, the band played many residencies, and played for the short-lived musical 'Swingin' The Dream' in November 1939. They disbanded in July 1940, and Bud toured with his own big band before joining Joe Marsala in October 1940. Moved to Chicago, led own big band, then own small group played residencies in Chicago, at The Drum, etc. Service in U.S. Army from June 1943 until 1945, led service band at Fort George, Maryland, then led big band in the Aleutians. From summer of 1945 led own quartet, played at Eddie Condon's (late 1946 until early 1947), then in February 1947 took own trio to play residency at Copacabana Hotel, Rio de Janeiro. From late 1947 regularly led own groups in U.S.A., during 1949 worked mainly in Chicago, long residency at own Gaffer Club. Played in Chile and Peru (1952-3), led own trio at The Metropole, New York, etc. (1954), continued prolific free-lance recording activities, including regular sessions with Eddie Condon. Continued leading own small groups throughout the 1950s and 1960s, regularly featured at major jazz festivals throughout the U.S.A. Was temporarily out of action for six months (late 1967 to spring 1968) after a car smash. Toured U.S.A. and overseas in packages organised by pianist George Wein. Made several solo visits to Great Britain, also toured Europe with 'Jazz from a Swinging Era' in 1967. Extensive recording career including free-lance sessions with: Buck Clayton, Gene Gifford, Wingy Manone, Mezz Mezzrow, Adrian Rollini, Lee Wiley, Muggsy Spanier, Jess Stacy, Jack Teagarden, Joe Venuti, Teddy Wilson, etc. With The World's Greatest Jazz Band (1969-71). Spent a good deal of the 1970s working in Europe. Author of two books of reminiscences. Lived in London during the mid 1970s, then moved back to the U.S.A., and made Chicago his base, played at various festivals during the early 1980s.

FRIEDMAN, 'Izzy' Irving — *Born: Linton, Indiana, 25th December 1903*
clarinet/saxes

Studied clarinet with a local teacher, then played in a theatre orchestra in Terra Haute, Indiana, before moving to Chicago in 1923. Studied with Chicago Symphony's principal clarinettist, played residency at The Moulin Rouge Club. Moved to New York in late 1924, studied composition and conducting, continued gigging until joining Vincent Lopez from 1925 until summer of 1926. Played with many bands in New York and took part in many free-lance recording sessions before joining Paul Whiteman from February 1928 until June 1930. During this period also made records with Bix Beiderbecke, Ed Lang, Frank Trumbauer, etc. After taking part in the Paul Whiteman film 'The King of Jazz', Izzy settled in Hollywood and began working as a musician in the Warner Brothers' Studios. In 1932 organised first of Warner Brothers' permanent studio orchestras; from 1934 until 1943 was Assistant Head of Music Department at Warner Brothers, continued to play and conduct. Occupied similar position at M.G.M. Studios 1943-6; from 1946 until 1949 was Head of Music for Eagle-Lion Studios. In April 1950 formed own 'Primrose' company, which provided music (and sound effects) for hundreds of films and thousands of television programmes. In 1963 Izzy sold the business, and since that date has lived in retirement in Beverly Hills, California.

FROEBA, Frank
piano

Born: New Orleans, Louisiana, August 1907
Died: Miami, Florida, 18th February 1981

Father was a professional pianist. Began on piano at a very early age, whilst still in his teens played in local theatres and worked with Johnny Wiggs and John Tobin's Band. Moved to New York in 1924 with Johnny De Droit's Orchestra, played residency at New York Ballroom, then led own band at Silver Slipper, Atlantic City. From 1927 played mainly in New York for various leaders: violinist Frank Cornwell, Enoch Light, Jerry Freeman, briefly with Casa Loma Band. With Irving Aaronson (1933), then with Will Osborne until December 1934. With Benny Goodman from 1934 until summer of 1935. Briefly with Mike Riley-Ed Farley Band. Played long residency at 18 Club, New York, from 1935-44, also led own recording bands and played occasionally in the Milt Herth Trio. Throughout these years Froeba was also active as a house musician for Decca. Solo residency at Governor Clinton Hotel, New York (summer 1944), then solo spot at Ryan's (early 1945). Regularly featured on station WNEW from 1941 until the early 1950s. In the 1950s worked under the name Froba and enjoyed considerable commercial success on record. Made permanent move to Miami, Florida, in 1955, mainly active as solo pianist.

FRYE, Carl B.
alto sax/clarinet

Born: Boston, Massachusetts, 22nd April 1907

Studied at local Hampton Institute. First professional work with Clarence Johnson Band in North Carolina (1928). With Earle Howard (1929-30). Occasionally with Fats Waller, then Willie Bryant (1937-8), Don Redman (1939), Benny Carter (1940), Louis Armstrong from September 1940 until 1942. Left full-time music, but continues to gig in New York.

FRYE, 'Don' Donald O.
piano/vocals

Born: Springfield, Ohio, 1903
Died: New York City, 9th February 1981

Began on piano at 13, worked with Cecil and Lloyd Scott whilst still in high school and went with them to New York in 1924. Remained with the band until the early 1930s, then played for several years in Freddy Moore's Trio (with Pete Brown). Was original member of John Kirby Sextet (May 1937), then worked with Lucky Millinder until joining Frankie Newton in 1939. With Zutty Singleton Trio and Sextet from October 1940, played in Los Angeles with Zutty in 1943. Returned to New York and took up residency as house pianist at Jimmy Ryan's. Has continued to work as a soloist.

FULBRIGHT, 'Dick' Richard W.
string bass/tuba

Born: Paris, Texas, 1901
Died: New York City, 17th November 1962

Toured with the Virginia Minstrels before joining Alonzo Ross and his De Luxe Syncopators (1926-8), played season in Florida with Luckey Roberts, then settled in New York. With Lou Henry's Band (directed by Lt. J. Tim Brymn), then with Bingie Madison (summer 1929). With Charlie Skeete's Band (late 1929), then again worked with Bingie Madison. With Elmer Snowden (1931-2), then regularly with Teddy Hill until late 1937 (including 1937 tour of Europe). With Billy Hicks at St. Regis Hotel, New York, then with pianist Dave Martin at St. George Hotel, New York. Joined Zutty Singleton December 1939, with Zutty in 1940, then rejoined Dave Martin in 1941. With Alberto Soccaras (1943-7), then freelanced in New York—worked with Noble Sissle at Diamond Horseshoe, etc. Retired from music in 1958, last regular work with Buck Washington.

F

FULFORD, Tommy — *Born: 1912*
piano — *Died: New York City, 16th December 1956*

With Bobby Neal's Band (c. 1935), with Blanche Calloway in Indianapolis (1936), then moved to New York, with Snub Mosley in spring 1936 until joining Chick Webb in summer of 1936. Remained after that leader's death to work with Ella Fitzgerald until late 1939, left the band briefly, then rejoined until 1942. Worked mainly as a solo pianist during the 1940s and early 1950s, played with Tony Parenti at The Metropole (1955-6), and Neopolitan City, New York. Continued gigging until shortly before his death, which occurred a few months after his wife had died.

FULLER, 'Bob' Robert — *Born: New York. c. 1898*
reeds

Did coast-to-coast tour with Mamie Smith during the early 1920s, thereafter undertook prolific free-lance recording dates, working with Bessie Smith, Clarence Williams, etc. During the late 1920s led own band for long residency at 125th Street Dance Hall in New York. Left full-time music to work for New York City Police Department as a turnkey.

FULLER, Walter — *Born: Dyersburg, Tennessee, 15th February 1910*
trumpet/vocals

His father was a mellophone player. Left home at 14 to tour with a medicine show. With Sammy Stewart from c. 1927 until spring 1930, left the band at Savoy Ballroom, New York, returned to Chicago to join Irene Eadie and her Vogue Vagabonds. Joined Earl Hines in 1931, left to work with Horace Henderson from August 1937 until August 1938, then rejoined Earl Hines until September 1940. Led own band at new Grand Terrace, Chicago (1941) and other venues. Led own band at Radio Room, Los Angeles (late 1944), Downbeat, Chicago (spring 1945). Moved to California; from 1946 led own band in San Diego, including 12-year residency at Club Royal. Continues to play regularly, also undertakes solo vocal engagements.

GABRIEL, Percy Julian
string bass

Born: New Orleans, Louisiana, 11th July 1915

Father Martin Gabriel (1876-1932) was a noted musician, several of Percy's brothers and sisters also played. Worked in family band during adolescence. Played jobs in New Orleans on tenor sax and string bass from 1935. With brother Clarence's Trio prior to working with Kid Rena, then played on boats sailing to New York with Harold Dejan, left band in New York. Worked in Harlem with Bob Robinson's Trio, then to Florida with vocalist Jack Sneed, back to New Orleans, worked there with Herbert Leary, Papa Celestin, Sidney Desvigne and A. J. Piron. To Texas with Don Albert, then led own band in New Orleans. Worked in Chicago with Lee Collins and Henry Allen. Toured with Jay McShann, left band in California and worked there with Jesse Price. To New Orleans with Paul Barbarin then toured with Lucky Millinder, Danny Barker and Blue Lu Barker. Moved to Detroit in 1950, gigged extensively before forming band that he co-led with brother Martin (clarinet), and then worked regularly in Detroit during the 1970s.

GAILLARD, 'Slim' Bulee
vocals/guitar/piano/vibes/tenor sax/composer

Born: Detroit, Michigan, 4th January 1916

Father was a steward on a liner, Slim travelled with him during school holidays and was accidentally left behind on the island of Crete—remained there for six months. Entered show business in the early 1930s as a solo variety act—he played guitar and tap-danced simultaneously. Moved to New York in 1937, appeared as a single on radio talent contest, then formed double act with 'Slam' Steward (in which Slim sang and played guitar). This duo achieved considerable success, they gained a long series on radio WNEW, and made a big-selling record of their composition 'Flat Foot Floogie'. By early 1940 Slim was leading his own quintet in Chicago, but the duo played together occasionally until Slim joined the Army in 1943. He was released during the following year and led own trio at various clubs in Los Angeles, including Billy Berg's, The Swing Club, etc. During the 1950s and 1960s did single work as a vocalist, master of ceremonies, and comedian. Managed a motel in San Diego (1962), left to play residencies in New York and San Jose, California (1963). Worked in Los Angeles (1970-1), brief reunion with Slam Stewart at 1970 Monterey Jazz Festival. Active throughout the 1970s, several tours of Europe during the early 1980s.

'Slim' Gaillard has appeared in many films, including: 'Star Spangled Rhythm', 'Hellzapoppin', 'Almost Married', 'Go, Man, Go', 'Two Joes from Brooklyn', etc.

GAINES, Charlie
trumpet

Born: Philadelphia, Pennsylvania, 8th August 1900

His son, Stanley, is a bassist; another son, the late Charlie Jr., was a trumpeter. Played in local brass bands until 1917, then worked in Philadelphia and Atlantic City with Charlie Taylor's Band, also worked in Atlantic City with Charlie Johnson. Moved to New York in 1920, played in Wilbur Sweatman's Orchestra, also joined Clarence Williams' recording staff. Gigged at The Garden of Joy with various leaders, joined Sam Wooding at The Nest (c. 1923). Toured with Earl Walton's Band before joining LeRoy Smith in 1925, for the next five years worked regularly with LeRoy Smith (including 'Hot Chocolates' revue), also free-lanced in New York; occasionally with Charlie Johnson, also recorded with Fats Waller in 1929. In 1930 returned to Philadelphia to lead own band, briefly rejoined Le Roy Smith in 1931, then again led own band in Philadelphia (accompanying Louis Armstrong in 1932). Brief excursion to New York in 1934 to record own composition 'Ants in my Pants' with Clarence Williams, then resumed leading in Philadelphia. During the 1940s continued long residency at Carroll's; led own trio at the Hangover Club in Philadelphia during the late 1960s. Gigging in the mid-1970s with own quartet.

GALBREATH, Frank
trumpet/vocals

Born: Roberson County, North Carolina, 2nd September 1913
Died: Atlantic City, New Jersey, 2nd November 1971

Raised in Washington, N.C. Took up trumpet at 15, played with local Domino Five until July 1929, then joined Kelly's Jazz Hounds (from Fayetteville) until April 1930. Played with The Florida Blossoms Minstrel Show for six months, then early in 1931 joined the Kinston Night Hawks. In April 1933 played at Chicago World's Fair with Smiling Billy Steward's Floridians; left Billy Steward in November 1934 and moved to New York. Gigged with various leaders including: Fletcher Henderson, Jelly Roll Morton, Willie Bryant, Edgar Hayes, etc. From 1937 until 1938 worked in Philadelphia with Lonnie Slappey's Swingsters, returned to New York with Lucky Millinder (1939), Jimmy Mundy (late 1939), and Lucky Millinder (1940), then with Louis Armstrong Orchestra from September 1940 until October 1943. Few weeks with Charlie Barnet, then service in U.S. Army until November 1944. With Luis Russell (late 1944-5), Willie Bryant (1946), Tab Smith (1946-7), also worked briefly with Billy Eckstine and Sy Oliver in 1947. Mainly with Lucky Millinder from 1948 until 1952, visited Britain on U.S.O. tour with Snub Mosley (summer 1952), then for 10 years did regular overseas U.S.O. tours. During this period also briefly led own band at Savoy, and worked with Red Prysock (1955-6), Paul Williams (1957-8), Benny Goodman (April-June 1959), Reuben Phillips (1959-60), Ray Charles (1960), and Fats Domino (1961). In June 1963 left the Sammy Davis Show and settled in Atlantic City. Continued to play regularly until illness in summer of 1969.

GANDEE, 'Al' Albert — *Born: 1900*
trombone — *Died: Cincinnati, 3rd June 1944*

Best remembered for his work with The Wolverines. Joined that band in Cincinnati in January 1924, after touring and recording left the band to recommence work at his own dairy business. Continued to play regularly including long spell of theatre work with Dave Piet's Orchestra in Cincinnati. Lost his life in a car crash.

GANT, 'Willie' William D. — *Born: New York City. c. 1900*
piano — *Died: New York, February 1979*

Known as 'The Tiger'. Began playing piano at the age of 12. First professional work at William Bank's Cafe, New York (c. 1917). Formed own band in 1921 which featured many well-known jazz soloists, led for long residencies in New York, Small's, etc. Mainly solo work from 1927, played in New York, California, etc., during the 1930s and 1940s. Has worked mainly in New York during the last 30 years of his life, long residencies at Hotel Fairfax, Cerutti's, etc.

GARCIA, 'King' Louis K. — *Born: Juncos, Puerto Rico, 25th August 1905*
trumpet — *Died: Los Angeles, California, 9th April 1983*

Began on trumpet whilst at local school, later played in Municipal Band of San Juan (directed by Juan Tizol's uncle, Manuel). Played in the Victor Recording Orchestra, then settled in U.S.A. in the early 1920s, worked in Original Dixieland Jazz Band at Melody Lane Club, New York (c. 1926), then spent many years in orchestra led by Emil Coleman. Extensive recording work in the 1930s, several sessions with the Dorsey Brothers, also led own recording band and recorded with vocaliste Amanda Randolph. With Vic Berton Orchestra (1935), Richard Himber (1936), Nat Brandwyne (1937-8), and Louis Prima Big Band (1939). Continued studio work in the 1940s, regularly with Emil Coleman Orchestra. Led own Latin-American band in New York from the late 1940s. Moved to California in 1960, soon afterwards ill health caused him to cease playing.

Not related to Russell or Richard Garcia.

GARDNER, 'Jack' Francis Henry — *Born: Joliet, Illinois, 14th August 1903*
piano/composer — *Died: Dallas, Texas, 26th November 1957*

Also known as 'Jumbo Jack'. Began on piano at the age of eight; later, when his family moved to Denver, Colorado, he worked in a music store and joined Doc Becker's Blue Devils at the Coronado Club. Worked with Boyd Senter before moving to Chicago in 1923, joined George 'Spike' Hamilton's Band for a brief spell, then worked with Art Cope's Band at the Vanity Fair Cafe. Led own band at Commercial Theatre, Chicago (1927), also toured with own band; made recordings with Wingy Manone (1928). Brief spell with Jean Goldkette in Detroit (c. 1929), also toured theatres as accompanist for vocalist Gene Austin. Worked mainly in Chicago during the early 1930s with: Fred Hamm, Phil Spitalny, Maurice Sherman, etc., recorded with Jimmy McPartland in 1936. Moved to New York in 1937, played in orchestra led by violinist 'Sandy' Williams, then joined Harry James from 1939 until 1940. Moved back to Chicago, led own trio at Silver Palms, etc., extensive work as soloist and accompanist, recorded with Baby Dodds in 1944. Gigged with various jazz groups in Chicago for many years before moving to Texas. Enjoyed early success with a hit tune 'Bye, Bye, Pretty Baby', later composed show tunes, some in collaboration with lyricist Rex Roberts.

GARLAND, 'Montudi' Edward Bertram

Born: New Orleans, Louisiana, 9th January 1885?
Died: Los Angeles, California, 22nd January 1980

Began on drums, played snare and bass drum for parade work. Switched to tuba and mellophone during his teens and continued to play marching gigs. Later switched to string bass and worked with The Imperial Orchestra and with John Robichaux. Continued to double on brass bass and did parade work with the Eagle, Security, Excelsior, and Superior Bands before moving to Chicago in 1914. Led own band on Orpheum Circuit accompanying Mabel Lee Lane, then returned to Chicago and joined Manuel Perez, subsequently worked with Lawrence Duhé and Freddie Keppard. Joined King Oliver in Chicago and moved to West Coast with the band (1921); remained in California and joined Kid Ory. Left to work in Black and Tan Orchestra (late 1923), then rejoined Kid Ory, and worked with Mutt Carey after Ory left for Chicago (late 1925). From c. 1927 led own band for long residency at 111 Dance Hall, Los Angeles. Continued to lead own groups until rejoining Kid Ory in 1944 (gigged with Jelly Roll Morton in Los Angeles in late 1940). Remained with Kid Ory until spring 1955, left the band abruptly and joined Andrew Blakeney. With Earl Hines in San Francisco from September 1955 until June 1956. Spell with trombonist Turk Murphy and free-lancing. Worked with Joe Darensbourg from 1960, free-lanced in Los Angeles, then regularly with Andrew Blakeney in the mid-1960s, appeared with Blakeney in the 1966 film 'Hotel'. Played in Young Men of New Orleans (1969). Brief return to New Orleans for April 1971 Jazz Fest. Continued to play regularly during the 1970s, including international tours with The Legends of Jazz.

GARLAND, 'Joe' Joseph Copeland
tenor/baritone/bass saxes/arranger/composer/clarinet

Born: Norfolk, Virginia, 15th August 1903
Died: Teaneck, New Jersey, 21st April 1977

Brother of trumpeter Moses Garland. Began playing whilst at school in Oxford, North Carolina, later studied at Aeolian Conservatory in Baltimore (played in A. Jack Thomas Concert Band in 1921) and at Shaw University. Played in concert bands and orchestras until 1924, then joined pianist Graham Jackson's Seminole Syncopators. Joined Elmer Snowden on alto and baritone in 1925, following year worked with Joe Steele's Orchestra, then briefly with Henri Saparo. Worked in New York and South America with Leon Abbey (1927). In 1928 with Charlie Skeete, then worked and recorded with Jelly Roll Morton, rejoined Joe Steele. With Bobby Neal in 1931, then joined the Mills Blue Rhythm Band in 1932, remained with the band (working under Lucky Millinder) until 1936—also recorded with Duke Ellington in 1933. With Edgar Hayes in 1937, Don Redman in late 1938, then with Louis Armstrong Orchestra from early 1939 until 1942 (musical director from May 1940). In 1943 and 1944 free-lanced in New York—spell with Claude Hopkins in late 1944; rejoined Louis Armstrong as musical director in May 1945, remained until Louis disbanded in 1947, worked in big band led by Herbie Fields, then rejoined Claude Hopkins (1947). Musical director for Earl Hines Big Band (late 1948). Left full-time music in the early 1950s, but continued to lead own small band regularly, occasionally forming big bands for specific engagements.

GENTRY, 'Chuck' Charles *Born: Belgrade, Nebraska, 14th December 1911*
all saxes/clarinet

Originally a clarinettist, began playing in school band in Sterling, Colorado, and continued whilst studying at Colorado State Teachers' College. Professional debut with Ken Baker in Los Angeles (1935). Joined Vido Musso's Band in 1939, then with Harry James (1940-1). Joined Benny Goodman from July 1941 until early 1942, then worked with Jimmy Dorsey until serving in Glenn Miller's U.S. Air Force Band (1943-4). After demobilisation played with Artie Shaw, Jan Savitt, and with Benny Goodman from late 1946 until late 1947, then concentrated on studio work. Since the late 1940s has been a baritone sax specialist, employed in West Coast studio bands.

GEORGE,, Karl Curtis *Born: St. Louis, Missouri, 26th April 1913*
trumpet

Worked with McKinney's Cotton Pickers (c. 1933) and with Cecil Lee's Band in Detroit, then joined Jeter-Pillars Orchestra. First came to prominence as a member of Teddy Wilson Orchestra (April 1939 to April 1940). Played with Lionel Hampton in 1941-2, then service in U.S. Army. Released in early 1943, remained on West Coast, spent over a year in Stan Kenton Orchestra, then worked with Benny Carter Band on West Coast. Short spell with Count Basie from spring 1945, during that year also led own recording band. Regular member of Happy Johnson Band in Los Angeles during 1946. Has for many years been in very poor health, spending his unfortunate retirement in St. Louis.

GIBBS, 'Eddie' Edward Leroy *Born: New Haven, Connecticut, 25th December 1908*
bass/guitar/banjo

Family moved to New York in 1918. Originally played banjo; studied guitar with Elmer Snowden. During late 1920s to early 1930s, with Wilbur Sweatman, Billy Fowler, Eubie Blake, Charlie Johnson, etc. Then regularly with Edgar Hayes (1937-8), including tour of Europe (1938). Briefly with Teddy Wilson, then regular member of Eddie South Group in 1940-1. Long spell with pianist Dave Martin (from February 1941) before playing with Luis Russell and Claude Hopkins. Own trio at Village Vanguard, then with Cedric Wallace Trio. Reverted to banjo for three-year stint with Wilbur de Paris (1952-5). In 1959 changed to string bass and, after tuition from Ernest 'Bass' Hill, began working regularly on that instrument, but played banjo at New York World's Fair in 1965. During late 1969 worked regularly in The Jazz Family on bass and banjo.

GIBSON, 'Andy' Albert Andrew *Born: Zanesville, Ohio, 6th November 1913*
arranger/composer *Died: Cincinnati, Ohio, 10th February 1961*

Played violin as a child, then changed to trumpet. Played with Zack Whyte Band in 1932-3, subsequently with Blanche Calloway, McKinney's Cotton Pickers, etc. Moved to New York in mid-1930s, played with Lucky Millinder. From 1937 concentrated on full-time arranging, scored for Duke Ellington, Count Basie, Charlie Barnet, etc., etc. Led own band during U.S. Army Service (1942-5). Returned to arranging after release from service. From 1955 active as musical director for King Records. Moved back to his home state in 1960. Andy's later work was performed on a recording session organised by Stanley Dance in December 1959.

GIFFORD, 'Gene' Harold Eugene *Born: Americus, Georgia, 31st May 1908*
guitar/arranger *Died: Memphis, Tennessee, 12th November 1970*

Raised in Memphis, Tennessee. Started arranging whilst playing banjo in high school band. With Bob Foster Band in El Dorado, Arkansas, then touring with Lloyd Williams' Band and Watson's Bell Hops. Made record debut in Chicago (1927), subsequently led own band for tour of Texas, then with band led by Blue Steele (real name: Gene Staples); whilst with that band began concentrating on guitar. With Henry Cato's Vanities Orchestra (early 1928). Regularly arranged for several of Jean Goldkette's Bands, and in 1929 joined Orange Blossoms (a Goldkette unit then directed by Hank Biagnini). This band formed nucleus of the Casa Loma Band. Gifford became principal arranger, but continued playing guitar and banjo with the band until December 1933 when his place was taken by Jacques 'Jack' Blanchette, enabling Gifford to work as full-time staff arranger. Throughout the late 1930s and 1940s very active as free-lance arranger for many famous big bands. Was on WWL staff in New Orleans in 1945; then, after U.S.O. tours in 1945 and 1946, returned to work under Glen Gray in 1948 and 1949. During 1950s worked outside of music as an audio-consultant and radio engineer, but continued to arrange. Moved to Memphis in 1969, taught music there.

GILLESPIE, 'Dizzy' John Birks — *Born: Cheraw, South Carolina, 21st October 1917*
trumpet/vocals/composer

Father was a mason who played several musical instruments. Began playing trumpet in early teens. Played with own trio (trumpet, piano and drums), gained scholarship to Laurinburg Institute, N.C., but left before his last year and moved to Philadelphia in 1935, worked there with Frank Fairfax. Moved to New York and joined Teddy Hill's Band at the Savoy Ballroom in 1937, toured Europe with Hill later that year. Joined Cab Calloway in 1939 for two years, then worked briefly with big bands led by Ella Fitzgerald, Claude Hopkins, Les Hite, Lucky Millinder, Charlie Barnet, Fletcher Henderson and Benny Carter. Led own small band at Down Beat Club in Philadelphia (late 1942) prior to joining Earl Hines for several months. Briefly with Duke Ellington in New York in late 1943. Co-led small band at Onyx Club, N.Y. with bassist Oscar Pettiford, also brief spells in several other small bands, including John Kirby's Sextet. During this period gained reputation of being one of the leading exponents of what was then called 'be-bop' (along with alto saxophonist Charlie Parker, b. 1920). Joined Billy Eckstine's Big Band in June 1944, then again led own small band (1945) which later that year was augmented into a big band. During the late 1940s, 1950s and 1960s, Dizzy alternated between leading small and big bands. Did several wide-ranging international tours with big band, including some for U.S. State Department. His quintet also performed a vast number of international engagements. Dizzy also did concert tours as a soloist with the 'Jazz At The Philharmonic' presentations. In 1971-72, he also guested in an all-star touring line-up called The Giants of Jazz. Continued to do widespread touring during the late 1970s, mainly with a quintet, many overseas visits including Africa, Australia, Cuba, Europe. Working schedule undiminished during the early 1980s.

'To Be Or Not To Bop', Dizzy Gillespie's autobiography (with Al Fraser) first published in 1979.

GLENN, Lloyd — *Born: San Antonio, Texas, 21st November 1909*
piano/arranger

First professional work at the age of 19 in Millard McNeal's Melody Boys, moved to Dallas a year later. Played with The Royal Aces (led by trombonist George Corley) and The De Luxe Melody Boys before joining Terrence Holder. Stayed until this unit disbanded in 1932, returned to San Antonio and joined band led by drummer Clifford 'Boots' Douglas—Boots and his Buddies. Left during the summer of 1934 to join Don Albert, then resident at Shadowland in San Antonio. Left Don Albert in 1937—from 1938-42 gigged in San Antonio and did occasional teaching. Moved to California in 1942, did a spell of day work at the Douglas Aircraft Factory, then joined Walter Johnson Trio in 1944. Following year moved to Los Angeles, regular gigs and own recording groups—joined Kid Ory Band in autumn 1949, left in 1953, formed own trio which recorded regularly through the late 1950s and early 1960s. Has remained on West Coast. Is an 'a. and r.' man for Down Beat Records. During the 1970s did several tours with vocalist Joe Turner, and own touring in Europe.

GLENN, 'Tyree' Evans Tyree — *Born: Corsicana, Texas, 23rd November 1912*
trombone/vibes/vocals — *Died: Englewood, New Jersey, 18th May 1974*

Tyree Jr. is a tenor saxist. During late teens played with local bands in Texas, then regularly with band led by drummer Tommy Myles in Washington, D.C., and Virginia (1934-6). With Charlie Echols' Band in Los Angeles in 1936, also with Eddie Barefield on

West Coast, then joined Eddie Mallory's Band (accompanying Ethel Waters), remained with this band until 1939, except for time lost through being injured in a band-coach crash. With Benny Carter Big Band from March 1939 until December 1939, then joined Cab Calloway. With Cab until 1946, then in September of that year to Europe as a member of Don Redman Orchestra. Remained in Europe for solo engagements until April 1947, then back to New York—subbed for Lawrence Brown in Duke Ellington Band in May 1947—shortly afterwards joined Duke Ellington on a regular basis until 1951 (absent for 1950 European tour). Returned to Scandinavia for solo engagements in late 1951. From 1952 mainly active in studio work, radio, and television, usually on vibes and trombone—occasionally undertaking acting roles. From 1955 combined studio work with leading own quintet (usually featuring Harold Baker). Joined Louis Armstrong All Stars in spring 1965, remained until Louis' 1968 illness. Led own group at The Roundtable, New York (1969). With Louis Armstrong (September 1970-March 1971), depped with Duke Ellington (summer 1971).

GOLDKETTE, Jean — *Born: Valenciennes, France, 18th March 1899*
leader/piano — *Died: Santa Barbara, California, 24th March 1962*

After living in Greece and Russia, moved with his family to U.S.A. in 1911. Began playing professionally in Chicago, then with Andrew Raymonds' Band in Detroit in 1921. Shortly afterwards formed own band—by the late 1920s his organisation controlled over 20 bands. Goldkette himself did not play in any of these aggregations. Today he is chiefly remembered as the employer of many famous jazz musicians including: Bix Beiderbecke, Steve Brown, Jimmy and Tommy Dorsey, Ed Lang, Danny Polo, Joe Venuti, etc., etc. Goldkette appeared as piano soloist with the Detroit Symphony Orchestra in 1930. By the early 1930s had relinquished his nominal interest in all his bands, also ceased to act as entrepreneur for McKinney's Cotton Pickers, he worked as an agent for many years. Re-formed bands in the mid-1940s and 1950s, but was mainly active as a classical pianist. Moved from Detroit to Santa Monica in 1961.

GOODMAN, 'Benny' Benjamin David — *Born: Chicago, Illinois, 30th May 1909*
clarinet/alto sax

At 10 began music studies at local synagogue, took up clarinet, at 12 studied at Hull House under Johnny Sylvester, also received private tuition from Franz Schoepp. During 1921 took part in a talent contest at Chicago's Central Theatre; he imitated Ted Lewis (accompanied by Benny Meroff's Orchestra). Joined the musicians' union at the age of 13, and during the early 1920s played in bands with various local boys including: Jimmy McPartland, Dave Tough, Art Hodes, etc. From the age of thirteen worked semi-regularly with bands led by Charles 'Murph' Podalsky, also gigged with various bands including Chuck Walker's Meteorgnomes. During summer of 1923 worked occasionally in bands playing for excursions on the Great Lakes steamboats, his first meeting with Bix Beiderbecke took place during one of these gigs. From the autumn of 1923 worked regularly at Guyon's Paradise (where Jules Herbevaux conducted the orchestra), continued at Guyon's until late 1923, then joined Arnold Johnson at the Green Mill Gardens. From autumn 1924 until August 1925 played in Art Kassel's Band at the Midway Gardens, then signed with Ben Pollack in Chicago and travelled to California with him to join the band at the Venice Ballroom, Los Angeles (replacing Fud Livingston, who had temporarily left the band). Returned to Chicago with Ben Pollack in January 1926; at this time regular work for the Pollack Band was scarce, and Benny Goodman did various free-lance gigs and a spell with Benny Meroff at the Granada Theatre, Chicago. Worked on and off with Pollack during 1926, rejoined the band regularly c. February 1927 at the Southmoor Hotel and travelled to the West Coast with the band during summer of 1927. He left the band in Chicago late in 1927 and worked for two months with Isham Jones at the Million Dollar Rainbow Gardens, then rejoined Pollack and moved with him to New York in March 1928. Left Pollack in September 1929, worked for a month in Paramount Theatre Orchestra, then joined Red Nichols from October 1929 until January 1930. Prolific free-lance activities from 1930, played for various Broadway shows, did extensive radio-studio work (for Don Voorhees, David Rubinoff, Andre Kostelanetz, Paul Whiteman, etc., etc.) and regular recording dates (with Ben Selvin, Red Nichols, Ted Lewis, Ben Pollack, Ed Lang-Joe Venuti, etc., etc.). Led own recording band and occasionally led bands for outside engagements. During the spring and summer of 1932 played regularly in band he organised to accompany vocalist Russ Columbo. Formed first regular band for residency at Billy Rose's Music Hall, New York (1st June to 17th October 1934). The band was featured regularly on the National Biscuit Company's 'Let's Dance' coast-to-coast radio show from December 1934 until May 1935, during this period the band played outside jobs—mostly in the New York area. They began their first national tour in July 1935, on 21st August 1935 they began a residency at the Palomar Ballroom (Los Angeles) which was to prove the turning point in Goodman's career. The band quickly achieved national, then international, fame. After a long residency at the Congress Hotel, Chicago (from November 1935 until May 1936), the band returned to New York and proceeded to go from success to success. In 1936 the band made its first film, 'The Big Broadcast of 1937', during that year Benny Goodman introduced his racially-integrated quartet to the public (featuring Goodman, Lionel Hampton, Gene Krupa, and Teddy Wilson). On 3rd March 1937 the band began its brief, but phenomenally successful, first stay at the Paramount Theatre, New York. On 16th January 1938 Benny Goodman with his orchestra and several famous guest stars played one of their most celebrated engagements: The Carnegie Hall Jazz Concert. In the summer of 1938 Goodman took a vacation in Europe, briefly visiting London in July. He resumed leading until forced by illness to disband in July 1940. (In August 1939 Goodman had signed Charlie Christian, who was in the first of Goodman's famous sextets.) After undergoing an operation for the relief of his sciatica he gigged with his own sextet in October 1940, and re-formed big band for debut on 25th October. Throughout the 1940s, 1950s, and 1960s, Benny Goodman continued to lead his own highly successful big (and small) groups. He also continued to appear as clarinet soloist with various classical ensembles. In the summer of 1949 he topped the bill at the London Palladium (accompanied by pianist Buddy Greco, a specially formed sextet, and the augmented Skyrockets' Orchestra). Subsequent overseas tours include: Europe (April-June 1950), Japan, Thailand, Burma (December 1956 to January 1957), Europe, including Brussels' World Fair (May 1958), Europe (October to early November 1959), U.S.S.R. (May-July 1962), Japan—quartet (February-March 1964), Belgium (August 1966). Three tours of Europe (early 1970, spring 1971 and autumn 1971) leading big band comprised mainly of British musicians. Continued throughout the 1970s and led own band for tours of Europe in 1981 and 1982.

Early in his career Benny Goodman regularly doubled on alto sax, he also occasionally played tenor, soprano, and baritone saxes; in 1927 and 1928 he recorded on trumpet. Post-1940 he rarely played sax, he did however broadcast on tenor sax (briefly, on a borrowed instrument) in March 1941, and in the spring of 1943 occasionally played alto sax during his band's stay on the West Coast. In 1955 a semi-biographical film, 'The Benny Goodman Story' was made. Other films featuring Benny Goodman's Orchestra include: 'The Big Broadcast of 1937', 'Hollywood Hotel', 'Stage Door Canteen', 'Sweet and Lowdown', 'The Powers Girl', etc., etc. Benny Goodman also appeared in 'A Song is Born'. For a complete summary of Benny Goodman's recordings, films, etc., the reader is advised to consult the magnificent bio-discography 'B.G. On the Record', by D. Russell Connor and Warren W. Hicks (published in 1969). 'The Kingdom of Swing', by Benny Goodman and Irving Kolodin was first published in 1939.

GOODWIN, Henry Clay
trumpet

Born: Columbia, South Carolina, 2nd January 1910
Died: New York City, 2nd July 1979

Mother was a pianiste. Played drums, tuba, and trumpet in local Armstrong High School Band. Worked in Washington with pianist Sam Taylor's Band, then with Claude Hopkins during summer 1925. Sailed to Europe in September 1925 with Hopkins' Band (as part of Josephine Baker Revue), left the show in Berlin, returned to New York, then sailed to Argentina with Paul Wyer. Returned to New York, worked with Elmer Snowden and Cliff Jackson's Krazy Kats in late 1920s. To Europe in June 1933 as member of Lucky

Millinder Band, worked with Willie Bryant in New York before spending two years with Charlie Johnson's Band. Worked briefly with Cab Calloway, then with Edgar Hayes in 1937-8. With Hayes until 1940, worked with Sidney Bechet, then joined Cecil Scott Band at Ubangi Club in 1942. Left in 1944, briefly with Gene Sedric, free-lancing in New York, then with Art Hodes (1946). To Europe in February 1948, played at Nice Jazz Festival, returned to U.S.A., worked regularly with Bob Wilbur Band in Boston (late 1948-9). With Jimmy Archey small band from 1950 until forced to leave through illness in 1951—toured Europe with Archey (late 1952). In autumn of 1956 worked in San Francisco with Earl Hines, returned to New York and continued to play regularly through the 1960s.

GOUDIE, 'Big Boy' Frank
tenor sax/clarinet/trumpet

Born: Royville (Youngsville), Louisiana, 13th September 1899
Died: San Francisco, California, 9th January 1964

Family moved to New Orleans when Frank was eight. Began by playing a home-made fiddle, then played cornet in school band. Became apprentice at a barber's shop, but also played piano for silent movies whilst still in his early teens. Occasionally experimented with sax and clarinet, but worked mostly on cornet during his days in New Orleans. Played with Papa Celestin's Original Tuxedo Band, the Magnolia Band, Arnold DuPas, and Jack Carey. From 1921 began touring with a minstrel show, for the next four years worked in Texas, Louisiana, New Mexico, and California with a variety of bands including Frank Matthews' and The Louisiana High Browns. Quit touring in Tampico, Mexico, and sailed to Europe. Lived in France from 1925, concentrated on tenor sax and clarinet, but occasionally played trumpet; worked in France, Portugal, Spain, Belgium, Switzerland, and Holland with Benny Peyton, Louis Mitchell, Sam Wooding, Noble Sissle, and Freddy Johnson. With Willie Lewis from April 1935 until October 1938, then joined Oscar Aleman Band. Remained in Paris until 1940, then spent duration of World War II in Brazil and Argentina. Whilst in South America played with various bands including spell with Booker Pittman Orchestra, also led own small bands. Returned to France in 1946, worked with pianist Charlie Lewis, Arthur Briggs, and Harry Cooper. With Glyn Paque in Switzerland during 1948, left in April 1949, for next two years spells with Bill Coleman Band. From 1951 until 1956 led own band in Berlin. Moved back to U.S.A. in summer of 1957, lived in San Francisco where he ran own business (which was part of an inheritance from his uncle). Continued to play clarinet regularly—worked with Marty Marsala, Earl Hines, Burt Bales, Dick Oxtot, Eddie Smith, Bill Erickson, etc.

GOWANS, 'Brad' Arthur Bradford
valve-trombone/clarinet/cornet/saxes

Born: Billerica, Massachusetts, 3rd December 1903
Died: Los Angeles, California, 8th September 1954

Showed his skill as a multi-instrumentalist whilst at high school. First professional work as a clarinettist, played slide-trombone in Rhapsody Makers Band with clarinettist Jim Moynahan, then reverted to clarinet to replace Sidney Arodin in Tommy De Rosa's New Orleans Jazz Band, also worked in Perley Breed's Orchestra. Switched to cornet, work with Joe Venuti in 1926; later that year joined band led by Jimmy 'Schnozzle' Durante. Spent two years in Mal Hallett's Band, then worked in Bert Lown's Orchestra. Left professional music, worked at a variety of jobs before joining Bobby Hackett Band at Theatrical Club, Boston, in 1936. Played in Boston with Frank Ward's Orchestra, then to New York in April 1938 to join Wingy Manone—on valve-trombone. Rejoined Bobby Hackett in summer of 1938, doubling valve-trombone and fourth sax. Worked briefly with Joe Marsala, then with Bud Freeman's Summa Cum Laude Band in 1939, worked briefly with Joe Marsala until April 1940, then rejoined Bud Freeman until July 1940, then into Nick's. Worked with Ray McKinley's Big Band early in 1942; briefly with Art Hodes during 1943, regular spells at Nick's 1942-3. Reverted to clarinet to tour with Katherine Dunham Show. During following year temporarily left full-time music to work in a Boston defence plant. With Max Kaminsky in Boston (November-December 1945), then at Condon's until June 1946. With Jimmy Dorsey Big Band from spring of 1948, following year toured with Nappy Lamare's Band. With Nappy Lamare (1950), also free-lanced (mainly on West Coast). Worked in Las Vegas with tenorist Bernie Billings' Band (early 1951). With Eddie Skrivanek's Sextet from Hunger from spring of 1953, collapsed whilst playing with that band at the El Cortez Club in Las Vegas (January 1954)—was never able to return to work, long spell in hospital before dying of a malignant disease.

GRAUSO, Joe
drums

Born: New York City, 1897
Died: New York City, 11th June 1952

Professional musician from 1914, worked local jobs with pianist Frank Signorelli. From 1916 until 1918 toured with brass bands, circus shows, and carnivals. Formed own Happy Five Melody Boys in 1918 for year's residency at Arcadia Cabaret in Brooklyn, then worked for many years as percussionist in vaudeville theatres. Inactive through illness in late 1930s, worked for three years as a book-keeper, then in 1941 joined Art Hodes, then led own band for two-year stay at club in Forest Hills. Worked at Nick's from February 1944, recorded with Miff Mole, Eddie Condon, etc., regularly with Muggsy Spanier until early 1945. Worked in Billy Butterfield Band in 1948. His son Robert is a drummer.

GRAY, Glen
(real name: Glen Gray Knoblaugh)
saxes/leader

Born: Roanoke, Illinois, 7th June 1906
Died: Plymouth, Massachusetts, 23rd August 1963

Studied at Illinois Wesleyan College, left to work as a cashier for Santa Fe Railroad Company, began playing local gigs. Played with a Jean Goldkette unit called the Orange Blossom Band, this Detroit-based band moved to take a residency at the Casa Loma Hotel in Toronto, Canada. The band began touring, and in New York in 1929 registered as The Casa Loma Orchestra Inc.—Glen Gray was elected president of the company—he continued to play in the sax section whilst violinist Mel Jenssen fronted the band. From 1937 Glen began fronting the band, from then the band was billed as Glen Gray and the Casa Loma Orchestra. Retired from touring in 1950, from 1956 occasionally organised recording groups—re-recording material associated with the Casa Loma Band.

The Casa Loma Band appeared in 1943 film 'Girls Inc.'

GRAY, 'Tick' Thomas B.
trumpet

Born: c. 1905

Joined King Oliver in Chicago (February 1927), subsequently played in New York with Oliver in May 1927. Returned to Chicago, worked with Junie Cobb (1928), Boyd Atkins (late 1929), Midnight Revellers (1930), Fred Avendorph (1931 and 1932), also with Clarence Moore, Saxist Art Short and Jesse Stone's Cyclones during the 1930s. Left full-time music and ran own restaurant for some years, continued gigging with many bands in Chicago, including dates with Elgar's Marching Band. Is now reported to be farming in Michigan.

GREEN, Charlie
trombone

Born: Omaha, Nebraska. c. 1900
Died: New York, February 1936

Known as 'Big Green' and 'Long Boy.' Played with brass bands in Omaha and Tulsa. Worked with the Omaha Night Owls (c. 1920), subsequently with Frank 'Red' Perkins' Band at Broomfield Cabaret and at other venues in and around Omaha. Toured with carnival shows before settling in New York. Worked regularly with Fletcher Henderson from 1924 until 1927, thereafter worked occasionally with Henderson. Briefly with June Clark's Band at the Tango Gardens, then joined Fats Waller and James P. Johnson for Keep Shufflin' revue (early 1928), again worked with Henderson, left to play in Chicago, then returned to New York, continued recording with Bessie Smith. During summer of 1929 briefly with Zutty Singleton's Band at the Lafayette Theatre, New York, with Benny Carter from September 1929. During following year worked at the Saratoga Club, brief returns to Fletcher Henderson, also worked occasionally with Elmer Snowden and Chick Webb. With Jimmie Noone at the Savoy, New York, in June 1931, then brief spell with McKinney's Cotton Pickers. In 1932 gigged with Sam Wooding and Don Redman, then regularly with Chick Webb (late 1932-3), again with Benny Carter in 1933, then worked with Chick Webb for a while in 1934. Early in 1935 worked in Louis Metcalf's Band, then joined Kaiser Marshall's Band at the Ubangi Club in New York. Big Charlie died under tragic circumstances, he froze to death on a Harlem doorstep. He couldn't get into his home and decided to spend the night outdoors with fatal results.

During the late 1940s a rumour gained credence in British jazz circles that Charlie Green was still alive in Holland, having spent the war years in that country. This was untrue; the confusion arose because veteran American trombonist Jake Green had worked in Rotterdam during the 1930s.

GREEN, 'Freddie' Frederick William *Born: Charleston, South Carolina, 31st March 1911*
guitar

Began playing guitar at the age of 12, later went to New York to finish schooling. Whilst playing at Black Cat Cafe, New York, was heard by John Hammond who recommended him to Count Basie. First date with Count Basie in Philadelphia (March 1937), has worked regularly with Basie ever since—playing un-amplified guitar. Has taken part in many free-lance recording sessions with: Mildred Bailey, Emmett Berry, Benny Carter, Karl George, Benny Goodman, Lionel Hampton, Billie Holiday, Pee Wee Russell, Joe Sullivan, Earle Warren, Dicky Wells, Teddy Wilson, Lester Young, etc.

GREER, 'Sonny' William Alexander *Born: Long Branch, New Jersey, 13th December c. 1895*
drums *Died: New York, 23rd March 1982*

Started on drums whilst at high school, then worked with various bands in and around New Jersey including Wilbur Gardner, Mabel Ross, and in one of Harry Yerek's many orchestras. Whilst visiting Washington, D.C., took a job playing at the Howard Theatre with Marie Lucas Orchestra. Met Duke Ellington in 1919, during the following year—on 20th March 1920—did first gig with Duke. Shared early experiences with Duke Ellington (q.v.) and remained with the band until March 1951. Joined Johnny Hodges' Small Band until replaced by Joe Marshall in September 1951. From that time free-lanced in New York, playing for various leaders including: Louis Metcalf, Henry 'Red' Allen (1952-3, including trip to Bermuda), Tyree Glenn (1959), etc. Other than spell of inactivity through broken shoulder (1960) continued to play throughout the 1960s with Eddie Barefield, J.C. Higginbotham, etc. In 1967 led own band at 'The Garden Cafe', New York, during that year also took part in filming of 'The Night They Raided Minsky's'. Worked regularly with Brooks Kerr trio during the 1970s.

During Sonny's 31 years with Duke he was absent through illness for several short periods, his deps include: Tommy Benford, Kaiser Marshall, Fred Avendorph (1935), Cootie Williams (spring 1939), Lionel Hampton (early 1943), Hillard Brown (autumn 1944), Sid Catlett (1945), Ed McConney (spring 1947), Oliver Coleman (spring 1948), Bill Clark (early 1951).

GRIFFIN, 'Chris' Gordon *Born: Binghamton, N.Y., 31st October 1915*
trumpet

Began on piano at the age of five, lost interest two years later; took up trumpet at the age of 12. Played in school bands, then gave up playing for a while until forming a local band with a neighbour who played piano. At 15 did first professional work in a New York taxi-dance-hall, then with Scott Fisher's Band until joining Charlie Barnet (1933-4), did a summer season with Rudy Vallee, then worked again with Barnet (1935). Spell with Joe Haymes, then C.B.S. studio work before joining Benny Goodman from May 1936 until August 1939. Returned to C.B.S. in 1939. During the 1930s did free-lance recordings with: Miff Mole, Mildred Bailey, Teddy Wilson, etc. Worked briefly for Jimmy Dorsey in spring of 1940 and played on several of Benny Goodman's recordings during the 1940s and 1950s, but for over 30 years was staff musician at C.B.S. Studios. Partnered Pee Wee Erwin in running a trumpet-tuition school. Toured Europe with Warren Covington (1974).

GRIMES, 'Tiny' Lloyd *Born: Newport News, Virginia, 7th July 1916*
guitar/vocals

Played drums in Huntington High School Band, did some gigs on drums, then worked as a pianist and dancer in Washington, D.C. (1935). Continued with this work until 1939 (including residency at The Rhythm Club, New York, in 1938), then began playing guitar. Eight months later was working professionally (on amplified guitar) with The Cats and a Fiddle. Left in 1941 and worked in California, and there joined Art Tatum's Trio, worked with Tatum until 1944, then led own trio at the Tondelayo Club, New York. Led The Rocking Highlanders in New York and Cleveland during the late 1940s, long spell of touring with own group in the 1950s, then residencies in Philadelphia. Led at the Village Gate, New York (1962), Purple Manor (1963), etc., then inactive through illness, returned to regular playing at Copra Lounge, New York, in late 1966. Toured France in 1968 and 1970. Has played on many free-lance recording dates. Own trio in New York (1971). With Earl Hines (1972), led own group during the 1970s, also starred at many jazz festivals. Brief spell of inactivity through illness (1980) then resumed touring schedule.

GUARENTE, 'Frank' Francesco Saverio
trumpet

Born: Montemilleto, Southern Italy, 5th October 1893
Died: U.S.A., 21st July 1942

Began on trumpet during childhood. Emigrated to the U.S.A. in 1910 to join his brother in Allentown, Pennsylvania; played with local bands, then moved to New Orleans in 1914. Worked in a bank for a while, then became professional musician—swapped lessons with King Oliver. Played residencies at Kolb Restaurant, Tom Anderson's, Triangle Theatre Orchestra, and worked with the Mars Brass Band. Left New Orleans (c. 1916), did solo act in Texas, then played with Alabama Five prior to serving in the U.S. Army during World War I. Returned to Texas (c. 1919), then played with Charlie Kerr's Band in Philadelphia. Joined Paul Specht in 1921 and directed the orchestra's small group The Georgians. Visited Europe in 1922, then rejoined Specht until May 1924 (including residency in London—June-August 1923). Visited Europe in May 1924, from September 1924 led The New Georgians in Europe until joining pianist Carroll Gibbon's Savoy Orpheans in London (January 1927). Played with various leaders in London, then returned to U.S.A. in 1928 and rejoined Paul Specht for two years. Did studio work throughout the 1930s; worked with Victor Young's Orchestra, the Dorsey Brothers, Harry Salter's Orchestra, etc., etc. Illness forced retirement from playing in the early 1940s.

GUARNIERI, 'Johnny' John Albert
piano/composer

Born: New York City, 23rd March 1917

Brother of bassist Leo; their father was a violinist and violin maker. At 10 began taking music lessons from his father, later studied for a year at City College in New York. Gigged with local bands from 1935, with George Hall's Band (1937-8), also played two spells with Mike Riley's Band. With Benny Goodman (December 1939 to July 1940), then Artie Shaw until February 1941—took part in Gramercy Five recordings on harpsichord. Rejoined Benny Goodman until August 1941, then rejoined Artie Shaw. With Jimmy Dorsey (February 1942 until March 1943), then joined Raymond Scott at C.B.S. (doubled at The Onyx Club, in Cozy Cole Trio during 1943). Prolific free-lance recordings during the 1940s; continued with studio work in the 1940s and 1950s, with C.B.S. W.M.C.A., and N.B.C., also led own group on television shows. Moved to California in 1963, long residency at Hollywood Plaza Hotel until summer of 1966, then worked at Charter House Hotel, Anaheim. Has many compositions to his credit. Continued to work regularly throughout the 1970s and early 1980s, toured Europe in 1983.

GUY, Fred
guitar/banjo

Born: Burkesville, Georgia, 23rd May 1897
Died: Chicago, Illinois, 22nd November 1971

Raised in New York City, first professional work with Joseph C. Smith Orchestra, then led own band at The Oriental, New York, before joining Duke Ellington (spring 1925) on banjo, switched to guitar c. 1934. Other than brief absences, remained with Duke Ellington until January 1949. Left full-time music and remained in Chicago, which had been his home city for many years. Managed a local ballroom for over 20 years. After a long illness he took his own life.

H

HACKETT, 'Bobby' Robert Leo
cornet/guitar

Born: Providence, Rhode Island, 31st January 1915
Died: Chatham, Massachusetts, 7th June 1976

One of nine children, his father was a railroad blacksmith. Played guitar, violin, and occasionally cornet whilst still at school. Left school at 14 to play in a local Chinese restaurant with Benny Resh's Sextet (on guitar), stayed for three months, then played banjo in Charlie Culverwell's Big Band at the Rhodes Ballroom. On guitar and violin with Billy Lossez's Band at the Hotel Biltmore, Providence, then with Herb Marsh Band at Onondaga Hotel, Syracuse. During summer of 1933 played guitar and violin in Payson Re's Band in Falmouth, Massachusetts, then in trio (with Pee Wee Russell and Teddy Roy) at The Crescent Club, Boston—mainly on cornet. Played cornet with Teddy Roy's Band during summer residency at Cape Cod (1934), later that year rejoined Billy Lossez's Band in Providence. Early in 1936 joined Herb Marsh's Septet at the Theatrical Club, Boston (on guitar and cornet), from May 1936 led own band at the same venue and specialised on cornet. Moved to New York, sat in with Joe Marsala in March 1937, then gigged with Lester and Howard Lanin, Meyer Davis, etc., before joining Marsala at the Hickory House on 10th October 1937 (on guitar, doubling cornet). Briefly with Red McKenzie, then led own band at Nick's, New York (1938), also guested at Benny Goodman's Carnegie Hall Concert (16th January 1938). Continued to work at Nick's, then led own big band at Famous Door and on tour (1939), disbanded and joined Horace Heidt in September 1939. Prolific free-lance recordings from 1937 including sessions organised by jazz critic Leonard Feather, was also featured in original radio production of 'Young Man with a Horn'. Remained with Horace Heidt until June 1940, went to West Coast to play soundtrack for Fred Astaire film 'Second Chorus', led band at Nick's from September 1940, brief return to Horace Heidt (November 1940), then led own 10-piece band in Boston. With Glenn Miller (on guitar, doubling cornet) from July 1941 until September 1942, then staff musician at N.B.C. until November 1943. Toured with the Katherine Dunham Revue, then rejoined Joe Marsala at Hickory House on 29th August 1944. With Glen Gray and the Casa Loma Band from 2nd October 1944 until 24th September 1946 (except for brief absences), then from 30th September became staff musician at A.B.C. Did studio work for several years, but also played regularly at Nick's, etc., and led own sextet in Boston, Philadelphia, etc., during the early 1950s. On 24th November 1956 began leading own band at the Henry Hudson Hotel, New York, continued at the Henry Hudson during 1957, also led the band for brief tours including Canada (summer 1957). Returned to studio work in the late 1950s, continued leading own quartet. With Benny Goodman from October 1962 until July 1963, also briefly fronted Ray McKinley's Band in summer of 1964 during that leader's short illness. In spring of 1965 began working with vocalist Tony Bennett, visited Europe with Bennett in 1965 and 1966. Led own sextet at Riverboat, New York (summer 1967). Led own quintet (1969-70), guested at jazz festivals (1970-1), residency in Hyannis (1970-1). Toured Japan with George Wein (1971). Continued to work regularly until shortly before his death. His son Ernie is a drummer.

HAGGART, 'Bob' Robert Sherwood
string bass/composer/arranger

Born: New York City, 13th March 1914

Spent childhood in Douglaston, Long Island, began playing banjo and guitar and took lessons from George Van Epps, also played trumpet and piano in school band in Salisbury, Connecticut, then switched to string bass whilst at high school. Played with Bert Brown and Bob Sperling, then became founder-member of the Bob Crosby Band (1935). Arranged and part-composed several of the band's big successes and was featured with Ray Bauduc on 'Big Noise from Winnetka', remained with the band until 1942, then worked as a studio musician in New York. For the past 28 years has continued to work in radio, television, and recording orchestras, and has enjoyed great success as an arranger. During the 1950s organised (with Yank Lawson) a regular series of small band recordings and also arranged many of the tunes for Louis Armstrong's four-volume L.P. recreation set made in 1956-7. During the late 1960s played frequently in bands organised by Bob Crosby, from 1968 worked with The World's Greatest Jazz Band. His son Bob Jr. plays drums. Continued to co-lead The World's Greatest Jazz Band during the 1970s. Played Nice Festival with Bob Crosby, 1981, later that year did solo tour of Europe. Toured

Europe co-leading Lawson-Haggart Band in 1982. Played regularly during the early 1980s, including leading own band at Rainbow Room, New York (1984).

HALL, Adelaide
vocals
Born: Brooklyn, New York, 20th October c. 1904

Father was a music teacher at Pratt Institute, after his death in the early 1920s Adelaide began her stage career. Was featured in 'Shuffle Along', then sailed to Europe in May 1925 with the 'Chocolate Kiddies' revue. Returned to New York and appeared in 'Desires of 1927', then starred in the 'Blackbirds' and visited Europe with this show. Recorded with Duke Ellington in October 1927. During the early 1930s did extensive touring in the U.S.A., regularly using jazz musicians as accompanists (Art Tatum, Joe Turner, Bernard Addison, etc.), also revisited Europe. Starred in 'Brown Bodies on Broadway', 'Cotton Club Revue', etc., returned to Europe in 1936, worked in France with Willie Lewis, Ray Ventura, etc. Moved to London to star in 'The Sun Never Sets' and had own radio series (accompanied by Joe Loss and his Orchestra), c. 1938. Has made her home in England ever since, has continued to work regularly, including world-wide touring. Recorded in London in February 1970. Toured regularly during the 1970s and early 1980s, including engagements in the U.S.A.

HALL, 'Al' Alfred Wesley
string bass
Born: Jacksonville, Florida, 18th March 1915

Attended school in Philadelphia. Began on cello at the age of eight, played in local orchestras, then switched to brass bass until specialising on string bass from 1932. Played with local bands in Philadelphia (1933-5), then worked with Billy Hicks' Sizzling Six in New York (1936-7). With Campbell 'Skeets' Tolbert until joining Teddy Wilson Big Band in April 1939, worked with Teddy Wilson's Sextet (1940 to May 1941). With pianist Ellis Larkins' Trio (1942-3), also worked in drummer Kenny Clarke's Band (early 1943). Staff musician at C.B.S. (1943-4), then worked for several years in Broadway theatre orchestras, continued to play club gigs including brief spell at Eddie Condon's Club early in 1947. Toured with Errol Garner, also worked briefly for Count Basie in 1952. Ran own Wax record company during the late 1940s. Throughout the 1950s and 1960s has continued to play for Broadway shows. Has studied television production and is active as video tape editor. Appeared with Eubie Blake at Newport Jazz Festival in 1960, also worked with Phil Moore (1965), Benny Goodman (1966) including dates in Belgium. Prolific free-lance recording career, also appeared in the film 'The Night They Raided Minsky's' (1967). In late 1969 played in the Hazel Scott Trio. With Tiny Grimes' Trio (1971). Extensive free-lancing during the 1970s, also toured Europe. With Alberta Hunter (1978).

HALL, Edmond
clarinet/baritone sax
Born: Cadiz Street, New Orleans, Louisiana, 15th May 1901
Died: Boston, Massachusetts, 11th February 1967

Brother of Herbert Hall, two other brothers, Robert and Clarence, also became musicians; their father, Edward, was a regular member of the Onward Brass Band. Edmond started on guitar, did local gigs, but after two years switched to clarinet. First worked (with Lee Collins) in Bud Roussell's Band (1919), then (with Lee) joined Jack Carey's Band in 1920. From 1921-3 worked in Buddie Petit's Band including tours to Houston and Galveston—whilst in Galveston bought his first alto sax. Left New Orleans, in band led by trumpeter Mack Thomas, played in Pensacola, Florida, then joined pianist Eagle Eye Shields' eight-piece band in Jacksonville (1924), after two years joined Alonzo Ross and his Deluxe Syncopators in Miami (featured on soprano sax). With this band made first recordings (August 1927) and first trip to New York (March 1928). After two weeks' work at the Rosemont Ballroom the Ross unit disbanded, Edmond and Cootie Williams joined drummer Arthur 'Happy' Ford's Band at Happyland, New York. In July 1929 Edmond went to Atlantic City to join Billy Fowler, returned to New York two months later and began working with Charlie Skeets at the Venetian Gardens, New York. By the end of 1929 Claude Hopkins had been appointed leader and the renamed band opened at the Savoy Ballroom in January 1930. Except for brief absences was with Claude Hopkins until 1935 (clarinet and baritone sax). With Lucky Millinder in 1936, with Billy Hicks' Sizzling Six for most of 1937, brief return to Millinder in late 1937. With Zutty Singleton Trio from early 1939, then joined Joe Sullivan in October 1939. With Henry 'Red' Allen Sextet for a year from late 1940, then with Teddy Wilson Small Band from late 1941 until 1944. (Declined offer to join Duke Ellington in June 1942.) Formed own sextet for long residencies at both Cafe Society clubs (September 1944 until autumn 1946), then led mainly in Boston until 1950. After a three-week spell in California returned to New York to work at Eddie Condon's Club from July 1950 until joining Louis Armstrong All Stars from September 1955 until July 1958. In autumn 1959 moved to Ghana and made plans to settle there, but returned to New York in December 1959. During the 1960s made several solo tours of Europe: Czechoslovakia, Germany, Great Britain, etc., also worked again at Eddie Condon's and played with Jimmy McPartland's Band (summer 1964). Toured Europe again in 1966, played at Carnegie Hall Jazz Concert in January 1967, was later featured at the Boston Globe Jazz Festival.

HALL, 'Herb' Herbert L.
clarinet/saxes

Born: Reserve, Louisiana, 28th March 1907

Began on banjo and, during 1923-5, worked regularly in Louisiana with Niles Jazz Band, switched to alto sax and clarinet whilst with trumpeter Augustin Victor's Band (1926-7). Briefly with Professor Holmes' Band in early 1928, then worked with Sidney Desvigne until joining Don Albert in late 1929. Remained with Don Albert until late 1937, then worked in Pittsburgh with trumpeter Jimmy Watkins (late 1937-8) and in Cleveland and Pittsburgh with pianiste Shudina Walker and her Band. Rejoined Don Albert from December 1938 until early 1940, remained in San Antonio after that band's temporary break up and worked mainly with drummer Fats Martin's Quartet until autumn 1945. Moved to Philadelphia and joined Herman Autrey's Band until 1947. With Cass Carr's Band briefly, then with trumpeter Harvey Davis' Band at Club Cinderella, New York, until 1954. Worked with Doc Cheatham in Boston (1955), toured Europe with Sam Price's Bluesicians (late 1955 to early 1956). Played at Ryan's in New York, then spent several years working mainly at Eddie Condon's Club. With Wild Bill Davison's Jazz Giants (1968-9), in late 1969 worked in The Jazz Family, again with Wild Bill Davison (spring 1970). With Don Ewell, Bob Greene, Red Balaban, etc., then moved to Texas. Extensive touring during early 1980s, including several tours of Europe.

HALL, 'Ram' Minor
drums

Born: Sellers, Louisiana, 2nd March 1897
Died: California, 23rd October 1959

Younger brother of Tubby Hall, related to the Humphrey family. Moved with family into New Orleans during the early 1900s. Studied at New Orleans University until 1914, did first paid gigs, 'depping' for Henry Martin in Kid Ory's Band, later worked regularly with bassist Oke Gaspard and the Superior Band. Moved with family to Chicago, replaced Tubby in Lawrence Duhé's Band at the De Luxe Cafe, then served in U.S. Army (1918-19). Moved from Chicago to play in San Francisco with King Oliver's Band, left after two months (replaced by Baby Dodds), returned to play in Chicago with Jimmie Noone's Band. Moved to California permanently and played with Mutt Carey's Jeffersonians from 1927 until 1932 (mainly in Culver City). Played regularly with Winslow Allen Band during the 1930s, spent six months in the U.S. Army from September 1942, was given honourable discharge and began working in the Douglas Aircraft factory. Returned to regular playing and joined Kid Ory's Band (1945), played regularly with Ory until being taken ill on European tour (1956). Suffered from cancer during the last years of his life, but played occasionally with the New Orleans Creole Jazz Band early in 1959 before entering Sautell Hospital, Los Angeles.

HALL, 'Skip' Archie
piano/organ/arranger

Born: Portsmouth, Virginia, 27th September 1909
Died: Ottawa, Canada, November 1980

Brother-in-law of Sy Oliver. Music lessons from his father, began playing piano and organ at the age of eight, subsequently studied music at the Martin-Smith College in New York. Gigged in New York, then led own band in Cleveland during the 1930s. Specialised in arranging during the early 1940s, then served in U.S. Army. Led own service band in

Europe. After demobilisation did long spell of free-lance session work and led own recording band, with Buddy Tate in the 1950s. Continued to play professionally during the 1960s, regularly with George James (1963), occasionally with Buddy Tate, toured Europe with Buddy Tate's Band in late 1968.

HALL, 'Tubby' Alfred — *Born: Sellers, Louisiana, 12th October 1895*
drums — *Died: Chicago, Illinois, 13th May 1946*

Elder brother of Minor Hall. Family moved to New Orleans in early 1900s. Drums from early teens, played with various marching bands, then worked regularly with the Crescent Orchestra from 1914, also worked with the Eagle Band and Silver Leaf. Moved to Chicago in March 1917, played in Sugar Johnny Smith's Band from May 1917. Served in U.S. Army for two years, then played in Chicago for various bandleaders including: King Oliver, Jimmie Noone, Tiny Parham, Clarence Black, Carroll Dickerson, Louis Armstrong-Earl Hines, Boyd Atkins. During the 1930s did several stints with Johnny Dodds and Jimmie Noone. Continued to play regularly until shortly before his death. Led own band at Ball of Fire in 1945.

HAMILTON, 'Bugs' John — *Born: St. Louis, Missouri, 8th March 1911*
trumpet — *Died: St. Louis, Missouri, 15th August 1947*

Played in New York in band led by trombonist Billy Kato (1930-1), also played briefly with Chick Webb's Band. With Kaiser Marshall's Band at the Ubangi Club, New York (1935), Bobby Neal (late 1935), with Fats Waller from 1938 until 1942, played in Eddie South's Band in summer of 1943. Died of tuberculosis.

HAMILTON, 'Jimmy' James — *Born: Dillon, South Carolina, 25th May 1917*
clarinet/tenor sax/arranger

Widower of pianiste Vivian Hamilton (née Jones) who recorded under the name of Vivian Smith. Raised in Philadelphia, started on baritone horn at seven, later studied piano, trumpet, and trombone. Worked on trombone and trumpet with several bandleaders in Philadelphia including Frank Fairfax and Lonnie Slappy, then concentrated on sax and clarinet. Brief spells with Lucky Millinder and Jimmy Mundy, then with Teddy Wilson from 1940 until 1942. Joined Eddie Heywood, then worked in Yank Porter's Band at Hotel St. George, New York, before joining Duke Ellington in May 1943, remained with Duke until summer of 1968. Led own group in U.S., then moved to St. Croix, Virgin Islands. Continued to play and teach throughout the 1970s. Worked with Mercer Ellington in the U.S.A. during the early 1980s, also toured Europe as a soloist.

HAMPTON, Lionel — *Born: Louisville, Kentucky, 12th April 1909*
vibes/drums/piano/vocals

His father worked as an entertainer before World War I. Lionel was raised by his mother in Birmingham, they then moved on to Chicago (c. 1916). Attended schools in Wisconsin and Chicago, began playing drums in Major N. Clark Smith's *Chicago Defender* Newsboys' Band. Received xylophone tuition from Jimmy Bertrand and some drum tuition from Snags Jones. Worked with various Chicago bands, including Detroit Shannon. After being stranded in Hastings, Nebraska, moved to California (c. 1927), worked with The Spikes' Brothers, then joined Paul Howard's Quality Serenaders—made record debut with Howard in 1929. Began long residency as house musician at Sebastian's Cotton Club, Culver City, worked there first with trumpeter Vernon Elkins, then long spell with Les Hite. Recorded on drums and vibes with Louis Armstrong (1930). Took part in many films with Les Hite's Band, also played in Nat Shilkret's Studio Orchestra. During this period studied music at the University of Southern California. Worked with Charlie Echols (late 1934), then formed own band for residencies in Oakland and Los Angeles, own band appeared in the Columbia film 'Depths Below', Hamp also appeared as the masked drummer with Louis Armstrong in the film 'Pennies From Heaven'. Led own big band at the Paradise Cafe, Hollywood (1936), then began appearing as guest star with Benny Goodman's Quartet. Worked for Goodman from November 1936 until July 1940, was featured in Goodman's small groups, also occasionally played drums with the big band. Regularly led own recording bands from 1937. Moved back to California in August 1940 to form own big band which made its official debut in Los Angeles on the 6th November 1940. From then until the present time Hamp has continued to lead his own highly successful touring band. From 1953 has undertaken many overseas tours, visiting Europe, Japan, Australia, Africa, the Middle East, etc., he also appeared as a soloist at London's Royal Festival Hall in October 1957. His only absence from regular playing was from October-December 1955, when he was recovering from injuries sustained in a band-bus crash. In October 1969 his band was featured at London's Jazz Expo. During the 1930s Hamp played for, and appeared in, many films; he was later featured in 'The Benny Goodman Story'. Very active during the 1970s mostly leading own small groups occasionally with own big band. Featured at President Jimmy Carter's White House Jazz Party (June 1978). Extensive overseas touring during early 1980s including visits to Europe and Japan.

HANDY, 'Captain' John
alto sax/clarinet

Born: Pass Christian, Mississippi, 24th June 1900
Died: 12th January 1971

Tried various instruments before becoming drummer in family band led by his violinist father—John's two brothers, Sylvester (bass) and Julius (guitar) also played in the band. Switched from drums to clarinet during his teens, moved to New Orleans c. 1918 and began working with band led by Tom 'Kid' Albert, worked on and off with Albert for several years including tour of Texas. Gigged in New Orleans with various leaders: Amos Riley, Chris Kelly, Kid Rena, John Casimir, etc. Led own band at The Entertainers' Club during the mid-1920s, also worked for two years in Baton Rouge with Tut Johnson's Band and toured with Kid Howard. Specialised on alto sax from the late 1920s. During the early 1930s toured Texas with own Louisiana Shakers, returned to New Orleans and led own band for long residency at the La Vida Dance Hall. During the 1960s continued to work regularly on alto sax; played on clarinet for a while with Kid Sheik's Band in 1961. Toured Europe as a soloist in 1966 and 1968, also visited Japan with Kid Sheik in 1967. Made several L.P.s during the 1960s. Featured at Newport Jazz Festival (July 1970). Died at his home in Pass Christian.

HANDY, William Christopher
composer/cornet/vocals

Born: Florence, Alabama, 16th November 1873
Died: New York City, 28th March 1958

Known as 'The Father of the Blues'. Was originally a cornetist, played for a while with the Bessemer Brass Band, then took a vocal quartet to Chicago for the Exposition of 1893. From 1896 was cornet soloist with Mahara's Minstrels, later became the troupe's musical director, toured on and off with this unit for seven years. During this period did extensive musical studies and also taught at Huntsville Agricultural and Mechanical College. Led own orchestra, mainly in the South, composed 'Memphis Blues' (first published in 1912), subsequently wrote many famous tunes including: 'St. Louis Blues', 'Yellow Dog Blues', 'Beale Street Blues', 'Ole Miss', 'Hesitating Blues', etc., etc. Took own orchestra to New York in 1917 for recordings, following year moved to New York with his partner Harry H. Pace and established a music publishing business. An eye disease caused Handy to go blind in the early 1920s, from then on he was mainly active as a music publisher-composer; however, he did front bands (occasionally playing cornet) on several occasions including brief tour with Jelly Roll Morton's Band through Iowa, Indiana, etc. (c. 1926). During the 1930s he toured with Clarence Davis' Band (1932), following year did theatre work with The Old Timers; led own orchestra (directed by violinist Billy Butler) at The Apollo, New York (1936). A concert commemorating Handy's 65th birthday was held at Carnegie Hall, New York, in 1938. In 1943 he sustained severe injuries when he fell on to the New York subway track, for the rest of his life he was a semi-invalid, but continued to work regularly at his publishing interests. In 1939 he recorded on cornet and vocals with J. C. Higginbotham, Edmond Hall, etc. In 1960 a statue of Handy was unveiled in Memphis, Tennessee. In 1969 a commemorative postage stamp was issued in the U.S.A. The film 'St. Louis Blues', which was loosely based on Handy's life, featured Nat 'King' Cole.

W. C. Handy's autobiography 'Father of the Blues' was first published in 1941.

HARDEE, John
tenor sax

Born: Corsicana, Texas, 20th December 1918

Both parents were musical, an uncle, Ashford Hardee, was a professional trombonist. Played piano at local dances, then saxophone with The Blue Moon Syncopators, Florenz O'Harris and Rick Calhoun. Played in Bishop College Band, then spent six months in Don Albert's Band (1937-38). Returned to college until 1941. Army service in Signal Corps Band, stationed near New York City. After leaving Army worked with Tiny Grimes then led own band. Played club dates in New York before moving to Dallas in 1949 to become a school band director. Led own group in Dallas, residency at Harmony Lounge until late 1950s, at Sky Room in early 1960s. Quit playing until late 1974, resumed, and worked at Nice Festival in France during summer of 1975.

HARDIN, Lil
(see Armstrong, Lillian)

HARDING, 'Buster' Lavere
piano/arranger

Born: Ontario, Canada, 19th March 1917
Died: New York City, 14th November 1965

Raised in Cleveland. Led own band in Cleveland during the early 1930s, then worked in Buffalo with Marion Sear's Band. Led own trio at the Savarin Cafe, Boston (1938). Played second piano and arranged for Teddy Wilson's Big Band (late 1939 to spring 1940), also arranged for Coleman Hawkins' Big Band (late 1939). Led own quartet at Nick's, New York (May 1940). Staff arranger for Cab Calloway (1941-2), then prolific free-lance arranging for: Artie Shaw, Count Basie, Dizzie Gillespie, Benny Goodman, etc., etc. Musical director (and occasionally accompanist) for Billie Holiday (c. 1954). Was seriously ill for the last few years of his life, continued to arrange, and worked occasionally in various small groups including brief spell with Jonah Jones in the 1960s.

HARDWICK, 'Toby' Otto
alto sax/bass sax/baritone sax

Born: Washington, D.C., 31st May 1904
Died: Washington, D.C., 5th August 1970

Started on string bass at the age of 14, worked with Carroll's Columbia Orchestra (c. 1920), then switched to 'C' melody sax. Began gigging with Duke Ellington in and around Washington, also worked for Elmer Snowden at Murray's Casino, Washington (c. 1922). Went to New York with Duke Ellington in 1923 and shared many of that leader's early experiences—including week with Wilbur Sweatman (March 1923) and residencies with Elmer Snowden—occasionally doubled violin and string bass in the mid-1920s, but specialised on alto sax. Worked regularly with Duke Ellington until the spring of 1928. Went to Paris, worked in band led by bassist John Ricks, led own band and played briefly with Noble Sissle and Nekka Shaw's Orchestra before returning to New York. Brief stint with Chick Webb (1929), then led own band at the 'Hot Feet' Club, New York (1930), subsequently led at Small's then worked with Elmer Snowden before rejoining Duke Ellington in spring 1932. Except for brief absences he remained with Duke until May 1946. Subsequently retired from music, worked in hotel management, also ran own farm in Maryland.

HARDY, Emmett Louis
cornet

Born: Gretna, New Orleans, Louisiana, 12th June 1903
Died: New Orleans, Louisiana, 16th June 1925

Both parents were musicians. Began on piano and guitar, then cornet from age of 12. At 14 began playing in Jack 'Papa' Laine's Band, later worked with Norman Brownlee's Orchestra. Left New Orleans in band accompanying variety artiste Bea Palmer. Left this band in Davenport, Iowa, and joined Carlisle Evans' Band on S.S. 'Capitol' for eight months (1919). Returned to New Orleans, led own band, then joined Tony Catalino's Band on S.S. 'Sydney'. Moved to Chicago to augment the New Orleans Rhythm Kings at Friars' Inn, after a dispute with Local A.F. of Musicians' Union he returned to New Orleans.

Played briefly with Norman Brownlee's Orchestra, then inactive for the last year of his life through pulmonary tuberculosis.

HARRINGTON, John David *Born: Denver, Colorado, 23rd May 1910*
clarinet/saxes

Brother of Seaton 'Jew' Harrington (alto sax). First professional work with George Morrison in Denver (1927-8), then joined T. Holder's Band, subsequently became a member of Andy Kirk's Band (1929). With Kirk until 1944 (except for brief absence through jaw injury late 1940), then with Skippy Williams (1945) and Claude Hopkins (1946). Moved back to Denver, where he and Seaton opened their own club, John later worked in a department store in Denver.

HARRIS, Arville S. *Born: St. Louis, Missouri, 1904*
saxes/clarinet *Died: New York, 1954*

Uncle of Le Roy Harris, Jr., brothers were Jimmie Harris (violinist and music teacher), and Le Roy Harris, Sr., who played banjo, guitar and flute. Arville played on riverboats from 1920, also with Hershal Brassfield's Band (c. 1921). With Bill Brown and Brownies (1925-8). Many recordings for Clarence Williams in the late 1920s. Joined Cab Calloway early 1931, with Cab until 1935 (including trip to Europe). With Jack Butler (1935), later worked regularly for LeRoy Smith. With Claude Hopkins (1937 and 1939), with pianist Maurice Rocco (1938). Led own band at Majestic Ballroom, N.Y., for the last ten years of his life. Died of a heart attack.

HARRIS, 'Dicky' Richard *Born: Birmingham, Alabama, 15th November 1918*
trombone

An uncle, William Harris, played trumpet. First teacher was W. W. Handy (a nephew of W. C. Handy). Began working with pianist Frank Hines in Birmingham (1937-39). Joined Erskine Hawkins in 1941, left in 1943 to join Army Air Force Band for two years. With J. C. Heard (1946-48), Joe Thomas (1948), Lucky Millinder (1949-50), then briefly with Buck Clayton and Illinois Jacquet. With Arnett Cobb from 1953-56. Free-lanced from 1958 onwards, since 1970 has specialised in playing for Broadway shows.

HARRIS, Le Roy W. Jr. *Born: St. Louis, Missouri, 12th February 1916*
alto/clarinet/flute/oboe/vocals

Son of Le Roy W. Harris (died 1969). Studied violin from 1921-5 with his uncle Jimmie. Took up sax and clarinet in 1928. Worked with Chick Finney's Band (1929). Moved to Chicago, with Burns Campbell (1930), Ray Nance (1931-6), Eddie Coles (1937), Earl Hines (1937-43). After serving in U.S. Navy Band (1943-4), with Bill Doggett, Bill Martin, Four Tons of Rhythm and Ben Thigpen, again with Earl Hines in the mid-1950s. With Archie Burnside in St. Louis (1957-60), with pianist Eddie Johnson's Trio in St. Louis County (1960-71).

HARRIS, 'Bill' Willard Palmer *Born: Philadelphia, Pennsylvania, 28th October 1916*
trombone *Died: Florida, 21st August 1973*

His half-brother, Bob Harris, was a professional bass player. Bill played piano as a child, then played tenor sax and trumpet before concentrating on trombone. Gigged in Philadelphia during the early 1930s (including some jobs with Charlie Ventura). From the age of 19 did two years in the merchant marine, returned to gig in Philadelphia. Professional musician from 1938. In 1942 played for one week with Gene Krupa, then brief spell with Ray McKinley, returned to do defence-plant work in Philadelphia, left to play for two months with Buddy Williams' Band in Dayton, Ohio. To New York with Bob Chester, then with Benny Goodman from August 1943 until March 1944—including soundtrack work for the film 'Sweet and Lowdown'. Remained in California, played briefly with Charlie Barnet

Louis Armstrong with Carroll Dickerson's Orchestra – 1929. (l. to r.) Fred Robinson, Mancy 'Peck' Carr, Homer Hobson, Jimmy Strong, Pete Briggs, Bernadine Curry, Gene Anderson, Crawford Wethington, Louis Armstrong, Zutty Singleton, Carroll Dickerson

Louis Armstrong. 1937

Louis Armstrong in Zurich – November 1934. Arita Day (vocaliste), Louis Armstrong, Herman Chittison (piano), Peter du Conge, Alcide Castellanos, Castor McCord (saxes)

Teddy Buckner

Lawrence Brown

Neil Reid and Joe Bishop

Wallace Bishop

Pete Brown

Louis Bacon and Johnny Russell

Emmett Berry

Charlie Barnet

Harold Baker and Jimmy Rushing

Count Basie

Sidney Bechet

Peter Bocage

Arthur Briggs

Sharkey Bonano

Joe Bushkin

Georg Brunis

Don Byas

Wingie Carpenter

Billy Butterfield

Bunny Berigan

June Clark

Bill Dillard

Charlie Christian

Wilbur and Sidney De Paris

Sterling Bose

Floyd Casey, Ed Allen

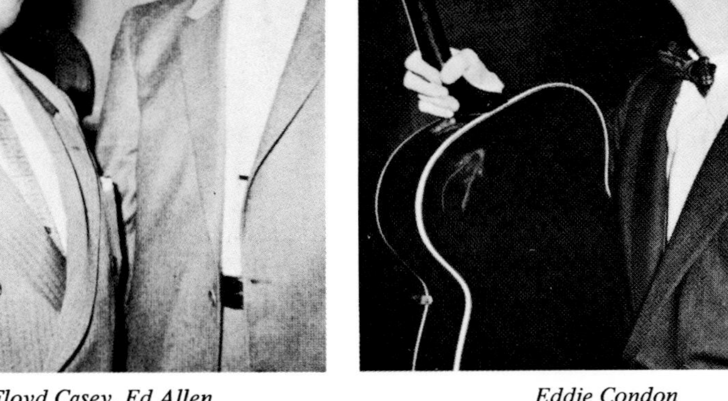

Eddie Condon

Al Cooper's Savoy Sultans – 1937. Grachan Moncur (bass), Alex 'Razz' Mitchell (drums), Cyril Haynes (piano), Pat Jenkins (trumpet), Sam Massenburg (trumpet), Rudy Williams (alto), Ed McNeil (tenor), Al Cooper (alto/clarinet).

(l. to r.) Freddy Jenkins, Sam Nanton, Cootie Williams, Harry White, Arthur Whetsol, Sonny Greer, Duke Ellington, Harry Carney, Fred Guy, Johnny Hodges, Wellman Braud, Barney Bigard

Milt Hinton

Teddy Hill

Bunk Johnson's Band – New York 1946. Bunk Johnson (trumpet), George Lewis (clarinet), Jim Robinson (trombone), Kaiser Marshall (drums), Alcide Pavageau (bass), Don Ewell (piano)

W. C. Handy

Darnell Howard

Earl Hines

Billie Holiday

Woody Herman, Mary Lou Williams, Sidney Bechet

Lucky Millinder

Grachan Moncur

Wingy Manone

Jack McVea

Benny Morton

Herb Morand

Snub Mosley (slide-saxophone)

Paul Mertz

Miff Mole

Al Morgan – 1969

Jelly Roll Morton

Jimmy McPartland, Bud Jacobson, Boyce Brown

Jimmy Thompson and Jelly Roll Morton

and Freddie Slack, then led own small group at Cafe Society Downtown, New York. Brief return to Bob Chester, then in August 1944 joined Woody Herman. Remained with Woody until 1946. Led own quartet at Three Deuces, New York (May 1947), then joined Charlie Ventura. Returned to Woody Herman (1948-50). From 1950 began regular touring with J.A.T.P. shows, also led own small groups and worked Oscar Pettiford (1952) and with Sauter-Finegan Orchestra (1953). Rejoined Woody Herman for two years from early 1956, returned to Florida and co-led groups with Flip Phillips, toured Europe with Woody in early 1959. With Benny Goodman from August until November 1959 (including European tour), then worked in Florida with Red Norvo. Continued to lead own small groups in Florida, then worked regularly with Charlie Teagarden's Band from spring of 1962 until 1964. With Norvo again from 1965 until summer of 1966, then joined house band at the Tropicana, Miami, also continued to do regular television work in Florida.

HARRIS, Joe
trombone/vocals

Born: Sedalia, Missouri, 1908
Died: Fresno, California, summer 1952

Took up trombone at 16, played with local bands in Oklahoma, then moved to Seminole, Texas (where he first met Jack Teagarden—1927). Played for a while in Canada, then temporarily gave up full-time music, but continued to gig in Sedalia, Missouri. Played in riverboat band on S.S. 'Idlewild', then joined Joe Haymes' Band in Springfield, Missouri, in late 1932 joined Frankie Trumbauer (residency in Chicago, then tour of Texas). Left to take Jack Teagarden's place in Ben Pollack's Band (then at Chez Paree, Chicago—May 1933). Free-lanced in New York, then became member of Bob Crosby's first band (1935), recorded with Benny Goodman (April 1935), then joined Benny Goodman from August 1935 until May 1936. Left to join M.G.M. studio staff in Hollywood, played for various leaders including George Stoll and Victor Young until February 1937, when he suffered a fractured skull in a car accident. Out of music until joining big band led by sax-arranger Lyle 'Spud' Murphy (February 1938). Studio work and a spell in Carl Hoff's Orchestra, then rejoined Ben Pollack from March until July 1940. In 1942 played for seven months in Pee Wee Erwin's Band, then three months with Bob Chester before returning to studio work. Rejoined Benny Goodman from spring 1943 until August 1943, then played in Eddie Miller's Big Band. Returned to studio work, during the late 1940s was gigging in California with various bands including Ted Jefferson's Mel-o-tones. He lost his life in a car smash.

HARRIS, Wynonie
vocals/composer

Born: Omaha, Nebraska. c. 1910
Died: Oakland, California, 14th June 1969

Started professional life as a buck-and-wing dancer, doubling on drums, worked under various names: 'Peppermint Cane', 'Mississippi Mockingbird', etc. Settled in Los Angeles during the early 1940s, worked with Lucky Millinder and Lionel Hampton. During the mid-1940s began making a series of highly successful rhythm-and-blues singles which gained him international fame. Despite this he worked mostly in California, occasionally visiting the East Coast, on his last tour, in 1967, he appeared at the Apollo in Harlem.

HARRISON, 'Jimmy' James Henry
trombone/vocals

Born: Louisville, Kentucky, 17th October 1900
Died: New York City, 23rd July 1931

Family moved to Detroit in 1906. Jimmy took up trombone at 15—mainly self-taught—worked locally, then moved with his father to Toledo, Ohio. Helped to run family restaurant, also played semi-professional baseball. Left home to play and sing in a touring minstrel show. In 1919 settled temporarily in Atlantic City: led trio at Philadelphia House Saloon, also played with Charlie Johnson at same venue and with Sam Wooding at Scott's Hotel. Left Wooding to join Hank Duncan's Kentucky Jazz Band at Hotel Ellwood in Detroit, also played with Roland Smith's Band in Detroit. Moved back to Toledo, did local work; first played with June Clark and James P. Johnson at Herman's Club, Toledo. From 1921-3 played in various touring shows, spell with Howard Jordan's Band, then to New York with Fess Williams. Played with pianist Charlie Smith's Band at Ed Small's

Cabaret Club, continued when June Clark was appointed leader (1924). Worked with June Clark at various venues including Palace Gardens and Tango Gardens, New York. During the years 1925 and 1926 Jimmy worked with Billy Fowler's Orchestra, briefly with Henri Saparo, Duke Ellington, and June Clark, then with Elmer Snowden at The Nest and Balconnades Ballroom. With Fletcher Henderson from early 1927, left to rejoin Charlie Johnson in 1928, then returned to Fletcher Henderson. Whilst on tour with Henderson during summer of 1930 taken ill in Harrisburg, Pennsylvania, returned to Henderson (1931), joined Chick Webb (spring 1931 to summer 1931). Succumbed to a stomach ailment in the Wiley Private Sanitorium, New York.

HART, Clyde
piano/arranger

Born: Baltimore, Maryland, 1910
Died: New York City, 19th March 1945

First professional work with Gene Coy's Band, then two years as pianist-arranger with Jap Allen's Band (1930 to April 1931). With Blanche Calloway until 1935, briefly with McKinney's Cotton Pickers (1935). Settled in New York (1936), led own quartet at the Brittwood Club, arranged for Andy Kirk, also played solo piano in various clubs and did recordings with Henry Allen, Billie Holiday, etc., etc. Joined Stuff Smith late 1936 until 1938, then with Roy Eldridge, Lester Young, Frankie Newton, before joining John Kirby in late 1942. Worked briefly with Wilbur de Paris and Walter 'Foots' Thomas, then several months in Tiny Grimes' Band (summer 1944). Led own band at the Tondelayo Club, New York, in autumn of 1944. With Don Byas until early 1945, then ill health curtailed regular playing, he then did arranging for Paul Baron's C.B.S. Orchestra. Died of tuberculosis.

HARTWELL, 'Jimmy' James
clarinet/alto sax/string bass

Born: c. 1900
Deceased

Mother was an organist. Played in Chicago with the Ten Foot Band and with Russ Wilkins' Melody Boys (c. 1922), then became a founder-member of The Wolverines. Remained with The Wolverines until spring of 1925, left them in Miami and began working locally on alto sax and clarinet. In the late 1920s led own band in Florida and also played in Joe Strum's Miami Beach Band. He suffered from asthma and during the 1930s switched to string bass. Played for several years at the Manhattan Hotel, Sarasota, Florida, later joined Carl Springer's Band at The Tropical, Sarasota (from 1942). No details available on date and place of his death.

HAUGHTON, Chauncey
clarinet/saxes/piano

Born: Chestertown, Maryland, 26th February 1909

Brother of John E. 'Shorty' Haughton (trombone) (1904-78) and of Clifton Haughton (trumpet), their father was also a musician. Began on piano at eight, took up clarinet whilst at high school in Baltimore. Later played clarinet and sax in the Morgan College Band. First professional work in 1927 with Ike Dixon's Band, then worked with Elmer Calloway (brother of Cab) and the White Brothers' Band, came to New York (1932) with Gene Kennedy's Band. Worked with Blanche Calloway until 1935, then with Claude Hopkins, Noble Sissle, and Fletcher Henderson before joining Chick Webb. Left Chick in November 1937 to join Cab Calloway. Left Cab in January 1940 to join band led by Ella Fitzgerald, remained with Ella until 1942. With Duke Ellington from summer of 1942 until being called up on 10th April 1943. After demobilisation did long U.S.O. tour (winter 1945 to summer 1946) with vocaliste Frances Brock, then to Europe in Don Redman's Band (September 1946). After that unit disbanded in Europe Chauncey played briefly in Scandinavia during 1947, then returned to the U.S.A. Brief return to Cab Calloway in the late 1940s, then left full-time music.

HAWKINS, Coleman Randolph
tenor sax

Born: St. Joseph, Missouri, 21st November c. 1901
Died: New York City, 19th May 1969

Junior School in St. Joseph and in Kansas City, Missouri, then studied music at Washburn College, Topeka, Kansas, and in Chicago. Originally played piano and cello; tenor saxophone from the age of nine. Gigged with school bands at 11, at 16 was playing professionally in and around Kansas City. Was playing in a 12th Street theatre orchestra in Kansas City, Missouri, when signed by Mamie Smith to join her Jazz Hounds (summer of 1921). Did extensive touring with Mamie Smith until early in 1923, left in New York, gigged with various bands and worked at The Garden of Joy with pianist Ginger Jones, also did free-lance recordings with Fletcher Henderson. Regular member of Fletcher Henderson's Orchestra from 1924 until early 1934—occasionally doubled on bass sax and very occasionally soloed on clarinet. Left Fletcher Henderson to tour Europe as a soloist. Arrived in England on 29th March 1934, remained in Europe until July 1939. During this period worked in Britain, France, Holland, Switzerland, Belgium, Scandinavia, etc. Various accompaniments included: Jack Hylton's Orchestra, Mrs. Jack Hylton's Orchestra, The Ramblers, Jean Omer's Orchestra, The Berries, Freddy Johnson, etc. Recorded in Europe with The Ramblers (Holland), The Berries, led by Berry Perritz (Switzerland), Jack Hylton (England), Freddy Johnson (Holland), Michel Warlop (France), Benny Carter, Django Reinhardt, etc., also appeared in the British film short 'In Town To-night'. Toured Britain from April 1939, returned to New York in July 1939. Led own band at Kelly's Stables, New York. Formed own big band for debut at the Arcadia Ballroom, New York (November 1939). Led big band at the Golden Gate Ballroom, New York, The Apollo Theatre, Savoy Ballroom, etc., until February 1941, then reverted to small band. Toured with own mixed band in 1943. Led own sextet in California for most of 1945, the sextet appeared in the film 'The Crimson Canary'. In 1946 took part in first national 'Jazz at the Philharmonic' tour. Returned to Europe in May 1948 for appearances at Paris Jazz Festival, again visited Europe in late 1949-50. During the 1950s did extensive touring with Norman Granz's J.A.T.P. including several trips to Europe. Played solo guest-star appearances at Cafe Society, Terrassi's, etc., also co-led successful quintet with Roy Eldridge. Toured American Service Bases in Europe with Illinois Jacquet's Band (autumn 1954). Prolific free-lance recordings; was featured at all major jazz festivals in U.S.A., also appeared in the 'Seven Ages of Jazz' presentations in Canada. During the 1960s was also featured at The Metropole, New York, and the Village Gate, etc. In 1962 recorded with Duke Ellington. During the last years of his life made many appearances at the Village Vanguard, New York, toured Britain as a soloist in November 1967. Continued to work regularly until a few weeks before his death, appeared with Roy Eldridge on Chicago television show early in 1969.

HAWKINS, Erskine Ramsay — *Born: Birmingham, Alabama, 26th July 1914*
trumpet/composer

Father was killed in action during World War I. Started playing drums at the age of seven, switched to trombone, then specialised on trumpet from the age of 13. Spent several years at the State Teachers' College in Montgomery, Alabama, and was appointed leader of the 'Bama State Collegians. The band originally came to New York in 1934, fronted by J. B. Sims, but subsequently worked under Erskine Hawkins' name. Throughout the 1940s and 1950s the band retained its big following, particularly at the Savoy Ballroom, N.Y. In the 1960s occasionally led big band for specific bookings (and May 1971 recording), but worked mainly with own quartet, long residency at Concord Hotel, N.Y. (1971). In 1947 received Hon. Doctorate of Music from Alabama State College. Continued to lead own band during the 1970s, made guest appearance of Nice Jazz Festival in 1979.

HAYES, 'Clancy' Clarence Leonard — *Born: Caney, nr. Parsons, Kansas, 14th November 1908*
banjo/vocals/composer — *Died: San Francisco, California, 13th March 1972*

Was originally a drummer, later played guitar then switched to banjo. Moved to San Francisco in 1926, and soon began appearing on local radio, and working with California bands. Worked regularly with Lu Watters from 1938 through until Watters disbanded in 1950, during the early 1940s sometimes played drums with Watters. During the 1950s spent some years with Bob Scobey's Band, before playing long residency at Turk Murphy's Earthquake McGoon's Club as vocalist-banjoist. Guested with many bands, including The World's Greatest Jazz Band during last years of his life, also featured at many jazz festivals, including Pasadena, Manassas and Washington, D.C. Died of cancer.

H

HAYES, **Edgar Junius**
piano/arranger

Born: Lexington, Kentucky, 23rd May 1904
Died: Riverside, California, 28th June 1979

Gained Bachelor of Music degree at Wilberforce. At 18 toured the South with Fess Williams, later led own Blue Grass Buddies in Ohio (1924), then worked with Lois B. Deppe's Orchestra (1925). In late 1925 led own band at Ritz Cafe, Cleveland, Ohio, then played in Madison's Commodore Orchestra in Buffalo (1926). In spring of 1927 led own Eight Black Pirates for the touring show 'Rarin to Go'; from August 1927 until 1930 led own Symphonic Harmonists at Alhambra, New York, etc. Played and arranged for the Mills Blue Rhythm Band from 1931, remained to work under?'Baron Lee' (Jimmy Ferguson) and Lucky Millinder until 1936. In 1937 formed own big band (with several ex-members of Lucky Millinder's Band), continued to lead until 1941 including tour of Belgium and Scandinavia in March and April 1938. Moved to California in summer of 1942 and began long residency at Somerset House, Riverside, until early 1946, led own quartet The Stardusters in California until the early 1950s. From 1954 until 1959 played solo residency at Diamond's Lounge in San Bernardino; in the 1960s played in Tustin and Newport Beach. Residency in Riverside (1970).

HAYMAN, **'Joe' Joseph**
alto sax/clarinet/baritone

Born: Little Rock, Arkansas, 7th June 1903
Died: New York, November 1981

Played in bands led by Alex Hill and Eugene Crook during the early 1920s. Sailed to Europe in September 1925 as a member of Claude Hopkins' Band accompanying Josephine Baker Revue, subsequently toured Europe with Hopkins before returning to New York in 1926. With Claude Hopkins (1926), Wilbur de Paris (1927-8), with Eugene Kennedy in New York (early 1929), then joined the 'Blackbirds' revue and returned to Europe in May 1929, returned to U.S.A. in 1931. Worked in Europe with Willie Lewis from 1934 until December 1938, then with Bill Coleman, etc., played in Egypt with the Harlem Rhythm Makers. Returned to U.S.A. in early 1940, worked with Louis Armstrong's Big Band, and with Claude Hopkins then left full-time music and became a pharmacist at a New York hospital.

HAYMER, **'Herbie' Herbert**
tenor sax/clarinet

Born: Jersey City, 24th July 1915
Died: Santa Monica, California, 11th April 1949

Began on alto sax at the age of 15. Changed to tenor sax five years later and worked with Carl Sears-Johnny Watson Band at Yoeng's Chinese Restaurant in New York. Briefly with Rudy Vallee and Charlie Barnet, then with Red Norvo from spring 1936 until joining Jimmy Dorsey in February 1938. Left in March 1941, worked with Woody Herman for almost a year, then with Kay Kyser until summer of 1943, then brief spell with Benny Goodman. Joined Dave Hudkin's Band in Los Angeles in autumn of 1943—continued to work occasionally with that band for several years. Brief spell in U.S. Navy in 1944, after release was mainly active as a studio musician in Hollywood, but also worked with Red Nichols (1945), Benny Goodman (1947), etc. Played in various orchestras led by Axel Stordahl, Paul Weston, etc., etc. Was killed in a car crash whilst driving home from a Frank Sinatra recording session.

HAYMES, **Joe**
piano/arranger

Born: Marshfield, Missouri, 1908

Whilst in his teens he worked with a travelling circus as a trapeze artist, also played bass drum in the circus band. Later worked as a self-taught pianist and arranger. Joined Ted Weems as staff arranger before forming own band, which came to New York in the early 1930s for residencies at the Roseland Ballroom, Empire Ballroom, etc. The band did many recordings; some were issued under Haymes' name, many were pseudonymous. In 1934 Haymes turned the band over to Buddy Rogers, but later re-formed a band, 12 members of which became the original Tommy Dorsey Band (1935). Haymes again re-formed and continued recording. Continued leading in the 1930s, but occasionally fronted other bands (including tour with Les Brown in 1938). During the 1940s he lived for a while in Oklahoma, then worked in Hollywood Studios before joining C.B.S. in New York.

HAYNES, Cyril
piano/arranger/composer

Born: Panama Canal Zone. c. 1915

Brother of saxophonist Ronald Haynes, who died in March 1938. Raised in New York City, started on piano before he was 10, gigged with local teenagers, George Foster, Charlie Shavers, etc. Worked with local bands, played in band led by guitarist Benny Benjamin. Majored in music at Columbia University. Did brief road tour with 'Dixie on Parade' revue before joining Billy Hick's Sizzling Six until September 1937. Joined Al Cooper's Savoy Sultans in late November 1937 and worked regularly with the band until 1943, then with Frankie Newton, George James, etc. Played residencies as house pianist at Cafe Society, Onyx, etc. Led own recording groups, also recorded with Barney Bigard (1944). With the Al Casey Trio (1944). In 1947 worked for a while as accompanist for vocaliste Lena Horne; solo residencies in California (1948-50). With Noble Sissle in 1950, then played solo piano at The Reuben Bleu in New York. Played with various bands in the 1950s including Andy Kirk, Cab Calloway and Reuben Phillips' Big Band. Did several annual tours (accompanying Cab Calloway) with the 'Harlem Globetrotters' show during the 1960s. Played at Uncle John's Straw Hat, New York (April 1970). Regularly at Jimmy Ryan's Club, New York (1978).

HAYTON, 'Lennie' Leonard George
piano/arranger

Born: New York City, 13th February 1908
Died: California, 24th April 1971

Began on piano at the age of six, studied at the De Witt Clinton School in New York. In 1926 worked with Spencer Clark in the Little Ramblers, early in 1927 joined Cass Hagen Orchestra at the Hotel Manger, New York. With Paul Whiteman from September 1928 until May 1930. Prolific free-lance recording and arranging during the late 1920s and 1930s with Bix Beiderbecke, Red Nichols, Frankie Trumbauer, Joe Venuti, etc., etc., also played tympani on a Bix recording session. During the 1930s led own band, also worked regularly as musical director for Bing Crosby. Spent over 10 years as musical director at the M.G.M. Studios in Hollywood, was also musical director for his wife, Lena Horne. Died in Desert Hospital, Palm Springs.

HAYWOOD, Cedric
piano/arranger

Born: Houston, Texas, 1914
Died: Houston, Texas, 9th September 1969

Played in high school band alongside Arnett Cobb. Joined Chester Boone's Band in 1934, then with Milton Larkin's Band from 1935 until 1940. With Floyd Ray Band in 1940, Lionel Hampton in 1941, briefly rejoined Milton Larkin in 1942, also worked with Sidney Bechet in 1942. Moved to California in 1943, gigged with local bands, then served in U.S. Army during World War II, after release worked with various bands with Saunders King (1948), then three years mainly with Illinois Jacquet. Returned to San Francisco, then worked with Cal Tjader Quartet (1952), prolific arranging and free-lancing, then joined Kid Ory in 1955, worked mainly with Ory for several years including two tours of Europe. Regularly with tenorist Brew Moore in the early 1960s, moved back to Houston in the summer of 1963. Led own big band a Club Ebony, Houston, from 1964.

HAZEL, 'Monk' Arthur
drums/cornet/mellophone

Born: Harvey, Louisiana, 15th August 1903
Died: New Orleans, Louisiana, 5th March 1968

Originally specialised on drums (his father was a drummer), whilst still in his teens he gigged with Emmett Hardy, who gave him a cornet. He worked mainly on drums, but doubled throughout his career. During the 1920s worked with many bandleaders in and around New Orleans: Emile 'Stalebread Charley' Lacoume (in Bucktown), Abbe Brunies, Happy Schilling, Tony Parenti, Jules Bauduc, Johnny Wiggs, etc. During the late 1920s and early 1930s led own Bienville Roof Orchestra in New Orleans, also worked in Red Bolman's Orchestra and with Weenie White in Shreeveport. Toured as accompanist to vocalist Gene Austin, returned to New Orleans, was featured on trumpet and drums with Joe Caprano's Band in 1937. Long spell in Lloyd Danton's Quintet until U.S. Army service

in 1942. Was released during the following year, drove a truck in New Orleans, but continued to do local gigs. From 1948 he worked often with Sharkey Bonano, also played for George Girard, Roy Liberto, Mike Lala, and Santa Pecora.

HEARD, 'J.C.' James Charles *Born: Dayton, Ohio, 8th October 1917*
drums/vocals

Family moved to Detroit when 'J.C.' was two years old. Worked with local bands including long spell with trumpeter Bill Johnson, also worked in Detroit with Sam Price's Trio. Regularly with Milton Larkin's Band before joining Teddy Wilson's Big Band in April 1939, was forced by illness to leave Wilson temporarily in 1940, joined that pianist's sextet from December 1940 until summer of 1942. Briefly with Benny Carter, then mainly with Cab Calloway from autumn 1942 until September 1945, also did dates with other leaders (including Count Basie—spring 1944). Briefly in Benny Morton's Sextet, then led own band at Cafe Society, New York, from early 1946. From 1946 did regular work with Norman Granz's 'Jazz at the Philharmonic' shows, led own band at Cafe Society and in Detroit (1947). Briefly subbed for Jo Jones with Count Basie (summer 1947). Led own small group, active free-lancing and regular overseas tours with J.A.T.P. during the 1950s. From 1953 until 1957 lived in Japan, led own group there, also toured the Pacific area including Australia. Returned to U.S.A. in late 1957, again led own group, toured Europe with Sam Price from October 1958. Returned to New York, did free-lance studio work and gigged with Lester Lanin's Orchestras. With Coleman Hawkins at The Metropole, New York (1959). With Teddy Wilson Trio (1961), pianiste Dorothy Donegan (1963), with Red Norvo in Las Vegas (1964), then regularly led own trio. Moved to Detroit in 1966, led trio at local Playboy Club. Own band at Sheraton Metro Inn (1971). Widespread touring (including Europe) during the 1970s and 1980s.

HEGAMIN, Lucille *Born: Macon, Georgia, 1897*
(née Nelson) *Died: New York City, 1st March 1970*
vocals

Was married to pianist William 'Bill' Hegamin from 1914 until 1923. Sang in church choir and local theatre before leaving home at 15 to tour with a Leonard Harper Revue. Was stranded in Peoria, Illinois, made her way to Chicago (c. 1914), sang at various clubs accompanied by Bill Hegamin, then moved to West Coast with own band—played long residency in Seattle, Washington. Moved to New York in late 1919, began recording career in 1920. Toured with own Blue Flame Syncopators in the early 1920s; solo residency at The Shuffle Inn (late 1921), subsequently fronted own Dixie Daisies. Worked with The Sunnyland Cottonpickers (1926 and 1927); John C. Fullerton regular accompanying pianist. Played in several Broadway shows during the 1920s—was then known as 'The Cameo Girl'. Worked with George 'Doc' Hyder's Southernaires in the late 1920s, subsequently left the profession. In 1933 and 1934 did seasons at The Paradise in Atlantic City, then retired from music. Became a registered nurse in 1938. Appeared at several charity benefits during the early 1960s and recorded again in 1962.

HEMPHILL, 'Scad' Shelton *Born: Birmingham, Alabama, 16th March 1906*
trumpet *Died: New York, December 1959*

Attended Industrial High School in Birmingham, was taught by 'Fess' Whatley. Toured with pianist Fred Longshaw's Band accompanying Bessie Smith (early 1924), later that year enrolled at Wilberforce College and became a member of Horace Henderson's Collegians. With Benny Carter in New York (late 1928-9), then joined Chick Webb (1930-1). In the Mills Blue Rhythm Band from 1931 until 1937, with Louis Armstrong Orchestra from December 1937 until joining Duke Ellington early in 1944. Remained with Duke until September 1949, then free-lanced in New York until forced to quit playing due to ill health.

HENDERSON, 'Bobby' Robert Bolden
piano/vocals/occasionally trumpet

Born: New York City, 15th March 1910
Died: Albany, New York, 9th December 1969

Was also known as Jody Bolden. Played piano from the age of nine, later attended School of Commerce in New York studying book-keeping, whilst at this school began doing local gigs, then played residency at Pod's and Jerry's. Received some tuition from Fats Waller. Played in Washington, D.C., in band led by drummer Tommy Myles, then toured with the Boston bandleader Joe Neville. Regularly accompanied Billie Holiday (1933), played residency at The Onyx Club, then left New York City for solo residencies in Utica, St. Lawrence, Syracuse, etc. Played trumpet in U.S. Army Band during World War II, after demobilisation again played solo residencies. Was resident at The Kerry Blue in Albany for most of the 1950s, appeared at Newport Jazz Festival in 1957. Played in Puerto Rico (1960-1), residency in Schenectady (1963). Resident in Albany during last years of his life—died of cancer.

HENDERSON, Horace
piano/arranger/composer

Born: Cuthbert, Georgia, 22nd November 1904

Brother of Fletcher. Began piano studies at 14, spent a year at Atlanta University, then studied at Wilberforce College for three years (gained A.B. degree). Formed own student band The Collegians. During summer vacation of 1924 the band worked at the Bamville Club, New York, during the following year they played residency at Lawrence, Massachusetts, then began regular touring (using the Wilberforce campus as its base until summer of 1926). Regular tours and residencies in 1927, began working as The Dixie Stompers in 1928. Horace temporarily disbanded and worked with Sammy Stewart (late 1928). Re-formed for touring in 1929, played further residencies in New York (1929-31), Rockland Palace, Connie's Inn, etc., relinquished leadership to Don Redman, continued to work with Redman until early 1933 (worked for a week in Duke Ellington's Orchestra in New York—November 1932). Played in Fletcher Henderson's Band from early 1933 until late 1934, again led own band, then worked with Vernon Andrade in New York from spring 1935. Rejoined Fletcher early in 1936, left to form own big band for residency at Swingland, Chicago (July 1937), led on and off there for over a year, the band then played at the Savoy, Chicago (1938), and toured. At Grand Terrace, Chicago, from January 1939, subsequently at the 5100 Club. Disbanded, then re-formed big band using most of Nat Towles' personnel until December 1940. Served in U.S. Army from November 1942 until August 1943, rejoined Fletcher in Chicago. Left Fletcher in New York (May 1944), became accompanist for vocaliste Lena Horne, re-formed big band in July 1945, debut at Plantation, Los Angeles, then long residency at the Million Dollar Theatre, Los Angeles (1947-9). Led own small group in Chicago from September 1949 until spring 1950. During the 1950s led own band in Minneapolis, Las Vegas, California, etc. Worked with the 'Billy Williams' Revue' in the early 1960s, also toured with own big band. During the late 1960s has worked mainly in Denver, Colorado. Arranger for many bandleaders including: Fletcher Henderson, Benny Goodman, Charlie Barnet, The Casa Loma Orchestra, Tommy Dorsey, Earl Hines, Jimmie Lunceford, etc.

HENDERSON, 'Smack' Fletcher Hamilton
piano/arranger/composer

Born: Cuthbert, Georgia, 18th December 1897
Died: New York City, 28th December 1952

Brother of Horace. Piano from the age of six. Local schools, then studied at Atlanta University College from 1916, gained degree in chemistry. Moved to New York in 1920 intending to do post-graduate research there, instead became a song demonstrator for the Pace-Handy Music Company. Later left the company and became recording manager for the Black Swan Recording Company, organised first band to tour acompanying Ethel Waters' The Black Swan Troubadours (autumn 1921 to summer 1922). Returned to New York, Became house pianist for recording companies, played gigs with violinist Shrimp Jones' Band at Broadway Jones' Club in New York. Was then elected leader of band newly formed for residency at the Club Alabam, New York (early 1924), took up residency at the Roseland Ballroom, New York (late summer 1924). For the next 10 years Henderson's Band appeared regularly at the Roseland, but also played at many other

New York ballrooms and theatres, did regular touring and played dates in other cities (leader briefly out of action through August 1928 car accident). Despite many personnel changes and at least two complete reshuffles Henderson continued to lead regularly until 1939. Early in the 1930s he had commenced regular arranging. Long residency at Grand Terrace, Chicago, in 1936; later led in Boston, New York, California, etc., until joining Benny Goodman as arranger (and sextet pianist) in June 1939. From late 1939 ceased playing piano for Goodman and worked solely as staff arranger. Formed own big band for residency at Roseland, New York, from 31st January 1941, subsequently toured for a while before disbanding. Re-formed for dates at the Appollo Theatre, New York (spring 1943), then toured with own mixed band, played in New York with this unit in spring 1944. Formed new band for residency at Rhumboogie, Chicago (May 1945), then moved to California (c. August 1945), returned to Chicago for long stint at the Club DeLisa from c. February 1946 until May 1947. Disbanded and again worked as staff arranger for Benny Goodman. Toured as accompanist for Ethel Waters (summer 1948 until December 1949). With composer-pianist J. C. Johnson wrote the 'Jazz Train' revue and led own band for that show at Bop City, New York. Led own sextet at Cafe Society, New York, in December 1950. Suffered a stroke on 21st December 1950. Suffered partial paralysis and was hospitalised for long periods; was never able to resume playing. Arranged for many bandleaders including: Teddy Hill, Will Bradley, Isham Jones, Jack Hylton, The Casa Loma Orchestra, etc., etc.

'Hendersonia'—a bio-discography by Walter C. Allen was first published in 1973.

HENDERSON, Rosa
(née Deschamps)
vocals

Born: Kentucky, 24th November 1896
Died: New York City, 6th April 1968

Not related to Fletcher or Edmonia Henderson. In 1913 began touring with her uncle's carnival troupe, toured (mainly in Texas) until 1918. Married 'Slim' Henderson and toured for several years in the Mason-Henderson Show. During the 1920s was featured in several New York musical comedies. Began prolific recording career in 1923—some of her records being issued under various pseudonyms: Flora Dale, Mamie Harris, Sarah Johnson, Sally Ritz, Josephine Thomas, and Gladys White. Left the profession in the late 1920s, played occasional engagements during the 1930s, but worked for many years in a New York department store. During the 1960s sang occasionally at charity benefits.

HENKE, 'Mel' Melvin E.
piano

Born: Chicago, Illinois, 4th August 1915
Died: Los Angeles, California, 31st March 1979

Student of the Chicago College of Music. Played with many bands in Chicago including: Frank Snyder, Maurice Stein, Steve Leonard, and Bud Freeman (1942). In 1944 moved to New York for club residencies, briefly with Horace Heidt (autumn 1944), then returned to Chicago. Long solo residencies in Chicago and studio work for A.B.C. and N.B.C., then moved to California to do studio work and composing for films.

HENRY, 'Haywood' Frank
saxes/clarinet/flute

Born: Birmingham, Alabama, 10th January 1913

Originally a clarinettist, played in 'Bama State Collegians. Left the band to go to New York, played in 131st Street Church Band, then worked with Leon Englund's Band at Arcadia Ballroom before rejoining the 'Bama State Collegians which subsequently became Erskine Hawkins' Band—remained with that band from 1935 until the early 1950s. Worked with Tiny Grimes in the early 1950s, then active free-lance work on all saxes, played baritone in Henderson Re-union Band in 1957 and 1958, worked occasionally on clarinet with Wilbur de Paris in the early 1960s. Regularly with Earl Hines from late 1969 until early 1971 (including tour of Europe). (Worked with various leaders during the 1970s, toured Europe with Sy Oliver, and with New York Jazz Repertory Company. Toured Europe during the early 1980s, including work on tenor-sax with Panama Francis and his Savoy Sultans.

HERBERT, Arthur *Born: Brooklyn, New York, 28th May 1907*
drums

Both parents from Trinidad; Arthur is the uncle of drummer Herbie Lovelle. Did first gigs at the Grassy Point Hotel, Long Island, in 1930, during following year worked in Brooklyn and at Dickie Wells' Club in Harlem. Did day job at a silver and gold refinery in New York, but played regularly for various bandleaders: Henry Miller, Fess Gittens, Duncan-Holder Orchestra, etc. First professional work with Eddie Williams' band at Savoy, New York (1935). Led own Rhythm Masters in New York, joined Edgar Hayes in 1938. With Pete Brown (1939), Coleman Hawkins (late 1939-40), Eddie Durham (late 1940), Hot Lips Page (1941), Sidney Bechet (1941), George James (1942-3), Mezz Mezzrow (1943), Pete Brown (1946), etc. Left full-time music, runs own exterminator business, but has continued to play regularly, frequently with Lem Johnson in the 1960s.

HERFURT, 'Skeets' Arthur *Born: Cincinnati, Ohio, 28th May 1911*
alto/tenor/clarinet/vocals

Raised in Denver, Colorado, began playing in bands whilst at the University of Colorado. With Smith Ballew (1934), Dorsey Brothers (summer 1934-5), Jimmy Dorsey (1936), left in January 1937, brief spells with George Stoll Orchestra and Ray Noble, then with Tommy Dorsey (1937 to October 1939). Settled on West Coast, worked with Alvino Rey until service in U.S. Army (1944-5). Studio work in Hollywood, with Benny Goodman (December 1946 to spring 1947), resumed studio work, also led own band. During the early 1950s worked regularly in Frank DeVol's Studio Orchestra, also with Billy May (1952-3). Has continued with studio work, also with Benny Goodman in 1961 and 1964.

HERMAN, 'Woody' Woodrow Charles *Born: Milwaukee, Wisconsin, 16th May 1913*
clarinet/alto/vocals

Sang in vaudeville theatres from early childhood, took up sax at 11 and clarinet at 14 and incorporated them in his variety act. Worked with Myron Stewart's Band and toured Texas with Joe Lichter's Band (c. 1928), then briefly became a student at Marquette University. With Tom Gerun (Gerunovitch) from 1929-34. Spent eight months in Harry Sosnick Band (1934), two months with Gus Arnheim, gigged with Joe Moss until joining Isham Jones' Juniors. Joined the band in Denver (c. late 1934), and remained with it until Jones disbanded in late summer of 1936. Woody and five other ex-members formed the nucleus of a co-operative band—with Woody as leader. This unit played first at the Schroeder Hotel in Milwaukee, but made its official debut at the Roseland in Brooklyn. The orchestra (billed as 'The Band That Plays The Blues') gradually achieved popularity, its box-office appeal greatly enhanced by the success of 'The Woodchoppers Ball' recording. Woody also recorded with The King's Jesters in 1938. In the early 1940s, after extensive personnel changes, the band became known as The First Herd; this unit first performed Stravinsky's specially written 'Ebony Concerto' at Carnegie Hall in March 1946, they disbanded in December of that year. Woody re-formed in 1947, but cut down to a small band in late 1949. During the 1950s Woody continued leading various Herds; in spring 1954 his band did their first European tour. During the late 1950s and 1960s Woody has, for several months each year, led own big bands, usually specially assembled for specific tours. In spring of 1959 he brought a few star sidemen to Europe and toured with an Anglo-American band; during the 1960s he toured Europe several times. Woody has appeared in many films. Extensive touring throughout the 1970s, recovered from serious auto crash in 1977, and continued fulfilling international touring schedule during the early 1980s.

HEYWOOD, 'Eddie' Edward Jr. *Born Atlanta, Georgia, 4th December 1915*
piano/composer/arranger

His father, Eddie Sr., a graduate of the Boston Conservatory of Music, was a famous bandleader-pianist in the 1920s and 1930s. Eddie Jr. was the nephew of bandleader LeRoy Smith. Received first lessons from his father at the age of eight; at 14 was playing piano in the local 81 Theatre Orchestra, remained in Atlanta until c. 1932, then joined

Wayman Carver's Ramblers. With Ralph Porter (1934), then joined Clarence Love (1934), and eventually came to New York with this band in 1937. Gigged in New York, then joined Benny Carter Orchestra from January 1939 until July 1940. Worked in Zutty Singleton Trio from July 1940, briefly with Leonard Ware and Don Redman before leading own band at Village Vanguard, New York, in 1941. His sextet played several residencies in New York—Cafe Society Downtown, Three Deuces, etc.—before working in California (late 1944-5). During their stay in Hollywood they appeared in the films 'The Dark Corner' and 'High School Kids'. Led sextet in New York for most of 1946, returned to West Coast early in 1947, soon afterwards was forced by partial paralysis to quit playing for almost three years. Resumed regular playing in spring of 1950 and since then has led own trio. Achieved considerable success with his composition 'Canadian Sunset'. Suffered recurrence of hand paralysis in late 1960s. Recovered, and played many concerts in the 1970s, also club dates in New York and New England.

HICKS, Henry
trombone

Born: Birmingham, Alabama. c. 1904
Died: New York City. c. 1950

Attended Wilberforce College, played in Edgar Hayes' Blue Grass Buddies (c. 1924), then played regularly in Horace Henderson's Collegians from 1925 to 1928. With Benny Carter's Band in 1929, briefly with Bingie Madison, then with the Mills Blue Rhythm Band from 1930 until 1934.

Not related to the trumpeter-bandleader Billy Hicks, who in 1971 was living in Puerto Rico.

HIGGINBOTHAM, J. C.
trombone

Born: Social Circle, near Atlanta, Georgia, 11th May 1906
Died: New York, 26th May 1973

Two brothers were also brass players—'Higgy's' niece is song-writer Irene Higginbotham. He first played bugle, then his sister bought him his first trombone. Worked in family restaurant, also played with Neal Montgomery Orchestra (1921) and gigged with pianist Harvey Quiggs. Moved to Cincinnati to learn tailoring at a training school, left to work as mechanic at the General Motors factory. Joined Wesley Helvey's Band (c. 1924), led own band, also gigged with Wingie Carpenter. In late 1925 toured with pianist Eugene Landrum's Jazz Band in the 'Ragtime Steppers' show. In 1926 he was sent for by Wingie Carpenter and joined drummer Eugene Primus' Band in Buffalo, New York, after seven months he joined another band in Buffalo led by a pianist named Jimmy Harrison. Whilst on a visit to New York in September 1928 he sat in at the Savoy Ballroom with Chick Webb and with drummer Willie Lynch's Band, was subsequently signed by Luis Russell and remained with Russell until 1931—during this period played for two brief spells with Chick Webb (no recordings). With Fletcher Henderson from spring 1932, then with Benny Carter in autumn of 1933. Brief absence from music scene until summer 1934, then joined the Mills Blue Rhythm Band (directed by Lucky Millinder). Left in late 1936, briefly with Fletcher Henderson early in 1937, then with Louis Armstrong Big Band until November 1940. Joined Henry 'Red' Allen Sextet (as co-leader) in December 1940 and worked regularly with Henry Allen until February 1947 (during this period appeared with Louis Armstrong and Sidney Bechet at a New Orleans Jazz Foundation Concert in January 1945). During the late 1940s and early 1950s worked mainly in Boston, occasionally led own band, also featured with Joe Thomas, Rex Stewart, etc. Worked in Cleveland and Boston in 1955, then from 1956 began regular appearances at Central Plaza, New York, soon moved into The Metropole and worked there on and off throughout the late 1950s (including several stints with Henry Allen). Took part in Fletcher Henderson re-union in 1957, also did extensive free-lance recordings, to Europe with Sam Price in October 1958 (sharing trombone duties with Elmer Crumbley). During the 1960s has regularly led own band, various residencies in New York including Freedomland, Room at the Bottom, The Purple Onion, etc., also played many gigs with trumpeter Joe Thomas. Was featured at Newport Jazz Festival in 1963; also played in Scandinavia. In December 1966 he briefly returned to his home town in Atlanta to record an L.P. Continued to play regularly in the late 1960s. Spent several months in hospital (1971).

HIGHTOWER, 'Willie'
trumpet

Born: Nashville, Tennessee, October 1889
Died: Chicago, Illinois, December 1959

Husband of pianiste Lottie Hightower. Led own seven-piece band in New Orleans—The American Stars—for several years from c. 1916, moved to Chicago in 1921. Played in Carroll Dickerson's Band, then worked in his wife's big band—Lottie E. Hightower's Night Hawks—later rejoined Carroll Dickerson. Did theatre work during the 1930s including spell with Andrew Hilaire's Band in 1933, then retired from full-time music.

HILAIRE, Andrew H.
drums

Born: New Orleans, Louisiana. c. 1900
Died: Chicago, Illinois. c. 1936

Chiefly remembered for his recordings with Jelly Roll Morton. Worked for most of his life in Chicago. With Lil Hardin's Band (c. 1921), with Doc Cooke from 1924 until 1927. Regular theatre work in late 1920s. With Jerome Pasquall (1930), briefly with Eddie South (1931). Led own band in Chicago (1933), with Robert Dade Orchestra (1934), own band at Indiana Theatre (spring 1935). Suffered from chronic asthma.

HILL, Alex
piano/arranger/composer/vocalist

Born: Little Rock, Arkansas, 19th April 1906
Died: Little Rock, Arkansas, 1937

First piano lessons from his mother. Worked with Alphonso Trent. Organised own band in 1924 and began touring. Became musical director of a travelling revue, left the show in Los Angeles (c. 1927). Did studio work in Hollywood (playing atmosphere music on silent-film sets), also gigged with various bands including Mutt Carey's Jeffersonians. Moved to Chicago, worked with Jimmy Wade, Carroll Dickerson, Jerome Don Pasquall, etc., replaced Jerome Carrington in Jimmie Noone's Band (1928). Left Noone in the summer of 1929, worked with Sammy Stewart and played Savoy, New York, residency with Stewart in spring of 1930. Brief spell with Andy Kirk, then worked in New York as a free-lance arranger before becoming staff arranger for Irving Mills' organisation. Arranged for Claude Hopkins, Paul Whiteman, Duke Ellington, etc. Briefly deputised for Duke Ellington on piano in spring of 1935, left Irving Mills and organised own big band which made its debut at the Savoy Ballroom, New York, in November 1935. Was soon forced to disband due to ill health, entered hospital early in 1936, a few months later did solo work in New York; advanced tuberculosis forced him to retire to his brother's home in Little Rock. Also arranged for Paul Howard's Quality Serenaders, Fats Waller's Big Band, Eddie Condon, Willie Bryant, etc.

HILL, 'Chippie' Bertha
vocals

Born: Charleston, South Carolina. c. 1900
Died: New York City, 7th May 1950

Was one of 16 children. Began professional career as a dancer at LeRoy's in Harlem (1916), later toured as a singer and dancer with Ma Rainey's troupe. Worked as a solo act on T.O.B.A. circuit before settling in Chicago (c. 1925). Prolific recordings, accompanied by Louis Armstrong, Richard M. Jones, Lonnie Johnson, etc. Worked regularly in Chicago clubs and theatres until 1930, then left full-time music to raise her seven children. During the 1930s and early 1940s occasionally sang in Chicago theatres, also did long residency at the Club DeLisa, but was working in a bakery when rediscovered by writer Rudi Blesh in 1946. Starred in the 'This Is Jazz' radio series, started residency at the Village Vanguard, New York, on 5th September 1947, later worked regularly at Jimmy Ryan's. Appeared at Carnegie Hall (with Kid Ory) on 30th April 1948. Went to France in May 1948 to appear at the Paris Jazz Festival (accompanied by pianist Claude Bolling). Returned to work at Ryan's, last Chicago appearance was at the Blue Note Club in February 1950, then returned to Ryan's. Was knocked down and killed by a car in Harlem.

HILL, 'Bass' Ernest
string bass/tuba

Born: Pittsburgh, Pennsylvania, 14th March 1900
Died: New York City, 16th September 1964

Worked with Claude Hopkins during the summer of 1924, sailed to Europe with Hopkins (accompanying Josephine Baker Revue) in September 1925. Returned to U.S.A. in 1926, again worked with Hopkins from 1926 until 1928. Played in LeRoy Smith's Orchestra, then worked with Bill Brown and his Brownies before joining Eugene Kennedy Orchestra (1929), briefly with Charlie Skeets' Band (1929). During the early 1930s again worked with LeRoy Smith, played for a few months in Chick Webb's Band, with Benny Carter's Band in 1931 and again 1933-4, briefly with Rex Stewart's Band at the Empire Ballroom, New York (summer 1933). With Willie Bryant's Band (1935), went to Europe with Bobby Martin's Band in June 1937, when Martin returned to U.S.A. (1939) remained with band—then renamed The Cotton Club Serenaders. Remained in Switzerland at outbreak of World War II, played for a few months with tenorist Mac Strittmatter's Band, then sailed back to U.S.A. in spring of 1940. With Maurice Hubbard's Band in New York (August 1940), then rejoined Claude Hopkins (1941-2). Worked in New York with Zutty Singleton, to California with Zutty in April 1943. Worked with Louis Armstrong in summer of 1943, then again with Claude Hopkins (late 1943 and 1944). With Cliff Jackson (autumn 1944), U.S.O. tour with Herbie 'Kat' Cowens (late 1945 to early 1946), then worked with pianiste Minto Kato. Returned to Europe in November 1949, worked with Bill Coleman in Switzerland and Italy and with Big Boy Goudie in Germany, returned to the U.S.A. in January 1952. Extensive gigging with Happy Caldwell, drummer Henry 'Chick' Morrison, altoist Wesley Fagan, Eli Logan, etc. From 1954 was also employed as a delegate in the New York offices of the American Federation of Musicians.

HILL, 'Teddy' Theodore *Born: Birmingham, Alabama, 7th December 1909*
tenor and soprano saxes/clarinet *Died: Cleveland, Ohio, 19th May 1978*

Played drums in school band, then switched to trumpet. Whilst studying at the Industrial High School in Birmingham, received tuition from 'Fess' Whatley, gave up trumpet and specialised on saxes and clarinet. Toured with the Whitman Sisters' show (1926-7), then joined drummer George Howe's Band (1927) at the Nest Club, New York, subsequently worked in Luis Russell's Band (1928-9), also assisted in management of Russell's Band. Worked with James P. Johnson (1932), regularly led own big band from 1932, residencies at Lafayette Theatre, Ubangi Club, Savoy Ballroom, New York, etc. Toured England and France in 1937, played at Moulin Rouge in Paris before touring Britain (including bookings at the London Palladium, July 1937). Returned to U.S.A., continued to lead band until 1940, was then active as manager of the famous 'early bop' club at Minton's in Harlem. Managed Minton's for many years.

HINES, 'Fatha' Earl Kenneth *Born: Duquesne District of Pittsburgh, Pennsylvania, 28th December 1903*
piano/vocals/composer *Died: Oakland, California, 22nd April 1983*

Earl's sister, Nancy, a pianiste, led her own band in Pittsburgh during the 1930s; their father, Joseph, played cornet in local brass bands; their mother, Mary, was an organist. Began playing cornet at an early age, piano studies from the age of nine. Majored in music at Schenley High School. Was spotted by vocalist Lois B. Deppe who secured him a place in Arthur Rideout's Orchestra. Later, Deppe organised the Pittsburgh Serenaders (which Hines directed) for residency at the Lieder House, Pittsburgh, toured with Lois Deppe (1923). Worked with Harry Collins' Orchestra in Pittsburgh then moved to Chicago, played residency at Entertainers' Club with violinist Vernie Robinson, later led at the same venue. Toured Pantages circuit for almost a year with Carroll Dickerson, returned to Chicago worked with Dickerson, Erskine Tate, and other leaders. Musical director for Louis Armstrong's Stompers at Sunset Cafe (1927), later that year, Louis, Earl and Zutty Singleton ran their own short-lived club at Warwick Hall, Chicago. In late 1927, Earl began working with Jimmie Noone at the Apex Club. Went to New York in December 1928 to record a solo session for the Q.R.S. Company, returned to Chicago, took own band into the Grand Terrace on 28th December 1928. Continued recording with Louis Armstrong in 1929. Throughout the 1930s Earl Hines and his Orchestra played many residencies at the Grand Terrace, they also did regular touring and occasionally played dates in New York. Whilst at the Grand Terrace Hines was given the nickname 'Fatha' by radio announcer Ted Pearson. Earl temporarily disbanded early in 1940, opened own Studio Club in Chicago, then re-formed big band for residencies in California (late 1940). He continued to lead own successful big bands until 1947, many of his young sidemen went on to gain considerable fame; one temporary innovation was the introduction of an all-girl string section in September 1943. In March 1944 Earl briefly fronted the Ellington Band whilst Duke was absent with tonsillitis. He disbanded in 1947 and again ran own club in Chicago. Joined Louis Armstrong All Stars from January 1948 until autumn 1951—late in 1948 Earl fronted his own big band which for a time travelled with the Armstrong All Stars. Led own sextet from late 1951, did residencies and touring. Led own small band for long residency at the Hangover Club, San Francisco, commencing September 1955 (Earl having first played at the club in June 1952). Visited Europe with all-star group (headed by Jack Teagarden and Earl Hines) in autumn of 1957. Worked mainly in California with own band throughout the late 1950s. Moved with his family to Oakland in 1960, did regular tours, also played residencies in San Francisco, ran own club in Oakland in 1963. Played highly successful New York dates in 1964 at the Little Theatre and at Birdland. Toured Europe in spring of 1965 and subsequently made several visits to Europe, toured Russia with a sextet in the summer of 1966. Featured with the 'Swinging Era' package in Europe (spring 1967), at London's Jazz Expo (1968). Continues to lead own quartet, occasionally undertakes solo engagements. Toured Europe again in 1969 and 1970. Extensive engagements throughout the 1970s, toured Europe, Japan, and Australia. Despite bouts of ill health, Hines continued to work regularly up until the weekend before he died.

Stanley Dance's book 'The World of Earl Hines' was published in 1977.

HINTON, Milton John *Born: Vicksburg, Mississippi, 23rd June 1910*
string bass

Received first music lessons from his mother. Learnt brass and string bass whilst at high school in Chicago. First professional work with Boyd Atkins Band, later worked with Tiny Parham before playing at the Show Boat Cabaret in Chicago with bands led by Jabbo Smith and Cassino Simpson. Worked with Eddie South in late 1931, briefly with Erskine Tate, then rejoined Eddie South for a long spell including California (late 1932). Worked with Zutty Singleton and Fate Marable, then in late 1936 joined Cab Calloway. Remained with Cab until 1951, then did extensive free-lance work in New York. Worked for two months with Count Basie, later with Louis Armstrong All Stars (summer 1953 and again in 1954). From then until the present time has been one of the busiest session men in New York. Visited Paris in November 1966, continues to play jazz dates, appeared at New Orleans Jazz Fest in 1969, and at House of Sounds Festival, Washington, D.C. (September 1971). Maintained very busy schedule during the 1970s, including overseas tours with Pearl Bailey, Bing Crosby, etc. Extensive freelance work during the early 1980s.

HITE, Les *Born: Duquoine, Illinois, 13th March 1903*
alto sax/piano/xylophone *Died: Santa Monica, California, 6th February 1962*

Attended local school in Urbana, then studied at University of Illinois. Played sax in family band, then worked with Detroit Shannon's Band before touring with the Helen Dewey Show. After the show folded in Los Angeles joined Spikes Brothers' Orchestra (1925), worked for various leaders: Mutt Carey, Paul Howard, Curtis Mosby, Vernon Elkins, drummer Henry 'Tin Can' Allen. Led own band at Solomon Penny's Dance Palace, etc. Circa September 1930, Hite began leading at Sebastian's Cotton Club (deposing trumpeter Vernon Elkins). Led band at Cotton Club for many years, accompanying many guest stars including Louis Armstrong and Fats Waller. The band also did a considerable amount of film-studio work, both soundtrack and visual. They did some touring and occasional residencies in New York (1937), Portland (1938), and Chicago (1940). Hite continued to lead in Los Angeles from 1942 until 1945 when he quit full-time playing to organise his own business. For the last five years of his life he managed a booking agency.

HODES, 'Art' Arthur W. *Born: Nikoliev, Russia, 14th November 1904*
piano

Family moved to U.S.A. when Art was six months old. Went to school in Chicago. Began gigging in late teens, played for dances at Hull House, Chicago, did a spell at Rainbow Gardens, Chicago, then toured with Dick Voynow's Wolverines (for part of the tour the band worked under the nominal leadership of Smith Ballew). Summer season at Delavan Lake, Wisconsin (1927), returned to Chicago to work in Dago Larry Mangano's Club. With Wingy Manone at Eldorado, Chicago (1928), whilst with Wingy made record debut (1928). Worked mainly in Chicago through the early 1930s, played with many bands including Floyd Town's and Frank Snyder's, also led own small groups and played solo piano at various venues including Capitol Dancing School, Harry's 'New York' Bar, and Liberty Inn. Moved to New York in April 1938, played at the Hickory House before working for several months at Ross's Tavern (1939). Short spell at The Pirate Den before briefly with Joe Marsala (late 1939). With Mezz Mezzrow Trio in spring 1940, then led own band at Child's Restaurant, New York. Led own band in 1941-2, also did disc-jockey shows on Radio WNYC. Worked in Joe Marsala Big Band in spring 1943, left to form a band for residency at Hofbrau, Lawrence, Massachusetts. (From February 1943 until November 1947 Art Hodes edited the fine magazine *Jazz Record.)* At the Hickory House again early in 1944. From 1945 until 1949 led own band for various residencies including Village Vanguard, Stuyvesant Casino, Ole South, Camp Unity, Jimmy Ryan's, Riviera, etc., etc. With Tony Parenti Band in summer of 1949. Moved back to Chicago (early 1950). During the 1950s and 1960s has played many residencies in Chicago: Rupneck's, Brass Rail, Jazz Ltd., etc., also dates in Toronto, St. Louis, etc., hosted educational TV series, and taught piano at Park Forest Conservatory. Played in Denmark (autumn 1970). Residency in Crete, Illinois (1971). Toured with Bigard, Condon, Davison in October 1971. Led own band during the 1970s, also did solo tour of Europe in 1977. Continued to work regularly during the early 1980s. 'Selections From The Gutter' (portraits from the Jazz Record, edited by Art Hodes and Chadwick Hansen was first published in 1977).

HODGES, 'Johnny' 'Rabbit'
real name: Cornelius Hodge
alto and soprano saxes/composer

Born: Cambridge, Massachusetts, 25th July 1907
Died: New York City, 11th May 1970

Brother-in-law of the late Don Kirkpatrick. Played drums and piano, then sax at the age of 14; through his sister, he got to know Sidney Bechet, who gave him lessons. He followed Bechet in Willie 'The Lion' Smith's Quartet at the Rhythm Club (c. 1924), then played with Bechet at the Club Basha (1925). Continued to live in Boston during the mid-1920s, travelling to New York for week-end gigs. Played with Bobby Sawyer (c. 1925) and Lloyd Scott (c. 1926), then from late 1926 worked regularly with Chick Webb at Paddock Club, Savoy Ballroom, etc. Briefly with Luckey Roberts' Orchestra, then joined Duke Ellington in May 1928. With Duke until March 1951 when formed own small band. (In summer of 1948, whilst Duke Ellington was on solo tour of Britain, Johnny led a quartet at the Apollo Club, New York.) Continued to lead own septet until spring 1955. After a spell of TV-studio work on the Ted Steele Show he rejoined Duke Ellington in August 1955, except for brief absences, remained with Duke until fatal heart attack. Few weeks' leave in spring 1958 to work in Florida with Billy Strayhorn. In spring of 1961, together with several band colleagues, toured Europe in the Ellington Giants. Regularly led own recording bands from 1937; prolific free-lance recordings.

HOLDER, Terrence
trumpet

Born: c. 1898

Worked in Alphonso Trent's Band during the early 1920s, then formed own band—The Dark Clouds of Joy—early in 1929 Holder was deposed and Andy Kirk voted leader of the band. Briefly led own small band, then (with Jesse Stone's assistance) formed new band (known as The Twelve Clouds of Joy). Continued leading during the 1930s, then left full-time music, during the 1940s worked with Nat Towles' Band and gigged in Billings, Montana.

HOLIDAY, Billie 'Lady Day'
vocals/composer

Born: Baltimore, Maryland, 7th April 1915
Died: New York City, 17th July 1959

Christian name was Eleanora; named 'Billie' after film star Billie Dove. Her father, Clarence Holiday (1900-37), was a professional guitarist who worked for many bandleaders including Billy Fowler, Fletcher Henderson, and Don Redman. Moved from Baltimore to

New York in 1928, shortly afterwards served for four months in a State Institution on Welfare Island. After release lived in Jamaica, Long Island, occasionally singing at the Elks' Club, moved back to New York City and lived with her mother on 145th Street, Harlem. Successfully auditioned for Jerry Preston and began working at the Log Cabin Club and various other venues in the 133rd Street area: Monette's, Mexico Club, The Bright Spot, etc. Was heard by John Hammond early in 1933; he subsequently arranged for her to make recording debut with Benny Goodman (November 1933). After residency at The Alhambra Grill did short season in Montreal, Canada, in band organised by Louis Metcalf. Returned to New York worked regularly at The Hot Cha Club (134th Street), also theatre appearances on Long Island and at The Apollo, New York. Began recording with own studio group, also made many sides with Teddy Wilson's Studio Band. Forced to leave 'Stars Over Broadway' revue at Connie's Inn (January 1936) because of ptomaine poisoning (Billie was replaced by Bessie Smith). After recovery did theatre dates with Jimmie Lunceford, then moved to Chicago for Grand Terrace Summer 1936 Revue—was accompanied for this production by Fletcher Henderson's Orchestra. After being dismissed from the show returned to New York, briefly at The Onyx Club during September 1936, then residencies at The Uptown House and Dicky Well's Shim-Sham Club. Joined Count Basie in March 1937, left in February 1938; almost immediately Billie joined Artie Shaw (then playing in Boston), but left the band during a New York residency in November 1938. During 1939 appeared regularly at Cafe Society, New York, during that summer again appeared in Chicago. In December 1939 began working at Kelly's Stables, New York. During the early 1940s worked long residencies in New York: Ernie's, Kelly's, Cafe Society, etc. In August 1942 residency at The Downbeat Club, Chicago. In spring 1943 cancelled bookings to visit the West Coast, returned to New York for theatre dates at The Apollo (May 1943) and Loew's (June 1943), then long residency at The Onyx Club. Moved into The Downbeat Club, New York (formerly The Famous Door), in August 1944; from December worked at The Spotlite Club. In spring 1945 worked in Los Angeles, then after a brief, unhappy, spell at The Plantation Club, St. Louis, returned to The Spotlite in New York. In late summer of 1945 toured with big band directed by trumpeter Joe Guy (1920-61), who was then married to Billie. Returned to Downbeat, New York, residency in October 1945. On 16th February 1946 Billie did her first solo concert at the New York Town Hall, continued residency at Downbeat until moving to Hollywood for the filming of 'New Orleans' (late 1946). Returned to New York, worked at The Downbeat, Cafe Society, and Club 18. Brief spell in hospital (spring 1947). Arrested in Philadelphia (May 1947) for violation of U.S. narcotics laws—in June 1947 was sentenced by the Philadelphia Federal Court to a year-and-a-day. After being released from the Federal Reformatory, Alderson, West Virginia, in February 1948, Billie returned to New York and gave concerts at Carnegie Hall during March 1948. In April 1948 played three weeks in the 'Holiday on Broadway' revue; began residency at The Strand Theatre, New York, from 16th July 1948. Residency at Billy Berg's Club, Los Angeles (late 1948), played dates in San Francisco and Northern California, was tried and acquitted in San Francisco on narcotics charges. Worked in Detroit (April 1949), then from July 1949 worked at Million Dollar Club, Los Angeles; Cafe Society, New York (October 1949); at Blue Note, Chicago (December 1949). Throughout the 1950s Billie worked as a solo attraction, starring at many clubs, theatres, and concert halls in the U.S.A. Club residencies in Washington, Chicago, San Francisco, Boston, etc., etc. Billie made several concert appearances in New York, but was forbidden by law from working in New York clubs. Early in 1954 she toured Europe with Leonard Feather's 'Jazz Club U.S.A.' package; in late 1958 played solo dates in Europe (including television work in Britain). Billie made her final public appearance at a concert at The Phoenix Theatre, New York (25th May 1959). She entered hospital and during her final illness was placed under arrest for possessing illicit drugs. She died at the Metropolitan Hospital in New York.

Billie Holiday appeared in the films 'Symphony in Black' (1935) and 'New Orleans' (1947), also (with Count Basie) in a Universal-International short (released 1950). Pianists who worked as Billie Holiday's regular accompanists include: Dot Hill (1933), Bobby Henderson (1933-4), Vivian Smith (1937), Sonny White (1939-40), Joe Springer (1946), Bobby Tucker (1947-8), Carl Drinkard (1949-53), Buster Harding (1952), Mal Waldron (1957-9).

'Billie's Blues' by John Chilton, first published in 1975.

H

HOLLAND, 'Peanuts' Herbert Lee
trumpet/vocals/composer

Born: Norfolk, Virginia, 9th February 1910
Died: Sweden, 7th February 1979

His brother, Charles, was a professional singer (Fletcher Henderson, etc.). Received trumpet tuition in Jenkins' Orphanage Band. Worked on and off with Alphonso Trent from 1928 until 1933, spell with Al Sears' Band in Buffalo (late 1932). Briefly with Jeter-Pillars, Willie Bryant, and Jimmie Lunceford, with Lil Armstrong's Big Band (1935-6). Led own band at Olcott Beach Ballroom, Buffalo (1938). Moved to New York City in 1939, joined Coleman Hawkins Band, then with Fletcher Henderson (early 1941); from 1941 until 1946 worked mainly with Charlie Barnet. Led own band in 1946 until going to Europe with Don Redman in September 1946. Has lived in Europe ever since, touring as a single and occasionally with own small group, worked mainly in Scandinavia from 1955 until 1959, then moved back to Paris. Later moved to Sweden.

HOLLON, 'Kenny' Kenneth Lynn
tenor sax

Born: Brooklyn, N.Y., 26th November 1909
Died: New York, 30th September 1974

Taught by cousin, Clifton Glover. First gigs with 'Hat' Hunter in 1931, then worked with The Louisana Stompers. Despite having a daytime government job was much in demand as a musician and during the 1930s and early 1940s worked with Luis Russell, Charlie Johnson, Teddy Hill, Claude Hopkins, Vernon Andrade, Frankie Newton, Fats Waller's Big Band, Don Redman, Buddy Johnson, and Louis Jordan, then long spell with Don Wilson's Orchestra from 1945 until 1969.

HOLMES, 'Bobby' Robert E.
alto and soprano saxes/clarinet

Died: January 1968

With Fess Williams in the late 1920s then joined band led by drummer Willie Lynch. Toured with King Oliver (summer 1930), with Fess Williams (summer 1931), worked with Mills Blue Rhythm Band and Chick Webb during the early 1930s, with Tiny Bradshaw (1934-5), pianist Maurice Rocco (1938).

HOLMES, 'Charlie' Charles William
alto and soprano saxes/clarinet/oboe/flute

Born: Boston, Massachusetts, 27th January 1910

Boyhood friend of Harry Carney and Johnny Hodges. Studied music with Joseph Wagner in Boston, played oboe with the Boston Civic Symphony Orchestra in 1926. Moved to New York (with Harry Carney) in 1927, briefly with Chick Webb, then joined Henri Saparo's at Bamboo Inn, worked at same venue with pianist Joe Steele. With drummer George Howe's Band at The Nest, remained when Luis Russell was appointed leader. Left Russell (c. mid-1928), joined Henri Saparo's Band at Bamboo Inn, New York, then worked with pianist Joe Steele at the same venue. Rejoined Luis Russell in 1929, with Mills Blue Rhythm Band (1932), then again worked with Luis Russell and later Louis Armstrong until September 1940. With Bobby Burnet in New York (February-March 1941), left music briefly in summer 1941 to return to Boston. With Cootie Williams' Big Band from early 1942 until 1945, then toured the Orient with Jesse Stone's U.S.O. Show. Briefly with John Kirby early in 1947, later that year worked in Billy Kyle's Sextet. Left full-time music to work in the offices of a Wall Street insurance broker. Continued to play gigs in the 1960s and 1970s, including occasional recordings.

HONORE, Gideon J.
piano

Born: New Orleans, Louisiana, 15th September 1904

Moved to Chicago in June 1921. Studied piano at Axel Christenson School of Jazz, received tuition from Kenneth Anderson, Professor Nicholson, and Mrs. Massey. First gigs with Palmer Cadiz at the Cascade Gardens, then solo piano dates in Chicago before forming own band, which played at Lakewood Hall and Huntington Hotel during the late 1920s. During the 1930s worked with many bandleaders in Chicago: Jimmie Noone (1936 and 1939), Tiny Parham, Hosea Duff (1933), Jesse Stone (1935), Eddie Coles

(1937), Preston Jackson, Floyd Campbell, etc., also solo work in U.S.A. and Canada. In 1940 led own quartet (featuring Darnell Howard) at 411 Club, Chicago, also with Sidney Bechet at Club Rio, Springfield, Illinois (1944), and with Dallas Bartley in Chicago (1945). Did theatre tours with Helena Jester (including Apollo, New York). Moved to California in July 1948, worked with Kid Ory at the Jade Room, Beverly Cavern, etc., and with Teddy Buckner at the 400 Club. Mainly with Albert Nicholas Quartet (1950-3). In the late 1960s worked regularly in duo with bassist Rocky Robinson, also taught piano. Often worked with Roger Jameson's New Orleanians during the 1970s.

HOOPER, 'Lou' Louis Stanley
piano/composer/violin

Born: near Chatham, Ontario, Canada, 18th May 1894
Died: Charlottetown, Canada, 17th September 1977

Father and brothers were musicians. Raised in Ypilsanti, Michigan, sang in church choir. Gained degree at Detroit Conservatory (1916). Moved to Harlem in 1921, played in silent cinemas, theatres, and accompanied singers, made many free-lance recordings. Moved back to Detroit in the early 1930s, later toured with Myron Sutton's Canadian Ambassadors. Moved to Montreal in 1933, joined Royal Canadian Artillery in 1939 as a musical director, did overseas tours during World War II. Returned to Detroit, led own band there, then moved back to Canada. Played many concerts in Canada during the 1960s and early 1970s.

HOPKINS, Claude Driskett
piano/leader/arranger/composer

Born: Alexandria, Virginia, 24th August 1903
Died: New York, 19th February 1984

Raised in Washington, D.C., where both his parents were on the staff of the Howard University. Began playing piano at the age of seven, later spent two years studying medicine and music at Howard University, gained AB degree and did further year's study at Washington Conservatory. Played in college orchestras, then led own band in Atlantic City (summer 1924), played briefly in New York with Wilbur Sweatman, then again organised own band. Sailed to Europe in September 1925, leading own band for the Josephine Baker revue, toured throughout Europe with the show, then led own band (comprised of Joe Hayman and several European musicians) in Italy and Spain (early 1926). Returned to New York in spring of 1926 and during that summer led own band at Smile-a-While, Asbury Park, New Jersey, played residencies in New York and Washington, then led own band for 'Ginger Snaps' touring revue (1927). Continued leading during the late 1920s at Roseland Ballroom, Asbury Park, Cocoanut Grove, New York, etc., was then appointed leader of the musicians then working with Charlie Skeete. Led the new band at the Savoy Ballroom, New York (1930), then long residencies at the Roseland Ballroom (1931-4), Cotton Club (late 1934-6), etc. (During the 1930s Claude Hopkins occasionally fronted the band, using Ray Durant, Mike Dishman, etc., as pianist.) From 1937 until 1940 did extensive touring, occasional residencies in New York, etc. Reorganised band in 1941, played on West Coast, New York, etc., until disbanding late in 1942. In 1943 worked as an inspector at the Eastern Aircraft factory in New Jersey and led the company's Wild Cat Band, also led own band on tour of Canada, Ohio, etc. (September-November 1943). In October 1944 formed new band for residency at Club Broadway, New York, etc., early in 1946 own big band into Zanzibar, New York. Formed own quintet in October 1947, played in Boston and The Place, New York (1948), then led own sextet at Club Zanzibar, New York (1950-1). Worked in Boston (1952), from 1954 began regular appearances with Henry 'Red' Allen at The Metropole, New York, also played in Herman Autrey's Trio in late 1950s and with clarinettist Sol Yaged in 1960. Regular recording sessions during the 1950s. From 1960-6 regularly led own small group, regular seasons at Nevele Country Club in the Catskills, Longwood Casino, etc. From late 1967-9 played with Wild Bill Davison in The Jazz Giants. Continues to play regularly, brief spell with Roy Eldridge at Jimmy Ryan's, New York (1970). Played many jazz festivals during the 1970s. Toured Europe with Earle Warren and Dicky Wells.

During the mid-1930s, Claude Hopkins' Orchestra appeared in the films 'Dance Team', 'Barbershop Blues', and 'Wayward'.

H

HORTON, Robert H. — *Born: Birmingham, Alabama, 8th September 1899*
trombone — *Deceased*

Also known as Redius, Everett, and 'Bob Mack'. Played in 'Fess' Whatley's Band at Industrial High School, Birmingham. Worked with Sam Wooding at The Nest, New York (1922-4), to South America with Leon Abbey in May 1927, returned to the U.S.A., joined Wilbur de Paris Orchestra at Pearl Theatre, Philadelphia (late 1927-8). With Chick Webb at The Renaissance, New York, etc. (1928-9), Gene Kennedy (1929). With Charlie Johnson (c. 1930), toured with Ralph Cooper's Kongo Knights (1932-3), Lucky Millinder (1933-4), Willie Bryant (1935-6), Edgar Hayes (1937-40) including tour of Europe. Worked on and off with Cootie Williams' Big Band during the 1940s, briefly with Claude Hopkins (March-June 1946). Retired from full-time music, worked for the New York City Park Department, but continued to gig in the late 1960s with Happy Caldwell, etc.

HOWARD, Bob — *Born: Newton, Massachusetts, 20th June 1906*
(real name: Howard Joyner)
vocals/piano

Moved to New York in 1926, worked as a solo act in various clubs, began recording career in 1931. Throughout the 1930s played long residencies in New York including: Tillie's, Park Central Hotel, Famous Door, The Hickory House, etc., also featured at Loew's State Theatre, The Apollo, Lafayette, etc. During the mid-1930s made a series of records with all-star jazz accompaniment and did successful tours of Europe as a solo artist. Had own radio series from 1935 and at one time was the only Negro artist having own commercial radio programme. During the late 1930s did long spell at Mamie's Chicken Shack, New York, where he also accompanied vocalist Billy Daniels. Had own television show on C.B.S. during the 1950s; also played residencies in Los Angeles, Las Vegas, Montreal, etc.

HOWARD, Darnell — *Born: Chicago, Illinois, 25th July. c. 1895*
clarinet/violin/saxes — *Died: San Francisco, California, 2nd September 1966*

His father, Sam Howard, played violin, cornet, and piano; Darnell's mother also played piano. Took up violin at the age of seven, lessons from Charlie Elgar; studied at John Farren School, Chicago. Joined musicians' union in 1912, played for six weeks with pianist Clarence Jones at the Panorama Theatre, Chicago, then resumed studies at high school. First professional work with John H. Wickcliffe's Ginger Orchestra: in Milwaukee (1913), Minneapolis (1914), Milwaukee (1915), Lamb's Cafe, Chicago (1916). To New York with W. C. Handy's Orchestra for first recordings (on violin)—September 1917. Returned to Chicago, led own band at Elite Cafe and Arcadia Ballroom, then toured Middle West with Charlie Elgar (1921), then (with several other Elgar sidemen) joined Plantation Days Band (led by James P. Johnson) for brief stay in London (March-May 1923). Returned to U.S.A., then revisited Europe with the five-piece Singing Syncopators (1924). Back to Chicago where he joined Carroll Dickerson, then with Dave Peyton before joining King Oliver's Dixie Syncopators. Played with Oliver (on alto/soprano/clarinet and violin) at the Plantation for seven months, then left U.S.A. with the New York Singing Syncopators (led by pianist William Hegamin). The N.Y.S.S. were based in Shanghai, but also toured the Philippines and Japan. Darnell returned to the U.S.A. and rejoined King Oliver in July 1926. Doubled with Erskine Tate at the Vendome Theatre (1926 to October 1927) and Carroll Dickerson at the Sunset Cafe (1927), briefly in Vaughn's Lucky Sambo Orchestra (March 1927), then joined Jimmy Wade's Dixielanders (1928). From summer 1928 led own quartet at the Club Ambassador in Chicago and doubled with Charlie Elgar's Band at the Savoy. In 1929-30 worked mainly with Dave Peyton at the Regal Theatre, also led own Jungle Band at the Ritz Cafe. Spell with Jerome Carrington's Orchestra (early 1931), then with Earl Hines' Big Band from 1931-7. Played with Eddie Cole's at 5100 Club, later led own group at various Chicago clubs including: 5100, Off-Beat (1939), and 308 Club (1940), also played briefly in Fletcher Henderson's Band and with Coleman Hawkins' Band in spring 1941. In 1943-5 continued to lead own group in Chicago (Tropical Isle, Pershing Lounge, etc.), but also owned own photographic and radio-repair shop. Played with Kid Ory in California (August-October 1945), then again led in Chicago, also played for various other leaders including 'Doc' Evans and Mel Grant. Moved back to California in late 1948 to join Muggsy Spanier, mainly with Muggsy Spanier until spring 1953, then joined trumpeter Bob Scobey. With Jimmy Archey Band in early 1954, then from 1955-62 worked with Earl Hines' Small Band. Recovered from serious illness (1962), led own small groups and also gigged with Elmer Snowden and pianist Burt Bales. Toured Europe with New Orleans All Stars early in 1966, returned to U.S.A. and entered hospital. Left hospital, then suffered a stroke in June 1966 which ended his playing days. He died in September 1966 of a brain tumour.

HOWARD, Earle
piano/vocals/composer/organ/guitar

Born: Petersburg, Virginia, 3rd June 1904
Died: Modena, Italy, December 1978

In 1918 moved with his parents to New York City, attended PS89 School with Fats Waller and played in boys' band with Charlie Irvis, Benny Carter, and Benny Morton. First professional work in 1920, playing for a show touring New England. Left in 1923, formed own septet in Hartford, Connecticut. By 1924 was leading own nine-piece Whispering Serenaders at Cinderella Ballroom, Hartford. After long spell of touring played residency at Strand Danceland, New York (autumn 1928 to spring 1929). (From 1927 did regular summer seasons in New England.) Worked in Bill Benford's Band (spring 1929 to spring 1930), then led own big band in Boston (1930) before New York residencies at Saratoga Club, Savoy Ballroom (1931), Rose Danceland (1932). After leading in Boston (1933) became musical director for Percy Nelson's Band (October 1933 to May 1934), then led own bands in New York through the 1930s. Toured South America with Baron Lee (Jimmy Ferguson) in summer of 1938, then played in New York with 'The Blackbirds Show' and Leon Abbey (1939). Worked as a solo entertainer throughout the 1940s. To Europe in late 1951, played long residencies in Switzerland, Italy, France, Austria, and Germany, then moved to make his home first in Finland and then Sweden. Now plays mostly in Stockholm and Malmo, regular TV and radio work. Moved to Italy in the 1970s.

HOWARD, 'Kid' Avery
trumpet

Born: New Orleans, Louisiana, 22nd April 1908
Died: New Orleans, Louisiana, 28th March 1966

Started on drums at 14, played with Andrew Morgan and Chris Kelly, then switched to cornet, did parade work for many years with the Eureka, Allen's Brass Band, and the Tuxedo. Organised own band in the late 1920s, residencies in New Orleans and touring as far as Chicago, also worked for Jack Carey, Sam Morgan, etc. During the 1930s did pit work in Palace, Gem, and Lincoln theatres, also regularly at La Vida Dance Hall and The Tavern. After recording with George Lewis in 1943, gigged in New Orleans for several years, worked regularly with Lewis from 1952 (including tour of Europe 1959). Recovered from serious illness in 1961 and played frequently at Preservation Hall and Dixieland Hall in New Orleans during last years of his life. He died of a cerebral haemorrhage.

HOWARD, Paul Leroy
tenor sax/clarinet

Born: Steubenville, Ohio, 1895
Died: Los Angeles, California, 18th February 1980

Father played cornet, mother piano and organ. Started on cornet, then began doubling on alto sax (also learnt clarinet, oboe, bassoon, flute, and piano). Moved to Los Angeles in 1911, first professional work in 1916 with Wood Wilson's Syncopators (on tenor sax), then with Satchel McVea's Howdy Band. Continued doubling cornet until 1917, worked for a while in San Diego, then long spell with Harry Southard's Black and Tan Band from 1918. During the early 1920s also played with King Oliver and Jelly Roll Morton on the West Coast. With the Quality Four (Harvey Brooks on piano) from 1923, then led own Quality Serenaders from 1924. Briefly with Sonny Clay Band, then re-formed Quality Serenaders. Two years' residency at Sebastian's Cotton Club from 1927, later at the Kentucky Club, Los Angeles. Disbanded in the early 1930s, then Paul worked in Ed Garland's 111 Band. Formed own trio (1934). Played in Lionel Hampton's Band (1935), then in Eddie Barefield's Big Band (1936-7). With Charlie Echols until re-forming own band in late 1939. Led own band at Virginia's, near Los Angeles, for 14 years until 1953. Since 1937 he has held the position of Financial Secretary with the Local 767 branch of the musicians' union. Continued to play throughout the 1950s.

HOWARD, Rosetta
vocals

Born: Chicago, Illinois. c. 1914
Died: Chicago, Illinois, 1974

Chiefly remembered for her recorded work with the Harlem Hamfats. Began singing professionally in 1932, worked in Chicago with Herb Morand and Odell Rand during the mid-1930s, went to New York with them in 1937 and 1938. With Eddie Smith's Band in Chicago (1938-9), visited New York again in 1939. With pianiste Lillian Allen at 333 Club, Chicago, then with Sonny Thompson's Band (1941). Solo work in the 1940s, then devoted herself to singing in the Pilgrim Baptist Church Choir.

HUCKO, 'Peanuts' Michael Andrew
clarinet/tenor sax

Born: Syracuse, New York, 7th April 1918

Played with Johnny Camarata Band before moving to New York in 1939. Briefly with Jack Jenney's Band, then joined Will Bradley in October 1939 (replacing Bernie Billings), short spell with Tommy Reynolds in summer 1940, then on tenor with Joe Marsala until rejoining Will Bradley September 1940. Left Bradley in 1941; with Bob Chester and Charlie Spivak, then joined U.S. Army Air Force. Served in Europe with Glenn Miller's A.A.F. Band. After demobilisation played in Benny Goodman's Band (late 1945 to early 1946), then with Ray McKinley from February 1946 until April 1947. Did radio work with Jack Teagarden's Sextet in New York (summer 1947), then joined Eddie Condon in October 1947. On and off with Condon until August 1950, briefly with Wild Bill Davison in San Francisco (1949), and with Joe Bushkin in New York (1950). C.B.S. studio work with pianist Bernie Leighton (late 1950-1), then A.B.C. studio musician from 1951-5. Toured Japan with Benny Goodman in late 1956 (as lead alto), then to Europe with Jack Teagarden-Earl Hines All Stars in autumn 1957. With Louis Armstrong All Stars from July 1958 until March 1960. A.B.C. studio work in the early 1960s, then led own group at Condon's Club 1964-6. Toured Britain as a soloist in May 1967. In 1967 married vocaliste Louise Tobin (who was once Mrs. Harry James), they made their home in Denver, Colorado, but returned East to appear together at the 1969 Newport Jazz Festival. Finished two-year residency at Navarre Club, Denver, in December 1969. Joined Lawrence Welk's Orchestra (late 1970). Featured with Glenn Miller Orchestra (1974), then played residencies in Denver, then resumed widespread international touring schedule.

HUDSON, Will
arranger/leader/composer

Born: Barstow, California, 8th March 1908
Died: S. Carolina, 1981

Studied arranging at high school in Detroit. Whilst working as a mail clerk he began arranging for McKinney's Cotton Pickers, also sold arrangements to Erskine Tate in Chicago. Brought to New York in 1932 by Cab Calloway, shortly afterwards became staff arranger for impressario Irving Mills, scored for Cab Calloway, Andy Kirk, Ina Ray Hutton, Don Redman, Louis Armstrong, etc. In late 1935 began co-leading big band with vocalist-songwriter Eddie de Lange, from May 1938 Hudson became sole leader. Continued leading until 1941, brief reconciliation with de Lange, then concentrated on free-lance arranging. Continued arranging and composing throughout the 1950s, but abandoned jazz arranging in the late 1940s.

HUG, Armand
piano

Born: New Orleans, Louisiana, 6th December 1910
Died: New Orleans, 19th March 1977

Taught piano by his mother. Began playing in public in 1923, by 1925 was fully professional, working residency at The Fern Club. During the 1920s and 1930s played many residencies in New Orleans, also worked with various bands including spell with the Owls in 1928. After wartime duties in the U.S. merchant marine he continued to work in New Orleans, long solo residency at the Rumpus Room, then into Musso's Club, 300 Club in Gretna, etc., also had own series on local television. Long residency at Golliwog Lounge, occasionally played in bands during the 1960s including stints with Johnny Wiggs and Sharkey Bonano. Was featured at the New Orleans Jazz Fest in June 1969. A prolific and successful composer.

HUMES, Helen
vocals/piano

Born: Louisville, Kentucky, 23rd June 1913
Died: Santa Monica, California, 9th September 1981

Moved to New York in her early teens, made record debut in Chicago (1927). In the early 1930s did theatre work and long spell with Vernon Andrade's Orchestra, then residency at Cotton Club, Cincinnati, before joining Count Basie in July 1938. Left Basie in the spring of 1941, did residency at the Village Vanguard, then (accompanied by Clarence Love's Orchestra) did extensive touring. After further residencies in New York moved to California in 1944. Scored with hit record of 'Be baba leba' in 1945, worked mainly on the West Coast, regular concert and television appearances, also worked in the play 'Simply Heavenly'. Toured Australia with Red Norvo in 1956 and worked occasionally with Norvo in the U.S.A. during the late 1950s. Did residency at Renaissance, Los Angeles, in summer of 1960, toured Europe 1962. Moved to Australia in June 1964, then returned to U.S.A. Left music temporarily c. 1967, moved back to Louisville, but resumed professional singing in 1973. Did U.S. residencies and international touring during the 1970s.

HUMPHREY, Willie James
clarinet/saxes

Born: New Orleans, Louisiana, 29th December 1900

Brother of Earl (trombone) and Percy (trumpet/drums); their father, Willie Sr. (died: 1964), was a clarinettist, their grandfather, 'Professor' Jim Humphrey was a celebrated music teacher. Started on violin at nine, switched to clarinet five years later, joined trumpeter George McCullum's Band, later worked in the Silver Leaf Orchestra. In 1919 played briefly on the riverboats, then moved to Chicago where he played with King Oliver, trombonist George Filhe, and Freddie Keppard. Returned to New Orleans in 1920, played for various leaders including: Amos Riley, Frankie Dusen, Zutty Singleton, Kid Rena, also led own band. Moved to St. Louis in 1925 and for the next seven years worked mainly with Fate Marable and Dewey Jackson. Taught music in New Orleans from 1932 until 1935, then joined Lucky Millinder's Band until June 1936. (During this period recorded with Henry 'Red' Allen.) Returned to New Orleans and played with Steve Lewis, Louis Dumaine, the N.O.L.A. Band, etc. Served in U.S. Naval Band during World War II. Worked with Young Tuxedo and Eureka Brass Bands, worked in his brother Percy's Band, then during early 1950s with Paul Barbarin, including New York residency in 1955. From the late 1950s led own Hot Four at Preservation Hall, also played regularly in Sweet Emma Barrett's Band. Toured Europe with Billie and Dede Pierce in 1967. In 1969 played in brother Percy's Band. Often toured with the Preservation Hall Jazz Band during the 1970s and early 1980s.

HUMPHRIES, 'Fat Man' Frank
trumpet/saxes

Born: Gracey, Kentucky, 8th April 1913
Died: Nyack, New York, 1st November 1978

Brother of Hildred (alto sax and trumpet), two nephews Teddy (piano) and Roger (drums) are professional musicians. Formed Original Humphries Play Boys in 1928, then (with Hildred) played with Vernon Stern (1929), Pittsburgh Harlemites (1931), Jack Spruce (1933-4) own orchestra (1935-38), 'Ham' Williams (1941), Christopher Columbus (1942). Whilst Hildred served in the Army, Frank worked with Lucky Millinder, Cootie Williams, Louis Jordan, Don Redman, Tab Smith, etc. Together in the mid-1940s they re-formed the Humphries Brothers' Band which played together for more than 30 years.

HUNT, George
trombone

Born: Kansas City, Missouri. c. 1906
Died: Chicago, Illinois. c. 1946

With Bennie Moten's Band from 1932. Worked with Count Basie at the Reno Club, Kansas

City, and travelled to New York with the band in 1936. Left Basie in 1937, worked with Fletcher Henderson (late 1937), then moved to Chicago, worked with Artie Starck's Band (1939), Erskine Tate (1940), and toured with Earl Hines (1941). He returned to Chicago and committed suicide there.

HUNT, 'Pee Wee' Walter
trombone/vocals

Born: Mt. Healthy, Ohio, 10th May 1907
Died: Plymouth, Massachusetts, 22nd June 1979

Both parents were musical; his father was a violinist, his mother a guitarist. After leaving high school in Columbus, Ohio, he studied at the Ohio State University. Began playing banjo at 17, later graduated from Cincinnati Conservatory. Played with local bands on banjo and trombone, then joined Jean Goldkette for residency at the Pla-Mor Ballroom, Kansas City (late 1927 to early 1928). Later worked in Hollywood Theatre Orchestra in Detroit, then in 1929 became a founder-member of the Casa Loma Band (directed by Glen Gray), heavily featured on vocals (including recorded duet with Louis Armstrong 1939). Left Glen Gray in May 1943 and became a disc-jockey in Hollywood, did regular free-lancing playing, after a spell with Freddie Fisher's Band he joined the U.S. Merchant Marine in early 1945. He formed his own small band in Los Angeles (1946) and achieved great success with his tongue-in-cheek record of 'Twelfth Street Rag' (1948).

HUNTER, Alberta
vocals

Born: Shelby County, Memphis, Tennessee, 1st April 1895

Ran away to Chicago at the age of 11, did first professional singing at Dago Frank's Club, left after 18 months and worked for three years at Hugh Hoskins', then featured at the Panama Club and Dreamland. Moved to New York and throughout the 1920s did regular recordings, occasionally using her sister's name, Josephine Beatty, as a pseudonym. Played regular club dates in New York, also did theatre work including the 'How Come' show. Worked in Europe during the early 1930s—co-starrring with Paul Robeson in the London production of 'Showboat'. Brief return to New York, then again in Paris and London in 1935. In 1936 returned to New York and was featured at Connie's Inn, returned to Europe, then back to U.S.A. in 1937. During the late 1930s played long residencies in New York, was also featured on N.B.C. radio series. During World War II did extensive touring for the U.S.O.—including Pacific and Europe. In Britain with Snub Mosley (1952), later toured Canada and played long residencies in Chicago, in 1954-5 understudied in the Broadway Show 'Mrs. Patterson'. In 1956 she left the music profession and began working as a professional nurse, resumed recording in the 1960s. Returned to full-time singing in October 1977 and began long residency at The Cookery in Greenwich Village.

HURLEY, Clyde L.
trumpet

Born: Fort Worth, Texas, 3rd September 1916
Died: September 1963

Mother was a professional pianiste/vocaliste. Started on piano, then switched to trumpet. Played for several years in local bands before joining Ben Pollack (then touring Texas) in 1937. Moved to California with Pollack, also did radio-studio work before joining Glenn Miller in the spring of 1939. Left in 1940, spent a year with Tommy Dorsey before joining Artie Shaw (1941). From 1942-9 worked in Hollywood film-studio bands, subsequently spent five years in N.B.C. television studios. From 1955 has free-lanced in California for film, television, radio, and record companies, worked in many films including: 'The Five Pennies', 'The Gene Krupa Story', etc., also featured in Matty Matlock's Rampart Street Paraders.

HUTCHENRIDER, Clarence Behrens
clarinet/saxes/flute

Born: Waco, Texas, 13th June 1908

Took up sax at the age of 14, led own band at high school, then played at the Adolphus Hotel, Dallas, in band led by Jack Gardner, subsequently with Dick Richardson and Claiborne Bryson Bands in Shreeveport, Louisiana, before joining Ross Gorman in 1928.

With Tommy Tucker (1929), then with Merle Jacobs in Cleveland (c. 1930). Spell with Austin Wylie, then joined Casa Loma Orchestra (directed by Glen Gray) in autumn of 1931. Featured mainly on clarinet with Casa Loma (occasionally on tenor: 'No Name Jive', etc.) until 1943. He suffered an illness in the spring of 1943, but returned to the band until December of that year. Did radio shows and tours with Jimmy Lytell's Band for three years, then illness enforced temporary retirement from full-time music. Returned to regular playing, worked with Glen Moore Band and Walter Davidson, then formed highly successful trio which, through the late 1950s and 1960s, played long residencies in New York at the Gaslight, Speakeasy, Stork, and Gay 90s. Continued to play regularly throughout the 1970s including dates with The New Orleans Nighthawks.

HUTTON, Ina Ray
(real name: Odessa Cowan)
leader/vocals

Born: Chicago, Illinois, 13th March 1916
Died: Ventura, California, 19th February 1984

Her mother (Marvel Ray) was a professional pianiste. During the early 1930s Ina sang and danced in several Broadway productions including: Lew Leslie's 'Clowns in Clover', George White's 'Melody Revue', and the Ziegfeld Follies. In late 1934 agent Irving Mills signed her to front a big all-girl orchestra (the outfit's first musical director and arranger was Alex Hill). Continued with all-girl band through the 1930s, then during the 1940s led own male band, disbanded in 1944, then re-formed using the alumni of Bob Alexander's Band. During the 1950s Ina occasionally fronted her own all-girl bands, but also did solo vocal work.

I

INGE, Edward Frederick *Born: Kansas City, Missouri, 7th May 1906*
clarinet/saxes/arranger

Clarinet from the age of 12, studied in conservatories in St. Louis and Madison, Wisconin. Professional debut with George Reynolds' Orchestra (1924), then with Dewey Jackson before joining Art Simms in Milwaukee, after Simms' death worked with Oscar 'Bernie' Young until late 1928. With McKinney's Cotton Pickers (late 1930-1), then long spell with Don Redman until 1939. Joined Andy Kirk in early 1940 (replacing Don Byas), left in 1943. Did regular arranging for Kirk, also scored for many bandleaders including Don Redman, Jimmie Lunceford, and Louis Armstrong. Led own band in Cleveland (1945), then settled in Buffalo to organise own business. Led own band in Buffalo in the 1950s and 1960s, also worked in Cecil Johnson's Band in the 1960s. With C. Q. Price's Band in Buffalo (1971).

IRISH, George *Born: Panama, 1910*
saxes/clarinet/arranger *Died: Boston, Massachusetts, 24th November 1959*

Raised in Boston, Massachusetts. Began professional career as sax/arranger with Blanche Calloway's Band (summer 1938), following year joined Teddy Wilson's Big Band, with Benny Carter (1940 to early 1941), then with Fletcher Henderson until 1942. Briefly with Don Redman (1943), then formed own band. Moved back to Boston and became a teacher at the Academy of Music in Arlington, Massachusetts, a position he held until his death.

IRVIS, Charlie *Born: New York City. c. 1899*
trombone *Died: New York City. c. 1939*

Brother of pianist Gibbie Irvis. Began playing in boys' band with Earle Howard, Bubber Miley, etc. With Lucille Hegamin's Blue Flame Syncopators (1920-1), then with Willie 'The Lion' Smith at Capitol Palace. Joined The Washingtonians (Duke Ellington, Elmer Snowden) in early 1924 (replacing John Anderson), with Duke Ellington and Elmer Snowden (1925-6). (During the 1920s took part in many Clarence Williams recording sessions.) With Charlie Johnson (1927-8), then toured with Jelly Roll Morton (1929-30), member of Bubber Miley's Band (1931).

IRWIN, Cecil *Born: Evanston, Illinois, 7th December 1902*
saxes/clarinet/arranger *Died: near Des Moines, Iowa, 3rd May 1935*

With Carroll Dickerson Orchestra (c. 1924-5), then with Erskine Tate, The Cafe de Paris Orchestra, Chicago (1927), and Junie Cobb before joining Earl Hines in December 1928 as tenor saxist/arranger. Prolific free-lance recordings in the 1920s. Other than brief absences he remained with Earl Hines until the time of his death in an accident. He was killed instantly when the Earl Hines' band coach was involved in a crash near Des Moines, Iowa.

JACKSON, 'Bull Moose' Benjamin Clarence — *Born: Cleveland, Ohio, 1919*
tenor sax/vocals

Began on violin, switched to tenor-sax in high school, worked in local band led by trumpeter Freddy Webster before joining Lucky Millinder (1944-45), then led own small group called The Buffalo Bearcats. Made a number of successful rhythm-and-blues singles during the late 1940s and early 1950s, also worked with Tiny Bradshaw's Band. Retired from full-time music in the late 1950s, but emerged to play tour of Middle East and Africa with Buck Clayton in 1977.

JACKSON, 'Chubby' Greig Stewart — *Born: New York City, 25th October 1918*
string bass

Both parents were in show business. Chubby's son is a drummer. Raised in Freeport, Long Island. Clarinet in school band at 16, then bought a bass from Arnold Fishkind. Studied at Ohio State University. Returned to New York (1937), joined Mike Riley's Band, subsequently with Johnny Messner, Raymond Scott, Jan Savitt, Terry Shand, and Henry Busse before working with Charlie Barnet (1941-3). Regularly with Woody Herman from September 1943-6, returned to the band several times in the late 1940s and 1950s. Worked with Charlie Ventura in 1947, late that year toured Scandinavia with his own band. Returned to Woody Herman in mid-1948, then again led own big band in New York. Disbanded and free-lanced in all-star units (including Charlie Ventura's Big Four), then moved to Chicago in 1953. Did five years' studio work and was resident compere on a children's TV programme, worked briefly in Louis Armstrong All Stars early in 1954. Moved back to New York in 1958, did extensive studio work, compered television shows, and was active as a successful song-writer. In the early 1960s organised own bands for specific engagements, but also worked with various small groups including Harold Baker Quartet (1963) and Joe Coleman's Big 4 (1965). In the late 1960s worked mainly in Florida with his own band. Moved to Los Angeles in summer of 1971, prolific free-lance work there, and in Las Vegas. Toured Europe during the 1970s, including work with Lionel Hampton (1979).

JACKSON, 'Cliff' Clifton Luther — *Born: Culpeper, Virginia, 19th July 1902*
piano — *Died: New York, 24th May 1970*

Played professionally in Washington and Atlantic City before moving to New York in 1923. Worked in Happy Rhone's Club Orchestra (1925), Lionel Howard's Musical Aces (1926), and with Elmer Snowden before forming own Krazy Kats in January 1927, the band played several residencies in New York: Capitol Palace, Murray's Roseland, Lenox Club, etc. Worked mainly as a soloist or vocal accompanist through the 1930s. With Sidney Bechet at Nick's in early 1940, then formed own trio for Cinderella Club, New York. From autumn of 1944 until 1951 was the house pianist at Cafe Society Downtown except for 1946 tour with Eddie Condon. During the 1950s was featured pianist at several other New York venues, also worked in Garvin Bushell Trio (1959), J. C. Higginbotham Band (1960), Joe Thomas Band (1962). From 1963 worked regularly in Tony Parenti's Trio at Ryan's, also took part in filming of 'The Night They Raided Minsky's'. His widow is Maxine Sullivan. Solo recordings in 1969. Played at the RX Room, Manhattan, until the night before he died.

JACKSON, Dewey — *Born: St. Louis, Missouri, 21st June 1900*
trumpet

Played in Odd Fellows Boys' Band during his early teens. First professional work with Tommy Evans' Band in St. Louis (1916-17), then played for a year with George Reynolds' Keystone Band before joining Charlie Creath on riverboat 'J.S.' (May 1919). Then from 1920 until 1923 led own Golden Melody Band. In spring 1924 joined Fate Marable on S.S. 'Capitol'. During the following year led The St. Louis Peacock Charleston Orchestra on the S.S. 'Capitol'. After working on the 'J.S.' steamer moved to New York in August 1926 and spent four months with violinist Andrew Preer's Orchestra at the Cotton Club, then travelled to New Orleans to rejoin Fate Marable on the S.S. 'St. Paul'. Again with Charlie Creath (summer 1927), led own band (1927-9), occasional dates with Marable, then led own band at Castle Ballroom, St. Louis, from September 1930 until May 1932. Rejoined Charlie Creath (1934), worked in band jointly led by Fate Marable and Charlie Creath (1936), then from 1937 led own Musical Ambassadors on riverboats during the summers and in St. Louis ballrooms during the winters. Continued on riverboats until 1941, then led at various local ballrooms and clubs during the 1940s. Left full-time music to work as a hotel commissionaire, but began playing regularly again in 1950. Worked in Singleton Palmer's Band, then with pianist Don Ewell's Trio in 1951, led own band again during the 1950s, played occasional dates in the 1960s.

JACKSON, Franz R. *Born: Rock Island, Illinois, 1st November 1912*
tenor sax/clarinet/arranger

Studied at Chicago Musical College. Gigged with various bands before working with Cassino Simpson (1931), Carroll Dickerson (1932), Frankie Jaxon (1932), drummer Fred Avendorph (late 1932). Toured with Reuben Reeves (spring 1933), with Eddie King and the Jesters (1933), Carroll Dickerson (1934), joined bassist William Lyles (August 1934). Worked for Jimmie Noone for a year, briefly with Fletcher Henderson, then joined Roy Eldridge in Chicago, worked with Roy in New York (1939-40). To California with Earl Hines in October 1940, following year worked with Fats Waller. With Cootie Williams in New York (early 1942), briefly with Pete Brown, then worked in Boston with Frankie Newton. Toured with Roy Eldridge Big Band in 1944, then (from late 1944) long spell with Wilbur de Paris Band. With Jesse Stone on U.S.O. tour of Pacific (1946), continued touring with U.S.O. shows in late 1940s and early 1950s, returned to Chicago where he formed his own 'Original Jass All Stars' in 1956. The band played long successful residencies at the Red Arrow, Stickney, Illinois, played in New York (December 1968), and undertook several overseas U.S.O. tours including tour of Vietnam in autumn 1969. Did widespread touring during the 1970s. Played residency in Schaumburg, Illinois during early 1980s, also made solo tour of Europe (1981).

JACKSON, Graham W. *Born: Portsmouth, Virginia, 22nd February 1903*
piano

A musical prodigy whose mother was a noted singer. After high school he travelled to Atlanta and worked in band at the Royal Theater, later led own band, The Seminole Syncopators, there. Studied organ at musical college in Chicago. Led own band for many years in and around Atlanta including long residency at the 81 Theater, also taught music at the Booker T. Washington School and Morris Brown College. Led own bands during the 1920s, 1930s, 1940s and 1950s. During the 1930s and early 1940s played regularly for President Franklin D. Roosevelt at the Little White House in Hot Springs. Has now retired from music.

JACKSON, Preston *Born: New Orleans, Louisiana, 3rd January 1902*
(real name: James Preston McDonald) *Died: Blytheville, Arkansas, 12th November 1983*
trombone

Took surname of his step-father. Studied at Thomas Lafon and McDonogh 25 schools and at New Orleans University. Moved to Chicago in 1917. Mother bought him first trombone in August 1920, took lessons from Chicago trombonist William Robertson, nine months later played in local chapel band. Gigged with trumpeter Tig Chambers, then joined newly formed band led by violinist Al Simeon (brother of Omer Simeon). Took lessons from Honore Dutrey and Roy Palmer, then joined Eli Rice in Milwaukee, also toured with Eli Rice, after 14 months returned to Chicago and worked briefly in Teddy Weatherford's Band at Dreamland. Joined Art Simms' Band at Wisconsin Rook, Milwaukee, c. 1925, mainly with Simms' Band subsequently led by Oscar 'Bernie' Young until spring of 1930, also led own recording band. Worked for eight months with Dave Peyton at the Regal Theatre (1930), then joined Erskine Tate at the Michigan Theatre before joining Louis Armstrong in January 1931. Toured with Louis until early 1932, then returned to Chicago, worked with trumpeter Johnny Long (1932), Frankie Jaxon (1933), also worked regularly with Carroll Dickerson. Briefly with Jimmy Bell (late 1934). Worked with Jimmie Noone,

Carroll Dickerson, and bassist William Lyle, then played for several years in Zilner Randolph's W.P.A. Band—also wrote a regular column for *Jazz Hot* and *Hot News*. Worked occasionally with Roy Eldridge and Walter Barnes, brief spell with Johnny Long's Band (late 1939). Left full-time music but continued gigging, served on board of directors of local A.F. of Musicians from 1934 until 1957. In the 1940s, led own band which recorded in 1946. Occasionally led own band during the 1950s, also active with several small bands including spell with Lil Armstrong in 1959. Continued playing and recording during the 1960s, worked in Little Brother Montgomery's Band in late 1969. Moved to New Orleans during the 1970s, continued to play regularly in the 1970s, including tours of Europe. Died whilst touring with the Preservation Hall Jazz Band.

JACKSON, 'Butter' Quentin Leonard
trombone/vocals/occasional string bass

Born: Springfield, Ohio, 13th January 1909
Died: New York, 2nd October 1976

Brother-in-law of Claude Jones. At six received piano lessons from his mother; violin at 12, played in school orchestra. Played trombone from age of 18, worked with Gerald Hobson Band and with Lloyd Byrd's Buckeye Melodians, then with Wesley Helvey Band from August 1929 until January 1930. Played in Zack Whyte's Chocolate Beau Brummels, then joined McKinney's Cotton Pickers as trombonist/vocalist from December 1930 until May 1932. Left to play in Don Redman's Orchestra, remained with Redman until December 1939. With Cab Calloway from January 1940 until August 1946, then toured Europe with Don Redman. Returned to U.S.A. in December 1946 and rejoined Cab Calloway until 1948. Briefly with Lucky Millinder, then in Duke Ellington's Orchestra from 21st October 1948 until 20th October 1959. Toured Europe in Quincey Jones' Band (1960), then joined Count Basie until autumn 1962. Later that year played with Charlie Mingus, rejoined Duke Ellington briefly in spring of 1963. Did some studio work and played in the house band at the Copacabana, New York, late 1964. From the mid-1960s played in several big bands specially formed in New York including Louis Bellson's (1964) and Gerald Wilson's (1966). Toured with Sammy Davis (1970), with Al Cohn Band, Jones-Lewis (1971). Suffered fatal heart attack whilst playing for Broadway show 'Guys and Dolls'.

JACKSON, 'Rudy' Rudolph
clarinet/saxes

Born: Fort Wayne, Indiana, 1901
Died: Chicago, Illinois, c. 1968

Raised in Chicago, both parents were musicians. Worked in local bands from 1918, regularly with Carroll Dickerson in the early 1920s, then with King Oliver (late 1923 to summer 1924), then long spell of touring with travelling shows. With Billy Butler in New York (1925), with Vaughn's Lucky Sambo Orchestra on tour (from June 1926). Briefly with King Oliver in February 1927, then recommenced touring with the 'Lucky Sambo' show. Joined Duke Ellington in June 1927, replaced by Barney Bigard in December 1927. Sailed to Europe with Noble Sissle (May 1929), returned to New York with Sissle, in 1931 again went with Sissle to Europe, long spells with Leon Abbey. Worked with Teddy Weatherford and Leon Abbey in India during the mid-1930s. Returned to Europe, then rejoined Teddy Weatherford in Colombo, Ceylon. Played regularly in India and Ceylon until after World War II, then returned to live in Chicago; ceased regular playing and began long period of employment for the Western Union Telegraph company.

JACKSON, 'Tony' Anthony
piano/vocals

Born: Amelia Street, New Orleans, Louisiana, 5th June 1876
Died: Chicago, Illinois, 20th April 1921

Played piano in New Orleans brothels before the turn of the century—also worked occaionally in Adam Olivier's Band. Worked in Louisville, Kentucky (1904), and for a time partnered Glover Compton, had previously worked as accompanist to the Whitman Sisters. Briefly in New Orleans in autumn of 1904 and again 1910-12, then moved to Chicago permanently (he returned to New Orleans in February 1914 to attend his mother's funeral). Played in duo with Glover Compton at Elite No. 1, as a solo entertainer in many Chicago clubs, also worked again as accompanist for the Whitman Sisters. Worked for several years at the De Luxe Cafe, then moved to the Pekin Cafe, continued working there until shortly before his death. A prolific composer; his most famous tune is 'Pretty Baby'.

J

For a detailed summary of Tony Jackson's career the reader is advised to read 'They All Played Ragtime', by Rudi Blesh and Harriet Janis.

JACOBS, 'Pete' Edward
drums

Born: Asbury Park, New Jersey, 7th May 1899
Died: c. 1952

Originally played in The Musical Aces, then joined Claude Hopkins (summer 1926-8), with Charlie Skeete in 1928. Worked regularly in Claude Hopkins' Band from 1930 until April 1937 when ill health caused premature retirement from the music profession.

JACOBSON, 'Bud' Orville Kenneth
clarinet/saxes/piano

Born: Milwaukee, Wisconsin, 22nd February 1906
Died: West Palm Beach, Florida, 12th April 1960

Raised in Chicago. Played various instruments before specialising on alto and clarinet, later he played both of these simultaneously in a family musical act with his parents. Attended Crane High School, played in school band and began playing in local trio at various venues including Colony Club, Oak Park. Later played in Russ's Melody Boys and did summer seasons at holiday resorts. Gigged in Chicago in 1924, then formed short-lived White City Band, following year worked in Detroit with Art Kassel. Then worked mostly in Chicago with various bands including: Chuck Walker (1926), Joe Kayser (1927), Thelma Terry (1928), Wingy Manone (in Toledo 1929 and Chicago 1930), Floyd Town (1929), Charlie Pearce (1930), Joe Kayser (1930-1). Gigged in Chicago and worked on lake steamers, then with Frank Melrose (1933). With Frank Snyder at The Subway Club from spring 1934 until summer 1935, then two-year spell on piano accompanying vocaliste Anita O'Day at the Ball of Fire Club. With drummer Joey Conrad's Band (1938-9), then long spell of gigging on sax and piano. Joined Earl Wiley on tenor/clarinet (1943-4), briefly led own band at The Famous Door, then with Mark Fisher's Band until summer 1945. With Jack Page in late 1945, also led own recording group The Jungle Kings during 1945. Then worked with own band at Vine Gardens and other clubs. Organised many jazz concerts in Chicago during late 1940s and early 1950s. Forced to quit regular playing through heart trouble, he moved to Florida in the mid-1950s.

JAFFE, Nat
piano

Born: New York City, 1918
Died: New York City, 5th August 1945

Lived in Germany 1921-32. Returned to New York, gigged with local bands before joining Jan Savitt, spell of studio work, then with Joe Marsala (spring 1938), Charlie Barnet (1938-9). With Jack Teagarden from January to July 1940, left to do solo work on 52nd Street, New York. Led own small groups in New York through the early 1940s, inactive in last months of his life through high blood pressure. He was the husband of vocaliste Shirley Lloyd.

JAMES, Elmer
string bass/tuba

Born: Yonkers, New York, 1910
Died: New York, 25th July 1954

Played tuba in Gene Rodgers' Revellers in 1928, then with June Clark Band for a year before joining Chick Webb until December 1932. Switched to string bass, worked briefly with Benny Carter, brief return to Chick Webb, then with Fletcher Henderson from spring 1934. With Lucky Millinder late 1934-6, then on and off with Edgar Hayes 1937-9 (also played in Mezz Mezzrow's Disciples of Swing—late 1937). With Claude Hopkins in 1940, then left music to become a bread salesman. Gigged with Zutty Singleton Trio in 1942, but never returned to full-time playing.

JAMES, George
alto/baritone/clarinet/flute

Born: Beggs, Oklahoma, 7th December 1906

High school in St. Louis. Played with Charlie Creath's No. 2 Band and with Johnny Neal's Syncopators. Moved to Chicago in 1928, worked briefly for many bandleaders including: Jimmie Noone, Sammy Stewart, Ida Marples, Doc Watson, Bert Hall, etc., then led own trio. With Jimmie Noone (1930 to early 1931), then toured with Louis Armstrong until December 1931, then stayed on in New York. Played in Savoy Bearcats (1932) before joining Charlie Turner's Arcadians, remained when this band became Fats Waller's Orchestra, with Fats until 1937. Played for 'Blackbirds Revue' in 1938-9, brief spell with James P. Johnson (spring 1940), later that year played for three months in Benny Carter's Band before joining Teddy Wilson. With Lucky Millinder from summer of 1941 until early 1942. In 1943 led own band in New York for residencies at The Famous Door and Cafe Society. Rejoined James P. Johnson in summer 1944, then led own band in Pittsburgh, Detroit, and New York before joining Claude Hopkins from March-October 1945. Spent two years in Noble Sissle's Orchestra, worked briefly in Basil Spears' Orchestra, then formed own band. Continued to lead own band through the 1960s, playing residencies in New York City, Jamaica, New York, and New Jersey. International touring with Clyde Bernhardt's Band during the 1970s. Toured with the Harlem Blues and Jazz Band during the early 1980s prior to moving to Columbus, Ohio.

JAMES, Harry Hagg
trumpet

Born: Albany, Georgia, 15th March 1916
Died: Las Vegas, Nevada, 5th July 1983

Parents worked with travelling circuses; Harry's father, Everett, conducted the band. Began on drums at the age of seven, at 10 began taking trumpet lessons from his father. In 1931 the family settled in Beaumont and Harry began playing in Texas with various bands including Old Phillips Friars, Logan Hancock, and Herman Waldman, also toured as far as New Orleans with band led by violinist Joe Gill. With Ben Pollack from 1935-6, then joined Benny Goodman in January 1937. Left Goodman in late December 1938 to form his own band which made its official debut in February 1939 at the Benjamin Franklin Hotel, Philadelphia. Previously he had led his own recording band and had taken part in pick-up studio recordings with Teddy Wilson, Lionel Hampton, etc. By the early 1940s Harry's band had an enormous following, several records featuring his trumpet playing became best-sellers. Continued to tour regularly until the early 1950s, then after a spell of semi-retirement in California he reorganised his band for residencies in the U.S. and a tour of Europe in late 1957. During the 1960s was not continually active as a bandleader, but regularly led for long seasons in Nevada. In 1960 he played engagements in New York after a seven-year absence from that locale, subsequently he returned to play in New York on several occasions including Carnegie Hall Concert in September 1964. Harry James was originally married to vocaliste Louise Tobin, subsequently he married actress Betty Grable in 1943, since their divorce he has remarried. Films include: 'Private Buckaroo', 'Mr. Co-Ed', 'A Tale of Two Sisters', 'Syncopation', 'Bathing Beauty', 'If I'm Lucky', 'Carnegie Hall', 'Springtime in the Rockies', 'Kitten on the Keys', 'Best Foot Forward', 'Two Girls and a Sailor', 'Do You Love Me', 'The Benny Goodman Story', etc. Harry James also soundtracked for actor Kirk Douglas in 'Young Man with a Horn'. Toured Europe with own big band in autumn 1970 and again in autumn 1971, also played residencies in the U.S.A. during 1970s. Starred in touring show 'The Big Broadcast of 1944' during the late 1970s. Continued touring in early 1980s, including visit to the Argentine in 1981. Played last date with his band in Los Angeles, 26th June 1983.

JAXON, 'Half Pint' Frankie
vocals/composer

Born: Montgomery, Alabama, 3rd February 1895

Gained nickname through being 5 ft. 2 in. Orphaned in early childhood, to Kansas City in 1906, attended Attuck Grammar School from 1906 until 1909. At 15 began singing in local clubs and cinemas, then toured with the McDaniel Company (organised by the father of famous vocaliste-actress Hattie McDaniel). From 1912 until 1914 toured in double act with Gallie De Gaston. Did solo work, then joined Whitley Brothers' show, in April 1916 began working as singer-producer at various clubs in Atlantic City. Appeared at Sunset Cafe in Chicago (April 1917), then played residency at the Paradise Cafe, Atlantic City. Worked each summer until 1926 at this venue, usually playing winter seasons in Chicago. Toured with white band, Mae Dix and her Chicago Harmonaders, then worked mainly in Chicago from 1927 until 1936. Occasionally did tours and sang in other cities (with Bennie Moten in Kansas City—June-September 1930, etc.), but mainly active in the 1930s leading own Quarts of Joy. From December 1931 featured regularly on radio WJJD, then station WBBM from 1933. Toured with own band in 1936, worked on WMAQ, WCFL stations, etc. Led own bands for hotel residencies (1937-41), also continued with radio work. In October 1941 became a government employee at the Pentagon in Washington, D.C., was transferred to California in 1944, continued working for the government until his retirement. He used his own composition 'Fan It' as his signature tune, this tune was later recorded by Woody Herman.

JEFFERSON, Hilton
alto sax

Born: Danbury, Connecticut, 30th July 1903
Died: New York City, 14th November 1968

Went to junior school in Boston, then high school in Providence, Rhode Island. First played banjo, on which he joined Julian Arthur's Orchestra at the Hay's Theatre, Philadelphia (summer 1925). Left to study alto sax, rejoined Julian Arthur (on sax) in late 1925 and went with the orchestra to New York. Left to work for five months with 'Banjo Bernie', then from May 1926 until 1928 worked mainly with Claude Hopkins. With Chick Webb from 1929 until late summer 1930, then toured with King Oliver. (From the late 1920s Hilton Jefferson worked for brief spells with many bands in New York including: Edgar Dowell, Bill Brown, Ginger Young, Charlie Skeete, and Elmer Snowden.) After touring with King Oliver returned to Chick Webb, then during 1931 spent a brief spell in McKinney's Cotton Pickers. Rejoined Claude Hopkins from May until August 1932. Briefly with Benny Carter, then with Fletcher Henderson from October 1932 until September 1934, again with Chick Webb in 1934. Combined free-lance work with Claude Hopkins dates until reverting to Chick Webb Band in autumn of 1936. From December 1936 until early 1938 worked mostly for Fletcher Henderson, yet again with Chick Webb in 1938, also worked for Claude Hopkins during 1939. With Ella Fitzgerald before joining Cab Calloway in January 1940. Left in 1949 and began two years as house man at Billy Rose's Diamond Horseshoe Club, New York. Briefly with Cab Calloway in 1951, then eight months with Duke Ellington (from summer 1952 until February 1953). Did autumn 1953 tour with vocaliste Pearl Bailey (Don Redman directing the orchestra), then left full-time music to work as a guard at a New York bank. Continued to do regular gigs including several recording sessions. Also long regular stints with Harry Dial's Quintet and Noble Sissle. Regular member of Wally Edwards' Uptown Concert Band from late 1950s, also worked in Mercer Ellington's Big Band.

JEFFERSON, Maceo B.
guitar/banjo

Born: Beaufort, South Carolina. c. 1898
Died: Bridgeport, Connecticut, 15th June 1974

Did first professional work with pianist Frank Clarke in Norfolk, Virginia, subsequently moved to New York, played with Wilbur Sweatman (1923) and various New York bands before sailing to Europe with the Plantation Orchestra (1926). Remained in Europe through the early 1930s, worked with Arthur Briggs and many bands including a spell accompanying Louis Armstrong (1934). Returned to the U.S.A. briefly, then back to Europe (1937), was imprisoned by the Nazis and was interned at Compiegne concentration camp until late 1944, was then repatriated to the U.S.A. Visited New York in the 1960s, then moved to Bridgeport, Connecticut, where he devoted considerable time to composing.

JENKINS, 'Freddie'/'Posey' Frederic Douglass
trumpet

Born: New York City, 10th October 1906
Died: Texas, 1978

Switched to playing left-handed whilst in his early teens. Taught by Lt. Eugene Mikell and played regularly in the 369th Regiment Cadet Band. Went to Wilberforce University in the early 1920s, played briefly with Edgar Hayes' Blue Grass Buddies, then regularly with Horace Henderson's Collegians from 1924 until 1928. Joined Duke Ellington in 1928 and remained until severe illness in late 1934 (occasionally doubling on E-flat cornet during 1934). Began playing again in 1935 at Adrian's Tap Room. From January 1936 spent a brief spell conducting the Luis Russell Band at Connie's Inn (in between Louis Armstrong's featured numbers), then became part-owner of the Brittwood Club, New York. By March 1937 had recovered sufficiently to play in The Cotton Club Floor Show with Duke Ellington. Left Duke in May 1938 to form own short-lived band (co-led with Hayes Alvis). Late in 1938 suffered a recurrence of severe lung ailment and spent many months in hospital. Never returned to professional playing, but was active as a song-writer, press agent, and musical adviser in Washington, New York, and California throughout the 1940s. During the 1960s worked in Texas as a disc-jockey and press correspondent.

JENKINS, George
drums

Born: Norfolk, Virginia, 25th July 1917
Died: San Francisco, California, 10th May 1967

Worked with Clint Turner, then spent four years with the Hardy Brothers' Band before joining Lionel Hampton from 1941 until 1943, brief tour with Lucky Millinder, then with Buddy Johnson (1944-5). Rejoined Lionel Hampton from late 1945 until summer 1946, then spell with Charlie Barnet until leading own band in Detroit. In late 1940s worked regularly at The Metropole, New York (briefly with Louis Armstrong All Stars in spring of 1949). Moved to California, with Benny Carter (1951), then leading own small bands and gigging with many bands. During the early 1960s mainly led own trios in California and Las Vegas, brief return to The Metropole. Brother of vocalist Bea Foote.

JENKINS, 'Pat' Sidney
trumpet

Born: Norfolk, Virginia, 25th December 1914

Played trumpet for five years before moving to New York in 1934. Regularly with alto saxist Al Cooper's Savoy Sultans from 1937 until 1944, then served in U.S. Army. After demobilisation worked in Tab Smith's Band for three years, led own band for a while, then joined Buddy Tate's Band in 1951. Continued to play regularly with Tate at the Celebrity Club, New York, but because of day-time work at a New York department store was unable to do foreign tours with Buddy Tate. Has now retired.

JENNEY, 'Jack' Truman Elliot
trombone

Born: Mason City, Iowa, 12th May 1910
Died: Los Angeles, California, 16th December 1945

His brother, Bob, was also a professional musician, their father taught music. Jack began playing trumpet at eight whilst at school in Cedar Rapids, then switched to trombone, by the age of 11 was playing gigs with his father's band. In 1923 joined Art Brown's Novelty Band in Dubuque, Iowa, then spent three years at Culver Military Academy. First professional work with Austin Wylie (1928), then briefly with Earl Hunt's Band, with Isham Jones' Juniors in early 1930s, then with Mal Hallett from spring to autumn of 1933—also worked briefly with Phil Harris Band at Hotel Pennsylvania. From 1934-8, regular studio work in New York (Victor Young, Fred Rich, N.B.C., C.B.S., etc.), led own studio band in 1938, then formed own unsuccessful big band which resulted in bankruptcy. Mainly with Artie Shaw from September 1940 until late 1941, then returned to session work. Briefly with Benny Goodman from late 1942 (including work in film 'Stage Door Canteen'), also appeared in the film 'Syncopation'. In 1943 briefly fronted Bobby Byrne's Band (when that leader joined U.S. Navy), then formed own band for work in California. Served in U.S. Navy from late 1943 until May 1944, then returned to West Coast studio work. Died in hospital from complications following appendectomy.

JEROME, Jerry
tenor sax/clarinet/flute/arranger

Born: Brooklyn, New York, 19th June 1912

Spent several years studying medicine, played regularly in college bands. Worked with Harry Reser's Band during college vacations (1935), then quit studies to become a professional musician. With Glenn Miller (1936-7), briefly with Red Norvo (early 1938), then worked as a studio musician. With Artie Shaw until joining Benny Goodman from November 1938 until July 1940, then rejoined Artie Shaw until March 1941. From 1942-6 worked as musical director and conductor at N.B.C. studios, then a. and r. executive for

Apollo and Keystone records before resuming at N.B.C. in 1948. Worked for many years as musical director for WPIX television company in New York.

JOHNAKINS, Leslie F. *Born: Newport News, Virginia, 1st October 1911*
baritone sax/reeds

Began playing clarinet in high school. Did paid musical work in 1928 prior to attending college in North Carolina, played there with Dave Taylor's Band (1929-30), and remained when band became Jimmy Gunn's Serenaders (1931-34). With Buddy Johnson (1935). Moved to New York and worked with Claude Hopkins (1936), Blanche Calloway (1937), Hot Lips Page (1938), Edgar Hayes (1939), Eddie Barefield (1941) and Earl Bostic (1941) before doing defence-plant work during World War II. Continued to play gigs during this period. In November 1975 celebrated 30 years as a member of Machito's Orchestra.

JOHNSON, Archie *Born: Ellisville, Mississippi, 5th December 1906*
trumpet

Raised in Pittsburgh. To New York with the Elite Serenaders (1926). Left New York to join Zack Whyte's Band in Cincinatti; remained with Whyte for over two years then joined Blanche Calloway's Band (also worked with Speed Webb, Horace Henderson and Banjo Bernie during the late 1920s-early 1930s). With Blanche Calloway (1934-35), then spell with Eddie Mallory's Band before working with Lucky Millinder during the late 1930s and early 1940s (also worked with Claude Hopkins and Benny Carter during the late 1930s). Continued to play during the 1980s, often with Bobby Booker's Band.

JOHNSON, 'Bill' William Manuel *Born: New Orleans, Louisiana, 10th August 1872*
string bass/guitar/banjo *Died: 1972*

Played guitar from the age of 15, took up string bass in 1900. Played locally at Tom Anderson's Cafe and with the Peerless Orchestra, Frankie Dusen's Eagle Band, etc.—doubled on tuba for parade work. Moved to California c.1909, and in 1914 sent for Freddie Keppard (and several other New Orleans musicians) to bring the Original Creole Orchestra to the West Coast. After working in California the band toured from coast to coast on the Orpheum Circuit—theatre residencies in New York, Chicago, etc. The original band broke up in New York, Johnson returned to Chicago and organised own band (1918). Later that year he led the Seven Kings of Ragtime in New York and again toured Orpheum circuit. Left to join King Oliver and remained with King Oliver until 1923. Led own band in Chicago for many years, also worked for several bandleaders including Johnny Dodds, Freddie Keppard, Jimmy Wade, and Clifford 'Klarinet' King. Long spell in the Smizer Trio (in the 1930s). Continued to play in Chicago until the 1950s. He gave up playing in the early 1960s and moved to Mexico.

JOHNSON, 'Bill' William K. *Born: Lexington, Kentucky. c. 1905*
banjo/guitar/vocals *Died: Lexington, Kentucky, summer 1955*

Played with local bands in and around Louisville. To New York with the Dixie Ramblers in late 1926, with drummer George Howe's Band (1927), subsequently with Luis Russell from 1927-32 (also recorded with King Oliver). Was occasionally featured on vocals (i.e. 'You Might Get Better'—Henry Allen Orchestra 1930). With Fess Williams 1933-4. Continued to work on guitar throughout the 1930s. Left full-time music in the 1940s and moved back to Lexington. He lost his life in a fire that destroyed his home.

JOHNSON, 'Bill' William *Born: Jacksonville, Florida, 30th September 1912*
alto sax/clarinet/arranger *Died: New York, 5th July 1960*

Originally a pianist, alto sax from age of 16. Worked with Smiling Billy Steward's Celery City Serenaders and with C. S. Belton's Band. Studied at Wisconsin Conservatory, Illinois Conservatory, and Marquette University, Milwaukee. Whilst in Milwaukee worked with

Jimmy Dudley and Jabbo Smith. Subsequently with Sam Marshall, Baron Lee, and Tiny Bradshaw. With Erskine Hawkins from 1936 until c. 1943. Arranged a great many numbers for Erskine Hawkins and was co-composer of Tuxedo Junction. He later moved to Canada, eventually returning to New York where he died of a lung ailment.

None of these three Bill Johnsons is connected with the trumpeter Bill Johnson (ex-McKinney's) who led his own band in Detroit for many years.

JOHNSON, 'Budd' Albert J. *Born: Dallas, Texas, 14th December 1910*
tenor sax/saxes/clarinet/arranger/vocals

Younger brother of 'Keg' Johnson. Given first music lessons by their father, who played cornet and organ; later studied with Booker Pittman's mother, Mrs. Portia Pittman (daughter of Booker T. Washington). Originally played piano, then gigged on drums and did brief spell with a touring show. Changed to tenor sax, played with local Blue Moon Chasers and occasionally in big band organised by Sammy Price. In 1927 joined William Holloway's Blue Syncopators, remained when Ben Smith became leader, toured Texas, then joined Eugene Coy's Happy Black Aces. Played briefly with Bretho Nelson's Band, later joined Terrence Holder in Dallas (early 1929). This band was later led by Jesse Stone, played in Stone's band in Missouri (including Kansas City), then, together with Stone, joined George E. Lee's Band. Moved to Chicago (1932), played with Clarence Shaw at the Grand Terrace, spells with various bands including Eddie Mallory's, then with Louis Armstrong until Louis disbanded July 1933. During 1934 did regular dep work for Cecil Irwin in Earl Hines' Band, worked with Jesse Stone's Cyclones 1934-5, then after Cecil Irwin's death (May 1935) joined Hines regularly. With Hines until 1936, then toured for a year as staff arranger for Gus Arnheim Orchestra. Returned as lead alto to Earl Hines (early 1937); briefly with Fletcher Henderson (as lead alto) in early 1938, then with Horace Henderson from April 1938. Back to Earl Hines on tenor (and musical director) in September 1938, remained with Earl until December 1942 (except for brief spell with Johnny Long Band in early 1940). Briefly with Don Redman in spring 1943, then U.S.O. tour with Al Sears' Band, also worked as staff arranger for Georgie Auld Band. In February 1944 joined Dizzy Gillespie at the Onyx Club, New York. From the mid-1940s did several spells with Dizzy Gillespie, also led own band at Three Deuces, etc. Pioneered the early days of bop by organising (and arranging for) several important small groups. Acted as musical director for Billy Eckstine's Orchestra, also arranged for Woody Herman, Buddy Rich, Boyd Raeburn, etc. Prolific free-lance recording activities, also with J. C. Heard Sextet (1946), Sy Oliver (1947), briefly with Machito (1949), trombonist Benny Green (1951), Snub Mosley's U.S.O. tour of Europe (summer 1952), Cab Calloway, etc., etc. In the early 1950s regularly led own small groups, also worked as musical director for Atlantic Records, organised own publishing company and continued free-lance playing and arranging. From February 1956 until spring 1957 with Benny Goodman (including tour of Asia). With Quincy Jones (1960), Count Basie (1961 to early 1962), led own band at Half Note, New York, etc. With Earl Hines (1965), Gerald Wilson Big Band in New York (early 1966), then to Russia with Earl Hines (summer 1966), also worked in Tommy Dorsey Band directed by trombonist Urbie Green. Featured with Earl Hines in overseas-touring 'Swinging Era' package (1967), later did a solo tour of Europe, again with Earl Hines in Europe (1968). Left Earl Hines in summer 1969 and formed JPJ Quartet (with Bill Pemberton, drummer Oliver Jackson, and pianist Dill Jones). Toured Europe with Charlie Shavers in February 1970. Widespread free-lance activities during the 1970s.

JOHNSON, 'Buddy' Woodrow Wilson *Born: Darlington, South Carolina, 10th January 1915*
piano/arranger/composer/vocals *Died: New York, 9th February 1977*

Brother of vocaliste Ella Johnson (born: 1923). Toured Europe with the Cotton Club Revue before World War II. Returned to New York in 1939, began recording career. Led own small band during the early 1940s, then formed big band, long residencies at the Savoy Ballroom, New York, and regular touring, achieved wide success in the rhythm-and-blues market. In the 1960s led a small band, was active in church welfare work.

J

JOHNSON, 'Bunk' Geary
trumpet

Born: New Orleans, Louisiana, 27th December 1889
Died: New Iberia, Louisiana, 7th July 1949

Usually gave his first name as William or Willie. Bunk's own accounts of his early career defy accurate sequential listings, but after writer Lawrence Gushee found evidence that Bunk was born ten years later than the 1879 that he claimed as his birth-date some of his movements could be charted more easily. Bunk married twice, his second wife, Maude, was related to clarinettist George Bacquet. Bunk began playing cornet during childhood, he studied with 'professor' Wallace Cutchey of the New Orleans University. During the early years of this century played in Adam Olivier's Orchestra, and c. 1905 worked in bands led by Buddy Bolden and Bob Russell. Bunk then claimed to have toured extensively with McCabe's Minstrels, Hagenbeck's and Wallace's Circus Band (visiting New York, San Francisco, and, so he said, London, England). He also said that he worked on liners sailing to the Orient, to Australia and to Europe. In between these trips he returned regularly to New Orleans and settled there c. 1910, working with Frankie Dusen's Eagle Band and Billy Marrero's Superior Band, the Old Excelsior, Allen's Brass Band, etc. Bunk also worked in Alexandria, Louisiana with Clarence Williams, and played regular dates at cabarets in New Orleans, including spell at Pete Lala's. Bunk left New Orleans, c. 1915, taught for a while in Florenceville and Mandeville, also worked with various bands in Baton Rouge, Bogalusa and Lake Charles. Left Louisiana to tour with minstrel shows and circus bands (newspaper reports cite him with P. G. Lowery's Band in 1918). Bunk later played in theatre orchestras and then toured with Dee Johnson's Band in the late 1920s. He settled temporarily in Texas (c. 1930) and worked with Sam Price at the Yellow Front Cafe in Kansas City, Missouri, c. 1930. He moved back to Louisiana, worked with Imperial Band in Lake Charles (pianiste Nellie Lutcher in the band), with Gus Fortinet's Band in New Iberia, the Yelping Hound Band in Crowley, and with trumpeter Evan Thomas' Black Eagle Band. In November 1931, Thomas was stabbed to death (by John Guillory) whilst playing at a dance in Rayne, unconfirmed reports say that Bunk's trumpet was damaged in the skirmish. Bunk continued gigging (despite dental problems) and played a one-nighter with Paul Barnes in 1933. Bunk settled in New Iberia and did various day-jobs, including caretaking and driving a truck-and-trailer for sugar and rice companies. He also undertook paid engagements as a whistler at local fairgrounds. In early 1939 he was contacted by William Russel and Frederic Ramsey Jr. after Louis Armstrong and Clarence Williams had mentioned Bunk during research interviews for the book 'Jazzmen'. From May 1940 until July 1941, Bunk was employed as a music teacher by the Works Progress Administration; the teaching schedule (which Bunk said involved 118 pupils) prevented his taking part in a 1940 recording session in New Orleans. A plan to record Bunk with Earl Hines and Sidney Bechet failed to materialise and Rex Stewart did the session. Bunk began gigging with local bands, moved into New Orleans temporarily, played one date with Allen's Brass Band. In June 1942 made first issued recordings. He returned to New Iberia to do haulage work before leaving for California. Played first concert in San Francisco on 12th April 1943. Did day-work in a drugstore, also gigged with Baker Millian and played Sunday afternoon sessions at the C.I.O. Hall with Lu Watters' sidemen (July 1943-January 1944). Played one date with Kid Ory, recorded for World Transcription Service just before leaving California (July 1944). Returned to Louisiana, did more recordings; also played dates in Opelousas with band led by pianist Tex Parker. Played at New Orleans Jazz Foundation Concert in January 1945. Moved to New York in March 1945, one date at Jimmy Ryan's prior to working with Sidney Bechet's Band at Savoy Cafe, Boston, from 12th March 1945. Bunk left the band on 11th April 1945 (temporarily replaced by Pete Bocage whose place was soon taken by Johnny Windhurst). Bunk returned to Louisiana to organise band for residency at Stuyvesant Casino, New York (28th September 1945-12th January 1946), returned to Louisiana, then again led at Stuyvesant Casino (10th April-31st May 1946). The unit disbanded and Bunk returned to New Iberia, played dates as a guest star including two concerts in Chicago (autumn 1946). Worked in and around Chicago from April until June 1947. Played concerts at New York Town Hall in autumn 1947, played gigs at Caravan Ballroom, New York City (October), organised own band using musicians resident in New York, led at Stuyvesant Casino (November). Made last recordings in December 1947 then returned to his home in New Iberia. In late 1948 he suffered a stroke which paralysed his left arm; for the rest of his life he was a semi-invalid.

JOHNSON, 'Charlie' Charles Wright
piano

Born: Philadelphia, Pennsylvania, 21st November 1891
Died: New York City, 13th December 1959

Raised in Lowell, Massachusetts. Began on trombone, played with various bands in New York c. 1914. Then moved to Atlantic City and concentrated on piano. Led own band in Atlantic City from c. 1918, brought band to New York to open at Small's Paradise on 22nd October 1925. For over a decade led resident band at Small's, occasionally returning to Atlantic City for summer seasons. Did some touring in the late 1930s, but ceased full-time leading in 1938. Gigged in New York through the 1940s, but long spell of ill health curtailed his activities in the 1950s. He died in the Harlem Hospital and was buried in the Frederic Douglass Cemetery.

Not to be confused with the one-time Duke Ellington trumpeter, Charlie Johnson, who died early in 1937.

JOHNSON, 'Countess' Margaret
piano

Born: Chanute, Kansas, 1919
Died: Kansas City, Kansas, summer 1939

First public appearance at 3, own band in Kansas City at 15, which later merged with Oliver Todd's Hottentots, when this band broke up, she joined Harlan Leonard. When Mary Lou Williams was taken ill in the spring of 1938 bandleader Andy Kirk wired the Kansas City musicians' union Local 627, for a temporary replacement, they sent Margaret Johnson to join Kirk's band at Missouri University, Columbia. Toured with Andy Kirk for four months, contracted tuberculosis, returned to Kansas City, did some local work before becoming critically ill in early 1939. Margaret's brother, Roy Johnson, was one of the pioneers of the bass guitar.

JOHNSON, 'Dink' Oliver
piano/clarinet/drums

Born: Biloxi, Mississippi, 28th October 1892
Died: Portland, Oregon, 29th November 1954

First played the drums, later began learning the piano. Worked on both during his early years. Played in Las Vegas c. 1913, then joined the Original Creole Orchestra on drums, after touring with them he left in Los Angeles and formed his own Louisiana Six. Worked for a while on drums with Jelly Roll Morton until replaced by Ben Borders, then began to learn the clarinet. With Kid Ory on clarinet and piano c. 1920; played clarinet on Ory's first recordings (1922). During early 1920s led own Five Hounds of Jazz in Los Angeles, renamed the band Los Angeles Six for Chicago residency in 1924. Returned to California, mainly active on piano. Retired from full-time music, ran own small restaurant in Los Angeles during the 1940s. Played occasionally during last years of his life including recording sessions in 1945.

JOHNSON, 'Eddie' Edward
piano

Born: East St. Louis, 8th March 1912

Piano from age of 10, taught by a cousin. First paid work in a St. Louis speakeasy (1929), two months later (in August 1929) joined Oliver Cobb's Orchestra. Cobb died in June 1930, and Johnson became the leader of the band which was renamed Eddie Johnson's Crackerjacks. The band began recording, and flourished during the 1930s and 1940s. During the 1960s and 1970s led own trio for long residencies in and around St. Louis, Missouri, combining this with the active ownership of a recording studio.

JOHNSON, Freddy
piano

Born: New York City, 12th March 1904
Died: New York City, 24th March 1961

Worked as Florence Mills' accompanist c. 1922 before forming own band in New York (1924). During 1925 worked with Elmer Snowden, joined Billy Fowler in 1926. Briefly with Henri Saparo (late 1927) and Noble Sissle, then joined Sam Wooding. To Europe with Wooding in June 1928, left Wooding in late 1929. Returned to play solo in Paris, long residency at Bricktop's, also led (assisted by Arthur Briggs) own band. Worked with Freddy Taylor's Band in late 1933, then in February 1934 left France to work in Belgium and Holland. Co-led band with Lex Van Spall, then played regularly at the Negro Palace in Amsterdam, including several long spells in trio with Coleman Hawkins. Joined Willie Lewis (then in Belgium) in spring of 1939. Remained in Holland when Lewis Band moved to Switzerland (1941). Worked at the Negro Palace, then opened own club La Cubana in Amsterdam until arrested by the Nazis on 11th December 1941. From January 1942 until February 1944 was interned in Bavaria, then repatriated to the U.S.A. in March 1944. Worked with George James, then joined Garvin Bushell's Band at Tony Pastor's Club, New York (August 1944). During the late 1940s and 1950s was mainly active as a piano teacher and vocal coach, also played solo residencies including residency at Well's, New York (1959). Went to Europe in late 1959 with the 'Free and Easy' show. By then he was very ill with cancer, but after leaving the show was able to play for several weeks in Holland (1960). After a spell in a Copenhagen hospital (autumn 1960) he returned to New York and shortly afterwards entered the St. Barnabas Hospital where he remained until his death.

JOHNSON, 'Gene' Eugene McClane
alto/clarinet

Born: Hartford, Connecticut, 1902
Died: New York, February 1958

Worked with several bands in New York from the mid-1920s including: Charlie Skeete, Bill Brown and his Brownies, Henri Saparo, Tommy Jones, and Earle Howard. With Claude Hopkins from 1930 until 1937—occasionally doubling baritone sax. Subsequently with Chick Webb and Erskine Hawkins, also did occasional gigs on drums. During the last years of his life he worked with the Latin-American band led by Machito.

JOHNSON, George
alto/clarinet

Born: Grand Rapids, Michigan, 25th April 1913

Worked with Zack Whyte and Benny Carter before sailing to Europe with Freddy Taylor in September 1935, late that year joined Willie Lewis in Paris, left in July 1937 to lead own band at the Villa d'Este, subsequent residencies with own Harlemites at the Chantilly Club and Au Boeuf sur la Toit (summer 1938). Returned to U.S.A. in 1939, worked with Frankie Newton in 1940 and 1941, then with Raymond Scott at C.B.S. from August 1942. Worked on and off with John Kirby Sextet during 1943-5. In Rex Stewart Band (summer 1946), then leading own group in Spain from November 1946. Remained in Europe for 10 years, working mostly in Switzerland, returned to New York in the mid-1950s, subsequently returned to live in Europe. Lived in France, led in France, Spain, Switzerland, etc., then moved to Holland.

JOHNSON, Gus
drums

Born: Tyler, Texas, 15th November 1913

Began playing piano, then studied drums and bass. Whilst at school in Dallas was featured on drums at the age of 10 at the Lincoln Theatre, Houston, played with McDavid's Blue Rhythm Boys c. 1925, joined Lloyd Hunter Band in Omaha, Nebraska (on drums), later played bass with the band, then reverted to drums. Worked for two years in band led by pianist Ernest 'Speck' Redd, then joined Jay McShann in Kansas City (1938). Remained until joining Army in 1943, after release with Jesse Miller Band in Chicago from spring 1945 until 1947. Worked with Earl Hines and Cootie Williams before joining Count Basie in late 1949, left Basie on 23rd December 1954. After an appendectomy began regular studio and session work. Brief spell working with vocaliste Lena Horne, then from 1957 regularly with Ella Fitzgerald. With Woody Herman in 1959. Continued to work with Ella Fitzgerald through the early 1960s including overseas tours, combined this with session work and frequent club appearances with jazz groups including regular work with baritone saxist Gerry Mulligan. Was featured on hundreds of recording sessions throughout the 1960s. In 1969 began long stay with The World's Greatest Jazz Band. Moved to Denver, Colorado during the 1970s, and made that his base for widespread freelance work, including tours to Europe during the 1970s and 1980s.

JOHNSON, 'Swan' Howard William
alto sax/clarinet/piano/arranger

Born: Boston, Massachusetts, 1st January 1908

Brother of the late 'Bobby' Johnson (guitar/banjo), who died in May 1964. Bobby, who played in many big bands including Charlie Johnson's and Chick Webb's, took part in many recording sessions including some with Bessie Smith, Taft Jordan, Red Norvo, etc. Howard worked with bands in Boston before moving to New York, played with Fess Williams, Billy Kato (1930-1), and James P. Johnson. With Elmer Snowden before joining Benny Carter's Orchestra (October 1932), then several years in Teddy Hill's Band (including trip to Europe in 1937). Spell with Claude Hopkins in the early 1940s and regular work as an arranger. With Dizzy Gillespie Big Band from 1946 until 1948. Continued to play through the 1950s and 1960s, working regularly in Lem Johnson's Band. During the 1970s worked with the Harlem Jazz and Blues Band, and also played many freelance dates.

Not related to the pianist Clarence Johnson.

JOHNSON, J. C.
piano/vocals/composer

Born: Chicago, Illinois, 14th September 1896
Died: New York, 27th February 1981

Attended Wendell Phillips High School in Chicago; played piano from an early age. Moved to New York, made first recording in 1923 accompanying Ethel Waters. Took part in many recording sessions during the 1920s, often accompanying singers, then concentrated on composing and writing for revues. Collaborated on several songs with Fats Waller and Andy Razaf. Served as an ambulance driver during World War II. Resumed composing and wrote part of 'The Jazz Train' (toured Europe with that show in 1955). From the late 1940s onwards was active as a civic leader in Harlem.

JOHNSON, 'James P.' James Price
piano/arranger/composer

Born: New Brunswick, New Jersey, 1st February 1894
Died: New York, 17th November 1955

Originally taught piano by his mother. Moved with family to Jersey City, then to New York. Played at local rent parties during his early teens, first professional work at Coney Island in summer of 1912. Subsequently played solo piano in various clubs in New York and Atlantic City, after touring Southern vaudeville circuit he returned to New York and played residencies at Leroy's, Barron Wilkin's, The Clef Club, etc., c. 1918. Again did theatre tour, left to play a residency in Toledo, Ohio (1919). In 1921 he began his prolific recording career, also worked as musical director for Dudley's 'Black Sensations/Smart Set' revues, led own Harmony Seven in New York (1922). To England with 'Plantation Days' show in March 1923. During the 1920s did many recording sessions with bands and accompanied singers (including Bessie Smith, Ethel Waters, etc.). By then he was firmly established as a successful composer, having written many tunes: 'Charleston', 'If I Could Be With You', 'Carolina Shout', etc. For the rest of his life he devoted a great deal of his time to composing. In 1923 he scored his own 'Runnin' Wild' revue; he premiered his extended work 'Yamecraw' at Carnegie Hall in July 1928. Worked in Keep Shufflin' with Fats Waller in 1928, during following year directed the orchestra for Bessie Smith's film 'St. Louis Blues'. During the 1930s he concentrated on composing, writing his 'Symphony Harlem' in 1932, and several works for the stage including the one-act work 'De Organizer' in collaboration with the famous poet Langston Hughes. He did, however, regularly lead his own orchestra during the early 1930s, also played occasionally in other bands ('Fess' Williams, 1936-7, etc.). In 1939 he began playing again regularly, did solo spot at Cafe Society (August), played for 'Swingin' the Dream' show (November), and led own band at Cafe Society (December). In 1940 he led at Elks' Rendezvous and Cafe Society, New York, until taken ill in summer of 1940. Returned to music the following year as musical director for 'Pinkard's Fantasies'. With Wild Bill Davison in Boston (early 1943), then led own band (and solos) in New York (1944). Took part in Eddie Condon's New York Town Hall concerts and also was featured as solo artist-composer at Carnegie Hall. Led at the Pied Piper (1945). Played at Eddie Condon's Club (1946) until suffering a stroke in October of that year. Active again in spring 1947. In 1949 worked in California production of his revue 'Sugar Hill', also played occasionally with Albert Nicholas Quartet. He returned to New York and continued working until suffering a severe stroke in 1951. He was an invalid for the rest of his life. He remained at his home for three years, but spent his last days in Queens Hospital.

JOHNSON, 'Keg' Frederic H.
trombone/guitar

Born: Dallas, Texas, 19th November 1908
Died: Chicago, Illinois, 8th November 1967

Was the elder brother of 'Budd' Johnson. First lessons from his father, a cornetist. Later studied with Booker Pittman's mother (Mrs. Portia Pittman, daughter of Booker T. Washington). Did day work in local Studebaker car factory and gigged on various instruments until specialising on trombone from 1927. Worked with the Blue Moon Chasers in Dallas and William Holloway's Merrymakers, then toured with Ben Smith's Blue Syncopators. With Terrence Holder's 12 Clouds of Joy in Dallas (early 1929), remained to play in Jesse Stone's Band. Later played in George E. Lee's Band, then worked with Grant Moore before settling in Chicago. Played in Eli Rice's Orchestra (1930), briefly with Jabbo Smith, then with Cassino Simpson's Band for 'Dixie on Parade' revue (1931). With Ralph Cooper's Orchestra at Regal Theatre, Chicago, and Clarence Moore (early 1932), then short spell with Eddie Mallory before touring (and recording) with Louis Armstrong until July 1933. Moved to New York, played in Benny Carter's Orchestra, then with Fletcher Henderson from January 1934 to December 1934. Joined Cab Calloway in January 1935 and remained wtih Cab until the summer of 1948 (except for brief absence early in 1940). With Lucky Millinder (1948-50)—short while with tenorist Gene Ammons in 1949. Worked in Eddie Wilcox Band (1951), then moved to California. With Benny Carter (1952) and briefly with Duke Ellington (1953) then left full-time music to work as a house decorator. Continued to do regular gigs (some on guitar) with various leaders including: Sammy Franklin, tenorist Wardell Gray, and Harvey Brooks, etc. Moved back to New York in late 1950s, with Eddie Barefield Band (late 1959), then with Gil Evans (1960), also depped for Wilbur de Paris in summer of 1960. In 1961 joined vocalist Ray Charles' Orchestra, remained in that band for six years, dying suddenly whilst on tour.

JOHNSON, 'Lem' Lemuel Charles
tenor sax/vocals/clarinet

Born: Oklahoma City, 6th August 1909

Also known as 'Deacon'. Attended Douglass High School, started on clarinet, gigged with local bands and played in Oklahoma City in The Jolly Harmony Boys led by Charlie Christian's brother, Edward. Switched to sax in 1928, received tuition from Walter Page whilst working summer season (1928) with The Blue Devils in Shawnee, Oklahoma. In 1929 did regular radio work with Sammy Price and Leonard Chadwick in Oklahoma. Spell with Gene Coy, then with 101 Ranch Show (1930). Played with various bands in Milwaukee including Grant Moore's and pianist Hobart Bank's, then three years with Eli Rice (mainly in Minneapolis). Brief return to Grant Moore, then short tour with Earl Hines before moving to New York (April 1937). With 'Fess' Williams, Luis Russell (briefly), Louis Jordan (late 1938 until early 1939), then formed own trio. Led own sextet during the early 1940s, but also brief spells with Buster Harding Quartet (spring 1940), Eddie Durham (1940), Edgar Hayes and Sidney Bechet (1941), Claude Hopkins (1942). Whilst doing defence-plant work at Douglas aircraft factory played in band organised by Claude Hopkins (1943). Then re-formed own sextet, residencies in New York City, Rochester, Keansbourg, New Jersey, etc., and overseas U.S.O. tours, also recorded with Hot Lips Page, Sy Oliver, etc. For many years worked during the day for the New York postal authorities, but through the 1950s and 1960s continued to lead own highly successful band which regularly featured many well-known musicians.

JOHNSON, 'Lonnie' Alonzo
guitar/vocals

Born: New Orleans, Louisiana, 8th February 1899 (?)
Died: Toronto, 16th June 1970

Brother of pianist James 'Steady Roll' Johnson. Did local gigs with his brother, also played violin and guitar in cafes and theatres in New Orleans. Sailed to Europe c. 1917, did revue work in London and theatre tours (the late Billy Mason, a well-known Scottish bandleader, once said that he briefly worked in Glasgow with Will Marion Cook in 1921—'Lonnie' was then with Cook on banjo). Returned to New Orleans to find that the 1918-19 flu epidemic had almost wiped out his entire family. Moved on to St. Louis (c. 1922), worked with Charlie Creath, Fate Marable, Nat Robinson, etc. (mainly on violin and piano). Worked in a steel foundry for two years, but continued gigging (mainly on violin and piano). Circa 1925 he entered and won a talent contest organised by the OKeh Record Company. Shortly afterwards he began his prolific recording career, worked as an OKeh staff musician until 1932. From this period onwards he specialised on guitar, but also did some recorded work on piano and violin. (During his OKeh years he recorded with countless artistes including: Louis Armstrong, Duke Ellington, Ed Lang, etc.) In 1932 he moved to Cleveland and played on and off for a few years with Putney Dandridge's Band. Played on numerous local radio shows, also did day work in a Galesburg tyre factory and in Cleveland steel mill. Moved to Chicago in 1937, worked with Johnny Dodds, then became house musician at the Three Deuces until 1939. Led own quartet at Boulevard Lounge, etc. (1940), Squyre's Club (1942). From the mid-1940s he began appearing as a solo vocalist, accompanying himself on amplified guitar. Recorded many singles and composed the best-seller 'To-morrow Night' (1948). He visited London, for a concert appearance in June 1952, returned to the U.S.A. and made Cincinnati his home base for several years until moving to Philadelphia where he worked for a time as a chef at the Benjamin Franklin Hotel until the early 1960s. He toured Europe in the autumn of 1963 as part of a 'blues package', earlier that year he had appeared with Duke Ellington in New York. From the mid-1960s he worked regularly in Toronto, Canada, also did some touring. In 1969 was injured in an accident, then suffered a stroke which sent him for many months to the Riversdale Hospital, Toronto. Sang at a Toronto blues concert in 1970.

JOHNSON, Manzie Isham

drums

Born: Putnam, Connecticut, 19th August 1906
Died: New York, 9th April 1971

Raised in New York from infancy. Studied violin and piano as a child, then specialised on drums. With Willie Gant's Ramblers (1926), also worked with June Clark and in Elmer Snowden's Westerners. With Henri Saparo (autumn 1927), then with Joe Steele. Joined Horace Henderson (1930). With Don Redman from 1931 until early 1937, with Willie Bryant from summer of 1937; led own band at the Palace, New York (late 1938). (During the 1930s Manzie did many studio sessions with Henry Allen, Lil Armstrong, Mezzrow-Ladnier, etc.) With Don Redman again early in 1940, then with James P. Johnson (summer 1940), then with Ovie Alston until brief spell with Fletcher Henderson in the spring of 1941. With Frankie Newton in Autumn of 1941, subsequently with Horace Henderson and long spells with Ovie Alston. Rejoined Don Redman until Army call-up in spring of 1944. After demobilisation again played with Ovie Alston's Band, also regularly led own small group for various residencies (including season at Camp Unity in summer of 1949). Left full-time music in the 1950s, but continued to gig regularly with Garvin Bushell, Happy Caldwell, Lem Johnson, etc. Played regularly during the 1960s.

JOHNSON, 'Money' Harold

trumpet/fluegel horn/vocals

Born: Tyler, Texas, 23rd February 1918
Died: Long Island, 28th March 1978

Began on trumpet at 15, lessons from local teacher, Leonard Parker. Soon did first professional work with Eddie and Sugar Lou's Hotel Tyler Orchestra, then played in Dallas for two years in a band led by his cousin, saxophonist Red Calhoun. Played with bands led by John White and Henry Thompson before joining Nat Towles in 1937. Remained with that band for seven years, then together with the rest of Towles' sidemen he joined Horace Henderson (1942-4). Then long spell in Rochester with Bob Dorsey's Band before rejoining Nat Towles at Rhumboogie in Chicago. Briefly with Count Basie in late 1944, then with Cootie Williams' Band in early 1945, alternated between Cootie's Band and Lucky Millinder during late 1940s. During the 1950s worked for many leaders including: Louis Jordan, Lucky Thompson, Panama Francis (in South America), Buddy Johnson, Cozy Cole, Mercer Ellington, etc., etc. Regularly with Reuben Phillips' Band at the Apollo, New York, during the 1960s, also prolific recording-studio work, toured Russia with Earl Hines in 1966, again toured Europe with Earl Hines in late 1968. Played occasionally with Duke Ellington in 1968, joined the band temporarily in June 1969, briefly with Sy Oliver (1970), then with Duke Ellington (1970-1). Active free-lancing until the night of his death.

JOHNSON, Otis
trumpet

Born: New York City, 13th January 1910

Worked with Gene Rodgers' Revellers in New York (1928), during 1928 worked with Henri Saparo, then with Eugene Kennedy's Band (summer 1929), Charlie Skeete's Band (autumn 1929), before working with Luis Russell (late 1929-30). Worked in New York and New England with Eugene Kennedy, then returned to Luis Russell (early 1932), with Benny Carter (1934). With Charlie Turner's Arcadians, then joined Willie Bryant (1935). Briefly with Eddie Condon-Joe Marsala Group in 1936, then with Don Redman from summer 1936 until September 1937 when he rejoined Charlie Turner. With Louis Armstrong's Orchestra (1938-9), then rejoined Don Redman (1940). With the onset of World War II he made the Army his career, having previously served in U.S. National Guard. Moved to Colorado Springs.

JOHNSON, Pete
piano

Born: Kansas City, Missouri, 24th March 1904
Died: Buffalo, N.Y., 23rd March 1967

Spent part of his childhood in an orphanage, left school at 12 and did a variety of jobs before learning to play the drums. Worked as a drummer from 1922-6 with various pianists including: Louis 'Good Bootie' Johnson and Ernest Nichols. After piano lessons from his uncle Charles 'Smash' Johnson (and others) he began to gig on piano (1926). First regular work with Clarence Love's Band, then solo pianist at many Kansas City clubs (from 1926-38) including: The Lone Star, The Grey Goose, The Backbiter's, The Hawaiian Gardens, The Kingfish, The Peacock Inn, and The Sunset. During this period began working regularly with vocalist Joe Turner. Also played occasionally with bands including Herman Walder's and drummer Abbie Price's. To New York in 1938 (with Joe Turner) for feature spot on Benny Goodman Radio Show, also appeared very briefly at the Apollo Theatre. Back to The Spinning Wheel, Kansas City, before returning to New York for Carnegie Hall 'Spirituals to Swing' concert (December 1938). Long residency at Cafe Society, New York (from 1939), together with Albert Ammons and Meade Lux Lewis made up the Boogie Woogie Trio, later worked in duo with Albert Ammons at the same venue and residencies in California (1947-8). During the 1940s also occasionally toured in duo with Meade Lux Lewis, played long solo residencies. Lived in Buffalo from 1950, did long spells of day work, but continued to play in local clubs—on national tour with the 'Piano Parade' package in 1952, later that year again briefly teamed with Meade Lux Lewis. In 1955 briefly reunited with Joe Turner, also worked as accompanist for Jimmy Rushing. To Europe in May 1958 in J.A.T.P. show (including Joe Turner), in July of that year also appeared at Newport Jazz Festival, returned to play at Johnny Ellicott's Grill in Buffalo until serious illness in autumn of 1958. For the rest of his life Pete Johnson suffered from ill health (heart trouble and diabetes), he did, however, go to New York in the summer of 1960 for recording sessions and did occasional work in Buffalo during the 1960s including concert appearance in November 1964.

Not related to the Kansas City drummer Murl Johnson (born: 22nd March 1903), who worked regularly with Pete during the 1920s and 1930s. In 1965 'The Pete Johnson Story' (compiled and edited by Hans J. Mauerer) was published in book form.

JOHNSON, Walter
drums

Born: New York City, 18th February 1904
Died: New York City, 26th April 1977

Worked with Freddie Johnson's Red Devils and Bobby Brown's Band before joining Elmer Snowden (1925), worked with Billy Fowler (1926), then again with Elmer Snowden until joining Fletcher Henderson in summer of 1929. With Henderson until autumn 1934 (except for spell in 1930), then with Sam Wooding until joining LeRoy Smith at Connie's

Inn (1935). Rejoined Fletcher Henderson for a year from summer of 1936, then with Lucky Millinder (1938-9), Claude Hopkins (1939), Edgar Hayes, Coleman Hawkins' Big Band (1940), Claude Hopkins (summer 1940). Again with Fletcher Henderson (1941-2), then worked in house band at the Elks' Rendezvous, New York. Mainly with Tab Smith from 1944 until 1954, shortly afterwards left full-time music to work as a bank guard, but continued to free-lance. During the 1960s continued to gig in New York, occasional work with pianist Orville Brown.

JONES, Claude B.
trombone/vocals

Born: Boley, Oklahoma, 11th February 1901
Died: Aboard the liner S.S. 'United States', 17th January 1962

Brother-in-law of Quentin Jackson. Trombone at 13, played in town band, then at Langston High School where he also doubled on trumpet and drums. Attended Wilberforce College, also served as a musician in the Students' Army Training Corps. Quit law studies at Wilberforce and subsequently joined the Synco Jazz Band in Springfield, Ohio (1922). This band later became McKinney's Cotton Pickers, remained with McKinney's until spring 1929. Joined Fletcher Henderson in May 1929 (originally for production of the show 'Great Day'—during Henderson's short stay with the show Claude Jones doubled on trombone and fourth trumpet). With Henderson in 1930 (also played occasionally in Chick Webb's Band). Joined Don Redman c. September 1931, left in September 1933 to rejoin Fletcher Henderson. Left Henderson (c. September 1934), played in Chick Webb's Band until joining Cab Calloway in late 1934 (occasional vocal features with Cab's Band including 'Jes Naturally Lazy'). Left Cab in January 1940 to join Coleman Hawkins' Big Band, with Zutty Singleton Band in New York (March-May 1940), then again with Hawkins before playing with Joe Sullivan's Band (November-December 1940). Briefly with Fletcher Henderson (1941), then left full-time music to manage own sausage-manufacturing company. Continued to do regular gigs, including spells wwth Herman 'Humpy' Flintall (1941), Benny Carter (1942), Don Redman, Cab Calloway (1943). Resumed full-time playing to join Duke Ellington (on valve trombone) in spring 1944. Left Duke in c. October 1948, with Machito Orchestra in May 1949, then studio work and brief spell with Fletcher Henderson (1950). Brief return to Duke Ellington from January-March 1951. Left music to become an Officers' Mess Steward on the liner S.S. 'United States', in this employment made many visits to England.

JONES, 'Hank' Henry
piano

Born: Pontiac, Michigan, 31st July 1918

All his family were musical, including his brothers, Thad Jones (trumpet/arranger) and Elvin Jones (drums). Studied piano with Pauline Frisbee (later known as the actress Carlotta Franzell). Played gigs whilst at high school prior to working in bands led by Benny Carew and altoist Ted Buckner. To New York in 1944. With Hot Lips Page, Andy Kirk, John Kirby (1945). Worked as accompanist for Billy Eckstine. In 1947 began long series of tours with 'Jazz At The Philharmonic' (including European trips in the 1950s). With Coleman Hawkins, Howard McGhee before becoming accompanist with Ella Fitzgerald (1948). Mainly with Ella for five years, then worked with Benny Goodman on and off during the late 1950s, including tour of the Orient (1956-57). From the late 1950s until the mid-1970s was on C.B.S. staff, during this period also did countless free-lance recordings, also worked in Thad Jones-Mel Lewis Big Band (1966). During the mid-1970s led own trio but continued to do prolific free-lance work. Conducted and played in 'Ain't Misbehavin'' show during the late 1970s and early 1980s, also undertook international touring including dates in Japan (1981).

JONES, Isham
saxes/string bass

Born: Coalton, Iowa, 31st January 1894
Died: Florida, 19th October 1956

Raised in Saginaw, Michigan. Led own band at 18, moved to Chicago in 1915, concentrated on tenor saxophone, led own trio at Mahoney's Club. Later led orchestra at Green Mill and Rainbow Gardens, subsequently his orchestra played long residency at Hotel Sherman from early 1920s. Appeared in New York before sailing to London in 1924.

Returned to U.S.A. and began establishing a national reputation. From 1926 until 1936 his orchestras enjoyed widespread popularity, his last band, Isham Jones' Juniors, contained the basic personnel for the orchestra formed by Isham Jones' sideman Woody Herman. The Juniors broke up in 1936. Jones decided to devote more time to composing, but during the pre-1939 years assembled several temporary bands and occasionally fronted other bands. Throughout the 1940s ran own general store in Colorado, moved to Florida in 1955, he died of cancer a year later. Prolific composer whose successes included: 'Spain', 'On the Alamo', 'I'll See You in My Dreams', 'It Had to Be You'.

JONES, 'Jimmy' James Henry
piano/arranger/composer

Born: Memphis, Tennessee, 30th December 1918
Died: Burbank, California, 29th April 1982

Originally a guitarist, switched to piano, worked in Chicago with Stuff Smith and moved to New York as part of that group. With J. C. Heard (1946-47) then worked as accompanist for singer Sarah Vaughan from October 1947 until April 1952. Inactive through illness, then resumed working with Sarah from October 1954 until January 1958. Prolific free-lance work during the 1960s as player and arranger, also led own trio. Worked as musical director and accompanist for Ella Fitzgerald during the late 1960s until moving to Los Angeles in 1969, where he composed for television and for movies as well as playing gigs with jazz groups during the late 1970s.

JONES, Jo' Jonathan
drums

Born: Illinois, 7th October 1911

Went to school in Alabama. Played trumpet, piano, and saxes from the age of 10. Left home to work in touring carnival shows, occasionally as singer and dancer. Played drums in Ted Adams' Band in the late 1920s, then joined Harold Jones' Brownskin Syncopators in Lincoln, Nebraska (1931). Briefly with Grant Moore, Jap Allen, Bennie Moten, then worked with Lloyd Hunter's Serenaders (out of Omaha, Nebraska) until 1933. Moved to Kansas City, joined Tommy Douglas Band (playing piano and vibes), briefly with Count Basie (1934), then worked with Rook Ganz in Minneapolis. Returned to Kansas City, left residency at the Amos and Andy Club to rejoin Count Basie (then playing in Topeka—late 1935). Left Basie early 1936 to work in St. Louis with the Jetar-Pillars Band, returned to Count Basie in early autumn of 1936. Remained with Count Basie until service in U.S. Army (October 1944), after release worked mainly with Basie (April 1946-February 1948). Toured with Norman Granz's 'Jazz At The Philharmonic' in 1947, with Illinois Jacquet (1948-50), also led own trio in 1948. In Lester Young's Band (1950), with J.A.T.P. in 1951, then two years in Joe Bushkin Quartet. Extensive free-lance work in New York throughout the 1950s, frequently led own trio including trip to Puerto Rico (1960), also worked regularly with Teddy Wilson, Claude Hopkins, pianist Ray Bryant, etc. Made several tours of Europe with 'Jazz At The Philharmonic'. In 1969 spent several months in Europe with Milt Buckner, returned to New York and resumed regular playing. Many free-lance recordings throughout his career with: Billie Holiday, Teddy Wilson, Duke Ellington, Johnny Hodges, Harry James, Benny Goodman, Lionel Hampton, etc. Was featured at many jazz festivals during the 1970s. His son Jo is also a drummer.

During Jo Jones' long stay with Count Basie he was absent through illness on a few occasions. Deputies included Harold West (early 1940) and Baby Lovette (spring 1942).

JONES, 'Jonah' Robert Elliot
trumpet/vocals

Born: Louisville, Kentucky, 31st December 1908

Husband of Elizabeth (sister of Russell Bowles). Jonah's brother James was formerly a trumpeter. During early teens played alto-horn in local Booker T. Washington Community Center Band, switched to trumpet, local work in bands led by Artie Jones and Othello Tinsley. First professional with trombonist Wallace Bryant's Band on riverboat 'Island Queen', returned to Louisville, worked with Johnny Montague and Clarence Muse. Joined Horace Henderson in Cleveland (1928), toured until band broke up in Buffalo. Gigged in Cleveland then back to Louisville. With Hardy Brothers' Orchestra in Indianapolis (from January 1930), then joined Wesley Helvey's Band until August 1930. Joined Horace

'Pops' Diemer's Band in Buffalo, several months with Jimmie Lunceford (1931) before joining Stuff Smith at Little Harlem Club, Buffalo. With Stuff 1932-4, including big band at Lafayette, New York (June 1934). With Lil Armstrong's Big Band (1935), briefly in McKinney's Cotton Pickers, then rejoined Stuff Smith at Silver Grill, Buffalo, prior to sextet taking up Onyx Club, New York, residency (February 1936). Remained with Stuff until joined Benny Carter in 1940, briefly with Fletcher Henderson (early 1941), then regularly with Cab Calloway from February 1941 until spring 1952—later did occasional work with Cab. With Earl Hines' sextet, then played in Broadway theatre orchestra for 'Porgy and Bess'. Toured France and Belgium as a soloist (1954), returned to New York, gigged with society orchestras led by Lester Lanin and Meyer Davis. Began leading own quartet in summer of 1955, after residencies at The Embers, New York, London House, Chicago, etc., the group began regular television work. They achieved international success and made many best-selling L.P.s. Long residencies at The Embers, The Rainbow Grill, etc., also played in Monaco and toured Australia. The group, enlarged to a quintet, maintained its popularity, early in 1970 they played in Honolulu and Thailand. Jonah visited England on vacation in 1970 and 1971. Featured at European jazz festivals (1978) Continued to lead own group during the early 1980s.

JONES, Reunald Sr.
trumpet

Born: Indianapolis, Indiana, 22nd December 1910

Cousin of Roy Eldridge. Two of his brothers, Reginald (bass) and Leopold, were professional musicians. Reunald Jr. is a noted trumpet player. Reunald's father was a music teacher at the Michigan Conservatory. Did local work in Minneapolis, then worked with saxist Leonard Gay and his Chocolate Playboys (1928), following year with Bill Warfield Band in Indiana, then joined Speed Webb in 1930. From 1931-46 worked for many bandleaders including: Charlie Johnson, The Savoy Bearcats, J. Frank Terry, Teddy Hill, Jimmie Lunceford, 'Fess' Williams, Sam Wooding, Claude Hopkins, Chick Webb, Willie Bryant, Don Redman, etc. With Duke Ellington for two months in spring of 1946, later that year briefly with Jimmie Lunceford. During late 1940s and early 1950s with Lucky Millinder, Erskine Hawkins, Ed Wilcox, and Sy Oliver. With Count Basie from February 1952 until October 1957 (including overseas tours). Session work in New York, then toured Europe with Woody Herman in spring 1959. Regularly with George Shearing Big Band from late 1959. With Nat 'King' Cole from January 1961 until that leader's final engagements in 1964 (including work in Europe). Worked with Phil Moore in New York (1965), then active free-lance work, occasionally touring with name vocalists. Moved to California during 1970s; his son Reunald Jr. is also a trumpeter.

JONES, 'Myknee' Richard Mariney
piano/composer

Born: Donaldsville, Louisiana, 13th June 1889
Died: Chicago, Illinois, 8th December 1945

At 12 became water-carrier for the Claiborne Williams Band and eventually played tuba with them, later played alto horn and cornet with the Eureka Brass Band. Had begun on piano during childhood, after tuition from Richard 'Fishing Bread' Barret he began playing professionally at Lulu White's Mahogany Hall and at Josie Arlington's. Later he led his own band at Jack Robison's Tent Cabaret (1910) and at Abadie's and George Fewclothes' Cabaret (c. 1912). He also played in various bands and orchestras in New Orleans including John Robichaux's and Armand Piron's. He began composing in 1915, one of his first tunes 'Lonesome Nobody Cares' was featured by vocaliste Sophie Tucker. After working with Papa Celestin in 1918 he moved to Chicago where he helped to organise the Chicago branch of Clarence Williams' publishing house and music shop. He played in bands led by Bernie Young and Willie Hightower, but was mainly active as manager of the 'race' department of Okeh records (a position he held until February 1927). During the 1920s recorded many sides with his Jazz Wizards and took part in many studio recordings. He continued to lead his own band during the 1930s, doing occasional tours. He occasionally led his own band in Louisiana during the early 1930s. By then he was established as a successful composer, he was also a talent scout for various record companies. During World War II he did defence-plant work at Foote Brothers' gear factory in Chicago, but continued to play regularly until the time of his death. During the last year of his life he was a talent scout for the Mercury Record Company.

J

JONES, 'Slick' Wilmore
drums

Born: Roanoke, Virginia, 13th April 1907
Died: New York City, 2nd November 1969

His brother Gil led own band in Virginia for many years, their father was also a musician. Worked with John Lockslayer's Band in 1925. Moved to New York, began studying at the Damrosch Conservatory. Played with Fletcher Henderson from spring 1935 until February 1936, then joined Fats Waller (replacing Arnold 'Scrippy' Boling). Worked on and off with Waller until 1942. With Stuff Smith (late 1942), Una Mae Carlisle Band (spring 1943), then joined Eddie South (July 1943). Worked with Claude Hopkins, Hazel Scott, Don Redman, before long spell with Gene Sedric's Band from late 1946. With Wilbur de Paris in 1954, during following year worked in Boston with Wilbur de Paris, Doc Cheatham, etc. In New York regularly after 1959, spell with Scoville Brown, then several years with Eddie Durham Band at Moby Dick's, Long Island. Was seriously ill in 1964, but temporarily recovered and resumed playing for a while.

JONES, 'Snags' Clifford
drums

Born: New Orleans, Louisiana. c. 1900
Died: Chicago, Illinois, 31st January 1947

His irregularly placed teeth inspired his nickname. Went to school with Lee Collins and Buddie Petit. Played for a year in Petit's Band, then joined Jack Carey's Band, later played in Papa Celestin's Band and Armand Piron's Orchestra. Moved to Chicago in 1922 to join trumpeter Tig Chambers at Joyland Park, during following year worked with Al Simeon's Hot Six, then toured with King Oliver (1924). Spent several years based in Milwaukee with Art Simms and Bernie Young until 1931. Briefly with Walter Barnes (late 1931). With Charlie Elgar, Freddie Williams (1933), Georgia Gorham (1933), then regular free-lance work mainly in Chicago. Worked at the Oahu Isle Club in Chicago in 1946, during that year played two concerts with Bunk Johnson in Chicago. In late 1946 he joined Darnell Howard's Trio at the Silhouette Club, Chicago, he worked at that job until the night before his death.

JONES, Wallace Leon
trumpet

Born: Baltimore, Maryland, 16th November 1906
Died: New York, 23rd March 1983

Cousin of Chick Webb. Played in Ike Dixon's Harmony Birds (1928-9), Percy Glascoe Kit Kat Orchestra (1930). Moved to New York. Briefly with Chick Webb, then regularly with Willie Bryant in 1936-7. With Duke Ellington from March 1938 until March 1944. Played with Benny Carter in New York (September 1945), during following year worked in Snub Mosely's Band, with John Kirby (early 1947). Left full-time music to become a mortician.

JONES, 'Preacher' Wardell
trumpet

Born: c. 1905

With Bill Brown and his Brownies at Alhambra Ballroom, New York (spring 1929), briefly with Benny Carter at Arcadian Ballroom (autumn 1929), then with Bingie Madison's Band until joining the Mills Blue Rhythm Band (1930), remained with that band until 1936, then played briefly in Fats Waller's Big Band. Worked in Hot Lips Page Big Band in spring of 1938. (No trace of musical activity after 1940.)

JOPLIN, Scott
piano/composer

Born: Texarkana, Texas, 24th November 1868
Died: New York City, 1st April 1917

Probably the most famous of the ragtime pianist-composers, in the 1890s he also played cornet in the Queen City Negro Band of Sedalia, Missouri. Worked for many years in the Texas Medley Vocal Quartet, whilst with them sold his first compositions (1895): 'Please Say You Will' and 'Picture of her Face'. Extensive touring and long spells in Kansas City, Sedalia, and St. Louis, before moving to New York in 1905. A prolific composer ('Maple Leaf Rag', 'Original Rag', etc.) of rags, waltzes, and songs, also wrote two operas, 'Treemonisha' and 'A Guest of Honour'.

An unconfirmed report suggests that Joplin visited Britain in 1901. For fuller biographical details of Joplin (and many other ragtime specialists) the reader is advised to consult 'They All Played Ragtime', by Harriet Janis and Rudi Blesh.

JORDAN, Louis
alto sax/saxes/vocals

Born: Brinkley, Arkansas, 8th July 1908
Died: Los Angeles, 4th February 1975

Father was a bandleader, and music teacher. Started on clarinet at the age of seven, went to school in Little Rock, Arkansas. Worked in pianist Jimmy Pryor's Imperial Serenaders (late 1929), then with Ruby Williams' Belvedere Orchestra in Hot Springs (1930), worked with various bands in that area, then moved to Philadelphia. Joined Charlie Gaines, also worked with tubaist Jim Winters' Band in Philadelphia (1932). To New York with Charlie Gaines in March 1934 where they both took part in Clarence Williams' recording session ('I Can't Dance . . .', etc.). Returned to Philadelphia with Gaines, then returned to New York to join Local 802, whilst awaiting entry to the union occasionally returned to Philadelphia to gig with Gaines. Played briefly with Kaiser Marshall's Band, then from summer 1935 worked with LeRoy Smith's Orchestra in New York, Cleveland, and Atlantic City. In summer of 1936 began two-year stay with Chick Webb's Band (featured on soprano, alto, and vocals). In August 1938 began leading own small band at the Elks' Rendezvous in New York; in December of that year his band (later to be called the Tympany Five) made their recording debut. Jordan's recordings enjoyed huge record sales throughout the 1940s—his 'Choo Choo Ch'Boogie' selling over two million copies. He occasionally worked as a soloist in the 1940s and also recorded with Louis Armstrong, Bing Crosby, Ella Fitzgerald, etc. Continued leading own small band until 1951 (except for absence through injuries January 1947 to February 1948). Briefly led own big band in early 1950s, then resumed with small group. Lived for many years in Phoenix, Arizona, then moved to Los Angeles in the early 1960s. Brief solo tour of Britain in late 1962, continued leading throughout the 1960s, including tours of Asia in 1967 and 1968.

Louis Jordan has appeared in several films; he was featured in the 1949 movie 'Shout Sister Shout'.

JORDAN, 'Steve' Stephen Philip
guitar

Born: New York City, 15th January 1919

Studied with Allan Reuss. With Will Bradley-Ray McKinley Band 1939-41, then year with Artie Shaw. One week with Teddy Powell's Band before joining U.S. Navy 1942-5, served in 'Saxie' Dowell's Service Band. After demobilisation worked with Bob Chester, with Freddie Slack until spring 1945, then joined Glen Gray and the Casa Loma Band. With Stan Kenton (1948), Boyd Raeburn (1949), then worked on production staff at N.B.C. for two years (1950-2). Long spells with Benny Goodman from summer 1954 until spring 1957. Worked as tailor in New York and Washington in late 1950s and early 1960s. In 1965 recommenced regular playing with group led by clarinettist/vibist Tom Gwaltney at the Blues Alley Club, in Washington, D.C. Played in house-band at Blues Alley (1971).

JORDAN, 'Taft' James
trumpet/vocals

Born: Florence, South Carolina, 15th February 1915
Died: 1st December 1981

Cousin of trumpeter Dave Riddick. Raised in Norfolk, Virginia. Played trumpet and baritone horn in St. Joseph's School Band—taught music by Dr. Josiah Bailey. Worked with Ben Jones' Band in Norfolk (1929), then moved to Philadephia for further education. Played professionally in band led by violinist Jimmy Gorham, later worked with George 'Doc' Hyder in Philadelphia and New York. During this period played in some Washboard Rhythm Kings and Washboard Rhythm Band recording sessions. Joined Chick Webb in September 1933. Except for a six-week stint in Willie Bryant's Band (1936), Taft remained with Chick Webb until the leader's death. Continued working under leadership of vocaliste Ella Fitzgerald until the summer of 1941. During following year led own eight-piece band at the Savoy Ballroom, New York, remaining there until temporary closure in April 1943. Joined Duke Ellington in May 1943, remained until the early summer of 1947. Played with various bands in New York including long spell in Lucille Dixon Orchestra at the Savannah Club (1949-53). Toured with Don Redman in autumn 1953. Studio work in New York, also co-led band with Dick Vance. In May 1958 played in Europe with Benny Goodman, remained with Goodman until July 1958. From 1960 led own quintet, also freelanced with various leaders and did studio work. For several years in 1960s played for the Broadway show 'Hello, Dolly', continued to gig, worked with Red Richards' Trio (1977).

KAHN, Roger Wolfe
leader/multi-instrumentalist

Born: Morristown, New Jersey, 19th October 1907
Died: New York, 12th July 1962

Son of millionaire-banker Otto Kahn. Began playing violin at seven, later learnt piano, woodwinds, and brass. Intensive classical studies during early teens. Led own orchestra in New York at 17 and on and off for the next decade, it occasionally featured well-known jazz musicians including: Miff Mole, Joe Venuti, Ed Lang, Stan King. After a long spell in the aviation industry he returned to conducting and composing.

KAMINSKY, Max
trumpet

Born: Brockton, Massachusetts, 7th September 1908

At 12 led own juvenile band in Boston—The Six Novelty Syncopators. During the early 1920s worked with various bands in his home state including spell with Art Karle's Band in Cape Cod. Temporary move to Chicago in 1928, played at Cinderella Ballroom (with George Wettling), returned to Boston before revisiting Chicago. To New York in 1929, toured with Red Nichols, then returned to Boston. Played with Leo Reisman at the Bradford Hotel, Boston, during the early 1930s and also gigged with various small bands. On his occasional trips to New York recorded with Mezz Mezzrow, Benny Goodman, and Eddie Condon. Worked with Joe Venuti Orchestra in New York (early 1934), then with Teddy Roy Band, Eddie Elkins, Jacques Renard, Jack Marshard, and Leo Reisman, before joining Tommy Dorsey (September-December 1936). In small band with Pee Wee Russell before playing briefly with Ray Noble's Band (early 1937), later that year worked in the short-lived Mezz Mezzrow's Disciples of Swing. With Artie Shaw from January-June 1938, then again with Pee Wee Russell before rejoining Tommy Dorsey in November 1938. With Bud Freeman Summa Cum Laude Band 1939-40, then joined Tony Pastor Band for a few months until March 1941 when he rejoined Artie Shaw. Left to join Alvino Rey (early 1942), then played with Joe Marsala's Big Band until joining the U.S. Navy in summer of 1942. Served in Artie Shaw's Naval Band, including tour of the Pacific area, during which he recorded with local jazzmen in Australia (1943). Returned to U.S.A. in December 1943, gained honourable discharge in March 1944. Led own band at Pied Piper, New York, until December 1944, played in Art Hodes' Band (1945), then from November 1945 until March 1946 led own band in Boston. With Eddie Condon until January 1947, then worked with Art Hodes and briefly with Jack Teagarden. Led own band at Village Vanguard from 1948. Through the 1950s combined small jazz-group work with regular stints in society orchestras. In autumn 1957 toured Europe with Jack Teagarden-Earl Hines All Stars, and in late 1958 began tour of the Orient with Jack Teagarden's Band. From 1960 has worked frequently in New York jazz groups, occasionally leading own small bands at various clubs including Eddie Condon's. During the late 1960s regularly featured at Jimmy Ryan's, New York. Visited London in March 1970. In 1963 Max's autobiography: 'My Life in Jazz' was published. During the 1940s, played at many of Eddie Condon's New York Town Hall Concerts. Prolific free-lance recording career. Left Ryan's (1970), active in New York (1970-1), toured Japan with George Wein (September 1971). Regularly at Jimmy Ryan's Club, New York City until 1983.

KARLE, 'Art' Arthur D.
tenor sax/clarinet

Born: Boston, Massachusetts. c. 1905
Died: Boston, Massachusetts, 21st December 1967

Led own band in Boston and Cape Cod areas during the 1920s. Moved to New York in the early 1930s, worked for various leaders including Benny Goodman, also led own recording bands. Worked with Hiram 'Hy' Jason's Band in the early 1940s, then moved back to Boston, did defence-plant work, but continued gigging during World War II. Occasionally led own bands in Boston during the 1950s—during the 1960s did 'society' work with the Jack Marshard and Herb Sulkin Orchestras.

KAZEBIER, 'Nate' Nathan Forrest
trumpet

Born: Lawrence, Kansas, 13th August 1912
Died: Reno, Nevada, 22nd October 1969

Raised in Cedar Rapids, Iowa; his brother played tenor sax. Trumpet from the age of nine, later played in high school orchestra. In 1930 joined Austin Wylie in Cleveland, with Jan

Garber (1931), subsequently with Slats Randall, worked with a succession of bands before joining Benny Goodman from April 1935 until August 1936. Worked in California with Ray Noble, briefly with Seger Ellis' Brass choir early in 1937. In February 1938 joined Lyle 'Spud' Murphy's Band, then worked again with Ray Noble and various studio orchestras before joining Gene Krupa in spring 1939. With Jimmy Dorsey from April 1940 until September 1943, left to resume studio work in Hollywood. Worked again with Benny Goodman from February 1946 until spring 1947, then settled in California. Continued studio work for many years, occasionally played jazz gigs including spell with Jess Stacy in the late 1940s. During the 1960s worked in Reno as a golf instructor, but continued to play trumpet regularly.

KEITH, Jimmy
tenor sax/clarinet

Born: San Antonio, Texas, 22nd February 1915
Died: Kansas City, Missouri, January 1969

Attended school in Kansas City, Missouri, then studied at the Vocational College in Topeka, Kansas. Returned to Kansas City, formed own band, then worked with Tommy Douglas (1935), again led own band until 1938, then with most of his sidemen joined Harlan Leonard. Worked with Harlan Leonard until the early 1940s, briefly with Count Basie in 1944, then led own sextet at the Sterling Club, Kansas City (1945), the Rialto, College Inn, etc. Led own band in and around Kansas City during the 1950s and 1960s, long residency at the Playmates Club, Kansas City.

KELLEY, 'Peck' John Dickson
piano

Born: Houston, Texas, 1898
Died: Houston, Texas, 26th December 1980

Led own 'Bad Boys' in and around Texas from the early 1920s; many famous jazzmen worked in the band including: Jack Teagarden, Leon Roppolo, Pee Wee Russell, Leon Prima, etc. During the 1920s and 1930s 'Peck' worked almost entirely in Texas—except for a brief spell in St. Louis (1925) and a trip to New Orleans with Joe Gill's Band (c. 1934). He steadfastly refused offers to join 'name bands and continued to play long residencies in Houston at Jerry's Inn, Rice Hotel Roof, and Southern Diners' Club. Brief spell in U.S. Army until March 1943, then returned to Houston. Eyesight problems caused temporary retirement (1946-8), then returned to play long residency at Dixie Bar, Houston, from December 1948. Retired from regular playing in the mid 1950s, continued to reside in Houston. Recordings of his work were finally issued posthumously.

KELLY, George
tenor sax/arranger

Born: Miami, Florida, 31st July 1915

Began playing piano at nine, switched to alto sax at 13, then to tenor. Led his own band, the Cavaliers, in Florida during the early 1930s which included Panama Francis and Grachan Moncur. Moved to New York, played in the Savoy Sultans from 1941 to 1944, then led own small group for many years (brief spell with Rex Stewart Band in 1946). In the late 1950s joined Cozy Cole's Band. Led own band in New York during the 1960s, also gigs with other leaders, usually plays in Buddy Tate's Band whilst Buddy is on solo tours. Toured Europe with Jay McShann (1970). Worked with Panama Francis and his Savoy Sultans during the 1970s, also led own band in U.S.A. and on international tours during the 1970s and 1980s.

KELLY, 'Guy' Edgar Guy
trumpet/vocals

Born: Scotlandville, Louisiana, 22nd November 1906
Died: Chicago, Illinois, 24th February 1940

Played with 'Toots' Johnson Band in Baton Rouge, then toured Texas before settling in New Orleans. Worked with Papa Celestin in 1927 and 1928 (including residency in Mobile). In 1929 began touring with Kid Howard's Band, left to live in Chicago. Toured with Boyd Atkins' Firecrackers (summer 1930). Played in Cassino Simpson's Band in 1931, then with Ed Carry (1932), Erskine Tate, Dave Peyton, Tiny Parham, Carroll Dickerson (1934), and Jimmie Noone, before joining Albert Ammons from 1935 until 1936. With Carroll Dickerson Big Band from February 1937, with Erskine Tate at Coliseum (early

1938), gigged in Chicago before rejoining Albert Ammons' Rhythm Kings early in 1939—this was his last regular job.

KEMP, 'Hal' James Harold
saxes/clarinet

Born: Marion, Alabama, 27th March 1905
Died: California, 21st December 1940

Began playing piano, originally taught by his sister. During early teens played in a movie theatre in Marion, then moved with family to Charlotte, North Carolina (1917). Played clarinet, led own band whilst at Alexander Graham High School—The Merry Makers. Took up alto sax whilst studying at the University of North Carolina, joined (and eventually led) The Caroline Club Orchestra, composed of students from the university. Travelled with this band to London during the summer of 1924 for residency at the Piccadilly Hotel. Returned to university, during 1925 led another band Hal Kemp and the Boys from the Hill, returned to university to graduate in summer of 1926. Following year launched professional career, appeared at New York Strand Roof in January 1927. Toured several states, had long residency in Miami before visiting Europe from May until August 1930. During these early years Hal Kemp's Band also made many records using the name The Carolina Club Orchestra. Throughout the 1930s Kemp continued to lead his own commercially successful big band until his untimely death; he died of pneumonia after being very seriously injured in a car crash.

KENTON, 'Stan' Stanley Newcomb
piano/arranger/composer

Born: Wichita, Kansas, 19th February 1912
Died: Los Angeles, California, 25th August 1979

Reared in Colorado, family moved to California in 1917. Began on piano in early teens, at 14 took lessons from local pianist Frank Hurst. Played in quartet at Bell High School, Los Angeles. Did six-week tour with the Flack Brothers' Sextet in 1930, then worked in Las Vegas prior to working with territory band in Arizona. Gigged in Los Angeles then joined Everett Hoaglund (1933-34) at Rendezvous Ballroom, Balboa Beach, worked with Russ Plummer's Band at same venue (1935), prior to stint in San Francisco with Hal Grayson's Orchestra. With Gus Arnheim in 1936. Worked with Vido Musso's Band at Villa Venice, L.A. from August 1938, in which Kenton acted as straw-boss. In 1939 worked in pit band at Earl Carroll's Vanities in L.A. until 1940, formed own rehearsal band which obtained bookings in 1941 at Huntingdon Beach, quickly followed by a summer season at the Rendezvous Ballroom, Balboa Beach. In November 1941 played their first date at the Hollywood Palladium. Since then Kenton has continued to lead highly successful big bands, despite several bouts of serious illness. He has undertaken many international tours, and in 1956 his became the first American big band to work unrestrictedly in Britain since 1937. His 1970s tours included Europe and Japan. During that decade he devoted a great deal of time and energy to taking his band to jazz clinics at various colleges and educational centres. Mainly inactive through a serious operation in 1977, Kenton had sufficiently recovered to appear at the Newport Jazz Festival's Silver Jubilee concert at Saratoga, N.Y. in June 1978. 'Straight Ahead—The Story of Stan Kenton'—by Carol Easton was first published in 1973.

KEPPARD, Freddie
cornet

Born: New Orleans, Louisiana, 27th February 1890
Died: Chicago, Illinois, 15tn July 1933

Brother of tuba-player and guitarist Louis Keppard (born: 1888). Both brothers began on fretted instruments: Freddie on mandolin, Louis on guitar. Freddie also played violin and accordion before switching exclusively to cornet. Originally taught by Adolphe Alexander. After playing a few local gigs he organised The Olympia Orchestra c. 1906—during the period 1907-11 he also worked in Frankie Dusen's Eagle Band. Played regularly in clubs and dance halls including: Pete Lala's, Groshell's, George Fewclothes (Focault's), Hanan's, etc. In 1914 (at bassist Bill Johnson's request) he and several colleagues travelled to Los Angeles, Keppard became frontman and co-leader of The Original Creole Orchestra. The orchestra toured the Orpheum Circuit for several years including visits to Chicago and New York (1915). The Original Creoles temporarily disbanded in 1917, but soon re-formed under Keppard's leadership they played a residency at the Logan Square Theatre, Chicago, then briefly toured the Orpheum Circuit again. Keppard then settled in Chicago, played residency at The Entertainers' Cafe, then toured with the 'Tan Town Topics'. Returned to play at The Entertainers' and at the De Luxe. (Jasper Taylor once said that Keppard worked with Lt. Tim Brymn in New York—this may have been in 1919). Briefly with King Oliver at the Royal Gardens (c. 1920), then worked at the Lorraine Club with Jimmie Noone, also doubled with Mae Brady's Band at Dreamland. Joined Doc Cooke at that venue in autumn 1922, remained for two years except for brief spell with Erskine Tate in 1923. During this two-year period also doubled in Ollie Powers' Band. From 1924 was regularly employed at Bert Kelly's Stables—this arrangement continued for several years, but Keppard had long leaves of absence. Rejoined Doc Cooke in late 1925 until c. early 1926, led own band, again worked at Bert Kelly's. Rejoined Doc Cooke from spring until September 1927, with Erskine Tate in early 1928, led own band at LaRue's Dreamland (spring 1928), later worked with Jerome Don Pasquall's Band at Harmon's Dreamland (late 1928). Toured Illinois and Indiana with own band, then worked with Charlie Elgar at the Savoy Ballroom. Lived in musical obscurity for the last years of his life, suffered from tuberculosis, after a long illness he died in the Cook County Hospital, Chicago.

KERSEY, 'Kenny' Kenneth Lyons
piano

Born: Harrow, Ontario, Canada, 3rd April 1916
Died: New York, 1st April 1983

Mother was a pianiste-music teacher, father a cellist. Studied at The Detroit Institute of Music and began doubling on trumpet. Moved to New York in 1936, began extensive gigging on piano and trumpet, then joined Lucky Millinder as replacement for Billy Kyle. Subsequently worked with Billy Hicks, Frankie Newton, and Roy Eldridge, before spending 10 months with Henry Allen in 1941. Short spell with Cootie Williams, then joined Andy Kirk in May 1942. Left Kirk to serve in the U.S. Army, played trumpet in Camp Kilmer Army Band, was stationed near New York City and was able to make regular guest appearances with Andy Kirk's Band. After being demobilised in January 1946 he joined Teddy McRae's Band, did regular tours with 'Jazz At The Philharmonic' from late 1946 until early 1949—during this period also worked with Roy Eldridge (late 1948) and with Buck Clayton's Sextet, did solo residencies at Lou Terrasi's Club. With Edmond Hall in Boston from May 1949 until 1950, Henry Allen (1951-2), Sol Yaged Trio (1952-4), Charlie Shavers (1955), again with Sol Yaged (1956-7). Suffered a severe illness in the late 1950s and was forced to quit regular playing.

KEYES, Joe
trumpet

Born: Houston, Texas. c. 1907
Died: New York, November 1950

From 1928 played with various bands in Houston including Johnson's Joymakers. With Eugene Coy (early 1930), then with Jap Allen (summer 1930), left Allen to join Blanche Calloway in April 1931. Joined Bennie Moten (1932), with Count Basie in Little Rock, Arkansas (early 1934), then briefly with Nat Towles before joining Rook Ganz in Minneapolis (1934). Rejoined Count Basie in Kansas City and travelled to New York with Basie in late 1936. Left in 1937, gigged with various bands including Hot Lips Page's. With Claude Hopkins at Meadowbrook in 1939, briefly with Eddie Durham's Band (1940), afterwards played for a short while with Fletcher Henderson and Fats Waller (1941). In 1943 worked in Wildcats Band, organised by Claude Hopkins at the Eastern Aircraft Factory. Because of drinking problems he did little regular playing in the last years of his life. Cab Calloway bought him a new trumpet and tried to get him to resume regular playing, but to no avail. On 6th November 1950 his body was found floating in the Harlem River; a mystery surrounds the manner of his death, it was formally described as drowning from undetermined circumstances. Shortly before his disappearance he had been showing people a roll of money that his mother had sent him to join her in Dallas, Texas.

KILLIAN, 'Al' Albert
trumpet

Born: Birmingham, Alabama, 15th October 1916
Died: Los Angeles, California, 5th September 1950

With Charlie Turner's Arcadians (c. 1935). Toured South America with Baron Lee (Jimmy Ferguson) in summer of 1937, then worked with Teddy Hill and Don Redman before ioining Count Basie in January 1940. With Charlie Barnet (1943), rejoined Count Basie, then with Lionel Hampton (spring 1945), rejoined Charlie Barnet (summer 1945), left in January 1946, returned to Barnet in June 1946. Led own band late 1946, with Billy Eckstine (spring 1947), also worked with Earle Spencer. With Boyd Raeburn in summer of 1948, joined Duke Ellington in late 1948, left Duke Ellington after 1950 European tour. Returned to Los Angeles, last engagement was a one-nighter with Charlie Barnet. Was murdered by a psychopathic landlord. Burial took place in Chicago.

KINCAIDE, 'Deane' Robert Deane
saxes/clarinet/trombone/flute/arranger

Born: Houston, Texas, 18th March 1911

Moved with his family to Decatur, Illinois, during childhood. Played in local band led by Byron Hart (1927). During his teens learnt to play piano, trombone, and flute, before concentrating on tenor saxophone. Worked in Nebraska and Peoria before joining Wingy Manone in Shreveport, Louisiana (1932). Returned to Chicago, with Ben Pollack from 1933 until 1935. Worked with Lennie Hayton's Band in summer of 1935, then became member of newly formed Bob Crosby Band, played in reed section until June 1936, then became band's staff arranger. Left Bob Crosby in spring 1937, spent six months as tenor sax-arranger with Woody Herman, then returned to Bob Crosby from September 1937 until January 1938. Two months with Wingy Manone, then joined Tommy Dorsey from March 1938 until January 1940. Briefly with Joe Marsala, then with Ray Noble (August-November 1940). Short spell with Glenn Miller, then arranged and played for Muggsy Spanier's Big Band (1941). Did free-lance arranging before serving in U.S. Naval Air Force (1942-5). Has been mainly employed as an arranger since the mid-1940s, but worked regularly with Ray McKinley's Band from 1948. During the 1950s did many arrangements for important television shows, played for a while in Ray McKinley's Small Band in 1956, also toured with Yank Lawson's Band in spring 1962. Based in Florida during the 1970s, continued playing and also active as musical director and arranger for many television shows. Retired from regular playing in January 1981.

KING, Stan
drums/percussion

Born: Hartford, Connecticut, 1900
Died: New York City, 19th November 1949

Played gigs with local bands from an early age, but continued working as a clerk in an insurance office until going to New York with Barney Rapp's Band. Regularly with the California Ramblers from 1922 until 1926, subsequently worked for Roger Wolfe Kahn, Jean Goldkette, Paul Whiteman, and Jack Albin's Orchestra (summer 1928). With Bert Lown and Hotel Biltmore Orchestra from late 1929 until summer of 1931, then worked with Dorsey Brothers' Pit Orchestra for the show 'Everybody's Welcome' before concentrating on radio and recording studio work. With Benny Goodman (1934), Joe Haymes (summer 1935), Three T's (Trumbauer, Jack and Charlie Teagarden) in late 1936, continued with free-lance studio work. With Chauncey Morehouse Band (1938), toured with Bob Zurke's Band (late 1939 to early 1940). Free-lanced before working for long spell with Chauncey Grey's Band at the El Morocco Club in New York.

KIRBY, John
string bass/tuba/arranger

Born: Baltimore, Maryland, 31st December 1908
Died: Hollywood, California, 14th June 1952

Orphaned at an early age. Learnt to play the trombone, moved to New York (c. 1925), whilst scuffling to find gigs he had his instrument stolen, worked at a variety of day jobs (including spell as a Pullman porter) before saving enough money to buy a tuba. With Bill Brown and his Brownies (1928-30), then joined Fletcher Henderson during 1930. Began doubling on string bass (lessons from Wellman Braud and Pops Foster). After switching from aluminium bass to wooden bass in 1933 he rarely played tuba. With Chick Webb from spring 1934, led own quartet at President Hotel, New York (1935), rejoined Fletcher Henderson in late 1935. Rejoined Chick Webb in summer 1936, then joined Lucky Millinder in autumn 1936. From 1938 until 1941 was married to Maxine Sullivan. Was an original member of the small band that went into Onyx Club (15th May 1937), later Kirby was appointed leader, and during the sextet's initial 11 month's residency they gained a wide reputation. During this period Kirby occasionally doubled on trombone. The sextet subsequently worked at many New York clubs including: The Famous Door, Fifi's, Monte Carlo Club, The Beachcomber, Hickory House, etc., also played at the New York World's Fair Zombie Club (summer 1940). The band also played residencies in Chicago, Los Angeles, etc. Personnel was virtually unchanged until 1942. New York residencies at Famous Door, Loew's Theatre, and Larchmont in 1943 and 1944, spell on West Coast from late 1944. In July 1945 Kirby returned to New York with an entirely different line-up, the surviving original members played together in New York early in 1946. Personnel changes were very frequent during the last years of the group, but the original sextet (with the exception of Sid Catlett, who played in place of the late O'Neill Spencer) re-formed for a Carnegie Hall concert on 20th December 1950. Kirby led own quartet (1950), then worked with Henry Allen at the Hickory Log, and with Buck Clayton at Terrasi's in the spring of 1951, later that year he moved to California. In early 1952 he played occasionally in Benny Carter's Band, then started to reorganise a new sextet (with arrangements by Gene Roland), but ill health forced him to abandon the project. He died in Los Angeles from diabetes and other complications.

KIRK, 'Andy' Andrew Dewey
bass sax/baritone sax/tuba

Born: Newport, Kentucky, 28th May 1898

Husband of pianiste Mary Colston; their son, Andy Kirk Jr. (deceased) played tenor sax. During childhood moved with his family to Denver, Colorado. Tentative efforts on piano, also sang in school choir, later took up tenor sax, tuition from Franz Rath, also received harmony lessons from Walter Light. Worked for ten years as a postman before joining 11-piece band led by violinist George Morrison (operating out of Denver)—Kirk working mainly on tuba and bass-sax. After touring and recording with Morrison, Kirk worked temporarily as a postman, then joined newly formed Terrence Holder Band in Dallas, Texas, this outfit was later known as the 'Dark Clouds of Joy'. In January 1929 Holder left, and Kirk was appointed the leader, the band was first fronted by vocalist Bill Massey, later by Pha Terrell. For one brief spell in 1931 the entire band worked under Blanche Calloway (in Philadelphia), they immediately reverted to their former billing for a residency at Winwood Beach, Kansas City. Throughout the early 1930s Andy Kirk and his Clouds of Joy steadily gained popularity, much of their work was in the Middle West, but as early as 1930 they had played dates in New York. Widespread touring from 1936. The band enjoyed an international reputation from 1936 until 1948 when it disbanded. Kirk moved to the West Coast for a while, then returned to New York to manage the Hotel Theresa. He continued to organise big bands for specific engagements during the 1960s. Visited Europe in the 1960s. Now works as a supervisor in stockroom of New York's Local 802, American Federation of Musicians.

KIRK, Wilbert
drums/harmonica

Born: St. Louis, Missouri, c. 1906
Died: New York City, 26th September 1983

Raised in New Orleans and Kansas City. Played in theatre orchestras. With Dewey Jackson (c. 1930) before doing regular seasons with Fate Marable. With Jeter-Pillars Band 1934 until early 1935, then joined Noble Sissle until 1943. Briefly with Don Redman in 1943. With Claude Hopkins (late 1944-5), then became house drummer at the Club Zanzibar in New York. Subsequently did widespread touring leading own family harmonica group, regular appearances on television. Joined Wilbur de Paris (on drums) in March 1956, spent several years with de Paris (including tour of Africa in 1960).

K

KIRKEBY, **'Ed' Wallace Theodore**
leader/manager

Born: Brooklyn, New York, 10th October 1891
Died: Mineola, Long Island, 12th June 1978

His father was a part-time banjo player. Ed played banjo, mandolin, and piano, but began work as a soap salesman before joining Columbia as a record promoter in 1916, later became assistant director of popular recordings, managed first dates for the Original Memphis Five, also worked in music publishing. In 1920 he began managing The California Ramblers, they soon began a long residency at the Post Lodge in Westchester and subsequently commenced their prolific recordings. They also did sessions under a variety of pseudonyms (The Goofus Five, University Six, Five Birmingham Babies, etc.). In 1926 Ed led a band for season at the Club Deauville, Miami, organised 'The McAlpineers' for residency at the Hotel McAlpin, New York (1928). During the 1920s and 1930s organised bands for prolific recordings and extensive broadcasting (pseudonyms included: Ted Wallace, Ed Loyd), subsequently managed the Pickens' Sisters and became an a. and r. man for RCA Victor. In 1938 became Fats Waller's manager and travelled with Fats for the last five years of the pianist's life, was with him on his last journey. Ed continued in management and for many years represented The Deep River Boys.

'Ain't Misbehavin' ', The Story of Fats Waller, by Ed Kirkeby (in collaboration with Duncan Schiedt and Sinclair Traill) was first published in 1966.

KIRKPATRICK, **'Don' Donald E.**
piano/arranger

Born: Charlotte, North Carolina, 17th June 1905
Died: New York City, 13th May 1956

Married Johnny Hodges' sister. Came to New York from Baltimore with drummer Johnny Ridgley's Band (summer 1926), soon began working for Chick Webb; worked mainly with Chick Webb until late 1932, then long spell with Don Redman from early 1933. During the late 1930s and 1940s was mainly active as an arranger, scoring for Chick Webb, Don Redman, Benny Goodman, Alvino Rey, Cootie Williams, Count Basie, etc., also gigged with various leaders including Zutty Singleton and Mezz Mezzrow. Left full-time music for a while, then did overseas tour with Herbie Cowens in 1943, worked at Nick's, New York, from mid-1944. Gigged with Bunk Johnson in New York in November 1947. With Wilbur de Paris from 1952-5, then played in Boston with Doc Cheatham (late 1955). Played gigs at Stuyvesant Casino, Central Plaza, and Hotel Theresa, New York, during the last few months of his life—died of lobar pneumonia.

KLEIN, **'Manny' Emmanuel**
trumpet

Born: New York City, 4th February 1908

Three of his brothers were professional musicians: Dave (trumpet), Sol (violin), and Merrill (string bass). Began playing trumpet during early childhood, later studied with Max Schlossberg. During his teens he played for B. F. Keith's Boys' Band, later played in the New York Junior Police Band. First professional work with Louis Katzman's Ambassador Orchestra. In December 1928 played in Al Goodman's Orchestra for the Broadway show 'Follow Thru', for the next nine years was one of the busiest free-lance musicians in New York—worked with Don Voorhees, Red Nichols, Fred Rich, Roger Wolfe Kahn, Benny Goodman, the Dorsey Brothers, Eddie Elkins, etc., etc. In 1932 visited England whilst on holiday, vacations in Hawaii (1934 and 1935). Moved to California in November 1937. From March 1938 worked in band co-led with Frank Trumbauer. With violinist Matty Malneck's Orchestra (1939), taking a role in the Bing Crosby film 'East Side of Heaven'. Throughout the 1940s (except for U.S. Army service) and 1950s did regular studio work for film and recording companies—occasionally played dates with outside bands including brief spell with Lionel Hampton in late 1940. Has played soundtracks for countless films—dubbed for actor Montgomery Clift in 'From Here to Eternity' and for an ailing Ziggy Elman in 'The Benny Goodman Story'. Not long after celebrating his 50th year as a musician he toured Japan with Percy Faith's Orchestra (1966). Made several visits to Europe during the 1970s, and was featured at the Breda, Holland, festival.

K

KLINK, 'Al' Albert
saxes

Born: Danbury, Connecticut, 28th December 1915

Studied with Frank Chase. With Charlie Boulanger's Band prior to working with Glenn Miller 1939-1942. With Benny Goodman from August 1942 until early 1943, and again from fall of 1943 until spring 1944, worked with Tommy Dorsey and other big bands prior to becoming studio musician in 1947, worked in the studios for many years. Active free-lance in the 1970s, played first of many dates with the World's Greatest Jazz Band in late 1974, toured Europe with W.G.J.B. Extensive free-lance work during the late 1970s and 1980s, including many international tours.

KNOWLING, Ransom
string bass/tuba/violin

Born: New Orleans, Louisiana, 24th June 1912
Died: Chicago, Illinois, 22nd October 1967

Worked in Sidney Desvigne's Orchestra during the late 1920s and early 1930s, then regularly with Joe Robichaux for several years. Settled in Chicago, and during the late 1930s and 1940s took part in many free-lance recordings. Worked with many bands in Chicago including spell with Little Brother Montgomery in the late 1950s.

KRESS, Carl
guitar

Born: Newark, New Jersey, 20th October 1907
Died: Reno, Nevada, 10th June 1965

Began on piano, switched to banjo, then guitar. Gigged with many bands in New York area, worked regularly with Eddie Elkins. From the late 1920s was mainly employed as a studio musician for radio and recordings—contracts with many leaders including Al Goodman, Peter Van Steeden, Ray Sinatra, etc. Throughout his lifetime made many jazz recordings with various leaders, and made a speciality of duetting with other guitarists: Ed Lang, Dick McDonough, and George Barnes. Worked on banjo with Clarence Hutchenrider's Trio (1960). Whilst appearing in Reno with George Barnes he suffered a fatal heart attack.

KRUEGER, 'Benny' Benjamen
saxes/clarinet

Born: Newark, N.J., 17th July 1899
Died: Orange, N.J. 29th July 1967

Chiefly remembered for his recorded work with The Original Dixieland Jazz Band in 1920 and 1921. From the mid-1920s was prominent as a rádio bandleader and contractor for radio stations—during the mid-1930s was musical director for singer Rudy Vallee.

KRUPA, Gene
drums

Born: Chicago, Illinois, 15th January 1909
Died: Yonkers, N.Y., 16th October 1973

Attended Bowen High School, later studied at St. Joseph's College in Indiana—during summer vacations played a season with The Frivolians in Madison, Wisconsin. In 1925 began studying percussion with teachers Al Silverman, Ed Straight, and Roy Knapp. During that year worked with Al Gale's Band and Joe Kayser, subsequently with Leo Shukin, Thelma Terry, Mezz Mezzrow, the Benson Orchestra, Eddie Neibauer's Seattle Harmony Kings, etc. Moved to New York (1929), began working for Red Nichols, and during next two years worked mainly in theatre bands directed by Nichols. During the early 1930s played in various commercial bands including Irving Aaronson's, Russ Colombo (1932), Mal Hallet (1933), and Buddy Rogers (1934). Starred with Benny Goodman from December 1934 until February 1938, then formed own big band for debut at Steel Pier, Atlantic City, in April 1938. Continued to lead own successful band until May 1943 when circumstances outside of music forced him to disband. In San Francisco for a short while, then returned to New York and studied harmony and composition. Rejoined Benny Goodman in September 1943 until mid-December 1943, then joined Tommy Dorsey in New York, remaining with that band until following July. Left to organise own big band which got under way late in 1944—initially it proved to be an enormous band hovering between the 30- and 40-piece mark—it settled down to a more usual format and enjoyed wide success until 1951. From September 1951 began to tour regularly in 'Jazz At The Philharmonic' shows—usually featured with own trio. Toured with own trio/quartet in the 1950s (including trips overseas), also appeared regularly at The Metropole, New York. Temporarily inactive in late 1960 due to heart strain, then resumed leading. In June 1963 led specially formed big band in Hollywood, a year later made second visit to Japan with own quartet. From 1954 Gene and Cozy Cole ran a drum-tuition school in New York. Continued leading own small groups during the 1960s. A supposedly biographical film 'The Gene Krupa Story' (retitled 'Drum Crazy' in some countries) was released in 1959, the role of Gene Krupa was played by actor Sal Mineo—Gene recorded the soundtrack. Semi-retirement from October 1967 until leading own quartet at Hotel Plaza, N.Y. (1970). Resumed regular playing, occasionally touring, continued playing until shortly before his death from leukemia.

Film appearances include: 'George White's Scandals', 'Some Like It Hot', 'Beat The Band', 'The Benny Goodman Story', etc.

KYLE, 'Billy' William Osborne *Born: Philadelphia, Pennsylvania, 14th July 1914*
piano/arranger *Died: Youngstown, Ohio, 23rd February 1966*

Pianist from the age of eight, played in school symphony orchestra whilst attending West Philadelphia High. Gigged with local bands from the age of 15. From 1932 until 1934 free-lanced in New York City and Syracuse, then played residency at the Memphis Club in Philadelphia, also worked as regular accompanist for Bon Bon Tunnell on Station KYW. Brief spell in Tiny Bradshaw's Band, then in 1936 organised own band in Baltimore; temporary lay-off due to broken arm. With Lucky Millinder from autumn 1936 until joining John Kirby in February 1938. With Kirby until being called up late in 1942, served in the Pacific area before being demobilised in late 1945. Brief return to John Kirby in early 1946, then toured with Sy Oliver, rejoined John Kirby, then again worked with Sy Oliver; led own trio, quartet, and sextet (1947-8), later did two-year stint playing for the Broadway show 'Guys and Dolls'. During the early 1950s was mainly occupied with free-lance studio work, joined Louis Armstrong's All Stars in autumn 1953. Remained with Louis (except for brief absences through illness) until the time of his death; was taken ill whilst the band was playing a one-nighter in Youngstown, Ohio. He was admitted to the South-side Hospital there and died a week later.

LACEY, Jack
trombone

Born: Lancaster, Pennsylvania, 1911
Died: New York City, 25th May 1965

Played in Philadelphia with Oliver Naylor's Orchestra in the late 1920s. Free-lanced in New York, then worked for a while with Talmadge Henry's Band. With Joe Reichmann's Band at the Arcadia Ballroom, New York, then joined Benny Goodman for a year from summer of 1934, left to do studio work. Other than time spent in the services during World War II, did regular studio work through to the 1960s. Last outside work was with the Merle Evans Band during the 1960s.

LADNIER, 'Tommy' Thomas J.
trumpet

Born: Florenceville, Louisiana, 28th May 1900
Died: New York City, 4th June 1939

Trumpet tuition from Bunk Johnson. Moved to Chicago c. 1917, subsequently toured in band led by drummer John H. Wickcliffe. Worked for Charlie Creath in St. Louis (c. 1921), then returned to Chicago; with violinist Milton Vassar at the Lincoln Gardens (1922), Ollie Powers (1923), etc. Recorded with Lovie Austin (1924), briefly with Fate Marable, then joined King Oliver. In spring 1925 was sent for by Sam Wooding, auditioned for Wooding in New York (April 1925) and subsequently sailed to join up with the band in Europe (June 1925). In June 1926 left Sam Wooding in Berlin and journeyed in to Poland as a member of the Louis Douglas Revue. By early August 1926 had arrived back in New York, later that month played in saxist Billy Fowler's Orchestra at Carlin's Park, Baltimore, returned to New York with Fowler and played residencies with him at The Cameo Club and at a Brooklyn dancing school. With Fletcher Henderson (c. October 1926), remained with Henderson throughout 1927, then toured with Sam Wooding from early 1928 and sailed to Europe again with Wooding in June 1928. Left Wooding in Nice (early 1929), joined Benton E. Peyton and toured Europe with Peyton for several months. With Harry Flemming's Blue Birds in Spain (October 1929), worked again with Louis Douglas then led own band in France (spring 1930). With Noble Sissle: in Paris (summer 1930), London (late 1930), New York (1931), Paris (spring 1931). Returned to U.S., worked accompanying The Berry Brothers' dancing act, then with Sidney Bechet formed The New Orleans Feetwarmers. The group played at the Saratoga Club, in White Plains and New Jersey, then opened at the Savoy Ballroom, New York, on 14th September 1932. After they disbanded in the spring of 1933, Ladnier and Bechet worked in their own 'Southern Tailor' shop in New York, when Bechet rejoined Noble Sissle, Ladnier left New York. Gigged for a while with own quintet in New Jersey, then did regular teaching, later worked in Buffalo. Was again in New York City in the early summer of 1937, then worked in Newburgh, N.Y. In late 1938, through the efforts of famous jazz critic Hugues Panassié, he was rediscovered and subsequently recorded with Mezzrow, Bechet, and Rosetta Crawford. Appeared with Sidney Bechet at the 'Spirituals to Swing' concert in New York (December 1938). Whilst staying at Mezz Mezzrow's apartment he suffered a fatal heart attack.

Walter C. Allen kindly sent details of an item that appeared in the Chicago Defender dated 21st September 1935, in which a trumpeter, Tommy Lardier, of 4527 Prairie Avenue, Chicago, is mentioned. None of the Chicago musicians that I have contacted remember a trumpeter of that name, and I feel that the man in question is most probably Tommy Ladnier. Tommy's cousin, Calvin, still plays trumpet in Chicago, he uses the original family name Ladner.

LAINE, Julian
trombone

Born: New Orleans, Louisiana, 1907
Died: New Orleans, Louisiana, 10th September 1957

With Prima-Sharkey Melody Masters (1928), worked with Johnny Bertucci's Band in Biloxi, Mississippi, during the late 1920s. Returned to New Orleans and played with Tony Almerico's Band on the riverboats. With Sharkey Bonano (1936), then with Red Bolman and Jules Bauduc. Was injured in car smash in 1937, but soon resumed regular playing. Joined Louis Prima in Chicago, later worked with Joe Venuti then returned to New Orleans and rejoined Tony Almerico. Formed own band in 1940, spent two years in U.S. Army (1942-4), then worked with Tony Almerico and Leon Prima, also gigged with Sharkey Bonano. Led own band at Three Deuces, New Orleans (1949), with Muggsy Spanier in Chicago and San Francisco (1950), also toured with Sharkey Bonano. Returned to gig in New Orleans, played occasionally with Johnny Wiggs, was then forced to quit playing through failing health. Not related to 'Papa Jack' Laine.

LAINE, 'Papa Jack' George Vital *Born: New Orleans, Louisiana, 21st September 1873*
drums/alto horn/leader *Died: New Orleans, Louisiana, 1st June 1966*

Father of Alfred Laine (1895-1957). Played drums, brass bass, and alto horn during childhood. Formed own ragtime band in New Orleans c. 1890. The success of his Reliance Band enabled him to form several other units bearing that name. These Reliance Bands worked throughout the Gulf Coast States during the early 1900s. In 1904 Laine led for three months in St. Louis, Missouri. He retired from music in 1917 and worked at own blacksmith's business, later he managed a garage for many years. During the 1940s he often attended meetings of the New Orleans Jazz Club, and in the early 1960s did taped sessions with Johnny Wiggs.

LAMARE, 'Nappy' Hilton Napoleon *Born: New Orleans, Louisiana, 14th June 1907*
guitar/banjo/vocals

His brother, Jimmy, is a sax player. Began playing whilst at Warren Easton High School. Toured with Johnny Bayersdorffer in 1925, worked in New Orleans with Sharkey Bonano, Monk Hazel, The Midnight Serenaders, Johnny Wiggs, New Orleans Owls, etc. Toured with Billy Lustig's Scranton Sirens. Joined Ben Pollack (on guitar) in September 1930, subsequently became founder-member of the Bob Crosby Band in 1935. Remained with Bob Crosby until late 1942 then, together with several colleagues, became part of Eddie Miller's Band in California (early 1943). Regularly led own small bands from the mid-1940s, worked with Jimmy Dorsey in 1948, then led own group at a night club that he part-owned. Has played regularly throughout the 1950s and 1960s, for many years co-led with Ray Bauduc; frequent tours throughout the U.S.A. (and to the Orient in late 1956). Temporarily inactive through car-crash injuries (early 1962), then resumed co-leading with Ray Bauduc. Worked with Bob Crosby; regularly with Joe Darensbourg (1969). Free-lancing in California during 1970s. Toured Europe with 'A Night in New Orleans' package (1975). Worked with Bob Crosby at Nice Festival (1981). Often worked with Joe Darensbourg (1983).

LAMBERT, 'Don' Donald *Born: Princeton, New Jersey, 1904*
piano *Died: Newark, New Jersey, 8th May 1962*

His mother, who led a band, gave him first piano tuition. Worked for most of his life as a solo pianist; in New York during the late 1920s and early 1920s, then played for many years at the Town House, Montclair, before long residency at Wallace's Bar in East Orange, New Jersey. Recorded for Bluebird in 1941 and for Solo Art in 1961. Featured at Newport Jazz Festival (July 1961).

LANG, Eddie *Born: Philadelphia, Pennsylvania, 25th October 1902*
(real name: Salvatore Massaro) *Died: New York, 26th March 1933*
guitar

His father was a fretted-instrument maker; Eddie's sister, Eadie, worked on guitar during the 1930s. Began on violin at age of seven, studied with teachers in Philadelphia. Whilst still at school became a friend of Joe Venuti, and for much of his career worked alongside him. First professional work on violin at L'Aiglon Restuarant, Philadelphia, worked on banjo with Chick Granese's Trio (c. 1918). With Charlie Kerr's Band (1920-3), on banjo and guitar (doubling violin). With Bert Estlow in Atlantic City, and Vic D'Ippolito (1923), brief variety tour with Frank Fay and Barbara Stanwyck. Six months with Billy Lustig's Scranton Sirens until summer 1924, then joined Mound City Blue Blowers, later that year visited London with M.C.B.B. Prolific free-lance radio and recording work on guitar from 1925. Summer season with Vic D'Ippolito (1926), with Joe Venuti's Band in New York (September 1926), two months later Lang and Venuti joined Roger Wolfe Kahn, they also did a series of theatre shows for Don Voorhees and played in Adrian Rollini's short-lived big band (October 1927). They co-led at Vanity Club, New York (autumn 1928); both worked with Paul Whiteman from May 1929 until May 1930, including appearances in the film 'King of Jazz'. Extensive free-lance work, again with Roger Wolfe Kahn (spring 1932). For the last year of his life Lang was mainly employed as accompanist to Bing Crosby; he died from complications following a tonsillectomy.

LANIGAN, 'Jim' James Wood
string bass/tuba

Born: Chicago, Illinois, 30th January 1902
Died: Elburn, Illinois, 9th April 1983

Both parents were musicians. Played violin and piano from an early age. Began gigging on piano and occasionally drums with the Austin High School Blue Friars, then switched to string bass and tuba. Worked with Husk O'Hare's Wolverines, then joined Bill Paley's Band (1926). Worked for a while with the Mound City Blue Blowers, then spent two years with Art Kassel. During the 1930s worked with many varied musical aggregations, mainly in Chicago, including almost four years with Ted Fio Rito. Was staff musician at N.B.C. Chicago studios from 1937, with WGN from 1948 until 1952—during this period also did regular jazz gigs with Bud Jacobson's Jungle Kings, etc., and played a good deal of classical work. During the 1950s played at several jazz concerts in Chicago. Left full-time music in the 1960s, continued to gig with Frank Chase Sextet, etc., in November 1965 played at Austin High as part of that school's 75th anniversary celebrations. Worked for fifteen years with Chicago Symphony Orchestra until 1968.

LANGONE, Frank C.
clarinet/saxes

Born: Philadelphia, Pennsylvania, 11th March 1907

Began playing at 12, originally taught by Abe Beloff in Philadelphia. Did theatre work in Philadelphia, then worked on liner cruises with Al Donahue's Orchestra, appeared with this band in Paris and Rome. From the mid-1930s worked for many leaders including: Buddy Rogers, Isham Jones, Bunny Berigan, Carmen Cavallaro, Bobby Hackett (Big Band), Mike Riley, Jan Savitt, Jimmy Dorsey, Howard Lanin, etc., also recorded with Bob Crosby and Tommy Dorsey. Continues to play regularly, worked with Jan Garber in 1969.

In some reference books Langone has been confused with Slats Long.

LANOUE, Conrad T.
piano/arranger

Born: Cohoes, New York, 18th October 1908
Died: Albany, New York, 15th October 1972

Began playing piano at the age of 10, studied at the Troy Conservatory. Did first gigs in the early 1920s at the Harmony Hotel, Cohoes, later worked for several years around the Capital district with Carmen Mastren and his brothers. Worked for Bernie Kane and Charles Randell then joined Mike Riley-Ed Farley Band (1935). Worked with Louis Prima, then long association with Wingy Manone (1936 until 1940); during this period also worked with Joe Haymes (early 1938), etc., and did arrangements for various big bands. From 1940 until the late 1960s did long stints with Hal Landsberry, Charles Peterson, and Lester Lanin, left full-time music in 1968 following a serious illness.

LARKIN, 'Tippy' Milton
trumpet/valve-trombone/vocals

Born: Houston, Texas, 10th October 1910

Milton Jr. is also a trumpeter. Taught himself to play trumpet after hearing Bunk Johnson (then working in a travelling show). Worked with Chester Boone's Band and with Giles Mitchell's Birmingham Blue Blowers, then formed own band in 1936 for debut at the Aragon Ballroom, Houston, subsequently the band did extensive touring through the territories, also played residencies at College Inn, Kansas City, Rhumboogie, Chicago (August 1941 to July 1942), Apollo Theatre, New York, etc. Served in U.S. Army from November 1943, began doubling on valve-trombone, played in Sy Oliver's Service Band. After demobilisation re-formed own band, led at Rhumboogie, Chicago (1946), did various tours, etc., later led small group (The X-Rays). Made his home in New York, has led small band for many years, residency upstairs at the Celebrity Club. In 1962 was injured in a car crash, but soon resumed regular playing prior to moving back to Houston.

L

LAROCCA, 'Nick' Dominic James
cornet/trumpet/composer

Born: New Orleans, Louisiana, 11th April 1889
Died: New Orleans, Louisiana, 22nd February 1961

Father was an amateur cornetist; Nick's son, James, is a trumpeter. Began on cornet whilst still at school, co-led juvenile band with violinist Henry Young during summer of 1905, later gigged in New Orleans with local string trios until forming own band in 1908. Later played briefly for various leaders including guitarist Dominic Barrocca (1911), trombonist Bill Gallity (1911), and the Brunies Brothers (1911). From 1912 until 1916 played regularly in Papa Laine's Reliance Bands; worked with drummer Johnny Stein (Hountha) at the Haymarket Cafe, New Orleans (1915) and subsequently left New Orleans for Chicago with Stein on 1st March 1916. In late May 1916 LaRocca and three of his colleagues left Stein and formed The Original Dixieland Jazz Band. The O.D.J.B. used a temporary drummer (Earl Carter) for their first engagement at the Hotel Normandy in Chicago—June 1916 (Tony Spargo joined them after two weeks). In January 1917 the band (with Larry Shields in place of Alcide Nunez) opened at Reisenweber's in New York, the band's Victor recording career began the following month. The O.D.J.B. arrived in England on 1st April 1919, after playing theatre and ballroom dates (and making records) they returned to the U.S.A. in July 1920. LaRocca continued to lead the O.D.J.B. for various residencies (Folies Bergere Cafe, New York, Balconades Ballroom, New York, etc.) until suffering a nervous breakdown in January 1925. He eventually returned to New Orleans and ran his own contracting business, but emerged from his retirement to the revived O.D.J.B. which began working in July 1936. The five-man line-up soon became a 14-piece band, then reverted to the small line-up until LaRocca disbanded in January 1938. After playing his final date on 1st February 1938, LaRocca returned to New Orleans to resume running his business and took no part in subsequent O.D.J.B. re-creations. LaRocca was composer and part-composer of many tunes that have become jazz standards including: 'At the Jazz Band Ball', 'Original Dixieland One-step', 'Fidgety Feet', 'Sensation Rag', etc., etc.

For a detailed account of LaRocca and his colleagues, the reader is advised to consult 'The Story of the Original Dixieland Jazz Band', by H. O. Brunn (first published in 1960).

LATTIMORE, Harlan
vocals

Born: Cincinnati, Ohio, 1908

Mother was an operatic soprano. Left Johnson C. Smith College and became professional singer on Station WLW in Cincinnati, later did a year's residency at the Regal Theatre, Chicago, before returning to WLW. Was signed by Don Redman in 1932, worked mainly with Don Redman throughout the 1930s. Served in U.S. Army during World War II, then left full-time music; is a resident of New York.

LAVERE, Charles
(real name: Charles LeVere Johnson)
piano/vocals/arranger/composer

Born: Salina, Kansas, 18th July 1910
Died: Ramona, California, 28th April 1983

Piano from the age of seven, began professional career with a cousin, Stan Weis, as 'Dan and Stan'. Moved to Oklahoma City, played alto sax (with Charlie Teagarden) in Herb Cook's Oklahoma Joy Boys. Left Oklahoma University with Frank Williams and his Oklahomans, was stranded in New York, worked as accompanist for Bert Froman, played in Pittsburgh with Etzi Covato's Band, then went to Bermuda with Sam Robbins' Orchestra. Subsequently toured with Marshall Van Pool, Tracy Brown, and Boyd Schreffler, also played trombone with Johnny Dorchester's Band. With Wingy Manone in Chicago (1933), also recorded with Jack Teagarden. Toured Texas with Eddie Neibauer, then worked with Dell Coon's Band in Chicago; led own all-star recording group in Chicago (1935): Jabbo Smith, Zutty Singleton, Joe Marsala, Boyce Brown, etc. Did radio work (on piano) with Rico Marcelli's Band, also played trumpet with Joe Sanders' Band. Worked in Chicago with Henry Busse, then moved to New York (1937) and joined Paul Whiteman until early 1938. Left in Los Angeles and joined Frank Trumbauer; in 1939 began working with Skinnay Ennis on radio shows, was also featured with John Scott Trotter and regularly accompanied Bing Crosby until 1947. Prolific studio work in Hollywood; had million-seller record as vocalist with Gordon Jenkins (1947): 'Maybe You'll Be There'. Led own Chicago Loopers on record and at 1949 Dixieland Jubilee, from 1950-4 played the Dixieland Jubilees with the Sextet from Hunger, worked regularly with Country Washburne's Band. Played for (and co-composed) 'Golden Horse Shoe Revue' at Disneyland (1955-9), worked as accompanist for comedian George Burns, then led own quintet in New York (late 1960) until moving to Las Vegas (1961-3), whilst there did solo residencies, also worked with Bob Crosby (late 1961 to early 1962) and with Wingy Manone (spring 1963). To Southern California in June 1963, solo spots, theatre work, and spell with Jack Coon's, also played on two cruises to Australia. Arranged and played for Russ Morgan in Las Vegas (1967), returned to Southern California where he organised own piano-repair and tuning service.

Compositions include: 'The Blues Have Got Me', 'Cuban Boogie Woogie', etc.

LAWRENCE, Charlie
clarinet/saxes/piano/arranger

Born: Los Angeles, California, 1905

First professional work in band co-led with Buster Wilson, this later became The Sunnyland Jazz Orchestra. Throughout the 1920s and 1930s worked and arranged for many bandleaders in California including Paul Howard and Les Hite—he arranged several of the tunes that Louis Armstrong recorded in California ('Ding Dong Daddy', 'If I Could Be With You', and 'I'm In The Market For You). Later specialised on piano, toured with Noble Sissle (1947), also worked with Kid Ory and with George Olsen's Orchestra. Led own trio for residency at Bamboo Club, Hollywood. In later years worked as a teacher, arranger, and solo pianist.

LAWSON, 'Big Jim' Harry
trumpet

Born: Round Rock, Texas, 25th December 1904

Began playing at 15, doubled trombone for several years, worked in circus and carnival bands before joining Terrence Holder, subsequently worked with Andy Kirk. Remained with Kirk until the early 1940s, left full-time music, but continued to play in Andy Kirk's occasionally formed big bands until 1956 when teeth trouble enforced retirement from playing.

LAWSON, 'Yank' John Rhea
trumpet

Born: Trenton, Missouri, 3rd May 1911

Mother was a pianiste. 'Yank' originally played saxophone and piano, but switched to trumpet during his teens. Played with bands at the University of Missouri, then gigged around Shreveport. With Ben Pollack (1933 to autumn 1934), worked with Will Osborne (early 1935), did free-lance studio work in New York, then became a founder-member of the Bob Crosby Band (1935). Worked with Bob Crosby until August 1938, then joined Tommy Dorsey until November 1939. Briefly with Abe Lyman, then few months with Richard Himber (early 1940); from summer 1940 until May 1941 played in theatre orchestra for the show 'Louisiana Purchase'. Rejoined Bob Crosby in May 1941, left to work briefly with Benny Goodman (December 1942), then worked for many years in New York studio bands, prolific free-lance recordings. Together with Bob Haggart led recording band which made several L.P.s in the 1950s. Toured with own band (spring 1962), worked with Peanuts Hucko at Eddie Condon's Club (1964-6), also took part in several Bob Crosby Band reunions including tour of Orient (late 1964) and residencies in New York in 1965 and 1966. Led at Condon's in late 1966. Real name is Lawson, and not, as is often printed, Lausen. Recovered from illness (1981) and co-led Lawson-Haggart Band in Europe (1982). Continued to play regularly during 1980s.

LAYLAN, Rollo
drums/percussion

Born: Wisconsin. c. 1910

First played in band led by his mother (who was a pianiste), Gert Laylan's Syncopators, then worked with Otto Anderson before joining Joe Mae's Jazz Band in Madison, Wisconsin. Briefly with Bunny Berigan early in 1938, then with Paul Whiteman from April 1938-40. Two months with Art Hodes (early 1941), then worked in Florida with Emery Deutsch. With Joe Marsala in 1944, then served in U.S. 3rd A.A.F. (1945). In 1946 worked as second drummer in Ray McKinley's Band, then returned to Florida and led own group. From 1951 his band became known as Preacher Rollo and the Saints, and as such achieved national fame. Continued to lead in Miami until 1965, played with pianist Don Ewell in summer of 1966, then worked in Chicago at Jazz Ltd. (early 1967). Left full-time music, moved to Florida (1971).

LEARY, Ford
trombone/vocals

Born: Lockport, New York, 5th September 1908
Died: New York City, 4th June 1949

Free-lanced in New York City before joining Bunny Berigan (late 1936-7), worked with Larry Clinton (1938-40) and Charlie Barnet (1940-1) before joining Mike Riley. Briefly with Muggsy Spanier Big Band from spring 1942. Later worked as a professional actor in the Broadway show 'Follow The Girls', then injured his back and was inactive for two years. Suffered a long illness, was admitted to Bellevue Hospital and died soon afterwards.

LEE, 'Buddy' George Oliver
trumpet

Born: Louisville, Kentucky, 8th May 1906
Died: Detroit, Michigan, 1971

Left Zack Whyte's Band to work with McKinney's Cotton Pickers 1930-31, moved from Detroit to New York and worked briefly with Teddy Hill, then moved back to Detroit and rejoined McKinney's Cotton Pickers from spring 1932 until summer of 1934. Was forced to quit playing because of a lung ailment, subsequently became a professional photographer.

LEE, George Ewing
saxes/piano/vocals

Born: Kansas City, Missouri, 28th April 1896
Died: 1959

Brother of Julia Lee. First played in a U.S. Army Band (1917) on baritone sax and piano. Returned to Kansas City to lead own small band—long residency with own trio at the Lyric Hall. During the late 1920s and early 1930s led own Singing Orchestra—brief spell co-leading with Bennie Moten (c. 1934), then re-formed own band for residencies in Kansas City including Brookside Club (1938) and Reno Club (1939). Quit professional music in the 1940s, moved to Detroit where he managed a tavern during the 1950s.

LEE, Julia
piano/vocals/composer

Born: Boonville, Missouri, 31st October 1902
Died: Kansas City, Missouri, 8th December 1958

Sister of George Lee, their father was a violinist. At 10 studied piano with Charles Williams and 'Scrap' Harris, during early teens sang in a kids' band together with bassist Walter Page. Professional work from 1916. Worked in her brother's band from c. 1920 until 1933, left several times to work as a soloist including spell in Chicago in 1923. Long residencies at Milton's in Kansas City from 1934 until 1948—brief tours and short residency at the Three Deuces, Chicago, in 1939. To California in August 1948 for recordings, club, and theatre work. Worked at Ciro's, Los Angeles, in 1949, late in 1950 left Tiffany's, Los Angeles, to return to Kansas City. Residency at the Cuban Room, Kansas City, from late 1950. Continued to work mainly in Kansas City during the 1950s (at the High Ball Bar in 1958). Died in her sleep from natural causes.

LEE, 'Sonny' Thomas Ball
trombone

Born: Huntsville, Texas, 26th August 1904

Studied at Texas State Teachers' College, worked with Peck Kelley in Texas. Continued studies in St. Louis, worked with the 'Scranton Sirens'. Whilst with Frank Trumbauer in St. Louis (1925) did occasional work for Charlie Creath including a recording session. With Gene Rodemich, Paul Specht, Harold Leonard, and Vincent Lopez, before joining Isham

Jones from 1933 until 1936. With Artie Shaw (1936), then worked in Gordon Jenkins' Theatre Orchestra until joining Bunny Berigan at the Pennsylvania Hotel in May 1937. Left Berigan in April 1938, long spell with Jimmy Dorsey from April 1938 until 1946.

LEEMAN, 'Cliff' Clifford
drums

Born: Portland, Maine, 10th September 1913

Played in local bands during his early teens, also played percussion with Portland Symphony. First professional work as a xylophonist on variety tour, returned to finish high school, did local gigs, then joined Dan Murphy in Boston (1933). With Hank Biagini (1935), then with Artie Shaw from April 1937 until late 1938 (except for absence through illness in summer of 1938). Briefly with Glenn Miller (April 1939), then worked with Tommy Dorsey from May until November 1939 before joining Charlie Barnet. Left Barnet early in 1943, worked briefly in Chicago with Johnny Long's Band (spring 1943), then joined Woody Herman. Few months' U.S. Army service early in 1944, returned to New York, worked with John Kirby, Don Byas, Raymond Scott, at C.B.S. and led own band (1944). Worked again with Kirby in 1945, also with Jimmy Dorsey's Band. Lived in Portland, Maine, in 1946, did local gigs, then worked with new Jean Goldkette Band in Atlantic City (1947), brief spell with Bobby Byrne's Band and with Glen Gray and the Casa Loma Band. Rejoined Charlie Barnet (1949), then with Bob Chester's Band until April 1950. Worked with Pee Wee Erwin, then rejoined Raymond Scott at C.B.S. (1951). Did regular studio work throughout the 1950s, occasional dates with Billy Butterfield, also played regularly at Nick's and Condon's with various leaders. With Bob Crosby in Las Vegas (1960), with Wild Bill Davison and touring with Yank Lawson (1962), Wild Bill Davison, Dukes of Dixieland (1963), also in group accompanying vocalist Dick Haymes (1963). Toured Japan, Australia, New Zealand, with Eddie Condon (spring 1964), worked with Dukes of Dixieland; from summer 1964 spent two years mainly with Peanuts Hucko in New York. In autumn 1966 worked with Yank Lawson at Condon's. Continued to play regularly in the late 1960s, with Joe Venuti (late 1968), in 1969 toured for a while with George Wein's Newport All Stars, then in late 1969 worked in New York with Joe Venuti. With Bobby Hackett (March 1970), season in Brielle, N.J. (summer 1970). Continues to play regularly, including dates at jazz festivals. Toured Europe with Kings of Jazz (1974), and with Wild Bill Davison (1976). With World's Greatest Jazz Band (1976-1977), also active free-lance. Continued to play regularly during early 1980s, often featured at various jazz festivals.

LEIBROOK, 'Min' Wilford F.
bass sax/tuba/string bass

Born: Hamilton, Ohio, 1903
Died: Los Angeles, California, 8th June 1943

Nicknamed 'Min' after a cartoon character. Started on cornet, switched to bass sax and tuba. Played tuba in the Ten Foot Band in Chicago, subsequently joined The Wolverines. Left early in 1925 to join band led by pianist Arnold Johnson. To New York, worked for Paul Whiteman from 1927 until 1931—except for brief spell early in 1930. (During this period did free-lance recordings including sessions on bass sax with Bix Beiderbecke.) Worked with pianist Eddie Duchin (1935), with Lennie Hayton Orchestra on bass sax and string bass; after playing in short-lived Three T's Band (Jack and Charlie Teagarden, Frankie Trumbauer—December 1936) moved to West Coast with Eddie Duchin. Several years of studio and theatre work on string bass; with Manny Strand's Orchestra at Earl Carroll Theatre, Los Angeles, until shortly before his death.

LEONARD, 'Mike' Harlan Quentin
alto, soprano, tenor saxes

Born: Kansas City, Missouri, 2nd July 1905

Played clarinet in Lincoln High School Band, taught by Major N. Clark Smith, later received tuition from George Wilkenson and Eric 'Paul' Tremaine. Briefly with George E. Lee's Band in Kansas City (1923), then with Bennie Moten from late 1923 until 1931. Together with trombonist Thamon Hayes he co-led The Kansas City Skyrockets, after working in and around Kansas City they moved to Chicago in 1934, soon afterwards

Hayes left to return to Kansas City, and Leonard became the sole leader. This unit disbanded in 1937. During the following year Leonard reorganised his own band, using several members of Jimmy Keith's Band. After playing residencies in Kansas City the band went to New York, appearing at the Savoy Ballroom and the Golden Gate Ballroom during 1940, then returned to the Middle West and later took up residency at Fairyland Park, Kansas City. In the spring of 1943 Leonard led the band for a residency at the Hollywood Club, Los Angeles, during this engagement he began fronting the band for the first time. He continued playing regularly until the mid-1940s, then took a permanent managerial position with the Los Angeles Internal Revenue Bureau. His brother, Walter, was a professional tenor saxist.

LESSEY, 'Bob' Robert *Born: British West Indies, 16th March 1910*
guitar

First professional work with trumpeter Tommy Jones Orchestra in New York (1931-3), then worked regularly with Bill Brown's Band (and occasionally with Sam Wooding) before joining Tiny Bradshaw in 1934. With Fletcher Henderson from 1935 until late 1936, then spent three years in Don Redman's Orchestra (1937-40). Did last professional playing with Lucky Millinder (in 1941), then left full-time music to work for New York City authorities. Continued to gig for many years.

LETMAN, 'Johnny' John Bernard *Born: McCormick, South Carolina, 6th September 1917*
trumpet/vocals

Raised in Chicago, played trumpet in local boys' club band, then played in high school band. Joined Nat 'King' Cole's Band c. 1934, worked with him for a year, then gigged with Gerald Valentine in Illinois before playing in Columbus, Ohio, with drummer Scat Man Carruther's Band. Worked for a year with Jimmy Raschelle's Band, then returned to Chicago and joined Delbert Bright's Band. Briefly with Bob Tinsley's Band and spell with Johnny Long Band, then formed own small group which was resident at Joe's De Luxe Cafe, Chicago, from early 1940 until early 1941. Later that year worked with Horace Henderson, then spent a year with Red Saunders' Band. In 1943 did defence-plant work in Detroit, also gigged with altoist Ted Buckner. Moved to New York in 1944, later that year began two-year stint with Phil Moore. Played with Cab Calloway, Milt Buckner, and Lucky Millinder, briefly with Count Basie in 1951—also worked in Sammy Benkin's group during 1951. Has regularly led own small bands during the 1950s and 1960s, also free-lance work for Sam 'The Man' Taylor, Eddie Condon, Wilbur de Paris, Claude Hopkins, Phil Moore, Conrad Janis, Eddie Barefield, Panama Francis, etc. Toured France in summer of 1968 with Tiny Grimes, Milt Buckner, and Wallace Bishop. Musically active throughout 1970s and early 1980s.

LEVINE, 'Hot Lips' Henry *Born: London, England, 26th November 1907*
trumpet

Lived in the U.S.A. from the age of six months. Began playing cornet in early childhood, received tuition from Max Schlossberg. During the summer of 1926 he began playing regularly with The Original Dixieland Jazz Band in New York, after the O.D.J.B.'s temporary break-up early in 1927 he joined Vincent Lopez, then worked in London with Ambrose from March to October 1927. Through the late 1920s and 1930s played for many Broadway shows and worked for various leaders including: Rudy Vallee, George Olson, Cass Hagen, Sam Lanin, etc., etc. Then long spell as staff man at New York's N.B.C. studios, early in 1940 began leading the N.B.C.'s jazz group—The Chamber Society of Lower Basin Street. Joined the U.S. Army in summer of 1942. Long spell of leading an Army band including service in Sicily and Italy. After demobilisation again led own band and did free-lance work in New York, musical director for Cleveland television station (1953), then moved to Florida. During the 1960s played long residencies at the Deauville Hotel, Miami, also led own band in Las Vegas. Visited England on vacation (1982).

LEWIS, 'Ed' Edward
trumpet

Born: Eagle City, Oklahoma, 22nd January 1909

Son of trumpeter Oscar Lewis. Family moved to Kansas City, Missouri, before Ed started school. Began on baritone horn and marched alongside his father in Shelly Bradford's Brass Band. Ceased playing temporarily until 1924, then again took up baritone horn and joined band led by Jerry Westbrook for a year. Switched to trumpet, two months in Paul Bank's Band, then worked with pianiste-vocaliste Laura Rucker before spending six years with Bennie Moten (1926-32). Left in February 1932 and joined newly formed Thamon Hayes and his Kansas City Skyrockets, did extensive touring and residencies in Chicago. Ed returned to Kansas City and worked for various leaders including Pete Johnson and Jay McShann. Joined Count Basie in February 1937 and remained until September 1948. Left music and worked as a cab-driver, later became motorman on New York subway. Resumed playing again in 1954, soon organised own 12-piece band which gigged in and around New York. Continues to play gigs in New York. Toured Europe with 'The Countsmen' (1983).

LEWIS, George
(real name: George Louis Francis Zeno)
clarinet/alto sax

Born: Dauphine Street, New Orleans, 13th July 1900
Died: Touro Infirmary, New Orleans, 31st December 1968

Bought a toy fife at the age of seven, saved hard and bought first clarinet at 16. By 1917 was playing in young musicians' band The Black Eagles, for the next five years worked with various leaders including: Buddie Petit, Henry 'Kid' Rena, Kid Ory, Chris Kelly, Leonard Parker, etc., also played in the Pacific Brass Band. Formed own band in 1923 and in the same year began long association with the Eureka Brass Band. Out of action in 1928 with a broken leg, then joined Arnold DuPas' Olympia Band until 1932, briefly with trumpeter Evan Thomas' Band in Crowley, Louisiana (Bunk Johnson played second trumpet) until the leader was murdered on the stand at a dance in Rayne (1932). Returned to New Orleans and worked as a stevedore, continued to gig, and play in parades with Kid Howard and The Eureka, then played residency at the Harmony Inn, New Orleans, mainly on alto sax. In 1942 he took part in the first Bunk Johnson recordings which placed him at the forefront of the traditional revival. Continued to lead own band in New Orleans including residency at the Gypsy Tea Room (1943), left New Orleans in September 1945 to work in New York with Bunk Johnson's Band, they disbanded in 1946 and George returned home and continued to lead own small groups. Residency at Manny's Tavern (1947-8) playing clarinet and alto sax. From 1949 until 1951 worked mainly on Bourbon Street, at El Morocco Club with trumpeter Elmer Talbot, and at the Dream Room, broadcast over WDSU in 1950 and 1951. In 1952 worked at Hangover Club in San Francisco with Lizzie Miles, then began regular touring, leading own band and occasionally working as a soloist. Consolidated his international reputation by touring Europe and Japan several times. For much of his later life he had to contend with failing health, but continued to play regularly until late 1968, last worked at the Preservation Hall, New Orleans.

The family name was originally Zenon. A biography 'Call Him George', by 'Jay Allison Stuart' (Dorothy Tait) was first published in 1961. In the summer of 1946 Lewis (with Kid Howard's Brass Band) took part in the filming of 'New Orleans'. The sequence was not used in the film. 'George Lewis' by Tom Bethell, first published in 1977.

LEWIS, Meade 'Lux' Anderson
piano/composer

Born: Chicago, Illinois, 4th September 1905
Died: Minneapolis, Minnesota, 7th June 1964

Nickname derived from the tag he was given as a child: 'The Duke of Luxembourg'. Son of a Pullman porter, spent part of childhood in Louisville, Kentucky. Attended South Division School in Chicago, first studied violin, then specialised on piano, played in many Chicago clubs and bars. During the early 1930s worked in a W.P.A. shovel gang, then began driving a taxi in Chicago. Was rediscovered by John Hammond in late 1935, as a result he re-recorded his famous 'Honky Tonk Train Blues'. By early 1936 he was again established as a full-time musician, after a residency at Doc Huggins' Club in Chicago

('Lux and his Chips') he moved to New York. Regular member of Boogie Woogie Trio with Pete Johnson and Albert Ammons. In August 1941 left New York to live in California, and from then used Los Angeles as his central base for touring. Long residencies in Hollywood and regular appearances on A.B.C. television. Died in a car crash after playing an engagement at the White House Restaurant, Minneapolis.

LEWIS, 'Sabby' William Sebastian — *Born: Middleburg, North Carolina, 1st November 1914*
piano/arranger

Raised in Philadelphia, moved to Boston in 1932 and began gigging on piano. First professional work with Tasker Crosson's Ten Statesmen (1934). In 1936 formed own seven-piece band for residency in Wilmington, Massachusetts, led small band in Boston and New York before augmenting in the early 1940s. Led own big band for several years including residency at Club Zanzibar, New York (1944). During the 1950s reverted to a small group, throughout the 1960s has continued to lead own band, mainly active in Boston. Temporary absence from music in 1963 due to injuries sustained in car smash. Working mainly in New England during the 1970s.

LEWIS, Steve — *Born: New Orleans, Louisiana, 19th March 1896*
piano/composer — *Died: Louisiana. c. 1941*

First regular work with the Silver Leaf Orchestra c. 1910, later worked in the Olympia Orchestra, left New Orleans in 1917 to tour with Billy and Mary Mack's Merrymakers Revue, returned to New Orleans in 1918 and joined Armand Piron's Orchestra, worked regularly with Piron until 1928 including residency in New York and recording sessions. Taught piano during the 1920s, one of his pupils was Luis Russell. During the 1930s worked for various leaders and led own band. Committed to an asylum in 1940.

LEWIS, Sylvester — *Born: Kansas City, Missouri, 19th October 1908*
trumpet — *Died: New York, 1974*

Attended Lincoln High School in Kansas City until 1924, then studied at Western University at Quindaro, Kansas (1925). Gigged in Kansas City, then began touring in 'Shake Your Feet' revue (with Herbie Cowens). Left the show in New York, gigged for a while, worked with Herbie Cowens' Big Band at Rockland Palace, New York (September 1928); recorded with Jelly Roll Morton. With Aubrey 'Bobbie' Neal's Ramblers (1929-30). Then with Claude Hopkins from 1930 until 1936. Worked in Billy Butler's Orchestra for 'Rhapsody in Black' revue; with Noble Sissle and Eubie Blake for U.S.O. 'Shuffle Along' revue from December 1941. Service in U.S. Army during World War II, led own band for tour of Pacific area. In 1948 studied Schillinger method at New York University. In 1949 became employee of the New York Transit Authority, worked for them for over 20 years.

LEWIS, Ted — *Born: Circleville, Ohio, 6th June 1892*
(real name: Theodore Leopold Friedman) — *Died: New York, 25th August 1971*
clarinet/vocals

Brother Edgar was a cornetist, they both played in local boys' band. Ted organised his first band in 1910. In 1915 he went to New York, worked at the College Arms Cabaret before joining Earl Fuller's Band. In 1917 he formed his first professional band—50 years later he was still fronting his own band. During that half-century he employed many famous jazz musicians including: Georg Brunis, Muggsy Spanier, Jimmy Dorsey, etc.

LEWIS, 'Willie' William T. — *Born: Cleburne, Texas, 10th June 1905*
alto sax/clarinet/vocals — *Died: New York, 13th January 1971*

Started on clarinet at 12, played in school orchestra, first gigs in a Dallas cinema, then whilst still at school played at the Ella Moore Variety Theatre in Dallas. Studied at New England Conservatory in Boston (1921), briefly with Will Marion Cook, then toured with variety act The Musical Spillers. Joined Sam Wooding in New York and sailed with Wooding to Europe in May 1925. When Wooding temporarily disbanded in Belgium in November 1931 and returned to the U.S.A., Lewis began leading own band for residency at the Merry Grill in Brussels, the band later played in Ostend, Cannes, Berlin, etc. Returned to New York with own band in January 1934, played residency at Park Avenue Restaurant, New York, then returned to Europe in April 1934. For the next five years the orchestra achieved great success in France, Holland, Belgium, and Egypt. There was a big reshuffle after a walk-out in late 1938, but by the summer of 1939 the band re-established itself with a season in Belgium. In 1940 the band was trapped by the Nazi invasion of Holland, they made their way to Switzerland, thence to play in Portugal before returning to the U.S.A. in October of 1941. Though Lewis occasionally made public appearances in post-war years—playing at various clubs and working as clarinet player in the Broadway show 'Angel in the Pawnshop' (1951)—he was mostly employed outside music as a bartender.

Not related to the Texas pianist Willis 'Willie' Lewis.

LINCOLN, 'Abe' Abraham
trombone

Born: Lancaster, Pennsylvania, 29th March 1907

Father was a musician; Abe began playing trombone at the age of five. Replaced Tommy Dorsey in The California Ramblers in 1926, also worked with Arthur Lange and Ace Brigode during the 1920s. With Roger Wolfe Kahn and Paul Whiteman before spending five years in Ozzie Nelson's Band c. 1934-9. Moved to Hollywood and played in studio orchestras for many years. With the onset of the Dixieland revival he also worked with small bands—played on many recordings during the 1940s and 1950s. Mainly active as a free-lance during the 1960s, brief spell with The Village Stompers, also worked with Wild Bill Davison in early 1967. Featured at Sacramento Dixieland Jubilee (1976).

LINDSEY, John
string bass/trombone

Born: Algiers, Louisiana, 23rd August 1894
Died: Chicago, Illinois, 3rd July 1950

Father was a guitarist, brother Herb a violinist. During his early teens began playing bass in the family band. After serving in U.S. Army during World War I began working in New Orleans on trombone. Played with John Robichaux Orchestra at Lyric Theatre, then joined Armand Piron—journeyed with them to New York. Left Piron in 1924 to tour with King Oliver, subsequently with Dewey Jackson (late 1925), settled in Chicago. Throughout the 1920s doubled on trombone and string bass with various leaders including: Willie Hightower, Carroll Dickerson, Lil Hardin, and Jimmy Bell. During this period made a series of recordings with Jelly Roll Morton. On tour with Louis Armstrong, March 1931 to March 1932 including residency in New Orleans. Returned to Chicago, worked with Jimmie Noone, Art Short, Richard M. Jones, and the Harlem Hamfats during the 1930s. During the last 10 years of his life worked on string bass, led own quartet at Music Bar, Chicago, also worked regularly with Darnell Howard and with guitarist Bob Tinsley's Orchestra, etc.

LINGLE, Paul
piano

Born: Denver, Colorado, 3rd December 1902
Died: Honolulu, Hawaii, 30th October 1962

Father, Curt Lingle, was professional cornet player. Began on piano at age of six, by 13 was working variety circuits accompanying his father. During the 1920s settled on West Coast, worked with many bands including Tom Gerun's, Jimmie Grier's, and Coffee Dan's. Played accompaniment for singer Al Jolson in several films including 'The Jazz Singer', 'Mammy', and 'Sonny Boy'. During the 1930s did studio work and resident spots on KPO radio station, San Francisco. Played occasionally with Lu Watter's Band at Mark Twain Hotel, San Francisco, in 1940, but for next 12 years worked mainly as a ragtime soloist in West Coast night clubs—long residencies at Hambone's in San Francisco and The Jug in Oakland. Moved to Honolulu in 1952, played in various clubs, organised own band and taught piano and harmony.

L

LIVINGSTON, 'Fud' Joseph Anthony
clarinet/saxes/arranger

Born: Charleston, South Carolina, 10th April 1906
Died: New York City, 25th March 1957

Brother, Walter (died: 1931), also a professional saxophonist—their parents owned a retail shoe business in Charleston. Fud played accordion and piano during childhood, then took up sax, worked with Talmadge Henry in Greensboro during summer of 1923. With Ben Pollack at the Venice Beach Ballroom, Los Angeles, left in summer 1925, worked with California Ramblers from October 1925, then joined Jean Goldkette (late 1925). Rejoined Ben Pollack in Chicago during summer of 1926, left in autumn 1927 to join Nat Schilkret in New York. In 1928 worked for Don Voorhees, Jan Garber, etc., prolific free-lance work in New York including recording sessions (usually on tenor and clarinet), many recordings with Red Nichols, Miff Mole, Joe Venuti, etc. Brief return to Ben Pollack, then to London in March 1929, joined Fred Elizalde at Savoy Hotel. Returned to New York in June 1929. Played for 'Almanac' revue (September 1929), then free-lanced until joining Paul Whiteman in June 1930. Left in September 1930 but continued to arrange for Whiteman. During early 1930s mainly active as an arranger, scoring for Ben Pollack, Al Goodman shows, etc., etc. Returned to full-time playing with Jimmy Dorsey (1935-7). Then worked as an arranger for various bands including Bob Zurke's short-lived Big Band, and staff work for Pinky Tomlin (1940). During the 1940s worked mainly in Hollywood. Returned to New York, did occasional arranging, but excessive drinking led to a deterioration in his health; he worked occasionally as a pianist in New York bars until shortly before his death.

LIVINGSTON, Ulysses
guitar

Born: Bristol, Tennessee, 29th January 1912

Played in the West Virginia State College Band, then travelled with the Horace Henderson Band as a valet. Returned to West Virginia, began playing professionally with touring carnival bands. In 1936 with Lil Armstrong's Band in Buffalo, then moved to New York. Gigged with Stuff Smith, Frankie Newton, and Sammy Price before joining Benny Carter (June 1939). Left that band in June 1940, then regularly with Ella Fitzgerald until early 1942. Free-lancing until short spell in U.S. Army, released in September 1943. Moved to West Coast, played with Spirits of Rhythm, led own group The Four Blazes for a while, to Hawaii with Cee Pee Johnson (October 1947), then free-lance session work which he combined with work as an electronics engineer. In recent years has concentrated on electric bass.

LOFTON, 'Cripple Clarence'
piano/vocals

Born: Kingsport, Tennessee, 28th March 1896
Died: Chicago, Illinois, 9th January 1957

Lived in Chicago from 1918. Worked professionally during the 1920s and early 1930s, usually as a solo pianist. Left full-time playing, then recommenced regular work until he was knocked down by a taxi in 1940. Occasionally made guest appearances during the last decade of his life.

LONG, Huey C.
guitar

Born: Sealy, Texas, 25th April 1904

Many relatives were musicians, including brothers Jewell, Herbert and Sam. Began on piano in 1922, played banjo from 1924. First gigs with Frank Davis's Louisiana Jazz Band in summer of 1925 prior to joining Dee Johnson's Merrymakers. Moved to Chicago in late 1926. Free-lance work before joining Ernesto Marrero (1929). During the early 1930s worked with Clarence Black, Willie Hightower, Mack Swain, Clarence 'Eddie' Moore. Switched from banjo to guitar in 1933. With Jesse Stone (1934), Zilner Randolph (1935-37), Johnny Long (1937-42), Fletcher Henderson (1942-43), Earl Hines (1943-44). Formed own trio in 1944, but also worked with Sonny Thompson (1950) and Snub Mosley (1951-52). Now has extensive teaching schedule at own studios in New York City, but also continues to lead own group which features vocaliste Margo Richards.

LONG, 'Slats' Don
clarinet

Born: Wichita, Kansas, 6th December 1906
Died: Wichita, Kansas, 13th March 1964

Worked with Cass Hagan in 1928. With Ed Farley—Mike Riley Band (1935), Red Norvo (spring 1936), Vincent Lopez (early 1937), Chauncey Morehouse's Band (spring 1938), with Bud Freeman at Kelly's, New York (1939), with Bobby Hackett's Band (late 1940), also worked with Ted Lewis and Raymond Scott. Prolific free-lance recordings during the 1930s. Left music to work in the aircraft industry from summer of 1943 until 1964. Died of a heart attack.

LOPEZ, 'Ray' Raymond
cornet

Born: New Orleans, Louisiana, 28th November 1889
Died: California, 27th April 1970

Played in street parades at 14, two years later began working with Papa Laine. Joined Tom Brown in 1912, and played in Chicago, and on tour with Brown until 1915. Led own band in Chicago (1916), there joined Blossom Sealey, accompanying her until 1920. Worked in Chicago with Clint Brush's Jazz Babies before joining Tommy Rogers. Moved to California in December 1920 and joined Abe Lyman, left Lyman to join Gus Arnheim from 1927 until 1929 (including tour of Europe). Left to form own band. Left full-time music in the late 1930s to work in the aircraft industry.

LORD, Jimmy
clarinet/tenor sax

Born: Chicago, Illinois. c. 1905
Died: New York City. c. October 1936

Worked with The Wolverines in Chicago during the summer of 1925. With Benny Meroff's Orchestra at Granada Theatre, Chicago, also worked with David Lewinter's Band at Crystal Ballroom, Chicago. Moved to New York, worked with Willard Robison, did free-lance arranging, also took part in recordings with Billy Banks (1932). Long lay-off from playing due to a lung illness, after recovering sufficiently to form his own band he contracted pneumonia which proved fatal.

LOVETT, 'Baby' Samuel
drums

Born: Alexandria, Louisiana. c. 1895

His elder brother Bud was also a drummer. Began playing drums at age of 11, was taught by Harry Walker. First gigs at Sky Roof Garden in Alexandria, then worked in and around Louisiana with various leaders before moving to Kansas City in the early 1920s. Became one of the stalwarts of the Kansas City music scene. With Thamon Hayes (1933) led own band and played long residency with Pete Johnson at the Sunset Club. Worked with Woody Walder and with Herman Walder in 1939. Deputised for Jo Jones in Count Basie Band (spring 1942). Worked for 15 years in Julia Lee's Group, in Kansas City and in California (1943-58). Formed own quartet which played regularly during the 1960s and early 1970s.

LOWE, 'Sammy' Samuel Milton
trumpet/arranger

Born: Birmingham, Alabama, 14th May 1918

Came from a musical family; his brother, James, played sax, his sister, Leatha, was a pianiste. Took up trumpet whilst at Lincoln Grammar School, began arranging whilst at high school. Studied with John 'Fess' Whatley, played in Paul Bascomb's Band, left school for six months to tour with Jean Calloway's Band. Whilst at Industrial College, Nashville, led Tennessee State Collegians. Moved to New York in 1936 to join the Bama State Collegians directed by Erskine Hawkins. Remained with Hawkins until 1955. Worked with various leaders including: Eddie Heywood, Cab Calloway, Earle Warren, Don Redman, Illinois Jacquet, Reuben Phillips, etc., before becoming musical director for several rock-and-roll bands. Occasionally records with own studio band. Prolific arranger, also a-and-r man for Platinum Records (1971).

L

LUCAS, 'Al' Albert B
string bass

Born: Windsor, Ontario, Canada, 16th November 1916
Died: New York City, 19th June 1983

Mother was a pianiste, father a bassist. Extensive piano tuition from his mother; played tuba and string bass from the age of 12. Moved to New York in 1933, worked with Kaiser Marshall, then long spell with the Sunset Royal Orchestra from 1933 until 1942. With Coleman Hawkins' Septet in 1942-3, with Hot Lips Page (June 1943). With Eddie Heywood (1944 to summer 1945). Briefly with Duke Ellington (sharing bass duties with Junior Raglin July-September 1945), then with various leaders: Eddie South, Hot Lips Page, Errol Garner, etc. Regularly with Mary Lou Williams during 1946, mainly with Illinois Jacquet from 1947 until 1953 (including European tour). With Eddie Heywood's Trio from the mid-1950s, also worked with other leaders including: Teddy Wilson, Coleman Hawkins, and Mary Lou Williams. During the 1960s mainly occupied with studio work, but continues to play jazz dates. Toured Japan with Sam 'The Man' Taylor (1970-1). Active free-lance during the 1970s.

LUCIE, Lawrence
guitar/vocals

Born: Emporia, Virginia, 18th December 1907

His wife, Susan King (guitar/vocals), recorded under the name of Nora Lee King. Father played violin, brother saxophone. Worked regularly in family hillbilly band. Specialised on guitar from 1931, worked on guitar and banjo with June Clark's Band in 1931, with Benny Carter (1932-3). During 1934 subbed for a week with Duke Ellington, then worked in pianist Dave Martin's Band before joining the Mills Blue Rhythm Band. With Fletcher Henderson from summer 1934 until late 1934, then worked again with the Mills Blue Rhythm Band (then led by Lucky Millinder), returned to Fletcher Henderson (late 1936); with Fletcher until 1938, rejoined Lucky Millinder. Joined Coleman Hawkins' Big Band in January 1940, then with Louis Armstrong's Big Band from May 1940 until 1944. Began leading own small group at 51 Club, New York (1944), subsequently toured with own band. Continued leading, then toured with band led by drummer Louis Bellson in 1959. From late 1950 until January 1961 worked in Cozy Cole's Band, left to concentrate on free-lance work. Has regularly led own quartet during the 1960s, also gigs with various leaders. Extensive studio work and teaching during the 1970s. Took part in W. C. Handy tribute concert at Carnegie Hall (1981).

LUNCEFORD, 'Jimmie' James Melvin
multi-instrumentalist/leader/arranger

Born: Fulton, Mississippi, 6th June 1902
Died: Seaside, Oregon, 12th July 1947

Father was a choir-master in Warren, Ohio. Went to high school in Denver, Colorado, where he studied music with Paul Whiteman's father (Wilberforce J. Whiteman). Played alto sax with George Morrison's Orchestra at the Empress Theatre (1922). Left Denver, gained Bachelor of Music degree at Fisk University (1926). During the mid-1920s also studied in New York and played dates there during college vacations with John C. Smith, Wilbur Sweatman, Elmer Snowden, and Deacon Johnson. From 1926 taught music at Manassa High School in Memphis, whilst there formed a band featuring his students. The band began to do regular summer seasons, then from 1929 (with three former Fisk students—Edwin Wilcox, Willie Smith, and Henry Wells—joining the band) became fully professional, residencies and broadcasts on WREC in Memphis. After touring and residencies in Cleveland and Buffalo the band moved into New York in September 1933 for dates at the Lafayette Theatre. After touring New England they returned to New York to take up residency at the Cotton Club from January 1934. Widespread touring from the mid-1930s; the band gradually built up a national reputation, and after a short tour of Scandinavia in February 1937 it consolidated its previous successes and became one of the most sought-after big bands in the U.S. Though Lunceford played all the saxes, guitar, and trombone, he rarely played with the band, but chose to conduct. He did, however, play trombone on the band's 1929 (Chickasaw Syncopators) recordings, and occasionally played alto in the early 1930s. He played flute on the 1939 version of Liza, and—because of call-up problems depleting the personnel—alto in the sax section in 1943. The band never regained their pre-war popularity, but continued to work regularly.

The leader collapsed whilst signing autographs during a personal appearance at a music store, he died shortly afterwards. The band was soon reorganised under the joint leadership of Eddie Wilcox and tenorist Joe Thomas, in 1948 Wilcox became sole leader.

The Lunceford Band appeared in several short films, also featured in 'Blues in the Night'.

LUGG, George
trombone

Born: Chicago, Illinois, 6th October 1898
Died: Bayside, Long Island, December 1946

Served in U.S. Navy during World War I. Played at the Camel Gardens, Chicago, in 1924. Toured (and recorded) with Jules Alberti and his Tennesseans (1925). In 1926 went to Europe with a band led by Canadian Gene Jones, played in Greece and France. Returned to Chicago (c. 1927) and worked on and off with Frank Snyder until 1935. Brief spells with Bobby Hackett's Band and with Charlie Barnet. Worked in New York with Mezz Mezzrow's Disciples of Swing (November 1937). During the early 1940s gigged with Dixieland bands in New York, last worked with Art Hodes at The Ole South, New York, in autumn 1946. Accidentally drowned whilst on his way home in darkness.

LYTELL, Jimmy
(real name: James Sarrapede)
clarinet

Born: New York City, 1st December 1904
Died: Long Island, 26th November 1972

Used the surname of film star Bert Lytell. Went to school in Brooklyn; during vacation of summer 1916 did first band work at a summer resort. With Original Indiana Five, autumn of 1921, then early in 1922 joined the Original Dixieland Jazz Band, then playing at The Balconades Ballroom, New York, left in March 1922 to join Original Memphis Five. Toured and recorded with that quintet until 1925, then joined Capitol Theatre Orchestra in New York—working under Eugene Ormandy. Free-lanced in late 1920s, then spent many years (from 1930) on the staff of N.B.C., eventually becoming a musical director in the 1940s. Took part in the re-formed Original Memphis Five during summer of 1949—throughout 1950s combined studio work with regular club and recording work with various bands. Led own band in Long Island (1971).

M

MACE, 'Tommy' Thomas F.
saxes/flute/oboe/clarinet

Born: Sicily, Italy, 27th July 1911

Moved to U.S.A. as an infant, began playing saxophone in 1919. Played first gigs in 1928 in home town of Hartford, Conn. During the 1930s worked for Red Norvo, Isham Jones, Wingy Manone, Joe Venuti, and Abe Lyman. Worked in 1940s for Paul Whiteman, Freddy Martin, Artie Shaw, Jimmy Grier, Anson Weeks, Jan Savitt and Charlie Ventura. From 1950 until 1966 specialised in playing for Broadway shows, then moved to do extensive free-lance work in Florida.

MACKEL, 'Billy' John William
guitar

Born: Baltimore, Maryland, 28th December 1912

Did first professional work on banjo, worked mainly in Baltimore during the 1930s. Led own band from 1940 until joining Lionel Hampton in 1944, has remained with the band ever since, during the 1960s dovetailed his work between Hampton and acting as accompanist for the Billy Williams' Quartet—a vocal group.

MADISON, Bingie S.
tenor/clarinet/piano/arranger

Born: Des Moines, Iowa, 1902
Died: New York City, July 1978

Originally a pianist, played for local movie houses and clubs from 1919, then similar work in California and Canada during 1921. Joined altoist Bobby Brown's Quartet in Canada. Later, in August 1922, rejoined Bobby Brown in Newark, New Jersey. With Brown until December 1925, then spent four months in Bernie Davis' Band—in which Bingie doubled piano and sax. First formed own band in 1926, then short spell with Cliff Jackson (on tenor) and with trombonist Lew Henry's Band (originally directed by Lt. Tim Brymn). Lew Henry left and Bingie became leader of the band—then resident at Tango Palace, New York. Disbanded c. 1930, worked in Elmer Snowden's Band, then formed own big band for residency at Broadway Danceland c. 1931. Short spells with Sam Wooding, Lucky Millinder, and Billy Fowler, before joining Luis Russell in New York (on tenor and clarinet). Remained to work under Louis Armstrong until 1940, then worked with various leaders including: Edgar Hayes, Ovie Alston, before playing for three and a half years with Alberto Socarras. Left in 1947, led own small band at Tango Palace until 1953.

MADISON, 'Kid Shots' Louis
trumpet

Born: New Orleans, Louisiana, 19th February 1899
Died: New Orleans, Louisiana, September 1948

Played drums in waifs' home band alongside Louis Armstrong and 'Kid' Rena. Was taught cornet by Joe Howard and Louis Dumaine, theory by David Jones. Worked with Oscar Celestin and recorded with Original Tuxedo Orchestra in 1925. Throughout the 1920s and 1930s worked regularly with various brass bands including: Young Tuxedo, Eureka, and W.P.A.—recorded with Bunk Johnson's Brass Band in 1945. During 1947 played residency at Cadillac Cafe, combined this with his day work for New Orleans Board of Health, also played at P. & L. Club on Lake Pontchartrain. Inactive after suffering a stroke in January 1948.

MALLORY, Eddie
trumpet/sax/arranger

Born: Chicago, Illinois. c. 1905
Died: New York City, 20th March 1961

Worked with The Alabamians from 1927 until early 1931 (mainly under Marion Hardy's leadership). Joined Tiny Parham in 1931, during the following year took over the band and led at the Granada Cafe and Villa Venice. Moved to New York in 1933, worked briefly with The Mills Blue Rhythm Band and Benny Carter, then joined bassist Charlie Turner's Arcadians (1934). Was for a time married to Ethel Waters, and from 1935 until 1939 directed her accompanying band. Led own bands during the 1940s, led for residency at Rhumboogie, Chicago (1945 until January 1946). In 1946 re-formed a band sponsored by boxer Joe Louis. Ceased playing, worked as an agent in Atlantic City, then became manager of a car sales unit in New York before resuming agency work in New York.

MANETTA, 'Fess' Manuel
multi-instrumentalist

Born: Algiers, Louisiana, 3rd October 1889
Died: New Orleans, Louisiana, 10th October 1969

Came from a family of distinguished brass players. Began on violin and guitar, but did first paid work as a pianist for Countess Willie Piazza. By 1910 had mastered cornet, saxophone, and trombone, played at Tuxedo Hall, also with Eagle Band. Then in Chicago for a short spell during 1913, returned to New Orleans, played locally for five years, then to Los Angeles in November 1919 to join Kid Ory. Returned home shortly afterwards—toured as pianist with Martels' Family Band, then piano in Ed Allen's Band on riverboats, settled down in New Orleans where his versatility and musicianship enabled him to work with many bands and orchestras including: Celestin's, Arnold Du Pas, and Manuel Perez's. In later years he became the most renowned teacher in New Orleans. Gave occasional public performances well into his seventies, making a specialty of playing two brass instruments simultaneously.

MANONE, 'Wingy' Joseph Matthews
trumpet/vocals

Born: New Orleans, Louisiana, 13th February 1900
Died: Las Vegas, 9th July 1982

Mother a pianiste, brother played clarinet and guitar. Wingy (so-called because he lost his right arm in a streetcar accident when he was a child) played kazoo and sang in kids' bands. Took up trumpet; by the age of 17 was proficient enough to work on the riverboats. Moved to Chicago and began working at the Valentino Inn. Then gigged in New York before joining Crescent City Jazzers in Mobile (1924), moved with them to St. Louis where they became known as The Arcadian Serenaders. Led own band in San Antonio, then short spell with Peck Kelley in Houston. Briefly with Ham Crawford's Band in late 1925, then with 'Doc' Ross playing in Texas, New Mexico, and California. Left in autumn 1926 and led own band in Biloxi, Mississippi. Moved to New York in late 1927, did gigs and recording date, then on to Chicago. Led own band and gigged with various leaders including Ray Miller and Charlie Straight. To New York to record with Benny Goodman (1929), also led own band in Ohio and guested with Speed Webb. During the late 1920s and early 1930s did a variety of musical jobs including touring in 'Estelle Taylor' show and 'Bernie Fields' show, also worked briefly in a Red-Indian Band. In 1930 led own band at 'My Cellar', Chicago, then gigged in St. Louis, Chicago, and New York. Led own band at Brewery Club in Chicago 1933, then after a spell in Milwaukee moved to New York. From late 1934 led own band in New York: Hickory House, Maria's, Famous Door, etc. After big success of his recording 'Isle of Capri' he played residencies in Chicago, Los Angeles, New Orleans, etc. Led in Florida from late 1939, then moved to Hollywood in 1940 to appear in the film 'Rhythm on the River'. Lived in California until 1954, did regular radio work with Bing Crosby and led at various clubs including: Streets of Paris, Billy Berg's, Royal Room, etc. Occasionally appeared in New York and Chicago. Played in Las Vegas (1954) and decided to settle there. Has led own bands through the late 1950s and 1960s, usually in Las Vegas. Occasional solo dates in New York and appearances at jazz festivals including Newport. Solo work in Europe 1966, 1967, and 1971. Led at Union Plaza, Las Vegas (1971). Occasional dates in U.S.A. and Canada during 1970s, also toured Europe with 'A Night in New Orleans' package (1975).

Films include: 'Rhythm on the River', 'Hi-Ya Sailor', 'Sarge Goes to College'
A biography 'Trumpet on the Wing,' by Wingy Manone and Paul Vandervoort II, was published in 1948.

MARABLE, Fate
piano/calliope/leader

Born: Paducah, Kentucky, 2nd December 1890
Died: St. Louis, Missouri, 16th January 1947

Taught by his mother, who played piano. Several brothers were musicians. First played in public at age of nine. Left home town at 17 to join the steamboat 'J.S.' (sailing from Little Rock, Arkansas). Worked a duo on this boat with violinist Emil Flindt. Worked regularly on riverboats for next 10 years, then formed own Kentucky Jazz Band. Throughout 1920s and early 1930s continued to lead on various Streckfus Line boats. Many of his sidemen subsequently became famous including: Louis Armstrong, Boyd Atkins, Henry 'Red' Allen, Earl Bostic, Jimmy Blanton, Johnny Dodds, Baby Dodds, Pops Foster, Al Morgan, Mouse Randolph, Eugene Sedric, Nat Storey, Zutty Singleton, etc., etc. During mid-1930s shared leader's duties with Charlie Creath, left steamers summer of 1940 when a badly infected finger caused a long lay-off from playing. In the mid-1940s played in St. Louis at the Club Windsor and at the Victorian Club, contracted pneumonia and died in the Homer G. Phillips Hospital.

MARES, **Paul Joseph**
trumpet/composer

Born: New Orleans, Louisiana, 15th June 1900
Died: Chicago, Illinois, 18th August 1949

Father was trumpeter Joseph P. Mares. At 16 worked with Leon Roppolo in Bucktown, Lake Pontchartrain. Worked with Tom Brown in New Orleans. Moved to Chicago in 1919 to join drummer Ragababy Stevens at the Camel Gardens, also worked in Chicago with Tom Brown. With Georg Brunis at Bert Kelly's Stables, later they both worked with Dixon's Band on the S.S. 'Capitol'. During a stay in Davenport, Iowa, they linked up with their boyhood friend Leon Roppolo—all three returned to Chicago to join Friars' Inn Orchestra—later known as the New Orleans Rhythm Kings. About 18 months later Mares and Roppolo went to New York to join Al Siegal at Mills Caprice in Greenwich Village. Mares returned to New Orleans and some months later reorganised the New Orleans Rhythm Kings (1925). He soon left full-time music to enter family fur business (wholesale muskrat pelts). Moved back to Chicago in 1934 and formed band for January 1935 debut at Harry Hepp's New York Bar, Chicago. Opened own barbecue restaurant in Chicago, later sold this and did defence-plant work in World War II. Musically active again from 1945. Formed new band for Chicago Blue Note in February 1948, played last engagements at Tin Pan Alley Club in summer of 1948.

MARGULIS, **'Charlie' Charles A.**
trumpet

Born: Minneapolis, Minnesota, 24th June 1903
Died: Minnesota, April 1967

First professional work in local movie theatre, then with Eddie Elkins, Paul Specht, and Sam Lanin before joining Jean Goldkette's Book-Cadillac Hotel Orchestra in Detroit (December 1924)—at that time the orchestra was directed by Joe Venuti. Left after a year and worked in Detroit and Chicago with Ray Miller. Stints with Russ Morgan and Ole Olsen before joining Paul Whiteman in September 1927. Left Whiteman in California (early 1930), moved back to New York, then suffered serious illness and returned to West Coast to recuperate. Returned to studio work in New York, did many sessions with the Dorsey Brothers, etc. Formed own band in spring 1937, joined Glenn Miller briefly early in 1938, then resumed own band before joining Jack Miller (1938), also ran own chicken farm in late 1930s. Formed new band in 1940, temporarily adopted the name Charlie Marlowe, played residencies in California (1941). Returned to New York in spring of 1942 and resumed studio work, continued free-lancing for many years.

MARRERO, **Lawrence Henry**
banjo/guitar

Born: New Orleans, Louisiana, 24th October 1900
Died: New Orleans, Louisiana, 5th June 1959

His brothers were Eddie (bass), John (banjo), and Simon (bass); their father, Billy, was a bassist. Laurence started on string bass, was then taught banjo by his elder brother, John. First regular work with Wooden Joe Nicholas in 1919, also played bass drum in the Young Tuxedo Band from 1920. Worked occasionally with trumpeter Chris Kelly and regularly with Frankie Dusen, Lee Collins, Pete Bocage, and John Robichaux. In 1942 made recordings with Bunk Johnson and was subsequently featured on many recordings, worked in New York with Bunk Johnson 1945-6, then worked in New Orleans with George Lewis (during 1947-8, residency at Manny's Tavern, played amplified guitar). Worked regularly with Lewis until ill health caused him to quit touring in late 1955. Later led own band, mainly in New Orleans.

Not related to the late Ernesto 'Ernie' Marrero, who played drums and washboard with Tiny Parham.

MARSALA, 'Joe' Joseph Francis
clarinet/saxes/composer

Born: Chicago, Illinois, 4th January 1907
Died: Santa Barbara, California, 4th March 1978

Brother of Marty; their father, Pete Marsala, was a valve-trombonist. In 1937 married harpist/pianiste/vocaliste Adele Girard. Started on clarinet at 15; worked at a variety of day jobs, including buyer for a shoe company, brass-foundry worker, mail-order clerk, and truck driver. Worked local club jobs at week-ends from 1925 with various pianists: Red Feilen, David Rose, Art Hodes, etc. Left Chicago in 1929 to join Wingy Manone in Akron, Ohio, the job folded after a week; Joe worked with Nelson Maple's Leviathan Orchestra in Cleveland before returning to Chicago. Joined Harold West's Orchestra for nine months, and gigged occasionally with Ben Pollack at Chez Paree. Short trip to Florida, then toured Montana and the Dakotas with a circus band (c. 1931). With Wingy Manone at Brewery Club (near site of Chicago's 1933 World Fair), then played in Florida (1934). Gigged in Cicero, Illinois, then joined Wingy Manone's Quartet at Adrian Rollini's Tap Room, New York (early 1935), with Wingy into the Hickory House, after Wingy left (1936), Joe Marsala became the leader. During July 1936 co-led (with Eddie Condon) one of the first 'mixed' groups to appear on 52nd Street, worked at Yacht Club, New York, with Red McKenzie, also at McKenzie's Club. Played gigs on sax with Joe Moss' Society Orchestra, also briefly led own band at the Hotel Pennsylvania, then in December 1936 played with band (including Marty Marsala and Eddie Condon) on the 'Empress of Britain' for cruise to Havana and Jamaica. Led at Paradise Restaurant, New York, then into Hickory House on 17th March 1937. Absent through illness in spring 1938, then again at Hickory House until June 1939. For the next nine years Joe Marsala played several long residencies at the Hickory House. In summer of 1939 he briefly toured leading own big band, also played at The Fiesta, New York, in late 1939, again led own big band at the Log Cabin, Armonk, New York, and Glen Island Casino in summer and autumn 1942. Reverted to leading small band. Played at opening of Eddie Condon's Club December 1945, then led briefly at the Copacabana (early 1946). Finally left the Hickory House in early 1948, toured Canada, then returned to New York and left full-time music. Lived in Colorado from 1949 until 1953, continued playing occasional dates, returned to New York in 1954 and ran own music-publishing business. Moved to Chicago in 1962 and became a vice-president of the Seeburg Music Corporation, worked with that company for six years, made business trips to Europe. Moved to California in November 1967, continues to play occasionally; recorded 'Sweet Lorraine' with vocalist Tony Bennett (and Bobby Hackett) in the mid-1960s. Led own All Stars in California (late 1969-70). Enjoyed considerable success with several compositions including: 'Little Sir Echo', 'Don't Cry Joe', 'And So to Sleep Again'.

MARSALA, 'Marty' Mario Salvatore
trumpet

Born: Chicago, Illinois, 2nd April 1909
Died: Chicago, Illinois, 27th April 1975

Brother of Joe. Was originally a drummer, worked in Chicago with bands led by pianist 'Red' Feilen, and with 'Joe Bananas'. Switched to trumpet in the late 1920s, gigged with many bands in Chicago, then moved to New York in 1936 to join Joe Marsala's Band. Except for short periods worked mainly with Joe until 1941 (briefly with Will Hudson—September 1937). Led own band at Nick's, New York, from August 1941, then toured in big band fronted by comedian Chico Marx (musical director, Ben Pollack) from spring 1942 until March 1943. Led own quintet in Chicago from April 1943. Served in U.S. Army from early 1944 until late 1945, rejoined Joe, then led own trio at Ryan's (December 1945), with Miff Mole at Nick's (February 1946), then spell with Tony Parenti in late 1946. Mainly active leading own band in Chicago and California in late 1940s and early 1950s. Moved to San Francisco (c. 1955), led own band at various clubs including: The Hangover, East Street, The Kewpie Doll, etc., also played for a while in Earl Hines' Small Band. From the late 1950s underwent long periods of inactivity through illness. Led own band at The Hangover, San Francisco, in spring 1962, then played three months' residency at

Jazz Ltd., Chicago. Worked at Saris in 1964, again seriously ill, then recommenced playing again in summer of 1965. During the late 1960s had suffered long bouts of illness.

MARSH, **George W.**
drums/percussion

Born: c. 1900
Died: Los Angeles, California, April 1962

From 1924 until the late 1920s worked mainly with Paul Whiteman, left the orchestra several times, was twice replaced by Johnny 'Gloom' MacDonald and once by Vic Berton (1927). Recorded with Frank Trumbauer, Bix Beiderbecke, Ed Lang, etc. Worked in Ferde Grofe's Orchestra (c. 1932-4), then moved to California to join film-studio orchestra. Other than spell of war work in Minneapolis in the 1940s he lived in Hollywood until his death.

MARSHALL, **'Joe' Joseph**
drums

Born: Pensacola, Florida, 7th December 1913

Mother was a pianiste. Raised in Chicago, attended Wendell Phillips High School, was taught music by Major N. Clark-Smith and Walter H. Dyett. First gigs with Henderson Smith's Band (1931-32). During the 1930s worked mainly in Chicago with Johnny Long, Erskine Tate, Nat Cole, Sax Mallard, and King Kolax. Toured with Burns Campbell Band (1935-38). With Walter Fuller (1940), Coleman Hawkins (1940), Milton Larkins (1941), Jimmie Lunceford (1942-47), Joe Thomas (1948). During the 1950s worked with Johnny Hodges, Lucky Millinder, etc., and spent six years with the Arthur Godfrey Show on C.B.S. Played for many television shows during the 1960s, also spent 3 years playing for 'Funny Girl' show, worked for Benny Goodman and toured Africa with Dick Vance in 1969. With Tyree Glenn's group during the early 1970s, then active freelance including television work and playing for shows.

MARSHALL, **'Kaiser' Joseph**
drums

Born: Savannah, Georgia, 11th June 1899
Died: New York City, 3rd January 1948

Raised in Boston, attended the English High School and ran regularly for college track team. Taught drums by George Stone and William Maloney. First professional work accompanying singer Jules Bledsoe. Gigged with Charlie Dixon in Boston and New York; worked at Broadway Jones' Night Club, then with violinist 'Shrimp' Jones at the Club Bamville. This unit forming the nucleus of the 1924 Fletcher Henderson Band. Remained with Fletcher until 1930 (except for brief absence in 1929). Led own Czars of Harmony (1931), briefly with LeRoy Smith, then with Ellsworth Reynolds co-led Kaiser and Reynolds' Bostonians (1932). During the early 1930s subbed in Duke Ellington's Band for a month, with Cab Calloway for two months, and with McKinney's Cotton Pickers. With Leon Englund's Band (c. 1934), then led own band at Ubangi Club, New York (summer 1935), Harlem Uproar House (1935), and at The Apollo Theatre (July 1936), etc. To Europe with Bobby Martin's Band (June 1937), returned to U.S.A. in following year, occasionally subbed for Chick Webb in late 1938. With Edgar Hayes from March until October 1939. Led own band and free-lanced during the early 1940s, with Wild Bill Davison's Band in Boston (early 1943), worked regularly with Art Hodes in 1943, 1944, 1946, and 1947, also briefly with Garvin Bushell (autumn 1944), Sidney Bechet (March 1945), and with Bunk Johnson at the Stuyvesant Casino, New York (spring 1946). To Chicago for recordings with Mezz Mezzrow and Sidney Bechet (18th-20th December 1947), played last gig at Jimmy Ryan's a few days before succumbing to pneumonia and other complications following a severe case of food poisoning.

MARTIN, **'Bobby' Robert**
trumpet

Born: Long Branch, New Jersey, 15th May 1903

Married to vocaliste Thelma Minor. Went to school with June Clark and Sonny Greer. With Sam Wooding at Club Alabam, New York (1925), sailed to Europe with Wooding in May 1925. Remained with Sam Wooding in U.S.A. and Europe until late 1931. Mainly with

Willie Lewis from 1932 until August 1936. Moved back to the U.S.A., formed band in New York and returned to Europe in June 1937. The band suffered a set-back when all its arrangements were lost in a fire at The Mephisto, Rotterdam, in spring 1938, but they continued touring Denmark, France, and Switzerland. Martin returned to the U.S.A. in the spring of 1939 and led own groups at various venues in New York: The Kit-Kat from May 1939, The Place (late 1939 and again in 1941), Jigg's (1940), and at own club, etc. Played residency at the Rose Room, New Jersey, from 1944, then left music to run family business in New Jersey and New York.

MARTIN, 'Chink'
(real name: Martin Abraham)
string bass/tuba/guitar

Born: New Orleans, Louisiana, 10th June 1886
Died: New Orleans, Louisiana, 7th January 1981

Father of string bassist Martin 'Little Chink' Abraham Jr. (born: 1918) and brother of Willie Abraham (banjo/guitar/bass). Originally a guitarist, then switched to tuba, worked with the Reliance Band and Jack Laine from c. 1910, began doubling on string bass and played with many bands in New Orleans, then to Chicago to join augmented New Orleans Rhythm Kings (1923). Returned to New Orleans in 1924, worked with Johnny Bayersdorffer and Freddie Newman, then worked in New Orleans with re-formed N.O.R.K. (1925). Regularly with the New Orleans Harmony Kings and later with the New Orleans Swing Kings, then became a staff musician with radio WSMB. Continued to free-lance with various bands in New Orleans in the 1940s and 1950s, regularly with Crawford-Ferguson Night Owls in the 1960s. Worked at Preservation Hall throughout the 1970s, and continued there until October 1980.

MARTIN, 'Dave' David
piano/cello/composer

Born: New York City, 5th October 1907
Died: New York, 4th May 1975

His father was a noted music-teacher who ran a conservatory. David's brother and sister were violinists. Played with many bands in New York during the late 1920s and early 1930s. Worked in Europe from the mid-1930s notably with Eddie South. Returned to the U.S.A. in 1939, led own band at St. George's Hotel in Brooklyn then rejoined Eddie South in May 1940. Left to serve in U.S. Army during World War II. Led own group from the mid-1940s which was featured at Cafe Society, New York in 1948. During the 1950s did prolific work as soloist and accompanist, including three months in London, England during summer of 1958. Own band during the 1960s, regularly with Sol Yaged during the early 1970s.

MASEK, 'Joe' Joseph
tenor sax/clarinet

Born: Chicago, 1912
Died: Chicago, Illinois, 3rd August 1975

Attended Harrison High School in Chicago. During the 1930s worked with Jack Chapman, Don Pedro, Tom Gentry, Tweet Hogan. Recorded with Charlie La Vera in 1935. Regularly with Henry Busse during the late 1930s until joining Jimmy McPartland at Offbeat Club in Chicago in spring 1939. Was active as a teacher during the 1940s and 1950s, continued to play professionally through to dates in the early 1970s with Hall Kartun's Band at Continental Plaza Hotel.

MASON, Norman
clarinet/alto sax/trumpet

Born: Miami, Florida, 1895
Died: St. Louis, Missouri, 29th July 1971

Brother of trumpeter Henry Mason. Raised in The Bahamas, started on trumpet at the age of eight, originally taught by his father. Returned to the U.S.A. and at 18 began touring with the Rabbit Foot Minstrel Show (playing alongside George Mitchell for a while). Joined Fate Marable in New Orleans (c. 1919), originally as a trumpeter, then switched to alto sax. Played in Ed Allen's Whispering Gold Band (1922), also led own Carolina Melodists during the 1920s. Worked mostly with Fate Marable from 1927 until 1933, brief spell with Ira Coffey's Walkathons (late 1933). Based in St. Louis throughout the 1930s, then moved to Chicago and began specialising on clarinet. Gigged in St. Louis during the early 1950s, played with Joe Smith and his Rampart Ramblers, then began long association with Singleton Palmer's Band. Continued working regularly with Palmer throughout the 1960s until he suffered a stroke in 1969.

MASTREN, Carmen Nicholas *Born: Cohoes, New York, 6th October 1913*
(real name: Mastandrea) *Died: Valley Stream, L.I., 31st March 1981*
guitar/banjo/violin

Younger brother is Al Mastren (trombone); three other brothers John, Frank, and Eddie (died: 1953) were also musicians. Carmen began on violin, switched to fretted instruments in early 1930s, worked regularly in his family band for several years. Joined Wingy Manone Quartet in 1935, following year began a long spell with Tommy Dorsey which concluded in spring 1940. With Joe Marsala until spring 1941, brief spell with Ernie Holst's Orchestra, then worked as an N.B.C. studio musician. Later worked with Raymond Scott and Bob Chester before serving in Glenn Miller's A.A.F. Band—including European tour. Returned to U.S.A. in 1945, recommenced studio work in 1946. From 1947 combined playing with conducting and arranging. From 1953 was a regular member of N.B.C. studio staff. Extensive free-lance work during the 1970s, often with New York Jazz Repertory Company.

MATHEWS, Emmett *Born: St. Louis, Missouri. c. 1902*
saxes/vocals

Worked with many bands in St. Louis during the early 1920s, toured with Wilson Robinson's Bostonians (1922-3). Moved to New York, worked with pianist Irvin Puggsley's Hot Six (1928) and with Edgar Hayes at the Alhambra Theatre (1929), led own band at that venue (1930), also worked with Bill Benford's Band (1930). Moved to Chicago in spring of 1931, led own band. Returned to New York, joined bassist Charlie Turner's Arcadians, remained with the band when they became accompanying unit for Fats Waller. Led own recording band in the mid-1930s—featured on vocals and soprano sax. Remained with Fats Waller until 1937, then re-formed own band which played many theatre dates including the Apollo, New York. Throughout the 1940s and 1950s regular member of Steve Gibson and his Red Caps—a very successful vocal and instrumental combo. Has now retired from full-time music.

MATLOCK, 'Matty' Julian Clifton *Born: Paducah, Kentucky, 27th April 1907*
clarinet/saxes/arranger *Died: Los Angeles, 14th June 1978*

Spent childhood in Nashville, Tennessee. Began playing clarinet at 12; worked with local bands (doubling sax) including five-year spell with Beasley Smith's Band, working mainly in Nashville. In 1928 worked several months in Jimmy Joy's Orchestra before returning briefly to Beasley Smith. Moved to Pittsburgh to join the Tracy-Brown Orchestra (1929), joined Ben Pollack in October 1929. Remained with Pollack until late 1934, free-lanced in New York, then together with several colleagues from the Pollack band began recording as Clark Randall's Orchestra (featuring vocalist Frank Tennile). Bob Crosby was subsequently brought in to front the band. Remained with Bob Crosby until late 1942 (prolific arranging for Crosby) except for brief spells with Ray Noble and Bunny Berigan. Worked with Eddie Miller in California in 1943, has lived on the West Coast ever since. Has regularly led own studio groups and bands in Los Angeles, Las Vegas, etc., also worked for many leaders including: Pee Wee Hunt, Red Nichols, Ben Pollack, Bill Williams, Rex Stewart, etc., etc. During the 1950s and 1960s took part in many of the re-formed Bob Crosby Bands including unit that toured the Orient in late 1964. Worked on Red Nichols' last engagement in Las Vegas (June 1965), long spell in Phil Harris' Orchestra. Played regularly, occasionally leading own band, until forced to retire by illness (1975).

MATTHEWS, 'Dave' David *Born: Chagrin Falls, Ohio, 6th June 1911*
saxes/arranger

Raised in McAlester, Oklahoma. His mother taught at the Chicago Music College, Dave studied there for five years, gaining his Bachelor degree in 1930. Originally specialised on alto sax, later doubled on tenor. With Ben Pollack from 1935 until autumn 1936, then joined Jimmy Dorsey. Left to work with Benny Goodman from March 1938 until January 1939. With Harry James from 1939 until late 1941, then joined Hal McIntyre Orchestra. Next with Woody Herman until spring 1943, following year worked with Stan Kenton and Charlie Barnet. Left to organise own band on West Coast (early 1945). Several spells with Charlie Barnet in the late 1940s. Worked mainly as an arranger during the 1950s, but also continued to lead own bands including work in Reno, Nevada, in the 1960s. With Don Conn Orchestra, Lake Tahoe (1971).

MATTHEWS, George
trombone

Born: Dominica, 23rd September 1912
Died: New York City, 28th June 1982

Father was a guitarist. Raised in New York, studied for four years at the Martin Smith School of Music (1927-31). Played with various bands in and around New York, then joined Tiny Bradshaw in 1934. With Willie Bryant (1935-7), then with Louis Armstrong before joining Chick Webb's Band, later worked under Ella Fitzgerald's leadership. With Count Basie from early 1946 until late 1949. With Erskine Hawkins during the early 1950s. Featured with Lucille Dixon's Band during the early 1960s. Freelanced during the 1960s and 1970s.

MAXEY, Leroy
drums

Born: Kansas City, Missouri, 6th June 1904

Attended Lincoln High School in Kansas City. During the early 1920s worked with Bennie Moten and with Dave Lewis' Jazz Boys at Troost Dancing Academy, Kansas City, then to St. Louis to join violinist Wilson Robinson's Syncopators (replacing 'Lige' Shaw—1923). After extensive touring this band became resident at the Cotton Club, New York, under the leadership of violinist Andrew Preer (died: 1927). The band later worked as The Missourians before becoming Cab Calloway's Orchestra. Leroy remained with Cab until November 1938 when serious illness forced him to retire from full-time music. Has lived for many years in Flint, Michigan.

MAXWELL, 'Jimmy' James K.
trumpet

Born: Stockton, California, 9th January 1917

Both parents were amateur musicians. Began playing cornet as a child, later studied trumpet with Arnold Graham, Herbert L. Clarke, Lloyd Reese and Benny Baker. Played local gigs at 15, worked in band co-led by Gil Evans 1933-34. With Jimmy Dorsey (1936), Maxine Sullivan (1937), Skinnay Ennis (1938), Benny Goodman (1939-43). With staff orchestra at C.B.S. (1943-45). From 1945-63 played regularly for Perry Como Show, and from 1963-73 for the Tonight Show with Johnny Carson. During these years played substitute dates in bands led by Woody Herman, Count Basie, Will Bradley, etc., also played in N.B.C. Symphony Orchestra and on countless recordings. Worked occasionally for Duke Ellington 1961-74. Toured Russia with Benny Goodman (1962). During the 1960s worked with Quincy Jones, Oliver Nelson and Gerry Mulligan. During the 1970s played U.S. and international dates with New York Jazz Repertory Company. During the late 1970s played full schedule with many various ensembles, including Dick Sudhalter's New Californians. As a sideline Jimmy plays bagpipes. Full working schedule during early 1980s, including leading own band in Europe and the Far East. Jim Maxwell's instruction manual 'The First Trumpeter' first published in 1982.

MAY, 'Billy' William E.
trumpet/arranger

Born: Pittsburgh, Pennsylvania, 10th November 1916

Professional work at 17 with George Olsen's Polish-American Orchestra, played with Al Howard's Band, Lee River, Barron Elliot, etc., before joining Charlie Barnet in 1939—arranged several of Barnet's most popular numbers. With Glenn Miller (1940-1), worked as trumpeter-arranger with Les Brown in autumn 1942, then moved to California. Played in Alvino Rey's Band (early 1943) and doubled defence work at the Vega plant. Continued playing trumpet through the 1940s, also did arranging and conducting for radio shows.

The success of his 1951 studio-band recordings for Capitol encouraged him to lead a big touring band; he quit touring in late 1953, the band later worked under the direction of Sam Donahue. Billy May resumed his work as a successful free-lance arranger in Hollywood, scoring for films, television shows, and recording sessions. He continued to work regularly throughout the 1960s except for a brief spell of inactivity following a mild heart attack late in 1963. Continued composing and arranging during the 1970s. Visited Europe in 1983.

McCLUNG, 'Gus' Augustus

trumpet

Born: Chattanooga, Tennessee, 1905

Worked with Cecil and Lloyd Scott in Springfield, Ohio, and New York (1922-25). With Clarence Paige (1926), McKinney's Cotton Pickers (1926-27). During the 1930s worked with: Horace Henderson, Claude Hopkins, Charlie Johnson, Kaiser Marshall, Noble Sissle, Tiny Bradshaw, etc. With Buddy Johnson (1940-41), then left music in 1942 for health reasons.

McCONVILLE, Leo

trumpet

Born: Baltimore, Maryland, 1900
Died: Baltimore, Maryland, February 1968

From 1914 began playing with bands in the Baltimore area, professional debut with Louisiana Five in 1919. In the early 1920s joined Jean Goldkette at the Greystone Ballroom, Detroit, then vaudeville tours, worked with Paul Specht before joining Roger Wolfe Kahn. From 1928-31 worked mainly with Don Voorhees, but also did extensive work in radio and recording studios. Session work until the mid-1930s, then moved to Reisterstown in Maryland where he began chicken farming. Continued to play with local bands through the late 1930s and 1940s—long spells with Bob Craig Band and Bob Iula's Orchestra.

McCORD, Castor

tenor sax/clarinet

Born: Birmingham, Alabama, 17th May 1907
Died: New York City, 14th February 1963

Twin brother of saxophonist Theodore Jobetus McCord, both played in Edgar Hayes' Blue Grass Buddies (1924). Whilst studying at Wilberforce University, Xenia, Ohio, became a member of student band led by Horace Henderson—took up professional music with that band, played residency in Atlantic City, then into New York. With Mills Blue Rhythm Band (1929-30)—dates with Louis Armstrong—with Eubie Blake Band until joining Charlie Matson Orchestra in New York (1932). Regularly with Mills Blue Rhythm Band until journeying to Europe in band playing with Blackbirds of 1934 (August 1934). Settled in Paris, played in band accompanying Louis Armstrong and Coleman Hawkins, then spent a year and a half in Leon Abbey Band including two trips to India in 1936. Led own trio in Amsterdam in spring 1937, later that year with Fletcher Allen's Band in Paris. After playing with Walter Rains' Band in Rotterdam (early in 1938) Castor returned to the U.S.A. With Leon Abbey in New York, then joined Benny Carter Big Band at Savoy early in 1939, played with Eddie Mallory during following year. From 1941 until 1942 was a member of Claude Hopkins' Band. Left professional music in the 1940s and became a hairdresser, continued in that employment until shortly before his death.

McCRACKEN, 'Bob' Robert Edward

clarinet/saxes

Born: Dallas, Texas, 23rd November 1904
Died: California, 4th July 1972

Studied piano as a child, then changed to clarinet. Played with Eddie Whitley Band at 17. Then (together with Jack Teagarden) played in The Southern Trumpeters, they both joined Doc Ross and his Jazz Bandits, with that band to Los Angeles where they were known as Doc Ross and his Texas Cowboy Band—they disbanded in New Orleans. McCracken and Teagarden then travelled to New York. McCracken played with Johnny Johnston and also recorded with The Levee Loungers (a Willard Robison unit). Returned to Texas, played with Ligon Smith, then toured with Joe Gill (1934), rejoined Doc Ross until 1935. With Joe Venuti, Frankie Trumbauer, before moving to Chicago with Leonard Keller's Band (1939). PLayed with Jimmy McPartland and with Wingy Manone (1940). Left in 1941, brief spell with Benny Goodman, then with Russ Morgan for two years, similar period with Wayne King Orchestra. Worked mostly in Chicago until touring Europe with Louis Armstrong All Stars in September 1952 until early 1953. Moved to West Coast, worked with Kid Ory, Ben Pollack, Pete Daily during 1950s—played regularly with Jack Teagarden in 1954 and 1956. Toured Europe with Kid Ory in autumn of 1959, returned to West Coast where he combined business interests with regular playing—worked on tenor and clarinet with Jack Teagarden again in 1962. With Wild Bill Davison (1967), the Russ Morgan Orchestra (early 1969), etc.

McDONOUGH, 'Dick' Richard
guitar/banjo

Born: 1904
Died: New York City, 25th May 1938

Originally a banjoist. Throughout the late 1920s and 1930s was one of the busiest session men in New York—took part in hundreds of recordings with various leaders including: Red Nichols, Sam Lanin, Dorsey Brothers, etc., etc. His first recording was with Don Voorhees ('Baby Blue'). Enjoyed a noted partnership with guitarist Carl Kress during 1930s, also led own radio and recording band. Collapsed whilst working at the N.B.C. studios in New York, was taken to hospital where an emergency operation failed to save his life.

McEACHERN, Murray
trombone/alto sax/trumpet

Born: Toronto, Canada, 1915
Died: Los Angeles, California, 28th April 1982

Played violin from the age of five, at 12 gave a solo recital at Massey Hall, Toronto. Then took up clarinet and alto, switched to tenor at 15, then trumpet, trombone, and tuba. Did a novelty instrumental act in Chicago, then joined Benny Goodman on trombone in May 1936, played with Goodman until November 1937. Free-lanced for a while, then joined Casa Loma Band on alto and trombone from January 1938 until January 1941. At that time was appointed assistant conductor of Paul Whiteman Orchestra, remained in that position until December 1941, then moved to West Coast. Regular studio work throughout the 1940s and 1950s—occasionally played with outside bands, i.e. with Harry James in 1943, but generally employed on film soundtracks. Solo work heard in many movies including 'The Glenn Miller Story' and 'The Benny Goodman Story'. Regular recording sessions on trombone and alto sax, at one time was featured in regular TV show performing on these two instruments and trumpet. Briefly with Duke Ellington (1973), led Tommy Dorsey Band during mid-1970s.

McGARITY, 'Lou' Robert Louis
trombone/violin/vocals

Born: Athens, Georgia, 22nd July 1917
Died: Alexandria, Virginia, 28th August 1971

Began playing violin at the age of seven, 10 years later won State high school contest on violin and shortly afterwards began specialising on trombone. Gigged with various bands whilst studying at the University of Georgia (1934-6), then joined Kirk DeVore's Band in Atlanta (1936). During 1937 worked with saxist Nye Mayhew's Band in New York and Boston. With Ben Bernie from early 1938 until joining Benny Goodman in October 1940. Left Goodman in autumn 1942, worked with Raymond Scott at C.B.S. before serving in the U.S. Navy. Rejoined Benny Goodman from early 1946 until August 1946. Left Goodman on West Coast, did regular studio work, also worked with Red Nichols at the El Morocco Club, Los Angeles. Moved back to New York in June 1947, worked regularly as a studio musician (including another spell with Raymond Scott), but frequently appeared with Eddie Condon's Band for club dates and recordings. Ill health temporarily curtailed activities from 1957, but returned to full schedule in the 1960s. Toured Far East with Bob Crosby (late 1964), also with Crosby in New York (1966). With World's Greatest Jazz Band (1968-70). Resumed studio work, also played jazz dates. Heart attack whilst at Blues Alley, Washington, D.C.

McGHEE, Howard B.
trumpet/composer

Born: Tulsa, Oklahoma, 6th February 1918

Family moved to Detroit during Howard's infancy. Played clarinet in high school band then switched to trumpet. Worked with saxist Leonard Gay (1939), Jimmy Rachel (1940), own band at Club Congo, Detroit (1941), prior to joining Lionel Hampton for two months in September 1941, with Andy Kirk from November 1941 until joining Charlie Barnet in August 1942 for a year. Rejoined Andy Kirk until summer of 1944 then brief spells with Billy Eckstine and Count Basie. With Coleman Hawkins in New York and California November 1944 to March 1945. Led own small band 1945-47, also took part in free-lance recordings, and worked with George Auld's Band. Did several 'Jazz At The Philharmonic' tours in the late 1940s, took own small band to Europe in May 1948, later that year led own short-lived big band. Toured Pacific area, Japan and Korea with small band led by Oscar Pettiford (November 1951), remained briefly with the band after Pettiford was deposed in January 1952. Played occasional club dates during the 1950s, and some gigs with Machito's Band, but often underwent enforced periods of absence from professional music. During the 1960s was again active, played various jazz festivals, toured Europe in fall of 1964, worked briefly with Duke Ellington (1965), and formed own big band (1966), toured Europe as soloist (1967). During the 1970s was featured with own quintet, and with own big band, also arranging and composing.

McGRATH, 'Fidgey' David Fulton
piano/arranger

Born: Superior, Wisconsin, 6th December 1907
Died: Los Angeles, California 1st January 1958

Was father-in-law of multi-instrumentalist Victor Feldman. Worked with Red Nichols at the Park Central Hotel (summer 1931), regular studio work for radio and recordings, worked regularly with the Dorsey Brothers. Mainly with Lennie Hayton's studio orchestra from 1935-7. Briefly with Bunny Berigan from January 1938, worked with Chauncey Morehouse Band in spring of 1938. N.B.C. house musician from 1939 until late 1943. Moved to Hollywood for film-studio work. During the 1930s was featured on recordings with many leaders: Joe Venuti, The Dorsey Brothers, Red Nichols, etc. Composed 'Mandy Is Two'.

McHARGUE, 'Rosy' James Eugene
clarinet/saxes

Born: Danville, Illinois, 6th April 1907

First musical tuition from his mother, who was a pianiste. Played 'C' melody sax before concentrating on clarinet. Worked with The Wolverines in Indianapolis (late 1925). Following year with Seattle Harmony Kings. Played with Floyd Town, long spell with Maurice Sherman Band, then with Ted Weems as sax/clarinet/staff arranger until late 1942. Moved to Los Angeles. Played in Eddie Miller's Band (spring 1943), briefly with Benny Goodman, then joined Kay Kyser from June 1943 until 1946. Worked on and off with Red Nichols from 1947 until summer of 1951. Own band from early 1950s, worked several years at Hangover Club, then long residencies in California.

McKENDRICK, 'Little Mike' Gilbert Michael
banjo/guitar/vocals

Born: Paris, Tennessee. c. 1903
Died: Chicago, Illinois, early 1961

Raised in Paducah. His father, Gilbert Sr., was a violinist who doubled trombone. In the early 1920s 'Little Mike' and his four brothers, Reuben Michael (guitar/banjo), Richard Michael (trombone), Daniel Michael (violin), and James Michael (piano), all moved to Chicago. To the utter confusion of discographers and this writer, they all, at one time or another, worked as Mike McKendrick. 'Little Mike' was with Hughie Swift's Orchestra in the mid-1920s, then with Doc Cooke before joining Joe Jordan's Sharps and Flats. Briefly led own band in Chicago, then to Europe with Eddie South in 1928. Left South in Europe (c. 1931) and for the next eight years worked with own International Band, mainly in France and Spain. During the late 1920s was temporarily absent from the music scene after being involved in a shooting incident with Sidney Bechet. Returned to the U.S.A. in October 1939, worked briefly in New York, then returned to Chicago where he formed his own International Trio, continued to lead own band through the 1950s.

McKENDRICK, 'Big Mike' Reuben Michael

guitar/banjo/vocals

Born: Paris, Tennessee, 1901
Died: Chicago, Illinois, 22nd March 1965

Brother of Gilbert 'Little Mike' McKendrick (q.v.). Worked on and off for several years with Oscar 'Bernie' Young in the 1920s, with Edgar Hayes' 8 Black Pirates (April-May 1927), Dave Peyton (summer 1927), again with Bernie Young (1928 to spring 1930), also worked with Tiny Parham in 1929. With Jerome Carrington's Orchestra (early 1931), then from spring 1931 until March 1932 (and again in 1933) acted as band manager for Louis Armstrong. Led own band in the 1930s, also worked with Erskine Tate (1934) and Zutty Singleton, Cleo Brown (1934-5). Continued to lead own band, also worked regularly in duo with Ikey Robinson. During the 1950s and early 1960s subbed in Franz Jackson's Band. Worked with clarinettist Brian Shanley's Band (early 1962), then long spell as house musician at Jazz Ltd., Chicago, until early 1965 when he entered hospital suffering from a circulatory ailment.

McKENZIE, 'Red' William

vocals/kazoo

Born: St. Louis, Missouri, 14th October 1899
Died: New York City, 7th February 1948

Raised in Washington, D.C. After both his parents died he moved back to St. Louis. Worked at various jobs including a spell as a professional jockey, then together with Jack Bland and Dick Slevin formed a novelty musical act which was subsequently named The Mound City Blue Blowers. At the instigation of bandleader Gene Rodemich they travelled to Chicago for recording debut (February 1924). Their initial release 'Arkansas Blues' was a huge seller and they began a long series of theatre tours. Eddie Lang joined the group in Atlantic City and later worked with them during their trip to London. They returned to the U.S.A. in 1925 and recommenced touring. Despite personnel changes, McKenzie continued to lead the group until 1932, playing long residencies in New York and Florida. In 1932 he signed a three-year contract to appear with Paul Whiteman's Orchestra. During his stint with Whiteman he also led his own band and sang on various recording sessions with other leaders. Left Whiteman to reorganise 'M.C.B.B.' in spring 1933. In 1935 he organised his own club on 52nd Street, New York, and revived The Mount City Blue Blowers name for recording sessions. After the death of his first wife, Marie, he left New York in 1937 and moved back to St. Louis. Returned briefly to New York early in 1939 for a residency at Kelly's, then returned to St. Louis. He spent several years working for a St. Louis brewery and was musically inactive until working at an Eddie Condon Town Hall Concert in New York (1944). Suffered ill health during the last few years of his life. After spending six weeks in St. Clair's Hospital, New York, he succumbed to cirrhosis of the liver.

During the late 1920s Red McKenzie was active as a talent scout for recording companies, he was largely responsible for gaining recording contracts for Bix Beiderbecke, The Chicago Rhythm Kings, and The Spirits of Rhythm.

McKIBBON, 'Al' Alfred B.

string bass

Born: Chicago, Illinois, 1st January 1919

Father and brother were musicians. Raised in Detroit, attended Cass Technical High School. Did early gigs with McKinney's Cotton Pickers (1935), then worked with Kelly Martin, and altoist Ted Buckner before moving to New York. With Lucky Millinder (1943), Tab Smith (1945-46), Coleman Hawkins (1946-47), J. C. Heard (1947), Dizzy Gillespie (1947-49), Count Basie (1950), George Shearing (1951-58), Cal Tjader (1958-59). During the 1960s worked mainly in Los Angeles, mainly free-lance club and concert dates, and recordings, also worked regularly at N.B.C. studios. Toured extensively with The Giants of Jazz in 1971-72, also did widespread work with vocalist Sammy Davis in the 1970s.

McKINLEY, 'Ray' Raymond Frederick

drums/vocal

Born: Fort Worth, Texas, 18th June 1910

Worked with Duncan Marion's Orchestra and the Tracy-Brown Band before joining Smith Ballew in 1932, then with the Dorsey Brothers in 1934, after the brothers split up Ray remained with Jimmy Dorsey until June 1939. Then (together with Will Bradley) organised a big band that made its debut in September 1939, continued co-leading until February 1942, left to form own big band. Joined the U.S.A.A.F. and served in Europe with Glenn Miller's Band, after Miller's death he acted as the band's unofficial leader until return to U.S.A. in July 1945, then led until November 1945. Led own big band 1946-50, then worked as a solo vocalist, but continued to lead own band for specific engagements. In the spring of 1956, at the invitation of Glenn Miller's widow, he organised a new Glenn Miller Orchestra, during the following year he led the band on an extensive tour of Europe. Continued to lead with considerable success until early 1966, McKinley then resigned as leader, his place being taken by clarinettist Buddy De Franco. Period of semi-retirement in Connecticut, then re-formed own band in the late 1960s, residency at Riverboat, New York (late 1969 to early 1970). Continued to play during the 1970s.

McKINNEY, 'Bill' William
drums/leader

Born: Cynthiana, Kentucky, 17th September 1895
Died: Cynthiana, Kentucky, 14th October 1969

Served in U.S. Army during World War I, then worked as a circus drummer until settling in Springfield, Ohio. In Springfield he took over the leadership of the Synco Septet, the group later worked as The Synco Jazz Band. McKinney relinquished the drum chair to Cuba Austin in order to become the band's business manager. They played residencies in Michigan, Toledo, Baltimore, and at the Arcadia Ballroom, Detroit (1926), before being signed by Jean Goldkette for residency at the Greystone Ballroom, Detroit. From then on the band was billed as McKinney's Cotton Pickers. Detroit was to be the band's home base for several years, they also did regular wide-ranging tours reaching New York, Philadelphia, Atlantic City, Ohio, Illinois, Minneapolis, etc. In June 1927 Don Redman was appointed musical director of the band. In 1930 the band ceased working under the auspices of Jean Goldkette, they left Detroit, toured down to Kansas City before taking up residency at Frank Sebastian's Cotton Club, Culver City, California (May 1931). Then after a tour of the Middle West the band split into two factions, several members leaving to form the nucleus of Don Redman's Band. Benny Carter became the new musical director in the summer of 1931. The band continued touring before taking up residencies in Detroit. After Benny Carter had left (1932), the band recommenced a long spell of touring before breaking up in Baltimore (1934). Several bands began operating as The Cotton Pickers, but McKinney himself was inactive until he re-formed a band for residency at the Recreation Ballroom, Boston, in January 1935. This band continued operating on and off for the next year (in various locations). Then in 1937 McKinney began managing the Cosy Cafe in Detroit, throughout the late 1930s he continued to act as manager-leader for bands working under his name including one that was resident at Plantation Cafe in Detroit (1939). In the 1940s he severed his connections with the music business and worked in the Ford factory in Detroit. He retired in the 1950s and suffered from poor health for many years.

'McKinney's Music' by John Chilton, first published in 1978.

McKINNEY, Nina Mae
vocals

Born: Lancaster, South Carolina, 1912
Died: New York City, May 1967

Raised in Philadelphia, came to New York as a dancer, worked in 'Blackbirds of 1928' and was picked for a starring role in the film 'Hallelujah'. During the late 1920s and 1930s she appeared in many films including: 'Safe in Hell', 'Reckless', 'The Lost Lady', 'In Old Kentucky', etc. She did extensive tours as a solo artiste, first appearing in Europe from December 1932 (accompanied by Garland Wilson). During one of her visits to Britain she co-starred with Paul Robeson in 'Sanders of the River'. During the early 1940s she specialised in theatre and cabaret work, then returned to regular filming, appearing in 'Without Love', 'Dark Waters', 'Night Train to Memphis', etc.

McLIN, 'Jimmy' James A.
guitar

Born: Brookesville, Florida, 27th June 1908
Died: St. Petersburg, Florida, 15th December 1983

His father was a minister, his mother a school-teacher. Began playing piano at seven, taught by Professor Bell. Then self-taught banjo from the age of 10, later played guitar and doubled throughout the 1920s and early 1930s. First gigs in St. Petersburg, Florida, with pianist Roy Graham. Worked with Eagle Eye Shields in Jacksonville from c. 1926. Moved to New York in 1928, gigged with various bands, then worked regularly with James P. Johnson from 1931-4. Brief spells with various bandleaders including: Roy Eldridge, Ward Pinkett, Bobby Henderson, Billy Hicks, etc., then working mainly with Claude Hopkins from 1941-2. (During the 1930s also recorded with many 'names' including: Buster Bailey, Billie Holiday, Willie 'The Lion' Smith, Buddy Johnson, etc.) also played with Sidney Bechet at Nick's (spring 1940), Dave Nelson (early 1941), and briefly with Jimmie Lunceford. Three years' service in U.S. Navy, during which time he played regularly, mainly on trombone and mellophone. Rejoined Claude Hopkins in late 1945, then three years' advanced studies at Harnett's School of Music, again with Claude Hopkins (1950-1). Continued free-lance work, playing on many recording sessions, then began working as accompanist to The Ink Spots vocal group.

McPARTLAND, 'Jimmy' James Dougald *Born: Chicago, Illinois, 15th March 1907*
trumpet

Brother of banjoist/guitarist Richard 'Dick' McPartland (1905-57), their father was a music teacher. Started on violin at five, then switched to cornet in early 1920s. Formed band with his brother and several of their friends (Jim Lanigan, Bud Freeman, Frank Teschemacher, Dave Tough and pianist Dave North). This group was subsequently known as The Austin High Gang (though not all of them attended that school), they gigged as The Blue Friars. Jimmy did first professional work with Al Haid's Band in 1923, subsequently worked with 'Frisco' Hasse, Charles 'Murph' Podolsky, and the Maroon Five before moving to New York to join The Wolverines. Played alongside Bix Beiderbecke for five nights until Bix left to join Jean Goldkette. Left New York with The Wolverines to play in Miami, Florida, and Chicago; the band played in Chicago under Dick Voynow's leadership, later Jimmy fronted the band when they were billed in Des Moines and Chicago as Husk O'Hare's Wolverines (May 1926). Then worked in Detroit with Art Kassel before joining drummer Bill Paley's Band at Friars' Inn, Chicago (late 1926). Returned to Art Kassel before joining Ben Pollack at The Blackhawk, Chicago, subsequently went to New York with Pollack. Played on many free-lance recording sessions, finally left Pollack in autumn 1929. Short spell with Arnold Johnson's Orchestra, played for Broadway show 'Sons O' Guns', then with Roger Wolfe Kahn for 'Sweet and Low' production. Toured with Russ Colombo, then briefly with Smith Ballew and Horace Heidt, before working with Harry Reser's Band on South American cruises. Played in New York with Charles Drury Band, then back to Chicago (c. 1934) to join his brother's Embassy Four. After long spell of touring (and residencies in New Orleans, Chicago, etc.) he left to form his own band. From 1937 until 1940 played mainly in Chicago, led own band at Three Deuces, Hotel Sherman, etc., then to Nick's New York (early 1941). Brief return to Chicago, then with Jack Teagarden until joining U.S. Army in late 1942. Served in Europe, took part in Normandy invasion, then played in service show 'Bandwagon' where he met and married pianiste Marian Page (February 1945). Brief visit to England, then back to U.S.A. and began leading own quartet in Chicago. Throughout the late 1940s and early 1950s led own bands in Chicago, Wisconsin, etc., also visited Britain in 1949 and 1954. Began to work regularly in New York from 1953, long spells at Nick's, The Metropole, etc., also acted in television play 'The Magic Horn'. Has continued to work regularly throughout the 1960s, mainly with own groups, but also spells with Bud Freeman, Peanuts Hucko, etc., etc. (on 20th November 1965 took part in the concert to commemorate the 75th anniversary of the Austin High School). With Tony Parenti (1969), continues regular playing, often at Jimmy Ryan's (1970-1). Played solo dates in South Africa (1972). Continued to play regularly during the 1970s. Featured with Marian McPartland at Newport Jazz Festival (1978). Active schedule during early 1980s, including tour of Britain (1981).

McRAE, 'Teddy' Theodore *Born: Philadelphia, Pennsylvania, 22nd January 1908*
tenor sax/arranger

Brother of Bobby (guitar/trumpet) and Dave (alto/baritone saxes). Worked in family band whilst studying medicine, also doubled regularly on guitar and trumpet. With June Clark on and off from 1926, led own band at the Club Ebony, New York, in 1927. Spells with

Chick Webb, Charlie Johnson, and June Clark. Joined Elmer Snowden (1932). Briefly with Stuff Smith (1934), with Lil Armstrong (1935), Chick Webb in spring 1936. Remained after the leader's death to work for Ella Fitzgerald (briefly as musical director) until late 1941. Worked with Cab Calloway, then briefly with Jimmie Lunceford in late 1942. Worked as staff arranger for Artie Shaw, then two stints (on alto and tenor) with Lionel Hampton in 1943. Musical director of Louis Armstrong's Big Band for a year from spring 1944, then formed own band in 1945. During the 1950s and 1960s has arranged for many bands, also for a time (in partnership with Eddie Wilcox) ran the record company RaeCox.

McSHANN, 'Jay' James Columbus *Born: Muskogee, Oklahoma, 12th January 1909*
piano/vocals

His cousin, Pete McShann, played drums. Piano from age of 12. Spent two months at Fisk University, returned home, then went to Tulsa to play in Al Dennis Band for four months. Briefly led own band in Arkansas before year's study at Winfield College, Kansas, left to tour Arizona and New Mexico in Eddy Hill's Band. Whilst on a trip to visit relatives in Iowa he stopped off at Kansas City and began playing in local clubs. During the mid-1930s worked in many Kansas City night-spots, then after residency at Monroe Inn he joined band led by trumpeter Dee 'Prince' Stewart (1937). Three months later began leading own band at Martin's, Kansas City (which included altoist Charlie Parker). In early 1939 worked for four months in Chicago with own trio, then back to leading band at Martin's. After a residency at the Century Room, Kansas City (February-June 1940) the band began regular touring, leading eventually to its successful debut in New York. Continued to lead own big band until Army call-up in late 1943. He was released a year later and re-formed band which early in 1945 was resident at The Downbeat Club in New York. In June 1946 he took own band to Los Angeles for various residencies including Susie Q Club and Cobra Club. During the 1950s and 1960s led own group in Kansas City, long bookings at the Club Flamingo, Kismet Lounge, Barbary Coast Club, etc. Worked extensively in Europe during 1969—in March led specially formed band in France and Holland, subsequently appearing as a soloist at London's 'Jazz Expo' (October 1969). Toured Europe (autumn 1970). Own Band in Kansas (1971), dates in Toronto (June 1971). At Monterey Festival (September 1971). World-wide touring in the 1970s, often with own trio: Claude Williams (violin and guitar) and Paul Gunther (drums). During the 1980s, worked as a soloist and with own band, widespread international touring.

McVEA, Jack *Born: Los Angeles, California, 5th November 1914*
tenor, alto sax/clarinet

His father, Isaac 'Satchel' McVea (died: 1960), was a banjoist who led his own band for many years. Jack began on banjo and by the age of 11 was playing regularly in his father's band—began doubling on sax in 1927. After leaving Jefferson High School in 1932 he played professionally with Walter 'Dootsie' Williams' Harlem Dukes. In 1923 and 1934 was in band led by trumpeter Charlie Echols, worked briefly under Lorenzo Flennoy's leadership, then with Charlie Echols again (1935). With Claude Kennedy, Edyth Turnham, and Cee Pee Johnson, before joining Eddie Barefield's Big Band (1936). During the late 1930s played for many West Coast leaders and occasionally led own band. With Lionel Hampton (on baritone sax) from 1940 until January 1943. Returned to California and joined Snub Mosley's Band (April 1943). From 1944 led own band, but also appeared on several of Norman Granz's 'Jazz At The Philharmonic' concerts and broadcast with Count Basie. In 1946 his own band scored with a commercial hit single 'Open the Door Richard', he continued to lead through the 1950s, including residencies in Honolulu in 1951 and 1954. Worked briefly on M.G.M. studio staff and played on many free-lance recording dates. Led in Las Vegas in 1955, then briefly with Benny Carter until re-forming own band, with organist Perry Lee Blackwell's Trio (1959). During the 1960s has continued to lead own small groups in California and Oregon, combining this with various recording commitments. Led own trio (on clarinet) at Disneyland.

Jack McVea's Band was featured in the film 'Sarge Goes to College'.

MELROSE, **'Frank' Franklyn Taft**
piano

Born: Sumner, Illinois, 26th December 1907
Died: near Hammond, Indiana, early September 1941

His two brothers, Walter and Lester, were music publishers and talent scouts for recording companies. Frank began on violin, later specialised on piano, but did occasional gigs on violin. Worked with various leaders in and around Chicago in the late 1920s. During this period recorded under the pseudonym 'Kansas City Frank', also did sessions with the Dodds Brothers, Jimmy Bertrand, etc. Worked in New York, Kansas City, St. Louis, and Detroit; played with Bud Jacobson at the Chicago World's Fair (1933). Left full-time music for several years, did teaching and gigs in the late 1930s, then residency at Paddock and Derby Clubs in Calumet City until March 1940. In Chicago for a brief spell with Pete Daily, then worked as a machinist in a pressed-steel factory, continued to do club work including spell with Joe Sheets in Cedar Lake district. After a Labor Day weekend visit to Chicago, his mutilated body was found near Hammond, Indiana.

MENDEL, **Johnny**
trumpet

Born: Connecticut, 1905
Died: Chicago, Illinois, 11th October 1966

After touring with various bands, including spell with Henri Gendron and his Orchestra (1926), settled in Chicago. Was a plunger-mute specialist and received some tuition from King Oliver. Recorded with Bud Freeman (1929), worked mostly in Chicago during the early 1930s with Joe Kayser, Eddie Neibauer, etc. With Jimmy Dorsey, Charlie Barnet (1938 to mid-1939). Left full-time music, but continued regular playing with Jim Jackson Band (1944), Bud Jacobson (1945), etc. Briefly with Bud Freeman in 1949, during the following year worked at Jazz Ltd. Active as a teacher in the 1950s, continued playing in the 1960s, occasionally with Frank Chase Sextet, own Chicagoans and appearances at local jazz concerts, also sat in with Duke Ellington's Orchestra.

MERTZ, **Paul Madeira**
piano/arranger

Born: Reading, Pennsylvania, 1st September 1904

In 1918 began playing local gigs with theatre orchestras, dance bands, etc. Graduated from Reading High School in 1921, following year toured with the Dorsey Brothers' Wild Canaries, left to play residency at Hotel Addison, Detroit (September 1922) and matriculated at the University of Detroit. In January 1923 joined Jean Goldkette's Graystone Ballroom Band, in 1925 was transferred to Goldkette's Book-Cadillac Orchestra, also recorded with Bix Beiderbecke in 1925. Late in 1926 was shifted back to Goldkette's Graystone Band (which then included Bix Beiderbecke and Frank Trumbauer); arranged for Goldkette and Red Nichols' groups. Remained with Goldkette until February 1927, also recorded with Frank Trumbauer, then joined Fred Waring's Pennsylvanians February 1927 until March 1929 (including 1928 trip to Paris). Rejoined Jean Goldkette in March 1929 for several months, then moved to Hollywood, arranging for Paramount. Joined Irving Aaronson's Commanders from January 1920 until spring 1931, worked with them in Florida, Hollywood, and New York. Briefly with Red Nichols' Orchestra at Park Central Hotel, New York, then played piano-duo with Henry Vannicelli for 'Laugh Parade' Broadway Show. From January 1932 until July 1933 was pianist and chief arranger for Horace Heidt, then moved to Hollywood to work for Paramount Pictures. Joined Columbia Pictures in October 1936, and other than World War II service as a radio technician, remained with Columbia until 1954. (Wrote the hit tune 'I'm Glad There is You', published in 1942 under pen-name Paul Madeira.) Worked for M.G.M. Films (1958-60), but since 1954 has been mainly active as a free-lance arranger-composer and music co-ordinator for the film industry.

METCALF, **Louis**
trumpet/vocals

Born: St. Louis, Missouri, 28th February 1905
Died: Jamaica, L.I., 27th October 1981

Played drums, then switched to cornet—taught by P. G. Lankford. Played in local Knights of Phythias Brass Band, then several years on and off with Charlie Creath, also gigged in Warnie Long's Kid Jazz Band. To New York in summer of 1923 playing in Jimmie Cooper's revue. During following year spent several months with Willie 'The Lion' Smith at the Rhythm Club, New York. Early in 1925 joined Andrew Preer and his Cotton Club Syncopators, left to accompany Johnny Hudgins' variety act. Briefly with Elmer Snowden Band, then from February until August 1926 with Charlie Johnson Band. With Duke Ellington during late 1926-7. Worked with Jelly Roll Morton in New York during 1928, later that year joined the Luis Russell Orchestra. From autumn 1929 until summer 1930 worked in Connie's Inn Revue, then joined Vernon Andrade's Orchestra. Spent three years in Canada during the early 1930s, mainly leading own band. Returned to New York and joined Fletcher Henderson in March 1935, led own band before returning to St. Louis to play briefly with Dewey Jackson on the S.S. St. Paul. Moved on to Chicago, worked with Dave Peyton, then briefly with Zutty Singleton Band before returning to New York to reorganise own band. From 1936 onwards led own band (except for a brief spell with Noble Sissle in Cleveland). Ran own Heatwave Club in New York during late 1930s and early 1940s, led in Philadelphia (1945). Left New York in 1947, moved to Canada and organised and directed his own International Band until 1950. Brief spell away from the music scene, then returned to New York in 1951 and began leading own small groups; residencies at various clubs including: The Metropole, Baby Grand, Howard's, The Embers. Led own band at The Alibaba for several years during the 1960s. Recovered from serious illness during 1969 and once again formed own small band.

MEZZROW, 'Mezz'
(real name: Milton Mesirow)
clarinet/saxes

Born: Chicago, Illinois, 9th November 1899
Died: Paris, France, 5th August 1972

First played saxophone in 1917 whilst serving a brief jail sentence. Began gigging in and around Chicago from c. 1923, later did various summer seasons including leading own band at the Martinique Inn, Indiana Harbor, during summer of 1924. Gigged with the Austin High Gang (Jimmie McPartland, Frank Teschemacher, etc.), also with Irving Rothschild (1925) and Husk O'Hare's Wolverines (1926). Recorded with the Jungle Kings and Chicago Rhythm Kings and led own short-lived Purple Grackle Orchestra in 1928. Moved to New York, subbed for Gil Rodin in Ben Pollack's Band (June-July 1928) and recorded with Eddie Condon in October 1928. Gigged in New York, then sailed to Europe in March 1929, briefly led own quartet at L'Ermitage Muscovite in Paris, then returned to New York in April 1929. Toured with Red Nichols, then worked with Jack Levy's Orchestra at Minsky's, New York. During the 1930s Mezz occasionally played clarinet and tenor sax, but was more active in other pursuits. He organised own recording bands in 1933 and 1934 and took part in 1938 sessions supervised by Hugues Panassié. On 20th November 1937 his mixed band The Disciples of Swing began a brief residency at the Harlem Uproar House, they also played at the Savoy Ballroom in December 1937. In late 1938 Mezz played briefly in Manzie Johnson's Band at The Palace, New York. In 1939 and 1940 Mezz occasionally led own small groups, but in 1941 and 1942 he suffered a two-year absence from the music scene. Led own band at Kelly's Stables, New York, in spring 1943, then worked on and off with Art Hodes (1943-4). From early 1945 occasionally led own small group at Jimmy Ryan's; organised own record company King Jazz which featured Mezz with Sidney Bechet, Hot Lips Page, Sam Price, Kaiser Marshall, etc. Took own band to Europe for Nice Festival (February 1948), brief tour of France, then returned to U.S.A. Worked with Claude Luter at Au Vieux Colombier, Paris (1951), in late 1951 to early 1952 led own all-star band (Lee Collins, Zutty Singleton, etc.) for tour of Europe. In 1953 also led all-star band in Europe (Buck Clayton, Gene Sedric, etc.), toured late 1954 to early 1955 leading Lee Collins, Jimmy Archey, Freddie Moore, etc. During 1950s and 1960s made guest appearances throughout Europe. Visited New York early in 1970.

'Really The Blues', by Mezz Mezzrow and Bernard Wolfe was first published in 1946.

MIDDLETON, Velma
vocals

Born: St. Louis, Missouri, 1917
Died: Sierra Leone, 10th February 1961

Her brother, Emmanuel, was a string bassist. First toured with Connie McLean's Orchestra in 'Cotton Club Show', visited South America with this company c. 1938. Worked mainly as a solo entertainer until joining Louis Armstrong in 1942. Sang with Louis Armstrong's Big Band, later worked regularly with Louis' All Stars. In January 1961, whilst touring Africa with Louis, she was taken ill and died three weeks later in a hospital in Sierra Leone.

MIKELL, F. Eugene Sr.
trumpet/multi-instrumentalist/composer

Born: Charleston, South Carolina, 1880
Died: Brooklyn, New York, January 1932

Remarkably successful music teacher; some of his pupils were: Arthur Briggs, Pete Briggs, Freddy Jenkins, Russell Procope, Jerry Blake, Rudy Powell, Bobbie Stark, etc. Both his sons, Otto and Eugene Jr., became professional sax players. Eugene Jr., who plays alto sax and clarinet, worked with many name bands and still plays regularly in New York City. Eugene Sr. was one of the original music teachers at the Jenkins' Orphanage, South Carolina, he later became assistant leader for Jim Europe's 369th Infantry Band, then as a First Lieutenant became bandmaster of the 15th Infantry Regiment Band. After leaving the U.S. Army he became Director of Music at the Bordentown Industrial School in New Jersey, subsequently he did extensive teaching and band coaching in New York City.

It is beyond the scope of this work to present a detailed study of successful music teachers, but I felt that some tribute is due to the following tutors, whose names figure prominently in many entries in this book: Major N. Clark-Smith (Tuskegee, Kansas City, and Chicago); P. G. Lankford (St. Louis); Manuel Manetta (New Orleans); Mrs. Portia Pittman (Dallas); John 'Fess' Whatley (Birmingham, Alabama).

MILES, Lizzie
(real name: Elizabeth Mary Pajaud—née Landreaux)
vocals

Born: New Orleans, Louisiana, 31st March 1895
Died: New Orleans, Louisiana, 17th March 1963

Step-sister of Herb Morand (trumpet) and Maurice Morand (drums). Left New Orleans (c. 1909) with the Jones' Brothers' Circus, worked originally as a novelty performer—riding animals, etc. For the next eight years travelled with circuses and minstrel shows, occasionally doing solo-vocal act on theatre circuits. Temporarily left the profession in 1918 through illness, then worked in Chicago—sang with Freddie Keppard, Glover Compton, Charlie Elgar, etc. Began recording career in New York (early 1922). Resident at Herman's Inn, New York (1924), Capitol Palace, New York (1926). Visited Europe with Alexander Shargenski's troupe (c. 1925), did solo features at Chez Michele in Paris. Continued to work regularly until the early 1930s, suffered a serious illness, then resumed professional work in the 1930s. During the early 1950s temporarily lived in California, featured at the Hangover Club, San Francisco (1952), worked with trumpeter Bob Scobey's Band regularly from c. 1955 until spring 1957, returned to New Orleans, worked with Freddie Kohlman's Band, etc., then again to California. With Joe Darensbourg (1958), featured at Monterey Festivals (1958 and 1959). Retired from professional singing in 1959 and devoted much time to religious studies.

MILEY, 'Bubber' James Wesley
trumpet/composer

Born: Aiken, South Carolina, 3rd April 1903
Died: Welfare Island, N.Y., 20th May 1932

Family moved to New York City in 1909. His father, Valentine Miley, was an amateur guitarist; his three sisters, Connie, Rose, and Murdis, were professional singers (known as the South Carolina Trio). Was taught trombone whilst at school, then switched to cornet. Joined the U.S. Navy as a boy entrant in 1918, served for 18 months, then worked in New York with The Carolina Five before joining Willie Gant's Band at Lee's Cabaret, New York. Toured with Mamie Smith (autumn 1921), later played residency with house band at John O'Connor's Club, New York (winter 1922 until late 1923), also played for cabaret at Reisenweber's, New York. Toured the South with the 'Sunny South' revue, then again briefly with Mamie Smith. Worked in the Washingtonians (then led by Elmer Snowden—September 1923), remained to work with Duke Ellington (1924). Other than brief absences Bubber worked with Duke until January 1929. Gigged in New York, then sailed to France with Noble Sissle in May 1929, returned to New York after a fortnight in Paris, worked with Zutty Singleton's Band at the Lafayette Theatre, then joined Allie Ross Band at Connie's Inn. From early 1930 worked occasionally for Leo Reisman, sometimes dressed as an usher he would join the band from the audience; where segregation problems prevented visible participation, Miley played with the orchestra, but was hidden from view by a screen. In January 1931 he accompanied noted writer Roger Pryor Dodge (then a professional dancer) for the 'Sweet and Low' revue, remained for four months. In late 1931 Miley (financed by Irving Mills) formed his own band, they played in the 'Harlem Scandals' show in Philadelphia, then opened in New York (January 1932). Shortly afterwards Miley, ill with tuberculosis, was forced to stop playing. He entered hospital on the 18th April 1932 and died just over a month later.

MILLER, 'Eddie' Edward Raymond
(original name: Müller)
tenor sax/clarinet/vocals

Born: New Orleans, Louisiana, 23rd June 1911

Did first local gigs whilst still in his early teens, worked at the Silver Slipper and Halfway House in New Orleans. With the New Orleans Owls in 1928, subsequently moved to New York, worked on alto sax with various bandleaders for eight months. Left Julie Wintz to join Ben Pollack in September 1930, switched to tenor sax. Studied with Howard Vorhees, also worked in New York with Ralph Watkin's Band and gigged with Dorsey Brothers' pick-up band which included Bix Beiderbecke, Bunny Berigan, Bill Moore, and Larry Binyon. After break up of Ben Pollack's Band (1934), Eddie Miller became founder-member of band that eventually became Bob Crosby's Band. Remained with Bob Crosby until the unit disbanded in late 1942. From early 1943 led own band on West Coast (featuring several ex-Bob Crosby musicians). Very briefly in U.S. Army until August 1944, then again led own band in California before becoming a studio musician. Appeared with own band in Donald O'Connor film 'You Can't Ration Love' (1943), also prominently featured as a soloist on many film soundtracks including: 'The Girls He Left Behind', 'Mr. Big', 'You Were Meant For Me', 'No Way Out', 'Panic in the Streets', etc., etc. Played many dates with Nappy Lamare (1945-7) and took part in many Bob Crosby reunions during the 1950s and 1960s; to Japan with Bob Crosby in late 1964, also dates in Las Vegas and New York with Crosby. Occasionally worked in New Orleans during the 1960s, was also featured at many jazz festivals. Worked in Red Nichols' Five Pennies on Nichols' last engagement (Las Vegas, June 1965). Toured Britain as a soloist in spring 1967. Featured at New Orleans Jazz Fest (1969). With Pete Fountain from summer of 1967 until August 1976, worked mostly in New Orleans. Moved back to California and resumed prolific free-lance activities including touring Europe with World's Greatest Jazz Band, and working at Nice Festival with Bob Crosby (1981).

MILLER, 'Glenn' Alton Glenn
trombone/arranger/composer

Born: Clarinda, Iowa, 1st March 1904
Died: Reported missing after flight from England, 15th December 1944

His younger brother, Herb (a trumpeter), has led his own band for many years. Family moved to North Platte, Nebraska, in 1909. Glenn began on cornet and mandolin. After family moved to Grant City, Missouri, in 1916, he specialised on trombone and began playing in the Grant City Town Band. Attended Fort Morgan High School in Colorado, left before graduation and joined Boyd Senter in late 1921. Left Senter in 1922 to attend University of Colorado, continued gigging and began regular arranging. Joined Max Fischer's Band in Denver and moved with them to California, there joined Ben Pollack (1926) and returned East. Left Pollack in New York (summer 1928), worked briefly with Paul Ash, then active as a free-lance arranger, also took part in many free-lance recordings. Played in theatre orchestras for several Broadway shows: 'Strike Up The Band', 'Whopee', 'Girl Crazy', etc. Briefly with Bert Lown's Orchestra (1930), continued free-lance playing and arranging. On tour as musical director for Smith Ballew in the early 1930s, then free-lancing before joining the Dorsey Brothers' Orchestra (spring 1934)—continued to study arranging with Dr. Joseph Schillinger. Early in 1935 left the Dorseys to work in first American band organised by Ray Noble. During the following year arranged for Glen Gray and the Casa Loma Band and Ozzie Nelson until forming own band in

January 1937. After a year of touring and residency in New Orleans (June-August 1937) Miller temporarily disbanded. Re-formed in March 1938, after a slow start the band gradually gained popularity and moved steadily on to become one of the highest-paid bands in the U.S.A. They were featured in two films: 'Sun Valley Serenade' and 'Orchestra Wives'. In mid-1942 Glenn Miller volunteered for sevice in the U.S. Army. Joined in October 1942 with the rank of Captain. He assembled an all-star service personnel band and toured the U.S.A. on recruiting drives before being posted overseas in 1944. Led A.E.F. Orchestra in England (Major Glenn Miller and his A.E.F. Orchestra). Flew from an R.A.F. station near Bedford, England, to precede orchestra on posting to Paris. The single-engined Norseman aircraft never reached France, and a year later Major Glenn Miller was reported officially dead by the U.S. Army authorities. A posthumous film tribute 'The Glenn Miller Story' was released in 1953.

George T. Simon's book 'Glenn Miller', first published in 1974.

MILLER, Max
vibes/piano/guitar/bass/drums

Born: New Philadelphia, Ohio, 17th November 1911

At 16 was playing guitar with various territory bands, then played vibes and guitar with Vincent Lopez. Became staff musician for radio stations in the late 1930s, playing for WIND in Gary, Indiana, and WJJD in Chicago. Led own small group in Cleveland. Began working mainly on piano during the early 1940s, led own band for various Chicago club residencies, co-led short-lived band with Shorty Sherock in Chicago (late 1942) then defence plant work 1943-45. Returned to full-time music and was for many years one of the leading figures on the Chicago jazz scene.

MILLER, 'Punch' Ernest
(real name: Ernest Burden)
trumpet/vocals

Born: Raceland, Louisiana, 14th June 1894
Died: New Orleans, Louisiana, 2nd December 1971

Gained nickname by having a twin sister, Ernestine Judy. Played bass drum in his teens, then baritone horn and trombone before specialising on cornet. Played in Paul Rossier's Band and in Spencer Taylor's Brass Band. Visited New Orleans before joining the U.S. Army. Member of Army band and bugler at Camp Beauregard. After release (1919) lived in New Orleans. Gigged with Kid Ory, then worked regularly with Jack Carey's Band (including touring), subsequently formed own band. Played a week-end date with Fate Marable. During the early 1920s toured with own band, also toured with William McBride's 'Mack's Merry Makers' Revue'. Left that show in Houston, Texas, and worked with band led by drummer Frank Davis. In late 1926, moved (with guitarist Huey Long) to Chicago. Gigged at the La Salle Book Store, then worked with Hugh C. Swift's Band at Jeffrey Tavern. Played dates at the Monogram and Grand Theatres, also toured with Jelly Roll Morton (c. 1927). Worked for various leaders in Chicago: Al Wynn, Tiny Parham and Erskine Tate at the Vendome (1927), Freddie Keppard at LaRue's Dreamland (spring 1928). Subbed in Earl Hines' Band for one night (1929). From autumn of 1929 worked regularly in band led by New Orleans drummer François Moseley (Frankie Franko and his Louisianians). Briefly led own Harlem Club Four (1933), then again with Frankie Franko including tour in October 1934. In late 1934 to early 1935 played in New York with Leonard Reed's Orchestra at the Harlem Playhouse, then returned to work with Frankie Franko at the Golden Lily, Chicago (1935), after the club closed did dates with Zilner Randolph's W.P.A. Band and toured with Walter Barnes. During the early 1940s led own small band and trio at various Chicago clubs including the H. and T. Tavern and The Dipsy Doodle, gigged in band led by 'Sir' Oliver Bibbs. With Jasper Taylor at the 900 Club, Chicago (1945). Then long spells of touring with various carnival shows, including 'Cavalcade of Amusement'. Appeared on Rudi Blesh's 'This is Jazz' radio show in 1947, toured with the Bronze Mannekins (1948), then worked in circus bands and travelling rock-and-roll revues. Returned to New Orleans in late 1956, gigged with various bands until suffering serious illness in 1959. Resumed regular playing in 1960, led own band in Cleveland for four months, toured Japan with George Lewis early in 1964, worked with Lewis in New Orleans (1965). Was the subject of a 1971 film 'Till The Butcher Cut Him Down'.

M

MILLIAN, Baker
tenor sax

Born: Crowley, Louisiana, 1908

Originally played piano, switched to alto and 'C' melody saxes before specialising on tenor. Started with the Yelping Hound Band in Crowley, then played in New Orleans with Chris Kelly before moving back to Crowley to rejoin the Yelping Hound Band, also worked with Evan Thomas' Black Eagle Band from 1927 until 1929. Moved to Texas in 1929, played in the Buffalo Rhythm Stompers before working in New Mexico, subsequently joined Giles Mitchell Band in Houston, Texas (1931). Late the following year joined Chester Boone's Band at the Harlem Grill, Houston. From 1933 until 1938 was the featured tenor sax soloist with Boots and his Buddies, led by drummer Clifford 'Boots' Douglas. Left to settle in California, became a post office worker, but continued to play regularly—during 1943 did occasional gigs with his old colleague Bunk Johnson. After service in the U.S. Army returned to California; continued to gig throughout the 1950s and 1960s, mainly in Oakland and San Francisco.

MILLINDER, 'Lucky' Lucius
leader

Born: Anniston, Alabama, 8th August 1900
Died: New York, 28th September 1966

Raised in Chicago, attended Wendell Phillips High School. Worked as a master of ceremonies at various ballrooms and clubs in Chicago during the late 1920s. Fronted band for tour of R.K.O. circuit in 1931, during the following spring he took over the leadership of 'Doc' Crawford's Big Band and led at the Harlem Uproar House, New York. In June 1933 he took a different personnel to Europe and played residencies in Monte Carlo and Paris before returning to New York in October 1933. During the following year he began fronting the Mills Blue Rhythm Band, which subsequently worked under his name. He continued leading until the spring of 1938, then toured fronting Bill Doggett's Band, he again led in New York until being declared bankrupt early in 1939. He re-formed in September 1940 and continued leading a big band on and off until the summer of 1952, he then left full-time music and worked as a salesman for a spirit distillery. Later he reorganised bands for stints at the Apollo, New York, and various tours, but was also active as a disc-jockey on radio WNEW and as a publicist and fortune-teller. In later years he occasionally fronted bands for specific engagements. Lucky's band played the soundtrack for the 1940 film 'Paradise in Harlem'.

MILLS, Lincoln
trumpet

Born: Chrisfield, Maryland, 1910
Died: c. 1957

Worked with Eugene Kennedy's Band at the Arcadia Ballroom, New York, in 1929, subsequently with Cliff Jackson, 'Doc' Hyder in Philadelphia, and Bobby Lee in Atlantic City before joining Tiny Bradshaw in 1934. With Eddie South's Orchestra in New York (summer 1935), then worked with Claude Hopkins until 1938. With Benny Carter's Big Band at Savoy, New York, early in 1939, joined Coleman Hawkins in June 1940, then rejoined Benny Carter (February 1941 until spring 1942). During the 1940s worked for several years in Gene Sedric's Band. Took his own life sometime in the late 1950s.

MINCE, Johnny
(real name: John H. Muenzenberger)
clarinet/saxes

Born: Chicago, Illinois, 8th July 1912

Joined Joe Haymes at the age of 17; to New York with Haymes in the early 1930s, remained when the band worked under the leadership of Buddy Rogers. With Ray Noble's original American band (spring 1935). Briefly with Bob Crosby in 1936, resumed playing for Ray Noble until March 1937, then joined Tommy Dorsey until early in 1941. Short spell in Bob Strong's Band, then U.S. Army service from spring of 1941. Played in band with 'This is the Army' show and did overseas tours (including playing in Britain in 1944). After demobilisation went into radio studio work, was later featured regularly in television orchestras. Has continued to play regularly during the 1960s, occasionally leads own small band—subbed for a few days with Louis Armstrong in April 1967. Guested at Dick Gibson's Jazz Party in Colorado (1971), often during the 1970s, toured

Europe with Kings of Jazz (1974). Extensive touring throughout late 1970s and 1980s, including trips to Europe with Lawson-Haggart (1982) and tours with Keith Smith.

MINOR, 'Piggy' Orville
trumpet

Born: Kansas City, Missouri, 23rd April 1912

Worked regularly with Jay McShann's small band in Kansas City during the late 1930s, became member of McShann's Big Band in the 1940s, also led own band in the 1930s, and worked with Dee Stewart, Clint Weaver, etc. Led own group in the 1950s and was featured on trumpet, valve trombone, and vibes. Remained active in Kansas City during the late 1970s, featuring a specialty of playing the trumpet and valve trombone at the same time.

MINOR, 'Slamfoot' Dan
trombone

Born: Dallas, Texas, 10th August 1909
Died: New York City, 11th April 1982

Began playing trombone in 1926. Played in a local church band, then joined The Blue Moon Chasers, playing in and around Dallas. First professional work with Walter Page's Blue Devils, worked with this band from 1927 until 1929, then joined Ben Smith's Blue Syncopators. Toured with Earl Dykes in 1930, worked with Gene Coy's Black Aces, Lloyd Hunter's Serenaders, and Alphonso Trent in 1931, later that year joined Bennie Moten and remained until 1934. Worked with Count Basie in Little Rock, Arkansas (1934), and in Kansas City (1936). Remained with Basie from 1936 until July 1941. Worked on and off with Buddy Johnson from 1941 until 1944, during this period also worked briefly with Cab Calloway (1942) whilst Tyree Glenn was ill. With Mercer Ellington's Band (1945), also with Lucky Millinder in 1945. Regularly with Willie Bryant in 1946, then began free-lancing. Left full-time music but continued to play gigs during the 1960s.

MITCHELL, George
cornet

Born: Louisville, Kentucky, 8th March 1899
Died: Chicago, 27th May 1972

Started on trumpet at the age of 12, received tuition from a neighbour, Mr. Fields. Joined St. Augustine School Band, then became a member of the Louisville Musical Club Brass Band (led by Wilbur Winstead), during the summer months did brief tours with this band (c. 1916-17), then left Louisville to join the Rabbit's Foot Minstrel Show in Mississippi. Toured the South with his show, playing under Mark Veal's leadership, left to work with A. G. Allen's Minstrels for almost a year—received tuition from the Kentucky-born trumpeter Bobby Williams. Returned to home town and continued to play with the L.M.C. Band and Orchestra, also worked in band led by trombonist John Emory. On the recommendation of Bobby Williams, he moved to Chicago in late 1919. Worked with Irving Miller's 'Brown Skin Models' at the Grand Theatre, also spent eight months at the Club Alvadere (later The Nest) with violinist Arthur Sims. Played at The Deluxe from late 1920 with Tony Jackson, Horace Diemer (clarinet), Tubby Hall, Ida Mae Marples, etc. Left Chicago in 1921 to tour with Clarence Miller's Band, this travelling show folded in Hamilton, Ontario, in 1922. Gigged in Detroit, then home to Louisville before joining Doc Holly's Band in Milwaukee. Returned to Chicago in 1923 to join John Wickliffe's Band, then joined Carroll Dickerson at the Sunset Cafe, later worked with Dickerson at the Mahjong Club. In late summer of 1924 joined Doc Cooke, worked at Harmon's Dreamland and at the White City, doubled with Jimmie Noone at the Paradise Gardens, and whilst playing there made the permanent change from trumpet to trumpet-cornet (made by Harry B. Jay). Left Doc Cooke in summer of 1925, then joined Lil Armstrong's Band at Dreamland until spring of 1926. Free-lance recordings included sessions with Jelly Roll Morton's Red Hot Peppers, The New Orleans Wanderers, etc. During 1926 also worked with saxist Vernon Roulette's Band at various Chicago venues including: Jeffrey's Tavern, Hollywood Barn, Cafe de Paris. Worked for Dave Peyton in spring of 1927; then doubled with saxist Verona Biggs at the Owl Theatre until rejoining Doc Cooke's Orchestra in September 1927. With Earl Hines, summer 1929-spring 1930, and summer 1930-spring 1931. With banjoist Jack Ellis (summer 1931). Played club jobs, then left full-time music to become a bank-messenger, gigged with Freddie Williams' Gold Coast Orchestra (1934). During the 1930s played occasional summer park engagements with the W.P.A. Band, also with Elgar's Federal Concert Orchestra (June 1936), but was never a member of the Chicago Symphony Orchestra—as reported elsewhere. Retired from day job in the early 1960s.

MITCHELL, John *Born: Baltimore, Maryland, 1902*
guitar/banjo

Moved to New York in 1921, played with Johnny Dunn in band accompanying vocaliste Edith Wilson, from February 1922 until May 1923 worked with The Plantation Orchestra, left before the band's initial trip to London. Gigged in New York, then joined Sam Wooding Orchestra, subsequently sailed to Europe with Wooding in May 1925. After that unit disbanded in late 1931 became a member of Willie Lewis' Band. Remained with Lewis until 1941, left the band in Holland and was later interned by the Nazis. Was repatriated to the U.S.A. in spring of 1944, soon joined Jimmie Lunceford and remained until April 1946. Left full-time music, has ceased playing; in 1969 was superintendent at a New York apartment block.

MITCHELL, Louis A. *Born: Philadelphia, Pennsylvania, 1885*
drums *Died: Washington, D.C., 2nd September 1957*

Originally worked as an entertainer, playing drums and bandoline. To New York in 1912, formed Southern Symphonists' Quintet, to Europe in summer of 1914. Residency at Piccadilly Restaurant, then back to U.S.A. Returned to Britain in May 1915 with Don Kildare, later toured in variety act 'Jordan and Mitchell', then did solo act playing drums. In January 1917 formed Syncopating Septette which made its debut in Glasgow, that summer reorganised band which subsequently played at the London Palladium before appearing in France. Returned to U.S.A. in 1918, after singing with Jim Europe's Band, organised own Jazz Kings and once again worked in Europe. During the 1920s the band played long residencies in Paris, including a five-year spell at the Casino de Paris. During the 1930s Mitchell organised several business ventures in Europe including ownership of the Grand Duc Club, which he reportedly won in a crap game, then returned to U.S.A.

MOLE, 'Miff' Irving Milfred *Born: Roosevelt, Long Island, N.Y., 11th March 1898*
trombone *Died: New York City, 29th April 1961*

Father was a violinist who led part-time band The Mole Timers (Miff's grandfather was a Londoner). Began on violin at 11, took lessons for three years, during this period also learnt to play piano. At 14 played piano at local movie theatre. After short spell on the alto horn switched to trombone. First professional work at the College Arms, Brooklyn, with Gus Sharp's Orchestra; remained at this job for two years during which time studied with Charlie Randall. Brief stay at the Alamo Club, New York, in band led by pianist-comedian Jimmy Durante, then joined newly organised Original Memphis Five and began working with them at the Harvard Inn, Coney Island. Later the group went on the Orpheum Circuit to Los Angeles (via Chicago) accompanying the entertainers Quinn and Farnum. Four of the Original Memphis Five returned to New York, but Miff remained in California playing in theatre bands, later he spent several months with Abe Lyman at the Sunset Inn, Santa Monica. Rejoined Original Memphis Five at the Dance Caprice, New York, replacing Charlie Panelli. The group played a five-month residency at the Bluebird Cafe, Montreal, Canada, then returned to New York for Rosemont Ballroom residency. Miff left and was replaced by Charlie Panelli. Worked with Sam Lanin before joining Ray Miller in May 1924 for a year, in July 1925 joined Ross Gorman Orchestra, playing for Earl Carroll Vanities Revue, and thus met Red Nichols. During the following years made many recordings in small groups directed by Red Nichols. Played for Roger Wolfe Kahn from c. early 1926 until May 1927, prolific free-lance activities. From September 1927 was staff musician on radio WOR (originally in group directed by Don Voorhees), in 1929 became studio musician for N.B.C. Remained with N.B.C. until 1938 (during this nine-year period

Miff's work varied from working under Toscanini to directing accompanying group for Bessie Smith's broadcasts). Briefly with Charlie Margulis Band from August 1938, then signed for Paul Whiteman and joined the orchestra in December 1938. Left in 1940, ill with stomach ulcer, returned to N.B.C. for a while, began regular teaching. With Benny Goodman from c. August 1942 until August 1943, later that month took own sextet for brief run at Top Hat Club, Toronto. Led own sextet at Nick's, New York, from 31st October 1943, underwent surgery early in 1945, returned to Nick's until illness in spring of 1947. From late 1947 worked mainly in Chicago, led own band at Jazz Ltd., the Bee Hive, the Blue Note, etc., also regular dates with Muggsy Spanier. Returned to New York in 1954, long periods of inactivity, underwent several operations on his hip, began gigging again in 1956. In later years of his life worked at various jobs outside of music, played occasionally during last years of his life. Last gig was with Pee Wee Russell at Sherwood Inn, Long Island, on 12th June 1960.

MONCUR, Grachan — *Born: Miami, Florida, 2nd September 1915*
string bass

His half-brother was Savoy Sultans' leader Al Cooper (Lofton Alfonso Cooper, 1911-81). His son is trombonist Grachan Moncur III. Began playing string-bass, tuba, and trombone during his early teens. Worked with George Kelly's Band in Miami, then moved with his family to Newark, New Jersey. Tuition from Milton Bauzea, specialised on string bass. Began professional career at the Star Ballroom, Newark, subsequently worked with the Matinee Idols on Newark radio station. John Hammond heard a broadcast by this band and arranged for Grachan to take part in several all-star recordings. Became a founder-member of the Savoy Sultans (1937) and remained until they disbanded in 1945. Led own small band with pianist Ace Harris (autumn 1947), then joined band led by tenorist Joe Thomas (1948). Moved to Miami in the 1950s, continues to play regularly. During the late 1960s worked regularly in the Myrtle Jones Trio in Miami Beach, Florida. Noted for his recorded work with Teddy Wilson, Mildred Bailey, Billie Holiday, etc.

MONDELLO, 'Toots' Nuncio — *Born: Boston, Massachusetts. c. 1910*
alto sax/clarinet/arranger

His brother, Peter, and cousin, Victor, were professional musicians. First professional work with Mal Hallett's Band in June 1927. Mainly with Hallett until 1933, also worked with Irving Aaronson. With Joe Haymes and Buddy Rogers (1934), later that year briefly with Benny Goodman, then with Ray Noble and Phil Harris before becoming a studio musician, prolific free-lance recordings and long spell as lead alto with Andre Kostelanetz Radio Orchestra. Rejoined Benny Goodman from May 1939 until July 1940, then resumed studio work until joining U.S. Army in 1943. After release returned to studio work.

MONK, Thelonious Sphere — *Born: Rocky Mount, North Carolina, 10th October 1917*
(original name: Thelious Junior Monk) — *Died: Englewood, New Jersey, 17th February 1982*
piano/composer

His son Thelonious Monk Jr. is a drummer. Began playing piano at age of 11. Accompanied his mother's singing at local Baptist church in New York City where the family had moved during Monk's infancy. In the late 1930s played piano with a travelling evangelist's show, also gigged in and around New York. Worked with Keg Purnell's quartet (c. 1939) prior to becoming house pianist at Minton's Club in New York. Worked with Kenny Clarke's small band at Kelly's Stables, New York (late 1942), worked briefly with Lucky Millinder. With altoist 'Scotty' Scott's Band at Minton's Club (early 1943). With Cootie Williams (1944) and with Coleman Hawkins (1944), then led own small groups until forming own big band in 1959. Because of the 'cabaret card' law then in force Monk was not able to undertake club engagements in New York during the period 1951-57. During the 1960s was mainly active leading own quartet (which featured tenor saxist Charlie Rouse), the big band was occasionally re-assembled. In 1971 and 1972 toured world with The Giants of Jazz with Dizzy Gillespie, saxist Sonny Stitt, etc. Made occasional public appearances during the mid-1970s, activities restricted in the late 1970s by immobility. Received special tribute at President Jimmy Carter's 1978 White House jazz party.

MONTGOMERY, Leo Born: Allenton, Alabama, 9th November 1907
piano

Both parents were amateur musicians. Was raised in Chicago. First gigs with Hayes Alvis at Melrose Park, Illinois c. 1927. During the 1930s worked often with Johnny and Baby Dodds. With Gerald Casey and his Musical Ambassadors (1931), several years with Erskine Tate, briefly with Carroll Dickerson and Freddie Williams. During World War II organised own dancing studios, and began producing floor shows. Played occasionally as late as 1972.

MONTGOMERY, 'Little Brother' Eurreal Wilford Born: Kentwood, Louisiana, 18th April 1906
piano/vocals

Spent early childhood in Vicksburg, Mississippi, and New Orleans. Piano from the age of five, left home at 11, began playing in Holden, Louisiana. Worked in Plaquemine and Freiden, then moved back to New Orleans to play residency at Do Do's Club, later worked with Lee Collins at The Entertainers and with Leonard Parker's Band in Slipdale, Louisiana. Spell in Tallulah (1922), then worked at the Princess Theatre in Vicksburg and doubled in local clubs. Residencies in Jackson, Mississippi, in duo with drummer Henry Russ, subsequently worked in Arkansas City, then worked with Eugene Hutt's Serenaders. In 1928 began touring with Clarence Desdune's Orchestra, left them in Omaha, Nebraska, and travelled to Chicago, subsequently made first recordings for Paramount. From 1931 until 1939 mainly active as leader of own touring band 'The Southland Troubadors' (based in Jackson, Mississippi). Worked in Beaumont, Texas, and in Hattiesburg, then moved to Chicago early in 1942. Solo spots at many clubs including residency at Tin Pan Alley Club, then regularly with Lee Collins at the Victory Club (1945-8), also toured with Kid Ory in 1948. Played many solo residencies throughout the 1950s, occasionally led own band, also worked with Franz Jackson, Chris Clifton, etc. Visited Britain as solo artist in summer of 1960, returned to Chicago, long residency at A Touch of Olde, also worked with the Gold Coast Jazz Band, Franz Jackson, etc. Toured Europe with Blues Package in autumn 1966. Continues to play regularly in Chicago, sometimes leading own band, does occasional touring. Not related to the pianist Leo Montgomery, q.v.

MOORE, 'Bill' William Henry Born: Brooklyn, New York, 1901
trumpet Died: New York, 17th June 1964

Played in the California Ramblers during the early 1920s and was featured on many of their recordings. Long spell with Ben Bernie, combining this with studio work, appearing on many small studio-group recordings. Worked with Don Voorhees, Bert Lown, Lester Lanin, etc., then spent many years in radio-studio orchestras.

MOORE, 'Billy' William Born: Parkersburg, West Virginia, 7th December 1917
(piano/arranger)

Family moved to New York in 1932. Worked in a meat market for several years, began free-lance arranging. From 1939 arranged regularly for Jimmie Lunceford, then scored for Charlie Barnet, Tommy Dorsey, Jan Savitt, etc. Worked as a music publisher in the 1940s, continued regular arranging. Toured with the Peters Sisters as pianist-arranger from 1953 until 1960, then lived in Germany, worked as staff arranger for Berliner Rundfunk Radio (1960-3). In 1964 began touring as accompanist to the Delta Rhythm Boys, then settled in Denmark and worked as a free-lance arranger during the 1970s.

MOORE, 'Bobby' Robert
trumpet

Born: New York City, 1919

Played trumpet from an early age, made debut at Apollo Theatre, New York, during summer of 1935, playing in a talent contest accompanied by Willie Bryant's Orchestra. Subsequently played at the Black Cat, New York, until joining Count Basie (then in Pittsburgh) in March 1937, remaining with the band until c. October 1937. Played briefly with Hot Lips Page Band in 1938; during following year worked in the short-lived band organised by Jimmy Mundy and for a short while in Benny Carter Big Band. Early in 1940 he suffered a complete nervous breakdown, and after spending a short time in Bellevue Hospital, New York, he was committed to the Matteawan Institution. Never returned to professional music.

MOORE, Charles Victor
trumpet

Born: Louisville, Kentucky, 19th February 1908

Mother played piano and trombone. Cornet at 10, moved to Detroit, changed to trumpet. Own band at high school, then worked with Bob Cruzett (1924), Howard Bunts (1924). Organised own band, Chocolate Dandies, in 1926 which played residencies in Detroit and Canada. With Billy Minor's Melodians (1929-32). Joined McKinney's Cotton Pickers early in 1932, left in 1935. Active free-lance, then organised own band in 1945 which was still operating in the 1970s, also played gigs with the Gabriel Brothers New Orleans Jazz Band in and around Detroit during the late 1970s.

MOORE, Freddie
drums/vocals

Born: Washington, North Carolina, 20th August 1900

Played drums from the age of 12, worked in A. G. Allen's Minstrels, then played at the Frolic Theatre, Birmingham, Alabama, before doing extensive touring with travelling shows through Louisiana, Florida, and Cuba. Toured with William Benbow's 'Get Happy' revue (late 1926), then worked with Charlie Creath in St. Louis (c. 1927). Led own seven-piece band at the Savoy, Detroit, before working in New York with Wilbur Sweatman for three years from spring 1928. Briefly with Richard Chetman's Band, then toured with King Oliver (late 1931 to spring 1932). From 1933 until 1937 worked with own trio (Pete Brown and Don Frye) mainly at the Victoria Cafe, New York. Briefly with John Kirby, then free-lancing, four months with Lem Johnson, them again led at the Victoria Cafe in 1940. Worked regularly with Art Hodes in the mid-1940s, also with Sidney Bechet (1945 and 1947) and occasionally with Wilbur de Paris, briefly with Bob Wilbur (1948). Worked in Chicago with Art Hodes (1950), with Conrad Janis in New York (1951), with Wilbur de Paris (1952-4). Toured Europe with Mezz Mezzrow (late 1954 to early 1955), returned to Europe with Sam Price in late 1955. Continued to play during 1960s. With Tony Parenti (1968-70), with Roy Eldridge at Ryan's (summer 1971). Worked often with Graham Stewart during the 1970s, active as a free-lance during early 1980s.

MOORE, Monette
vocals

Born: Gainesville, Texas, May 1902
Died: California, November 1962

School in Kansas City, Missouri. Moved to New York in the early 1920s, made recording debut in 1923, prolific recording career including many sessions issued under pseudonyms. During the 1920s worked in Chicago, Dallas, Oklahoma City, etc., then appeared regularly with Charlie Johnson's Band at Small's, New York. Did vaudeville and club work during the 1930s including three years as understudy to Ethel Waters. In 1937 worked in Chicago with Zinky Cohn. Residency at 721 Club Harlem in 1941, then played dates in Cleveland and Detroit before moving to California in November 1942. Long residency at The Casablanca in Hollywood, then worked at the Streets of Paris, Hollywood, from 1945. Appeared in New York in 1947, then returned to West Coast, featured in James P. Johnson's 'Sugar Hill' show in California. During the 1950s left the profession and worked as a housemaid and women's room attendant in Los Angeles, continued to play local engagements. From summer of 1961 sang with the Young Men of New Orleans, whilst appearing with that group at Disneyland suffered a fatal heart attack.

Film appearances include: 'Yes Sir Mr. Bones' (1951) and 'The Outsider'.

MOORE, Oscar Frederic
guitar

Born: Austin, Texas, 25th December 1912
Died: Las Vegas, 8th October 1981

At 16 he and his guitarist brother, Johnny, formed their own band. Joined Nat 'King' Cole in autumn of 1937 and remained with him for 10 years, except for a very brief spell in the U.S. Army during the spring of 1944. In September 1947 left to work in Los Angeles with his brother's group The Three Blazers, then did extensive free-lance work, including leading own recording groups. During the late 1950s left full-time music to work as a bricklayer, then returned to professional playing.

MOORE, 'Big Chief' Russell
trombone/vocals

Born: On an Indian reservation near Sacaton, Arizona, 13th August 1912
Died: Nyack, New York, 15th December 1983

At 12 moved to Blue Island, Illinois, and began studying music with his uncle, William T. Moore. Tutored on trumpet, trombone, and french horn, then specialised on trombone. Worked on railroads, then did further studies at Sherman Institute in California. With Tony Corral's Band in Tucson, then worked in Lionel Hampton's Band (1935). Briefly in Eddie Barefield's Big Band in summer of 1936. Gigged in California, then long tour with Eli Rice which ended abruptly in Monroe, Louisiana. Worked with Papa Celestin (1939), then briefly with Harlan Leonard and Ernie Fields, with Noble Sissle (1939-41). With Louis Armstrong's Big Band from 1944 until summer of 1947. Worked occasionally with Sidney Bechet (1947-9 and 1951). To Europe for Paris Jazz Festival (May 1949). Led own band, then worked with Pee Wee Russell and Ruby Braff in late 1952. Toured Europe with Mezz Mezzrow from February 1953. Led own band during the 1950s, also worked with Eddie Condon, Wild Bill Davison, Tony Parenti, etc. During the 1960s continued to play regularly; with Louis Armstrong's All Stars from January 1964 until spring 1965, spell in hospital (late 1965). Resumed leading own band, also guest dates in Canada, also worked with Lester Lanin's Orchestra. Despite ill health maintained working schedule during 1981 and 1982, including tour of Europe with Keith Smith.

MOORE, 'Slim' Alton
trombone

Born: Selma, Alabama, 7th October 1908
Died: New York, 1978

Began on baritone horn, taught by Professor William Bolton, then switched to trombone. At 17 played in the band led by John Collins' mother, Georgia Barlowe. From 1926-7 worked with travelling medicine shows, then toured with Eddie Lemon's Dashing Dinah Show. Early in 1928 worked briefly with Gonzelle White Show, then touring with various bands until joining Gene Coy's Band in Dallas (October 1929 to March 1930). With Jesse Stone and Jap Allen's Band until joining Blanche Calloway in April 1931. Left after three years to settle in New York, joined Jack Butler's Band at Circle Ballroom, New York, in late 1934. In the following year worked with Charlie Skeete before joining Bobby Neal's Band. Played in Jackie Jackson's Band in Boston in 1936 before rejoining Blanche Calloway briefly. During 1937 played with pianist Maurice Rocco's Band, then spent several months with Leon Gross Orchestra including trip to Cuba. In 1939 played with various bands including: Hot Lips Page's, Charlie Johnson's, and Tiny Bradshaw's. Toured with Fats Waller in 1940 before joining Coleman Hawkins' Big Band. Worked with Horace Henderson for two months in autumn of 1941, then a year with Ella Fitzgerald Band before working in New York and California with Benny Carter (including appearance in 'Stormy Weather' film). Several stints with Hot Lips Page during mid-1940s, worked for various leaders including: Dizzy Gillespie, Herman 'Humpy' Flintall, Lucky Millinder, and Rex Stewart. With Louis Armstrong Big Band from 1946 until July 1947, then briefly with Herbie Fields' Band. Two years (1948-9) working mainly with Stafford 'Pazuza' Simon, then similar time with tenorist Freddie Mitchell Band. A year of free-lancing before leaving full-time music in 1952. Continued gigging, including participation in the Fletcher Henderson Reunion Bands in 1957. During the 1960s played trombone and euphonium in the Prince Hall Symphonic Band in New York and trombone with Edgar Battle.

M

MORAND, Herb
trumpet/vocals

Born: New Orleans, Louisiana, 1905
Died: New Orleans, Louisiana, 23rd February 1952

Brother of Maurice (drums); their step-sister was vocaliste Lizzie Miles. Began playing trumpet at the age of 13, at 18 did first professional work with Nat Towle's Creole Harmony Kings, worked in Oklahoma with this New Orleans Band for almost a year. After a brief return to New Orleans he left to tour Mexico in a band he co-led with bassist Charlie Towles (Nat's father). Then to New York, played jobs accompanying Lizzie Miles and spent several months in Cliff Jackson's Krazy Cats (no recordings). Returned to New Orleans, played regularly in Chris Kelly's Band, led own band and did various parade gigs. Moved to Chicago in the late 1920s, joined J. Frank Terry's Chicago Nightingales with W. McDonald and his Chicago Ramblers (1932), then long spell with pianist William Barbee and drummer 'Little' Joe Lindsey at Tony's Tavern (1934), also did recordings with Johnny Dodds and Frank Melrose. Then played regularly in the Harlem Hamfats (mostly in Chicago); this group made many recordings from 1936-8. Also played on the lake steamer S.S. North Shore and at Bratton's Rendezvous with Meade 'Lux' Lewis. Teamed up with Jimmy Bertrand for residency at The Firehouse, Chicago (1941), then returned to New Orleans. Led own band through the 1940s, including residencies at Mama Lou's, Lake Pontchartrain, and at the Rainbow Inn, but also gigged with George Lewis, becoming a regular member of his band in spring 1948 for job at Manny's Tavern. Led own band at The Rainbow Inn in spring of 1950—also did recordings early in 1950, then ill health caused his retirement. For most of his later life he was beset by weight problems—at one time he tipped the scales at over 300 pounds.

MOREHOUSE, Chauncey
drums/percussion

Born: Niagara Falls, New York, 11th March 1902
Died: Medford, New Jersey, 31st October 1980

Lived in Chambersburg, Pennsylvania, from 1906 to 1921. Whilst still at school played in duo with his pianist father for silent movies, also played in high school orchestra and with local Queen City Band. In 1919 formed own Versatile Five (which included Art Weems), left high school to travel to Pittsburgh with the Harrison and Hollins Group, then gigged for a year before joining Paul Specht's Society Serenaders for their debut in Detroit (1922). Remained with Specht for almost three years, then brief spells with Howard Lanin and Ted Weems before joining Jean Goldkette Orchestra at Graystone Ballroom, Detroit, in 1925. With Goldkette until summer of 1927—during this period recorded with Bix Beiderbecke, Frank Trumbauer, etc., etc. Was a member of short-lived Adrian Rollini Band at New Yorker Restaurant (September 1927), then joined Don Voorhees for theatre and radio work. Worked mostly as a studio musician from 1929 onwards, regular radio work and prolific recordings. In spring 1938 briefly led his own band in New York, during which he featured his own specially designed, chromatically tuned percussion (Stan King sharing drum duties). Continued to work as a studio musician for over 30 years. During the late 1960s played bass drum each summer with the Goldman Band for their appearances at the New York Central Park summer concerts. Appeared at several jazz festivals during the 1970s.

MORGAN, 'Al' Albert
string bass/tuba/vocals

Born: New Orleans, Louisiana, 19th August 1908
Died: Los Angeles, California, 14th April 1974

Brother of bandleader-trumpeter Sam Morgan (1895-1936), other brothers: Isaiah (trumpet), 1897-1966, and Andrew (sax/clarinet), born: 1903. Early efforts on clarinet and drums, then started playing on a three-string bass (c. 1918)—lessons from Simon Marrero. Did first gigs in band led by his brother, Isaiah—never worked with his brother Sam. Travelled to Pensacola, Florida, in 1923 with Lee Collins, whilst in Florida worked with trumpeter Mack Thomas and with the Pensacola Jazzers, then returned to New Orleans. Joined Davey Jones' Astoria Strutters on string bass then, after tuition from Jones, began doubling on double B-flat tuba. Left to work for two weeks in Sidney Desvigne's Orchestra on the S.S. Island Queen, then returned to New Orleans before joining Fate Marable on S.S. Capitol (1925). Remained with Marable for four years, during which time he studied under St. Louis bassist Cecil Scott. Left Marable at close of summer season 1929, returned to New Orleans, recorded with Jones-Collins Astoria Eight, then journeyed to New York. Recorded with the Mound City Blue Blowers. With Otto Hardwick's Band at the Hot Feet Club, New York (c. 1930), then with Vernon Andrade's Orchestra until joining Cab Calloway from June 1932 until the spring of 1936 (including tour of Europe 1934). Left Cab in California, organised band with Eddie Barefield, later led own band and worked with Fats Waller and with Louis Armstrong in the film 'Going Places'. Regularly with Les Hite during the late 1930s and with that band to New York in 1940. Left in spring 1941 to join Zutty Singleton's Trio, also did many free-lance recordings in various small groups. With Sabby Lewis Band from March 1942 until March 1944, then a year with Louis Jordan before rejoining Sabby Lewis. Remained with Lewis for over 10 years, occasionally worked for other leaders in Boston. Moved to California in February 1957; worked with Joe Darensbourg, Jack McVea, and pianiste-vocaliste Nellie Lutcher, also appeared in the films 'The Gene Krupa Story' ('Drum Crazy') and 'King Creole'. In 1960 began working with pianist Buddy Banks, throughout the late 1960s this duo was resident at the Tudor Inn, Norwalk, California.

MORGAN, Loumell
piano

Born: Raleigh, North Carolina, 28th October 1919
Died: New York City, 11th December 1983

Sister Ella Mae Morgan also plays piano, she was Loumell's first teacher. First gigs with Capitol City Aces in North Carolina. First professional work was touring with C. S. Belton's Band in the mid-1930s, then worked with Tiny Bradshaw, Baron Lee, Slim Gaillard & Slam Stewart, and Chris Columbus before forming own highly successful trio in the 1940s, which played from coast-to-coast for many years and recorded. During the 1970s continued to lead own group which worked mainly in the New York metropolitan area.

MORGAN, Russ
trombone/arranger

Born: Scranton, Pennsylvania, 28th April 1904
Died: Las Vegas, Nevada, 7th August 1969

Both sons are musicians: Jack (trombone) and David (guitar). Sold first arrangements whilst still in his teens. Worked with Paul Specht during the early 1920s (including tour of Europe), also with Billy Lustig's Scranton Sirens and Eddie Gilligan's Band before working as a musical director for Jean Goldkette's organisation. Led the Book-Cadillac Hotel Orchestra, Capitol Theatre Orchestra, etc. Later worked for Vincent Lopez, Phil Spitalny, Ted Fio Rito, etc., etc. Prolific free-lance arranger for various bands including Fletcher Henderson (also arranged 'Body and Soul' for Louis Armstrong). Recording executive from the 1930s, from 1935 led own big commercial band.

MORR, 'Skip'
(real name: Charles William Coolidge)
trombone

Born: Chicago, Illinois, 28th March 1912
Died: Ross, California, 1962

From a musical family. Began on drums, changed to trombone whilst at high school in California. Graduated Northwestern University in 1934, worked with Ted Weems, Bill Hogan and Henry Busse. To Hollywood in 1942, worked with Artie Shaw, Charlie Barnet, etc., then worked in studio orchestras. During the 1950s, worked in many Dixieland bands with Wingy Manone, Marty Marsala, Muggsy Spanier, etc.

MORRIS, Marlowe
piano/organ/arranger

Born: New York City, 16th May 1915
Died: New York c.1977

Nephew of Thomas Morris. First musical tuition from his father; played drums, harmonica, and ukelele before beginning on piano. Worked with June Clark's Band (late 1935 to early 1936), then solo piano at various clubs in New York. During 1939 worked with The Spirits of Rhythm at the Herock Club, New York, with Eric Henry's Band in 1940, then joined Coleman Hawkins' Band in late 1940 until Army call-up in February 1941. After release worked with Scoville Browne (1942), then with Al Sears at Renaissance Ballroom, New York, and on summer 1943 U.S.O. tour. Then worked with Sid Catlett until October 1944.

With 'Doc' (Moran) Wheeler in summer of 1945, then worked with Eddie South until joining Tiny Grimes early in 1946. Led own trio for a while, then temporarily left full-time music to do post office work for two years. In 1949-50 worked in Atlantic City and began specialising on organ. During the 1950s and 1960s worked mainly solo, New York residencies at Basie's Club, Small's, Shalimar, etc. Worked for New York Post Office (1971).

Marlowe Morris was featured in the film 'Jammin' the Blues'.

MORRIS, Thomas — *Born: New York City. c. 1898*
cornet — *Deceased*

Uncle of Marlowe Morris. Led own band in New York during the 1920s, also featured on several Clarence Williams recordings. Toured with the Mildred Franklin Show in 1927. During the late 1930s worked as a red cap at Grand Central Station, New York, then as Brother Pierre joined a religious sect headed by Father Divine.

MORROW, Buddy — *Born: New Haven, Connecticut, 8th February 1919*
(real name: Muni 'Moe' Zudekoff)
trombone

His brother, 'Al', is a professional trumpeter. Played trombone from age of 12, did local gigs, then joined the Yale Collegians. Moved to New York, studied at Juilliard and began gigging, recorded with Sharkey Bonano (1936). Briefly with Eddie Duchin's Orchestra before joining Artie Shaw in late 1936, subsequently with Vincent Lopez, Bunny Berigan, and Richard Himber, then joined Tommy Dorsey (summer 1938). With Paul Whiteman for a year from early 1939, then radio-studio work until joining Bob Crosby from summer 1941 until summer 1942. Served in the U.S. Navy as a bandsman until December 1944. Returned to studio work, then joined Jimmy Dorsey in May 1945 until forming own band (and adopting new name) in late 1945. Disbanded in 1946, returned to studio work, then in 1951 re-formed own band which achieved considerable commercial success. Few dates with World's Greatest Jazz Band (1970). Prolific session work, visited England in summer of 1971. Led the 'Tommy Dorsey' Orchestra during the 1970s and 1980s.

MORTON, 'Benny' Henry Sterling — *Born: New York City, 31st January 1907*
trombone

Step-father was a violinist. Studied at Textile High School in New York and began gigging with school friends. Spent several years on and off with Billy Fowler's Orchestra from 1924. With Fletcher Henderson (1926-8). With Chick Webb (1930-1), then rejoined Fletcher Henderson (March 1931). With Don Redman from 1932 until 1937, joined Count Basie in October 1937. Left Basie in January 1940 to join Joe Sullivan's Band at Cafe Society. With Teddy Wilson Sextet from July 1940 until 1943, then worked in Ed Hall's Sextet until forming own band in September 1944 (had previously led own recording-studio band in 1933). Disbanded in January 1946 and worked for several years playing in Broadway theatre orchestras. Did studio work in late 1950s and 1960s, also free-lanced with many bandleaders including Henry Allen at The Metropole (1960), in Las Vegas with Ted Lewis (summer 1964), later that year toured Africa with Paul Taubman's Concert Orchestra. In 1967 subbed for Vic Dickenson in the Saints and Sinners, also toured Europe with the Top Brass package. With Wild Bill Davison (1968), then again with Saints and Sinners with Bobby Hackett (spring 1970), Sy Oliver (1970-1), Ray Nance (autumn 1971). With World's Greatest Jazz Band (1973-1974), playing curtailed by illness (1977), resumed gigging (1978).

MORTON, 'Jelly Roll' — *Born: New Orleans, Louisiana, 20th October 1890*
real name: Ferdinand Lemott — *Died: Los Angeles, California, 10th July 1941*
piano/composer/arranger/vocals

Morton's imagination led him to apply a smoke-screen around hard-and-fast details of his origins. He gave his original name as Ferdinand Joseph La Menthe, and said that he had taken the name Morton from a step-father. Following Morton's words his birth-date was usually given as Freeport, Louisiana, 20th September 1885, but thanks to inspired research by Lawrence Gushee it became clear that Morton was born in New Orleans in 1890, and that his original family name was LaMothe. He was baptised Lemott; his step father's name was actually Mouton. None of these revelations diminish the man's superb talents. He played guitar and trombone a little before specialising on piano. He played in New Orleans sporting houses c. 1906, then moved temporarily to Biloxi, and Meridian Mississippi, and played in those towns before returning to New Orleans. He spent a couple of years pool-hustling and playing piano through Louisiana and Mississippi then gradually worked further afield visiting Missouri, Illinois, California, New York, etc. Some of his time was spent working with a touring vaudeville troupe, for a while he worked as a comedian-musician in a double act with a partner called Rose, he was part of McCabe's Troubadours. Morton gigged in Kansas City and St. Louis then moved to Chicago c. late 1914 for residencies at the Deluxe and Elite No. 2, led own band. In 1915 went to San Francisco to appear at the Exposition, returned to Chicago, later played solo piano at the Fairfax Hotel, Detroit. Did a bout of touring, playing piano and also engaging in several non-musical enterprises. Returned to California (c. 1917) and played at various clubs in and around Los Angeles including Cadillac Cafe, Baron Long's in Watts, and the U.S. Grand Hotel. Ran own club-hotel in Los Angeles, then organised own small band for residency at the Regent Hotel, Vancouver. After a vacation in Alaska, worked in Caspar, Wyoming, then briefly with George Morrison's Band in Denver, Colorado. Returned to Los Angeles, organised band that toured throughout California, reverted to solo piano for brief sojourn in Tijuana, worked in San Diego (1921), then returned to Los Angeles, gigged at the Jump Steady Club and led a short-lived career as a boxing promoter. Moved back to Chicago in 1923, recorded with The New Orleans Rhythm Kings (July 1923). During the next five years remained based in Chicago, regularly organised own recording sessions including the first of the Red Hot Peppers and for a time worked as staff arranger for the Melrose Publishing House. During this period Morton rarely played in Chicago, he did, however, do regular touring, usually fronting a band, very occasionally working as a sideman under other leaders. He toured briefly as second pianist in Fate Marable's Band (c. 1924) and for one short period worked in South Bend, Indiana, Davenport, Iowa, etc., with W. C. Handy, who fronted Morton's Band (and occasionally played cornet). Later, Morton did regular tours on the M.C.A. circuit, fronting bands led by pianist Gene Anderson, pianist Henry Crowder (summer 1927). Later that year fronted The Alabamians on tour. Moved to New York (c. February 1928), played residency at the Rose Danceland during summer of 1928 and did extensive recording. In late 1928 organised own big touring band, during 1929 and 1930 did extensive touring: York, Pennsylvania; Pittsburgh; Baltimore; through the New England States and Ohio, etc. The band was variously billed as the Red Hot Peppers or Jelly Roll Morton and his Chicago Syncopators. Morton settled in New York during the early 1930s, lost most of his money in an ill-fated cosmetics business, but continued to play regularly. Led own Orchestra at the Checker Club, Harlem (April 1931), headed own 'Speeding Along' revue, Jamaica Theatre, New York (May 1931), led at the Lido Ballroom, New York (October 1932), also accompanied Lillyn Brown in 'Headin' for Harlem' show and played briefly in Laura Prampin's Orchestra at Coney Island. Played occasionally at Pod's and Jerry's, New York, then became resident pianist at The Red Apple Club (7th Avenue and 135th Street), whilst working there took part in recording session organised by Wingy Manone (August 1934). Again led own touring band in 1935-6, then settled in Washington, D.C. After a period of musical inactivity he began playing at the Jungle Club in Washington from late 1936 until a brief return to New York in September 1938. (From May until July 1938 took part in regular recording sessions for the Library of Congress.) Settled in New York from late 1938, organised publishing company and did several recording sessions, also did occasional gigs leading own small band until forced to restrict activities through ill health. Moved to California in late 1940, formed new music company and organised own small group (this led to a dispute with the local musicians' union and Morton was subsequently fined $45). Early in 1941 his health began to fail rapidly, he entered a private sanatorium in June 1941, but soon returned home. He was subsequently admitted to the Los Angeles County General Hospital shortly before his death.

'Mr Jelly Roll' by Alan Lomax first published in 1950.

'Mr Jelly Lord' by Laurie Wright first published in 1980.

MORTON, **'Flutes' Norvel E.**
saxes/clarinet/flute

Born: c. 1900
Died: Detroit, Michigan, 1962

Lived in Chicago for many years, worked regularly with Erskine Tate and Dave Peyton, briefly with Louis Armstrong and Earl Hines. With Eddie King's Band (1932), with Reuben Reeves (1933-4), brief spell with Noble Sissle. His brother, Benny, was a saxophone-clarinet player; wrongly referred to as Benny Moten.

MOSBY, **Curtis**
drums/leader

Born: Kansas City, Missouri, 1895
Died: California. c. 1960

Toured with Tennessee Ten, then led own band in Chicago (c. 1918). Moved to California, led own band (and ran music shop) in Oakland (1921), then toured with Mamie Smith's Jazz Hounds until 1923. Led own Kansas City Blue Blowers in Los Angeles for many years including residencies at Solomon's Dance Hall, Lincoln Gardens, and Apex Club, etc., occasionally played violin. Fronted own band for 'Change Your Luck' touring show during the early 1930s. During the 1930s and 1940s ran own clubs and acted as a promoter. Absent from the music scene (1947-9), then opened own Oasis Club (1949).

MOSLEY, **'Snub'**
(real name: Lawrence Leo Mosely)
trombone/slide-sax/vocals

Born: Little Rock, Arkansas, 29th December 1905
Died: New York City, 21st July 1981

Studied in Cincinnati. With Eugene Crook, then joined Alphonso Trent—remained with Trent from 1926 until 1933. Worked with Claude Hopkins (1934-6), Fats Waller (1935), Louis Armstrong (1937), led own band in 1936; from 1938 led own band regularly. Many long residencies including: Pelham Heath Inn (1938), Woodmere Country Club, Long Island (1939), Queen's Terrace, Long Island (1940), California and Chicago (1942-3), Duluth, Minneapolis (1944), etc., etc. During the 1940s and 1950s did many U.S.O. tours including visit to Great Britain in 1952. Has continued to lead own small groups in the U.S.A., regular appearances at the Stagecoach, New Jersey, The Frolic Inn, New York, etc., etc. Has for many years played an instrument that he designed himself—the slide-saxophone. Toured Europe (1978).

MOTEN, **Bennie**
piano/leader/composer

Born: Kansas City, Missouri, 13th November 1894
Died: Kansas City, Missouri, 2nd April 1935

Uncle of pianist-accordionist Ira 'Buster' Moten (1904-65). Bennie's mother was a pianiste, at 12 he played baritone horn in Lacy Blackburn's Juvenile Brass Band for a year, then specialised on piano. Gigged with local bands, then became founder-member of B.B. and D. Band in Kansas City, later formed own band. During the early 1920s this operated originally as a five-piece unit, then Moten gradually augmented it until by the late 1920s it had become a big band. The band began recording in 1923, but worked mainly through the Middle West until the late 1920s when they played residencies at the Paradise Ballroom, Buffalo, Celeron Park Ballroom, New York, and Lafayette, New York. They returned to Kansas City for summer residency, then again visited New York. The band did wide-ranging tours in the late 1920s and early 1930s, during this period Moten had several bands working under his auspices. Owing to diminishing success he temporarily combined forces with George E. Lee, then again led own band. He died from complications following a tonsillectomy. The remnants of his band were taken over by Count Basie.

Two other musicians were also known as Benny Moten: a sax/clarinet player and a bassist—Clarence Lemont Moten q.v.

MOTEN, **'Benny' Clarence Lemont**
string-bass

Born: New York City, 30th November 1916
Died: New Orleans, Louisiana, 27th March 1977

Worked with Hot Lips Page, Jerry Jerome in 1941. In 1942 began working with Henry Allen, with whom he worked for long periods during the 1950s and 1960s. Left Henry

Allen in 1949, worked in Chicago with Eddie South, and with Stuff Smith (1950-51), then with pianist Ivory Joe Hunter (1952), Arnett Cobb (1953-54). With Ella Fitzgerald (1956). Toured Africa with Wilbur de Paris in spring of 1957, also worked with de Paris in New York. During the early 1960s accompanied vocaliste Dakota Staton prior to rejoining Henry Allen. Active free-lance during the late 1960s and early 1970s. Died of a heart attack whilst preparing to sail on a cruise as part of Earle Warren's Band.

MUELLER, 'Gus' Gustave
clarinet

Born: New Orleans, Louisiana, 17th April 1890
Died: California, 16th December 1965

Played regularly in Papa Laine's Reliance Bands before moving to Chicago with Tom Brown's Band in May 1915. Left Brown in August 1915, subsequently worked for Baron Long. Service in U.S. Army during World War I. Joined Paul Whiteman in California (c. 1919), worked briefly under trumpeter Henry Busse's leadership at the Alexandria Hotel then, together with the rest of the band, followed Whiteman East. Featured with Whiteman until c. 1924, then moved back to California. Continued to play during the 1940s, mostly gigging with hill-billy bands.

MULLENS, 'Moon' Edward
trumpet/arranger

Born: Mayhew, Mississippi, 11th May 1916
Died: 7th April 1977

Raised in Chicago. Worked with Frankie Jaxon, Willy Guy, etc., before moving to New York. With Chris Columbus, Hot Lips Page (1938), Earl Bostic, again with Chris Columbus (1941), then worked for Benny Carter before and after serving in U.S. Army. With Louis Armstrong Big Band (1946-7), then joined Cab Calloway. With tenorist Joe Thomas before joining Lionel Hampton in December 1949. Left Hampton in late 1959 to join Duke Ellington. Left Duke to run own photographic business.

MUNDY, 'Jimmy' James
tenor sax/violin/arranger/composer

Born: Cincinnati, Ohio, 28th June 1907
Died: New York, 24th April 1983

Began playing violin during early childhood, by the age of 12 was touring with an evangelist orchestra, playing a variety of instruments. Settled in Chicago, worked with Erskine Tate, Carroll Dickerson, etc. Moved to Washington, D.C., specialised on tenor sax and arranging, worked with the White Brothers (1926), Elmer Calloway, pianist Eddie White's Band (1929), Duke Eglin's Bell Hops (1930), then joined band led by drummer Tommy Myles. Whilst with Myles sold some arrangements to Earl Hines, subsequently joined Earl Hines from late 1932 until 1936. Arranged for Benny Goodman from 1935, worked as staff arranger for Goodman from 1936. Led own short-lived big band in 1939, then free-lance arranging for many leaders including: Count Basie, Paul Whiteman, Gene Krupa, Bob Crosby, Glen Gray, etc. After service in U.S. Army continued regular arranging. From 1959 worked in France as musical director for Barclay Records, returned to New York and resumed free-lance arranging.

MURPHY, 'Spud' Lyle
arranger/composer/saxes/clarinet

Born: Salt Lake City, Utah, 19th August 1908

Played clarinet, trumpet, trombone, and mellophone during school days. Mostly self-taught as an arranger. Worked in Mexico City on tenor and clarinet (1925), then did a stint in ship's band sailing to China. With Jimmy Joy (1927-8), Russ Gorman (1928), Tracy Brown in Pittsburgh (1929-30), Austin Wylie in Cleveland (1930-1), Jan Garber (1931-2), Mal Hallett (1933), Joe Haymes (1934). Staff arranger for Benny Goodman (1935-7), also scored regularly for Glen Gray. Worked on staff of publishing house, then moved to California. Led own band (mainly in Hollywood) during the late 1930s and early 1940s, then prolific free-lance arranging. Later made extensive studies of the 12-tone system.

MURPHY, 'Turk' Melvin *Born: Palermo, California, 16th December 1915*
trombone/composer

Helped Lu Watters organize the Yerba Buena Band in the late 1930s, worked regularly with Watters during the 1940s. With Marty Marsala in 1951, then worked consistently with own band which played long residencies in California during the 1950s, and also played dates in New Orleans, New York City, etc. From September 1960 thru February 1978 led band at own club in San Francisco (Earthquake McGoon's). During that period his band played at various other venues including Disneyland, they also toured Australia and Europe in 1974. Murphy was featured at the St. Louis, Missouri, Ragtime Festival in 1977. Band featured at Breda, Holland, Festival 1981. During the 1980s continued to play residency at Earthquake McGoon's (by then established at a new venue).

'Just For The Record' (a survey of Turk Murphy's career) by Jim Coggin was first published in 1982.

MURRAY, Don *Born: Joliet, Illinois, 7th June 1904*
clarinet/saxes/violin *Died: Los Angeles, California, 2nd June 1929*

Son of a minister, attended Englewood High School in Chicago, later studied at Northwestern University. Played tenor with the New Orleans Rhythm Kings (c. 1923), then moved to Detroit to join Jean Goldkette (doubling baritone), except for absences through illness, remained with Jean Goldkette until September 1927. During this period made recordings with Bix Beiderbecke, later did extensive free-lance recordings. Worked in brief-lived Adrian Rollini Big Band (September-October 1927), then regular work in Broadway theatre orchestras, mainly under direction of Don Voorhees (1928). Joined Ted Lewis; as a member of Lewis' Band, took part in the filming of 'Is Everybody Happy' at the Warner Brothers' Studio, Hollywood. Whilst working on this film Murray met his death. He was found unconscious, the head injuries that he sustained were alleged to have resulted from his falling against a parked car. He was taken to hospital and appeared to be making a recovery, but died shortly afterwards.

MUSSO, Vido William *Born: Carrini, Sicily, 17th January 1913*
tenor sax/clarinet *Died: Rancho Mirage, California, 9th January 1982*

Family emigrated to Detroit in 1920. Began playing clarinet in the late 1920s, moved to Los Angeles in 1930. Worked with Everett Hoagland (1933), then spells with various leaders including trip to Hawaii with Rube Wolff's Band. Led own band early in 1936, then worked in band led by arranger-pianist Gil Evans before joining Benny Goodman in August 1936. Left Goodman in December 1937, worked with Gene Krupa (April-June 1938), then led own band (brief return to Goodman in October 1939). With Harry James from January 1940 until April 1941, re-formed own band, then rejoined Benny Goodman until June 1942, then began leading the band that had been working under Bunny Berigan's leadership. With Woody Herman late 1942 to October 1943. Spell in U.S. Marines, then did defence-plant work before joining Tommy Dorsey (spring 1945), left Dorsey in late 1945, re-formed own band. Mainly with Stan Kenton from 1946 until spring 1947. From then onwards was mainly active leading own bands on the West Coast. Underwent operation on his hip in 1975, but resumed playing and recording.

MUSSULLI, 'Boots' Henry W. *Born: Milford, Massachusetts, 18th November 1917*
saxes *Died: Norfolk, Massachusetts, 23rd September 1967*

Played clarinet at 12. Worked in Massachusetts with Mal Hallett's Band. Joined Teddy Powell in 1943, with Stan Kenton (1944-47), then worked with Vido Musso, Gene Krupa, and Charlie Ventura before rejoining Stan Kenton in 1954. During the late 1950s worked with bands led by pianist Toshiko Akiyoshi and trumpeter Herb Pomeroy. During the 1960s led own group, and taught in his home state, regular free-lance activities restricted by onset of cancer.

M

MYERS, 'Bumps' Hubert Maxwell
tenor, alto, baritone saxes

Born: Clarksburg, West Virginia, 22nd August 1912
Died: Los Angeles, California, 9th April 1968

Family moved to California in 1921. First professional work at 17 with Earl Whaley's Band in Seattle. During the early 1930s worked for many bandleaders in Los Angeles: Lorenzo Flennoy, Curtis Mosby, Jim Wyn, Charlie Echols, Leon Herriford. With Buck Clayton's Big Band to Shanghai in 1934. Returned to Los Angeles in 1936, worked with Lionel Hampton and again with Charlie Echols before long spell in Les Hite's Band. Played in small band led by Lee Young and remained on tenor when Lester Young joined the band as co-leader (May 1941). Briefly with Jimmie Lunceford in 1942, then again with Lee and Lester Young in New York. Joined Benny Carter's Band in Los Angeles (spring 1943), few months in U.S. Army, then rejoined Carter in September 1943. Brief return to Jimmie Lunceford in summer of 1945, also recorded with Sid Catlett. From the late 1940s was frequently employed as a free-lance session musician, also played regularly for Benny Carter and worked occasionally in California with Jake Porter and Tommy Stewart. In December 1961 began three months of touring with Horace Henderson's Band. Inactive through poor health during last years of his life.

Was once the husband of vocaliste Evelyne Myers, they were divorced, and Evelyne later became Mrs. Marshall Royal.

MYERS, 'Serious' Wilson Ernest
string bass/guitar/arranger/vocals

Born: Germantown, Pennsylvania, 7th October 1906

Gained nickname because of deep interest in classical music. Originally a drummer, played in touring show backing Bessie Smith, also learnt clarinet and trombone. Switched to guitar and banjo in 1925; worked with King Oliver in 1931. Changed to string bass, regularly with Bechet-Ladnier New Orleans Feetwarmers from September 1932. Following year to France with Lucky Millinder—in 1934 with Willie Bryant Band. Long spell with Spirits of Rhythm until sailing to France in spring of 1937 to join Roger Devereaux at Chez Florence, Paris. Joined Willie Lewis in The Hague during April 1938, left to lead own band in Chamonix during winter of 1938—continued to lead own band until returning to U.S.A. late in 1939. With Sidney Bechet Quartet at Nick's New York, early in 1940, then rejoined Spirits of Rhythm in June 1940. Arranged for Jimmy Dorsey, then led own quartet in Hartford, Connecticut, before joining Everett Barksdale (late 1942). Played with Mezz Mezzrow at Nick's from May 1943, then extensive gigging before playing in trio Plink, Plank, Plunk (with pianist Bob Mosley and drummer 'Tiger' Haynes) early in 1944. Briefly with De Paris Brothers in late 1944, also with pianist Sinclair Brooks Trio before joining Rex Stewart Small Band early in 1946, left to join Duke Ellington in Baltimore 8th March 1946, left two months later to rejoin Rex Stewart. Then formed own small band which operated for many years, mainly in Philadelphia; left professional music and devoted a great deal of time propagating his religious beliefs.

N

NANCE, 'Ray' Willis
trumpet/violin/vocals/dancer

Born: Chicago, Illinois, 10th December 1913
Died: New York, 28th January 1976

Began on piano at six, three years later began studying violin, studied for seven years at Chicago Music College with Max Fishel. Attended Wendell Phillips High School and began doubling on trumpet, tuition from Major N. Clark-Smith. Studied for a term at Lane College, Jackson, Tennessee, played and broadcast with college band The Rhythm Rascals. Sang and played in Chicago night clubs from 1932, led own sextet at Dave's Cafe for several years, also played residency at Midnite Club (1935) and did short stints in Buffalo, East St. Louis, etc. Joined Earl Hines from February 1937 until December 1938, then with Horace Henderson (doubling violin and trumpet) from January 1939 until March 1940. Played at Joe Hughe's De Luxe Club before joining Duke Ellington in November 1940. Left Duke in 1944 to lead own small group, also worked briefly as a single in late 1945; returned to Duke and was a regular member of the band until September 1963—temporary absence from music in late 1961. (In 1948 Ray Nance, Duke Ellington, and vocaliste Kay Davis toured British variety theatres.) Ray switched to cornet in 1961. Led own small band in 1964, also worked for Paul Lavalle at New York's World Fair (1964 and 1965). Made solo tour of Europe in summer of 1966, worked with Henri Chaix's Band in Switzerland (1967). From late 1966-9 worked regularly with clarinettist Sol Yaged. Occasionally with Duke Ellington (1965-71), dates with George Wein (1970-1). Own quartet (autumn 1971).

NANTON, 'Tricky Sam' Joe
real name: Joseph N. Irish
trombone

Born: New York City, 1st February 1904
Died: San Francisco, California, 20th July 1946

Both parents from the West Indies. First professional work with Cliff Jackson, then two years mainly in pianist Earl Frazier's Harmony Five, in 1925 rejoined Cliff Jackson's Westerners. Worked with Elmer Snowden before joining Duke Ellington in 1926. Given nickname by Otto Hardwicke. Noted for 'wah-wah' effects he created with rubber plunger. Except for absence through pneumonia in October 1937, Tricky remained with Duke until suffering a stroke in late 1945. He resumed working with Duke (c. May 1946) and accompanied the band on a California tour, but died on that tour in a room at the Scragg's Hotel.

NAPOLEON, Phil
(real name: Filippo Napoli)
trumpet

Born: Boston, Massachusetts, 2nd September 1901

His brother, Ted, was a drummer, he is the uncle of Teddy and Marty Napoleon. Gave first public performance at the age of five. Recorded in 1916 as a cornet soloist. Became founder-member of the Original Memphis Five, some of whose prolific recordings were issued under a variety of pseudonyms, later led own band at Rosemont Ballroom (1927). Many years of studio work with Sam Lanin, Joe Rines, Leo Reisman, B. A. Rolfe, etc., left N.B.C. in 1936. From 1938 led own big band in New York, Chicago, etc., then resumed free-lance studio activities. Spell with Jimmy Dorsey in 1943. Led re-formed Memphis Five at Nick's, New York, from May 1949. Led own band at that venue for many years until moving to Florida in June 1956 where business interests included own club. Brief return to New York in July 1959, during that month appeared at Newport Jazz Festival. Continued to lead own band at his Napoleon's Retreat in Miami Beach, Florida.

NAPOLEON, 'Teddy' George
piano

Born: Brooklyn, New York, 23rd January 1914
Died: 5th July 1964

Nephew of Phil Napoleon, brother of pianist Marty (born: 1921). Did first professional work in 1933. Gigged with many bands, then worked for a long time with Tommy Tompkins' Band, subsequently with Johnny Messner, Bob Chester, etc. Joined Gene Krupa in 1944, several periods away from the band, but was regularly featured with Gene Krupa Trio until 1958 (including overseas tours in the 1950s). Briefly with Tex Beneke, then moved to Florida, led own trio and worked occasionally with Bill Harris and Flip Phillips.

N

NATOLI, 'Nat' Born: Boston, Massachusetts. c.1902
trumpet Deceased

Went on tour to Montreal, Canada, with Original Memphis Five (c.1924), worked regularly with Henry Thies Orchestra. With Jean Goldkette at Pla-Mor Ballroom in Kansas City (November 1927 to April 1928). With Paul Whiteman from summer of 1930 until autumn of 1934, left to work in studio orchestras. Continued to play regularly through the 1940s, from then on was more active as a musical contractor for studio musicians.

NELSON, 'Dave' Davidson C. Born: Donaldsonville, Louisiana, 1905
trumpet/piano/arranger Died: New York City, 7th April 1946

Nephew of Joe 'King' Oliver. Both parents played piano. First played violin and piano, then took up trumpet. First professional work with Marie Lucas Orchestra at Lincoln Gardens in Chicago. Played in Ma Rainey's Georgia Jazz Band, also did M.C.A. tour with Jelly Roll Morton. Worked with Richard M. Jones, who taught him arranging, member of Edgar Hayes' Eight Black Pirates (spring 1927). Led own band at Dreamland in 1927, worked briefly with Jimmie Noone at The Apex Club, with Leroy Pickett Orchestra (late 1928), then toured with own band before settling in New York. Few months with Luis Russell (1929), toured with King Oliver (June-October 1930), then led own big band (late 1930). Again worked with King Oliver. Led own Hot Shots Band which toured with Mae West in 'The Constant Sinner' (1931), then led own band for residencies in New York and New Jersey: Pelham Heath Inn, Laurel Gardens, Roebling Ballroom, Cedar Theatre, etc. From the mid-1930s played piano in own small band, worked on trumpet with own sextet during the early 1940s. During his last four years he was a staff arranger for the Lewis Publishing Co. Continued gigging (on trumpet and piano) until shortly before suffering a fatal heart attack.

NELSON, 'Big Eye' Louis Born: New Orleans, Louisiana, 28th January 1885
clarinet Died: New Orleans, Louisiana, 20th August 1949

Also known as Louis DeLisle. Father was an accordionist, taught Louis to play the accordion, he later played violin, string bass, and guitar, but specialised on clarinet from 1904. Tuition from Lorenzo Tio Sr. Worked in Imperial Orchestra (c.1905), with Golden Rule Orchestra (1907), with Manuel Perez in Imperial Band (c.1910), Superior Orchestra (c.1912), also worked with the Eagle Band and with Papa Celestin. Left New Orleans in June 1916 to join the Original Creole Orchestra, left the following spring during temporary break up and returned to New Orleans. Worked in Lyric Theatre Orchestra (1918), then worked on and off with John Robichaux from late 1918 until 1924. Worked with Willie Pajeaud (c.1925), several stints with Sidney Desvigne in the late 1920s, continued to play regularly during the 1930s. Recorded with Kid Rena in 1940. Led own quartet at Luthjen's Bistro in New Orleans from 1939 until 1948. Recorded in the summer of 1949.

NELSON, Louis Born: New Orleans, Louisiana, 17th September 1902
trombone

Brother of sax-player George Nelson. Raised in Napoleonville from the age of two. First played alto horn, then switched to trombone in the early 1920s. Worked with Joe Gabriel's Band in Thibodeaux, then in New Orleans with Kid Rena, Original Tuxedo Orchestra, etc. With trumpeter Kid Harris, then long spell with Sidney Desvigne's Big Band in the 1930s, from 1944 worked regularly with Kid Thomas. During the 1950s did extensive touring with George Lewis including visits to Japan and Europe, also made solo tour of Europe. Continues to play regularly, mainly in New Orleans, at Preservation Hall, etc., appeared at Jazz Fest in June 1969. International touring with Legends of Jazz during the 1970s. Continued to work prolifically during the early 1980s, including international touring.

NELSON, Percy Born: Hartford, Connecticut, 1902
clarinet/saxes/flute Died: Hartford, Connecticut, 12th March 1983

Originally a drummer, switched to sax in 1922. Gigged around Hartford on sax and clarinet, then to New York in late 1920s, formed own big band The Night Hawks which played 18-month residency at The Hotel Bond, then did widespread touring through New England, Pennsylvania, Canada, etc. Returned to Hartford in early 1940s, quit full-time music, but continued to lead own bands. During the late 1960s played clarinet regularly with Paul McGeary's Gin Bottle 5 plus 1.

NESBITT, John
trumpet/arranger

Born: Norfolk, Virginia, c.1900
Died: Boston, Massachusetts, 1935

With Lillian 'Jones' Jazz Hounds, then with Amanda Randolph before joining McKinney's Syncop Septette (c.1925), remained with the band (subsequently named McKinney's Cotton Pickers) until 1930, arranged many tunes for the Cotton Pickers including: 'Shim-Me-Sha-Wabble', 'Crying and Sighing', 'Plain Dirt', etc. Lived temporarily in New York, arranged for Fletcher Henderson, Luis Russell, etc. Brief spells with Zack Whyte's Chocolate Beau Brummels, Speed Webb; gigged with Earle Warren's Band in the early 1930s. Incapacitated by a stomach ailment during last years of his life.

NEWTON, 'Frankie' William Frank
trumpet

Born: Emory, Virginia, 4th January 1906
Died: New York City, 11th March 1954

Worked with Clarence Paige, before joining Lloyd Scott's Band (then on tour) early in 1927, worked mainly with Lloyd Scott (in New York and on tours) until early 1929, also worked with Elmer Snowden (summer 1927). With Eugene Kennedy's Band (early 1929), then rejoined Scott's Band (then led by Cecil Scott), was occasionally featured as a vocalist ('Lawd, Lawd', etc.). With Cecil Scott (early 1930), then worked with Chick Webb, Charlie Johnson, and Elmer Snowden. Worked briefly with Garland Wilson on radio WEVD (1932), left New York for a while, then worked with Sam Wooding. Recorded with Bessie Smith in 1933, with Charlie Johnson from c. September 1933 until entering hospital in late 1935. Brief return to Charlie Johnson, then with Teddy Hill from spring 1936 until spring 1937. Complications followed a tonsillectomy (May 1937), worked with John Kirby from July until September 1937, recovered from injured back, played in brief-lived Mezz Mezzrow Disciples of Swing (November 1937). From December 1937 until February 1938 with Lucky Millinder, then formed own band. Led at Cafe Society, New York from 28th December 1938 until 1939 (absent through illness February 1939). Led own band at Kelly's Stables, New York, from February 1940, briefly with Edgar Hayes, then led own band for summer season. In spring 1941 led mixed sextet at Green Mansions, Lake George, own quintet at Hotel Pilgrim, Plymouth, Massachusetts (summer 1941), own big band at Mimo Club, New York (autumn 1941), then own small band at Kelly's Stables (late 1941). Led band in Boston (November 1942 to February 1943), then at Cafe Society Downtown, New York, from March 1943. Own quartet at George's, New York (June 1944), then worked with James P. Johnson at the Pied Piper (August 1944 to early 1945). Led own band in Boston, then played at Little Casino, New York (early 1946), briefly with Sid Catlett Band at Downbeat Club, New York (early 1947). Ill again in spring 1947, in late 1947 worked with Ted Goddard's Band at Savoy, Boston. In summer 1948 suffered a serious setback when his home (and trumpet) were lost in a fire. Gigged in Boston, then worked with Ed Hall's Band in Boston (summer 1949). Led own band at Savoy, Boston, from May 1950. Occasionally sat in at Stuyvesant Casino, New York, in 1951, but for last years of his life did little regular playing, lived in Greenwich Village, devoting considerable time to painting and politics.

NICHOLAS, Albert
clarinet/saxes

Born: New Orleans, Louisiana, 27th May 1900
Died: Basle, Switzerland, 3rd September 1973

Nephew of cornet and clarinet player 'Wooden Joe' Nicholas (1883-1957). Played clarinet from the age of 10, at 14 took lessons from Lorenzo Tio Jnr. Started work as a bank messenger, gigged with Buddie Petit, Joe Oliver, and Manuel Perez. Service in U.S. merchant marine from November 1916 until December 1919. Subsequently played in the Maple Leaf Band led by Oke Gaspard, did various gigs, then joined Arnold DuPas Orchestra at Cadillac Club (September 1921); with Manuel Perez from spring 1922. From early 1923 led own six-piece band at Tom Anderson's Cabaret, then left New Orleans in

May 1924 for seven-week tour with King Oliver. Returned home to lead at Tom Anderson's, then rejoined King Oliver in Chicago (December 1924). Left Oliver in August 1926, went with drummer Jack Carter's Band to Plaza Hotel, Shanghai. After a year with Carter, Albert and banjoist Frank Ethridge made their way to Egypt and worked with Guido Curti's Band in Cairo (December 1927) and Benedetti's Six Crackerjacks in Alexandria. Moved to Paris, played briefly in Louis Douglas Revue at Theatre de la Porte St. Martin, then returned to U.S.A., arriving on 9th November 1928. Joined Luis Russell in late November 1928 and remained with that band until December 1933. Worked for six months with Chick Webb, then did five months with Sam Wooding (mainly at Cotton Club, Philadelphia). In late 1934 joined The Blue Chips in New York, short absence from music, then worked in Bernard Addison's Group and John Kirby's Quartet at Adrian's Tap Room, New York. Later led own small group at same venue. From spring 1937 until spring 1939 worked with Louis Armstrong's Orchestra, with Zutty Singleton's Group (December 1939 to October 1940), briefly in Bob Burnet's Band (spring 1941), subbed in John Kirby Sextet for Buster Bailey in summer of 1941. In late 1941 left full-time music to work as a guard on New York subway, then worked for the U.S. government in Washington, D.C. Returned to New York in late 1945, worked for Art Hodes, also played with Bunk Johnson's Band for three dates. In February 1946 flew to California to join Kid Ory, came back to New York in September 1946, began working at Jimmy Ryan's. Worked in pianist Ralph Sutton's Trio (1948); from 1949 until 1953 mainly led own groups in and around Los Angeles. Worked for six weeks in Boston with Rex Stewart, then went to France (1953). Lived in Europe, made many tours all over the Continent including solo appearances in Britain in 1967. Returned to the U.S.A. for playing visits in 1959 and 1960. Was featured at the 'Jazz Expo' in London (October 1969). Visited New Orleans late 1969 to early 1970.

NICHOLS, 'Herbie' Herbert Horatio

piano/composer

Born: New York City, 3rd January 1919
Died: New York City, 12th April 1963

Piano at 8, studied with Charles Beck for 7 years. With Royal Baron Orchestra (1937), Floyd Williams (1938). In U.S. Infantry from September 1941 until August 1943. With sax-player Walter Dennis prior to joining Bobby Booker in 1944. With Herman Autrey (1945), Hal Singer, Freddie Moore (1946). Toured with Illinois Jacquet then worked on and off with John Kirby during 1948 and 1949. During the 1950s worked with Snub Mosley, Edgar Sampson, Milton Larkin, Arnett Cobb, Wilbur de Paris, Conrad Janis, etc. During the early 1960s played various club residencies in New York, played with Archie Shepp in 1962, and toured Scandinavia in 1962. Died of leukemia.

NICHOLS, 'Red' Ernest Loring

cornet

Born: Ogden, Utah, 8th May 1905
Died: Las Vegas, Nevada, 28th June 1965

His father taught all instruments, but specialised on clarinet. Red started on bugle at the age of four, cornet at five; at 12 was featured in family musical act and in his father's brass band. Gigged with local bandleaders including Lillian Fletcher, then gained scholarship to Culver Military Academy (December 1919). Played cornet, violin, and piano at the Academy until being dismissed in September 1920. Returned to Utah, played in pit orchestras, then joined Ray Stilson (on cornet, doubling violin) in 1922; later that year joined the Syncopating Five (a seven-piece group); made first (private) recordings. He was soon appointed leader of the band, and billed as The Royal Palms Orchestra, they began residency in Atlantic City (early 1923) and Lake James, Indiana. Briefly with Joe Thomas Band in Ohio, then worked in Asbury Park and New York with Malcolm 'Johnny' Johnson (from September 1923). In 1924 Johnson left full-time music and appointed Nichols as leader of the band which subsequently played at Pelham Heath Inn for three months; in late 1924 Nichols joined Sam Lanin in New York. From 1924 worked for many bandleaders including: Harry Reser, Benny Krueger, Ross Gorman, Henry Halstead, Vincent Lopez, Don Voorhees, etc., also with the California Ramblers. Regularly led own recording studio groups and took part in countless free-lance sessions. Briefly with Paul Whiteman from late April until 1st June 1927, then again worked with Don Voorhees. Led own bands and orchestras during 1928-30, played for several Broadway shows, occasional touring and trip to California (late 1928 to early 1929). Continued to lead own studio groups: The Five Pennies, The Redheads, Charleston Chasers, etc., etc. Led own band at Hollywood Hotel and Park Central during the early 1930s, numerous residencies in other cities and occasional touring (appendectomy early 1932). Mostly active leading a big swing band during the mid-1930s (featured on cornet and vocals); regular radio series. Featured at Famous Door, New York, in 1940, then widespread touring. Except for short breaks, continued to lead own band until spring of 1942, when he sold the band to Anson Weeks. Moved to California, left music to do defence work in the shipyards (except for brief spell fronting Henry Busse's Band during that leader's illness). With Glen Gray and the Casa Loma Band from February until June 1944, then formed own sextet—residency at Hayward Hotel, Los Angeles, from September 1944. During following spring began long residency at the El Morocco Club in Los Angeles, then at Hangover Club, San Francisco, from summer of 1948 until 1951. (During this last period Red and his band appeared in the Mickey Rooney film 'Quicksand'.) Residency at Playroom, Los Angeles, from December 1951 until January 1953. Worked mainly in California during the 1950s, including long stay at Marineland, Los Angeles. 'The Five Pennies', a film very loosely based on Red's career (starring actor Danny Kaye), was released in 1959—the story was from the book of the same name by author Grady Johnson. Red was a subject of the American television program 'This is Your Life'; he also appeared in the film 'The Gene Krupa Story' ('Drum Crazy'). These promotions encouraged Red Nichols to continue leading his own successful Five Pennies, the group played many important residencies throughout the U.S.A. and did overseas tours in 1960 and 1964. Whilst fulfilling residency at the Las Vegas casino Top of the Mint, Red suffered a fatal heart attack at a nearby hotel.

A wealth of information on Red Nichols' career (compiled by Woody Backensto) is contained in the April-May 1957 and April 1969 issues of Record Research.

NOONE, Jimmie *Born: Cut-Off, Louisiana, 23rd April 1895*
clarinet/soprano and alto saxes *Died: Los Angeles, California, 19th April 1944*

Born on family farm 10 miles from New Orleans. Started playing guitar at the age of 10, clarinet from 15. Family moved into New Orleans in late 1910, and Jimmie began taking lessons from Sidney Bechet. First paid work depping for Bechet in Freddie Keppard's Band (1913), subsequently worked with Keppard for a year then, together with Buddie Petit, formed the Young Olympia Band. Noone also led a trio at the Pythian Temple Roof Gardens during the summers of 1916 and 1917 and gigged with Kid Ory and Papa Celestin. In late 1917 moved to Chicago to join Freddie Keppard in the Original Creole Band, played residency at Logan Square Theatre and toured until the group disbanded in spring 1918. Returned to New Orleans, gigged with various bands, then returned to Chicago in autumn of 1918 (with King Oliver) to join band at the Royal Gardens (then led by bassist Bill Johnson). Soon afterwards began doubling by playing late-night residency with own small group at The Edelweiss. Remained at Royal Gardens until summer of 1920, then joined Doc Cooke's Orchestra (on clarinet and soprano sax), worked regularly with Doc Cooke until autumn of 1926, also continued doubling with own small group at various Chicago clubs (including The Nest) from summer of 1926. In autumn 1926 The Nest was renamed The Apex Club, and Noone led resident band there until it closed in spring of 1928—also worked again with Doc Cooke in 1927. From 1928-31 continued to lead at Chicago venues including: The Club Ambassador, El Rado, Alvin Dansant, during this period also played residency with augmented band at the Greystone Ballroom, Detroit. On 31st May 1931 began month's residency at The Savoy Ballroom, New York, returned to Chicago and led at Club Dixie (1932), The Lido (1933), Midnite (1934), etc. Moved to New York early in 1935 and formed band with bassist Wellman Braud which played at their short-lived Vodvil Club on 132nd Street. Noone returned to Chicago and led own band at Platinum Lounge (1937), Swingland (1938), etc., from autumn of 1938 did extensive touring (including dates in New Orleans). Played at Club DeLisa and The Cabin Inn (1939), also led own big broadcasting band in late 1939. Led at The Coach (1940-1), Yes Yes Club (1941), Downbeat-Garrick (1942), etc., left Chicago for residencies in Omaha, Nebraska, and with own quartet at The Tropics, San Antonio, Texas (May-June 1943). Moved to California; resident with own small group at Streets of Paris, Hollywood, from August 1943.

Did radio and record dates with Kid Ory, but continued leading own band. Died in his home from a sudden heart attack.

Jimmie Noone appeared (with The East Side Kids) in the 1944 Monogram film 'The Block Busters'.

NORMAN, Fred *Born: Leesburg, Florida, 5th October 1910*
trombone/arranger/vocals

Mother was a pianiste. Began on trombone at 14, studied at Fessender Academy and played in school orchestra, toured Florida with school band. Worked with local bands before moving to Washington, D.C., in 1930. Worked briefly with Duke Eglin's Bell Hops and Booker Coleman's Band, then joined Elmer Calloway's Band. With Claude Hopkins' Orchestra from 1932 until 1938, did many arrangements for the band. From 1938 mainly active as free-lance arranger-composer, doing scores for big-band leaders Bunny Berigan, Tommy Dorsey, Jimmy Dorsey, Benny Goodman, Isham Jones, Gene Krupa, Glenn Miller, Artie Shaw, Charlie Spivak, Jack Teagarden, etc. From 1950 worked as musical director for many stars. Overseas tour with singer Brook Benton (September 1971). Prolific arranging during the 1970s.

NORRIS, 'Al' Albert *Born: Kane, Pennsylvania, 4th September 1908*
guitar/violin *Died: 26th December 1974*

Raised in Olean, N.Y. Played violin from the age of 14; worked on banjo with various bands in and around Buffalo from 1927. Joined Jimmie Lunceford on banjo in 1932; specialised on guitar from 1934 (occasionally featured on violin). Remained with Lunceford until that leader's death (1947), except for service in U.S. Army during World War II. Subsequently worked with Ed Wilcox-Joe Thomas Band, then with Ed Wilcox. Retired from full-time music and began working for New York postal authorities.

NORVO, 'Red' *Born: Beardstown, Illinois, 31st March 1908*
(real name: Kenneth Norville)
vibes/xylophone/marimba/piano

Piano from early childhood, then studied xylophone; in 1925 toured the Middle West with a marimba band called The Collegians. Left them in Chicago, worked with Paul Ash and Ben Bernie and played regularly in local radio station, then enrolled as a student (mining engineer) at University of Missouri (1926-7). Returned to full-time music, led own band on Station KSTP and worked with Victor Young's Radio Orchestra in Chicago. Regularly featured with Paul Whiteman until mid-1932 (in late 1933 Red married Mildred Bailey; the marriage lasted for 12 years). Extensive free-lance recordings, worked occasionally with Charlie Barnet. From October 1935 led own band at Famous Door, New York, in May 1936 augmented the group from 6 to 10 pieces for Hotel Commodore engagement. During 1936 Red made several recordings on piano under the pseudonym Ken Kenny. From 1937-44 led bands of varying sizes including 10-piece unit at Palisades, New York, in 1940. In late 1944 he disbanded his sextet and joined Benny Goodman, from this period onwards worked mainly on vibraphone. Left Goodman in December 1945, with Woody Herman until December 1946. Moved to California in 1947, working as a free-lance and leading own group, returned to New York in September 1949 with own sextet. Began leading own trio in 1950. Toured Europe early in 1954, then led own small groups in U.S.A. After touring Australia in 1956 opened own club in Santa Monica, California, led in Las Vegas 1957-8. Featured with Benny Goodman tour in late 1959 (including Europe), also worked in Benny Goodman Sextet in spring 1961. During the 1960s rarely played in New York, worked mainly in California, Las Vegas, and Nevada, long residencies at the Sands Hotel. Out of action through ear operation (March-July 1968), then toured Europe as a soloist in late 1968. With George Wein's Newport All Stars (1969). Led own trio (1970-72), year's sabbatical, then resumed playing. Extensive schedule during early 1980s, including touring Europe.

N

NUNEZ, **'Yellow' Alcide**
clarinet

Born: New Orleans, Louisiana, 17th March 1884
Died: New Orleans, Louisiana, 2nd September 1934

Originally a guitarist, worked with violinist John Spriccio, switched to clarinet in 1902, together with trumpeter Frank Christian worked in the Right at Em's Razz Band. Subsequently worked regularly with many New Orleans Bands including: Papa Jack Laine's Reliance, Frank Christian's Ragtime Band, and Tom Brown's Band. Journeyed to Chicago in March 1916 with drummer Johnny Stein's Band, left with three other members of that band and became founder-member of the Original Dixieland Jazz Band. After a dispute with Nick LaRocca he ceased working with the O.D.J.B. on 31st October 1916. Led own band for a while, then toured the B. F. Keith Circuit with Bert Kelly's Band (accompanying Joe Frisco and Loretta McDermott) before joining Anton Lada's Louisiana Five. Toured with own quartet in the mid-1920s including residencies in Oklahoma and Texas. Returned to New Orleans in 1927, worked locally for several leaders, also played in the Police Band.

O'BRIEN, Floyd
trombone

Born: Chicago, Illinois, 7th May 1904
Died: Chicago, Illinois, 26th November 1968

From the early 1920s worked for many Chicago bandleaders including: Floyd Town, Charles Pierce, Thelma Terry, Joe Kayser, Husk O'Hare, etc. During the early 1930s worked in a theatre orchestra in Des Moines, Iowa, then with Floyd Town, Mal Hallet, Joe Venuti, Smith Ballew, Mike Durso's Band 1933-4. With drummer-vocalist-comedian Phil Harris from 1935 until early 1939. With Gene Krupa from April 1939 until joining Bob Crosby from May 1940 until late 1942. Worked in California with Eddie Miller's Band (early 1943), then free-lanced on West Coast, organized own photographic-record shop in Los Angeles, worked in Shorty Sherock's Band in 1945. Moved back to Chicago in late 1948, briefly with Bud Freeman, then with Isbell Dixielanders, Jack Ivett (1949), regular work with Art Hodes, also taught music and worked as a piano tuner. Moved back to West Coast, gigged with many bands, later worked with Smokey Stover's Band. Moved back to Chicago in 1962, continued to play with various bands, mostly in Chicago. In November 1965 played at Austin High School 75th Anniversary Concert.

O'BRIEN, Jack
piano

Born: Middletown, Connecticut, 13th December 1906

Began on piano at 8. Played college gigs around New England with Allie Wrubel (1921-25). To Miami in 1925, worked there with Jimmy Hartwell, violinist Milt Shaw and with Ray Miller's Band. With Enoch Light (1926), in Europe with George Carhart (1927-30), worked briefly in Paris with Mezz Mezzrow's Trio, also briefly with Lud Gluskin in Berlin. With Tony Pastor in Connecticut 1930-33, with Smith Ballew (1934-35). Settled down in Connecticut and continued to play there regularly through to the 1970s. Not connected with pianist Jack O'Brien who played for some years in Ted Weems' Band.

O'BRYANT, Jimmy
clarinet/saxes

Born: Louisville, Kentucky?
Died: Chicago, Illinois, 25th June 1928

It has been suggested that this extensively recorded musician was from St. Louis, but this is not corroborated by veteran musicians from that city. He is said to have toured extensively before settling in Chicago.

> *I am indebted to Walter C. Allen for supplying me with information culled from the* Chicago Defender *dated 30th June 1928. The paper reports that O'Bryant died in the County Hospital, Chicago.*

O'DAY, Anita
real name: Anita Belle Colton
vocals

Born: Chicago, Illinois, 18th October 1919

With Max Miller Band at Off-Beat Club, Chicago from January 1939, then at Three Deuces Club with same band for a year. Joined Gene Krupa early in 1941 for two years. Brief spell with Woody Herman, then with Stan Kenton 1944-45, rejoined Gene Krupa, left that band in Hollywood (spring 1946). Worked mainly as a solo act in late 1940s and 1950s, several long periods of enforced absence from music. Great resurgence of activity in the late 1950s, was featured at Newport Jazz Festival in 1958, toured Europe with Benny Goodman (1959). During the 1960s made many tours of Europe, and twice toured Japan, played club dates throughout U.S. including long residency at the Half Note Club, N.Y. in 1969. Did many overseas tours during the 1970s, also continued undertaking club and concert work in the U.S.A. Has appeared in several films; notably outstanding in 'Jazz on a Summer's Day'. Auto-biography 'High Times, Hard Times' first published in 1981.

OHMS, Fred
trombone

Born: 1918
Died: New York City, 5th May 1956

Had worked with Fred Waring's Pennsylvanians before joining Eddie Condon in June 1946. Briefly with Muggsy Spanier in 1947, with Billy Butterfield in 1948. During the early 1950s was mainly employed as a studio musician, but continued to play jazz gigs whenever possible. After a very brief illness he succumbed to double pneumonia.

OLDHAM, 'Bill' William *Born: Chattanooga, Tennessee, 1st June 1909*
tuba/string bass/baritone sax/trombone/composer

Brother of the saxophonist George D. Oldham, who died on the 21st June 1947. Moved with family to Chicago in 1919, played tuba from 1923, joined Major N. Clark Smith's *Chicago Defender* Boys' Band in 1925. Worked with the Midnight Revellers before working with Louis Armstrong Big Band (on string bass and tuba) in 1931 and again in 1933 and July-October 1935. Continued to work regularly in Chicago during the 1930s and 1940s, also gained Bachelor of Music at Chicago Conservatory, composed several extended works. Worked for many years with Franz Jackson, played in New York with that band in December 1968.

OLIVER, 'King' Joe *Born: Louisiana, 11th May 1885*
cornet/composer *Died: Savannah, Georgia, 10th April 1938*

Uncle of Dave Nelson. There is some doubt about the actual birthplace of King Oliver, he was certainly raised in New Orleans. Began on trombone, then switched to cornet, did early work in Walter Kinchin's Band and with the Melrose Band. During adolescence he permanently lost the sight in one eye through an accident. During the years 1908-17 did parade work, gigs, and occasional tours with various bands including: The Olympia, The Onward Brass Band, The Magnolia, The Eagle, The Original Superior, and Allen's Brass Band, was also employed as a butler. Worked at the Abadie Brothers' Cabaret in Richard M. Jones' Four Hot Hounds (c. 1912), with Kid Ory at Pete Lala's, also led own band at the same venue and at the 101 Ranch, etc. Rejoined Kid Ory in 1917, left c. March 1919, moved to Chicago to join clarinettist Lawrence Duhé's Band, doubled for a while in band led by bassist Bill Johnson. Later became leader of Duhé's Band and played residencies at Deluxe Cafe, Pekin Cabaret, and Dreamland (1920 to May 1921). Took band to San Francisco, led at the Pergola Dancing Pavilion (from June 1921), later worked in Oakland, Leak's Lake, etc. Returned to Chicago in April 1922, led own Creole Jazz Band at Lincoln Gardens (from 17th June 1922), subsequently toured and made record debut in April 1923. Solo visit to New York (September 1924), returned to Lincoln Gardens until December 1924. Guested with Dave Peyton in December 1924, led own Dixie Syncopators at Plantation Cafe from February 1925 until spring 1927, then played dates in Milwaukee, Detroit, and St. Louis before working at the Savoy Ballroom, New York, in May 1927. Toured before disbanding in autumn of 1927, played on Clarence Williams' recording sessions (1928) and led own studio bands for recordings, occasionally formed bands for specific engagements. Reformed regular band for touring in 1930. Left New York and lived for a while in Nashville, Tennessee. Formed new band in 1931, recommenced touring, despite personnel changes and a series of misfortunes. King Oliver continued leading bands until 1937. He then ran a fruit stall in Savannah, Georgia, for a while before working as a pool-room attendant. He died in Savannah, but was buried in New York. His many compositions include: 'Dipper Mouth Blues', 'Canal Street Blues', 'Dr. Jazz'. The excellent 'King Joe Oliver' (by Walter C. Allen and Brian A. L. Rust) was first published in 1955.

OLIVER, 'Sy' Melvin James *Born: Battle Creek, Michigan, 17th December 1910*
trumpet/arranger/vocalist/composer

Brother-in-law of pianist Archie 'Skip' Hall. Raised in Zanesville, Ohio. Both parents were music teachers. Played trumpet from the age of 12, played in local Knights of Pythias Band whilst in his teens. Whilst still at high school joined Cliff Barnett's Club Royal Serenaders, with Barnett on and off for about three years, then left Ohio at 17 to join Zack Whyte and his Chocolate Beau Brummels (then in Huntington, West Virginia). Left Whyte to join Alphonso Trent, left after a few months to rejoin Zack Whyte briefly (1930), then settled in Columbus, Ohio, and began teaching and arranging. After submitting arrangements to Jimmie Lunceford was invited to join the band, and travelled to New York with them in late 1933 for their debut at the Lafayette Theatre. With Lunceford as principal arranger for six years, playing regularly in trumpet section, then to Tommy Dorsey in summer of 1939, working mainly as staff arranger-composer, occasionally featured on vocals. Army service from 1943 until late 1945, serving as a bandmaster. Worked again as free-lance arranger, regular arranging commissions for Tommy Dorsey. Led own big band in 1946, touring and residency at Zanzibar Club, New York, then 10 years as musical director and record supervisor at leading record companies, including Decca. During the 1950s and 1960s regular free-lance arranging, led own recording bands. Visited Europe in 1969. Led own big band in New York (summer 1970). Toured Europe with Warren Covington (1974), led own band for long residency in New York City during the late 1970s and 1980s.

ORCHARD, 'Frank' Francis H.
trombone/valve trombone

Born: Chicago, Illinois, 21st September 1914
Died: New York, 27th December 1983

Played violin as a child, switched to banjo before playing tuba and trombone in high school band. Did a year's study at Juilliard, left in 1933, played in Stanley Melba's Band, then left music to work as a salesman until joining Jimmie McPartland at Nick's in March 1941. Worked with Bobby Hackett (late 1942), with Max Kaminsky (1944). Left Kaminsky in September 1944 to join Johnny Morris Band. Free-lanced in New York during the 1940s, occasionally organised sessions in St. Louis during the late 1950s. Mainly active in New York during the 1960s, gigged with Billy Butterfield in late 1969. Often sat in at Jimmy Ryan's, New York (1970-1).

ORENDORFF, George Robert
trumpet

Born: Atlanta, Georgia, 18th March 1906
Died: California, 1984

Moved with his family to Chicago in 1915. Started on guitar, then began playing cornet. Whilst at Wendell Phillips High School met Lionel Hampton, Eddie South, Wallace Bishop, and several other boys who later became professional musicians. Worked in Detroit Shannon's Band at Riverview Park Ballroom, Chicago (1923), also toured with Shannon accompanying Ben Harney. Did gigs in Chicago including one-night dep for King Oliver. Left Chicago in April 1925 in band accompanying the Helen Dewey Show. Left in Los Angeles, did one gig with the Spikes Brothers Band (July 1925), then worked regularly with Paul Howard until 1930. Joined Les Hite at the Cotton Club, Culver City, played on recordings with Louis Armstrong (1931-2), also did regular film-studio work with Hite. Left Hite in 1939, worked with guitarist Ceele Burke before joining U.S. Army in 1943. After demobilisation left full-time music to work for the postal authorities. Continued to play regularly (including recording sessions), acted as an American Federation of Musicians' official for several years. Continued to play occasionally, worked with Ben Pollack and with the Peppy Prince Orchestra. Has had many poems published.

ORY, 'Kid' Edward
trombone/string bass/cornet/alto sax/vocals

Born: La Place, Louisiana, 25th December 1886
Died: Hawaii, 23rd January 1973

Played banjo from the age of 10, led boys' band in La Place, then began doubling on valve trombone before specialising on slide trombone. Made regular visits to New Orleans before making his home there, from c. 1912 until 1919 led one of the most successful bands in the city. A doctor advised Ory to live in a humid climate, and he moved to California in 1919. He soon sent for several New Orleans musicians and formed his own band on the West Coast in November 1919, they played residencies in San Francisco, Los Angeles, and Oakland, and in 1922 became the first black small band to have recordings issued. In late 1925 Ory handed over the leadership to Mutt Carey and moved to Chicago for recording dates with Louis Armstrong, he then joined King Oliver (playing alto sax for six weeks until trombonist George Filhe worked out his notice). Left Chicago with Oliver, played briefly with the band in New York (May 1927), then moved back to Chicago to join Dave Peyton in June 1927. During the following year he worked with Clarence Black at The Savoy, then in 1929 played in Boyd Atkins' Chicago Vagabonds at the Sunset Cafe. Returned to Los Angeles in 1930, played in Mutt Carey's Jeffersonians for a few months, then toured Pantages Theatre circuit with Leon Rene Orchestra. Briefly with Emerson Scott's Band in Los Angeles, then two months in Freddie Washington's Band at Club Araby (1931), worked with Charlie Echols' Ebony Serenaders, then left music to help his brother run a chicken farm (1933). Visited New York in September 1939, returned to Los Angeles and worked in a railroad office. Began regular playing again by joining Barney Bigard's Band at Trouville Club, Los Angeles (summer 1942). In 1943-4 was mostly active on string bass and alto sax, own quartet resident at Tiptoe Inn (late 1943). Reverted to trombone after success of Orson Wells' radio series (1944). Led own highly successful band for many West Coast residencies including: Jade Palace, Beverly Cavern, etc., did national concert tour in 1948. Occasionally doubled on cornet during the mid-1940s. The band occasionally worked outside of California; played residency at Child's, New York (spring 1955). Ill health forced Ory to temporarily disband in the summer of 1955, he soon re-formed and led his band on several overseas tours including visits to Europe in 1956 and 1959. From 1954 until 1961 he played often at his own club On The Levee, San Francisco. He continued to play regularly during the early 1960s, but after recurring bouts of illness moved to Hawaii in the summer of 1966. Pneumonia threatened his life early in 1969. After recovering, he lived in quiet retirement. Played at New Orleans Jazz Fest (April 1971).

Kid Ory appeared in several films including: 'New Orleans' (with Louis Armstrong) and with own band in 'Crossfire', 'Mahogany Magic', 'Disneyland After Dawn', 'The Benny Goodman Story'.

P

PAGE, 'Hot Lips' Oran Thaddeus
trumpet/mellophone/vocals

Born: Dallas, Texas, 27th January 1908
Died: New York City, 5th November 1954

First music lessons from his mother, a former school-teacher. Early efforts on clarinet and saxophone, specialised on trumpet from the age of 12. Joined kids' band led by bass drummer Lux Alexander. Left music temporarily, attended high school in Corsicana, Texas, left to do manual work in Seminole oil fields in Texas. Became regular member of band accompanying Ma Rainey, made first visit to New York with Ma Rainey for bookings at the Lincoln Theatre. Worked with a T.O.B.A. circuit touring band, accompanied Bessie Smith, Ida Cox, etc. Joined Troy Floyd Band in San Antonio, also worked in Texas with Sugar Lou and Eddie's Hotel Tyler Band. Was heard with this band by bassist Walter Page (no relation) and subsequently joined the Blue Devils early in 1928. Left the band in 1931 to join Bennie Moten's Band, worked mainly with Moten until 1935, after that leader's death (April 1935) led own quintet in and around Kansas City. Worked as a speciality act with Count Basie at the Reno Club, Kansas City (1936), was signed by manager Joe Glaser and moved to New York. Short spell with Louis Metcalf's Band at Bedford Ballroom, New York, and subbed for ailing Frankie Newton at Onyx Club (spring 1937). Formed own big band which opened at Small's Paradise, New York, in August 1937, in May 1938 the band began residency at the Plantation Club, later that year Lips fronted a smaller unit at the Brick Club, New York. Made solo appearances, then led own band at Kelly's Stables and Golden Gate Ballroom, New York (late 1939). Featured on tour with Bud Freeman's Big Band (July 1940), with Joe Marsala (October 1940), then from November led own big band at West End Theatre Club, New York. Led own septet at Kelly's Stables from May 1941, then joined Artie Shaw from 15th August 1941 until January 1942. Led own big band in New York, Boston, Chicago, etc. From summer of 1943 until early 1949 Lips usually led own small band (Onyx, Famous Door, New York; Savoy, Boston; Hotel Sherman, Chicago; etc.), during this period he occasionally formed big bands for specific engagements (Apollo, Spotlite, New York, tours, etc.). During 1944 he made several guest appearances at Eddie Condon's New York Town Hall Concerts, also played for Don Redman at the Apollo, New York (summer 1945) and worked as accompanist for Ethel Waters in New York (spring 1946). In May 1949 made first trip to Europe for Paris Jazz Festival, returned to U.S.A., continued leading own small band in New York, Chicago, Minneapolis, etc. Shared highly successful recorded single with Pearl Bailey—'The Hucklebuck'/'Baby it's Cold Outside' (1949). From July until October 1951 Lips played in Europe (Knokke, Belgium; Holland, Scandinavia, and France), returned to U.S.A., worked as a single on theatre dates, toured with jazz packages. In summer 1952 returned to Europe, played in Belgium, France, and Scandinavia. Featured at Cafe Society, New York (May-June 1953), worked mainly as a single during last year of his life. Suffered a heart attack on 27th October 1954, died in the Harlem Hospital nine days later.

PAGE, Walter Sylvester
string bass

Born: Gallatin, Missouri, 9th February 1900
Died: New York City, 20th December 1957

Played tuba, bass drum in local brass bands. Later, at high school, was taught string bass by Major N. Clark Smith. Whilst taking a teachers' course at Kansas University began playing in saxist Dave Lewis' Band, later worked with Bennie Moten in Kansas City. Regularly doubled on baritone sax throughout the 1920s. In January 1923 joined Billy King's Road Show, working in band led by trombonist Emir Coleman, during 1925 the outfit disbanded in Oklahoma City and Walter Page took the nucleus of the band to form his Blue Devils (Emir Coleman remaining to work for a while with Page). In 1931 he turned the band over to trumpeter James Simpson and worked with small bands in and around Kansas City before joining Bennie Moten. The Original Blue Devils (as they were then called) continued to work under various leaders including: drummer Earnest Williams, altoist Buster Smith, and trumpeter Leroy 'Snake' White. Walter Page remained with Moten until 1934, then worked in band led by Count Basie before joining Jeter-Pillars' Band in St. Louis (autumn 1934). Returned to Kansas City to rejoin Count Basie (c. early 1936). Remained with Basie until September 1942. Toured with Nat Towle's Band (spring 1945), then worked with Jesse Price's Band in Joplin, Missouri. Returned to Count Basie from summer 1946 until spring 1949, then joined Hot Lips Page. Worked with Jimmy Rushing (1951), then extensive free-lance work mainly in New York. Spell with Jimmy McPartland. Regular dates at Eddie Condon's Club and with trumpeter Ruby Braff. Toured with Wild Bill Davison (summer 1956), with Roy Eldridge (late 1956). Continued to work regularly until shortly before his death. He contracted pneumonia, and resultant complications caused his death.

Not related to Hot Lips Page or to trumpeter Dave Page (1914-51) or to tuba-player Vernon Page.

PALAO, 'Jimmy' James A.
violin/saxophone/alto horn

Born: New Orleans, Louisiana. c. 1885
Died: Chicago, Illinois. c. 1925 (?)

Played violin with The Imperial Orchestra from c. 1907, also worked on alto horn with Allen's Brass Band. Played in various clubs in New Orleans, left the city in 1914 to tour with the Original Creole Orchestra (doubling saxophone and violin). Remained in Chicago when the band broke up, worked with Lawrence Duhé and Lil Hardin, then moved to California with King Oliver (1921). Left Oliver to return to Chicago, later joined Fess Williams' touring band accompanying the vaudeville act Dave and Tressie (early 1924).

PALMER, Roy
trombone

Born: New Orleans, Louisiana, 1892
Died: Chicago, 22nd December 1963

Played guitar in Roseal's Orchestra (1906), switched to trumpet, but later specialised on trombone. Worked with Richard M. Jones at George Fewclothes' Cabaret in 1911, later member of Willie Hightower's American Stars at the Cadillac Club (1914-15). In 1917 left New Orleans with Lawrence Duhé to play residency in Sugar Johnny Smith's Band. After Sugar Johnny's death, King Oliver became leader and Palmer left the group. Subsequently joined trumpeter Tig Chambers. During the 1920s worked with many bandleaders in Chicago: Doc Watson, Hughie Swift, etc., also played briefly with W. C. Handy. Left full-time music in the early 1930s, worked for the Mazola Oil Company and played regularly in that company's brass band. In summer of 1940 moved to South State Street, Chicago, and opened own laundry business. During the early 1920s his pupils included Albert Wynn and Preston Jackson. In the 1950s he continued to teach trumpet, trombone, and theory at his Chicago home.

PALMER, Singleton Nathaniel
string bass/sousaphone

Born: St. Louis, Missouri, 13th November 1913

Originally a pianist. Active on sousaphone in St. Louis during the early 1930s with Dewey Jackson, Oliver Cobb, with Eddie Johnson's Crackerjacks from 1933 (doubling string bass). Worked with George Hudson's Band from 1940 until 1948. Joined Count Basie for a year from April 1949. Returned to St. Louis and formed own 'Dixieland Six', which worked regularly thereafter. Long residency at the Opera House, St. Louis.

PAQUE, 'Glyn' Eric Glyn
alto sax/clarinet

Born: Poplar Bluff, Missouri, 29th August 1907
Died: Basle, Switzerland, 29th August 1953

Two years younger than his nephew, saxophonist Bernadine 'Bert' Curry. Started on piccolo at eight, clarinet at 10. Moved to New York in 1926, professional work with trumpeter Dave Alford, then with Beaty Conner Quarter (1927). Subsequently with Henri Saparo (1928), The Missourians (late 1928-9), Warren Adams, Eugene Kennedy, Charlie Skeets (1929). With White Brothers' Orchestra (1929-30), Emmett Mathews (spring 1930), also gigged with King Oliver, toured with Oliver (June-August 1930). During the early 1930s worked for Dave Nelson, Walter Pichon, Cass Carr, The Savoy Bearcats, Benny Carter, also gigged with Jelly Roll Morton, Luis Russell, Claude Hopkins, Elmer Snowden, etc. With Willie Bryant from late 1934 until 1937. To Europe with Bobby Martin's Orchestra (June 1937), after Martin returned to U.S.A. (1939), Paque led the band, renamed The Cotton Club Serenaders. Settled in Switzerland, worked with Fred Boehler (1940-5), briefly with French bandleader Jerry Thomas and Philippe Brun, etc. Later led own sextet in

Berne, Basle, Geneva, and Zurich, toured with the Nicholas Brothers in 1948. Died of a heart attack on his birthday.

PARENTI, 'Tony' Anthony
clarinet/saxes

Born: New Orleans, Louisiana, 6th August 1900
Died: New York, 17th April 1972

Uncle of drummer August 'Augie' Schellang (1905-58). Both parents were from Sicily, father was a musician in the Italian Peasant Army. Tony first played violin, then changed to clarinet. Studied at St. Philips School, New Orleans, later received tuition from Professor Joseph Taverno and played in his Italian Band for 18 months. Deputised for Alcide Nunez in Papa Laine's Band, also gigged with Nick LaRocca and drummer Johnny Stein. Worked in Johnny De Droit's Band at the Grunewald Hotel (c. 1916), later joined the S.S. 'Majestic' Trio. Worked at the Triangle Movie House and at the Pup Club. Led own successful band in New Orleans (record debut: January 1925). Played regularly in Liberty Theatre Orchestra, also worked with Saenger Theatre Symphony Orchestra. Moved to New York in the late 1920s, worked with Paul Ash, Arnold Johnson, Fred Rich, Meyer Davis, Nat Brusiloff, B. A. Rolfe, etc., long spell as a C.B.S. staff musician, led own saxophone quartet on radio and in short Warner Brothers' film. Spent four years with Radio City Symphony Orchestra, left in 1939 to join Ted Lewis. Remained with Ted Lewis until summer of 1945. With Eddie Condon from January 1946, joined Georg Brunis in June 1946, led own band at Jimmy Ryan's from November 1946, led at Nick's, then again worked for Eddie Condon. Worked in Chicago with Muggsy Spanier (late 1947), then with Miff Mole in Chicago until January 1949. During the early 1950s worked for four years in Florida, mainly with Preacher Rollo Laylan's Five Saints, briefly with the Dukes of Dixieland in 1952. Moved back to New York in 1954, worked regularly at The Metropole and Central Plaza, also led own band in New York State, Boston, and Canada. Depped for two weeks in George Lewis Band (when Lewis was ailing) in 1959. Worked at Eddie Condon's Club (1962), also led own band at Cove Club, Greenwood (summer 1963). Led own group at Jimmy Ryan's from late 1963 until 1969, appeared at New Orleans Jazz Fest in June 1969. In autumn 1969 continued leading band at own club in New York. Active in New York area (1970-1).

PARHAM, 'Truck' Charles Valdez
string bass

Born: Chicago, Illinois, 25th January 1913

Was once a professional footballer with the Chicago Negro All Stars. Originally played drums, switched to string bass, took lessons from Walter Page. Worked with Zack Whyte—mainly in Cincinnati (1932-4), then moved back to Chicago. With Jimmy Bell's Tampa Tunesters (spring 1935), Zutty Singleton (summer 1935), then with Roy Eldridge from late 1936 until 1938—also did dates in Chicago with Art Tatum (1936). Briefly in Bob Shoffner Big Band (1940), then went to West Coast with Earl Hines (October 1940). Remained with Hines until 1942, then with Jimmie Lunceford for five years. Free-lanced in Chicago, then mainly with Muggsy Spanier from 1950 until 1955, briefly with altoist Gigi Gryce in 1954. With Herbie Fields from late 1956 until June 1957, briefly with Earl Hines (1958), worked with drummer Louis Bellson. After 1960 worked mainly in Chicago, often with Art Hodes, with Roy Eldridge (March 1971), also active as sports coach. Played regularly throughout the 1970s, featured at New York Jazz Fest 1981.

PARHAM, 'Tiny' Hartzell Strathdene
piano/organ/arranger/composer

Born: Winnipeg, Manitoba, 25th February 1900
Died: Wisconsin, 4th April 1943

Raised in Kansas City, attended Lincoln High School. Worked at Eblon Theatre, K.C. (1923), toured Pantages circuit with big band (1925). Moved to Chicago, co-led Syncopators with violinist Leroy Pickett (1926-7), then own band at: La Rue's Dreamland (1928), Sunset Cafe (late 1930), Granada (1931), Merry Gardens (1931-2), El Rado, Golden Lily, etc., summer seasons in Atlantic City, Baltimore. Arranged for Frolic Club's floor shows. Led own Savoy Band (1934-5), led at Club Havana, Chicago (1936), from then on usually worked as an organist in theatres and cinemas, for two years (1939 and 1940) played organ at the Savoy Roller-skating Rink in Chicago. Mainly touring during last two years of his life, he died in his dressing-room whilst fulfilling an engagement in Milwaukee.

PARKER, 'Knocky' John W.
piano

Born: Palmer, Texas, 8th August 1918

Recorded in Texas with The Wanderers in 1935. Subsequently worked with The Light Crust Doughboys and recorded with them from June 1937 until June 1939. After Army service in World War II worked with Albert Nicholas and Zutty Singleton in California. Thereafter combined his work as an English teacher with his roles as jazz lecturer and pianist. During the 1950s worked with a specially formed trio (with Omer Simeon and Arthur Herbert), recorded in New Orleans in 1959. Featured with Doc Evans (1960). Visited Britain in 1952. Played regularly throughout 1970s, featured at New Orleans Jazz Fest, 1983.

PARRISH, Avery
piano/arranger

Born: Birmingham, Alabama, 24th January 1917
Died: New York City, December 1959

Cousin of pianiste-vocaliste Gladys Palmer. Avery's mother was also a pianiste. Attended Alabama State College and whilst there began working with Erskine Hawkins, to New York in 1934. Left Erskine Hawkins (c. 1941), worked in California until suffering severe injuries in a Los Angeles bar skirmish in 1942. Suffered partial paralysis and never again played professionally. He worked day jobs for the rest of his life which ended under mysterious circumstances in New York. Composed the much-recorded blues 'After Hours'.

PASQUALL, Jerome Don
saxes/clarinet

Born: Fulton, Kentucky, 20th September 1902
Died: 18th October 1971

Family moved to St. Louis in 1903. During boyhood played mellophone in the Old Fellows' Brass Band. In August 1918 joined the U.S. Army, played mellophone in the 10th Cavalry Band, then switched to clarinet. Demobilised in 1919 wo ked with Ed Allen in St. Louis, they both left to work with pianist Ralph Stevenson's Band at the Alhambra Cafe, Seattle. Worked with Charlie Creath in St. Louis (1921), then began working for Fate Marable on the riverboats (1921), later that year studied in Chicago at the American Conservatory, also gigged on clarinet and 'C' melody sax with Milton Vassar, Doc Watson, etc. Two years (mainly on tenor sax) with Doc Cooke and his Dreamland Orchestra, left Chicago to study at the New England Conservatory in Boston, Massachusetts, gigged with local bands, in the summer of 1925 worked in New York, but continued full-time studies until graduating on the 27th June 1927, then joined Fletcher Henderson on lead alto, left in late 1928, lived in Chicago and led own band at Harmon's Dreamland, Club Ambassadeur. Toured with Keppard. Joined Dave Peyton in 1930, during following year worked in Jabbo Smith's Band, then worked with Tiny Parham (late 1931 to early 1932), Eddie Mallory took over Parham's Band and Jerome moved to New York. Worked briefly with Charlie Matson and Fess Williams before sailing to Europe with the 'Blackbirds of 1934' revue (August 1934). After return to New York worked with Fess Williams, LeRoy Smith, and Eddie South before spending six months with Fletcher Henderson (1936). With Noble Sissle from 1937 until 1944, except for a short spell in 1943. Quit touring and settled in New York, active as a free-lance musician and arranger, worked regularly with Tony Ambrose's Orchestra.

PASTOR, Tony
(real name: Antonio Pestritto)
tenor sax/vocals

Born: Middletown, Connecticut, 1907
Died: New London, Connecticut, 31st October 1969

His brother, 'Stubby', was a trumpeter. Began playing 'C' melody sax whilst at high school. Worked with various local bands including John Cavallaro (1927), then with Irving Aaronson (1928-30), also worked with Austin Wylie (c. 1930). Led own band in Hartford, Connecticut (1931-4), then touring with Smith Ballew until 1935. Worked briefly with Joe Venuti and Vincent Lopez before becoming a mainstay of Artie Shaw's bands from 1936 until 1940. Formed own band in late 1940 and achieved considerable success, continued to lead own band until 1959. From then onwards appeared with family vocal group which also featured his sons Tony Jr., Guy, and John. In the spring of 1968 he was forced to retire through ill health.

P

PAVAGEAU, 'Slow Drag' Alcide
string bass

Born: New Orleans, Louisiana, 7th March 1888
Died: New Orleans, Louisiana, 19th January 1969

Originally a guitarist, he gigged on that instrument with various bands including The Undertakers Band; he was, however, best known in New Orleans during his early days as a spectacular dancer. During the late 1920s he took up string bass and worked with various leaders including: Buddie Petit, Herb Morand, Elmer Talbot, Emil Barnes, etc. Worked regularly with George Lewis from 1943, went to New York with Bunk Johnson in 1945, subsequently worked regularly with George Lewis, with whom he made overseas tours. During the last few years of his life he regularly marched in parades as the Grand Marshal and played at Preservation Hall. His wife, Anne, recorded as a pianiste and vocaliste.

PAYNE, 'Bennie' Benjamin E.
piano/vocals

Born: Philadelphia, Pennsylvania, 18th June 1907

Began playing piano at 12, by the age of 16 was organist at the local church. Professional debut as pianist-vocalist at the Cotton Club, Philadelphia (1926). Worked with various bands before spending six months with Wilbur Sweatman in 1928. Received piano tuition from Fats Waller, worked as regular accompanist for vocaliste Elizabeth Welch. Joined 'Blackbirds of 1929' and came to Europe with this revue in 1929. Returned to New York, played in the 'Hot Chocolates' show, then worked as accompanist for Gladys Bentley. Joined Cab Calloway in November 1931, remained with Cab until service in U.S. Army from late 1943. (Visited Europe with Cab in 1934.) After service in U.S.A.F., rejoined Calloway until August 1946. With Pearl Bailey, then led own trio. From 1950 Bennie worked as accompanist and musical director for vocalist Billy Daniels, in this capacity made several trips to Europe, during his 1956 visit he recorded with British musicians. Settled in Los Angeles.

PECORA, Santo Joseph
(real name: Pecoraro)
trombone

Born: New Orleans, Louisiana, 31st March 1902
Died: New Orleans, Louisiana, 29th May 1984

His nephew, Santo Pecoraro (born: 1906), was a drummer. Originally played french horn, changed to trombone in his early teens. Played with Johnny De Droit's Band and with Leon Roppolo at Toro's Club before first professional work with Joe Fulco in a cinema orchestra. Left New Orleans in group accompanying vocaliste Bea Palmer, subsequently worked with the New Orleans Rhythm Kings (1924-5). With Johnny Bayersdorffer (1926) and with the Triangle Jazz Band before moving to Chicago, worked with Louis Panico in Chicago (late 1926), played for several years in theatre orchestras. During the 1930s worked with various big bands led by: Buddy Rogers, Will Osborne, Benny Meroff, and Ben Pollack. With Paul Mares at Harry's Bar in Chicago (1935), during following year worked with Sharkey Bonano in New York. Worked briefly with Charlie Barnet (late 1937), then settled in California. With Lyle 'Spud' Murphy's Band from April 1938, later that year worked with Wingy Manone in Los Angeles. Was a studio musician in Hollywood from 1939 until 1942, then after leading own big band returned to New Orleans. From 1942 led own band for various engagements including spell on riverboats, also did a great deal of work with Sharkey Bonano during late 1940s and 1950s. Led own band in Chicago (1959), then returned to New Orleans and resumed residency at the Famous Door, Bourbon Street. During the 1960s played long residencies at the Dream Room, New Orleans, before moving back to the Famous Door.

PEER, Beverly
string bass

Born: New York City, 7th October 1912

Was originally a pianist. Worked regularly on piano before switching to string bass. Joined Chick Webb in summer of 1936. After Webb's death (1939) remained with the band to work under Ella Fitzgerald's leadership until 1942. With Taft Jordan (1942) Sabby Lewis (1944). During the 1950s and 1960s worked regularly, including spells with Harry Dial, pianiste Barbara Carroll, singers Sarah Vaughan and Lena Horne. Spent over eight years with Jimmy Lyon at the Blue Angel Club. Worked regularly with pianist Bobby Short during the 1970s.

PEMBERTON, 'Bill' William McLane — *Born: New York City, 5th March 1918*
string bass

Began studying violin at the age of eight, switched to string bass at 18, after two years' study began working professionally. Worked with Frankie Newton before joining Mercer Ellington's Band (1946), subsequently with Billy Kyle's Quartet (1948), Herman Chittison, Eddie South, Art Tatum, Johnny Hodges, Billy Strayhorn, Lucky Millinder, etc. During the 1960s worked on many occasions with Earl Hines (including overseas tours—toured Russia with Earl in 1966). Also worked regularly in small groups led by Budd Johnson. With Claude Hopkins (1966). Toured with Earl Hines (1968-9). In late 1969, together with Budd Johnson, drummer Oliver Jackson, and pianist Dill Jones, worked in the J.P.J. Quartet. Active during the 1970s. Often worked with Panama Francis and his Savoy Sultans during the early 1980s, including engagements in Europe.

PEREZ, Manuel — *Born: New Orleans, Louisiana, 1879*
cornet — *Died: c. 1946*

Active with the Onward Brass Band from the turn of the century, also organised the Imperial Orchestra (c. 1900). In the years before World War I he was in constant demand for parade and dance work, during this period he occasionally doubled on cello. In 1915 he left New Orleans for a residency at the Arsonia Cafe in Chicago, also played at the Pekin Cafe, Royal Gardens, and with Arthur Sims Band in Chicago. Returned to New Orleans, played for one summer aboard S.S. 'Capitol', then took a residency at Oasis cabaret and Pelican Ballroom, also played parades with Maple Leaf Orchestra. During the late 1920s he returned to play in Chicago, worked with Charles Elgar at the Savoy (1928). Back in New Orleans he continued to work with the Onward Brass Band and also led own orchestra at Pythian Temple Roof Garden until the early 1930s. In later years he returned to his original trade (cigar making); a series of strokes prevented him from making any attempt to play cornet during his declining years.

PERRY, Ray — *Born: Boston, Massachusetts, 25th February 1915*
alto sax/violin — *Died: New York City, autumn 1950*

Two brothers, Joe (baritone sax) and Bay (drums) were professional musicians. Began on violin and made a feature of singing and bowing in unison, this inspired Slam Stewart (q.v.) to experiment. Worked on alto and violin with Dean Earl's Band from 1935, with Clarence 'Chic' Carter from 1937 until 1939. Joined Blanche Calloway from January until September 1940, then with Lionel Hampton from September 1940 until October 1943 when he was forced to quit through illness. With J. C. Heard's Band early in 1946, in summer 1946 led own band at The Spotlight, Ontario, Canada. Led own band in 1947, worked with Sabby Lewis in 1948, re-formed own band in late 1948. During the last few months of his life he worked in octet led by tenorist Illinois Jacquet.

PETERSON, 'Chuck' Charles — *Born: Detroit, Michigan, 1915*
trumpet — *Died: Michigan, 21st January 1978*

Spent part of childhood in Hearne, Texas. High school in Detroit, playing French horn and trombone in school band. Studied journalism and began working for local paper, switched to trumpet, worked for several local bands before joining Hank Biagini. With Artie Shaw (1937-early 1939), Tommy Dorsey (1939), Tony Pastor (1939-41), Woody Herman (1941-42). After Army service returned to live and work in Detroit.

PETIT, Buddy — *Born: White Castle, Louisiana, c. 1897*
cornet — *Died: New Orleans, Louisiana, 4th July 1931*

Went to school with Albert Nicholas and 'Snags' Jones. Was originally known as Joseph Crawford, but adopted surname of his step-father (valve-trombonist Joseph Petit). In 1916 co-led band with Jimmie Noone, in 1917 went to Los Angeles to join Jelly Roll Morton, but soon returned to New Orleans to lead Young Olympians. Throughout early 1920s did extensive touring in Gulf Coast area with his own band, also playing with Toots Johnson

Band in Baton Rouge. By the late 1920s was working on S.S. 'Madison'. Continued playing until the day before his death.

PETTIS, Jack — *Born: Danville, Illinois, 1902*
tenor sax

Originally played 'C' melody sax. Moved to Chicago during teens, played with Elmer Schoebel at the Eerie Club, then after a spell in Dixon's Band on the S.S. 'Capitol' joined New Orleans Rhythm Kings. Formed own band which accompanied vocaliste Ann Pennington on vaudeville circuits, stayed in New York after Palace engagements. Joined Ben Bernie, later worked under Bernie's auspices as leader aboard S.S. 'Leviathan' (the Atlantic pleasure liner). After leading band accompanying Morton Downey, did long residencies at Hotel New Yorker and in Hollywood. Retired from music many years ago.

PEYTON, 'Benny' Benton E. — *Born: c. 1890.*
drums — *Died: New York City, 24th January 1965*

In 1919 came to Europe as a member of Will Marion Cook's Southern Syncopated Orchestra, subsequently formed own band from members of the orchestra and led own Jazz Kings at Hammersmith Palais, London, etc. (1921), later led own band on the Continent, then toured Russia with trombonist Frank Withers and Sidney Bechet (1926). Continued to lead own band in Europe during the 1920s and 1930s, residencies in Hungary, Belgium, France, Switzerland, etc. Returned to New York in 1939, served for many years as a union delegate for the Local 802 of the A.F. of M. During the 1950s regularly played percussion in Wally Edwards' Rehearsal Band at Prince's Hall in Harlem.

PEYTON, Dave — *Born: c. 1885*
piano/arranger — *Died: Chicago, Illinois, 1956*

Worked in Wilbur Sweatman's Trio at the Grand Theatre, Chicago (c. 1908-12). Led own band for many years in Chicago, playing residencies at the Grand Theatre, Cafe De Paris, Plantation, Club Baghdad, Pershing Palace, Regal Theatre, etc., also acted as a band contractor, supplying musicians for specific engagements. Led own orchestra at the Regal Theatre during the mid-1930s, later worked mainly as a solo pianist. Played residency at the Spot O' Fun, Chicago, in the late 1940s, ran own dry-cleaning business during the 1950s.

PHILBURN, 'Al' Michael Aloysius — *Born: Newark, New Jersey, 24th August 1902*
trombone — *Died: Long Island, 29th February 1972*

Began on trombone at the age of 14, taught by Ernest Clarke. Worked casual engagements in and around Newark before joining Eddie Elkins' Band at Club Richman in 1924, following year with Paul Specht orchestra. Spent two years working with Cass Hagen and Red Nichols, then three years (1927-30) working mainly for Ed Kirkeby including many California Ramblers' sessions. From 1929 worked for several years in Bert Lown's Orchestra, then free-lance studio work before becoming staff musician at WNGW and N.B.C. (1936-48). Extensive recordings during this period. Did occasional jazz gigs during the 1950s, but was mainly occupied with session work. Briefly with Tony Parenti at Condon's in late 1962, then leading own Dixieland band at Freedomland until 1964, played with Paul Lavalle at that venue until 1965. In 1969 with a Lester Lanin band (led by Willis Kelly) at El Morocco in New York.

PHILLIPS, 'Flip'
(real name: Joseph Edward Filipelli) — *Born: Brooklyn, New York, 26th February 1915*
tenor sax/clarinet

Originally a clarinettist, received tuition from his cousin, Frank Reda. From 1934 until 1939 worked mainly at Schneider's Lobster House in Brooklyn, played clarinet and alto sax (some tuition from Pete Brown). On clarinet with Frankie Newton at Kelly's Stables, New York in February 1940, 1940 summer season with Newton, then played short season at Lake George with Newton in spring 1941. Specialised on tenor sax from 1942, worked with Larry Bennett in New York (1942), briefly with Benny Goodman (late 1942), then joined Wingy Manone. Briefly with Red Norvo from October 1943, then with Woody Herman until 1946; for the next 10 years was a regular member of Norman Granz's 'Jazz At The Philharmonic' tours, several visits to Europe. Worked in Gene Krupa's Trio in 1952 (including trip to Europe). Moved to Florida in the late 1950s, worked regularly with Bill Harris. Toured Europe with Benny Goodman in late 1959. During the 1960s played occasionally in New York, but mainly active leading own quartet in Pompano Beach, Florida. Began undertaking more widespread work in the 1970s, featured at Newport Jazz Festival (1978). Worked regularly throughout late 1970s and early 1980s, including tour of Europe 1982.

PHILLIPS, 'Lloyd' Benjamin Lloyd
piano/arranger

Born: Richmond, Virginia. c. 1905
Died: California, March 1974

Began studying piano during last year at school. First professional work accompanying a touring show through New England. Settled in New York in 1926. With trumpeter Dave Alford's Orchestra (early 1927), then worked for a long time in bands led by June Clark until 1930. Subsequently toured briefly with Dave Nelson's Band (1931), later worked with Nelson at The Nest club, New York (1932), also deputised for Joe Steele in Chick Webb's Band. In 1933 and 1934 with Fess Williams before touring Europe with Lew Leslie's 'Blackbirds' Revue. Returned to New York in 1935, spent two years in LeRoy Smith's Orchestra, then began specialising in accompanying solo singers. Continued to specialise in work as an accompanist through the 1940s, but also did regular jazz work with Sidney Bechet (1940), Snub Mosley, Everett Barksdale (1942), George James (1942-3), duo with Don Kirkpatrick (1943-6), Mezz Mezzrow, Sidney Bechet (1947-8), etc. From 1951 was regular accompanist for Pearl Bailey. During the 1960s recorded for Edgar Battle's Cosmopolitan label.

PHIPPS, 'Jimmy' James
piano

Born: New York City, 3rd July 1912

Began playing at age of 9, first teacher was William Francis. Played first gigs at the Balconnades Ballroom, New York in spring of 1929. During the early 1930s worked with Reggie Johnson's Band. With Doc Wheeler's Sunset Royals (1941), Benny Carter (1942), Erskine Hawkins (1943-4), Gus Aiken (1946), rejoined Erskine Hawkins (1946-47). With Henry Allen (1948-49). Left full-time music, but continued to play weekend gigs during the 1970s.

PICHON, 'Fats' Walter
piano/vocals/arranger

Born: New Orleans, Louisiana, 1906
Died: Chicago, Illinois, 25th February 1967

Began playing piano as a child. Moved to New York (c. 1922), subsequently played a summer season with a quartet at the Atlantic Hotel, Belmar, New Jersey. Moved on to Boston where he studied for four years at the New England Conservatory. After touring Mexico with the Eleven Aces (from Dallas, Texas) he returned to New Orleans. Worked with Sidney Desvigne (summer 1926), led own band at Pelican Cafe (1927), then worked with Desvigne on the riverboats. Returned to New York late in 1928, did recording sessions under own name, also sang on Luis Russell recording and arranging for various bands. Worked in Texas with the Dusky Stevedores (late 1929). Back to New York, worked with Elmer Snowden and toured with Fess Williams (1931). Returned to New Orleans (c. 1932). Worked with Sidney Desvigne, Armand Piron, etc., also led own band on riverboats—led own band in Memphis (1935), also toured briefly with Mamie Smith. In 1941 began long residencies at The Absinthe House, New Orleans, played solo dates there regularly in the 1940s and 1950s, also worked at Cafe Society in New York in 1944 and 1948, toured the Caribbean in 1952. During the 1960s soloed in Chicago, Milwaukee, New Orleans, etc., but was inactive for long spells whilst receiving treatment for failing eyesight.

P

PICOU, **Alphonse Floristan**
clarinet/composer

Born: New Orleans, Louisiana, 19th October 1878
Died: New Orleans, Louisiana, 4th February 1961

Was originally a guitarist starting at 14, began playing clarinet at 15, and was a full-fledged musician at the age of 16. First regular work in band led by trombonist Bouboul Fortunea Augustat, worked with the Accordiana Band, later led own Independence Band. During the late 1890s played regularly in the Lyre Club Symphony Orchestra, also worked with Oscar DuConge, Bunk Johnson, Dave Peyton, Wooden Joe Nicholas and Manuel Perez. Between 1900 and 1915 worked with many bands in New Orleans including: the Excelsior Brass Band, Freddie Keppard's Olympia Band, George Moret's Band, etc. Played briefly in Chicago with Manuel Perez at the Arsonia Cafe (c. 1917), returned to New Orleans, worked for John Robichaux, the Camelia Orchestra, the Golden Leaf Orchestra, also regular dates with the Tuxedo Brass Band. Composed tunes for King Oliver's Creole Jazz Band. (In one interview claimed to have recorded with Clarence Williams during the 1920s.) Played regularly until 1932, then returned to his original trade as a tin-smith. More active from the early 1940s, residency at the Club Pig Pen from 1944, in the late 1940s worked with Papa Celestin. Made records with Kid Rena and Papa Celestin featuring the famous clarinet solo from the march, *High Society,* for which he was noted. With Richard Alexis' Tuxedo Band in the early 1950s, also led own small group at The Paddock. Made special appearances with the Eureka Band in the late 1950s, but was mainly active in helping his daughter manage the various properties that he owned in New Orleans. His funeral was one of the most elaborate ever seen in the city.

PIERCE, **'Billie'**
(née Wilhelmina Goodson)
piano/vocals

Born: Marianna, Florida, 8th June 1907
Died: New Orleans, 29th September 1974

Wife of trumpeter Dee Dee Pierce. Accompanied various singers during the 1920s, then settled in New Orleans. During the 1960s and early 1970s did widespread touring with her husband throughout the U.S.A., Europe and the Orient.

PIERCE, **'Dee Dee'**
(real name: Joseph De Lacrois)
trumpet/vocals

Born: New Orleans, Louisiana, 18th February 1904
Died: New Orleans, Louisiana, 23rd November 1973

Played with many New Orleans' bands during the 1920s. Long period working as a bricklayer until forced to retire through blindness. Began working in a duo with his wife, Billie Pierce. After establishing themselves in New Orleans they went on to gain international fame during world-wide tours, often with the Preservation Hall Jazz Band. Touring restricted by onset of cancer.

PIRON, **Armand John**
violin/composer

Born: New Orleans, Louisiana, 16th August 1888
Died: New Orleans, Louisiana, 17th February 1943

At the age of seven he badly injured his right hip in a fall and was unable to walk for five years. Received musical tuition from his father, who was an orchestra leader, began playing professionally in 1904. First led own band in 1908, worked in the Peerless Orchestra (c. 1912), fronted the Olympia Orchestra from 1912. Partnered Clarence Williams in a publishing company, did promotional tours with Williams, including appearances with W. C. Handy's Orchestra (c. 1917). Began working in New Orleans with Papa Celestin (c. 1916). Formed own band in 1918 which played long residencies at Tranchina's Restaurant on Lake Pontchartrain and at the New Orleans Country Club. The band played briefly in New York in 1923, returned in 1924 to play residency at the Roseland Ballroom. Piron returned to New Orleans, again led at Tranchina's, later played long spells on the riverboats. During the last years of his life he led his own small night-club group. Died in the Charity Hospital, New Orleans.

During the band's New York bookings publicity photographs were taken billing them as Williams' Ten Jazz Kings.

PINKETT, 'Ward' William Ward
trumpet/vocals

Born: Newport News, Virginia, 29th April 1906
Died: New York City, 15th March 1937

His sister, Loretta (a saxophoniste), once led her own band in Newport News; their father (a tailor) played cornet as a hobby. Started on trumpet at the age of 10, later went to Hampton Institute, Virginia, and played in the school band; to New Haven Conservatory of Music in Meridian, Mississippi, for further studies. Joined White Brothers Orchestra in Washington, D.C., then went to New York with a travelling show. Briefly with Charlie Johnson at Small's, New York, then joined Willie Gant's Orchestra (summer 1926), with Billy Fowler Orchestra before becoming resident musician at James Hogan's Joyland. Worked at Bamboo Inn with bands led by Henri Saparo and Joe Steele, then played for Charlie Skeete and Jelly Roll Morton. Worked with Chick Webb at Bottomland and Renaissance in New York, then with Bingie Madison at Rose Danceland, New York (1931). With bassist Earl Magee's Orchestra before joining Rex Stewart's Band at the Empress Ballroom (summer 1933). With Teddy Hill's Band at Lafayette Theatre (1934). During 1935 worked with Albert Nicholas and Bernard Addison at Adrian Rollini's Tap Room, also played briefly in Louis Metcalf's Big Band at the Bedford Ballroom, New York. Died of pneumonia, was buried in his home town.

PITTMAN, Booker Taliaferro
saxes/clarinet/vocals

Born: Fairmont Heights, Maryland, 3rd October 1909
Died: Brazil, 13th October 1969

Raised in Dallas, Texas. His mother, Mrs. Portia Pittman (a daughter of Booker T. Washington) was a noted music teacher, her pupils included Budd and Keg Johnson, Sam Price, etc. Played with the Blue Moon Chasers in Dallas (1927), then toured with Gene Coy's Happy Black Aces (1928). With Fred Cooper Orchestra early in 1929, with Terrence Holder from spring of 1929. Moved to Kansas City, worked with Jesse Stone, Count Basie Trio, Bennie Moten, and Jap Allen, then joined Blanche Calloway in April 1931. Worked in Ralph Cooper's Kongo Knights (1932), then joined Lucky Millinder and travelled to Europe with Lucky in June 1933. Remained in Europe, worked with pianist Romeo Silva's Orchestra in summer of 1934, then brief spells with several bands before going to Rio de Janeiro, Brazil, in 1936 with Romeo Silva. In 1937 worked with guitarist David Washington in The Swing Stars at Rambia Hotel, Buenos Aires, then led own Swing Stars at the Chaumière, Buenos Aires (1937). Continued to work in Argentina until 1946, then returned to Brazil, continued leading own bands, then spent 10 years out of music running a farm in Sao Paulo. Resumed regular playing, visited the U.S.A. in summer of 1962, made guest appearances playing alto and soprano saxes. Played in Brazil and Argentina in 1963, then formed successful variety act with his step-daughter, vocaliste Eliana. Made television appearances in New York in late 1964, then returned to South America.

PLATER, 'Bobby' Robert
alto sax/flute

Born: Newark, New Jersey, 13th May 1914
Died: Lake Tahoe, Nevada, 20th November 1982

First professional work with the Savoy Dictators (1937), then worked with Tiny Bradshaw for three years before joining U.S. Army. Led the 93rd Division Band until 1945. Briefly with Cootie Williams' Big Band, then joined Lionel Hampton in 1946. Regularly with Hampton until 1964 (briefly out of action through sustaining broken legs in Hampton band-coach crash in October 1955). Joined Count Basie in autumn 1964, and remained with Basie until suffering a fatal heart attack whilst on tour with the band.

PLETCHER, 'Stew' Stewart F.
trumpet/mellophone

Born: 1907
Died: U.S.A., 29th November 1978

Studied at Yale, went to France with student band in summer of 1928. Led own band in U.S.A. during early 1930s. Worked outside of professional music for several long periods; is best known for his work with Red Norvo (1936-7). Left Norvo in July 1937, rejoined the band from September until December 1937. Briefly with Tony Pastor in 1939, then worked with Billy Bissett's Band in Salt Lake City (1939). Worked with Jack Teagarden (1945), with Nappy Lamare's Band in late 1949, again briefly with Jack Teagarden in 1955. Ill health in the 1970s. His son Tom plays cornet.

P

POLLACK, Ben
drums

Born: Chicago, 22nd June 1903
Died: Palm Springs, 7th June 1971

Played drums in Chicago school bands: Harrison High and Crane Technical. Did occasional jobs with gig bands organised by Husk O'Hare's Agency, but first regular work with Dick Schoenberg (in 1921) at Navy Pier, Chicago. Spell with pianist Izzy Wagner in Fox Lakes, Wisconsin, then joined Friars' Inn Orchestra (New Orleans Rhythm Kings). Then to Los Angeles, worked for a week with Larry Shields before joining Harry Bastin Band for 11 months including playing at Venice Ballroom. Returned to Chicago intending to work in family fur business, but abandoned the idea. Journeyed to New York, whilst there received offer to take over Bastin Band in Los Angeles. After making personnel changes remained on West Coast for almost a year from October 1924. Returned to Chicago, band work scarce, Pollack played as a sideman in Art Kassel's Band, then from May 1926 led own band in Chicago—first at the Southmoor Hotel, later at The Blackhawk (from May 1927). Band worked on West Coast in late 1927, moved to New York and opened at Little Club in March 1928. Summer season in Atlantic City, then returned to New York for residency at Park Central Hotel from late September 1928, doubled in Broadway show 'Hello Daddy' from late 1928—during this period temporarily forsook drums to conduct—Ray Bauduc joining as percussionist. Throughout early 1930s leading own band for long residencies including Silver Slipper, Chicago. Band broke up in California in December 1934, most of his sidemen formed nucleus of the first Bob Crosby Band. Led in New Orleans (1935), Chicago, Los Angeles (1936), etc., continued to lead own bands until 1942, then from May 1942 directing touring band for comedian Chico Marx. From August 1943 ran own booking agency and record company (Jewel), very little playing until successful appearance at Second Annual Dixieland Jubilee in 1949, then formed own sextet for residency at Beverly Cavern. Led own bands on West Coast, later opened own club in Los Angeles. Appeared as himself in film 'The Benny Goodman Story' (1956). Occasional guest appearances during 1960s, but mainly occupied running own restaurant in Palm Springs, California. Committed suicide by hanging.

POLLOCK, Edward
reeds/clarinet/vocals

Born: New Orleans, Louisiana, 9th May 1899

Moved to Chicago in the early 1920s, was taught saxophone by Erskine Tate. First gigs in a Robins, Illinois speakeasy in July 1925. In September 1925 joined Detroit Shannon. During the late 1920s and 1930s worked with Bert Hall, Charlie Elgar, Clifford King, Erskine Tate, Sammy Stewart, Eddie South, Jimmie Noone, Tiny Parham & Carroll Dickerson, recorded with several of these bands, and also recorded with Ma Rainey. Worked mainly in Chicago throughout career, but did national tour with Carl White's group in 1927 accompanying singer Al Jolson. Led own band during 1940s, including long residency at the Du Sable Lounge, Chicago. Left music and became a real estate broker.

POLO, Danny
clarinet/saxes

Born: Toluca, Illinois, 22nd December 1901
Died: Chicago, Illinois, 11th July 1949

Raised in Clinton, India. Father a clarinettist. Aged eight, joined marching band. Later formed novelty duo with young pianist Claude Thornhill. First professional work with Elmer Schoebel's Band at Midway Gardens, Chicago (c. 1923), then with Merritt Brunies' Band including trip to New Orleans. With Arnold Johnson in Florida, then joined Ben Bernie. In winter of 1926 'subbed' three months for Don Murray in Jean Goldkette's Band, then joined Paul Ash. Left U.S.A. (with Dave Tough) in summer of 1927, worked with George Carhart throughout Europe before leading own band in Paris, also worked with Arthur Briggs and Lud Gluskin. To London to join Ambrose's Orchestra (April 1930), summer 1930 vacation in U.S.A., again with Ambrose. Worked again with Lud Gluskin in 1932, rejoined Ambrose in October 1932. Returned to U.S.A. in December 1935. Returned to Britain, rejoined Ambrose from April until August 1938, then went to Paris; worked with Ray Ventura's Orchestra for 11 months from October 1938. Returned to New York in October 1939, soon joined Joe Sullivan's Band at Cafe Society on tenor and clarinet. With Jack Teagarden from July 1940 until January 1942 (including playing for soundtrack of 'Birth of the Blues'). With

Claude Thornhill from February 1942 until that leader joined U.S. Navy. Led own bands during the mid-1940s including long residencies in Flint, Michigan, and Newport, Kentucky. Rejoined Claude Thornhill on alto sax and clarinet in May 1947, regularly with Thornhill until March 1949, rejoined in June 1949 and was working with that band at the Edgewater Hotel, Chicago, when suddenly taken ill; he died the following day in the Illinois Masonic Hospital.

PORTER, 'Gene' Eugene
saxes/clarinet/flute/vocals

Born: Jackson, Mississippi, 7th June 1910

Both parents were non-professional guitarists. Started on cornet, had instrument stolen, bought a 'C' melody sax. Moved to Chicago in 1927 to attend high school, played bass clarinet in Reserve Officers' Training Corps Band. Bought an alto sax and began gigging in band led by trumpeter Billy King, quit school in September 1929, took clarinet lessons from Omer Simeon. Played on excursion train to New Orleans with Billy King (band booked to play for dancing in the baggage car), left in New Orleans and returned to Jackson. Whilst finishing studies gigged with local bands. Left home in April 1931 with Clarence Desdune's Orchestra, returned to New Orleans with Desdunes, subsequently worked with Papa Celestin before joining Joe Robichaux from 1933. Joined Sidney Desvigne on riverboat S.S. 'St. Paul' (April 1935), left in St. Louis, played in Tab Smith's Band for a month, then joined Jeter-Pillars' Band in October 1935. Left to work with Don Redman from February until September 1937, then rejoined Jeter-Pillars until June 1942. With Jimmie Lunceford from June-September 1942, then joined Benny Carter, moved with Carter to Hollywood (November 1942). Played in Los Angeles with Benny Carter (appeared in the film 'Stormy Weather'), was assistant leader with Carter, also played in various studio orchestras, appearing in the films 'The Gang's All Here', 'As Thousands Cheer', etc., etc. Army service from October 1944, was solo clarinettist in 103rd Army Band, after release in June 1945 rejoined Benny Carter for a while, then worked with Jake Porter (no relation). With guitarist Gene Phillips (late 1947), then joined Walter Fuller at Club Royal, San Diego (January 1948). Remained with Fuller until June 1960, then formed own small group. From 1967 resident at the Bronze Room, La Mesce, California (saxes, clarinet, flute, drums, and vocals).

PORTER, 'Jake' Vernon
cornet

Born California, 3rd August 1916

Raised in Oakland. Began on violin in 1923, specialised on cornet from 1925. First jobs with Melvin Parks' Band in 1931. Joined Wesley Peoples' Band in 1934, during the next six years worked in California for various bandleaders including: Ben Watkins, Clem Raymond, Saunders King, Lionel Hampton, etc. Moved to Los Angeles in May 1940, worked with Al Adams, C. P. Johnson, Leo Davis, Slim Gaillard, and Slam Stewart before serving in U.S. Army Cavalry Band from December 1942 until May 1943. After release played for Benny Carter and Fats Waller (1943). Following year with Noble Sissle, before playing for Fletcher Henderson and Horace Henderson in 1945. Formed own band, working on West Coast until 1951 (briefly with Benny Goodman in 1947). Quit full-time playing in 1951 to organise Combo recording company; after seven-year lay-off recommenced playing in 1958. Worked in Canada with Mike Riley in 1964, then worked mainly in California; during summer of 1969 toured with the vocalist Little Richard. Active as union official (1970). Active free-lancing during the 1970s, including film studio work. Toured Europe in 1978. Worked regularly during early 1980s, including organising own record label, and supplying music for various television productions.

PORTER, 'Yank' Allen
drums

Born: Norfolk, Virginia. c. 1895
Died: New York City, 22nd March 1944

Toured with 'Lucky Sambo' Vaughan revue before settling in New York in 1926. Worked mainly with Cliff Jackson from 1926 until 1930. With Charlie Matson Orchestra (1932), with Louis Armstrong (January and February 1933), then toured with Bud Harris (1933). Worked with James P. Johnson (1934). Regularly with Fats Waller from autumn 1935 until spring 1936, later that year joined pianist Dave Martin's Band at Hotel St. George in Brooklyn. With James P. Johnson Band (late 1939), with Joe Sullivan at Cafe Society (spring 1940), then with Teddy Wilson Small Band (July until December 1940), free-lance recordings with Benny Carter and Art Tatum. Returned to Hotel St. George in 1943, led own band there until shortly before his death.

POSTON, 'Doc' Joseph E. — *Born: Alexandria, Louisiana. c. 1895*
alto sax/clarinet/vocals — *Died: Illinois, May 1942*

Chiefly remembered for his work with Jimmie Noone. Regular member of Doc Cooke's Dreamland Orchestra from 1922 until 1924, then worked on riverboats with Fate Marable. Returned to Doc Cooke (1927), then worked with Jimmie Noone's Band from 1928 until 1930, brief return to Doc Cooke. Illness enforced premature retirement, spent the last eight years of his life in a sanatorium.

POTTER, 'Tommy' Charles Thomas — *Born: Philadelphia, Pennsylvania, 21st September 1918*
string bass

Raised in New Jersey, worked on piano and guitar before taking up string bass in 1940. Worked with Trummy Young, Billy Eckstine, John Hardee, etc., before spending two years with alto saxophonist Charlie Parker (b. 1920). Left Parker in 1949, worked briefly with Stan Getz and Count Basie. During the 1950s worked with Earl Hines, Artie Shaw, Eddie Heywood, Bud Powell, toured Sweden with trumpeter Rolf Ericson in summer of 1956, with Tyree Glenn (1958-59), with Harry Edison (1959-61). During the 1960s worked with Buck Clayton, Buddy Tate, Jimmy McPartland, etc., then left full-time music to work in civil service assisting in hospital recreation. Continued to free-lance during the 1970s.

POWELL, 'Jimmie' James Theodore — *Born: New York City, 24th October 1914*
alto sax/clarinet/flute

Played violin as a child, gave recital at New York Town Hall at 14, later studied music at DeWitt Clinton High School. Gigged with many bands in New York from the mid-1930s, regularly with Benny Carter (1939 to early 1940), briefly in Sidney Bechet Band at Mimo Club (February 1940). Toured with Fats Waller (1940-1). With Count Basie from summer of 1943 until early 1946, then with Willie Bryant. In the late 1940s and 1950s worked with Hot Lips Page, Don Redman, Eddie Heywood, Lucky Millinder, etc. Overseas tour with Dizzy Gillespie in 1956, also toured with Machito. From 1959 through the 1960s worked regularly with Reuben Phillips Band at the Apollo Theatre, New York, also with Bill Doggett. Worked with singer Aretha Franklin during early 1970s. Long spell with Sy Oliver's Band beginning 1975.

POWELL, 'Rudy' Everard Stephen — *Born: New York City, 28th October 1907*
alto sax/clarinet — *Died: 30th October 1976*

Started on piano, violin, and sax during early childhood, received saxophone tuition from Lt. Eugene Mikell Sr. and played in the 369th Cadet Band. Gigged with June Clark before joining Gene Rodger's Revellers in 1928, later that year joined Cliff Jackson's Krazy Kats, remained until summer of 1931, then joined band led by trombonist Billy Kato. Played with Elmer Snowden, Dave Nelson, Sam Wooding, and Kaiser Marshall Trio before working with Rex Stewart Band at Empire Ballroom, New York (1933). Briefly in pianist Dave Martin's Orchestra in 1934, then joined Fats Waller in 1934, worked regularly with Fats until January 1937. From March 1937 until late 1938 with Edgar Hayes (including European tour). Four months with Claude Hopkins, then with Teddy Wilson Orchestra from April 1939. In 1940 joined Andy Kirk for nine months, then with Fletcher Henderson from early 1941 until summer of 1942. With Eddie South for 15 months, then Don Redman from June 1943. Briefly with Chris Columbus Band in 1944, then rejoined Claude Hopkins for residency at the Zanzibar, New York (late 1944). With Cab Calloway from April 1945 until May 1948, then with Lucky Millinder for two years except for brief stint with Charlie Ventura Orchestra. Year with Jimmy Rushing's Kansas City Seven (1951-2), with Buddy Tate in 1953, then

Jack Purvis

Sam Price

Benny Peyton's Band – Switzerland 1935: (l. to r.) Peter du Conge, Harry Cooper, Zaidee Jackson, Frank Ethridge, Benny Peyton

Luis Russell's Orchestra: (l. to r.) **Bill Coleman, Jimmy Archey, Bill Dillard, Henry Allen, Will K. Johnson, Luis Russell, Paul Barbarin,**

Andrew Blakeney, Joe Darensbourg, Kid Ory

Kid Ory, Minor Hall, Alvin Alcorn, Albert Burbank, Ed Garland

Eddie Edwards, Larry Shields, Tony Sbarbaro, J. Russell Robinson, Nick LaRocca

Rudy Powell

Vernon 'Jake' Porter

Cozy Cole (drums), Pete Brown (trumpet/alto), Joe Marsala (clarinet), Benny Carter (alto), and Bobby Hackett (guitar) at a recording session organised by Leonard Feather (1939)

Bobby Martin's All Stars – 1937

Tony Parenti

Russell Procope

Eugene Porter

(l. to r.) Vido Musso (tenor), Ben Pollack (drums), Red Norvo (vibes), Russ Morgan (trombone), Jack Fina (piano), Joe Venuti (violin), Red Nichols (cornet)

Louis Prima

Alphonse Picou

Zutty Singleton and Hot Lips Page

Glyn Paque

Ike Quebec

Alton Purnell

Pee Wee Russell

Howdy Quicksell

Eugene Sedric, Garvin Bushell

The Spirits of Rhythm: (l. to r.) Virgil Scroggins, Leo Watson, Wellman Braud, Teddy Bunn

Charlie Spivak

Victoria Spivey

Rex Stewart

Johnny St. Cyr

Stuff Smith and his Onyx Club Band (1936): (Top, l. to r.) Clyde Hart, Cozy Cole, Mack Walker; (Bottom, l. to r.) Jonah Jones, Bobby Bennett, Stuff Smith

Elmer Snowden

Cyrus St. Clair

Muggsy Spanier

Art Tatum

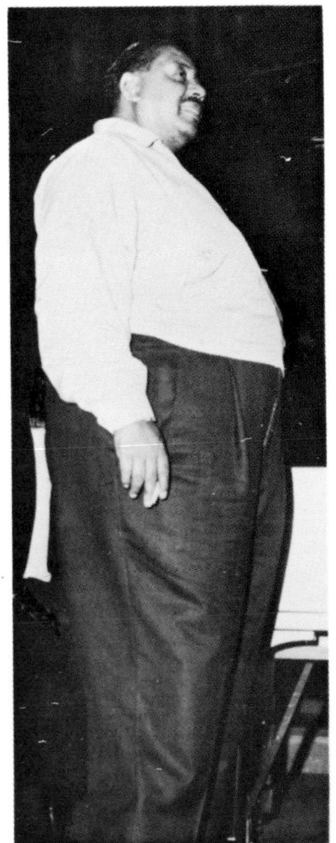

Joe Turner (vocals)

Joe Turner (piano)

Joe Sullivan's Cafe Society Band – 1939: Johnny Wells (drums), Edward Anderson (trumpet), Ed Hall (clarinet), Danny Polo (tenor sax), Henry Turner (bass), Joe Sullivan (piano)

Sam Wooding

Dicky Wells

Cootie Williams

Trummy Young

Bob Zurke's Big Band (1939) featuring Sterling Bose (trumpet) and Stan King (drums)

Clarence Williams

Spencer Williams

Lester Young and Benny Goodman

joined pianist Benton Heath's New Garden Ballroom Orchestra for eight-year spell ending in 1961. On tour with Ray Charles Orchestra, left in 1962 and worked with Buddy Johnson, Bobby Green, Joe Marshall, etc. From August 1965 played regularly with The Saints and Sinners until 1969 illness. Played week-end gigs in and around New York (1971), occasionally on tenor sax.

POWELL, 'Teddy' Theodore
(real name: Alfred Paolella)
violin/vocals/guitar/arranger/leader

Born: Oakland, California, 1st March 1905

Began on violin at the age of eight, doubled on banjo from 14, formed own band at 15. Worked in Los Angeles with Lou Singer Band, then whilst playing guitar in Ray West's Orchestra in Los Angeles (1927) was signed by bandleader Abe Lyman. Worked regularly with Lyman until 1934 (as banjoist/guitarist/violinist/vocalist/arranger), then under Lyman's auspices did extensive work organising bands for advertising agency radio contracts. Finally left Lyman in 1938, following year formed own band which made official debut at Donahue's in New Jersey. Played residencies at the Arcadia, Famous Door, etc., then after nine months' residency at Rustic Cabin, New Jersey, the band lost all its instruments in a fire (October 1941). Powell soon reorganised and continued leading big bands until 1944. From 1945 concentrated on composing and arranging, scored for several New York shows and wrote several big hits (including 'Bewildered', 'If My Heart Could Only Talk', etc.—some under the pen-name of Freddy James). Temporary absence from music for 15 months from late 1945, settled in Connecticut, continued to lead own band in the late 1940s and 1950s (usually on violin), played regular residencies in Miami, New York, Chicago, etc. From 1957 mainly active with own music-publishing business.

POWERS, Ollie
(Powers was the correct surname, not Powell as has been suggested)
drums/vocals

Born: Louisville, Kentucky. c 1890
Died: Chicago, Illinois, 14th April 1928

Worked as drummer-vocalist with Panama Trio in Chicago from 1914, then in duo with Shelton Brooks. With Fields' Crackerjack Band in the early 1920s, then led own Harmony Band at Dreamland (early 1924), also worked in Chicago as a solo act and occasionally in duo with vocaliste May Alix. Last engagement was with Jimmie Noone at the Apex Club from autumn 1926 until three weeks before he died. His death (from diabetes mellitus) took place in the Cook County Hospital.

PRATHER, Harry
string bass/tuba

Born: Cuthbert, Georgia, 1906
Died: Charlotte, North Carolina, 15th September 1981

Began playing tuba (c. 1920). Worked in carnivals, circuses, and theatre orchestras, then with George Baquet in Philadelphia (1928). Joined Jelly Roll Morton in early 1929 (then on tour in Harrisburg, Pennsylvania) and worked on and off with Morton until August 1930. With Dave Taylor's Dixie Serenaders (1931), subsequently with Jimmy Gunn Band (mostly in the Carolinas), changed to string bass in 1933. Moved to Chicago, worked with Punch Miller and Albert Wynn, then to New York in 1937. Played with Sidney Bechet, Frankie Newton, and Louis Jordan, then with Leon Abbey Orchestra (1941). With Harvey Davis Orchestra (1943), then on U.S.O. tour with Herman 'Humpy' Flintall's Band, again with Leon Abbey from 1945, also occasionally with Snub Mosely, Wilbur De Paris, etc. Freelanced in Canada during the early 1950s, then regularly in group accompanying the vocal group The Ink Spots (including tour of Europe). During the late 1950s and early 1960s with the Sabby Lewis Band. Settled in New York, continued to play regularly.

PRATT, Alfred
tenor sax/clarinet/vocals

Born: New Orleans, Louisiana, 19th December 1908
Died: South America. c. 1960

Moved to New York as a child. Professional from the age of 18, led own small band and gigged in Philadelphia, Baltimore, Washington, etc. With Bubber Miley's Band (1930), on tour with King Oliver from early 1931 until early 1932, then toured with Ralph Cooper's

Kongo Knights. To Europe with Lucky Millinder in June 1933; remained in Paris and played club residencies. Toured Europe with Louis Armstrong (1934), also worked with Romeo Silva's Orchestra and with Freddy Johnson. Left Europe (c. 1936) and settled in South America, worked in Santiago, Chile, early in 1937, then long residencies in Rio de Janeiro, Buenos Aires, etc.

PRICE, Jesse *Born: Memphis, Tennessee, 1st May 1909*
drums/vocalist *Died: Los Angeles, 19th April 1974*

Worked with George E. Lee's Band, Thamon Hayes, and Count Basie during the early 1930s. Led own band in Kansas City, then with trumpeter Dee 'Prince' Stewart (early 1938), moved to Chicago for two months, then led own band at Reno Club, Kansas City, in summer of 1938. Left to tour with Ida Cox, then rejoined Dee Stewart late in 1938. With Bill Martin's Band in Kansas City (spring 1939), then joined Harlan Leonard in late 1939 until short spell in Ella Fitzgerald Band (summer 1941). Own band (1942-3) except for brief spell with Walter Fuller in Chicago (August 1942). In spring of 1943 rejoined Harlan Leonard at the Hollywood Club, Los Angeles. Few months with Louis Armstrong from July 1943. Very briefly with Stan Kenton Orchestra (May 1944), short spell with Count Basie (October-November 1944). Led own band in Joplin, Missouri (1945), then returned to California. With Benny Carter (autumn 1948), with Slim Gaillard in Chicago (spring 1949), then with Jay McShann in Kansas City. Throughout the 1950s and 1960s worked regularly on the West Coast until illness in 1969. Led band at Monterey Festival (September 1971).

PRICE, 'Sam' Samuel Blythe *Born: Honey Grove, Texas, 6th October 1908*
piano/vocals

Not related to pianist Jimmy Blythe. Started on alto horn in local boys' band in Waco, Texas (taught by Professor Cobb). Family moved to Dallas in 1918; Sam began playing piano—studying with Mrs. Portia Pittman (daughter of Booker T. Washington). At 15 won a State contest as a Charleston dancer, and as a result toured as a featured attraction with Alphonso Trent's Band. Returned to Dallas to work in a music store, his employer, R. T. Ashford, was also a talent scout for recording companies, and thus got Sam jobs as an accompanist. First professional playing in Athens, Texas, in late 1925, then returned to Dallas. Led own big band, also played regularly at the Ella B. Moore Theatre and with Lee Collins at Riverside Park. Left Texas in 1927 to tour theatre circuits accompanying Happy Donovan and Travis Tucker in the 'Let's Go' show. Played in band led by trombonist Benny Long (1928); in 1929 pioneered jazz broadcasting in Oklahoma City with Lem Johnson and trumpeter Leonard Chadwick. From 1930-3 worked mainly in Kansas City, Missouri—played long residency at the Yellow Front Cafe (during which time he worked briefly with Bunk Johnson). After a spell at the Derby Cafe, Chicago (late 1933), he moved on to Detroit where he joined band led by trumpeter Bill Johnson at the Cave, later played with Johnson at the Harlem Club, then led own small group at Chequers Barbeque, etc. Worked at the Tuxedo Club, first with Bennie Pippin, then again with Bill Johnson. Moved to New York in late 1937 and soon joined Decca recording staff as house pianist and supervisor. During Sam Price's years with Decca he recorded with numerous vocalists including: Blue Lu Barker, Bea Booze, Lee Brown, Trixie Smith, Rosetta Tharpe, Evelyn Knight, Olie Shepherd, Peetie Wheatstraw, etc., also led own all-star Bluesicians. During the 1940s did solo residencies at various New York clubs including: The Famous Door, The Downbeat, Cafe Society, Eddie Condon's, Doherty's, etc., also in duo with pianist Arthur Gibbs for Tallulah Bankhead's play 'Clash by Night'. In February 1948 played in Europe at the Nice Jazz Festival (with Mezz Mezzrow), brief tour of France with Mezzrow, then returned to U.S.A. Worked regularly with Sidney Bechet during the late 1940s. From 1951 until late 1954 lived in Dallas, long residency at Cain's Hitching-Post and active with own business enterprises which included an undertaking company and two night clubs. Recorded with Jimmy Rushing soon after returning to New York. From late 1955 until spring 1956 toured Europe with own Bluesicians. In 1957 worked for a month in Zurich, Switzerland, with George Johnson. During the late 1950s and 1960s worked very often with Henry 'Red' Allen in New York. Toured Europe (including appearances at European

Jazz Festival) in summer of 1958. Toured France and Italy with own band (October 1958). In 1960 did extensive touring with the 'Tambourines to Glory' production, long spell at Eddie Condon's Club with Tony Parenti (1962-3). Featured at Antibes Jazz Festival (1963). Continued regular playing throughout the 1960s in addition to running own successful Down Home Meat Products company and taking active interest in local politics. Toured Europe (including Great Britain) in late 1969. Worked on a book on the history of jazz. Played dates at The Cookery, Greenwich Village (1971). Did several tours of Europe during the 1970s and 1980s.

PRIMA, Louis
trumpet/vocals

Born: New Orleans, Louisiana, 7th December 1911
Died: New Orleans, Louisiana, 24th August 1978

Younger brother of trumpeter Leon Prima (born: 1907), their sister, Mary Ann, was a pianiste. Played violin from the age of seven; then, in 1925, whilst his brother was in Texas with Peck Kelley, he taught himself to play trumpet on Leon's spare instrument. After he left Jesuit high school he began leading his own band for local night club residency, then played regularly in Saenger Theatre Orchestra. Worked mainly in New Orleans in the late 1920s and early 1930s; brief spell with Red Nichols in Cleveland (c. 1932). Led own band in New York from August of 1934, returned briefly to Saenger Theatre, New Orleans, then again in New York from 1935. Played many residencies in New York, Chicago, and Los Angeles during the 1930s. Led own big band in the 1940s, mainly active with own small show band in the 1950s and 1960s, achieved widespread commercial success. Was married to vocaliste Keely Smith from 1952 until 1961. Suffered serious illness in 1975.

Many film appearances including: 'You Can't Have Everything', 'Rose of Washington Square', etc., also played and sang on soundtrack of 'The Jungle Book' (1968).

PRIVIN, 'Bernie' Bernard
trumpet

Born: Brooklyn, New York, 12th February 1919

Did local gigs from the age of 16, with Harry Reser (1937), then with Bunny Berigan, Tommy Dorsey, Jan Savitt. With Artie Shaw (late 1938-9), Charlie Barnet (1940-1), Mal Hallett (1941), Benny Goodman (late 1941 to June 1942), Jerry Wald Band (1942), then again with Charlie Barnet. In armed forces from June 1943 until January 1946, served in Glenn Miller's A.A.F. Band (including Europe). With Benny Goodman until summer of 1946, then joined N.B.C. studio staff, with C.B.S. from 1950. Did regular studio work throughout the 1960s. Made several tours of Europe during the 1970s, some as a soloist.

PROCOPE, Russell
alto sax/clarinet

Born: New York City, 11th August 1908
Died: New York City, 21st January 1981

His brother, Bill, played violin, sax, and clarinet; their father was a violinist, their mother a pianiste. At six started on violin, played in junior high school orchestra, then began doubling on clarinet, studied with Lt. Eugene Mikell and played in the 369th Cadet Band. Played with Willie Freeman's Band in 1926, during same year also did a spell with drummer Jimmy Campbell's Band in Albany (on sax and violin). Residency at 116th Street Dancing School in New York, then with Henri Saparo at Bamboo Inn, with Charlie Skeete (1927) and trombonist Billy Kato (late 1927-8). Worked with Jelly Roll Morton at Rose Danceland in summer of 1928. In 1929 in Benny Carter's Band at Arcadia Ballroom, then with Chick Webb (1929-31). With Fletcher Henderson (spring 1931-4), then with Tiny Bradshaw (late 1934-5) in New York and Chicago. In Teddy Hill's Band (1936-7) including tour of Europe, worked with Willie Bryant, then with John Kirby Sextet from May 1938 until called up for service in U.S. Army in late 1943. Demobilised in late 1945, rejoined John Kirby in December 1945. Joined Duke Ellington in spring of 1946. Temporary absence through illness (1971), returned to tour Europe with Duke (autumn 1971), and remained with the band until Duke's death. Often with Brooks Kerr Trio, and free-lancing during the 1970s.

P

PROFIT, **Clarence**
piano

Born: New York City, 26th June 1912
Died: New York City, 22nd October 1944

His father, Herman Profit, was professional pianist; his cousin was pianist Sinclair Mills. Played piano from the age of three, led own 10-piece band during his teens, playing various New York residencies including Bamboo Inn, Renaissance, and the Alhambra. In 1930 and 1931 worked with Teddy Bunn in the Washboard Serenaders. In the early 1930s visited his grandparents in Antigua, remained in the West Indies for a few years, led own band in Antigua, Bermuda, etc. Returned to New York in November 1936 and began leading own successful trio at many New York clubs including: George's Tavern (1937-9), Ritz Carlton, Boston (1938), Yeah Man Club and Cafe Society (1939), Village Vanguard (1940), Kelly's (1940-3), Performers' and Music Guild Club (1942), Village Vanguard (1944). Was part-composer (with Edgar Sampson) of 'Lullaby in Rhythm'.

PURNELL, **Alton**
piano/vocals

Born: New Orleans, Louisiana, 16th April 1911

His brother, Theodore Nathaniel 'Wiggles' Purnell (1908-74) was a distinguished clarinet and saxophone player. Worked as a singer before playing gigs on piano (c. 1928). Played residency at the Pelican Annex before joining Isaiah Morgan's Band, subsequently worked with Alphonse Picou, 'Big Eye' Louis Nelson, and other leaders before joining Sidney Desvigne. Worked with 'Smiling' Joe Pleasants at the Famous Door in New Orleans in the early 1940s. Came to prominence with Bunk Johnson's Band in 1945, then worked regularly with George Lewis until early 1957. Moved to California in 1957, played many solo residencies, during the 1960s worked with Joe Darensbourg, Kid Ory, Andrew Blakeney, Teddy Buckner, Ben Pollack, Barney Bigard, and in the Young Men of New Orleans. Solo tour of Europe in late 1964, toured Australia in late 1965, then toured Europe with New Orleans All Stars early in 1966. During late 1960s continued to play solo residencies, also worked in the Young Men of New Orleans. Solo tour of Europe early in 1970. Was President of the Southern California Jazz Society. Widespread international touring during 1970s.

PURNELL, **'Keg' William**
drums

Born: Charleston, West Virginia, 7th January 1915
Died: New York City, 25th June 1965

Attended West Virginia State College, played with pianist Chappie Willett's Campus Revellers (1932-4). With King Oliver from December 1934 until autumn of 1935. Led own trio in New York during the late 1930s, also worked in Thelonius Monk Quartet in 1939. With Benny Carter Big Band (1939-40), with Claude Hopkins (1941-2). Joined Eddie Heywood in late 1942, with Heywood until 1948 (except for brief spell in U.S. Army from August 1944 and illness in late 1945). Returned to Eddie Heywood (1951-2), then free-lanced in New York and New Jersey for several years, worked mainly with Snub Mosley from early 1957 until shortly before his death.

PURTILL, **'Moe' Maurice**
drums

Born: Huntington, Long Island, N.Y., 4th May 1916

Gigged with several local bands before joining Red Norvo (1936-7), briefly with Glenn Miller (late 1937), Tommy Dorsey (January 1938-9) before rejoining Glenn Miller (1939-42). With Kay Kyser from 1942 until joining U.S. Navy in 1944. After demobilisation in 1946 played with Tex Beneke Band, then with Richard Himber in 1948 before beginning long spell as a studio musician in New York.

PURVIS, **Jack**
trumpet/trombone/vocals/piano/
multi-instrumentalist/composer

Born: Kokomo, Indiana, 11th December 1906
Died: San Francisco, California, 30th March 1962

Characters abound in the jazz world, but surely Jack Purvis must rank as the most eccentric jazzman of them all. A summary of his exploits is given here, a full account—if available—would probably fill the volume.

His father was an estate agent; Jack's mother died during his childhood, and he spent several years in a boys' training school where he first received musical tuition. He returned to Kokomo and played trumpet and trombone in local high school orchestras and dance bands (c. 1921), then worked for a long spell in the Original Kentucky Night Hawks—based in Lexington, Kentucky. He took time out to qualify as a pilot and also studied music in Chicago. He left the Original Kentucky Night Hawks in autumn 1926 to work as a free-lance arranger and trumpeter. Is said to have joined Whitey Kaufman's Original Pennsylvanians and worked with them in New York and Pennsylvania. In July 1928 he sailed to Europe with George Carhart's Band (playing trumpet and trombone). Only played with the band during their first evening aboard the 'Ile de France', then moved into a first-class lounge with fellow-aviators Levine and Acosta. Rejoined the band in France and played with them in Aix-les-Bains and Nice. Some weeks later he left his colleagues (somewhat hurriedly) via the roof of their Paris hotel. Back in the U.S.A. he joined Hal Kemp on trombone (c. October 1929), then switched to trumpet and remained with the band until the spring of 1930. He *did not* travel to Europe with Kemp's Band, but met up with them briefly in Paris during the summer of 1930. By September 1930 he was back in New York playing with the California Ramblers at a restaurant on 47th Street. Through 1931 he continued to play in Ed Kirkeby's radio and recording bands, doing broadcasting from the Ferenze Restaurant six nights a week, also did free-lance recordings with the Dorsey Brothers, Boswell Sisters, etc. He occasionally sat in as fourth trumpeter with Fletcher Henderson's Band. Mainly with Fred Waring in 1932 and 1933, during this period he very briefly became a harpist. He played in Kilgore, Texas (c. 1933)—Charlie Barnet also in the band. He set out for California with Barnet, but left him in El Paso. At this time it seems he utilised his skill as a pilot by flying cargo between Mexico and the U.S.A. His exploits as a mercenary in South America and as a chef in Bali are, as yet, undated. In 1933 he joined Charlie Barnet's Band for the last week of their residency at the Paramount Grill, New York, then worked in California, arranging for George Stoll's Orchestra and scoring for Warner Brothers' studio orchestras. One of his compositions, 'Legends of Haiti', was written for a 110-piece ensemble, he also worked as a chef in San Francisco! In 1935 he drove back to New York in a baby Austin (hauling a trailer full of cookery books and orchestral scores). He led his own quartet at the Club 18 and The Looking Glass, also recorded with Frank Froeba in December 1935. After touring for two weeks in Joe Haymes' Band he again disappeared. (Possibly at this juncture he organised his ill-fated School of Grecian Dancing in Miami.) In 1937 he worked briefly in Los Angeles, then played in Marysville, California, with a night-club quintet. After a temporary absence from music he rejoined the quintet in Medford, Oregon, but left after two weeks. Next worked (under the name Jack Jackson) with Johnnie Wynn's Band in San Pedro, California, left after a week and later played in a Fresno burlesque hall. In June 1937 he began serving a prison sentence for robbery at El Paso, Texas. In prison he directed (and played piano with) The Rhythmic Swingsters who broadcasted on Station WBAP in 1938. He was temporarily released from prison, but violated his parole and returned to Huntsville prison until his release in May 1947. It is rumoured that he resumed regular flying in Florida, but in the spring of 1948 a man resembling Purvis's description was seen sitting in a garden in Royal Place, Honolulu, giving renderings of the 'Flight of the Bumblebee' alternately on trumpet *and* trombone. In 1949 he lived briefly in Pittsburgh, the city in which his daughter, Betty Lou, was then working for a local radio station. After working as a carpenter he visited Spencer Clark prior to taking a job as a chef on a boat sailing from Baltimore. The last part of his life was spent working as a radio-repair man in San Francisco. Aliases used during his days in that city were: Mark Haelrigg, J. T. Lowry, Jack Pegler and Wallace Rhinehart. During 1937 he served briefly in the U.S. Army.

QUEALEY, Chelsea
trumpet

Born: Hartford, Connecticut, 1905
Died: Las Vegas, Nevada, 6th May 1950

Boyhood friend of saxist Bobby Davis (died: 1949). Quealey started on sax, then switched to trumpet. Worked with Jan Garber Orchestra (c. 1925), then with California Ramblers (1926-7). Sailed to England in December 1927 to join Fred Elizalde, illness forced sudden return to the U.S.A. in June 1929. Later that year joined the Paramount Theatre Orchestra in New York, following year with Don Voorhees for various Broadway shows. Again worked with California Ramblers in 1931. After a serious illness played briefly with Paul Whiteman, then joined Ben Pollack in Chicago and moved to California with Pollack. With Isham Jones' Juniors (early 1935-6), then with Red McKenzie and Joe Marsala for Coney Island residency (summer 1936); with Joe Marsala at Yacht Club, New York (autumn 1936). Joined Frankie Trumbauer Band in January 1937. Following spring worked briefly in Chauncey Morehouse Band, then free-lanced before joining Bob Zurke Big Band from September 1939 until early 1940. Left Zurke to join Jack Crawford's Band in Texas. Returned to New York and played regularly at Nick's with Georg Brunis, Brad Gowans, Miff Mole, etc. Moved back to California (c. 1946), worked for a while at various day jobs, then moved on to Las Vegas. Died of heart trouble.

QUEBEC, Ike Abrams
tenor sax/piano

Born: Newark, New Jersey, 17th August 1918
Died: New York City, 16th January 1963

Nickname was 'Jim Dawgs'. Gigged on piano as a teenager, also worked as a dancer. First professional work in tenor sax with the Barons of Rhythm in 1940. During the 1940s played with many small bands (usually in New York) including: Frankie Newton, Benny Carter, Coleman Hawkins, Kenny Clarke, Hot Lips Page, Trummy Young, Roy Eldridge Quintet, etc., etc. On and off with Cab Calloway from June 1944 until early 1951. Led own band in the 1950s; also worked as a chauffeur from the late 1950s. Made last recordings in 1961, then illness forced him to quit playing. He died of lung cancer.

QUICKSELL, 'Howdy' Howard
banjo

Born: 1901
Died: Pontiac, Michigan, 30th October 1953

Featured with Jean Goldkette from 1922 until 1927, during this period he also recorded with Bix Beiderbecke and Frankie Trumbauer (he composed the tune 'Sorry' which was recorded by Bix). He left full-time music in the 1930s and worked for many years for a Michigan distillery, later lived in Des Moines, Iowa.

QUINICHETTE, Paul
tenor sax

Born: Denver, Colorado (?) 17th May 1916
Died: New York City, 25th May 1983

Began playing clarinet and alto sax during childhood, switched to tenor sax and played local gigs before touring with Nat Towles and Lloyd Hunter. Worked with Ernie Fields, and with Shorty Sherock's Band then joined Jay McShann's Band in the early 1940s. Left McShann in California and joined Johnny Otis. Briefly with Benny Carter's Band and with Sid Catlett's Quartet before moving to New York as a member of Louis Jordan's Band. Worked with Lucky Millinder, J. C. Heard, Henry 'Red' Allen, and Eddie Wilcox, Hot Lips Page, etc., then spent the early 1950s with Count Basie. Made recordings under own name and became known as 'Vice-Pres' because of his Lester Young-like qualities. Worked with Benny Goodman in 1955, also with Nat Pierce, and toured briefly with Billie Holiday. Left full-time music in the 1960s and worked as an electronics technician. Resumed regular playing in 1973, worked with Brooks Kerr, Sammy Price, etc., but latter-day activities were restricted by long bouts of ill health.

QUINN, 'Snoozer' Edwin McIntosh
guitar/banjo/violin/vocals

Born: McComb, Mississippi, 18th October 1906
Died: New Orleans, Louisiana, 1952 (?)

Mandolin, guitar, and violin from the age of seven. Worked in a trio in Bogalusa, then toured with Paul English Travelling Shows. Joined Claude Blanchard's Orchestra in Houston,

Texas, then worked with Jack Wilrich Orchestra. With Peck Kelley's Bad Boys (1925), with Wingy Manone (summer 1925), then toured with Mart Britt Band. Worked with Louisiana Ramblers in Mexico (1927), then gigged around San Antonio, Texas (early 1928), moved to New Orleans, later that year joined Paul Whiteman for about nine months. Worked with hillbilly-singer Jimmy Davis (1931), then back to New Orleans, long spell with Earl Crumb's Band at Beverley Gardens, New Orleans. Forced by illness to quit full-time playing (c. 1940); from 1945 began playing more regularly, appeared at the New Orleans National Jazz Foundation Concert in April 1948. Advanced tuberculosis caused him to spend the last part of his life in hospital; he recorded in the hospital ward with Johnny Wiggs. The exact date of his death is unavailable, however the August 1949 issue of 'Jazz Notes' (Australia) gave the date as May 1949.

R

RAGLIN, 'Junior' Alvin Redrick
string bass

Born: Omaha, Nebraska, 16th March 1917
Died: Boston, Massachusetts, 10th November 1955

Originally a guitarist. Played string bass with Eugene Coy's Band in Oregon (1938-41) before joining Duke Ellington in California (late 1941)—played briefly in two-bass set-up until Jimmy Blanton entered hospital. Remained with Duke until brief U.S. Army service in early 1944. Gigged in New York, then rejoined Duke until November 1945. Worked briefly in Ray Nance's small group, then led own quartet before joining trio led by pianist Dave Rivera. Returned to Duke Ellington, sharing bass duties with Oscar Pettiford (late 1946-7). Illness caused premature retirement, he again worked briefly with Duke Ellington early in 1955.

RAINEY, Ma
(née Gertrude Malissa Nix Pridgett)
vocals

Born: Columbus, Georgia, 26th April 1886
Died: Georgia, 22nd December 1939

Made first public appearance at the age of 12 as part of a local show 'A Bunch of Blackberries' playing at the Springer Opera House, Columbus, Georgia. In 1904, she married William 'Pa' Rainey, toured with the Rabbit Foot Minstrels and Tolliver's Circus. During the early 1920s regularly accompanied by pianist Troy Snapps. After achieving considerable success with her recordings she headed her own show, which featured her Georgia Jazz Band. Did theatre and tent-show tours throughout the 1920s, except for a brief spell of retirement in Mexico. Bessie Smith, who early in life had been a protégée of Ma Rainey, shared the bill with her at a Fort Worth Stock Show early in the 1930s. After the death of her sister and her mother (in 1933) Ma retired and lived for the rest of her life in Rome, Georgia.

'Mother of The Blues' (a study of Ma Rainey) by Sandra Lieb, first published in 1981.

RAMEY, 'Gene' Eugene Glasco
string bass

Born: Austin, Texas, 4th April 1913

Played trumpet in college band, then worked on sousaphone in George Corley's Royal Aces (c. 1929). With the Moonlight Serenaders and Terrence Holder before moving to Kansas City, Missouri, in August 1932. Switched to string bass, received tuition from Walter Page. Led own bands for several years, also worked with Oliver Todd's Band and Margaret 'Countess' Johnson. With Jay McShann early in 1938, left, then rejoined the band at Martin's Inn (summer 1938). Remained with McShann until leader's call up (1943), then returned to Kansas City. Moved to New York in 1944 and for the next 10 years worked with many leaders including: Ben Webster, Coleman Hawkins, Charlie Parker, John Hardee, Eddie 'Lockjaw' Davis, Miles Davis, Dizzy Gillespie, Hot Lips Page, Tiny Grimes, Lester Young, etc. Few months with Count Basie from November 1952. Worked in group led by drummer Art Blakey (1954), accompanied vocaliste Eartha Kitt (1955), then varied free-lance work in New York including prolific recordings. Toured Europe with Buck Clayton in 1959 and 1961. During the 1960s worked with many leaders: Muggsy Spanier (1962), Teddy Wilson (1963), pianist Dick Wellstood, Jimmy Rushing, Peanuts Hucko, etc. Worked in Europe with Jay McShann and Eddie Vinson (March 1969). Continues to play regularly, early in 1970 worked with pianist Nat Pierce, Lem Johnson, etc. Moved to Texas in 1976. Toured Europe with Jay McShann (1979).

RAMIREZ, 'Ram' Roger
piano/organ/composer

Born: San Juan, Puerto Rico, 15th September 1913

Raised in the San Juan Hill section of New York. Began playing piano at the age of eight, five years later joined the musicians' union. Worked with the Louisiana Stompers in New York during the early 1930s, briefly accompanied Monette Moore early in 1933. Left the Louisiana Stompers to join Rex Stewart's Band at the Empire Ballroom, New York (summer 1933). Worked with the Spirits of Rhythm in 1934, joined Willie Bryant early in 1935. To

Europe with Bobby Martin's Band in June 1937, returned to New York in late 1939. Led own small group for Asbury Park residency, then worked with Ella Fitzgerald and Frankie Newton before spending a year with Charlie Barnet (1942). Rejoined Frankie Newton (1943), then with John Kirby's Sextet from early 1944 until joining Sid Catlett's Band at the Down Beat Club, New York (1944). From the late 1940s has usually worked with own trio, long residencies at Well's, Village Vanguard, Basin Street East, the Shalimar, and at Frank's Steak House, Long Island. Played organ extensively from 1953. Returned to tour Europe in spring 1968 (accompanying T-Bone Walker). Continues to work regularly. Composed 'Lover Man', 'Mad About You', etc. Active throughout the 1970s, including tours. Briefly with Harlem Blues and Jazz Band, including tour of Europe (1980). Played regularly during early 1980s.

RAND, Odell
clarinet

Born: c. 1905
Died: Chicago, Illinois, 22nd June 1960

Together with Herb Morland made up the front line of the much-recorded Harlem Hamfats—Rand played the E-flat clarinet for these recordings. Led own band (The Ebonites) for many years, long residencies in Chicago at the Rock Cellar Gardens, The Blinkin' Pup, etc. Continued to play until shortly before his death, gigged with Baby Dodds (1957) and with Lil Armstrong (1959).

RANDALL, William
saxes/arranger

Born: Chicago, Illinois, 1st September 1911
Deceased

Began on violin, changed to saxophone. Studied music with Major N. Clarksmith and played in high school orchestra. Did some touring in 1932 then worked in Chicago with Charlie Elgar, Eddie South, Dave Peyton, etc., before joining Earl Hines from 1936-39. Left to work briefly with Horace Henderson then rejoined Hines from 1940 until 1942. Defence work and Army service during World War II. Prolific arranging, freelance playing, and leading own group during the 1950s.

RANDOLPH, 'Mouse' Irving
trumpet

Born: St. Louis, Missouri, 22nd June 1909

First professional work with Fate Marable's Band, then joined Norman Mason's Carolina Melodists. With drummer Floyd Campbell's Orchestra (1928), then worked with Alphonso Trent and J. Frank Terry's Band before joining Andy Kirk from 1931-3, played occasionally for Fletcher Henderson early in 1934, spell with Benny Carter; then became regular member of Fletcher Henderson's Band from July 1934. Joined Cab Calloway from spring 1935 until late 1939, when he joined Ella Fitzgerald. With Don Redman from May 1943, then with Ed Hall Sextet throughout the late 1940s. With Eddie Barefield Sextet (1950), then long spell of touring with Marcelino Guerra's Latin American Orchestra. Played at Savoy Ballroom with Bobby Medera's Band (1955). From 1958 was a regular member of Henry 'Chick' Morrison's Orchestra in New York, also took part in free-lance recordings including sessions with Harry Dial's Bluesicians in 1961.

RANDOLPH, Zilner Trenton
trumpet/piano/arranger

Born: Dermott, Arkansas, 28th January 1899

Studied at the Biddle University in North Carolina, later spent several years studying music at the Kreuger Conservatory in St. Louis and at the Wisconsin Conservatory in Milwaukee. Played with many bands in and around Milwaukee including almost four years with Bernie Young's Band at Wisconsin Roof Ballroom and touring. Moved to Chicago, musical director for Louis Armstrong (March 1931 to March 1932) and again in 1933 and July to October 1935. With Carroll Dickerson and Dave Peyton in 1934. Formed own big band in Chicago (1936), continued to lead through the 1930s, also active as an arranger for Earl Hines, Woody Herman, Fletcher Henderson, Duke Ellington, Blanche Calloway, Ted

Weems, etc., etc. During the 1940s led own quartet in Gary, Indiana; Chicago, etc. From 1949 worked with his three children in family musical act (his son was christened Louis Armstrong Randolph). Recorded on piano in 1951. Ran own teaching studio in Englewood, Illinois during the 1970s.

RANK, 'Bill' William C.
trombone

Born: Lafayette, Indiana, 8th June 1904
Died: Cincinnati, Ohio, 20th May 1979

Came from a musical family—his brother was formerly a professional drummer. In 1921 Bill worked in Florida with 'Collin's Jazz Band', then moved on to Indianapolis to join Tade Dolan's Singing Orchestra. Joined Jean Goldkette in Detroit (1923)—first recording 'In the Evening'. Remained until the summer of 1927—during this period recording many sides with his colleague Bix Beiderbecke. Played in the short-lived band that Adrian Rollini led at the New Yorker Restaurant (1st September to 27th October 1927). Free-lance recording work with Sam Lanin, Roger Wolfe Kahn, and Nat Shilkret, then joined Paul Whiteman on 10th December 1927. Except for brief absences was with Whiteman until 1938. Spent four years playing in Hollywood studio orchestras, then moved to Cincinnati. Through the 1940s led own band in Cincinnati including residency with a 10-piece outfit at the Lookout House, then combined gigging with his day work in insurance. Has continued playing through the 1960s, on the first of two vacations to Europe (1968 and 1969) he recorded in England. Played gigs with Gene Mayl's Dixieland Rhythm Kings (1971). Appeared at numerous jazz festivals during the 1970s, and played last gig at a Coon-Saunders Festival two days before he died.

RAPPOLO
See Leon J. Roppolo

RASKIN, 'Milt' Milton William
piano/composer

Born: Boston, Massachusetts, 27th January 1916
Died: Los Angeles, California, 16th October 1977

Played saxophone during childhood; piano from 11, studied at New England Conservatory during the early 1930s. Played first gigs in School of Practical Art Band. Regularly on local radio stations, then moved to New York, played for a month with Wingy Manone's Band prior to joining Gene Krupa (early 1938-late 1939), then joined Teddy Powell prior to working with Alvino Rey (summer 1940). With Tommy Dorsey (1942-44) then moved to Los Angeles to work as a studio musician, later became successful studio orchestra conductor and musical director.

REARDON, Casper
harp

Born: Little Falls, N.Y., 15th April 1907
Died: New York City, 9th March 1941

Graduate of the Curtis Institute of Music, Philadelphia, studied with Carlos Salzeda. Played piano in parents' vaudeville act as a child, record debut in 1931, playing piano for tap-dance accompaniment. Specialised on harp from early teens, made professional debut with Philadelphia Symphony Orchestra, then spent five years as principal harpist with Cincinnati Symphony Orchestra—during this period also did radio work as a jazz harpist using the pseudonym Arpeggio Glissandi. Recorded with Jack Teagarden in 1934 and through the mid-1930s made guest appearances with Paul Whiteman, Casa Loma Band, Jack Denny Orchestra, and Abe Lyman. Worked in short-lived Three T's Band in New York late 1936. Following year to Hollywood to appear in 'Broadway Jamboree' film. Returned to New York, led own small groups, then moved to Chicago for residencies at Hotel Sherman and Ambassador Hotel. Resident at Le Ruban Bleu, New York, until shortly before his death.

REDMAN, 'Don' Donald Matthew
alto, soprano saxes/multi-instrumentalist/ vocals/arranger/composer

Born: Piedmont, West Virginia, 29th July 1900
Died: New York City, 30th November 1964

Don's brother, Lewis, led a band in Cumberland, Maryland, for many years, their father was a noted music-teacher. He began playing trumpet at the age of three, and before he was 12 could play proficiently on all wind instruments including oboe. After intensive musical studies at Storer's College, Harper's Ferry and the Chicago and Boston conservatories, he joined Billy Paige's Broadway Syncopators and went to New York with them in March 1923. Later that year began recording with Fletcher Henderson and subsequently joined the band early in 1924. With Henderson on sax and as staff arranger until June 1927. Moved to Detroit to take appointment as musical director for McKinney's Cotton Pickers, a position he held until summer 1931. During this period arranged and recorded with Louis Armstrong studio groups in Chicago. In October 1931 his first band was formed by combining a nucleus of ex-McKinney members with several musicians from Horace Henderson's Band. The band began their first long residency at Connie's Inn in 1932 and subsequently worked regularly throughout the 1930s until disbanding in January 1940. The band consolidated its considerable success by appearing on many important radio shows; they also appeared in one short film made by National in 1935. Throughout the 1930s Redman also arranged for Paul Whiteman, Ben Pollack, Isham Jones, Nat Shilkret, etc., etc., and also produced specially commissioned orchestrations for Bing Crosby. After his original band broke up in January 1940 he concentrated on free-lance arranging, then re-formed again in December 1940. In February 1941 he toured briefly fronting the Snookum Russell Band, then returned to New York to become staff arranger for Bobby Byrne. Returned to free-lance arranging, scoring for many name bands—providing Jimmy Dorsey with the arrangement of his big hit 'Deep Purple'. Re-formed big band for residency at The Zanzibar, New York (1943), then resumed full-time arranging for: Count Basie, Harry James, N.B.C. studio bands, etc. Formed band for European tour commencing September 1946, he remained in Europe after the band broke up and returned to the U.S.A. in August 1947. Own series on C.B.S. television in autumn 1949. From 1951 worked as musical director for vocaliste Pearl Bailey. Rarely played in public during the last few years of his life, but recorded on alto, soprano, and piano in 1958-9. Played piano at Georgia Minstrels concert in June 1962 and soprano sax for the Sissle-Blake Grass Roots concert in September 1964. During his later life worked on several extended compositions, which, so far, have not been publicly performed.

REESE, Rostelle

trumpet

Born: Illinois, 15th December 1914

Brother of trombonist Arthur Reese. Played in East Aurora High School Band, won junior state solo trumpet contest. Toured with Charlie Crusoe's Cotton Pickers 1934-35, and with Nat Cole's Band (1937). With Fletcher Henderson (1938), Leonard Reid, Erskine Tate, Earl Hines (1940-41). With Benny Carter (late 1941), Cootie Williams (1942), Jimmie Lunceford (1946-47). During the early 1950s worked with Claude Hopkins, Billy Eckstine, and Buddy Johnson. Brief spell in John Kirby's Sextet. Now an active free-lance in Los Angeles.

REEVES, 'Red' Reuben

trumpet

Born: Evansville, Indiana, 25th October 1905
Died: New York City, September 1975

Also known as 'River', brother of the late trombonist Gerald Reeves. Began playing trumpet at local Frederic Douglass High School, toured with Bill Smith and his Orchestra in 1923. Moved to New York in 1924 to study dentistry, gigged at Small's. To Chicago in January 1925, played at the Oriental Cafe and London Cabaret, then joined Erskine Tate (1926). Studied at the American Conservatory in Chicago and gained master's degree. Returned home for several months, then joined Dave Peyton at the Grand Theatre (autumn 1927), soon rejoined Erskine Tate. Left Tate in January 1928 to rejoin Dave Peyton, worked with Peyton 1928-30, also led own recording groups in 1929 and taught music at Wendell Phillips High School. With pianist-organist Jerome Carrington (early 1931), then moved to New York to join Cab Calloway, left Calloway in summer of 1931. Subsequently returned to Chicago, led own touring band from 1933-5, toured with Connie's 'Hot Chocolates' revue, then returned to New York. Worked in combo led by drummer Dick Ward and free-lanced.

During the late 1930s joined the U.S. National Guard and played regularly in the 369th Infantry Band. Served in U.S. Army throughout World War II, led 299th 7th Division Band in U.S. and for tour of the Pacific. After demobilisation joined Harry Dial's Band (1946). Left full-time music in 1952 to work as a bank guard, but continued gigging with Harry Dial and other leaders.

REEVES, Talcott
guitar/banjo

Born: Little Rock, Arkansas, 15th June 1904

Took up banjo at the age of 20, taught by Ralph Wilson. Went to Wilberforce College and joined Horace Henderson (1925), worked mainly with Horace Henderson until 1930. With Lockwood Lewis (1930). Played in Benny Carter's Orchestra in 1930 and 1932, then with Don Redman from 1932 until 1940 and again in 1943. Left full-time music, but has continued to free-lance in and around New York.

REID, Neil
trombone

Born: Arkansas, 16th January 1912

Played in Virgil Howard Band at the age of 12, then played with Dick Cisne Band before studying at University of Illinois. Worked in Isham Jones Juniors before joining Woody Herman. Left Herman in 1944 to join the U.S. Marines, served in the Pacific Area and played in Bob Crosby's Service Band. After being released early in 1946 moved to California and formed own construction company.

REISMAN, Leo Frank
violin/multi-instrumentalist

Born: Boston, Massachusetts, 11th October 1897
Died: 18th December 1961

Violin from the age of 10, public performances at 12. Played in local symphony orchestras and did hotel work before forming own band in 1919. Residency at the Hotel Brunswick until 1929, then Central Park Casino, New York (1929). Continued to lead own highly successful commercial orchestra in the 1930s and 1940s, long contracts at Waldorf Astoria, New York. Took band to Paris for 1937 International Exposition. Mainly active as a conductor during last 15 years of his life.

Max Kaminsky and Lee Wiley worked regularly with Leo Reisman during the early 1930s, Bubber Miley and Johnny Dunn were also briefly featured with his orchestra.

RENA, 'Kid' Henry
(original spelling: René)
trumpet

Born: New Orleans, Louisiana, 30th August 1898
Died: New Orleans, Louisiana, 25th April 1949

Brother of drummer Joe Rena. Played in waifs' home band with Louis Armstrong, later replaced Louis in Kid Ory's Band (1919). Led own band at Sans Souci Hall, also played in the Tuxedo Band, then organised own Dixieland Jazz Band, took own band on excursions to Chicago several times during the early 1920s (is said to be the originator of the trumpet ride-out chorus in the tune 'Panama'). Played for many years in the Tuxedo Brass Band, then formed own Pacific Brass Band marching band. Later he led small groups in various New Orleans clubs. Residency at Gypsy Tea Rooms in mid-1930s, then leading at the Budweiser taxi-dance-hall (1940). In 1940 organised band for recording session in New Orleans. Played at the Brown Derby until 1947, then ill health caused him to quit playing.

REUSS, Allan
guitar

Born: New York City, 15th June 1915

Did first gig at the age of 12, shortly after taking up banjo. Worked on guitar during the early 1930s and studied with George Van Epps. With Benny Goodman from April-June 1935, then regularly with Goodman (August 1936 until March 1938). Organised own teaching studio in New York and took part in many pick-up recording sessions. With Jack Teagarden from January until June 1939, joined Paul Whiteman autumn 1939. With Ted Weems from spring of 1941 until joining Jimmy Dorsey in March 1942, then did studio work for N.B.C. in Chicago until rejoining Benny Goodman from June 1943 until June 1944. With Harry James until May 1945, led own trio in Los Angeles, then concentrated on free-lance session work in Hollywood, also did regular teaching.

REYNOLDS, 'Jimmy' James Russel — *Born: c. 1907*
piano — *Died: New York City, 16th February 1963*

Resident at the Hollywood Cafe, New York, for many years in the 1930s and 1940s. Led own band, but occasionally worked with other leaders including Kaiser Marshall (1935), Hot Lips Page (1938), also recorded with Henry 'Red' Allen and Jabbo Smith. Worked with Harry Dial and Lester Boone in the early 1960s.

RHODES, Todd Washington — *Born: Hopkinsville, Kentucky, 31st August 1900*
piano/arranger — *Died: Flint, Michigan, 1965*

Family moved to Springfield, Ohio, when Todd was four months old. Studied at the Springfield School of Music (1915-17), then four years at the Erie Conservatory in Pennsylvania. Moved back to Springfield in 1921 and joined newly organised Synco Septette (which subsequently became McKinney's Cotton Pickers). Remained with the Cotton Pickers until 1934 (working in the latter stages under Cuba Austin's leadership). Gigged with local bands in Detroit until the early 1940s, then did war work in Detroit car factories, continued gigging, mainly as a solo pianist. Formed own quartet in 1946, following year increased to a seven-piece, began recording and playing long residencies in Detroit. Made several successful singles and began widespread touring, playing regular seasons in Florida.

RICCI, Paul J. — *Born: New York City, 6th April 1914*
clarinet/saxes

Father also a clarinettist. Began playing at 12, worked in New York taxi-dance-halls for four years, then during the early 1930s worked with Lud Gluskin, Gene Kardos, Red McKenzie, Adrian Rollini, Joe Venuti. With Red Nichols and Joe Haymes in 1934, then became a house musician for Decca/Brunswick recording studios, later worked for Columbia, RCA-Victor, and Capitol. Many years on N.B.C. studio staff from 1940 including regular work with Andre Kostelanetz. From 1950-66 did film-studio sessions for Paramount and Universal. Prolific free-lance recordings, also took part in Original Dixieland Jazz Band re-creation for special 'Chicago, and all that Jazz' television programme. Settled in Miami where he worked regularly on the Jackie Gleason television show and did free-lance studio work.

RICH, 'Buddy' Bernard — *Born: New York, 30th September 1917*
drums/vocals

Appeared in his parents' vaudeville act 'Wilson and Rich' before he was two years old. Tap-danced and played drums in Broadway show at the age of four. From the age of six began touring the U.S.A. and Australia as a single act ('Traps the Drum Wonder'), at 11 led own stage band. He began gigging with Art Shapiro (c. 1936) and received first jazz notice after sitting in with Hot Lips Page's Band in September 1937. With Joe Marsala from October 1937 until June 1938, briefly led own band at Piccadilly Roof, New York, then with Bunny Berigan until joining Harry James in December 1938. Worked with Artie Shaw, then with Tommy Dorsey from November 1939 until 1942. Played in Los Angeles with Benny Carter, service in the U.S. Marines until June 1944. Rejoined Tommy Dorsey June 1944 until October 1945 (whilst filming with Dorsey in Hollywood played for two weeks with Count Basie at the Club Plantation, Los Angeles). Formed own band in late 1945, continued to lead until January 1947, then in February did first of many tours with Norman Granz's 'Jazz At The Philharmonic'. Led own band intermittently during late 1940s. Joined

Les Brown in June 1949, left in September to resume work with J.A.T.P. Led own band in 1950, in 1951 led own band for 'Josephine Baker' show, then worked in Charlie Ventura's Big Four until November 1951. With Harry James for a year from spring 1953, then resumed with Tommy Dorsey until April 1955. With Harry James 1956-7 including tour of Europe, then formed own small group, also acted on television and worked briefly as a solo vocalist in autumn 1959. Whilst on tour with his own quintet in November 1959 he suffered a mild heart attack, but resumed leading small band in New York (spring 1960) and later led on a tour of Asia. From late 1961 until spring 1966 worked regularly with Harry James, also did many guest spots on television shows, concerts, etc. Formed own big band in 1966 which rapidly achieved international success, several overseas tours including 'Command Performance' in London (November 1969). Played on many Condon television shows (1948-9). Led own big band in early 1970s, small group (1974), then re-formed own highly successful big band which continued to play international tours during the late 1970s and 1980s.

RICH, Fred
piano/composer/leader

Born: Warsaw, Poland, 3rd January 1898
Died: California, 8th September 1956

Led own big commercial bands in the 1920s, toured Europe in 1925-6 and 1927-8. Played long residency at the Hotel Astor Roof in New York, then began leading own studio bands which featured many jazz musicians including: Bunny Berigan, Benny Goodman, The Dorsey Brothers, Tony Parenti, Joe Venuti, etc., etc. Musical director for various radio stations in the late 1930s, then on United Artistes' musical staff from 1942. In 1945 was badly injured in a fall and suffered partial paralysis, but continued studio duties through the 1940s and 1950s. Suffered long illness.

RICHARDS, 'Red' Charles
piano/vocals

Born: Brooklyn, New York, 19th October 1912

Made recording debut with Campbell 'Skeets' Tolbert. Subsequently worked with Roy Eldridge, Bobby Hackett, Jimmy McPartland. Spent four years with Tab Smith. With Sidney Bechet (1951), also Bob Wilbur (1951). To Europe in February 1953, toured with Mezz Mezzrow. Mainly with Muggsy Spanier from 1953 until 1957, then played solo dates in Columbus, Ohio (spring 1958). Took part in Fletcher Henderson reunion bands (1957 and 1958). Worked with Wild Bill Davison (1958-9), also again with Muggsy Spanier (1959). Played at Eddie Condon's (1961), again with Wild Bill Davison (1962). Since 1964 has led the Saints and Sinners, toured Europe in 1968 and 1969. Solo work in White Plains (1971). Led own group throughout the 1970s. Made many tours of Europe during the 1970s and 1980s, some with Panama Francis and his Savoy Sultans.

RICHARDSON, 'Ben'
clarinet/saxes

Born: Ep, near Belfry, Kentucky, 1906

Worked with J. Frank Terry, Zack Whyte, Speed Webb, and Blanche Calloway before settling in New York. Subsequently with Claude Hopkins, Louis Armstrong Big Band, also served in National Guard's 369th Regimental Band. Has worked for many years in band led by Buddy Tate, left music temporarily in 1966 when he underwent operation for amputation of a leg, but soon resumed playing with Buddy Tate and toured Europe with Tate's Band in late 1968. Toured Europe during the 1970s.

RICHARDSON, Rodney V.
string-bass

Born: New Orleans, Louisiana, 1917

Moved to Chattanooga, Tennessee, did local gigs on guitar and string-bass, later worked in Nashville with the Royal Knights (on guitar) and in Chattanooga with pianist Jimmy Edwards (on bass). Worked in riverboat band (led by pianist King Purdue) and began specialising on string-bass. Joined Harlan Leonard's Band in Kansas City and moved with them to California in 1943. Did club dates in Los Angeles, then worked with Count Basie from 1943 to 1946. First recordings with Lester Young in 1944, later worked in Lester Young's Band and also with Roy Eldridge, Tiny Grimes, etc. Moved to Los Angeles, continued playing regularly throughout the 1970s, including tour of Europe with Duke Barrell's Louisiana Shakers (1975).

RICHMOND, June
vocals

Born: Chicago, Illinois, 9th July 1915
Died: Gothenburg, Sweden, 14th August 1962

Worked with Les Hite in California, then joined Jimmy Dorsey's Band early in 1938, later sang with Andy Kirk's Band (1940) and Cab Calloway, then worked as a solo vocaliste. Worked in Europe from 1948, principally in France, then mainly in Scandinavia during the late 1950s and early 1960s. She died of a heart attack.

RILEY, 'Mike' Michael
trombone/trumpet/vocals

Born: Fall River, Massachusetts, 5th January 1904
Died: Torrance, California, 2nd September 1984

Worked on trumpet in Jimmy Durante's Band at Parody Club, New York, in 1927, later played trombone in several big bands including Irving Aaronson's and Will Osborne's. Came to national fame with the small band he briefly co-led with Eddie Farley, their 1935 recording of 'The Music Goes Round and Around' became a best-seller. This unit broke up after residency at The Onyx Club, New York, and both partners formed their own bands. Riley led for long spells in New York during the 1930s: Club Caliente, New York Tavern, Hickory House, etc.; and in Chicago and Hollywood in the 1940s. Played in Johnny Lane's Band in Chicago (1951), then resumed leading his own revue band, tours throughout U.S.A. and Canada during the 1950s and 1960s.

ROANE, Kenneth A.
trumpet/saxes/clarinet/oboe/arranger

Born: Hartford, Connecticut. c. 1902
Died: New York City, 3rd March 1984

Brother of trumpeter Eddie Roane (1911-46). Raised in Springfield, Massachusetts. Was already proficient on trumpet, clarinet, saxes, and oboe when he moved to New York in 1923. Worked with Lloyd and Cecil Scott, Fess Williams (including recordings on oboe in 1928), Jelly Roll Morton, Charlie Skeete, etc., during the 1920s, also occasionally subbed in Duke Ellington's Orchestra. With Joe Jordan's Orchestra (1930), then led own band during the 1930s, also played for five Broadway shows and worked regularly with Charlie Johnson, Sammy Stewart, and Sam Wooding (U.S.A. only). Later with Eddie Deas in Boston, Al Jenkins in Buffalo, and on tour with Danny Logan's Band. Member of Wen Talbot's Harlem Symphonic Society Orchestra. Played and recorded with Sidney Bechet (1939), then worked for various leaders including: Noble Sissle, Louis Jordan, Buddy Johnson, Claude Hopkins, Fats Waller, Marcellino Guerra, etc. Continues to be an active musician, gives tuition on all instruments, and does regular arranging and composing. Did administrative work for Local 802 for many years.

ROBERTS, 'Luckey', Charles Luckyeth
piano/composer

Born: Philadelphia, Pennsylvania, 7th August 1887
Died: New York City, 5th February 1968

Began stage career in early infancy, toured with Gus Seekes' Pickaninnies and Mayne Remington's Ethiopian Prodigies. Began playing piano (c. 1900). Played regular summer seasons and worked in the winter in a bicycle and juggling act. Settled in New York (c. 1910), began playing at Little Savoy Club and had first composition 'Junk Man Rag' published in 1913. Played residency at Barron Wilkins and toured vaudeville circuits with own band. In the 1920s and 1930s was known principally as a society bandleader and composer; he played many private engagements in New York, Boston, Washington, etc., and did regular summer seasons in Palm Beach, Florida. By 1930 he had seen 14 of his own musical comedies produced. During the early 1940s he conducted a large orchestra for public performances of his extended compositions—he was also featured on Rudi Blesh's 'This is Jazz' radio programme. From 1940-54 he owned his own Rendezvous club in New York. In later life he survived two strokes and a car crash. Continued composing until shortly before his death.

R

ROBERTSON, Dick *Born: Brooklyn, New York, 3rd July 1903*
vocals/composer

Worked as a solo artiste and partnered Ed Smalle before beginning prolific recording career in 1928. Free-lance recordings with many leaders including: Red Nichols, Eubie Blake, Fletcher Henderson, The Mills Blue Rhythm Band, Duke Ellington, Benny Goodman, Andy Kirk, Ben Pollack, Ben Bernie, Ben Selvin, Clarence Williams, etc., etc. Also recorded under various pseudonyms. Regularly led own studio bands during the 1930s and early 1940s, then quit full-time singing to concentrate on composing. Wrote: 'We Three', 'I'm a Little on the Lonely Side', etc.

ROBERTSON, 'Zue' C. Alvin *Born: New Orleans, Louisiana, 7th March 1891*
trombone *Died: Watts, near Los Angeles, California, 1943*

Played piano at the age of five, switched to trombone at 13, received tuition from his cousin, Baptiste Delisle. Did first jobs with the Cherry Blossom Band led by drummer Cornelius Tillman. Went on tour (c. 1910) playing in band accompanying the Kit Carson Wild West Show. Played at opening of Pete Lala's Cafe in New Orleans (c. 1912), during following year travelled to Chicago with a road show, then returned to play in New Orleans. Joined Olympia Band, replacing Ed Vinson, worked on trombone with Manuel Perez, also with Richard M. Jones at George Fewclothes' Club. Occasional work with John Robichaux on trombone and P. G. Loral Band on euphonium. Moved to Chicago in 1917 to work at De Luxe Cafe, with Jelly Roll Morton in 1923 and on tour with King Oliver in 1924. Extensive touring with W. C. Handy, then returned to Chicago to join Dave Peyton at Grand Theatre before further touring in the Drake and Walker Show. Settled in New York from spring 1929 and worked mostly on piano and organ (including Lincoln and Lafayette Theatres)—gave up trombone entirely in 1930. Moved to California (c. 1932), worked on piano and string bass throughout the 1930s. Collapsed and died after suffering a pulmonary haemorrhage.

It has been suggested that the correct nickname was 'Zoo', gained whilst Robertson was working with travelling circuses.

ROBESON, Orlando *Born: Tulsa, Oklahoma, 4th March 1909*
(real name: Roberson)
vocals

Chiefly remembered for his work with Claude Hopkins. Regularly with Hopkins in 1934, left early in 1935 to tour as featured act in a revue, returned to Hopkins. Briefly with Louis Metcalf's Band in New York (1936), then in band co-led with Clarence Love, mainly touring until August 1937, then led own band for residency at Cotton Club, Birmingham, Alabama. Rejoined Claude Hopkins on several occasions during the late 1930s. Army service during World War II, sang with service band in Phoenix, Arizona (1943). After demobilisation moved to the West Coast.

ROBICHAUX, Joseph *Born: New Orleans, Louisiana, 8th March 1900*
piano *Died: New Orleans, Louisiana, 17th January 1965*

A nephew of the famous New Orleans leader John Robichaux, was also related to the Dodds Brothers. Tuition from Steve Lewis. Began gigging at local house parties in 1917, during the following year went to Chicago for summer season with trumpeter Tig Chambers. Returned home in autumn 1918, worked with Papa Celestin and William Ridgley before joining Davey Jones, worked regularly with Lee Collins, also with Willie O'Connor, Kid Rena, The Black Eagle Band, and travelling carnivals before organising own band in 1931. In 1933 the band travelled to New York, but union restrictions prevented them from accepting regular work, they did, however, do five recording sessions. Continued to lead own New Orleans Rhythm Boys throughout the 1930s (including tour of Cuba), by 1939 they were operating as a 14-piece band. Worked mainly as a solo pianist in the 1940s, long residencies at The Absinthe House, New Orleans. During the 1950s worked in California accompanying Lizzie Miles, joined George Lewis in spring 1957, and other than brief absences worked with Lewis until late 1964 including tours of Europe and Japan. Played at Preservation Hall during the last week of his life.

ROBINSON, Eli
trombone

Born: Greensville, Georgia, 23rd June 1908
Died: New York, 24th December 1972

Family moved to Charleston, West Virginia, in 1920. Took up trombone in February 1925, by the following Christmas was gigging in high school band. Worked with Andy McKee's Band, then after leaving high school in 1928 moved to Detroit. Gigged with various bands, then moved to Cincinnati and worked with Alex Jackson (1930). For the next six years worked with many bands including: Speed Webb, Zack Whyte, J. Frank Terry, McKinney's Cotton Pickers, Blanche Calloway, etc. With Willie Bryant early in 1937, then with Mills Blue Rhythm Band directed by Lucky Millinder. Worked with Teddy Hill, then returned to Lucky Millinder. Briefly with Roy Eldridge in late 1939, then again with Lucky Millinder until joining Count Basie in July 1941. Left Basie in 1947, worked with various leaders, several stints with Lucky Millinder before joining Buddy Tate in 1954. Continued to work with Buddy Tate throughout the 1960s, but was absent from the band through illness in autumn 1969, rejoined the band in 1970.

ROBINSON, 'Fred' Frederick L.
trombone

Born: Memphis, Tennessee, 20th February 1901
Died: New York City, 11th April 1984

Began playing whilst at school in Memphis, subsequently to Dana's Musical Institute in Warren, Ohio, for further studies. Moved to Chicago in 1927, played with Carroll Dickerson at the Savoy, regular recordings with Louis Armstrong. Moved with Dickerson and Louis Armstrong to New York (spring 1929). With Edgar Hayes at the Alhambra Theatre (late 1929-30), then with Marion Hardy's Alabamians (1931), joined Charlie Turner's Arcadians, with the band for subsequent touring with Fats Waller until 1937. During the early 1930s also worked briefly for other leaders including: Benny Carter, Fletcher Henderson, and Don Redman. With Andy Kirk in 1939, left in August 1940. With Fletcher Henderson in 1941, and through the early 1940s worked for brief spells with Henderson. Worked with George James' Band in 1943, with Cab Calloway in 1945. Regular work for Sy Oliver from 1946 until 1950, then spent a year with Noble Sissle. Left full-time music in 1954 to work on New York subway system but continued to gig throughout the 1960s.

ROBINSON, 'Banjo' Ikey L.
banjo/guitar/piano/clarinet

Born: Dublin, Virginia, 28th July 1904

Both parents were musicians. Started work as a barber, but led own part-time band from 1918. Became professional musician in 1922—banjo-vocals with Harry Watkins' Orchestra in Virginia. Left in 1924, short spell with Harry McLain, then two years with Bud Jenkins' Virginia Ravens. Left to live in Chicago (1926), gigged with various bands, then worked with the Alabamians—also played for a brief spell with Jelly Roll Morton. With Clarence Moore (late 1928 to early 1929), then joined Sammy Stewart and eventually went to New York with that band in February 1930. Remained in New York, worked for Wilbur Sweatman and with Noble Sissle at Park Central Hotel (1931), also did numerous recordings with Clarence Williams. Led for Darktown Scandals and led own quartet at Casa Mia Club before returning to Chicago in 1934. With Carroll Dickerson at Sunset Cafe and Erskine Tate Orchestra before forming own band in 1935. Led own small bands in Chicago through the 1940s, also worked regularly in a double act with 'Little Mike' McKendrick ('Ike and Mike') until 1960; also gigged with Junie Cobb. Replaced Lawrence Dixon in the Franz Jackson Original Jazz All Stars and has worked with Jackson through the late 1960s including tour of U.S. Army Bases in Vietnam during autumn of 1969. Toured Europe during the 1970s. Worked mostly in Chicago during the late 1970s and early 1980s.

ROBINSON, J. Russel
piano

Born: Indianapolis, Indiana, 8th July 1892
Died: Palmdale, California, 30th September 1963

At 14 formed a piano and drum act with his brother, they toured (mostly through the South) until 1914—during this time he had sold his first composition 'Sapho Rag' and composed 'Eccentric'. Played solo piano in Indiana before moving to Chicago to play with the New Orleans Jazz Band led by Henry and Merritt Brunies. Moved to New York, joined the Original Dixieland Jazz Band in January 1919. Left the O.D.J.B. during their stay in London and returned to New York in October 1919. Worked as W. C. Handy's professional manager; rejoined O.D.J.B. for their residency at the Folies Bergère in New York (September 1920). Left in spring 1921 to work as accompanist for various singers including Marion Harris, Lucille Hegamin, and Lizzie Miles, then quit professional playing to work as a full-time composer. Took part in the revived O.D.J.B. in 1936, then moved back to the West Coast to resume composing. One of his most famous tunes is 'Margie', he also wrote the lyrics for 'Memphis Blues' and 'Ole Miss'.

ROBINSON, 'Jim' Nathan
trombone

Born: Deer Range, Louisiana, 25th December 1890
Died: New Orleans, Louisiana, 4th May 1976

In 1917 began playing the trombone whilst serving with the U.S. Army in France, was taught theory by Pops Foster's brother, Willard. Returned to New Orleans in 1919. Gave up playing temporarily. Resumed after a few months and subsequently played gigs with Kid Rena, then did part-time work in Jessie Jackson's Golden Leaf Orchestra and the Tuxedo Brass Band, but continued to work as a longshoreman. Joined Isaiah Morgan's Band in 1923 and remained with the band when it was subsequently led by Sam Morgan—played with Sam's band throughout the 1920s including engagements at the Warwick Hall, Chicago, in June 1929 (also worked with Papa Celestin for residency at the Gomez Auditorium in late 1927). Played at La Vida Dance Hall, New Orleans, during the 1930s, first in John Handy's Band, then leading own band before becoming a Kid Howard sideman. Also played regularly with Kid Howard's Brass Band in late 1930s. In 1940 took part in recording sessions with Kid Rena, subsequently recorded with Bunk Johnson and became a regular member of Bunk's Band for trip to New York in September 1945. After the band's second residency in New York Jim returned to New Orleans in June 1946. He recommenced parade work and played occasionally in George Lewis's Band. Worked more regularly with George Lewis in the 1950s including several overseas tours, also worked with Octave Crosby's Band in California (1954). Continued to play regularly throughout the 1960s, worked mainly in New Orleans, occasionally travelled for guest appearances with various bands including the Hall Brothers. Toured with Billie and DeDe Pierce (1966-7). Appeared at New Orleans Jazz Fest (June 1969), toured with the Preservation Hall Jazz Band (1969). Made several L.P.s under own name during the 1960s. Is now known as 'Big Jim', his nephew, Sidney Brown (string bass/tuba), being 'Little Jim'.

ROBINSON, Prince
clarinet/tenor sax

Born: Portsmouth (near Norfolk), Virginia, 7th June 1902
Died: New York City, 23rd July 1960

Clarinet from the age of 14, mostly self-taught. First worked in Lilian Jones' Jazz Hounds (1919-21), then with pianist Quentin Redd's Band in Atlantic City (1922), went to New York to join Lionel Howard's Musical Aces (1923). Two years mainly with Elmer Snowden, occasionally with June Clark, then worked with Duke Ellington from spring 1925. With Billy Fowler's Band (from summer 1926) before going to South America with violinist Leon Abbey's Band (May 1927). Regularly with McKinney's Cotton Pickers from 1928 until summer 1931, rejoined McKinney's from 1932 until early 1935. With Blanche Calloway's Band from summer 1935 until early 1937. With Willie Bryant from April 1937 until joining Roy Eldridge in November 1938. With Roy until 1940, then with Louis Armstrong's Big Band (1940-2), Lucky Millinder (1942-3), left Lucky to free-lance in New York. With Benny Morton at Cafe Society Downtown autumn 1944. In 1945 began working regularly with Claude Hopkins, worked on and off with Hopkins until 1952. Led own small group for residencies on Long Island, toured with Henry 'Red' Allen in 1954, regular dates with Freddie Washington's Dixiecrats in Bayside, Long Island, until summer of 1959. Took part in Fletcher Henderson reunion band in July 1958. Was hospitalised with cancer for the last few months of his life.

RODGERS, 'Gene' Eugene R.
piano/arranger

Born: New York City, 5th March 1910

Father was a music teacher at the Boston Conservatory. Played piano from the age of 14.

In 1928 led own Revellers in New York, played with Billy Fowler's Band and Chick Webb, then worked with Bingie Madison until 1931. During this period recorded with Clarence Williams, King Oliver, etc. Worked with Kaiser Marshall's Band and with Teddy Hill, then, together with Frank Radcliffe, formed the variety act Radcliffe and Rodgers Piano Removers. They toured with the 'Hot Chocolates', etc., and played variety halls in Britain in 1936—during this tour Rodgers recorded with Benny Carter in London, also made solo record in London. The act also toured Australia. In the late 1930s he returned to regular band work, played and arranged for Coleman Hawkins' Big Band (late 1939-40), also arranged for Fats Waller's Big Band. Worked in Zutty Singleton's Trio in New York (1940), then short spell of U.S. Army service. With Erskine Hawkins (1943), then moved to California for solo residencies: Hollywood Swing Club (late 1943), The Florentine, etc., whilst in Hollywood appeared in the films 'Sensations of 1945', 'That's My Baby', and 'I'll Tell the World'. Returned to New York, played at The Three Deuces (early 1945), Cotton Club (1946), then solo spots at Lindsay's Sky Bar, Cleveland (early 1947), Detroit (late 1947), Cafe Society, New York (spring 1948), etc. Widespread touring as a soloist in U.S.A. and Canada during the early 1950s. Led own trio for residency at the Broadway Lounge, Astor Hotel, New York, during the late 1950s. During the 1960s and 1970s has continued to work regularly as a soloist, residencies in New York, Vermont, Hartford, Connecticut, etc. Worked with Harlem Blues and Jazz Band (1981-2), including tours of Europe.

RODIN, 'Gil' Gilbert A.
saxes/clarinet/flute

Born: Russia, 9th December 1906
Died: Palm Springs, California, 17th June 1974

Played saxes, trumpet, and flute during early teens. Worked with Art Kahn in Chicago (1924-5), then moved to California; worked with Harry Bastin's Band, subsequently joined Ben Pollack on the West Coast. Except for brief absences, remained with Pollack until 1934. Did studio work in New York including a spell in Red Nichol's radio orchestra, then organised a unit that was to become the Bob Crosby Band (1935). Rodin was the president and musical director of the Crosby Band until he volunteered for the Coast Artillery in September 1942. Played in the Coast Artillery Band until Army release in late 1944. Co-led band with drummer Ray Bauduc in 1945, then quit playing to concentrate on management; helped Bob Crosby organise various bands during the late 1940s and 1950s. Worked as a radio producer during the 1950s then moved into television and successfully produced many important shows during the 1960s, in the U.S.A. and in Australia.

RODRIGUEZ, 'Rod' Nicholas Goodwin
piano

Born: Havana, Cuba, 10th September 1906

Toured and recorded as second pianist with Jelly Roll Morton (1929-30). During the early 1930s played in New York with the San Domingans; worked with Benny Carter (1933). Toured in band fronted by athlete Jesse Owens (1937), worked with Don Redman (1938), then with Alberto Socarras at Glen Island Casino (1939). Rejoined Don Redman in 1940. With Campbell 'Skeets' Tolbert (1943), from late 1945 until June 1946 did overseas U.S.O. tour accompanying vocaliste Frances Brock. Worked with Herbie 'Kat' Cowens in 1946. During the 1950s and 1960s has taught piano in New York, but continues to free-lance. Worked in Atlantic City with Johnny Coles (1953), long spell with Doc Cheatham at the International, New York, during the mid-1960s, also subbed for Billy Kyle in Louis Armstrong's All Stars (April 1961).

ROLLINI, Adrian
bass sax/vibraphone

Born: New York City, 28th June 1904
Died: Homestead, Florida, 15th May 1956

Brother of Arthur. A child prodigy on piano; at four, he gave a Chopin recital at the Waldorf Astoria Hotel, New York. At 14 led own band in New York—doubling piano and xylophone. Worked with the California Ramblers in early 1920s, whilst with this band bought his first bass sax and within a fortnight was playing it in public. Specialised on bass sax for several years. To London in December 1927 to join Fred Elizalde at the Savoy Hotel, other than two brief vacations in the U.S.A. (spring 1928 and winter 1928) he remained in London until December 1929. Returned to New York, joined Bert Lown's Orchestra and remained until spring 1931. Short spell playing in a re-formed California Ramblers in 1931, then mostly active on free-lance recording sessions (throughout the 1920s and early 1930s he participated in countless pick-up recording groups, mostly on bass sax, sometimes on hot fountain pen. In 1935 organised own club—'Adrian's Tap Room' at the Hotel President, New York, from this time onwards specialised on vibraphone, but did some recordings on piano and drums. Doubled with Richard Himber's Orchestra in mid-1930s, but continued to lead own small groups for long residencies at various hotels including: Piccadilly (New York), Park Sheraton (New York), and Blackstone (Chicago). Continued to lead own trio throughout the 1940s, then in the early 1950s moved to Florida where he opened his own hotel The Driftwood Lodge (in Tavernier). Continued to play various residencies in Miami, last worked at the Eden Roc Hotel in September 1955. Died of pneumonia and complications following a liver ailment.

ROLLINI, Arthur *Born: New York City, 13th February 1912*
tenor sax/clarinet

Brother of Adrian. Played piano at 12, switched to tenor sax, attended Columbia University where he led students' band. Worked with California Ramblers, then to London to join Fred Elizalde in March 1929, returned to U.S.A. in December 1929. (Whilst in London studied with clarinet virtuoso Jack Thurston.) Played in New York with Bert Lown, then in re-formed California Ramblers (1931). Played briefly with Paul Whiteman, then with George Olsen until joining Benny Goodman in summer of 1934. Remained with Goodman until May 1939, left to free-lance. Joined Will Bradley Orchestra in July 1941. Worked briefly with Benny Goodman in summer of 1944, but from 1943 until late 1958 worked as a staff musician for A.B.C. Studios, New York. In spring 1959 opened own laundromat business on Long Island, but from then until the present time has continued to free-lance, including regular session work.

ROPPOLO, Leon J. *Born: Lutcher, Louisiana, 16th March 1902*
clarinet/composer *Died: Louisiana, 14th October 1943*

First music lessons from his father, who was a clarinettist, also learnt guitar which he played occasionally throughout his career. His cousin Feno was also a clarinettist. Did early gigs at Bucktown, Lake Pontchartrain, with Georg Brunis, later worked with pianist Eddie Shields and with Santo Pecora in various clubs in New Orleans, played residency at Toro's Club (c. 1917). Left New Orleans in band accompanying vocaliste Bea Palmer, subsequently worked with Carlisle Evans' Band on riverboats and played residencies in Davenport, Iowa. Moved to Chicago with boyhood friends Georg Brunis and Paul Mares to join the Friars' Inn Society Orchestra (c. 1921), later named The New Orleans Rhythm Kings. After 18 months moved to New York with Paul Mares and joined Al Siegal's Orchestra at Mills Caprice in Greenwich Village. Moved to Texas and joined Peck Kelley's Bad Boys (summer 1924), then rejoined Carlisle Evans in St. Paul, was taken ill at Marigold Gardens, Minnesota, and returned to New Orleans. Played in a revived New Orleans Rhythm Kings (with Paul Mares) in New Orleans (spring 1925), subsequently suffered severe breakdown and was committed to a Louisiana mental home. Continued to play regularly, mainly on tenor sax; organised band in the mental home. Was temporarily released in the early 1940s, returned home to New Orleans, played two nights for Santo Pecora on the S.S. Capitol and sat in with Abbie Brunies on tenor sax.

ROWLES, 'Jimmy' James George *Born: Spokane, Washington, 19th August 1918*
piano/composer

Began playing piano at 14, attended Gonzaga College and University of Washington in Seattle. Gigged in Spokane before moving to Los Angeles in 1940. Worked with Garwood Van, and Dick Peterson before joining Slim Gaillard and Slam Stewart (early 1942), worked with Lee and Lester Young prior to brief spell with Benny Goodman in fall of 1942. With Woody Herman (late 1942-43), then joined service and played in Skinnay Ennis's Army Band. After demobilisation worked with Woody Herman, Les Brown, Tommy Dorsey, Benny Goodman, etc. During the late 1940s did regular radio shows with Bob Crosby's Band. Active free-lance in California during the 1950s and 1960s, many record dates and regular movie and television studio work. Moved to the East Coast in the 1970s, was featured on concert and club dates, led own small groups and was often featured with Zoot Sims. Did many free-lance recordings, was also featured at Newport Jazz Festival in the 1970s, also featured at Nice Festival 1978 and 1979. Continued to play regularly during the early 1980s.

ROY, 'Teddy' Theodore Gerald
piano

Born: Duquoin, Illinois, 9th April 1905
Died: New York City, 31st August 1966

Also known as 'Pappa'. Originally played cornet, then specialised on piano. Made record debut in 1927, worked with Coon-Saunders in Chicago before joining Jean Goldkette. Worked in New York with Leo Reisman, Vincent Lopez, Nat Shilkret, Willard Robison, etc., during the 1930s, also with Bobby Hackett and Pee Wee Russell in Boston (1933), led own band for summer residency at Cape Cod, Massachusetts (1934). Left full-time music in the early 1940s, served in U.S. Army (1943-5), worked with Max Kaminsky in Boston (late 1945 to early 1946), then free-lanced in New York, playing solo spots in various clubs including Eddie Condon's. With Pee Wee Russell (1951). Gigged with Miff Mole, Max Kaminsky, Wingy Manone during the late 1950s.

ROYAL, Marshall Walton
alto sax/clarinet

Born: Sapulpa, Oklahoma, 5th December 1912

Brother of trumpeter Ernie Royal (1921-83). Raised in Los Angeles, his father was a music teacher and bandleader, mother played piano. Started on violin, then guitar and clarinet before taking up alto sax. Played in local bands from the age of 13, with Curtis Mosby from 1929-31, then joined Les Hite. Remained with Hite until 1939, worked with Cee Pee Johnson's Band until joining Lionel Hampton's Band from October 1940 until September 1942 (occasionally doubling violin). Joined U.S. Navy and led own service band, after demobilisation played with Eddie Heywood in New York (spring 1946), then returned to California. Did studio work for five years and gigged with various bands in Los Angeles. In spring of 1951 joined Count Basie's Septet on clarinet (replacing Buddy De Franco), remained with Basie when he re-formed big band (playing lead alto). Worked for Count Basie until early 1970. Studio work in California (1971), dates with Earl Hines (September 1971). (In 1934, Marshall briefly subbed for Otto Hardwick in Duke Ellington's Orchestra.) Active free-lance during the 1970s. Played regularly during early 1980s including European tours.

RUSHING, 'Jimmy' James Andrew
vocals/piano

Born: Oklahoma, 26th August 1902
Died: New York, 8th June 1972

Nicknamed 'Mister Five by Five'. From a musical family; father played trumpet, mother and brother were singers. Early efforts on violin, then taught piano by his cousin, Wesley Manning. Studied music at Douglass High School in Oklahoma City and began singing around the Middle West. In California (1923-4), sang at the Jump Steady club (occasionally accompanied by Jelly Roll Morton) and at the Quality Club with Paul Howard and Harvey Brooks. Returned home in 1925 and helped his family run their luncheonette business. Toured with the Billy King Revue (Walter Page in accompanying band), later joining Walter Page's Blue Devils (1927). Remained with the Blue Devils until joining Bennie Moten in late 1929, worked with that band until the leader's death in April 1935, briefly with Buster Moten, then joined Count Basie in Kansas City (1935). Worked at the Reno Club, Kansas City, with Basie, subsequently went to New York with the band and remained as featured vocalist until October 1948 (also recorded with Benny Goodman, Bob Crosby, and Johnny Otis). Worked occasionally with Basie in 1949-50, but then formed own small band which played residency at Savoy Ballroom, New York, from late 1950-2 and also toured. Worked as a single from June 1952, residencies in New York, Newark, Kansas City, Cleveland, Oakland, California, Canada, etc. To Europe as solo artist in September 1957, following year with Benny Goodman at the Brussels World Fair (May 1958). To Europe with Buck Clayton (September 1959). Frequent guest appearances with Count Basie in the 1950s and 1960s, also regularly featured at important jazz festivals. Toured with Harry James, briefly with the Benny Goodman Sextet in spring of 1961, played long residency in Miami in 1962, toured Japan and Australia with Eddie Condon in spring 1964. Later that year toured Europe with Count Basie. In 1965 and 1966 worked regularly at the Half -Note in New York; continued to work as a single, featured in the 1969 film 'The Learning Tree'. Regular week-end dates at the Half-Note, N.Y. (1971), also sang in Toronto (1971), temporarily inactive through illness (August 1971), appeared at Kansas City jazz festival (1972).

RUSHTON, 'Joe' Joseph Augustine
bass sax/clarinet

Born: Evanston, Illinois, 7th November 1907
Died: California, 2nd March 1964

Played drums first, then clarinet before specialising on bass saxophone. Worked occasionally with the California Ramblers, led own band in Chicago from 1928-31, then left full-time music to work in an aircraft factory. With Ted Weems in 1934, and through the 1930s worked for many Chicago bandleaders, occasionally returned to aircraft work. With Jimmy McPartland from spring 1940, to California with Benny Goodman from November 1942 until September 1943, worked for Horace Heidt (February 1944 until spring 1945), then resumed work in aeronautics, continued gigging. Worked with Red Nichols from early 1947 until spring 1963 (including overseas tour). Suffered a fatal heart attack whilst driving home from a San Francisco jazz club.

RUSSELL, 'Johnny' John W.
tenor sax/clarinet/violin

Born: Charlotte, North Carolina, 4th June 1909

Raised in New York; mother played the organ. Began studying violin at nine, taught by David Martin Sr. at the Martin Smith Music School. Began doubling on tenor sax. First professional work at 17 in Albany, N.Y., with drummer Jimmy Campbell's Band (on violin and tenor), played summer season in Asbury Park, then joined Earle Howard's Band at the Strand Danceland, New York (late summer 1926). Left Howard in late 1927 to join band led by trombonist Billy Kato, then worked in Harry 'Father' White's Band at Nest Club, and Lenox Club, etc., also gigged with the Cass Carr Orchestra. Rejoined Billy Kato in 1930 for residencies at Broadway Danceland and Savoy, worked in Charlie Matson Orchestra, then joined Benny Carter's Orchestra (replacing Chu Berry). With Carter until joining Willie Bryant (1935-6), then to Europe with Bobby Martin's Band. After playing Paris (June 1937) the band did widespread touring in Europe. Joined Willie Lewis early in 1939 and remained in Europe with Lewis until September 1941, playing last residency in Lisbon, Portugal. Returned to the U.S.A., played in Philadelphia in Garvin Bushell's Band (1942), then called up for service in U.S. Army. Led the 93rd Division Military Band, then became assistant leader of Russell Wooding's 115th A.G.F. Band. Overseas service in France and Belgium with the 115th (then directed by Bill Graham). Demobilised in 1945, joined Cecil Scott at the Savoy Ballroom, worked with Eddie Cornelius before leaving music to work as a salesman. Continued to play free-lance club engagements.

Johnny Russell's playing was featured in the pre-war Erich Von Stroheim film 'Alibi'.

RUSSELL, Luis Carl
piano/arranger

Born: Careening Clay, near Bocas Del Toro, Panama, 6th August 1902
Died: New York City, 11th December 1963

His father, Felix Alexander Russell, was a pianist, organist, and music teacher. Luis studied guitar, violin, organ, and piano. First worked accompanying silent films in a

Panama cinema (1917), then played in the Casino Club, Colon, Panama. In 1919 he won $3,000 in a lottery and moved with his mother and sister to New Orleans. Gigged in various clubs and took lessons from Steve Lewis. Joined Arnold Du Pas Orchestra at Cadillac Club in late 1921-2. Worked at Tom Anderson's Cabaret in Albert Nicholas' Band (1923), later when Nicholas left, Luis Russell became the band's leader until late 1924 when he accepted an offer to join Doc Cooke in Chicago. Whilst waiting for union clearance he gigged with King Oliver. Worked with Doc Cooke for several months (on piano and organ), also doubled at the late-night clubs, then joined King Oliver (1925). Long spell at the Plantation with Oliver, also did intensive musical studies, left Chicago with King Oliver, after playing in Milwaukee, Detroit, and St. Louis, the band played at the Savoy Ballroom in May 1927. He left King Oliver in the summer of 1927 and joined drummer George Howe's Band at the Nest Club, New York. In October 1927 Russell was appointed leader of the band and they remained resident there for a year. During the late 1920s the band played many New York residencies including: Saratoga Club, Arcadia Ballroom, Savoy, Connie's Inn, etc., etc. In 1929 the band also accompanied Louis Armstrong for several months. During the early 1930s the band continued to play long residencies in New York, also did extensive touring. From September 1935 the band became the regular accompanying unit for Louis Armstrong and from then on was billed as Louis Armstrong's Orchestra—during the late 1930s Luis Russell occasionally doubled on trombone. Though most of the original Russell Band had left by 1940, Luis continued working for Louis Armstrong until 1943. He then formed his own big band which did widespread touring as well as residencies in New York (Savoy, Apollo, etc.) and Atlantic City, etc. He left full-time music in 1948 and became a shopkeeper (stationery, toys, sweets, etc.), occasionally gigged with his own small bands and continued to teach piano and organ. In 1959 he made his first return visit to Panama (after an absence of almost 40 years), whilst in Bocas del Toro he gave a classical piano recital. During the early 1960s he worked as a chauffeur, but continued teaching until shortly before his death. He died of cancer.

RUSSELL, 'Pee Wee' Charles Ellsworth
clarinet/saxes

Born: Maple Wood, Missouri, 27th March 1906
Died: Alexandria, Virginia, 15th February, 1969

During early childhood moved with his family from St. Louis to Muskogee, Oklahoma, where he attended Central High School. Took lessons on violin, piano, and drums, then studied clarinet with Charlie Merrill; first jazz inspiration was Alcide Nunez. Did gigs with the Perkins Brothers' Band near Muskogee, later worked briefly on an Arkansas riverboat with the Deep River Jazzband. Family moved back to St. Louis (c. 1920) and Pee Wee enrolled at Western Military Academy in Alton, Illinois (15th September 1920 until 21st October 1921). Later attended University of Missouri, but spent most of his time playing aboard riverboats, about this time played some dates with Herbert Berger's St. Louis Club Orchestra. Further clarinet studies with Tony Sarlie of the St. Louis Symphony Orchestra. Toured with the Allen Brothers tent show (c. 1922) before rejoining Herbert Berger in Juarez, Mexico (c. 1923), later worked with Floyd Robinson's Band in El Paso, Texas, then worked with Herbert Berger in Arizona and California, also worked in Houston with Peck Kelley's Bad Boys (1924). Back in St. Louis, Pee Wee worked again with Herb Berger (making his record debut with Berger in November 1924), also brief spells with Gene Rodemich, Joe Gill, Ray Lodwig, and Joe Johnson. In late 1925 worked in Frank Trumbauer's Band (with Bix Beiderbecke) at the Arcadia Ballroom in St. Louis. In summer of 1926 worked with Trumbauer and Beiderbecke in a Jean Goldkette band resident at Hudson Lake, near South Bend, Indiana. Early in 1927 Pee Wee went to New York to join Red Nichols, worked with Nichols on many occasions during the late 1920s and early 1930s, also took part in many pick-up recording groups and worked on soprano, alto, tenor saxes, and bass clarinet with several bandleaders including: Paul Specht, Cass Hagen, Don Voorhees, Austin Wylie, Ben Pollack, etc. In summer of 1933 worked in Payson Re Band (with Bobby Hackett) in Falmouth, Massachusetts, then in winter 1933-4 played at The Crescent Club, Boston (with Hackett and Teddy Roy). Moved back to New York, gigged for a while, then worked with Louis Prima in New York, Hollywood, Chicago, etc., from spring 1935 until early 1937. After a brief illness worked with Parker's Playboys in

Chicago (April 1937). In 1937 began long on and off residencies at Nick's, in Greenwich Village, New York. In Bobby Hackett's Big Band in 1938 (except for two weeks in November 1938 when he led own small group at Little Club, New York), with Hackett until July 1939 (doubling alto sax). With Bud Freeman's Summa Cum Laude Band and bands led by Eddie Condon until summer of 1940, then resumed at Nick's, played briefly in quartet led by accordionist Tony Ambrose. Spell with Jack Bland's Trio (early 1941), then Nick's until lay-off through illness (spring 1942). Many dates at Jimmy Ryan's in 1942, then from January 1943 with Georg Brunis and Wild Bill Davison, later several months with Brad Gowans and short stay in revue headed by dancer Katherine Dunham. Took part in most of the Town Hall Concerts organised by Eddie Condon. From November 1943 long spells with Miff Mole's Band at Nick's, in August 1944 worked with James P. Johnson at the Pied Piper Club, led own band in Boston (late 1945). A year with Eddie Condon from October 1946, then back to Nick's working under various leaders including Billy Butterfield (1948). With Muggsy Spanier and Miff Mole in Chicago (autumn 1948). In spring 1949 led own trio and worked with Art Hodes at the Riviera Club, New York, played many sessions at Central Plaza before working in Chicago in Art Hodes' Band (with Lee Collins, Georg Brunis). Moved to San Francisco in summer of 1950, became critically ill whilst working at Coffee Dan's Club (December 1950) and was taken to the San Francisco County Hospital, later underwent major operation at Franklin Hospital. Louis Armstrong, Jack Teagarden, Eddie Condon, Art Hodes, and many others rallied to his aid by playing at big benefit concerts. Pee Wee returned to New York in March 1951, sat in with Eddie Condon in July, but did not resume full playing schedule until opening with own band in Denver, Colorado (October 1951), led in Boston (1952), Jack Dempsey's Club, New York (1953), etc., then resumed playing for other leaders. Worked at Condon's from October 1955 until late 1956. Made solo appearances at jazz festivals and often worked with groups organised by George Wein. During the 1960s made appearances at many major jazz festivals in U.S.A. with the Newport All Stars, first trip to Europe with that unit in spring of 1961. Formed successful quartet with valve trombonist Marshall Brown in autumn of 1962, recorded with this group, they also played dates in Toronto and at Village Vanguard, New York. Toured Australia, New Zealand, and Japan with Eddie Condon in spring 1964. Visited Europe again with George Wein in autumn 1964, returned to play solo tour of Britain. In 1965, at his wife Mary's suggestion, he took up oil painting. Did several dates with Bobby Hackett including engagement at New York's Riverboat in July 1967, later that year worked in California with Eddie Condon's All Stars. In October 1968 headlined concert at New York Town Hall. Played on several occasions at Blues Alley, Washington, D.C. Last job was with George Wein's All Stars at President Nixon's inaugural ball (21st Jan. 1969). Died in an Alexandria, Virginia, hospital; burial in Union; N.J.

I am indebted to Pee Wee's friend, Jeff Atterton, for much of the previously unpublished information that is contained in this entry.

RUSSIN, 'Babe' Irving
tenor sax/clarinet

Born: Pittsburgh, Pennsylvania, 18th June 1911
Died: Panorama City, California, 4th August 1984

Brother of pianist Jack Russin (who sometimes worked under the name of Rusin), their sister, 'Sunny', was a professional pianiste. Babe's first professional work was with the California Ramblers (1926), worked with Smith Ballew (1926-7). Went to Europe with George Carhart (July 1928), returned to New York, worked occasionally for Roger Wolfe Kahn, regularly with Red Nichols. With Ben Pollack (1930), prolific free-lance recordings. Mainly with Red Nichols (summer 1930-2), with Russ Colombo's Band (late 1932-3). On C.B.S. staff from 1934 until December 1937, joined Benny Goodman for three months, resumed studio work, then worked for Tommy Dorsey from October 1938 until forming own band 1940-1 (residencies in New York, Florida, etc.). With Jimmy Dorsey from May 1942 until February 1944. Served in U.S. Army until early 1946, played in the A.F.R.S. service orchestra. Several brief stints with Benny Goodman in the late 1940s and 1950s including appearance in the film 'The Benny Goodman Story', but has been mainly occupied as a studio musician in Hollywood. Was given star billing for his part in the film 'The Glenn Miller Story'.

RUTHERFORD, 'Rudy' Elman
saxes/clarinet

Born: Detroit, Michigan, c. 1912

Worked mainly in Detroit before joining Lionel Hampton, left Hampton in June 1943, rejoined the band briefly in November 1943, then with Count Basie (1944-5—on baritone sax and clarinet), mainly on alto clarinet with Basie (1946-7). In spring 1947 joined altoist Ted Buckner's Band in Detroit, subsequently mainly active leading own small bands. Brief return to Count Basie (early 1951), during the 1950s and 1960s led own groups at Basie's Club, Milton's, Steak Out, New York, Ramopa Country Club, etc., also worked with Ram Ramirez Trio (1959) and with Buddy Tate (1964), etc. Active free-lance during the 1970s, also played with Earl Hines (1975).

S

ST. CLAIR, Cyrus
sousaphone

Born: Cambridge, Maryland, 1890
Died: New York City, 1955

Father and uncle were tuba players. Began playing cornet in the Merry Concert Band in Maryland, later switched to tuba. Moved to New York (c. 1925), worked with Wilbur de Paris Band and with Bobby Lee's Cotton Pickers, also played residency at Leroy's Club, New York. Spent five years with Charlie Johnson's Band from 1926; during this period played on many Clarence Williams' recording sessions including accompanying Bessie Smith, etc. Worked in Cozy Cole's Hot Cinders (1930), and gigged in New York. Musically inactive for several years, returned to regular playing for Rudi Blesh's 'This is Jazz' radio series (1947), recorded with Tony Parenti's Ragtimers. Worked for Buildings and Grounds Department of Columbia University until shortly before his death.

ST. CYR, 'Johnny' John Alexander
banjo/guitar

Born: New Orleans, Louisiana, 17th April 1890
Died: Los Angeles, California, 17th June 1966

His father, Jules Firmin St. Cyr (died: 1901), played guitar and flute. Johnny began playing on a home-made, 'cigar-box' guitar, then graduated to Spanish guitar. Formed own Consumers' Trio (named after a local brewery), then began gigging with Jules Baptiste and Manuel Gabriel (c. 1905-8). Played in Freddie Keppard's Band (and also with Keppard in The Olympia Band), but continued working during the day as a plasterer. Played briefly with Papa Celestin, then with Kid Ory. With Armand Piron (c. 1914), subsequently with pianist Arthur Campbell until 1916. Brief spell in King Oliver's Magnolia Band before rejoining Armand Piron. Left plastering trade to join Fate Marable on the riverboats (summer 1918 until summer of 1920). Again with Armand Piron, then riverboat work with Ed Allen's Whispering Gold Band and Charlie Creath before returning to New Orleans (c. September 1921). Returned to day work as a plasterer, did occasional parade work on alto horn. Played briefly with Amos White, then joined Manuel Perez at the Pythian Roof Gardens (1923). Moved to Chicago in September 1923, played briefly with King Oliver, then two months in Darnell Howard's Band before joining Doc Cooke's Dreamland Orchestra (from January 1924 until November 1929). During this period regularly doubled at various late-night clubs including spell with Jimmie Noone at The Apex. Also took part in many free-lance recording sessions with Louis Armstrong, Jelly Roll Morton, etc., etc. Left Doc Cooke in November 1929, gigged for a while in Indiana before returning to New Orleans (via Chicago). Worked as a plasterer throughout the 1930s and 1940s, continued regular part-time playing with Paul Barnes, Chester Zardis, Steve Lewis, etc. Spell with Alphonse Picou at The Paddock during the early 1950s, continued gigging, then regularly with Paul Barbarin. Played in California with Barbarin in 1955, from then on made his permanent home on the West Coast. Guested with many bands, played regularly with New Orleans Creole Jazz Band in Los Angeles (1959), then played with (and later led) The Young Men of New Orleans during the early 1960s. Survived a bad car crash during the summer of 1965, but was forced by illness to restrict regular playing during last years of his life. He died of leukaemia in the Los Angeles County General Hospital.

SAFRANSKI, 'Eddie' Edward
string bass

Born: Pittsburgh, Pennsylvania, 25th December 1918
Died: Los Angeles, California, 9th January 1974

Played violin during early childhood, switched to double bass in high school. First professional work with Harty Gregor in 1937, then played (and arranged for) Herman Middleman's Band in Pittsburgh (1937-38), also arranged for Artie Shaw's Band (1937). With Hal McIntyre's Orchestra (1941-45), then with Stan Kenton (1945-48), Charlie Barnet (1948-49). During the 1950s and 1960s worked as a staff musician for N.B.C. studios in New York City, moved to Los Angeles in late 1960s, where continued to do studio work, also free-lance dates with many varying small groups.

SAMEL, Morey
trombone

Born: Newark, New Jersey, 27th March 1909

Studied at New Jersey Technical College, took up trombone at the age of 16. Worked with bands in New Jersey, then worked for Roger Wolfe Kahn, Red Nichols, Ben Bernie,

Richard Himber, Nat Shilkret, Rudy Vallee, Paul Whiteman, etc., also did several Al Goodman shows. With Lenny Hayton's Orchestra 1936-7, joined Bunny Berigan in spring 1937 for several months. Did studio work, then brief spell with Jack Teagarden's Orchestra (early 1939), also worked briefly for Bob Crosby. With Artie Shaw (1941-2), Bob Chester (1942-3), then mainly active as a studio musician.

SAMPSON, 'The Lamb' Edgar Melvin
saxes/violin/arranger/composer

Born: New York City, 31st August 1907
Died: New Jersey, 16th January 1973

His daughter, Gladys, is a successful composer. Began on violin at the age of six, doubled alto sax from early teens. Led own high school band, then began working with pianist Joe Coleman in New York (1924). Did a season with Duke Ellington at the Kentucky Club, then with Bingie Madison and Billy Fowler (1926) before playing at Savoy Ballroom with Arthur Gibbs. With Charlie Johnson Band from 1928 until 1930, with Alex Jackson (c. 1930), then joined Fletcher Henderson (1931-2). Briefly with Rex Stewart's Big Band (1933). Joined Chick Webb in 1934, whilst with Chick he composed many tunes that were to become jazz standards. Left the band in July 1936 and began a long stint as busy free-lance arranger, scoring for Artie Shaw, Red Norvo, Teddy Hill, Benny Goodman, Teddy Wilson, etc., etc. Brief return to full-time playing: as musical director of Ella Fitzgerald Band from July-November 1939 and on alto/baritone with Al Sears (1943). Resumed regular playing in late 1940s, led own band in New York (1949-51)—mostly on tenor sax. Then arranging for, and playing with, several Latin-American bands including Marcellino Guerra, Tino Puente, and Rodriguez. Led own small band through the late 1950s and early 1960s, also gigged regularly with Harry Dial's Bluesicians. Inactive in the late 1960s through severe illness which necessitated the amputation of a leg.

SANDERS, 'Joe' Joseph L.
piano/vocals/arranger

Born: Thayer, Kansas, 15th October 1896
Died: Kansas City, Missouri, 14th May 1965

Nicknamed 'The Old Left Hander'. Shared leadership of Coon-Sanders Night Hawks with drummer Carleton A. Coon. After U.S. Army service in World War I they formed a small band that operated in Kansas City. After broadcasting debut in 1921 they began gradually augmenting and secured residencies in Chicago (1924). From 1926 they appeared regularly at The Blackhawk, Chicago, also did extensive touring during summer months. In May 1932 co-leader Carleton Coon died, Sanders continued to lead the band from then billed as Joe Sanders Original Nighthawks, long residencies at The Blackhawk Cafe through 1930s. During the 1940s did extensive studio work in Hollywood, also led band at The Trianon Ballroom, occasional returns to The Blackhawk. During the 1950s he was a regular member of the Kansas City Opera Company. After suffering for many years with eyesight problems he had a stroke in 1964.

SANDS, Bobby
tenor sax

Born: Brooklyn, New York, 28th January 1907

With Billy Fowler's Strand Roof Orchestra (c. 1927), with Charlie Skeets in 1929, then became member of Claude Hopkins' Band in 1930, worked with Hopkins throughout the 1930s. Left music in the 1940s and worked as a printer for many years.

SANNELLA, 'Andy' Anthony
violin/piano/alto/clarinet/guitar/banjo/vibes/vocals

Born: New York City, 11th March 1900
Died: c. 1961

At 10 started on guitar and violin, played in school orchestra. Then joined U.S. Army, was released through being under age, later served in U.S. Navy during World War I. Played violin and alto sax in orchestras in Panama City (1920-2), then returned to New York and joined Dan Gregory's Orchestra. Played with Mike Marker Orchestra, Ray Miller Orchestra, etc., then worked as musical director for many Broadway shows. Prolific free-lance radio and recording work from the mid-1920s; working regularly on all of the above-listed instruments. In later years he worked mostly on piano and organ—featured in a C.B.S. television series in the late 1940s.

S

SAUNDERS, 'Red' Theodore *Born: Memphis, Tennessee, 2nd March 1912*
drums/vibes/tympani *Died: Chicago, Illinois, 5th March 1981*

Began playing drums whilst attending school in Milwaukee. Did local work, then moved to Chicago, joined pianist Stomp King, then worked with Tiny Parham at the Savoy Ballroom (c. 1934). Began leading own band at the Club DeLisa, Chicago, in 1937, led own big band there for 18-year residency—during this period also subbed with Louis Armstrong All Stars, Duke Ellington, Woody Herman, etc. Led at the Regal, Chicago, from 1960 until 1967. Continued to play during the late 1960s, appeared with Art Hodes at the New Orleans Jazz Fest in 1968, worked with Little Brother Montgomery (1969). Occasionally led own big band (1970). Active during the 1970s.

SAUTER, 'Eddie' Edward Ernest *Born: Brooklyn, New York, 2nd December 1914*
arranger/trumpet *Died: Nyack, New York, 21st April 1981*

Raised in Nyack, N.Y. Originally played drums, studied at Columbia University and played and arranged for Columbia Blue Lions. Played trumpet with bands working on Atlantic liners. Travelled extensively throughout Europe, then settled in New York. Worked with Archie Bleyer in 1932, also brief spell with Charlie Barnet, continued studying arranging and composition at Juilliard School. Played trumpet and occasionally mellophone with Red Norvo in late 1935, but was mainly active as Red's staff arranger until June 1939 when he began arranging regularly for Benny Goodman. Scored for many big bands during the 1940s including Woody Herman, Tommy Dorsey, etc., also spell as staff arranger for Ray McKinley. After three long spells in hospital (suffering from a lung ailment) he got together with pianist-arranger Bill Finegan to form the Sauter-Finegan Orchestra (1952). The band was originally a studio unit, but later did tours and residencies before disbanding in 1957. Sauter then worked in Germany as musical director for Sudwestfunk until autumn of 1958. During the 1960s continued composing and arranging including scoring for the film 'Mickey One' in 1965.

SAYLES, 'Manny' Emanuel René *Born: Donaldsonville, Louisiana, 31st January 1907*
guitar/banjo/vocals

Son of musician George Sayles. First studied violin and viola with Dave Perkins, then self-taught banjo and guitar. Went to high school in Pensacola, Florida, for two years, then moved to New Orleans, joined William Ridgley's Tuxedo Orchestra. Worked with Fate Marable on S.S. 'Capitol' (1928), recorded with Jones-Collins Astoria Hot Eight (1929), also with Armand Piron and Sidney Desvigne on the riverboats. Moved to Chicago in 1933, led own small group and played for many leaders including bassist John Lindsey, recorded with Roosevelt Sykes. Moved back to New Orleans in 1949, continued to play regularly. Worked in Cleveland with Punch Miller (1960). Joined George Lewis and toured Japan with Lewis (1963-4). In 1964 toured with pianiste Sweet Emma Barrett. In 1965 returned to Chicago to work as house musician at Bill Reinhardt's Jazz Ltd. Returned to New Orleans in 1968, played regularly at Preservation Hall, etc. Did solo work in Britain in 1969. Toured Australia with Preservation Hall Band (1971), also toured Europe, worked mainly in New Orleans during the 1970s. Toured Russia with Preservation Hall Band (1979). Continued to play regularly during the early 1980s including tours of Europe.

SCHOEBEL, Elmer *Born: East St. Louis, Illinois, 8th September 1896*
piano *Died: Florida, 14th December 1970*

At 14 began playing piano accompaniment in silent-movie house in Champaign, Illinois, then long spell on tour accompanying various variety acts. In 1920 played in Chicago with the 20th Century Jazz Band. From 1922 until 1923 played regularly in the Friars' Society Orchestra (the N.O.R.K.), then formed own band for residency at Midway Gardens, Chicago. To New York with Isham Jones in 1925, returned to Chicago, led own band and through the late 1920s played for various leaders including Louis Panico, Art Kassel, etc. During this period also did regular arranging and transcribing for the Melrose Publishing House. Achieved great success as a composer ('Nobody's Sweetheart', 'Farewell Blues', etc.) and worked mainly at arranging and composing through the 1930s until becoming chief musical arranger for Warner Brothers' New York publishing company. Played regularly in late 1940s. With Conrad Janis Band in early 1950s. Moved to Florida, briefly with Blue Steele's Rhythm Rebels (1958), regular gigs in St. Petersburg. Worked with Arnie Mossler's Suncoaters two days before his death.

SCHROEDER, 'Gene' Eugene Charles
piano

Born: Madison, Wisconsin, 5th February 1915
Died: Madison, Wisconsin, 16th February 1975

Mother was a pianiste, father played trumpet and led own local band. Began studying at the Wisconsin School of Music, at 11 gigged with his father's band on piano, later doubled clarinet in high school orchestra (c. 1930). Spent a year at University of Wisconsin Music School (1932), then moved to Milwaukee in 1933. Played mainly in Milwaukee for several years, led own quintet, played for various leaders including Wild Bill Davison (occasionally) and long spell with Stan Jacobson's Band at the Wisconsin Roof Ballroom, also did summer seasons at the Chanticleer in Madison. Moved to New York in 1939, played at One Fifth Avenue, briefly with the Wes Westerfield Trio, then own group at Town Topics Club. In November 1940 joined Joe Marsala at the Hickory House, year later with Marty Marsala Band at Nick's. From summer of 1942 worked with Wild Bill Davison in Chicago, Boston, and New York, then into Nick's October 1943, working originally with Miff Mole. Began working with Eddie Condon and played at opening of Eddie's Club in December 1945. For the following 17 years worked almost exclusively for Condon (including trip to Britain in 1957). Free-lanced in New York, then briefly with The Dukes of Dixieland (including tour of Japan in summer of 1964). Later worked with Tony Parenti then moved back to Wisconsin. Played a season at Mt Telemark, Wisconsin in 1967, but ill health restricted activities during last years of his life.

SCHUTT, Arthur
piano/arranger

Born: Reading, Pennsylvania, 21st November 1902
Died: San Francisco, California, 28th January 1965

Taught piano by his father. Played piano in local movie houses from the age of 13, was heard by leader Paul Specht, who signed him for his orchestra (c. 1918). For the next six years Schutt worked mainly for Specht including trip to London in 1923. Worked for Roger Wolfe Kahn and Don Voorhees, then long spell of studio and recording work with Joe Rines' Orchestra, Fred Rich, Nat Shilkret, etc. During the late 1920s and early 1930s took part in countless free-lance recording sessions with Red Nichols, Frank Trumbauer, Bix Beiderbecke, Joe Venuti, Benny Goodman, etc. Led own band in New York in late 1930s, played briefly with Bud Freeman at Kelly's Stables in spring of 1939, then again led own band. During the 1940s and 1950s was mainly active as a studio musician in Hollywood, working for M.G.M., Columbia, etc. In 1961 he played piano at a bowling alley social club in Los Angeles, then long spell of ill health.

SCOBEY, Robert Alexander
trumpet

Born: Tucumcari, New Mexico, 9th December 1916
Died: Montreal, Canada, 12th June 1963

Family moved to Stockton, California in 1918. Cornet from age of 9, trumpet from 14. Studied at Berkeley College. Professional music from age of 20. One of co-founders of Lu Watters' Yerba Buena Band in late 1930s, played cornet alongside Watters until Army service 1942-46. Played in Army Band. Rejoined Watters until 1949. During the 1950s led own band in California, before moving to Chicago. Continued success throughout the early 1960s, including tour of Europe as part of the Harlem Globetrotters' package (1962). Continued playing dates with own band until weeks before dying of cancer. Former wife Jan's book 'He Rambled 'Til Cancer Cut Him Down,' which summarises Scobey's life, was first published in 1976.

SCOTT, 'Bud' Arthur
guitar/banjo/vocals/violin

Born: New Orleans, Louisiana, 11th January 1890 (?)
Died: Los Angeles, California, 2nd July 1949

Played guitar and violin from early childhood. Professionally active from the turn of the century, worked with John Robichaux's Orchestra (c. 1904), also played briefly in Freddie

Keppard's Olympia Orchestra. Left New Orleans in January 1913 as featured violinist with the Billy King Travelling Show. Worked in Mobile and Washington, then moved to New York in 1915. Played in various theatre orchestras, also worked in Baltimore (1917) as banjoist with Bob Young's Band. Did many engagements as vocalist with the Clef Club including appearance at Carnegie Hall in 1919. With Will Marion Cook's Orchestra (1921), left New York to move to Chicago, worked for three months with King Oliver in late 1923, then moved to California to join Kid Ory for a brief time. Back to Chicago to work for King Oliver, then again to West Coast playing with Kid Ory and Curtis Mosby's Blue Blowers. Rejoined King Oliver at the Plantation, Chicago, until 1926, then worked with Erskine Tate before joining Dave Peyton in late 1926. Continued to work with Peyton (on violin) for over two years, but also worked as manager (and banjoist) at the Cafe de Paris, Chicago, in 1927 before brief return to Erskine Tate, then with Jimmie Noone at the Apex Club (1928). Also did extensive free-lance recordings including sessions for Jelly Roll Morton. With Fess Williams in Chicago (January 1929), Dave Peyton (summer 1929). Left Chicago in September 1929 to make his home in Los Angeles. Worked with Leon Herriford Band and also (during the early 1930s) with Mutt Carey's Jeffersonians. Led own trio for several years and did movie-extra work, then rejoined Kid Ory in 1944. Continued to work with Ory until late 1948 when ill health forced him to quit regular playing. He continued to sit in occasionally with Ory during early 1949. Appeared in the film 'New Orleans'.

SCOTT, Cecil Xavier
clarinet/saxes

Born: Springfield, Ohio, 22nd November 1905
Died: New York City, 5th January 1964

Brother of drummer Lloyd W. Scott (born: 1902); their father was a violinist. Cecil Scott Jr. was a saxophonist. In 1919, whilst at high school, formed a trio with Lloyd and pianist Don Frye. By 1922 they were operating as a seven-piece—Scott's Symphonic Syncopators, they toured around Ohio until early 1924, then played at The Royal Gardens, Pittsburgh, prior to residency at Herman's Inn, New York, from June-October 1924. The band played in Ohio before returning to New York (1926-early 1927), dates at the Capitol Palace, etc. Back to Ohio, then played in Canada, Buffalo, Pittsburgh, again to Ohio before taking residency at Savoy Ballroom, N.Y., in December 1927. Long stay at the Savoy, also dates in Pittsburgh, Detroit, etc. In June 1929, Cecil became leader of the band, and his Bright Boys toured (and played many New York residencies) until the early 1930s: Savoy Ballroom, Renaissance Casino, etc. With Earle Howard (1932). In the early 1930s Cecil suffered a serious accident and was forced to disband. After his recovery he did extensive recording work for Clarence Williams, also did occasional work with Fletcher Henderson and played regularly with Vernon Andrade's Orchestra during the mid-1930s. With Teddy Hill in 1936 and 1937 (in New York and on tour), then long spell with band led by Alberto Socarras until forming own band for residency at the Ubangi Club from 1942. Worked with Hot Lips Page in Chicago (c. 1944), then from the mid-1940s regular spells with Art Hodes' small groups, later led own trio at Ryan's. Continued regular free-lance recordings through the 1940s. Worked mainly with Henry 'Chick' Morrison's Band in 1950-2, then with Jimmy McPartland's Band before leading own small group at various New York venues including: Central Plaza, Stuyvesant Casino, and Jimmy Ryan's. Played at the Great South Bay Festival in 1957 and 1958, also worked occasionally for other leaders including cornetist Jack Fine. In August 1959 played in Canada with Willie 'The Lion' Smith. During the early 1960s he continued to play regularly in New York.

Cecil Scott was the proud father of 13 children. During the early 1930s Cecil badly damaged his ankle in a fall; the resultant complications caused the amputation of a leg. The New York Rehabilitation Centre regularly called on Cecil to demonstrate, and lecture on, his adept use of an artificial limb.

SCOTT, 'Lannie' Lannice
piano

Born: Louisville, Kentucky, 1908
Deceased

Raised in Cleveland and Detroit, played regularly in those cities before moving to New York. Worked with Washboard Serenaders (1932), later played long residency at Paradise Inn, Detroit, prior to moving back to Cleveland for club residencies in the early 1940s.

Worked mainly as a soloist during the 1940s, and 1950s, and did some composing (Art Tatum recorded his tune 'The Shout'). During the early 1960s worked regularly with Henry Allen, later worked in the Jonah Jones Quartet.

SCOTT, Leon
trumpet

Born: Demopolis, Alabama, 15th August 1904
Died: Chicago, Illinois, 2nd January 1974

Father played baritone horn. Leon's daughter Julie L. Scott plays French horn and piano. Began on trumpet, was taught by John Whatley in Birmingham, Alabama. Moved to Chicago, studied music with Major N. Clark-Smith. Played gigs with John Wycliffe and Ida Mae Marples prior to working with Lester Boone's Band (1925). With John Morrisett (1926), Tiny Parham (1927), Sammy Stewart (1928-29), Walter Barnes (late 1929). In 1930-31 toured France and Belgium with Earl Moss. Worked with Lucky Millinder in Chicago and New York (1931), prior to brief return to Tiny Parham's Band. Worked often with Carroll Dickerson during the 1930s, with Horace Henderson c. 1933, then led own band. With Jimmie Noone (1937-39), also with Earl Hines (1938). Worked in Hawaii (1941-late 1945) with Andrew Blakeney, and with Eddie Sereno's Band. With Bardu Ali's Band in Los Angeles (1946). Worked with Benny Carter and Eddie Heywood in California, then moved back to Chicago in the late 1940s. Extensive free-lance activities in Chicago during the 1950s and 1960s, many dates with Franz Jackson from 1965 (including overseas tours). Ill health caused an end to regular playing during the early 1970s.

SCOTT, Raymond
(real name: Harold Warnow)
leader/pianist

Born: Brooklyn, New York, 10th September 1910

Brother of violinist Mark Warnow. Studied at New York's Institute of Musical Art during the early 1930s, then began working at C.B.S. studios in New York. During the mid-1930s he led a studio novelty quintet, then after leading on the West Coast (and scoring for and appearing in several films) he formed his own big band in 1939. The band did regular touring and also played several residencies including The Blackhawk, Chicago, in 1940. He returned to C.B.S. staff in 1942 and from August of that year began directing an all-star studio group which at various times included: Charlie Shavers, Cozy Cole, Ben Webster, Emmett Berry, Johnny Guarneri, George Johnson, Jerry Jerome, etc. During the 1950s and 1960s mainly active as an arranger-composer and musical director. Own electronics laboratory in Farmingdale (1971). In early 1970s moved to Van Nuys, California.

SEALS, Warner A.
reeds

Born: Huntington, West Virginia, 25th October 1901
Deceased

First worked in trio (with pianist Hazel Powell and drummer Kemper Royal) at local Douglass High School (1918-20). First professional work was playing in band aboard the S.S. 'Island Queen'. With Tom Howard's Melody Lads and Joe Steward's Band before joining Marion Hardy's Alabamians. With Alabamians for several years, including period in 1927 when Jelly Roll Morton fronted the band. Moved to New York with the Alabamians in 1929. During the 1930s worked with: Bill Brown, Eddie South, Billy Elmore, etc. Left full-time music to work as a receptionist at a Wall Street broker's office. Continued to play gigs during the 1960s, was for many years Corresponding Secretary of the New Amsterdam Musical Association. Died during the 1970s, his widow Gladys plays alto sax.

SEARS, 'Al' Albert Omega
tenor sax/saxes

Born: Macomb, Illinois, 22nd February 1910

Brother of sax-playing leader Marion Sears. Al originally specialised on alto and baritone saxes. First professional work in Buffalo with the Tynesta Club Quartet, then with Cliff Barnett's Royal Club Serenaders and Paul Craig's Band before moving to New York to replace Johnny Hodges in Chick Webb's Band (1928). Toured in 'Keep Shufflin' revue, led own band, then played with Zack Whyte, Bernie Young, before joining Elmer Snowden in New York (1931). Forced to leave Snowden through bout of pneumonia (spring 1932), returned to Buffalo and re-formed own band. Toured with Bud Harris and his Rhythm Rascals (early 1933), then led own band for several years in the 1930s (left music temporarily in 1935 to study business management course), band played residencies in Buffalo, Cincinnati, Newport, Kentucky, etc. Also worked briefly in Vernon Andrade's Orchestra in late 1938. Joined Andy Kirk from February 1941 until summer of 1942, then formed own band which played at Renaissance Casino, New York, and did long U.S.O. tour in 1943. Joined Lionel Hampton for four months from December 1943, then with Duke Ellington from May 1944 until September 1949 (brief absence in early 1949). In Johnny Hodges' small band from March 1951 until October 1952. After the success of the composition 'Castle Rock' he formed his own music-publishing company which became his major occupation. Continued to record through the 1950s, also occasionally played with Duke Ellington's Orchestra.

SECREST, Andy
trumpet

Born: Muncie, Indiana, 2nd August 1907
Died: California, 1977

Worked in Freda Sanker's Orchestra in Cincinnati, then with Ted Weems and Ray Miller Orchestra before joining Jean Goldkette, left after residency at Pla-Mor Ballroom, Kansas City (November 1927 to April 1928). With Paul Whiteman from November 1928 until 1932, then moved to California to work in Hollywood as a studio musician. Was featured in many studio orchestras including: Victor Young's, John Scott Trotter's, and Billy Mills' Radio Orchestra, etc. Occasionally did outside work including spell with Ben Pollack in spring 1938. In the early 1950s played at several West Coast Jazz Festivals. Left full-time music to work in real estate.

Has sometimes been confused with trumpeter Frank D. Siegrist (1900-47), who also worked with Paul Whiteman.

SEDRIC, 'Honey Bear' Eugene P.
tenor sax/clarinet

Born: St. Louis, Missouri, 17th June 1907
Died: New York City, 3rd April 1963

Eugene gained his nickname in the 1930s; at the time he wore an exotic camel-hair overcoat. His father, Paul 'Con Con' Sedric, was a professional ragtime pianist. As a boy he played in the local Knights of Pythias Band. First professional work at the Alamac Hall with Charlie Creath. Subsequently with Fate Marable and Dewey Jackson before joining Ed Allen's Band in late 1922. In September 1923 joined Julian Arthur's Band accompanying Jimmy Cooper's 'Black and White Revue'. Then gigged in New York until joining Sam Wooding. Sailed to Europe with Wooding in May 1925, remained with Wooding until October 1931 (when the band temporarily disbanded). Returned to New York and played again with Wooding in summer of 1932. Brief spell with Fletcher Henderson, then regular work with Fats Waller from 1934 until 1942. During Fats Waller's solo tours Sedric worked with various bands including: Mezz Mezzrow's Disciples of Swing (November 1937) and Don Redman (1938-9). Led own small group from March 1943—the band, which was originally resident at The Place, New York, later worked in Chicago, New Jersey, Boston, and Detroit. Recovered from serious illness, then worked briefly in the Phil Moore Four in late 1944 before touring with the Hazel Scott Show in late 1945. In the summer of 1946 he again formed his own band which played several New York residencies including: The Place, Cafe Society, and Small's. In the spring of 1951 he toured with Bobby Hackett's Band, then after a spell with Jimmy McPartland he sailed to Europe in February 1953 to tour with Mezz Mezzrow. From August 1953 worked regularly in band led by Conrad Janis, frequent appearances at the Central Plaza, etc. Did many free-lance recording sessions in the 1950s. Illness forced him to give up playing for the last 18 months of his life. He died after a long stay in the Goldwater Memorial Home.

SENIOR, Milton
alto/tenor/clarinet

Born: Springfield, Ohio, c. 1900
Died: c. 1948

After working in Springfield with the Willis and Wormack Band, in 1921 he became a founder-member of the Synco Septette (later called The Synco Jazz Band) which was taken over by William McKinney. Remained with McKinney's Cotton Pickers until autumn 1928. During the following spring he joined Wes Helvey's Band, then moved on to Toledo, Ohio (1930), where he led a band through the early 1930s (Art Tatum, then Teddy Wilson played in his Toledo Band). Long after leaving full-time music he took his own life.

SENTER, Boyd Langdon *Born: Lyons, Nebraska, 30th November 1899*
clarinet/multi-instrumentalist

His father was an orchestra conductor, his mother a professional singer. At nine he began playing violin and drums. During his early teens he learnt to play a great variety of instruments and did local theatre work from the age of 17. In 1920 he joined the Marie Hart Saxophone Quartet, led his own band in Atlantic City (1921-2), then worked in Myers' Sax Band before playing in the Chicago De Luxe Orchestra (1923). He then formed his own band and through the 1920s made many popular recordings, most of them featuring his unusual clarinet style. Many of his recordings were made with studio musicians (sometimes billed as his Senterpedes). During the 1930s he worked mainly in Detroit, long spell directing the orchestra at the Colonial Theatre. In World War II he ran his own aircraft-component company, then returned to lead at Scotty's Bar during the late 1940s. He continued playing in the 1950s and also ran his own 'Sports Senter'. In the early 1960s he was still playing regularly in Mio, Michigan.

SHAPIRO, 'Art' Arthur *Born: Denver, Colorado, 1916*
string bass

Lived in New York City from the age of five. Began playing trumpet at 13, switched to string bass at 18, but continued to do occasional gigs on trumpet during his teens. Joined Wingy Manone in New York (1935-6), left to do commercial work in Washington, D.C., then joined Joe Marsala (1937-8). From the mid-1930s recorded regularly with many studio groups and leaders including: Frank Froeba, Sharkey Bonano, Eddie Condon, Chu Berry, Tommy Dorsey, etc., etc. Joined Paul Whiteman in late 1938, left in 1940, worked with Joe Marsala and Bobby Hackett, then rejoined Whiteman until spring 1941. Moved to free-lance in Hollywood and continued making jazz record dates with Jack Teagarden, Joe Sullivan, Eddie Miller, etc. After service in U.S. Army returned to studio work, played with Benny Goodman from August-December 1947. Then mainly active as a studio musician. Settled in California.

SHAVERS, 'Charlie' Charles James *Born: New York City, 3rd August 1917*
trumpet/arranger/vocals/composer *Died: New York City, 8th July 1971*

Father was a trumpet player; Charlie was a distant relative of trumpeter Fats Navarro. Began playing piano and banjo, then switched to trumpet. Played occasionally with pianist Willie Gant in New York; first work away from New York was with Frankie Fairfax Band in Philadelphia (1935). Returned to New York and joined Tiny Bradshaw, then with Lucky Millinder from early 1937. In November 1937 joined John Kirby at the Onyx Club (replacing Frankie Newton). He soon became the sextet's principal arranger and composed 'Undecided', 'Pastel Blue', etc., whilst with the group. He finally left John Kirby in 1944, doubling with Raymond Scott at C.B.S. during his last year. In February 1945 he first joined Tommy Dorsey—for the next 11 years he left and rejoined the band many times. Occasionally with John Kirby early in 1946. In 1950 he co-led a sextet with drummer Louis Bellson and vibes-player Terry Gibbs, then several stints with Norman Granz's 'Jazz At The Philharmonic' tours including trips to Europe. Worked with Benny Goodman for several months from July 1954. During the 1960s regularly led own quartet including residencies at The Embers, The Metropole, etc., also did regular tours with Sam Donahue (then fronting The Tommy Dorsey Orchestra), visited Europe with this unit in 1964. From 1965 was extensively featured with The Frank Sinatra Jr. touring show including tours to Japan, Vietnam, Hong Kong, Canada, and South America, also did wide variety of recorded work. In late 1969 toured Europe (including Britain) as a soloist. Toured Europe again in 1970. Died of throat cancer; last gig with J.P.J. Quartet at Half-Note, N.Y. (23rd May 1971). Was an accomplished pianist.

S

SHAW, Artie
(real name: Arthur Jacob Arshawsky)
clarinet/saxes/composer

Born: New York City, 23rd May 1910

Raised in New Haven, Connecticut, from the age of seven. Played ukelele from age of 10, started on saxophone at 12. Joined New Haven High School Band; won local talent contest with banjoist Gene Beecher. Formed own band The Bellevue Ramblers for local gigs at Liberty Pier, Savin Rock, and Banham Lake. Left home at 15 to work in Kentucky, the job failed to materialise, worked his way home playing in a travelling band. With Don 'Johnny' Cavallaro in New Haven and Florida, then with Joe Cantor and Merle Jacobs in Cleveland. With violinist Austin Wylie's Band on and off from 1927-9, then joined Irving Aaronson's Commanders (switching to tenor sax). Moved to New York, sat in regularly with Willie 'The Lion' Smith at Pod's and Jerry's whilst awaiting Local 802 card, then with Paul Specht, Vincent Lopez, and Roger Wolfe Kahn, before season with Red Nichols at Park Central Hotel, New York (1931), then studio work with Fred Rich for a year from autumn 1931. Rejoined Roger Wolfe Kahn and did summer 1933 tour with that band. Did free-lance radio and recording work, then left music for a year to run a farm in Bucks County, Pennsylvania (1934). Moved back to New York for free-lance work. Led small group (clarinet, strings, and three rhythm) for concert at the Imperial Theatre in May 1936. The success of this one-shot venture eventually gained Shaw financial backing, and in 1936 he began touring with his own big band (including strings), this unit disbanded and during the following year Shaw reorganised with a conventional big-band line-up for April 1937 debut in Boston. With the help of a hit record ('Begin the Beguine') the band became one of the most popular of the swing-era bands. Shaw was absent through a tonsillectomy in the summer of 1939, then in November 1939 he suddenly disbanded and moved to Mexico for two months. He re-formed a big band in the late summer of 1940 and began recording with his own Gramercy Five, disbanded and re-formed again in 1941. Joined U.S. Navy in spring 1942 and led own specially picked service band, extensive tour of Pacific area, returned to U.S.A. in November 1943 and was given medical discharge in February 1944. Formed new big band in late 1944; throughout the late 1940s spasmodically led own bands. Studied classical guitar and clarinet in New York and guested at Carnegie Hall with National Symphony Orchestra in February 1949. In spring 1949 led own string orchestra for short residency at Bop City. From September 1949 again led big touring band, continued leading in the early 1950s, also re-formed a short-lived Gramercy Five in late 1953. Ran own dairy farm in Skekomeko, N.Y., then in 1955 moved to Spain and lived for several years in Gerona, by this time he had ceased playing and was mainly active as a writer. Moved back to the U.S.A. in 1960, finally sold property in Spain 1962. Married to actress Evelyn Keyes for many years. Mainly active writing and adapting for the theatre, and working outside of music business, but a band bearing his name (led by Dick Johnson) was formed in 1983.

Artie Shaw appeared in several films, he also had an abundance of non-simultaneous wives. His autobiography 'The Trouble With Cinderella' was first published in 1952, later he wrote a novel 'I Love You, I Hate You, Drop Dead'.

SHAW, 'Lige' Elijah W.
drums/percussion

Born: Jackson, Tennessee, 9th September 1900
Died: St. Louis, Missouri, 1982

One of a very large family. Worked as a tap-dancer at 11; moved to Memphis in 1914, worked at mechanical dentistry, began gigging on drums. In September 1917 joined Bowen and Blondins' Dandy Dixie Minstrels, then toured for four years with the Alabama Minstrels except for brief spell with Huntington's Mighty Minstrels. From March 1921 toured with the Original Georgia Minstrel Band including trip to West Coast. Worked at Booker T. Washington Theatre, St. Louis, then in June 1922 joined violinist Wilson Robinson's Bostonians, after touring Illinois, Iowa, and Nebraska, the band returned to St. Louis, Lige left and was replaced by Leroy Maxey. Worked in trio at Booker T. Washington Vaudeville House, then five years playing at the Criterion Theatre, St. Louis (1924-9). Moved to Mississippi (spring 1929), joined F. S. Wolcott's 'Hi-Brown Follies', briefly in '101 Wild West Show', (1930), then toured with Will E. Moore's Midnight Ramblers. Returned to St. Louis in 1931, did club dates, then a year at Club Plantation with trumpeter Walter

'Crack' Stanley. With Charlie Creath (1933-4)—Arcadia Ballroom and on S.S. 'St. Paul', then briefly with Dewey Jackson. Played regularly throughout the late 1930s, served long term as President of A.F. of M. Local 197. Recommenced touring in 1941 with the Ringling Brothers' Circus Band. With pianist Eddie Johnson at Delmar and Taylor Club, St. Louis (1943), later led own band at same venue. Again served as President of Local 197 from 1944 until 1957. Regular playing again from 1949, worked with Singleton Palmer throughout the 1950s (including recordings). Settled in St. Louis where he had his own well-established piano tuning-repair service. Played on Streckfus boat 'Admiral' (October 1971).

SHEARING, George Albert *Born: London, England, 13th August 1919*
piano/composer

Blind from birth. During teens played in blind students' band led by Claude Bampton prior to joining Ambrose. During World War II played regularly in Harry Parry's Radio Rhythm Club Band, doubled on accordion in Frank Weir's Orchestra in 1947. Moved to the U.S.A. in 1948, led own trio and quartet before forming quintet in 1949 which was to bring international fame to Shearing. The quintet (with varying personnel) was still operating in 1977, but during the intervening years Shearing also led a trio and had his own big band. He has also guested with several major symphony orchestras. Continued to maintain widespread touring schedule during the 1970s, often appeared in a duo (with bass) in 1978, during that year was presented with the 'Horatio Alger' award. Full working schedule during early 1980s including overseas tours.

SHEPHERD, 'Shep' Berisford *Born: Honduras, Central America, 19th January 1917*
drums/arranger

Parents moved to Philadelphia when 'Shep' was five months old. Two of his cousins were musicians: Sid Francis (bass) and Mike Headley (tenor sax). Attended Reynolds Junior High School, then majored in music at the Mastbaum Conservatory. From 1932 until 1941 worked with Jimmy Gorham's Band in and around Philadelphia, then with Benny Carter (1941-2)—also recorded with Artie Shaw (in June 1941). In U.S. Army from 1943-6, did extensive arranging, also played trombone in service bands and percussion in orchestras. Did short tour with Cab Calloway in 1946, with Buck Clayton Sextet (1947), then three years with Earl Bostic, returned to Philadelphia 1950-2, arranging and copying for publishers, also local recording sessions. With Bill Doggett's Group from 1952 until 1959 (co-composer of Bill Doggett's hit 'Honky Tonk'), then prolific free-lance recordings as percussionist. Played for many Broadway shows including: 'Mr. Kicks and Co.', 'America Be Seated', 'Jericho Jim Crow', etc., recordings with Sy Oliver, also worked occasionally with Erskine Hawkins. Toured with 'Here's Love' show in 1964, then settled in San Francisco. Long stay in local 'Chi-Chi' club; continued free-lance activities, also played trombone in local 49'ers Band.

SHERMAN, 'Jimmy' James Benjamin *Born: Williamsport, Pennsylvania, 17th August 1908*
piano/arranger *Died: Philadelphia, Pennsylvania, 11th October 1975*

Originally taught piano by his sister, then studied with private teachers. Did first gigs for local high school dances, then played occasionally with Jimmy Gorham's Band. First professional work with Alphonso Trent on Great Lakes steamer (1930), then with Peanuts Holland (1931), Al Sears (1932), Stuff Smith (1933-4). With Lil Armstrong's Big Band (1935), rejoined Stuff Smith in New York (1936). In 1936 and 1937 also recorded with Putney Dandridge, Lil Armstrong, Mildred Bailey, and Billie Holiday. From 1938 until 1952 worked as accompanist-arranger for the vocal group The Charioteers (including tour of Europe in 1948), then returned to Pennsylvania. Played for three years at The Tally Ho motel near Valley Forge, then in 1960 began long residency at Miss Jeanne's Crossroad Tavern, played there regularly for over a decade.

S

SHEROCK, 'Shorty'

(real name: Clarence Francis Cherock)
trumpet

Born: Minneapolis, Minnesota, 17th November 1915
Died: North Ridge, California, 19th February 1980

Began playing cornet as a child, did local gigs whilst attending high school in Gary, Indiana. Attended Illinois Military Academy in Abington. Worked with Charlie Pierce and Dell Coon before joining Ben Pollack (1936). Worked briefly with Frankie Masters, Jacques Renard, Jack Pettis, Seger Ellis, and Santo Pecora, then with Jimmy Dorsey (1937-9). With Bob Crosby (summer 1939 to January 1940), Gene Krupa (January 1940 to March 1941), Tommy Dorsey (April-July 1941), Raymond Scott (summer 1941), then in Bud Freeman Band (late 1941). With Bob Strong Band until joining Alvino Rey in July 1942. With Horace Heidt until March 1945, then led own band until June 1946, disbanded but re-formed again in 1948. Settled in California, rejoined Jimmy Dorsey for a brief spell in 1950, then worked as a free-lance studio musician in Hollywood. Worked with George Auld in 1954 in Los Angeles, but during the 1950s and 1960s was mainly active as a studio musician.

SHIELDS, Larry

clarinet

Born: New Orleans, Louisiana, 13th September 1893
Died: Los Angeies, California, 21st November 1953

Brother of clarinettist Harry (1899-1971), two other brothers, Eddie (piano) and Pat (guitar) were also distinguished musicians. Larry played clarinet from the age of 14, during his teens he occasionally played with Nick LaRocca in New Orleans. To Chicago (c. June 1915) to join Bert Kelly's Band, swapped places with Gus Mueller and in August 1915 joined Tom Brown's Band, with Brown to New York working as The Kings of Ragtime and The Five Rubes, the group disbanded in February 1916. Shields went back to New Orleans, returned to Chicago in November 1916 to join the Original Dixieland Jazz Band. Remained with the O.D.J.B. until December 1921—including long residencies in New York and trip to London. Briefly with Paul Whiteman, then moved to West Coast, led own bands at various venues including Tent Cafe and 400 Club in Los Angeles. During late 1920s did some touring through California, also appeared briefly in several films. Moved back to New Orleans during the 1930s, worked at jobs outside of music. Occasionally played clarinet including short spell at Subway Club, Chicago in summer 1935. Took part in re-formed Original Dixieland Five from July 1936 until February 1938—except for short absence in late 1936. During this period played briefly at Nick's, New York, with Georg Brunis. After O.D.J.B. break up in February 1938, Shields continued to work with Eddie Edwards and Frank Signorelli in new version of the O.D.J.B., but left to return to California (via New Orleans where he did some subbing for his brother Harry at The Dog House). Lived in California for the rest of his life, retired from active music. He made regular visits to New Orleans during the last few years of his life, died of a heart attack.

SHIRLEY, 'Jimmy' James Arthur

guitar/electric bass

Born: Union, South Carolina, 31st May 1913

Spent childhood in Cleveland, Ohio, was originally taught music by his father. Worked with J. Frank Terry's Band and with Hal Draper in Cincinnati (1934-6), then led own quartet in Cleveland before moving to New York. With Clarence Profit 1937-41, then two years accompanying Ella Fitzgerald. Joined Herman Chittison's Trio in 1944 and for the next 10 years played for long spells with Chittison, also led own small group from the mid-1940s, residencies at The Tondelaya (1945), The Onyx (1946), etc. Temporarily used a 'vibrola' attachment on his guitar. During the 1940s and 1950s also worked with Phil Moore, pianist Oliver 'Toy' Wilson, Vin Strong, Billy Williams, The Four Keys, etc. From the early 1960s regularly doubled on Fender Bass—with George James' Band in 1963 and Buddy Tate (1967), continued to work mainly in New York.

SHOFFNER, 'Bob' Robert Lee

trumpet

Born: Bessie, Tennessee, 30th April 1900
Died: Chicago, Illinois, 5th March 1983

Family moved to St. Louis in 1902. At nine began playing drums, then bugle, in the local Knights of Phythias Band. Did summer tours in this boys' band, then switched to trumpet in

1911, taught by 'Professor' Blue, also began playing piano. His first wife, 'Auzie' Shoffner, was a professional pianiste. Enlisted in the U.S. Army and spent two years with the 10th Cavalry in Arizona, eventually playing trumpet in the division band. After release (1919) worked in St. Louis and on the riverboats with Charlie Creath, then toured Ohio and Oklahoma with Tommy Parker's Band. In 1921 visited an aunt in Chicago and decided to work there, joined John H. Wickcliffe's Band, then worked with Everett Robbins and his Jazz Screamers (1921), subsequently joined Mae Brady's Band at Dreamland Cafe, then returned to St. Louis to play a season with Charlie Creath (1922). Settled in Chicago, with Honore Dutrey's Band at the Lincoln Gardens, then from June 1924 worked with King Oliver. Briefly with Dave Peyton and Lottie Hightower's Nighthawks (1925), then again with Oliver from May 1925 until February 1927. Returned to St. Louis for minor operation on his lip, back to Chicago, rejoined Dave Peyton in April 1927, then with violinist Wyatt Houston from May 1927. Lip problems again enforced lay-off from playing, joined Charles Elgar at the Savoy (1928), then worked with Erskine Tate at the Metropolitan Theatre. With Jerome Carrington (early 1931), then toured with McKinney's Cotton Pickers (summer 1931), due to union restrictions was unable to work with McKinney's in Detroit, returned to Chicago. Rejoined Erskine Tate and worked regularly with Frankie Jaxon in 1932, also worked in various theatre orchestras and subbed in Earl Hines' Band. Spell in band led by bassist William Lyle (November 1934), then moved to New York to join Fess Williams. Left Williams to free-lance in New York, two weeks with Fletcher Henderson at the Roseland Ballroom, also worked with Ovie Alston and Kaiser Marshall before joining Hot Lips Page at Small's, New York, in March 1938. Moved back to Chicago, joined Johnny Long's Band, left in January 1940 to organise own short-lived big band. Joined Autrey McKissick's Band in Chicago (November 1940), then left full-time music to work in the administrative offices of the State of Illinois for many years. Continued gigging until the mid-1940s, recommenced playing in 1957, regular local gigs, then joined Franz Jackson's Original Jazz All Stars, also organised own concert brass band. Forced by illness to quit regular playing in 1963, played occasionally in the mid-1960s.

SHU, Eddie
(real name: Edward Shulman)
reeds/trumpet/harmonica/vocals/composer

Born: Brooklyn, New York, 18th August 1918

Toured vaudeville circuits as a harmonica-playing ventriloquist. During service in U.S. Army (November 1942-November 1945), played saxophone, clarinet and trumpet in military bands. After demobilisation worked with Tadd Dameron, George Shearing, Johnny Bothwell, Buddy Rich, and Les Elgart prior to spell with Lionel Hampton 1949-50. During the 1950s was with Charlie Barnet, Chubby Jackson before working in Gene Krupa's Trio from 1954-58. Moved to Florida, led own group and worked as a solo act. Toured with Louis Armstrong All Stars, playing clarinet, in 1964 and 1965. Worked again with Lionel Hampton and Gene Krupa in the 1960s. During the 1970s active free-lance work based in New York City.

SIGNORELLI, Frank
piano/composer

Born: New York City, 24th May 1901
Died: Brooklyn, New York, 9th December 1975

Originally taught piano by his cousin, Pasquale Signorelli. Founder-member of Original Memphis Five (from 1917), worked briefly in the Original Dixieland Jazz Band in 1921, then resumed with Original Memphis Five. From the mid-1920s did prolific free-lance work for radio, recording, and theatre. Left Original Memphis Five in September 1926, joined Joe Venuti. Member of Adrian Rollini's short-lived New Yorker Band—September-October 1927. Recorded with Joe Venuti, Ed Lang, Bix Beiderbecke, etc., in late 1920s and early 1930s, enjoyed great success as a composer. Played in re-formed O.D.J.B., then from summer of 1938 joined Paul Whiteman. During the 1940s and 1950s continued to play regularly; worked with Bobby Hackett at Nick's in 1947, then at same venue with Phil Napoleon from late 1940s. Took part in television shows with specially re-formed Original Memphis Five. During the late 1950s played solo spots in Greenwich Village.

S

SILLAWAY, Ward
trombone

Born: Grand Rapids, Michigan, 29th March 1909
Died: Chicago, Illinois, 1st October 1965

Worked with Joe Haymes' Band in the early 1930s, then long spell in Phil Harris Orchestra before joining Bob Crosby. Left Bob Crosby in late 1938 to join Tommy Dorsey until spring 1940. Played for a while in pit orchestra for 'Louisiana Purchase' (1940), then long spell of studio work for C.B.S. (briefly with Benny Goodman in summer of 1944). Continued studio work in the 1950s, also long stay with Fred Waring's Pennsylvanians. In 1964 moved to Chicago and joined Local 10. Was married to ex-Dorsey vocaliste Kay Weber.

SIMEON, Omer Victor
clarinet/alto, baritone saxes

Born: New Orleans, Louisiana, 21st July 1902
Died: New York City, 17th September 1959

Family moved to Chicago in 1914. Began playing clarinet in Chicago, took lessons from Lorenzo Tio Jr. (then working in Chicago). In 1920 did first professional work in band led by his violinist brother—Al Simeon's Hot Six. Briefly with Jimmy Bell's Band, then with Charlie Elgar's Creole Band from 1923 until spring 1927 (working mostly in Milwaukee and Chicago). Took part in several pick-up recording sessions with Jelly Roll Morton in 1926. In spring 1927 joined King Oliver's Dixie Syncopators, brief tour, then Savoy, New York, residency in May 1927. Left King Oliver in Baltimore during summer of 1927 to rejoin Charlie Elgar at the Eagle Ballroom, Milwaukee, later worked at Dreamland, Chicago, with Elgar. Returned to New York in summer of 1928, joined Luis Russell at The Nest Club, then worked for a week with Jelly Roll Morton at the Rose Danceland before returning to Chicago. With Erskine Tate at Metropolitan Theatre from October 1928 until 1930 (occasionally doubling with Charlie Elgar at the Savoy). Gigged in Chicago, then three months with pianist Jerome Carrington's Orchestra at the Regal Theatre (early 1931) before joining Earl Hines. Remained with Earl Hines for 10 years—except for spell with Horace Henderson (March-August 1938) and briefly with Walter Fuller in 1940—also depped for Buster Bailey with Fletcher Henderson in 1936. Worked in Coleman Hawkins' Band from May 1941, then with Walter Fuller's Orchestra from late 1941 until summer of 1942. Joined Jimmie Lunceford in summer 1942 and remained with the band after the leader's death (1947), working under Eddie Wilcox's leadership until 1950. (Whilst with Lunceford made small band recordings with Kid Ory.) Gigged in New York, then regularly with Wilbur de Paris Band from autumn 1951 until shortly before dying of throat cancer (toured Africa with de Paris in spring of 1957).

In later life Simeon signed his name as Omer, however, several early reports give the name as Omar. The picture becomes more confused by a report that Simeon Sr. worked as a cigar maker, using the name Omer Simeon.

SIMMONS, John Jacob
string bass

Born: Haskell, Oklahoma, 1918
Died: Los Angeles, California, 19th September 1979

Went to school in Tulsa, then moved to California to complete studies. Played trumpet for two years until sustaining injuries in a football match, switched to string bass and within four months was gigging in Los Angeles. Worked with Nat 'King' Cole in California, then moved to Chicago. With Jimmy Bell, 'King Kolax' (trumpeter William Little), Floyd Campbell, etc., briefly in Johnny Letman's Band in late 1940, then joined Roy Eldridge in December 1940. With Benny Goodman from July-September 1941, with Cootie Williams' Big Band and Louis Armstrong in 1942 before joining C.B.S. Blue Network Orchestra. Briefly with Duke Ellington (c. October 1943), then returned to C.B.S. Prolific free-lance recordings. With Eddie Heywood in California (1945), brief absence from music, then returned to New York to join Illinois Jacquet (1946). Did session work during the late 1940s, then two years with pianist Errol Garner (1950-2), returned to studio work, then played regularly with Harry Edison in 1955, during following year worked in Scandinavia with Rolf Ericson-Duke Jordan Band. Long periods of inactivity due to illness, worked with pianist Phineas Newborn in 1960, but did little regular playing in the 1960s. Appeared in the film 'Jammin' The Blues'. Lived in California in the mid-1970s.

SIMMONS, 'Lonnie' Samuel
tenor sax/clarinet/piano/organ

Born: Charleston, South Carolina. c. 1915

With Fats Waller's Big Band, then worked with Hot Lips Page before joining the Savoy Sultans (led by alto/clarinettist Al Cooper) in 1939. Worked mainly with the Savoy Sultans until joining Ella Fitzgerald's Orchestra (1940-1). Formed own band, led U.S. Naval Band (1944-5), led in Hawaii (late 1945), own 10-piece band in Chicago from 1946, long residencies at the Pershing Lounge, Club Silhouette, etc., etc. Ran own restaurant in Chicago during the 1960s, worked on piano, and, during the late 1960s, the organ.

SIMON, 'Pazuza' Stafford
tenor sax/clarinet

Born: c. 1908
Died: New York, 1960

Worked with Willie Bryant and Louis Jordan before joining Benny Carter in 1940. With Louis Jordan (early 1941), then joined Lucky Millinder (1941-2). Led own band in 1943, then worked with George James (1944), briefly with Rex Stewart (1946). During the 1940s and 1950s regularly led own small band, died on the bandstand whilst working at the Savannah Club, Greenwich Village.

SIMPSON, Cassino Wendell
piano

Born: Chicago, Illinois, 22nd July 1909
Died: Elgin, Illinois, 27th March 1952

Received some tuition from Zinky Cohn. Played in The Moulin Rouge Orchestra in Chicago (c. 1925), then worked in Milwaukee and Chicago with Arthur Simm and his Orchestra, after that leader's death continued working with Oscar 'Bernie' Young—remained on and off with Young until spring of 1930, also worked with Erskine Tate and did extensive free-lance recordings. Briefly in Jabbo Smith's Band, then led own band in Chicago (c. 1931), continued to lead own bands until 1933. Worked as accompanist for Frankie Jaxon, this arrangement came to an abrupt end when Simpson was charged with attempting to manslaughter that singer, soon afterwards (in March 1935) Simpson was admitted to the Illinois State Hospital for Mental Diseases at Elgin, Illinois. He played bass drum in the hospital's marching band and piano and vibes in the 26-piece dance band. In 1944-5 he made solo-piano recordings at Elgin, but he was never released from the hospital and died there in March 1952.

I have never been able to ascertain where Cassino Simpson was born—some sources give Chicago, others Venice, Italy.

SINGER, 'Hal' Harold
tenor sax

Born: Tulsa, Oklahoma, 8th October 1919

Father was a guitarist. Took up violin at eight, later played saxophone and clarinet in high school band. Went to Hampton Institute, Virginia, in 1937 (where he later obtained degree in agriculture), but also did summer-vacation gigs in Oklahoma City with trumpeter James Simpson and in band led by Charlie Christian's brother, Edward. Professional with Ernie Fields' Band from summer of 1938, during the following year worked with Lloyd Hunter's Serenaders and with Nat Towles. In late 1939 joined Tommy Douglas Band; in 1941 became a member of Jay McShann's Band. Left to settle in New York (1942), extensive gigging, then with Hot Lips Page (1943), Jay McShann, Roy Eldridge Big Band (1944), Earl Bostic, Don Byas (1945), Henry 'Red' Allen Sextet (summer 1946), Sid Catlett (1947), Lucky Millinder (early 1948), then spent six months with Duke Ellington (1948). Through success of own best-selling single 'Cornbread'. formed own touring band 1949-58. Became house musician at The Metropole, New York, from May 1958. Led own band in New York (Baby Grand, etc.), during early 1960's, moved to Paris in 1965 and then worked regularly in Europe during the 1970s and early 1980s, including tour of England (1981).

SINGLETON, 'Zutty' Arthur James
drums

Born: Bunkie, Louisiana, 14th May 1898
Died: New York, 14th July 1975

Raised in New Orleans; uncle was Willie 'Bontin' Bontemps (bass/guitar/banjo). First professional work at Rosebud Theatre with Steve Lewis (1915), worked occasionally for

John Robichaux, then service in the U.S. Navy during World War I. After demobilisation returned to New Orleans, worked briefly as a chauffeur, then replaced Little Joe Lindsey in Tom's Roadhouse Band. Gigged with Papa Celestin and 'Big Eye' Louis Nelson, led own band at Orchard Cabaret, then played regularly with Luis Russell at the Cadillac (1921). With Fate Marable from late 1921 until 1923, then left riverboats to return to New Orleans. Did pit orchestra work for John Robichaux, then moved to St. Louis to join Charlie Creath (for over 40 years was married to Creath's piano-playing sister, Marge). Returned to New Orleans after a year, played there in band led by trombonist Charlie Lawson, then moved to Chicago. Subbed for Baby Dodds in Vernon Roulette's Band at Jeffrey's Tavern, worked with Doc Cooke and with Dave Peyton at Cafe de Paris (April 1927). With Jimmie Noone at The Nest before joining Clarence Jones' Band at the Metropolitan Theatre (with Louis Armstrong). Left in late 1927, played briefly at the Warwick Hall with Louis Armstrong and Earl Hines, then joined Dave Peyton at the Club Baghdad (late 1927), rejoined Jimmie Noone for a while, then joined Carroll Dickerson's Band (then featuring Louis Armstrong)—Zutty played on many of Louis' Savoy Ballroom small band recordings. Moved to New York with Dickerson and Louis Armstrong in spring of 1929. Later that year joined Allie Ross at Connie's Inn. Briefly led own band at the Lafayette Theatre, New York, then joined Vernon Andrade at the Renaissance. Returned to Connie's Inn with Fats Waller (late 1931). During the early 1930s also worked for several other leaders including Bubber Miley and Otto Hardwick. Together with Tommy Ladnier accompanied Berry Brothers' dancing act, then with 'Pike' Davis' Band backed Bill Robinson. Went on tour accompanying Norman and Irene Selby (c. 1933), the show ended its run in Chicago. Zutty settled in Chicago for several years, worked briefly with Jimmy Bell, then rejoined Carroll Dickerson at the Grand Terrace (1934). Led own band at the New Deal Club, then again worked for Dickerson. In May 1935 began leading own sextet at The Three Deuces, brief return to Carroll Dickerson, then led own band, first at The Flagship, then again at The Three Deuces. Remained at The Three Deuces and there became a member of Roy Eldridge's Band in September 1936, left during the following year to return to New York. Worked with the short-lived Mezz Mezzrow's Disciples of Swing in November 1937. Featured at Nick's from early 1938 (with Sidney Bechet until November 1938). In 1939 and 1940 led own trio and sextet at Nick's, also led at Village Vanguard and Kelly's before taking up long residency at Ryan's from March 1941 until early 1943. Moved to Los Angeles, led own quartet at Billy Berg's from April 1943, later that year did film-studio work and played with Paul Howard's Band and T-Bone Walker. Again led own band in 1944 and was regularly featured on Orson Welles' radio shows, also worked in Teddy Bunn's Group. With Slim Gaillard Trio in spring of 1945, then led own band at Streets of Paris, Hollywood. Continued to lead own bands through the 1940s, also played with other leaders including: Slim Gaillard (1946), Wingy Manone (1947), Eddie Condon (1948), Joe Marsala (1948), Nappy Lamare (1949). Worked with Art Hodes in Chicago (1950), then with Bobby Hackett (spring 1951) before joining Bernie Billings in Los Angeles (August 1951). Sailed to Europe in November 1951; after touring with Mezz Mezzrow worked with Hot Lips Page during summer of 1952 (at Knokke), then toured with Bill Coleman All Stars. Remained in Europe until February 1953. Settled in New York, was featured regularly at Stuyvesant Casino, Central Plaza, Metropole, etc., throughout the 1950s, briefly with Wilbur de Paris (late 1954). In late 1963, together with Tony Parenti, began long residency at Ryan's, left temporarily early in 1969, but soon returned to same venue (with Max Kaminsky). Brief return to New Orleans in June 1969 to play at the 'Jazz Fest'. Was forced to retire from full-time music after suffering a stroke in 1970.

Zutty's appearances in films include: 'Stormy Weather' (1943), 'New Orleans' (1946), and 'Turned-up Toes' (1949).

SISSLE, Noble Lee
leader/vocals/composer

Born: Indianapolis, Indiana, 10th July 1889
Died: Tampa, Florida, 17th December 1975

In 1914 formed first band for residency at Severin Hotel, Indianapolis. To Baltimore in 1915, worked in Bob Young's Band (with Eubie Blake-Luckey Roberts occasionally on second piano); later that year led own band at Cocoanut Grove, Palm Beach, Florida. Joined Jim Europe's Society Orchestra as guitarist-vocalist, then (with Europe) joined U.S.

Army in December 1916. Served as a lieutenant in 369th Division Band, acting as drum major, after service in France returned to the U.S.A. Toured with Jim Europe until that leader's death (1919), then formed highly successful duo with Eubie Blake; these two worked as partners for many years producing and composing for many shows including: 'Shuffle Along', 'Chocolate Dandies', etc., etc. In 1926 they played a residency in London at the Kit Kat Club, returned to U.S.A. in August 1926. Sissle returned to London in 1927, did solo act accompanied by pianist Harry Revel, then formed own band for residency at Les Ambassadeurs in Paris (summer 1928). Returned to U.S.A., then sailed again to Paris with own band in May 1929. Led in Paris, Monte Carlo, Ostend, etc., then played in London before returning to New York in December 1930. Residency at Park Central Hotel, again took band to Paris (1931), later it did extensive touring and residencies in Boston, St. Louis, etc. Noble Sissle continued touring during the mid-1930s (except for a spell of inactivity following injuries sustained in a car crash during summer of 1936). From 1938 led band at Billy Rose's Diamond Horseshoe in New York, continued this residency for over 12 years, but did touring for U.S.O. shows during World War II (including trip to Europe). During the 1960s continued to manage own publishing company (visited Europe on business in 1961), also continued to lead own bands and ran own night club, Noble's. Lived in Florida for the last years of his life.

Over the years Noble Sissle employed many famous jazz soloists including: Sidney Bechet, Buster Bailey, Harvey Boone, Johhny Dunn, Tommy Ladnier, etc., etc. In the 1920s and early 1930s Sissle appeared in at least three Vitaphone short films—two with Eubie Blake. 'Reminiscing With Sissle and Blake' by Kimball and Balcon, first published 1973.

SKERRITT, 'Freddie' Alfred A.
baritone sax/alto sax

Born: Montseratt, Leeward Isles, B.W.I., 1st May 1904

Raised in New York City. Started on drums, then changed to alto sax, lessons from Lt. Eugene Mikell. Worked with Willie Gant (1926), brief tour with Duke Ellington (1926) prior to joining Wardell Jones (1926). During the late 1920s worked with Bingie Madison, Cliff Jackson, etc. In the early 1930s with Billy Fowler, Frank Newton, Sam Wooding, Bud Harris, and Rex Stewart (at Empire Ballroom, New York, 1933). Led own trio in the late 1930s, also did brief tours with Fats Waller, and gigged with Machito's Orchestra. In U.S. Navy from August 1942 until July 1945. Rejoined Machito until 1956 then left full-time music. Played occasionally in the 1970s.

SLACK, 'Freddie' Frederic Charles
piano/composer

Born: near Westby, Wisconsin, 7th August 1910
Died: Hollywood, California, 10th August 1965

Led own band whilst at high school, playing drums. Moved to Chicago with parents in 1927, concentrated on piano, worked with Johnny Tobin's Band at Beach View Gardens, Chicago. Moved to Los Angeles in 1931, worked with Henry Halsted, Earl Burtnett, Archie Rosate and Lenny Hayton. Toured with Ben Pollack (1934-36). Returned to California in August 1936, worked briefly with Rube Wolf prior to long spell with Jimmy Dorsey (1936-39). Left Dorsey in August 1939, joined Will Bradley's Band, also worked with band co-led by Will Bradley and Ray McKinley. Led own band from the mid-1940s, appeared in several movies. Remained based in California during the 1950s and 1960s, activities were restricted during last years of his life by diabetes.

SMALLS, 'Cliff' Clifton Arnold
piano/trombone/arranger

Born: Charleston, South Carolina, 3rd March 1918

Began playing music as a child, father was also a musician. During high school played in local Royal Eight. Left Charleston with the Carolina Cotton Pickers, remained with them until joining Earl Hines in summer of 1942 (doubling trombone and second piano), left Hines in late 1946. With Billy Eckstine (1948-50) then with Earl Bostic until suffering serious injury in auto accident in 1951. Resumed touring in the mid-1950s, worked with trombonist Bennie Green, and with Paul Williams, also accompanied vocalist Clyde McPhatter. Musical director and accompanist for vocalist Brook Benton for seven years in late 1950s and early 1960s prior to becoming musical director for Smokey Robinson. During the 1960s also worked with Ella Fitzgerald, and with Reuben Phillips' Big Band at the Apollo Theater, N.Y. During the 1970s often worked with Sy Oliver's Band, also did work as accompanist, and made free-lance recordings. Toured Europe in Oliver Jackson Trio during early 1980s.

SMITH, 'Ben' Benjamin J. *Born: Memphis, Tennessee, 1st March 1905*
saxes/clarinet

Gigged with local bands, then joined Connor and McWilliams Boston Serenaders in Memphis (1926). Toured with carnival shows, then played in Texas with William Holloway's Merrymakers in 1927, subsequently led own Blue Syncopators until 1929. Gigged for a while in Omaha, then briefly led own band in Kansas City before working with George E. Lee (1930), Grant Moore, and Eli Rice's Plantation Cotton Pickers. In 1932 led own White Hut Orchestra in Pittsburgh and Philadelphia, then briefly with George 'Doc' Hyder, Blanche Calloway, and Charlie Gaines. Directed and played on Washboard recording sessions. Moved to New York (c. 1934), brief spell with Benny Carter Orchestra, then with Fess Williams, LeRoy Smith (1935), Claude Hopkins (c. 1936). Worked with Jabbo Smith in 1938, then year with Hot Lips Page. Stints with Lucky Millinder, Andy Kirk, and Snub Mosley during the 1940s, but mainly active leading own groups. Continued leading through the 1950s, also ran own arranging and copying service, and for a time organised own recording company.

SMITH, Bessie *Born: Chattanooga, Tennessee, 15th April 1895*
vocals *Died: Clarksdale, Mississippi, 26th September 1937*

Sang at local Ivory Theatre at an early age; began touring (c. 1912) with Fats Chappelle's Rabbit Foot Minstrels—which then featured Ma Rainey. Travelled with this troupe for a while, then toured the T.O.B.A. circuit with The Florida Cotton Pickers and as a solo act. Later she sang and danced in her own Liberty Belles act (c. 1919), about this time did regular seasons in Atlantic City, usually accompanied by Charlie Taylor's Band. On tour in 1921 including playing the Lyric Theatre in New Orleans, then worked in 'How Come' revue (1922)—made first (unissued) recording session. Played season in Philadelphia, then again to New York for first Columbia recordings in February 1923. Bessie soon established herself as one of the highest paid artistes on the theatre circuits. Toured regularly throughout the 1920s in various revues and tent shows (some of which she sponsored): 'Harlem Frolic Company', 'Midnight Follies', 'Midnight Steppers', 'High Brown Follies', etc., etc. She travelled with her own accompanying band—directed for several years by Kansas City pianist-organist Fred Longshaw, later by Bill Woods. The unit travelled in Bessie's own Pullman car, named Jackie Gee (her husband from 1923—they separated later). She went to New York regularly for recording sessions and to headline variety shows. In 1929 Bessie co-starred with Johnny Lee in the film 'St. Louis Blues'—music by James P. Johnson's Orchestra and W. C. Handy's Choir. Continued touring in the early 1930s, also appeared in New York, occasionally accompanied by Benny Carter's Orchestra, Teddy Hill, The Hardy Brothers, etc. Did radio series (c. 1933) accompanied by a studio band organised by Miff Mole. In November 1933 Bessie did her last recording session (supervised by John Hammond). Briefly in show at Connie's Inn, New York, from January 1936 (replacing Billie Holiday who was ill with ptomaine poisoning), then long spell at Art's Cafe, near her home in Philadelphia. Returned to New York in December 1936 to appear in 'The League of Rhythm' revue at the Apollo Theatre, then began touring with the 'Broadway Rastus' show. Bessie played her last engagement with this company in Darling, Mississippi, on the 25th September 1937, then began travelling overnight to the next night's booking. On Route 61, about 10 miles north of Clarksdale, Mississippi, the Packard, in which she was a passenger, hit the back of a stationary truck. The impact sliced off the roof of the car and turned the vehicle over onto its right side. Shortly afterwards the driver of the relatively undamaged truck drove from the scene of the accident to call for an ambulance. Dr. Hugh Smith, a noted surgeon from Memphis, who was driving to do some night fishing, came upon the scene of the accident. He found Bessie Smith lying in the road in a critical condition, having suffered severe injuries to her chest, abdomen, and right arm. Having rendered first aid to Bessie, Dr. Smith and his companion began clearing the back of his car to make room for the injured woman. Shortly afterwards they were forced to jump clear just before the back of his Chevrolet was rammed by another car—two passengers in the oncoming vehicle were both injured in the collision. Two ambulances arrived, one drove Bessie to the Afro-American Hospital in Clarksdale. After being operated on for the amputation of her right arm she died at 11:30 a.m. from a combination of shock and severe injuries. She was buried in the Mount Lawn Cemetery, near Darby, Pennsylvania.

In the spring of 1937 Bessie Smith, then on tour with Winsted's Minstrels in North Carolina, was unable to participate in New York recording session planned by John Hammond. Her death prevented her from fulfilling a contract to appear at the Savoy, New York, in October 1937. Chris Albertson's 'Bessie', first published in 1972.

SMITH, 'Buster' Henry *Born: Ellis County (near Dallas), Texas, 26th August 1904*
alto sax/clarinet/guitar/arranger

Brother of pianist Boston Smith. Began playing piano and organ, then switched to clarinet in late teens. Began working in Voddie White Trio (c. 1922), began doubling on alto sax. Gigged with many bands in Dallas, then to Oklahoma City in 1925 as a member of the Blue Devils (then led by trombonist Emir Coleman), remained to work under Walter Page's leadership. Remained with the Blue Devils until late 1933, then to Kansas City to join Bennie Moten-George E. Lee Band. Worked briefly with Ira 'Buster' Moten (1935), then with Count Basie co-led the Barons of Rhythm. Later led own band, left Kansas City late in 1936 to join Claude Hopkins (then in Iowa). Returned to work with Count Basie as staff arranger, worked briefly with Andy Kirk, then returned to Kansas City to lead own band. Worked with trumpeter Dee 'Prince' Stewart early in 1938, then from summer of 1938 led own band at The Antlers, Kansas City. Left Kansas City in September 1938, moved to New York, worked as an arranger for Gene Krupa and Hot Lips Page, also extensive gigging on alto and clarinet. Led own band in Virginia for a while in 1939, then worked in New York with Don Redman, Eddie Durham, Snub Mosley, etc. Returned to Kansas City in 1942, formed own band which played long residency at the Club Shangrila. From the 1940s on led own band in Texas, Oklahoma, and Arkansas—in 1959 his band recorded an L.P. at Fort Worth, Texas. During the 1970s lived in semi-retirement in South Dallas.

SMITH, Clara *Born: Spartanburg, South Carolina, 1894*
vocals *Died: Detroit, Michigan, February 1935*

Extensive work on theatre circuits from the early 1910s; began recording career in 1923. Made many records in the 1920s accompanied by all-star personnel: Fletcher Henderson, Louis Armstrong, James P. Johnson, etc. Appeared regularly at the Strollers' Club in New York during the early 1930s; played six-month residency at Orchestra Gardens, Detroit, then played dates in Cleveland. Died of heart trouble in the Parkside Hospital, Detroit.

I am grateful to Walter C. Allen for forwarding to me details of Clara Smith's obituary which was published in the Chicago Defender *dated 9th February 1935. Clara Smith was not related to Bessie Smith or to Trixie Smith (died: 21st September 1943) or to Laura Smith (died: February 1932).*

SMITH, Crickett *Born: Nashville, Tennessee, 15th August 1883*
trumpet/vocals *Deceased*

Uncle of Arthur Briggs. During the early years of this century toured with Mahara's Minstrels and worked with the Musical Spillers (1911). Settled in New York and worked for Ford Dabney for several years, took part in 'Ziegfeld Follies'. Worked with Jim Europe before World War I, to France in 1917 with Louis Mitchell for residency at Casino De Paris. Returned to New York, was soloist with Clef Club Orchestra in 1919. To Europe, again worked with Louis Mitchell, then worked for various leaders in Europe including Glover

Compton, Benny Peyton etc. also led own band. Worked in South America with Herb Flemming's International Rhythm Aces (1933), subsequently worked in Europe. Settled in India, and worked there with Leon Abbey, Teddy Weatherford, etc., also led own band in India and Ceylon.

SMITH, Floyd *Born: St. Louis, Missouri, 25th January 1917*
guitar *Died: Indianapolis, Indiana, 29th March 1982*

Father was a drummer. Floyd began on ukelele, then switched to guitar; studied theory a the Victor Hugo School in St. Louis. Played in Eddie Johnson's Crackerjacks and Dewe) Jackson's Band before working in the Jeter-Pillars Orchestra (1937-8). Joined the Sunsel Royal Orchestra in summer of 1938, left to work with the Brown Skin Models before joining Andy Kirk in January 1939. Served in Europe with U.S. Army during World War II, then returned to Andy Kirk in late 1945. Left Kirk in September 1946 to form own trio which played for several years at the Dusable Club in Chicago. In the mid-1950s worked with Wild Bill Davis, Chris Columbus, etc., led own group. To Europe with Bill Doggett in the early 1960s, again led own group. During the late 1960s in the Hank Marr duo in Atlantic City. Moved to Indianapolis during the 1970s.

SMITH, 'Howard' Harold *Born: Ardmore, Oklahoma, 19th October 1910*
piano/arranger

In 1919 moved with his family to Montreal, Canada; moved to New York in 1933. In 1934 played briefly with Benny Goodman at Billy Rose's Music Hall, then with Irving Aaronson and Ray Noble (1935) before joining Isham Jones' Juniors (1935 to early 1936). Took part in many free-lance recording dates, then with Tommy Dorsey from spring 1937 until January 1940, then joined C.B.S. staff in New York. Then regularly employed as a studio musician.

SMITH, 'Jabbo' Cladys *Born: Pembroke, Georgia, 24th December 1908*
trumpet/trombone/vocals

Father died when Jabbo was four years old; he moved with his mother to Savannah, then at six was placed in the Jenkins' Orphanage, Charleston, South Carolina. Was taught trumpet and trombone, at 10 began touring with the orphanage band. Ran away from the institution on several occasions, during one abscondence he played for three months in Florida with Eagle Eye Shields' Band (1922). He left the orphanage for good at the age of 16, travelled to Philadelphia and joined Harry Marsh's Band, later worked in Atlantic City with Gus Aiken. Worked with Charlie Johnson's Band in Atlantic City, subsequently in New York from autumn 1925 until early 1928, also sat in for recording session with Duke Ellington (November 1927). Joined James P. Johnson Orchestra and toured with 'Keep Shufflin'' revue from February 1928. The show folded in Chicago (November 1928) and Jabbo worked there for various leaders including: Carroll Dickerson, Sammy Stewart (briefly), Earl Hines, Erskine Tate (1929), Charlie Elgar, Tiny Parham (late 1930), also led own recording band. Led own band and worked with Cassino Simpson, then led at the Wisconsin Roof, Milwaukee, until spring 1932, also worked with Oscar 'Bernie' Young. With Fess Williams (1933), led own band in Milwaukee, then with Carroll Dickerson at the Sunset, Chicago, in the summer of 1934, toured with Eli Rice and with Red Perkins' Dixie Ramblers. Returned to Chicago, briefly led own band at Lamb's Cafe, briefly in Jesse Stone's Cyclones (April 1935), then toured with Eli Rice's Band before free-lancing in Detroit, worked briefly with Sam Price. Returned to his home town of Milwaukee and joined Claude Hopkins (then on tour) in 1936. With Hopkins for two years including residency at the Roseland, New York, in autumn 1936. Gigged with own band in New York, worked occasionally with Sidney Bechet (1939), then long residency at the Alcazar, Newark, New Jersey, first with own trio, then with saxist Larry Ringold's Band (1944). Brief return to Claude Hopkins, then moved back to Milwaukee, played with local bands and led own sextet at the Crystal Ballroom in the late 1940s. Left full-time music, but continued to play in the 1950s, including residency at The Down Under in 1958. Temporarily quit playing, but made comeback at Milwaukee Jazz Society concert in June 1961, resumed working with local bands and made a playing trip to Chicago. Continued day work with a car-hire company in Milwaukee, played valve trombone and piano at Tina's Lounge in 1966. Jabbo, a proficient pianist, became particularly interested in composing. Tours of Europe during the 1970s including London (1977). Played for 'One Mo' Time' show in New Orleans (1978), later worked in New York and touring production of that show during early 1980s. Overcame illness in 1982 and appeared at European festivals in 1983.

For many years a rumour persisted that there were two Jabbo Smiths, the confusion arose because one of Jabbo Smith's trumpet-playing colleagues was called 'Jabbo' Jenkins. In 1965 Richard Spottswood of Melodeon Records issued two L.P.s containing much of Jabbo Smith's best work.

SMITH, 'Joe' Joseph C.
trumpet

Born: Ripley, Ohio, 28th June 1902
Died: New York City, 2nd December 1937

Father was Luke Smith Sr., who led a big brass band in Cincinnati. Joe had six brothers—all trumpet players—the most famous was Russell T. Smith, another brother, Luke Jr., died in 1936; two others, George and Charlie, were also professional musicians. A cousin, Clarence Smith, played trumpet with Andy Kirk for a while. Joe was originally taught by his father, gigged with local bands, then left town with a travelling fair. Was subsequently stranded in Pittsburgh, whilst there he carved a unique wooden trumpet mouthpiece from a used cotton spool—for some years afterwards he occasionally used this for special effects. Travelled to New York (c. 1920) and worked with Kaiser Marshall at a 48th Street dancing school, returned to club work in Pittsburgh, then travelled to Chicago to join The Black Swan Jazz Masters (directed by Fletcher Henderson), then accompanying Ethel Waters (January 1922); on tour with this show until July 1922, returned to New York Left that city a few weeks later as member of Mamie Smith's Jazz Hounds. On tour (including bookings in California) until c. early 1923, then left Mamie Smith to free-lance in New York; with Billy Paige's Broadway Syncopators (1923), also extensive gigging and recording sessions (some with Fletcher Henderson). In March 1924 directed band for Noble Sissle and Eubie Blake revue 'In Bamville', remained with this show (later renamed 'The Chocolate Dandies') until November 1924. When the revue began touring Joe remained in New York, working as accompanist for comedian Johnny Hudgins until April 1925. Later that month joined Fletcher Henderson on a full-time basis. Remained with Henderson until October 1928—during this period recorded with many blues singers, notably Bessie Smith. Left Henderson to work in band led by violinist Allie Ross for the 'Blackbirds' revue. Joined McKinney's Cotton Pickers in Detroit (summer 1929), with that band until November 1930, left after being involved in the car accident in which George 'Fathead' Thomas suffered fatal injuries. Rejoined Fletcher Henderson in December 1930, worked in Boston with Kaiser Marshall's Band, then rejoined McKinney's (late 1931 to early 1932). Moved to Kansas City, Missouri, is said to have worked with Bennie Moten, was definitely with Clarence Love's Band at the El Torreon Ballroom in February 1933. In failing health, Joe Smith was picked up by the Fletcher Henderson Band in Kansas City, he attempted to play a job with them in Detroit, but was taken on to New York City where he soon entered a sanatorium in Long Island. His condition deteriorated steadily, and he was admitted to Bellevue Hospital where he died of paresis.

SMITH, John William
guitar

Born: Atlanta, Georgia, 27th November 1908

Played banjo in Neal Montgomery's Band during the late 1920s. Moved to New York, worked with Otto Hardwick (1930), studied with Edwin Colts. Joined Teddy Hill's Band in 1932, remained until 1939, including tour of Europe (1937). Worked with Fats Waller (1939-40), then toured with Mills Brothers until joining Benny Carter (late 1942). With Dizzy Gillespie's Band, then worked with Cab Calloway from 1946 until 1951. Did own solo act then worked with Wilbur De Paris from 1958 until c. 1966. Retired from music temporarily, but during the late 1970s began a long stay with Panama Francis and his Savoy Sultans.

S

SMITH, Mamie
(née Robinson)
vocals

Born: (Cincinnati, Ohio?), 1883
Died: New York City, 30th October 1946

Moved to New York in 1913 with a white vaudeville group The Four Mitchells. Later she worked in the show 'The Smart Set' and appeared at various New York clubs including Leroy's and Barron Wilkins'. In 1920 she became the first black blues singer to record solo; her version of 'Crazy Blues' (musical director Perry Bradford) sold a million copies within six months of issue. Mamie began touring accompanied by her Jazz Hounds. This group, originally directed by Ocey Williams, featured many jazz musicians in its fluctuating personnel: Coleman Hawkins, Joe Smith, Curtis Mosby, Amos White, etc. Her husband, William Smith, died on the 9th May 1928. Regular tours during the 1930s, occasionally accompanied by Fats Pichon's Band, Andy Kirk, etc. Led own Beale Street Boys at Town Casino, New York (1936). During the late 1930s and early 1940s appeared in several films. One of her last public appearances was at the Lido Ballroom, New York, where, on the 19th August 1944, she took part in a benefit concert; also appearing on the same bill was Billie Holiday. Mamie suffered a long illness in the Harlem Hospital; her burial took place in the Frederick Douglass Memorial Park, Staten Island, New York.

Films include: 'Jail House Blues', 'Paradise in Harlem', 'Murder on Lenox Avenue', and 'Sunday Sinners'.

SMITH, 'Pine Top' Clarence
piano/vocals

Born: Troy, Alabama, 11th June 1904
Died: Chicago, Illinois, 15th March 1929

Raised in Birmingham, Alabama. Worked as an entertainer in various Pittsburgh clubs before playing solo piano on T.O.B.A circuit, also worked for a time as accompanist to Ma Rainey. Settled in Chicago in the late 1920s. He was accidentally shot dead during a dance-hall fracas in Orleans Street, Chicago. He gained posthumous fame through his composition 'Pine Top's Boogie Woogie'—which he had recorded in 1928.

SMITH, 'Pops' Russell T.
trumpet

Born: Ripley, Ohio, 1890
Died: Los Angeles, California, 27th March 1966

Brother of Joe Smith (q.v.). Taught music by his father, started on alto horn, then trumpet from age of 14. First professional work in a Cincinnati theatre, then began touring with the Six Musical Spillers (c. 1910). Settled in New York and joined Ford Dabney at the Ziegfeld Roof. To Europe with Joe Jordan in 1914, returned to the U.S.A. and joined the Army, served as a musician in the 350th Field Artillery Band (directed by Lt. Tim Brymn). Sailed with this unit to France in 1917. After demobilisation he joined Jim Europe's Band in 1919, then spent four years working mainly with the 'Shuffle Along/Bamville' revue. Joined Fletcher Henderson regularly in late 1925. Was Henderson's first choice for lead trumpet work right through until 1942, during this period he also worked for many other leaders including: Claude Hopkins (1935-6), Benny Carter (1939-40), Horace Henderson, etc., etc. Was with Cab Calloway until summer of 1945, then began a long spell with Noble Sissle. Retired to California in the 1950s, played occasionally and also did some teaching.

SMITH, Richard J.
trumpet/arranger

Born: Kansas City, Missouri, 11th May 1909
Died: Kansas City, 15th November 1974

Played violin from the age of 10, whilst studying at the University of Iowa changed to trumpet (at the instigation of Eddie Thompkins). Played with college band—Cecil Bruton and his Blue Six—then, after graduating in 1931 with a B.Sc. in chemistry, played in Lincoln, Nebraska, with Harold Jones' Brownskin Syncopators. Subsequently joined band led by trombonist Thamon Hayes which eventually came under the leadership of Harlan Leonard, arranged many numbers for the band including 'My Gal Sal'. Left full-time music in 1939, taught music in Lincoln High School, also did war work. From 1946 until 1953 taught band and orchestra at Cole's G.I. Training School in Kansas City. Active in musicians' union work for many years, was elected local President in 1959. Represented Kansas City in the all-star orchestra at the inauguration of President Harry Truman. Continued to play regularly in and around Kansas City including long spell in septet led by pianist Willie Rice.

S

SMITH, **Robert** *Born: Providence, Rhode Island, 3rd January 1907*
alto sax/clarinet/composer

Played local gigs on drums before taking up the saxophone. Moved into New York City and joined Banjo Bernie's Band, later toured Florida with them. Joined The Sunset Royals for ten years from c. 1935 (remaining with them when they became Doc Wheeler's Sunset Orchestra). With Erskine Hawkins from 1944 to 1960, then moved to California, combining arranging with regular playing. Worked with Panama Francis and his Savoy Sultans during the late 1970s and early 1980s.

SMITH, **'Stuff' Hezekiah Leroy Gordon** *Born: Portsmouth, Ohio, 14th August 1909*
violin/vocals *Died: Munich, Germany, 25th September 1967*

His father, a barber and part-time boxer, also played all the string instruments and doubled on reeds. When Stuff was seven his father made him his first violin, at 12 he began playing in his father's band. At that time the family lived in Masillon, Ohio. Stuff won a musical scholarship to study at the Johnson C. Smith University in North Carolina, he left in 1924 to tour with the 'Aunt Jemima' Revue Band. After two years on the road he joined Alphonso Trent (then playing in Kentucky). Subsequently played with that band during their long residency at the Adolphus Hotel, Dallas. He moved to New York (with Edwin Swayzee) in 1928 to join Jelly Roll Morton, but soon returned to Alphonso Trent's Band. After various residencies and tours through Texas, Tennessee, Ohio, Canada, etc., he finally left Trent in Syracuse. Settled in Buffalo and led for residencies at Little Harlem Club, The Vendome Hotel, and The Silver Grill, he also briefly led own big band which played at The Lafayette, N.Y. (June 1934). Early in 1936, his sextet moved from Buffalo to New York for long residency at The Onyx Club (during this booking Stuff began to play amplified violin). The band played in Hollywood from summer 1937 until early 1938 then, facing union problems and a bankruptcy order, Stuff temporarily disbanded. He re-formed again later in 1938 and continued leading until the early 1940s. In 1942 he fronted the band that had previously been led by Fats Waller (Sammy Benskin on piano). This set-up ended when Stuff contracted pneumonia. After his recovery he led own trio at Garrick Lounge, Chicago (1943) and at The Onyx, New York (September 1944 to spring 1945), then moved to Chicago. He opened his own restaurant and formed a new trio for regular work in Chicago, the trio also played residencies in Milwaukee, Washington, New York, etc., then Stuff moved to California. Worked mainly on the West Coast during the 1950s, sometimes as a soloist. In the spring of 1957 his tour of Europe (with 'Jazz At The Philharmonic') was cut short by the recurrence of a serious stomach ailment. He returned to California and began leading own small group in early 1958. Continued to work regularly on West Coast (including appearance at Monterey Jazz Festival). Played for a year in Toronto, Canada, before working the Embers, New York, with Joe Bushkin (spring 1964). After a spell in California he began touring Europe early in 1965 (played residency in London during March 1965), he then did guest star appearances in Denmark, France, Belgium, Germany, etc. He died in Munich, but was buried in Denmark.

SMITH, **'Tab' Talmadge** *Born: Kinston, North Carolina, 11th January 1909*
saxes *Died: St. Louis, Missouri, 17th August 1971*

Mother and four sisters were all pianistes. Tab started on piano, then played 'C' melody sax before specialising on alto. Played with Ike Dixon's Band in Baltimore, then long spell with the Carolina Stompers before joining Eddie Johnson's Crackerjacks (1931-3). Played for a while on the riverboats with Fate Marable, then rejoined Eddie Johnson. Joined Lucky Millinder in June 1936, left in 1938 to join Frankie Newton, worked on tenor sax with Newton in 1939. Briefly on tenor with Teddy Wilson Big Band in spring 1940, then short stay with Count Basie before joining Eddie Durham Band in August 1940—left the following month to rejoin Lucky Millinder. Then with Count Basie from December 1940 until spring 1942, returned to Lucky Millinder until spring 1944, then formed own band. Continued to lead own small band through the 1940s, then moved back to St. Louis in 1951 to devote time to business interests—also led own band for residency at the 20th Century Club. In early 1952 (as a result of several best-selling singles) he resumed full-time music and continued leading own small group for several years. In the 1960s he returned to St. Louis, worked in real-estate, played gigs and taught music. In the last years of his life he played organ at a steak-house in East St. Louis.

SMITH, 'Tatti' Carl
trumpet

Born: Marshall, Texas. c. 1908

Son of a school teacher. Toured with road shows, then played in George Corley's Royal Aces (c. 1930), then a spell with Terrence Holder's Band (1931) before working mainly on West Coast with Gene Coy (1931-4). Returned to Kansas City, played with various bands before joining Count Basie at the Reno Club, with Basie to New York in late 1936. Left Basie early in 1937, then long spell with Campbell 'Skeets' Tolbert's Gentlemen of Swing (late 1938-40)—during this period also gigged with Hot Lips Page Big Band in late 1939. During the early 1940s played occasionally with Leon Abbey's Band and with Benny Carter, later with Roger Kay's Jumptet (late 1942-3). With Chris Columbus Band in 1944. After World War II he moved to South America and continued playing in Argentina and Brazil through the 1950s. Was formerly married to pianiste Vivian Smith (née Jones) who later married Jimmy Hamilton.

SMITH, Warren Doyle
trombone

Born: Middlebourne, West Virginia, 17th May 1908
Died: California, 28th August 1975

Began on piano at the age of seven. Family moved to Dallas in 1920. Lessons from his father on cornet and sax, then specialised on trombone. Continued doubling on sax for his first professional work with Harrison's Texans (1924-8). Long spell with Abe Lyman (1929-35). Joined Bob Crosby (summer 1936)—then in Indianapolis, and remained with that band until May 1940 when he briefly rejoined Abe Lyman. Worked mostly in Chicago from 1941-5, various leaders including: Wingy Manone, Bud Jacobson, Paul Jordan, etc. Moved to California in 1945, worked again with Bob Crosby, then long spell with Peter Daily in late 1940s. In 1950 with Jess Stacy, then briefly with Lu Watters before joining Nappy Lamare's Band (1951). Brief spell in New York with Duke Ellington (summer 1955). With Joe Darensbourg (1957-60), then with Wild Bill Davison, Ben Pollack, Johnny Lane, etc., before joining Red Nichols in the early 1960s—with Nichols to Japan in the summer of 1964. Continued to work regularly in California until the month of his death.

SMITH, 'Willie' William McLeish
alto, baritone sax/clarinet/vocals

Born: Charleston, South Carolina, 25th November 1910
Died: Los Angeles, California, 7th March 1967

Began on clarinet at 12, two years later played at local concerts accompanied by his sister on piano. Played in the Boston Serenaders in Memphis (c. 1926). Studied at the Case Technical College before attending Fisk University in Nashville, Tennessee. In 1927 during summer vacation worked in Belmar, New Jersey, with Beaty Conner Quartet. Whilst at Fisk he first met Jimmie Lunceford, after majoring in chemistry he left the college to join Jimmie Lunceford in Memphis (summer of 1929). Remained with Lunceford until the summer of 1942, then joined Charlie Spivak. In April 1943 he left Spivak to serve as a musical instructor in the U.S. Navy. After his release in late 1944 he joined Harry James, remained with James until March 1951 (except for brief absence in summer 1947). With Duke Ellington for a year from March 1951, left in spring 1952 to join Billy May's Orchestra. In early 1953 toured Europe with 'Jazz At The Philharmonic', then brief tour in Benny Goodman All-star Band (directed for most of the tour by Gene Krupa). Returned to California, did brief tours with Billy May, then led own band at the Oasis Club, Los Angeles. Rejoined Harry James in spring of 1954, remained with James until summer of 1963—during this period also worked regularly with Billy May and other West Coast studio orchestras. After a long spell of ill health he joined Johnny Catron's Band in Los Angeles (autumn 1964), worked with Johnny Rivers in Las Vegas during the following year, then returned to studio work. In late 1966 he played in New York in a big band specially formed by Charlie Barnet. The last few weeks of his life were spent in the Veterans' Administration Hospital in Los Angeles. He died of cancer.

SMITH, 'Willie the Lion'
William Henry Joseph Bonaparte Bertholoff
piano/composer/vocals

Born: Goshen, N.Y., 25th November 1897
Died: New York, 18th April 1973

Mother played piano and organ, Willie started on organ, then specialised on piano. From 1912 played many residencies in New York and Atlantic City until joining U.S. Army in November 1916. Saw active service in France, also played bass drum in Lt. Tim Brymn's Regimental Band. Demobilised in U.S.A. in late 1919. From 1920 began long residencies in New York including: Leroy's, Small's, Garden of Joy, etc. Did many free-lance recording sessions including accompanying Mamie Smith on 'Crazy Blues'. Toured theatre circuits and was also featured in 'Holiday in Dixieland' revue (1922-3). Led own band at Capitol Palace, Rhythm Club, Hooper's Club, etc., also played and acted in Broadway play 'The Four Walls' (1927-8). Featured pianist at Pod's and Jerry's in the late 1920s and early 1930s, also toured as accompanist for Nina Mae McKinney and took part in Clarence Williams' recording sessions. During the 1930s was featured at many venues in New York: The Onyx, Adrian's Tap Room, The Apollo, etc., etc., also led own recording groups and worked occasionally in the Milt Herth Trio. In the 1940s led own bands at Man About Town, Casablanca, Newark, Venetian Room, etc., etc. Toured Europe as a soloist late 1949 to early 1950. Played regularly at The Central Plaza sessions and took part in 'Jazz Dance' film. In the 1950s, 1960s and early 1970s appeared at many jazz festivals, including Newport (July 1971). Toured Europe in 1965 and 1966. Played many times in Canada, was the subject of two short films (1966).

Duke Ellington, one of Willie the Lion's most fervent admirers, dedicated 'Portrait of the Lion' to him. Willie the Lion was a very successful teacher, his pupils included: Joe Bushkin, Mel Powell, Howard Smith, Jack O'Brian (from Hartford, Connecticut), and Artie Shaw. 'Music on my Mind', by Willie 'The Lion' Smith and the late George Hoefer was published in 1965.

SNAER, Albert Joseph
trumpet

Born: New Orleans, Louisiana, 29th January 1902
Died: California. c. 1962

Studied with 'Professor' Paul Chaligny. Played locally with the Excelsior Brass Band, then worked for several years on the riverboats: with Dewey Jackson (1925-6), then co-led (with banjoist George Augustin) The Moonlight Serenaders, worked with Fate Marable in 1928. Moved to New York (c. 1930), briefly with Andy Kirk, then with Earle Howard in 1931. From 1932 until 1941 worked on and off with Claude Hopkins—during the mid-1930s also worked in LeRoy Smith's Orchestra. Left full-time music in 1942, and from then until the late 1950s ran own dry-cleaning business in Connecticut, he continued to play gigs and worked briefly with Sidney Bechet in 1949. In the early 1960s he moved to San Francisco and played occasionally with Big Boy Goudie; he lived to read the premature obituaries on him that were published in the summer of 1960.

SNOW, Valaida
trumpet/vocals

Born: Chattanooga, Tennessee or Washington, D.C., 2nd June c. 1900
Died: New York City, 30th May 1956

Sisters were Lavaida and Alvaida, their mother was a music teacher. Valaida's husband in the mid-1930s was dancer Ananias Berry (died: 1951), she later married Earle Edwards. Began professional career (c. 1920), appeared in Atlantic City and Philadelphia, residency at Barron Wilkins' during 1922, subsequently toured with Will Masten's Revue. Throughout the 1920s continued to sing, dance, and play trumpet in various shows in the U.S.A. In August 1926 sailed to Shanghai to work as a speciality act with Jack Carter's Band. Returned to U.S.A., worked in Chicago, then from 1929 toured through Russia, the Middle East, and Europe. After working in the 'Grand Terrace Revue' in 1933, was featured in the 'Blackbirds of 1934', and with this show arrived in England in August 1934. Returned to U.S.A., worked with Ananias Berry as double act in Los Angeles during the summer of 1935. Whilst in California appeared in two films: 'Take It From Me' and 'Irresistible You'. Valaida also appeared in the pre-war French film 'Alibi'. Toured the Far East again, then played The Apollo, New York in June 1936. Returned to Britain, from September 1936 began extensive touring in Europe: France, Belgium, Austria, Switzerland, Holland, Denmark and Sweden. After touring Sweden (summer 1941) was arrested by Swedish police and subsequently deported. Suffered harrowing experiences before resuming career at The Apollo, New York (April 1943). Did extensive tours of clubs and theatres then moved to California (1945). From 1946 until 1956 continued to work regularly as a vocaliste in concerts, shows, and clubs throughout the U.S.A., resumed regular recordings. Last engagement took place at the Palace Theatre, New York. Valaida collapsed at her home after suffering a cerebral haemorrhage; three weeks later she died in Kings County Hospital, New York.

SNOWDEN, Elmer Chester
guitar/banjo/saxes

Born: Baltimore, Maryland, 9th October 1900
Died: Philadelphia, 14th May 1973

Played banjo-mandolin and guitar from early childhood. First professional work with pianist Addie Booze (1914). Joined Eubie Blake in 1915, remained with the band when it was taken over by pianist Joe Rochester (1916). After Rochester's death in 1919 moved to Washington and played in trio led by Duke Ellington. In 1920 joined pianiste Gertie Wells (to whom he was married for some years), played briefly with Claude Hopkins (1921), then formed own band and began doubling on saxophone. After residencies in Washington and Atlantic City the band moved to New York in September 1923. Snowden originally led the Washingtonians in New York, from March 1924 he played in the Broadway Jones Band and was subsequently appointed leader, later that year he rejoined the Washingtonians, by that time led by Duke Ellington. After a spell in Ford Dabney's Orchestra, Snowden once again became a bandleader (autumn 1925), and at one time had five different bands working under his name in and around New York. During the late 1920s and early 1930s he led successful bands at several New York clubs including: The Hot Feet, The Bamville, The Nest, and Small's. During this last residency the band appeared in the Warner Brothers' film 'Smash Your Baggage' (Vitaphone 1932). After a dispute with the New York Local 802 Snowden moved to Philadelphia where he was mainly occupied teaching saxophone and fretted instruments. Some eight years later he returned to New York, organised a trio for a residency at The Samoa Club, then with the assistance of John Hammond gained exoneration from his dispute with the union and was readmitted. Moved into Cafe Society, Uptown, in June 1942, playing in Joe Sullivan Trio, some six months later organised own small group, residencies in New York and Philadelphia throughout the 1940s. From 1950 worked with own quartet which continued touring (including Canada) until 1957. Then three years combining music with a day job before forming own quartet for long residencies in Philadelphia and Springfield, Pennsylvania. Moved to California (1963), taught for three years at the Berkeley School of Music, worked in band led by trombonist Turk Murphy, then led own groups at The Cabale, Berkeley, and Coffee House, San Francisco, appeared at jazz festivals. Toured Europe in late 1967. Moved back to Philadelphia, continued to play occasionally in late 1969.

SOCARRAS, Alberto
flute/saxes/clarinet

Born: Oriente, Cuba, 19th September 1908

After playing with local orchestras moved to the U.S.A. and began a regular series of recordings with Clarence Williams. With 'Blackbirds' shows from 1928 until 1933, including tour of Europe. Briefly with Benny Carter in 1933, then formed own band, in 1934 again visited Europe, this time as musical director to an all-girls' band. With Sam Wooding in 1935, then again formed own band. Worked with Erskine Hawkins for '1937 Cotton Club Parade', then again formed band for residency at Harlem Uproar House from September 1937. From 1939 regularly led own band, residencies include: Glen Island Casino, Boston Beachcomber, Rendezvous Inn, etc., etc. For many years specialised in classical flute playing—gave solo performance at Carnegie Hall in 1945 and was solo flautist in first performance of Eddie Bonnemere's 'Missa Hoosierna' (1966). Active as a teacher throughout the 1970s.

SODJA, 'Joe' Joseph *Born: Cleveland, Ohio, 15th April 1911*
guitar

First instrument was a mandolin. Played local dances in family band with three brothers (1925). Did solo work on radio stations W.H.K. and W.T.A.M. in Cleveland, on guitar and banjo (1927-30). With Arcadian Melody Pilots (1926-30), Art Cook (1928), Nat Shilkret (1933), worked at C.B.S. Studios (1933-35). Led own all-star band for recordings in 1937. During the 1940s worked with Buddy Rogers, Don Bestor and Fred Waring, then worked for more than 30 years as a solo act.

SOPER, 'Tut' Oro *Born: 9th April 1910*
piano

For over 30 years was one of the leading pianists in his home city of Chicago. Worked for many leaders including: Bud Freeman, Wild Bill Davison, Boyce Brown, Bud Jacobson, Frank Snyder, George Olsen, Eddie Wiggins, Danny Alvin, Johnny Mendell, also played many solo residencies. Worked briefly in California with Muggsy Spanier (1950) and Marty Marsala during the early 1950s, toured with Eddie Condon in 1960, then returned to Chicago and worked with Georg Brunis. Continued to play in Chicago. Recorded with Baby Dodds (1944), Bud Freeman, Bill Dohler (1946).

SOUTH, Eddie *Born: Louisiana, Missouri, 27th November 1904*
violin *Died: Chicago, Illinois, 25th April 1962*

Family moved to Chicago when Eddie was three months old. A child prodigy on violin, first studied with Charles Elgar, then with Professor Powers, was later given jazz coaching by Darnell Howard. At 16 began working in Chicago, continued to study at the Chicago College of Music. Worked with Charles Elgar, Erskine Tate, and Mae Brady's Orchestra, then became front man and musical director for Jimmy Wade's Syncopators at Chicago's Moulin Rouge Cafe (c. 1924). Remained with Wade until 1927 including residencies in New York. Briefly with Erskine Tate until January 1928, with Gilbert 'Little Mike' McKendrick's Quartet, then to Europe leading own small group The Alabamians. Toured several European countries (including England in summer of 1930), also extensive musical studies in Paris and Budapest. Returned to lead own band in Chicago from autumn 1931, led in California (late 1932), then returned to Chicago. Did variety tours accompanying Bea Palmer, Gene Austin, etc. Returned to Europe in 1937, played long residency at the Club des Oiseaux, Paris, appeared in Holland (early 1938), returned to the U.S.A. in May 1938. Residencies in New York, Chicago, and Los Angeles during 1939. Continued to lead own groups (usually a quartet, occasionally big bands) during the 1940s and 1950s. Long engagements at Cafe Society, New York; Jigs, New York; The Garrick, Chicago; Trocadero, Hollywood; etc. Own radio series in the 1940s; regular television shows from Chicago during the 1950s. Suffered from ill health for many years, but continued to work professionally until a few weeks before his death, last worked at the DuSable Hotel in Chicago. Never used an amplified instrument; was known as 'The Dark Angel of the Violin'.

SPANIER, 'Muggsy' Francis Joseph *Born: Chicago, Illinois, 9th November 1906*
cornet *Died: Sausalito, California, 12th February 1967*

One of 10 children. Nicknamed after 'Muggsy' McGraw, a baseball manager. Started on drums, switched to cornet at 13. Played in Holy Name Cathedral School Band then, whilst working as a messenger boy, did semi-professional jobs with Elmer Schobel at the Blatz Palm Gardens, Chicago (1921). Tuition from Noah Tarintino, then professional debut with Sig Meyers' Band at White City, Chicago (1922), worked with Meyers until 1924. Briefly with clarinettist Johnny Lane's Band, Doc Rudder's Pershing Orchestra, and Charlie Straight. Mainly with tenorist Floyd Town's Band from late 1925 until 1928—during this period also worked in Sig Meyers' Druids and did occasional gigs with Charles Pierce. Two stints with Gene Green's Band. In 1928 played for four months in Joe Kayser's Band at the Merry Gardens, then in October 1928 joined Ray Miller's Orchestra at the College Inn,

Chicago. Was heard playing at this venue by Ted Lewis, Muggsy subsequently joined Ted Lewis in San Francisco (1929). Remained with Lewis until late 1936 (including European tour in 1930). Joined Ben Pollack from December 1936 until early 1938 when near-fatal illness enforced temporary retirement. Recommenced regular playing early in 1939; organised own Ragtimers for debut at Hotel Sherman, Chicago, on 29th April 1939. After residency at Nick's, New York, the group disbanded on 12th December 1939. Muggsy rejoined Ted Lewis from 22nd December 1939 until February 1940; he began sitting in with Bob Crosby's Band (then at The Blackhawk, Chicago) in May 1940 and soon after joined them. Left Crosby in February 1941 to organise own big band, which made its debut on 12th April 1941, continued to lead big band for the next two years, then formed own small band. Briefly out of action through injury incurred in car accident, then led own sextet at Capitol, Chicago. Returned to New York in March 1944, gigged with Art Hodes, etc., rejoined Ted Lewis from May-August 1944. Played on West Coast (October 1944), then joined MIFF MOLE at Nick's, New York. Worked mainly at Nick's until summer of 1947, then led at Blue Note, Chicago. Returned briefly to Nick's in February 1948, then led own band in Chicago, Denver, San Francisco, Los Angeles, etc., also did occasional dates with Georg Brunis at Jazz Ltd., Chicago. From 1951 until summer of 1959 worked on and off with Earl Hines in San Francisco. From 1957 made permanent home in California. Led at the Roundtable, New York (late 1959), Columbus, Ohio (early 1960), played at Essen Jazz Festival in Germany (spring 1960). Continued to lead and tour until 1964, frequent residencies in San Francisco: On the Levee, The Hangover, etc., also played season at Bourbon Street, New Orleans (1961). Not long after being featured at the 1964 Newport Jazz Festival he was forced to retire through ill health.

Muggsy's film appearances include: 'Sis Hopkins' (with Bob Crosby), 'Is Everybody Happy?', and 'Here Comes The Band' (both with Ted Lewis).

SPARGO, Tony
(real name: Antonio Sbarbaro)
drums/kazoo

Born: New Orleans, Louisiana, 27th June 1897
Died: Forest Hills, New York, 30th October 1969

At 14 began playing drums with the Frayle Brothers' Band, after a year began working with Ernest Giardina's Band, also did parade work in Papa Jack Laine's Reliance Bands. Whilst still working in a local office he continued playing with Giardina until 1915, then joined Merritt Brunies' Band at the Tango Place, also worked with pianist Carl Randall at the Black Cat Cabaret. Left New Orleans in June 1916 to join The Original Dixieland Jazz Band in Chicago. Continued to work under Nick LaRocca (q.v.) until early 1925, then became leader of The Original Dixieland Jazz Band for residency at The Cinderella Ballroom, New York. Led the small unit until early 1927, then led augmented band at Rose Danceland, New York, before working with Lacey Young's Orchestra (1927-8). Did a variety of musical work including again leading own band, then in 1936 took part in the re-creation of the O.D.J.B. (1936). Worked with LaRocca until early 1938, then continued with O.D.J.B. until 1940. Spargo began playing regularly at Nick's, New York, in 1939. Was featured at New York's World Fair in 1941. In 1943 toured in Katherine Dunham's Revue with Brad Gowans, etc., then resumed playing at Nick's. Regularly with Phil Napoleon at Nick's during the early 1950s, recorded with Connee Boswell in the 1950s. Retired from regular playing in the early 1960s.

SPENCER, 'O'Neill' William
drums/vocals

Born: Cedarville, Ohio, 25th November 1909
Died: New York City, 24th July 1944

His brother, Johnny, was a trumpeter. Attended school in Springfield, Ohio, played in local bands, then joined Al Sears in Buffalo (1930). Joined The Mills Blue Rhythm Band in 1931, subsequently worked under Baron Lee and Lucky Millinder. Joined John Kirby Sextet in July 1937 and worked regularly with the group until being taken ill with tuberculosis in 1941. Worked briefly with Louis Armstrong's Big Band (c. September 1941), rejoined John Kirby early in 1942. Suffered a relapse whilst working with John Kirby at The Apollo Theatre, New York (June 1943) and was forced to quit playing. Did many free-lance recordings during the 1930s including date (on drums and washboard) with Johnny Dodds (January 1938).

SPIVAK, 'Charlie' Charles
trumpet

Born: Kiev, Russia, 17th February 1907
Died: Greenville, S. Carolina, 1st March 1982

To U.S.A. at the age of three, raised in New Haven, Connecticut. Trumpet from age of 10, played in Hill House High School Band. Gigged with local Paragon Band then joined Don Cavallaro's Orchestra. Worked mainly with Paul Specht from 1924 until 1930. With Ben Pollack (1931-4), with the Dorsey Brothers from late 1934 until spring 1935, then joined Ray Noble. Did two years' studio work (including spell with Raymond Scott) then worked with Bob Crosby from November 1937 until August 1938. With Tommy Dorsey from August 1938 until c. June 1939, left to work as trumpeter/straw boss with Jack Teagarden's Band. Left in November 1939, formed own band which made debut in St. Paul. Disbanded a year or so later, subsequently took over Bill Downer's Band and with this new line-up gradually established the band as a major commercial success of the 1940s (they were featured in several films). Moved to Florida in the 1950s, continued to lead a band until suffering serious illness in 1963. After recovery led in Las Vegas, Miami, etc. In 1967 began an eleven-year residency at Ye Olde Fireplace in Greenville, South Carolina.

SPIVEY, 'Queen' Victoria
vocals/piano/organ/ukelele/composer

Born: Houston, Texas, 1906
Died: New York, 3rd October 1976

Raised in Dallas; one of eight children, sister of Addie 'Sweet Pea' and Elton. Played piano at local theatre from the age of 12, made record debut in St. Louis in 1926 (singing her own composition 'Black Snake Blues'). During the following year was featured at the Lincoln Theatre, New York, then gained important role in the film 'Hallelujah'. Made many recordings during the 1920s and 1930s accompanied by Louis Armstrong, Henry Allen, Lee Collins, Lonnie Johnson, etc. During the early 1930s directed Lloyd Hunter's Serenaders and was featured for a while with Jap Allen's Band, then worked as a solo artiste before forming successful duo with dancer Billy Adams (who was at that time her husband—Miss Spivey had previously been married to trumpeter Reuben Floyd). Tour with Olsen and Johnson's 'Hellzapoppin' show in the late 1940s, also guested with Henry Allen at The Stuyvesant Casino in 1950. In 1952 left full-time music and worked for a while as a church administrator. Returned to prominence in the 1960s, appeared at Jimmy Ryan's (1960), Gerde's Folk Centre (1961), did radio and television work and toured Europe with the American Folk Blues Festival in the autumn of 1963. During the late 1960s continued to organise own successful recording company in New York. Appeared with Turk Murphy's Band in San Francisco (September 1970). Featured at U.S. Blues Festivals (1971).

SPRINGER, 'Joe' Joseph
piano

Born: New York City, 22nd May 1916

Did first gigs on Coney Island in 1931. With Wingy Manone in 1935. Joined Louis Prima at Hickory House in N.Y. (1940), first recordings with Prima. With Buddy Rich's first band then worked with Gene Krupa (1942-3) prior to stints with Oscar Pettiford, Tiny Grimes, Henry Jerome, Ben Webster, Charlie Barnet, Raymond Scott and Jimmy McPartland, was also regular accompanist for Billie Holiday in the mid-1940s. Rejoined Buddy Rich briefly in 1952. Free-lanced in New York during the 1960s then moved to Florida.

SQUIRES, Bruce W.
trombone

Born: Berkeley, California, 21st January 1910
Died: North Hallywood, California, 8th May 1981

Originally taught by Warren Smith. Worked with Everett Hoagland's Band at Balboa Beach (1932). With Earl Burtnett (January 1933-May 1935), with Ben Pollack (May 1935-February 1937), Jimmy Dorsey (February 1937-January 1938), Gene Krupa (January 1938-March 1939), Benny Goodman (1939), Harry James (1939-40), Freddy Slack (1940-41), Bob Crosby (1942). Served in Ferry Command during World War II, then joined Opie Cates (1946), prior to working mainly in studio bands during the 1960s and 1970s.

S

STACY, Jess Alexandria
piano

Born: Bird's Point, Missouri, 11th August 1904

Started on drums, then switched to piano, mostly self-taught, some lessons from Mrs. Florina Morris. Played in local youth band: Peg Meyer's Original Melody Kings, then worked with Harvey Berry's Band on steamer S.S. 'Majestic' (1921), later played piano (and calliope) with Tony Catalano's Band on S.S. 'Capitol', also winter residencies at Coliseum Ballroom, Davenport, Iowa. Played residency with Al Katz and his Kittens at Atlantic Pier (spring 1926), later that year worked with Joe Kayser's Band in Ohio and at Arcadia Ballroom, Chicago. Worked mainly with Kayser until 1928, then long spell of varied work for many Chicago bandleaders: Danny Altier, Floyd Town, Louis Panico, Art Kassel, Eddie Neibauer, etc., also briefly led own Stacy's Aces. With Paul Mares at Harry's Bar (January 1935), Earl Burtnett's Band (March 1935), with Frank Snyder at Subway Club and with Maurie Stein at the Paramount Club (summer 1935). In July 1935, on the recommendation of John Hammond, he joined Benny Goodman, remained with Benny Goodman until July 1939 (also took part in many free-lance recordings). Went home to Missouri, then joined Bob Crosby in mid-September 1939, left Crosby to rejoin Benny Goodman in December 1942 until Goodman temporarily disbanded in March 1944. (Jess married vocaliste Lee Wiley in Los Angeles on the 7th June 1943—they were subsequently divorced.) Brief spell with Horace Heidt until 18th September 1944; joined Tommy Dorsey on 29th November 1944, left early in 1945 to organise own band. Disbanded early in 1946 and returned to Missouri. Rejoined Benny Goodman from November 1946 until March 1947, then formed own big band in California (May 1947). Disbanded in February 1948 and joined Billy Butterfield's Band at Nick's, New York. Free-lanced in New York, then moved to California, occasionally led own band, but worked mainly as a soloist at many clubs on the West Coast including: The Hangover, San Francisco (from February 1951), Brown Derby, Wilshire, Ile de France, Culver City, etc., etc. Brief reunion with Benny Goodman for special appearances December 1959 to January 1960. Left full-time music and after 1963 was an employee of the Max Factor Company. Played in all-star band at University Club of Pasadena on 2nd November 1969. Musically active during the 1970s, appeared at Newport Jazz Festival (1974), resumed recording, played in New Jersey (1979). Lives in California.

STAFFORD, George
drums

Born: c. 1898
Died: New York City, spring 1936

His sister was the vocaliste Mary Stafford. (A 1921 report suggests that Mary Stafford's real name was Annie Burns (from the Ozarks), this could, of course, mean that her brother also adopted the name Stafford for professional reasons.) Early work with Sam Wooding in Atlantic City, then to New York accompanying Madison Reid. Worked as accompanist for his sister, then joined Charlie Johnson's Band in Atlantic City (c. 1920). Worked regularly with Johnson until shortly before his death, also recorded with Henry Allen, Art Karle, Mezz Mezzrow, Eddie Condon.

STARK, 'Bobbie' Robert Victor
trumpet

Born: West 62nd St., New York City, 6th January 1906
Died: New York City, 29th December 1945

Began on the alto horn at 15, taught by Lt. Eugene Mikell Sr. at M.T. Industrial School, Bordentown, New Jersey, also studied piano and reed instruments before specialising on trumpet. First professional work subbing for June Clark at Small's, New York (late 1925), then played for many bandleaders in New York including: Edgar Dowell, Leon Abbey, Duncan Mayers, Bobbie Brown, Bobby Lee, Billy Butler, and Charley Turner, also worked briefly in McKinney's Cotton Pickers. Worked with Chick Webb on and off during 1926-7. Joined Fletcher Henderson early in 1928 and remained with that band until late 1933 except for a brief spell with Elmer Snowden in early 1932. With Chick Webb from 1934 until 1939. Free-lancing, then service in U.S. Army from 14th November 1942, played in Army band in Arizona, was invalided out of service on 19th November 1943. With Garvin Bushell's Band at Tony Pastor's Club, New York, from April until July 1944, then worked at Camp Unity with Cass Carr until joining Benny Morton's Sextet at Cafe Society (Downtown) New York in September 1944.

STEELE, 'Joe' Joseph A.
piano

Born: c. 1900
Died: New York City, 5th February 1964

Also known as 'Professor'. Graduate of the New England Conservatory. Worked (and recorded) with the Savoy Bearcats (1926). With Henri Saparo's Band at Bamboo Inn, New York (1927), then led own band in New York during the late 1920s. Toured with Pike Davis Orchestra for 'Rhapsody in Black' show (1931-2), then worked mainly with Chick Webb from 1932 until 1936.

STEGMEYER, 'Bill' William John
clarinet/saxes/arranger

Born: Detroit, Michigan, 8th October 1916
Died: Long Island, N.Y., 19th August 1968

Studied at the Transylvania College from 1934 until 1936, then with college friend Billy Butterfield joined Austin Wylie's Band in January 1937—worked as staff arranger for Wylie. Did regular work on Detroit radio station, then worked with Glenn Miller in 1938. With Bob Crosby from July 1939 until May 1940, then specialised in arranging, but also played for Billy Butterfield, Yank Lawson, Will Bradley, etc., and led own band at Kelly's Stables, New York. Was staff musician-arranger on Detroit radio station WXYZ from 1948 until 1950. Returned to New York, did regular arranging for television shows, became conductor at C.B.S. in 1960. Continued arranging until shortly before his death; he died of cancer in the Meadowbrook Hospital.

STEVENSON, George Edward
trombone

Born: Baltimore, Maryland, 20th June 1906
Died: New York, 21st September 1970

Father played piano, his brother, Cyrus, was also a pianist. George Jr. is a professional trombonist. At 15 studied saxophone and trombone with A. J. Thomas and joined his Baltimore Concert Band. At 19 joined pianist Harold Stepteau and his Melody Boys, then organised own 11-piece Baltimore Melody Boys. Disbanded in 1928 and moved to New York. Worked with Irwin Hughes' Orchestra at the Arcadia Ballroom (1930), then toured with Harold Stepteau and his Aristocrats. With Norwood Fennan and his Nubians (1931), with the Savoy Bearcats (spring 1932), then with Charlie Johnson (1932-3), Jimmy Smith and his Nighthawks (1934), Jack Butler (1934), Fletcher Henderson (1935), Claude Hopkins (1936), Ovie Alston (1937), drummer Jack Carter's Orchestra (1938), Lucky Millinder (1939-43), Cootie Williams and Roy Eldridge (1944), Cat Anderson (1947). From 1948 did extensive free-lancing including spells with Tony Parenti, Chris Columbus, and Don Redman. To Europe with Sam Price's Bluesicians (December 1955 until May 1956). Returned to New York, continued free-lancing, spell with cornetist Jack Fine (1957) and leading own band in Wantagh, New York. Worked with Joe Thomas, Lem Johnson, etc., during the 1960s. With Max Kaminsky at Jimmy Ryan's in 1969.

STEVENSON, 'Steve' Tommy
trumpet

Born: c. 1914
Died: New York, October 1944

With Jimmie Lunceford from 1933 until May 1935, then with Blanche Calloway from summer 1935 until mid-1936. With Don Redman 1939 to early 1940. Worked with Slim Gaillard's small band before joining Coleman Hawkins' Big Band in August 1940. Later worked with Lucky Millinder before joining Cootie Williams. Whilst working with Williams he contracted lobar pneumonia and died a few days after entering Bellevue Hospital, New York.

STEWART, Rex William
cornet

Born: Philadelphia, Pennsylvania, 22nd February 1907
Died: Los Angeles, California, 7th September 1967

Father played violin; mother was a pianiste. Family moved to Georgetown, near Washington, D.C., in 1914. Rex began on piano and violin, then after two years on alto horn switched to cornet. Played regularly in Danny Doyle's Boys' Band and received tuition from the leader. At 14 began doing gigs on Potomac riverboats. Left home to do a six-week tour with Ollie Blackwell and his Jazz Clowns, when this band folded he became a member of the Musical Spillers and made his first trip to New York with this act in October 1921. Remained with the Musical Spillers for over a year, playing cornet, trombone, tenor and soprano saxes, and xylophone. Quit the act to gig in various New York clubs including: Ed Small's, John O'Connor's, etc. (1923). Brief spells with Jimmy Cooper's Revue Band and Leon Abbey's Bluesicians, then three months with Billy Paige's Broadway Syncopators (spring 1924). Summer season at Asbury Park with subsequent work in Newark, New Jersey, with Bobby Brown's Society Orchestra. Returned to New York, joined Elmer Snowden's Band (1925). Left during the following year to join Fletcher Henderson, after a few months went to Wilberforce College to join Horace Henderson's Collegians. Rejoined Fletcher Henderson in 1928, left to work with Alex Jackson's Band (c. 1930), then spent several months in McKinney's Cotton Pickers (summer 1931), brief return to Fletcher Henderson, again with McKinney's (early 1932), then worked again with Fletcher Henderson until early 1933. Briefly with Fess Williams in New York in spring 1933, then led own big band at Empire Ballroom, New York, from c. June 1933 until autumn 1934. Spent a few months in Luis Russell's Band, then joined Duke Ellington in late December 1934. Except for short interludes, stayed with Duke until April 1943. Played in New Mexico in Dick Ballou Band (June 1943), gigged with Benny Carter in California (July 1943), then led own band in Los Angeles until rejoining Duke Ellington from October 1943 until December 1945. Formed own Rextet early in 1946, the band worked mainly in New York until leaving for Europe in October 1947. Disbanded in Europe and remained to do extensive work as a soloist, in that capacity appeared in Australia during summer of 1949. Returned to U.S.A. in spring 1950. Gigged around New York, then moved to Troy, New Jersey, to run own farm. Led own band in Boston during the early 1950s, also worked regularly as a disc-jockey on station WROW in Albany, N.Y. Organised (and recorded with) Fletcher Henderson Re-union Bands in 1957 and 1958. From February 1958 until July 1959 played at Eddie Condon's Club, subsequently moved to California. Continued disc-jockey work on local radio stations and began lecturing and writing on jazz history—articles appearing in *Down Beat, Playboy, Melody Maker, Jazz Journal,* etc. Did occasional spells of gigging in the 1960s and appeared at several jazz festivals. Toured Europe as a soloist twice in 1966, returned to play a few concerts in California, but by then was devoting most of his time to journalism. From 1934 regularly led own recording groups. Film appearances included: 'Scyncopation', 'Hellzapoppin'', 'Rendezvous in July'. Died suddenly from a brain haemorrhage. His book 'Jazz Masters Of The 30s' was published posthumously in 1972.

STEWART, Sammy
piano/organ/arranger

Born: Circleville, Ohio, 1890
Died: New York City, 5th August 1960

Raised in Columbus, Ohio. Formed own band in the early 1920s, played long residencies in Chicago from 1923, worked in New York (1926), also seasons of touring through Ohio, West Virginia, Michigan, etc. After playing the 1929 summer season at Wasaga Beach, Ontario, the band played a long string of one-nighters before opening in New York at the Savoy Ballroom on 22nd February 1930. The band played there for three months, then Stewart led at the Arcadia Ballroom, from then on he lived in New York. Led own band through the 1930s, also played in Ikey Robinson's Quartet in 1933. During the early 1940s he played organ at the Golden Gate Ballroom, continued to lead a sextet through the late 1940s. During the 1950s he taught piano and organ.

STEWART, 'Slam' Leroy Elliott
string bass/vocals

Born: Englewood, New Jersey, 21st September 1914

Began playing violin during childhood, switched to bass and worked with local bands including stint with Sonny Marshall, then studied at Boston Conservatory of Music. Whilst in Boston heard Ray Perry (on violin) singing and bowing in unison, later Slam began successfully experimenting with the idea of singing an octave above his bowed bass work. Worked with Peanuts Holland Band in Buffalo (1936-7), then moved to New York, met Slim Gaillard and formed duo. After their initial success on radio WNEW, the duo recorded the big-selling 'Flat Foot Floogie'. Slam worked with The Spirits of Rhythm (spring 1939), with Van Alexander's Orchestra (1940), also led own trio at Kelly's Stables, New York (late 1940), he continued to play specific engagements with Gaillard until Slim's call-up in 1942. Slam appeared in the 1943 film 'Stormy Weather', worked mainly with Art Tatum (1943-4). With Tiny Grimes' Quartet (autumn 1944), joined Benny Goodman in February 1945 and for next nine months did several brief interludes with Goodman. Worked with Art Tatum again in spring 1946, led own trio in the late 1940s, also played in France with Errol Garner in May 1948. Several short spells with Art Tatum in the early 1950s, with Roy Eldridge Quartet (1953). With pianiste Beryl Booker (1955-7), reunited with Slim Gaillard at Great South Bay Jazz Festival in summer 1958. In the late 1950s and 1960s worked mainly as accompanist for vocaliste-pianiste Rose Murphy (including European tour). Temporarily quit playing through illness. Led own trio in New York (late 1968), then led band at Binghamton television studios. Classical work with Lincoln String Quartet (August 1969). Toured Europe with Milt Buckner and Jo Jones (April 1971), worked often with Benny Goodman (1973-75), also active as a teacher of music. During 1978 appeared frequently on television in the 'Today' show, often in company with guitarist Bucky Pizzarelli. Continued to work regularly during the early 1980s, including tours of Europe.

STITZEL, 'Mel' Melville J.
piano/arranger/composer

Born: Germany, 9th January 1902
Died: Chicago, Illinois, 31st December 1952

Raised in Chicago. Worked with New Orleans Rhythm Kings (1923), then played and arranged for many bandleaders in Chicago: Floyd Town (1925), Bob Pacelli, Louis Panico, Maurice Sherman (1928). Worked in Benson Orchestra of Chicago (1929). Continued playing regularly during the 1930s. Led own band in the 1940s (including residency at the Green Mill Ballroom). Worked with Danny Alvin's Band in the early 1950s. Was composer of 'Tin Roof Blues', etc., also recorded with Bucktown Five (1925), Stomp Six (1925), and Benny Goodman Trio (1928).

STONE Jesse
piano/arranger

Born: Atchison, Kansas, 1901

Raised in St. Joseph and Kansas City, Missouri. Led own Blues Serenaders from 1920, later organised Blue Moon Chasers working in and around Dallas, Texas, worked with George E. Lee in Kansas City, then helped Terrence Holder organise new Clouds of Joy (1929). Musical director for George E. Lee (1930-1); then co-director of Thamon Hayes' Kansas City Rockets (1932-4). Led own band The Cyclones in Chicago from 1935, residencies at Morocco Club, etc. Continued to lead own bands in the 1940s, did U.S.O. overseas tour. From the early 1950s worked mainly as an a. and r. man for recording companies. Composer of 'Idaho'.

STORY, 'Nat' Nathaniel Edward

Born: Oak Station, Kentucky, 8th August 1904
Died: Evansville, Indiana, 21st November 1968

During the 1920s worked on riverboats with Fate Marable and with Floyd Campbell's Band. Lived in New York from the early 1930s, with Earle Howard (1931), toured with Bud Harris and his Rhythm Rascals (1933), with Luis Russell, Sam Wooding (1934). With Chick Webb from 1936, remained after that leader's death (1939) to work with Ella Fitzgerald until early 1940. Worked with Andy Kirk and Lucky Millinder, then left full-time music. Continued gigging in the 1960s, played regularly in Doc Stocker's Dixie Band in Indiana.

STOVALL, 'Don' Donald
alto sax/clarinet

Born: St. Louis, Missouri, 12th December 1913
Died: New York, 20th November 1970

Originally a violinist, then studied saxophone with St. Louis musician Jimmy Harris. During the early 1930s worked with Dewey Jackson, Fate Marable, etc. With Eddie Johnson's Crackerjacks (1932-3). With Lil Armstrong Band at Silver Grill, Buffalo (1936), then led own band in Buffalo for two years. Moved to New York in 1939, worked with Sam Price, Joe

Brown, Snub Mosely, Eddie Durham Big Band before joining Cootie Williams' Big Band in 1941. With Henry Allen's Sextet from autumn 1942 until 1950 except for stint with Peanuts Holland's Band in 1946. Left full-time music in 1950. Not related to pianist Tommy Stovall (from Gary, Indiana).

STRAYHORN, 'Billy' William
piano/arranger/composer

Born: Dayton, Ohio, 29th November 1915
Died: New York City, 31st May 1967

Early schooldays in Hillsboro, North Carolina, then attended high school in Pittsburgh, extensive musical studies. In December 1938 submitted work to Duke Ellington, Duke soon began recording Strayhorn's compositions, and a year later, after Billy had played piano for a while in Mercer Ellington's Band, he joined Duke on a permanent basis. From then until his death 28 years later, Strayhorn continued to compose and arrange for the Ellington Orchestra. He rarely appeared with them in public, but was responsible for many magnificient collaborations with Duke. His compositions include: 'Take the A Train', 'Lush Life', 'Chelsea Bridge', 'Johnny Come Lately', 'Raincheck', etc., etc; 'Blood Count', his final work, was written during the last stages of his fatal illness.

STRICKLER, Benny
trumpet

Born: Fayetteville, Arkansas. c. 1917
Died: Fayetteville, Arkansas, 1946

Played in local bands, then moved to California in 1936. Joined Seger Ellis Brass Choir in 1937, subsequently worked on West Coast with Rube Wolfe's Orchestra, Wingy Manone's short-lived big band, Joe Venuti, etc. With Bob Wills and his Texas Playboys (1941-2). In autumn 1942 replaced trumpeter Lu Watters (who had joined U.S. Navy) in Yerba Buena Band, a few weeks later he was taken ill with tuberculosis and spent the rest of his life in a sanatorium.

STRONG, Jimmy
clarinet/saxes

Born: 29th August 1906
Deceased

Chiefly remembered for his work on the Louis Armstrong Savoy Ballroom Five recordings. Active in Chicago from the early 1920s, worked in Lottie Hightower's Night Hawks, then toured with Helen Dewey Show (spring 1925), left the show in California, gigged with the Spikes Brothers' Orchestra and other bands, then returned to Chicago. With Clifford 'Klarinet' King Big Band (1928), Carroll Dickerson (1927 and 1929), Cassino Simpson (1931), led own band, then worked with Zinky Cohn (1937), Jimmie Noone's Big Band (1939). Moved to Jersey City, led own band at the Blue Room Club from October 1940.

STURGIS, 'Ted'
bass/piano/alto sax

Born: Cape Charles, Virginia, 25th April 1913

Began playing piano at age of 5. Moved to New York City, worked with Roy Eldridge, and with Jack Butler in 1935. With Blanche Calloway (1936), with Eddie Mallory—doubling on alto sax—(1937), again with Roy Eldridge (1939). During the 1940s worked with Bardu Ali, Louis Armstrong, Paul Bascomb, Don Byas, Benny Carter, Milt Buckner, Don Redman, Roy Eldridge, etc. Active free-lance during the 1950s and 1960s, did many U.S.O. tours (often playing piano). During the 1970s rejoined Roy Eldridge for long residency at Jimmy Ryan's Club in New York City.

SUGGS, Peter
drums/vibes

Born: Paducah, Kentucky, 12th March 1909

His father, W. Percie Suggs, played trumpet for many years with Fate Marable. Was taught piano by his mother, his brother also played sax and trumpet. In 1928 Pete began his professional career playing in a band led by Fate Marable's brother, Harold, then a spell with Wallace Bryant before moving to St. Louis (in 1931) to join Fate Marable on drums. Played in St. Louis ballrooms with Marable, but never worked on the riverboats with him.

Stayed in St. Louis until 1934, then moved to Buffalo, N.Y., to join Clarence Olden's Band at Vendome Hotel. Regularly with Lil Armstrong's Big Band in 1935, playing Detroit, New York, etc., then returned to Buffalo with clarinettist John Harris (1936). In autumn 1937 joined Fletcher Henderson in Chicago and remained with the band for almost two years—doubling on vibes. In 1940 joined 'Heads' Adams' Sextet in Buffalo, then led own band for several years until 1954 (interrupted by several spells in hospital). From 1954-65 worked regularly in Moe Balsom Band at Town Casino, Buffalo, also occasionally led own band and played in Edward Inge's Band. Then virtually retired from playing.

SULLIVAN, Joe
(real name: Joseph Michael Sullivan)
piano

Born: Chicago, Illinois, 4th November 1906
Died: San Francisco, California, 13th October 1971

Studied for two years at the Chicago Conservatory of Music. In the summer of 1923 led own quartet at Pine Point Resort in Indiana, then worked for 18 months on vaudeville circuit, beginning with Elmo Mack and his Purple Derbies (George Wettling also in the band). Then played mainly in Chicago (many jazz recordings) and regular radio work on WBBM, KYW, WENR. From the mid-1920s played with many bandleaders in Chicago including: Bob Pacelli, Earl Mace, Sig Meyers, Louis Panico, Enoch Light, Huston Ray, Coon-Saunders, etc., etc. Moved to New York in late 1920s, played with Red Nichols' Band at Hollywood Restaurant and on tour (1929). Played in Roger Wolfe Kahn's Orchestra, then regularly with Red McKenzie's Mound City Blue Blowers in 1931 and early 1932. Spell with Ozzie Nelson, then with Russ Colombo (late 1932) before rejoining Roger Wolfe Kahn in spring 1933. Did solo spot at The Onyx Club, New York, then moved to California. Played in George Stoll's studio orchestra and also worked regularly as Bing Crosby's accompanist (appeared with Bing in three films). Moved back to New York in summer 1936 and joined Bob Crosby's Band after they had finished residency at Hotel Lexington, New York. Remained with Bob Crosby until December 1936—a lung complaint was diagnosed and he spent the next 10 months in the Dore Sanitorium, N. Monravia, California. (In April 1937 a mammoth benefit concert was held in Chicago—featuring Bob Crosby's Band, Roy Eldridge, The Dodds Brothers, etc.) Joe subsequently recommended working as accompanist for Bing Crosby. In the summer of 1939 he briefly rejoined Bob Crosby as featured pianist (Norman 'Pete' Viera continued as band pianist). Left on 10th September 1939 and a month later began leading own mixed small band at New York's Cafe Society. Later played at Nick's, then residency at Famous Door until January 1941. Cut down to a trio, did further work at Cafe Society, then briefly with Bobby Hackett Band before moving to Los Angeles for residency at The Swanee Inn (spring 1943). Worked on the Coast until spring 1945, then featured at Hotel Sherman, Chicago, in duo with Meade Lux Lewis. Played regularly at Eddie Condon's in 1946-7, then made the West Coast his base for touring. During the 1950s appeared occasionally in New York, but played long residencies at The Hangover, San Francisco, brief spell with Louis Armstrong All Stars in early 1952. In 1961 he played briefly with Muggsy Spanier, then led own group at On the Levee Club. Played at Monterey Jazz Festival in 1963, during the following year was taken ill whilst appearing at the Newport Jazz Festival. Returned to California, playing solo residencies in San Francisco and Sausalito, also composed and performed the background music for the documentary 'Who's Enchanted'. In the late 1960s played occasional engagements. Sullivan composed many well-known jazz tunes including 'Little Rock Getaway', 'Gin Mill Blues', etc. Seriously ill in 1970.

Joe Sullivan appeared in many films in the 1930s, his sextet also recorded the music for the 1940 film 'Fight for Life'. In 1955 the original Bob Crosby Band assembled for a television tribute to Joe. As a joke, Sullivan and Eddie Condon once told a writer that the pianist's real name was Dennis Patrick Terence Joseph O'Sullivan, as a result this was often printed as Sullivan's actual name.

SULLIVAN, Maxine
(née Marietta Williams)
vocals/valve-trombone/fluegel horn

Born: Homestead, Pittsburgh, 13th May 1911

In early 1930s did radio work in Pittsburgh and sang locally with the Red Hot Peppers. Was heard by pianiste Gladys Mosier, who took her to the Onyx Club where Claude Thornhill (who worked briefly as her musical director) arranged her recording debut. Worked regularly with John Kirby (to whom she was married 1938-41) and recorded big-selling version of 'Loch Lomond'. In the late 1930s worked regularly on the West Coast before returning to New York. Toured with Benny Carter's Band in summer of 1941, then temporary retirement in Philadelphia from 1942. Returned to New York in mid-1940s and began long residencies at various clubs including: Ruban Bleu, Penthouse, Village Vanguard, etc. Worked in Europe in 1948 and 1954. Left music profession for a while and worked as a nurse, then from 1958 began successful comeback, also started featuring her valve-trombone playing. Many club appearances in the late 1960s. Sang on dates with The World's Greatest Jazz Band (1969). Was married to the late Cliff Jackson. Guested with World's Greatest Jazz Band often during the 1970s. Sang at many festivals during the 1970s and early 1980s, and continued with free-lance career.

Film appearances include: 'Going Places', 'St. Louis Blues', etc.

SWAYZEE, 'King' Edwin
trumpet/arranger

Born: Little Rock, Arkansas, 1903
Died: New York City, February 1935

Worked in local band led by Alex Hill, then joined Eugene Crook's Synco Six and subsequently became a member of Alphonso Trent's Band (1924). Toured with Sammie Lewis' Bamville Dandies (early 1925 to spring 1926). Worked on and off with Alphonso Trent, toured and recorded with Jelly Roll Morton, then brief return to Trent before going to New York. With Jelly Roll Morton in New York (1928), also with Charlie Skeet's Band. Worked and recorded with Chick Webb (1929) before sailing to Europe with Lew Leslie's 'Blackbirds' show. Left the 'Blackbirds' in Europe and worked in Herb Flemming's International Rhythm Aces (1930), later led The Plantation Band in Europe including residency at the Carlton Hotel, Amsterdam (summer 1930). Back to New York, worked for Chick Webb and with Sam Wooding (1932), then in summer of 1932 played and arranged for Eugene Kennedy's Band at the Arcadia Ballroom, New York. Joined Cab Calloway in autumn 1932 and remained with Cab (including trip to Europe) until the time of his death. Shortly after touring Canada with Cab he entered Mount Sinai Hospital in New York for an operation and died 36 hours later.

SWEATMAN, Wilbur C.
clarinets/arranger

Born: Brunswick, Missouri, 7th February 1882
Died: New York City, 9th March 1961

First played violin, then switched to clarinet. Toured with circus bands in the late 1890s, then with Mahara's Minstrels before forming own orchestra in Minneapolis (1902). Extensive tours on theatre circuits and several residencies in Chicago before moving to New York in 1913. Regularly at New York theatres (The Victoria, The Savoy, etc.), also played for the opening of Connie's Inn in 1923. Did a speciality feature during which he played three clarinets simultaneously. From the 1930s he concentrated on various business interests which included music publishing and acting as executor for Scott Joplin's estate. He continued to play fairly regularly in the 1940s, leading own trio for residency at Paddell's Club during the early 1940s. Late in his life he suffered severe injuries in a car accident, but was active until shortly before his death. A prolific composer, his most famous work is 'Down Home Rag'.

TAPP, Ferman
guitar/banjo

Born: Kentucky, 10th August 1897
Died: New York, 6th April 1975

Began on banjo at 14. Played first gig in Tennessee in 1916. Brother Jeff played guitar and harmonica. Formed own quartet, Tapp's Melody Lads in 1918. Moved to New York, led own Rain and Shine Boys during the 1920s. Joined Noble Sissle in 1929 and sailed to Europe with him. Remained with Sissle for a few months then returned to New York and re-formed own band which worked regularly during the 1930s and 1940s.

TARRANT, Raybon
drums

Born: Ennis, Texas, 25th December 1909

Began playing bass drum in uncle's brass band in Wichita Falls. First gigs with banjoist Otis Stafford's Band (1925-26), with Roy McCloud (1927-28) then with pianist Lafayette Thompson's Golden Dragon Orchestra from 1929-32, first in Texas then in Colorado. With Bert Johnson's Sharps and Flats (1933-4), Edith Turnham's Orchestra in San Diego (1936), G. L. 'Happy' Johnson's Orchestra (1937-8). With Cee Pee Johnson's Orchestra in Hollywood during early 1940s, then some years in Jack McVea's Band until forming own group in 1951 which continued to play regularly for many years.

TARTO, 'Joe'
(real name: Vincent Joseph Tortoriello)
string bass/tuba/arranger

Born: Newark, New Jersey, 22nd February 1902

Played trombone at 12, then switched to tuba. Gave false age and joined U.S. Army during World War I; to France playing tuba in Anniston Army Band. Wounded in action, returned to U.S.A., honourably discharged in May 1919. Formed own six-piece band, combining gigs with day work at the Edison Laboratories. Professional musician from October 1920, toured in band accompanying vocalist Cliff Edwards until joining Paul Specht from 1922 until spring 1924 (including tour of Europe). With Sam Lanin at Roseland Ballroom, New York, from spring 1924, during following year joined Vincent Lopez, again visited Europe, then returned to New York. Began playing for many Broadway shows, also did arranging for many bands including Chick Webb and Fletcher Henderson. Two years with Roger Wolfe Kahn, then from early 1930s specialised in recording and radio-studio work, has worked as a session man ever since. Continued to do occasional jazz gigs, working mainly during the 1970s, also active as an arranger.

TATE, 'Buddy' George Holmes
tenor sax/clarinet

Born: Sherman, Texas, 22nd February 1913

His brother, a saxophonist, gave Buddy an alto in 1925. Two years later began gigging with McCloud's Night Owls (led by his cousin, trumpeter Roy McCloud). In 1929 played for several months in Wichita Falls with the St. Louis Merrymakers, later that year joined Troy Floyd's Band in San Antonio. Briefly with Gene Coy's Band, then with Terrence Holder's 12 Clouds of Joy from 1930-3. Worked with E. J. Malone and his Rhythm Kings (early 1933), Wesley Smith's Band, Tan Town Topics, and Ethel May's Band before joining Count Basie in Little Rock, Arkansas (c. July 1934). From late 1934 until early summer 1935 with Andy Kirk, played with band at Wiley College, Texas, then long spell with Nat Towles until joining Count Basie in spring 1939. Remained with Basie until September 1948, brief return in early 1949, then for rest of that year worked mostly with Hot Lips Page, occasionally with Lucky Millinder. With Jimmy Rushing (1950-2), then formed own band in 1953. For the last 16 years has led regularly at the Celebrity Club, New York. Occasional reunions with Count Basie and to Europe with Buck Clayton's All Stars in 1959 and 1961. Visited Europe several times in the 1960s including tour with own band in late 1968. Played London's Jazz Expo (1969), then guested in Europe with Saints and Sinners, Toured Orient with Kat Cowens late 1970). Worked regularly throughout the 1970s and 1980s, undertaking many overseas tours.

T

TATE, Erskine
violin/multi-instrumentalist/leader

Born: Memphis, Tennessee, 19th December 1895
Died: Chicago, Illinois, 17th December 1978

Brother of the late James 'Jimmy' Tate (trumpet); their father was a music teacher. Studied music at the Lane College, Jackson, Tennessee, and at the American Conservatory in Chicago. Began playing violin professionally in Chicago (1912). In 1919 opened at The Vendome Theatre, Chicago, with a nine-piece band—Erskine Tate's Vendome Symphony Orchestra, by the mid-1920s this ensemble was a 15-piece unit. Remained at The Vendome until March 1928, then led at The Metropolitan Theatre for two years before working as the musical director of the Michigan Theatre until 1932. Throughout the 1930s continued to lead in Chicago theatres and ballrooms, long residency at The Cotton Club, Chicago, with a 12-piece band. In 1945 opened own music studio. In the 1950s and 1960s continued to be one of Chicago's leading music teachers, giving tuition on violin, saxophone, trumpet, guitar, piano, and drums.

Some of Erskine Tate's former sidemen include: Louis Armstrong, Boyd Atkins, Buster Bailey, Harold Baker, Wallace Bishop, 'Stump' Evans, Freddie Keppard, Earl Hines, Milt Hinton, George Hunt, Darnell Howard, Omer Simeon, 'Jabbo' Smith, Eddie South, Teddy Weatherford, etc., etc.

TATUM, 'Art' Arthur
piano

Born: Toledo, Ohio, 13th October 1909
Died: Los Angeles, California, 5th November 1956

Both parents were amateur musicians; mother played the piano, father the guitar. Art was born with cataracts on his eyes, despite undergoing several operations during his childhood, throughout his life he had only partial vision in one eye. Began on piano during early childhood, attended the Cousino School for the Blind, in Columbus, Ohio, also studied guitar and violin—regularly doubled on accordion during his early teens. Studied for two years at the Toledo School of Music under Overton G. Ramey. Formed own small band which worked in and around Toledo (c. 1926), spent a fortnight subbing for Herman Berry in Speed Webb's Band, later replaced Berry in Speed Webb's Band, but after three months was in turn replaced by Fitz Weston. Began working at clubs in Toledo including residency at Chicken Charlie's (c. 1928). In summer of 1929 started two-year residency on local WSPD radio station, continued working at local clubs: The Tabernella and the Chateau La France (from spring 1930), occasionally did short residencies in Cleveland. Worked with Milton Senior's Band at Chateau La France until mid-1931, did short local tours with own band, then continued playing at local clubs. In 1932 was heard by pianist Joe Turner, who recommended him for the job as Adelaide Hall's accompanist. Later in 1932 Art moved to New York to join Adelaide Hall, originally working in duo with pianist Francis Carter. Worked with Adelaide Hall for about 18 months, during this time also filled-in by playing at New York night spots; in 1933 subbed for two weeks in McKinney's Cotton Pickers (whilst pianist Todd Rhodes was ill). Worked mainly in Cleveland (1934 to mid-1935): Val's, Jimmy Jones', The Greasy Spoon, then long residency at the Three Deuces, Chicago (1935-6). To Hollywood in late 1936, Paramount Theatre, Club Alabam, etc. During 1937 worked mainly in Hollywood, also played further residency at Three Deuces, Chicago, to New York in late 1937. Played at the Famous Door before sailing to Europe in March 1938, appeared in England during March, playing in London at Ciro's, Paradise Club, etc. Worked mainly on West Coast (1939 to mid-1940), then residencies at Cafe Society and Kelly's, New York, etc. Continued working as a soloist until 1943, then began using trio format (original members Tiny Grimes and Slam Stewart), residencies at Three Deuces, New York (1943-4). In 1945 began first of annual concert tours, continued regular club appearances until 1954. In the last 18 months of his life mainly did concert work, played Black Hawk Club in San Francisco in 1955, during the same year also played in Toronto, Canada. During his later life he did prolific recordings for impressario Norman Granz. Last big concert appearance at the Hollywood Bowl on 15th August 1956, where he played for almost 19,000 people, by this time was very ill with uremia. He commenced a national concert tour, but was forced by illness to return to Los Angeles, he entered the Queen of Angels Hospital, Los Angeles, late on the 4th November and died early next morning. His burial took place at the Rosedale Cemetery, Hollywood.

An unconfirmed report says that Art Tatum visited New York before 1932 to guest on a Paul Whiteman radio show. Art Tatum appeared briefly in the film 'The Fabulous Dorseys' and also in a short 'March of Time' movie.

TAYLOR, 'Billy' William
string bass/tuba/composer

Born: Washington, D.C., 3rd April 1906

His son, Billy Taylor Jr., who died in 1977, was an accomplished bassist. Billy Sr. began playing tuba in 1919—originally taught by a policeman neighbour. Did local gigs, moved to New York in 1924, briefly with The Musical Spillers, then with Elmer Snowden (1925), Willie Gant (1926), Arthur Gibbs (1927-8), also with Charlie Johnson (1927-9). Regularly with McKinney's Cotton Pickers before rejoining Charlie Johnson (late 1932-3). Brief tour with Fats Waller, then with Fletcher Henderson (1934). With Duke Ellington from early 1935 (originally on tuba—duo work with Wellman Braud on string bass), switched to string bass and later shared bass duties with Hayes Alvis. Remained with Duke Ellington until January 1940—during the last two months of his stay with Duke he occasionally played tuba whilst Jimmy Blanton played string bass. Replaced Nick Fenton in Coleman Hawkins' Big Band early in 1940. With Henry 'Red' Allen Sextet (late 1940-1), then Joe Sullivan Trio (spring 1942) until joining Raymond Scott at C.B.S. studios in August 1942. Did N.B.C. studio work in 1943, during following year played with Cootie Williams' Big Band and with Barney Bigard's small group. With Benny Morton Band in 1945. Free-lanced in New York for several years (regularly with Cozy Cole in 1945 and 1949). Moved back to Washington, D.C. Played occasionally at Blues Alley Club in the 1960s.

TAYLOR, Eva
(née Irene Gibbons)
vocals

Born: 1896
Died: Jamaica, N.Y. 31st October 1977

Wife of Clarence Williams—made many records accompanied by her husband's studio bands—also did free-lance recordings. In 1922, at the invitation of Miss Vaughn de Leath ('The Original Radio Girl'), Eva began her long broadcasting career, she also appeared in many successful stage shows and revues. Her stage career began in infancy when she became a piccaninny in a travelling show, with this unit she visited Australia and New Zealand in 1900 and 1914, and Europe in 1906. During the late 1920s Eva had her own radio show on N.B.C., then worked for many years on radio WOR (guested on Paul Whiteman Radio Show in 1932). Retired from professional singing many years ago, but recorded in Britain during her 1968 summer vacation.

TAYLOR, Freddy
trumpet/vocals/guitar/dancer

Born: New York City, 1914

In the early 1930s worked as a dancer and entertainer at The Cotton Club, New York. During Lucky Millinder's 1933 tour of Europe he received trumpet tuition from Bill Coleman, for a while he played trumpet regularly and in September 1935 returned to Europe leading his own band. Stayed in Europe and led own band in Paris, Rotterdam, etc., also ran own night club in Montmartre, Paris, and worked throughout Europe as a solo act. He returned to the U.S.A. in the late 1930s and reverted to his role as an entertainer. Brief return to Paris in 1967.

TAYLOR, Jasper
drums/washboard/xylophone/vocals

Born: Texarkana, Texas, 1st January 1894
Died: Chicago, Illinois, 7th November 1964

Began playing drums whilst at local industrial school. Gigged with local pianiste and played in local theatres, then left Texas in 1912 to work with Young Buffalo Bill's Wild West Show. Later that year joined the Dandy Dixie Minstrels touring Mexico. Began studying xylophone, did theatre work in Memphis (c. 1913) and began working regularly with W. C. Handy. Whilst with Handy he got the idea of playing washboard after hearing a harmonica player accompany himself by strumming on bamboo strips, also gigged with Jelly Roll Morton in Memphis. Moved to Chicago in 1917, joined Clarence Jones at the Owl Theatre.

Served in France with the 365th Infantry Band, then worked with Will Marion Cook at the Clef Club in New York, again worked with W. C. Handy. Worked in the Chicago Novelty Orchestra (1922), then toured with Joe Jordan's Sharps and Flats, recorded with Clarence Williams in 1926, then settled in Chicago. With Dave Peyton and Fess Williams (1927-8), again with Peyton in 1929, also with Tiny Parham. During the 1920s led own recording band, also recorded with Freddie Keppard and Jimmy O'Bryant. Continued to do theatre and ballroom work during the 1930s, then left full-time music to work as a shoe mender. Resumed regular gigging in Chicago during the 1940s, with pianist Freddy Shayne (1944), Punch Miller at the 900 Club (1945), Natty Dominique at the Midnight Sun (1952), etc. Worked with Lil Armstrong at the Red Arrow Club in Stickney, Illinois (1959-60). Led own Creole Jazz Band in 1962.

TEAGARDEN, 'Charlie' Charles *Born: Vernon, Texas, 19th July 1913*
trumpet

Brother of Jack, Norma (born: 1911), and the late Clois (1915-69). Worked briefly as a Western Union messenger after leaving school, then played with Herb Book and his Oklahoma Joy Boys, subsequently toured with Frank Williams and his Oklahomans. After that band folded in New York he joined Ben Pollack from late 1929 until September 1930. Spent a year with Red Nichols, also did extensive free-lance studio work. With Roger Wolfe Kahn (1932), with Paul Whiteman from December 1933 until 1940—except for brief spell in the Three T's Band in late 1936. Worked in brother Jack's band in September 1940, left to play in theatre orchestra for Ethel Waters' show Cabin in the Sky, subsequently led own band until 1942. Played for a week with Jimmy Dorsey, then rejoined Jack's Band. Served in Ferry Command Service from late 1942. After demobilisation free-lanced in Los Angeles, then with Harry James (spring 1946), with Jack's band from June 1946, briefly led Jack's Band at the Susie-Q in Hollywood in December 1946. Worked on and off with Jimmy Dorsey from 1948 until 1950, with Ben Pollack late 1950 to spring 1951, brief return to Jack, then studio work with Jerry Gray, etc. Led own trio (with Ray Baudic and Jess Stacy) intermittently in 1951 and 1952. Studio work in Hollywood throughout the 1950s—regularly with Bob Crosby 1954-8. Subsequently moved to Las Vegas, continued extensive free-lance work, led own band for long residencies at the Cinderella Club, Las Vegas, during the 1960s. Active as official of Musicians' Union during 1970s.

TEAGARDEN, 'Jack' Weldon Leo *Born: Vernon, Texas, 29th August 1905*
trombone/vocals *Died: New Orleans, Louisiana, 15th January 1964*

Two brothers, Charlie—trumpet and Clois—drums (died: 1969) a sister Norma (piano). Piano from the age of five, his father (an amateur trumpeter) bought him a baritone horn two years later. By the age of 10 Jack was playing trombone. Moved with his family to Chappell, Nebraska (1918); briefly playing in local theatres accompanied by his mother on piano. After living in Oklahoma City Jack moved to live with his uncle in San Angelo and began gigging with local bands. Then played in quartet at Horn Palace Inn, near San Antonio, from late 1920 until September 1921 except for short summer season in Shreveport. Then from September 1921 until spring of 1923 with Peck Kelley's Bad Boys. Did manual work in Wichita Falls during summer of 1923, then toured with Marin's Southern Trumpeters before rejoining Peck Kelley. Briefly with Willard Robison from October 1924 before joining Doc Ross, brief spells with other bands, but remained with Doc Ross until November 1927 (including work on West Coast 1926 and first trip to New York). Dep work in 'Johnny' Johnson Band, including record debut (2nd December 1927), week's work with Wingy Manone, then gigging and six-week variety tour accompanying vocaliste Elizabeth Brice before joining Billy Lustig's Scranton Sirens at Roseland Ballroom, New York, in late February 1928. Joined Tommy Gott Orchestra for two months, then with Ben Pollack from late June 1928; with Pollack except for brief spells until leaving in Chicago during May of 1933. (During this period led own recording orchestra and took part in many studio sessions waxing with Benny Goodman, Red Nichols, Louis Armstrong, Eddie Condon, etc., etc.) Worked with Eddie Sheasby in Chicago (c. June 1933), then with Wingy Manone at Brewery Club, near Chicago World Fair Exhibition; subsequently joined Mal

Hallett in August 1933. Then with Paul Whiteman Orchestra from December 1933 until December 1938 except for month's engagement in New York from December 1936 with the Three T's (Jack and Charlie Teagarden and Frankie Trumbauer). Left Whiteman at Christmas 1938 and shortly afterwards began rehearsing own band which made its debut in New York (February 1939). From then until November 1946 Jack Teagarden led own big bands—which were successful musically rather than financially (during this period he acted and played in the film 'Birth of the Blues'). He did many free-lance recordings and was also featured at the Esquire Jazz Concert in January 1944. Led own sextet from late 1946 until joining Louis Armstrong All Stars from July 1947 until August 1951. Left to form own All Stars which he continued to lead until playing with Ben Pollack for several months in 1956. Re-formed own All Stars, also co-led (with Earl Hines) a sextet which visited Europe in autumn of 1957. Led own All Stars on tour of Asia (September 1958 to January 1959). Continued leading until the time of his death. He died of bronchial pneumonia at a New Orleans motel, having played his last engagement the previous night at The Dream Room, New Orleans.

A complete summary of Jack Teagarden's career, his recordings and film appearances, are contained in the excellent book 'Jack Teagarden's Music', by Howard J. Waters Jr. (Published in 1960 by Walter C. Allen in the Jazz Monograph Series.) A biography, Jack Teagarden, *by Jay D. Smith and Len Gutteridge was also first published in 1960.*

TEAGARDEN, Norma — *Born: Vernon, Texas, 28th April 1911*
piano

Sister of Jack, Charlie and Clois. Was taught piano by her mother, also learnt violin. Played gigs in Oklahoma City c. 1926, then moved to New Mexico in 1929 and spent five years playing in territory bands. Moved back to Oklahoma City in 1935, led own group there prior to working with bands in Texas. Moved to Long Beach, California in 1942, led own band there. Joined Jack Teagarden's Band in 1944, toured for two and a half years. Moved back to California, worked with Ben Pollack, Matty Matlock, Ada Leonard, Ted Vesley, Pete Daily and Ray Bauduc. Again with Jack Teagarden's Band from 1952 until remarrying in 1955. Moved to San Francisco in 1957, played many gigs there with Turk Murphy, Pete Daily, etc., also worked as a solo pianist. Toured Europe in Bob Mielke-Ev Farey Band (summer 1976).

TEAGUE, Thurman — *Born: Illinois, 1910*
string bass

Originally played banjo and guitar, gigged in Chicago, then worked regularly with Jack Goss in the early 1930s. Switched to string bass and began working with Ben Pollack, subsequently with Vincent Lopez and later with the King's Jesters. Regularly with Harry James from 1939 until 1944. Spell with Red Nichols in 1945-6, then mainly active as studio musician on West Coast, has lived in Raseda, California for many years.

TERRELL, Pha Elmer — *Born: Kansas City, Missouri, 25th May 1910*
vocals — *Died: Los Angeles, California, 14th October 1945*

Was working as a dancer/singer/compere at 18th Street Club in Kansas City when discovered by Andy Kirk. Sang with Andy Kirk's Band from 1933 until 1941, left to work in Indianapolis with Clarence Love's Orchestra. Toured for a while, then worked as a single on West Coast. Died of a kidney ailment in the Cedars of Lebanon Hospital in Los Angeles.

TESCHEMACHER, Frank — *Born: Kansas City, Missouri, 13th March 1906*
clarinet/alto/violin/arranger — *Died: Chicago, Illinois, 1st March 1932*

Raised in Chicago. Started on violin at 10, then learnt mandolin and banjo before taking up alto sax at the age of 14. Played violin in the Austin High School Orchestra and gigged on banjo, alto sax, and violin with school friends (Jimmy McPartland, Jim Lanigan, *et al.*) in

The Blue Friars. Worked on alto with Husk O'Hare's Red Dragons in 1924. During the following year, whilst playing a season at Lost Lake, Wisconsin, took up clarinet (some tuition from Bud Jacobson). Worked with Sig Meyers at White City, Chicago, then played briefly in Florida with Charlie Straight. From 1926 until 1928 worked mostly with Floyd Town's Band, also played with Charlie Straight and Art Kassel and did various recording sessions. To New York in June 1928 with the Chicago Gang, worked for a week accompanying variety act, then gigged around New York. Deputised for Gil Rodin in Ben Pollack's Band (July 1928), then played for a month in Atlantic City with Red Nichols in a Sam Lanin Band. Returned to Chicago October 1928. Played for various leaders in Chicago: Eddie Neibauer, Ted Lewis, Joe Kayser, Eddie Valzos, Charlie Straight, Floyd Town, Benny Meroff, and with Jess Stacy's Aces. Worked mainly on alto and violin during last two years of his life. On tour with Jan Garber in autumn 1931, left tour to return to Chicago, continued gigging, then joined Wild Bill Davison's newly formed big band. At 2 a.m. on the morning of 1st March 1932 he was fatally injured whilst travelling as a passenger in Wild Bill Davison's Packard. The car was in a crossroads collision with a taxi cab, 'Tesch' was taken to the Ravenswood Hospital where he died from multiple injuries shortly after admittance.

THIGPEN, 'Ben' Benjamin F.
drums/vocals

Born: Laurel, Mississippi, 16th November 1908
Died: St. Louis, Missouri, 5th October 1971

Began on piano, received tuition from his sister, Eva. Switched to drums and played first gigs in 1923, with Bobby Boswell in South Bend, Indiana. First professional work accompanying dancers Dave and Tressie, settled in Chicago and received percussion tuition from Jimmy Bertrand. Worked with Al Wynn (1925), Doc Cheatham (1926), and with Charlie Elgar's Creole Band in 1927-8 (did not record with Elgar). With J. Frank Terry's Band (mainly in Cleveland, Ohio) from late 1928 until 1930, then joined Andy Kirk. Featured with Andy Kirk until late 1947, then moved to St. Louis, Missouri. Led own quintet for a while, then regularly with Singleton Palmer throughout the 1960s. Ben was the father of famous drummer 'Ed' Thigpen; two other children are also musicians.

THOMAS, 'Fathead' George
saxes/vocals

Born: Charleston, West Virginia
Died: New Haven, Connecticut, November 1930

Featured vocalist with McKinney's Cotton Pickers from c. 1927 until the time of his death—also recorded with Duke Ellington in April 1926. He suffered fatal injuries in a car accident whilst travelling as a passenger with Joe Smith.

THOMAS, John L.
trombone

Born: Louisville, Kentucky, 18th September 1902.
Died: Chicago, 7th November, 1971

Attended Wendell Phillips High School in Chicago. First professional work with Clarence Miller's Orchestra (1923), toured with The Columbia Burlesque Wheel revue (c. 1925), returned to gig in Chicago. With Erskine Tate 1927-8 (recorded in Louis Armstrong's Hot Seven—May 1927). Worked with Dave Peyton (and Fess Williams) at the Regal Theatre (1928), with Jerome Pasquall (late 1928), then toured with Freddie Keppard. Joined Speed Webb in California, later worked with Leon Rene's Band in Los Angeles, returned to Chicago (c. 1930), rejoined Erskine Tate. With Cassino Simpson (1931), with Clarence Moore (early 1932). Toured with Reuben Reeves (early 1933), joined Ed Carry's Band (March 1933), then again worked with Reuben Reeves. In late 1934 briefly with McKinney's Cotton Pickers in Detroit and Buffalo, then joined Zack Whyte. Returned to Chicago, gigged for a while, then toured with Nat 'King' Cole's Band in 'Shuffle Along' revue (spring 1937). Gigged in Chicago before joining Erskine Tate (c. 1940), then worked with drummer Floyd Campbell's Band. Left full-time music and did defence-plant work in World War II. Worked briefly with guitarist Walter Dysett (1944), then quit playing for 10 years. Joined Franz Jackson's Original Jazz All Stars in late 1960, worked regularly with Jackson until the summer of 1965.

THOMAS, 'Joe' Joseph Lewis
trumpet

Born: Webster Grove, Missouri, 24th July 1909
Died: New York City, 6th August 1984

Wife is vocaliste Babe Matthews. Began playing trumpet whilst at school, taught by P. G. Lankford in St. Louis. First jobs with band led by St. Louis drummer Cecil 'Doggie' Scott (1928), then worked with Darrell Harris in Fort Wayne, Indiana (1929). With Eli Rice's Cotton Pickers (1930-2), Shuffle Abernathy (late 1932-33), and drummer Harold Flood in Milwaukee (1933). Worked with Ira Coffey at a Camden walkathon before going to New York. With Ferman Tapp's Band at Small's (c. May 1934). Joined Charlie Turner's Arcadians and remained with this band when it was taken over by Fats Waller. With Fletcher Henderson from summer of 1935. Joined Willie Bryant (1937), then worked regularly with Claude Hopkins before joining Benny Carter in May 1939. Briefly led own small band, then worked with James P. Johnson December 1939-November 1940. Led own sextet, briefly with Joe Sullivan, then worked with Teddy Wilson's Sextet from August 1942 until October 1943. With Barney Bigard until early 1945, also led own group in period 1943-45 and played for 'Blue Holidays' theatre production. Extensive free-lance recordings in mid-1940s, led own band prior to spell with Cozy Cole's Quintet (early 1948), with Bud Freeman's Band in Chicago for part of 1949. Continued to lead own group in the 1950s, also freelanced, including dates with Fletcher Henderson Re-union Band in 1957-58. During the 1960s led own band in New York, Boston, Toronto, etc., worked at Eddie Condon's Club in 1964, was also featured at Newport Jazz Festival that year. With Claude Hopkins in 1966. Played many gigs with J. C. Higginbotham during the 1960s. Continued to free-lance during the 1970s.

THOMAS, 'Joe' Joseph Vankert
tenor sax/clarinet/vocals

Born: Uniontown, Pennsylvania, 19th June 1909

Started on alto sax, worked with Earl Hood's Band in Columbus, Ohio, then began professional career with Horace Henderson (c. 1930). Worked with Stuff Smith in 1932, then played mainly in Buffalo; with drummer Guy Jackson before joining Jimmie Lunceford in 1933. After Lunceford's death in 1947 Joe Thomas co-led the band with Ed Wilcox. In November 1948 Joe Left to form his own band. During the early 1950s he left full-time music and moved to Kansas City where he now runs his own undertaking business. In July 1968 he made a brief return to New York and was successfully featured at the Newport Jazz Festival. Resumed recording, and played regularly during the 1970s.

Not related to Walter 'Foots' Thomas, or to the New Orleans reed-man Joe 'Cornbread' Thomas (1902-81).

THOMAS, Kid
(real name: Thomas Valentine)
trumpet

Born: Reserve, Louisiana, 3rd February 1896

Father (Fernand), was a trumpeter. Formed own band at age of 18 and played weekend dates at local Moran Club for several years, also gigged with Marshall Lawrence Band. Moved into New Orleans in 1922. Worked in Elton Theodore Band and later assumed leadership of the group. Led own band for long residencies in New Orleans. Was featured at Preservation Hall during the 1960s, later did extensive touring with the Preservation Hall Band. During the 1970s and early 1980s did a vast amount of international touring, some of it as a solo guest star.

THOMAS, 'Foots' Walter Purl
tenor sax/clarinet/flute/arranger

Born: Muskogee, Oklahoma, 10th February 1907
Died: Englewood, New Jersey, 26th August 1981

Brother Joe (born 1908) also a tenor saxophonist. Attended school in Topeka, Kansas, whilst studying at Kansas Vocational College began gigging with local bands. Moved to New York in 1927, worked with Jelly Roll Morton at Rose Danceland in 1928, then brief spells with Luis Russell and Joe Steele before joining The Missourians in 1929. Remained with the band when Cab Calloway became leader—stayed with Cab until 1943. Short spell with Don Redman (1943), then led own band at the Zanzibar, New York, in 1944. Ceased professional playing in 1948 and became agent-manager for many well-known artistes.

T

THOMPKINS, 'Eddie' Edward
trumpet/vocals

Born: Kansas City, Missouri, 1908
Died: Tennessee, 17th April 1943

Trumpet from an early age. Played with Terrence Holder, Eli Rice, Jesse Stone, and Grant Moore before entering Iowa University in 1926. Played with Cecil Bruton and his Blue Six whilst at university, also worked with George E. Lee during last year of his studies. Left university and briefly rejoined Grant Moore, then worked with T. Holder, Bennie Moten, Tommy Douglas, Eli Rice (1931), and trombonist Shuffle Abernathy (1932), before joining Jimmie Lunceford. Remained with Lunceford until December 1939. Whilst serving as a 2nd Lieutenant in the U.S. Army he was accidentally shot dead during maneouvres in Tennessee.

THOMPSON, 'Sir Charles' Charles Phillip
piano/organ/arranger

Born: Springfield, Ohio, 21st March 1918

Started on violin, then switched to piano. At 17 worked in a band led by Cecil Scott (not the tenor-player), left them in 1936 to join Lloyd Hunter's Serenaders. With Nat Towles from 1937, moved to California with Floyd Ray's Band, did studio sessions in Hollywood and also played in Lionel Hampton's Band (1940). Worked with George Clark's Band in Buffalo and in New York with the Harlem Dictators before joining Lee and Lester Young's Band at Cafe Society (1942). Gigged with many small bands on 52nd Street, also did arranging for Count Basie, Jimmy Dorsey, Lionel Hampton, Fletcher Henderson, etc. To California with Coleman Hawkins in 1944-5, with Lucky Millinder from January 1946. Co-led band with Illinois Jacquet 1947-8, did solo work in Washington, D.C., then joined Lennie Lewis Band in New York (1949). Occasionally with Jimmy Rushing (1950-2). Long solo residencies in Cleveland and in California, during which time began working regularly on organ, also worked again with Illinois Jacquet in 1952. Worked mainly as a soloist during the 1950s also did many free-lance recordings with various bands. Toured Europe with Buck Clayton in 1961. During the 1960s played many clubs in New York, also worked in Toronto, Puerto Rico, etc., toured Europe with 'Jazz from a Swinging Era' package in 1967. Worked in Toronto early in 1970. Inactive through illness (1974), resumed playing in 1975, regular European tours throughout the late 1970s and 1980s.

THORNHILL, Claude
piano/arranger

Born: Terre Haute, Indiana, 10th August 1909
Died: New York City, 1st July 1965

Started playing piano at the age of 10. Boyhood friend of Danny Polo, worked briefly in a duo with him. Did summer season on S.S. 'George Washington' with Heavy Elder's Riverboat Orchestra, then worked for a year with the Kentucky Colonels. Studied for two years at Cincinnati Conservatory, then worked for brief spells with Austin Wylie and Hal Kemp before settling in New York (c. 1931). Played for Don Voorhees, Freddy Martin, Jacques Renard, and Paul Whiteman before brief spell with Benny Goodman in 1934. Worked with Leo Reisman before joining Ray Noble in the spring of 1935. Left Ray Noble in 1936, joined Andre Kostelanetz for a while, led own small band in New York and acted as musical director for Maxine Sullivan. Moved to Hollywood in late 1937 for radio, film, and recording work, prolific free-lance arrangings, also helped Skinnay Ennis organise his first band. Formed own band in 1940 until joining U.S. Navy in 1942; player in Artie Shaw's Naval Band, later led own service band. After demobilisation in autumn of 1945 he began organising his own band which made its official debut in the spring of 1946, temporarily disbanded, but re-formed big band in 1949. During the 1950's he occasionally led a big band for specific engagements, but usually led a small group, in 1957 he worked for a while as musical director for vocalist Tony Bennett. In the 1960s he worked mainly as leader of a sextet, when not touring he lived in semi-retirement at his home in New Jersey. He died suddenly from a heart attack.

TIO, Lorenzo Jr.
clarinet/tenor sax/arranger/oboe

Born: New Orleans, Louisiana, 1884
Died: New York, 24th December 1933

His father, Lorenzo Sr., and his uncle, Luis, were also famous clarinettists. In 1897 he began playing regularly in the Lyre Club Symphony Orchestra. During the early 1900s worked with various small orchestras and trios, from c. 1910 played with the Onward Brass Band and began regular teaching, some of pupils include: Barney Bigard, Albert Burbank, Johnny Dodds, Albert Nicholas, Jimmie Noone, etc., etc. With Papa Celestin from c. 1913, then worked in Chicago with Manuel Perez in 1916. After a year he returned to New Orleans and rejoined Papa Celestin, worked with Armand Piron in 1918, then briefly with Oak Gaspard's Maple Leaf Orchestra. Rejoined Piron in 1919 and worked for that leader until 1928 (including New York residencies). Worked in New Orleans with the Tuxedo Brass Band, then returned to New York, gigged and free-lance arranging, also played for a while on the Albany-New York steamboats. Returned to New Orleans, again worked regularly with Armand Piron. Returned to New York and played residency at The Nest Club during the last few months of his life. His funeral took place in New Orleans.

TIZOL, 'Juan' Vincente Martinez
valve-trombone/arranger/composer

Born: San Juan, Puerto Rico, 22nd January 1900
Died: Inglewood, California, 23rd April 1984

Tuition from his uncle, Manuel Tizol. Played in the Municipal Band of San Juan during his late teens. To U.S.A. in 1920 with the Marie Lucas Orchestra, and played long residency at the Howard Theatre, Washington, D.C., with that orchestra, also worked with Bobby Lee's Cottonpickers and The White Brothers' Band. With Duke Ellington from August 1929 until April 1944 (except for absences through illness in late 1935 and September 1943), then with Harry James from April 1944 until March 1951 when he rejoined Duke Ellington. Left in late 1953 and worked with Harry James throughout remainder of 1950s, temporary return to Duke Ellington in spring of 1960. Lived in Los Angeles before moving to Las Vegas. Several of his famous compositions (including 'Perdido', and 'Caravan') were recorded originally by Duke Ellington.

TOLBERT, 'Skeets' Campbell A.
alto sax/clarinet/composer/arranger

Born: Charlotte, North Carolina, c. 1910

During the late 1920s and early 1930s (whilst at college) worked with Dave Taylor's Dixie Serenaders (recording with them in 1931). Later moved to New York to work as a musician with various small groups. Formed own 'Gentlemen of Swing'; made recordings and played long residencies in New York during the 1930s and early 1940s. Moved to Houston, Texas in the mid 1940s and worked as a teacher, also acted as a Musicians' Union official, later ran own musical instrument store in Houston.

TOMPKINS, Eddie
see THOMPKINS

TOUGH, 'Dave' David Jarvis
drums

Born: Oak Park, Illinois, 26th April 1908
Died: Newark, New Jersey, 6th December 1948

Attended Oak Park High School, then spent three years as a student at the Lewis Institute, Chicago—during this time played regular gigs with The Austin High Gang. Also spent summer vacations playing at holiday resorts: with pianist Bill Blaufuss (summer 1923) at Highland Hotel, Delavan, Missouri, with Lyman Woods' Trio (summer 1924) at the Calumet Inn, Sheboygan. Worked with various bandleaders in Chicago from 1925: Sig Meyers, Husk O'Hare's Wolverines, Art Kassel, Jack Gardner, etc., before sailing to Europe with Danny Polo in the summer of 1927. Worked mainly with George Carhart in Belgium, France, and Germany (recorded in Berlin, whilst playing a season at the Barbarrina Cabaret). Returned to New York playing aboard the S.S. Ile de France, free-lanced in New York briefly, then returned to Paris, worked with Mezz Mezzrow's Trio at L'Ermitage Muscovite (March 1929), rejoined George Carhart, then returned to the U.S.A. (c. May 1929). Worked occasionally in Benny Goodman pick-up bands, then toured with Red Nichols (autumn 1929). Serious illness enforced return to Chicago, recommenced local work, worked with Joe Kayser's Band (spring 1931), then musically inactive from 1932 except for occasional gigs at Liberty Inn and Capitol Dancing School. Returned to full-time music in late 1935, very brief spell with Ray Noble's Orchestra, then joined Tommy Dorsey in February 1936. Left Tommy Dorsey on 1st January 1938, few appearances with Red Norvo, then six weeks with Bunny Berigan, joined Benny Goodman in March 1938. Left in July 1938 to rejoin Tommy Dorsey, after two lay-offs through illness he quit Tommy Dorsey in early summer of 1939. Worked a few dates with Jimmy Dorsey, then joined Bud Freeman's Summa Cum Laude Band. With Jack Teagarden (August and September 1939), then spasmodic appearances with Bud Freeman until breakdown in health in January 1940. After recuperating at Tommy Dorsey's farm, returned to New York and worked with Mezz Mezzrow's group in May 1940. Joined Joe Marsala (September 1940), brief return to Benny Goodman (February-April 1941), then with Joe Marsala until joining Artie Shaw in August 1941. Briefly with Woody Herman, then into Charlie Spivak's Band in April 1942. Joined U.S. Navy and served as a member of Artie Shaw's Naval Band, after a tour of the Pacific area returned to the U.S.A. and was medically discharged in February 1944. Joined Woody Herman in April 1944, recurring illness caused several periods of absence, finally left Herman in September 1945. With Joe Marsala at the Gotham Dixie Club until January 1946—during this period worked briefly with Benny Goodman and played for opening night of Eddie Condon's Club (December 1945). On and off at Eddie Condon's from February until September 1946, dates with Jerry Gray's studio band (c. May 1946). Toured with J.A.T.P. in October 1946, returned to Eddie Condon's until 30th January 1947. With Charlie Ventura and Bill Harris from March until May 1947, then another spell in hospital. Gigged in New York, then to Chicago to work with Muggsy Spanier at the newly opened Blue Note Club (November 1947). Left Muggsy in January 1948, returned to New York before entering the New Jersey Veterans' Hospital at Lyons. During the time that he was an out-patient at that hospital he incurred fatal head injuries after falling down in a Newark street. His burial took place at Oak Park, Illinois.

TOWLES, Nat
string bass/leader

Born: New Orleans, Louisiana, 10th August 1905
Died: Berkeley, California, January 1963

Son of New Orleans bassist Phil 'Charlie' Towles. Originally played guitar and violin, then switched to string bass. First regular work with Gus Metcalf's Melody Jazz Band, then gigged with Buddie Petit, Henry 'Red' Allen, Jack Carey and the Original Tuxedo Orchestra before forming own Creole Harmony Kings—toured Oklahoma, Texas, and New Mexico from 1923-7, brief spell with Fate Marable (c. 1925). In 1929 left New Orleans with the Seven Black Aces led by banjoist Thomas Benton, then led own band 1930-3, based in Jackson, Mississippi. In 1934 worked for a while in band led by pianist Ethel Mays, briefly led own band in Dallas. In 1935 took over the Wiley College Students' Band in Austin, Texas, and resumed leading in Dallas, during the following year the band took up residency at the Dreamland Ballroom, Omaha, Nebraska. Throughout the late 1930s and 1940s his band toured regularly; in 1943 they played several residencies in and around New York including bookings at the Apollo Theatre in December 1943. Towles continued to lead his own band until moving to California in 1959; he ran his own tavern until suffering a fatal heart attack.

TRAPPIER, 'Traps' Arthur Benjamin
drums

Born: Georgetown, South Carolina, 28th May 1910
Died: New York, 17th May 1975

Lived in New York from early childhood. With Charlie Skeets from 1928, then worked with Tiny Bradshaw, Blanche Calloway, Skeets Tolbert and Buddy Johnson. With Fats Waller (1941-2), George James (1943), Wilbur de Paris (1944), Ed Hall (1944-5), Sy Oliver, Albert Nicholas (1947), Ralph Sutton (1948), Tony Parenti, Wingy Manone (1949), Hot Lips Page (1950-1), Sidney Bechet (1951), Sammy Benskin (1951). Regular dates at the Central Plaza during the early 1950s, led own trio during the 1950s and 1960s, also free-lanced with many small combos.

T

TRAYLOR, **'Rudy' Rudolph**
drums/vibes/piano/arranger

Born: Providence, Rhode Island, 1918

Played drums and piano in school band. Gigged in Philadelphia during the mid-1930s, then George Baquet got him a job as a house musician at a Philadelphia night club. Later played for two years with Lonnie Slappey and his Swingsters at Harlem Club, Philadelphia. Joined Earl Hines for a year from early 1941, worked with Hot Lips Page and Herman 'Humpy' Flintall before brief spell with Ella Fitzgerald Big Band. With George James in late 1942, then service in U.S. Army from December 1942 until February 1946. Studied at Juilliard, then two months with Jimmie Lunceford in 1947, with Noble Sissle from 1948 until 1951. Formed own band, then worked in Boston with trumpeter Joe Thomas, returned to New York and played in Broadway threatre orchestras. Worked for three years as studio musician for C.B.S., then a. and r. work for record companies, musical director for several vocal groups. Visited Europe in the late 1950s.

TREADWELL, **George McKinley**
trumpet/composer

Born: New Rochelle, New York, 21st December 1919
Died: New York, 14th May 1967

Worked in house band at Monroe's Uptown House in New York during the early 1940s. With Benny Carter (1942-43), then with Ace Harris and the Sunset Royals, and with Tiny Bradshaw before working with Cootie Williams (late 1943-early 1946). With J. C. Heard (1946-47), during this period married singer Sarah Vaughan, acted as musical director for Sarah Vaughan and did overseas tours with her. They were subsequently divorced but Treadwell carried on with managerial duties during the 1950s. When that arrangement ended he became an a. and r. man in the record business, and also had some success as a song-writer.

TRENT, **Alphonso E.**
piano/leader

Born: Fort Smith, Arkansas, 24th August 1905
Died: Fort Smith, Arkansas, 14th October 1959

Father was a high school principal. Piano lessons from W. O. Wiley during childhood. Gigged with local bands, then formed own band. Led in Muskogee, Oklahoma, during summer of 1923, studied at Shorter College in Little Rock, Arkansas, worked with Eugene Crook's Synco Six, was later appointed leader of the band (c. 1924). Gained long residency at Adolphus Hotel, Dallas, Texas, broadcast on WFAA, Dallas. Regular touring during the late 1920s including dates at the Savoy Ballroom, New York. Led for several brief seasons on Strekfus steamers and on the Great Lakes steamers. Retired from music temporarily in 1934. Led own small band regularly from 1938, concentrating mainly on territory work, later returned to his home town. During the last few years of his life did part-time playing including leading for residency at The Branding Iron.

TRISTANO, **'Lennie' Leonard Joseph**
piano/composer

Born: Chicago, Illinois, 19th March 1919
Died: New York, 18th November 1978

Began playing piano at age of 4. Lost eyesight during early childhood, spent almost ten years in a state institution for the blind in Illinois, whilst there learnt to play saxophone, clarinet and cello. Later studied at American Conservatory in Chicago and gained Bachelor of Music degree. During the early 1940s gigged in Chicago on piano and tenor saxophone. Moved to New York in August 1946, played gigs there and in California in late 1946 then settled on Long Island. Opened own studio in June 1951 where he instructed some of his musical colleagues, including altoist Lee Konitz, tenor saxist Warne Marsh and guitarist Billy Bauer. During the late 1940s he worked with Charlie Ventura but was mainly active leading own trio at the Three Deuces, N.Y., own quintet at The Royal Roost and own sextet at The Clique. During the 1950s, 1960s and 1970s was mainly active as a teacher, but played dates with Lee Konitz and Warne Marsh in the late 1950s and in the 1960s, also played solo dates in Canada, and in Europe in 1965 and 1968.

T

TRUEHEART, John
guitar/banjo

Born: Baltimore, Maryland, c. 1900
Died: New York, 1949

Close friend of Chick Webb. Worked with Chick in the local Jazzola Orchestra before moving to New York. Worked in all of Chick Webb's early bands and remained with him until suffering serious illness in 1937. Returned to Chick Webb in spring 1939; remained after that leader's death to work with Ella Fitzgerald until July 1940. Continued playing during the early 1940s including spell with Art Hodes in spring 1943, was then forced to retire through ill health.

TRUMBAUER, Frankie
'C' melody sax/multi-instrumentalist/vocals

Born: Carbondale, Illinois, 30th May 1901
Died: Kansas City, Missouri, 11th June 1956

His mother was a concert pianiste, his son, Bill, became a professional trumpet player and music teacher. Raised in St. Louis, during early teens played piano, trombone, flute, and violin before concentrating on 'C' melody sax (later in his career Trumbauer also recorded on cornet, alto sax, and bassoon). At 17 formed own band in St. Louis then, after service in U.S. Navy, returned to St. Louis to join Max Goldman's Orchestra. Subsequently with Ted Jansen's Band and Earl Fuller. Joined Gene Rodemich's Band and with them made recording debut, worked with Joe Kayser's Orchestra (1921), then joined Benson Orchestra in Chicago before playing with Ray Miller's Orchestra during 1923-4. Subsequently became a musical director for the Jean Goldkette Organisation and led a band at the Arcadia Ballroom which featured Bix Beiderbecke. Together with Bix played for Jean Goldkette until 1927, during this time these two musicians made many small band recordings together. They both worked in Adrian Rollini's short-lived big band (September-October 1927) and with Paul Whiteman's Orchestra; Trumbauer remained with Whiteman until the spring of 1932. Organised own band and did extensive touring before rejoining Whiteman in late 1933. Co-led the Three T's in late 1936 (with Jack and Charlie Teagarden), then left Whiteman and moved to West Coast, co-led band with Manny Klein, then worked with George Stoll (early 1938) before organising own big band (March 1938), using the name 'Trombar'. Left full-time music in March 1939 to become an Inspector for the Civil Aeronautics Authority in Kansas City. Led own band again in 1940. Worked as a test pilot throughout World War II. In late 1945 returned to music and worked with Russ Case's Studio group and with Raymond Paige's N.B.C. Orchestra in New York. Moved to Santa Monica in 1947, retired from full-time music. Again worked for Civil Aeronautical Authority in Kansas City, but continued to play occasionally and guested at Dixieland Jubilee Bix tribute in October 1952. Collapsed and died in the foyer of St. Mary's Hospital, Kansas City.

TUNNELL, 'Bon Bon' George N.
vocals/piano

Born: Reading, Pennsylvania, 1903
Died: Philadelphia, Pennsylvania, 20th May 1975

Led own vocal group: 'Bon Bon and his Buddies' in New York during the late 1920s and early 1930s, Connie's Inn, etc., then formed The Three Keys in Chester, Pennsylvania. The Three Keys ('Bon Bon', John 'Slim' Furness (guitar/vocals), and Bob Pease (string bass/vocals) moved to New York in summer of 1932 and began regular radio work. Regular touring and recordings during the 1930s; the trio appeared at the London Palladium in September 1933. 'Bon Bon' fronted his own band in 1940, was then featured with Jan Savitt until spring 1942. Quit professional singing and worked for many years in Yeadon, Pennsylvania and continued to sing with a re-formed Three Keys unit.

TURNER, Henry B.
string bass

Born: Quincy, Florida, 28th June 1904
Died: Brooklyn, N.Y., 26th July 1980

Began on double B-flat tuba in 1920, studied tuba and trombone for several years at Tuskegee Institute under Captain Frank Drye. Played first engagements with First R.O.T.C. Band at Tuskegee. First professional work with the Gurley Brothers' Band in Hartford, Connecticut (1925) on tuba and trombone. Played in New York with Banjo Bernie's Band and Charlie Skeet before joining Claude Hopkins at the Venetian Gardens, New York, in late 1929. Remained with Claude Hopkins until forced to quit through illness (1936), after recovery joined Snub Mosely (1937). Then worked with Sidney Bechet (1938), Joe Sullivan (1939-40), Louis Jordan (1940-1), George James (1942-3), Garvin Bushell (1944), Lem Johnson (1945—including overseas U.S.O. tour), Herman Chittison Trio (1946), Lem Johnson, Bobby Sands' Orchestra (1947-8), Harry Dial (1949-52), Big John Greer (1952-3), Buddy Lucas (1954), Wilbur de Paris (1957). From 1958 was actively engaged in free-lance, regular club and theatre dates, and TV and studio recordings.

Not related to the bassist-leader Charlie 'Fat Man' Turner (died: 27th October 1964).

TURNER, 'Big Joe' Joseph *Born: Kansas City, Missouri, 18th May 1911*
vocals

Father died in a car crash when Joe was 15 years old. He began working as a singing bartender at various clubs in Kansas City: The Hole in the Wall, The Black and Tan, etc. He teamed up with Pete Johnson at the Kingfisher Club and worked regularly with him for many years in Kansas City (including long stay at The Sunset). In 1938 they appeared together at Carnegie Hall and worked very briefly at Cafe Society, Famous Door, and the Apollo Theatre. They returned to Kansas City in August 1938 and took up residency at The Lone Star Club. Back to New York, then moved to California. In the summer of 1941 Joe sang with Duke Ellington's Band in the 'Jump for Joy' revue (Los Angeles), then worked in Hollywood clubs including long stay at Swanee Inn with various accompanists: Meade Lux Lewis (1943), Joe Sullivan (early 1944). Toured with Pete Johnson and Albert Ammons (1944) and with Luis Russell's Band (1945), but from mid-1940s was mainly active on West Coast. In late 1945 Joe Turner and Pete Johnson opened their own Blue Room Club in Los Angeles. In the 1950s recorded several big-selling singles including the 'Chains of Love', lived in Chicago, but continued touring and also appeared in 1956 film 'Shake, Rattle and Roll'. Toured Europe in 1958. During the 1960s moved to New Orleans, continued regular tours including visit to Britain in the spring of 1965. Worked mainly in Los Angeles 1969-71 (often with Johnny Otis). Featured at Monterey Festival (September 1971). Toured Europe with Milt Buckner (April 1971). Appeared at many jazz festivals during the mid 1970s. Temporarily inactive through illness 1980, but then resumed extensive touring.

TURNER, 'Joe' Joseph H. *Born: Baltimore, Maryland, 3rd November 1907*
piano/vocals

At five received first piano lessons from his mother, graduated to other teachers and entered first piano contest in 1923. After some tuition by pianist Frank Johnson he moved to New York (c. 1925). Began residency at Barron Wilkins with Hilton Jefferson, then joined June Clark's Band. Played at many solo spots in New York during late 1920s and also worked briefly with Benny Carter's Band (1929), Bingie Madison and Louis Armstrong (1930). During the 1930s spent many years working as accompanist for vocaliste Adelaide Hall (first in duo with Alex Hill, then with pianist Francis Carter). Toured Europe with Adelaide Hall in the mid-1930s, remained to play solo dates in Czechoslovakia (1936), Hungary, France, etc. In August 1939 was on his way to Turkey (via Switzerland), immediately returned from Turkey to France on outbreak of World War II and returned to the U.S.A. in October 1939. Worked as a single before service in U.S. Army, in 1944-5 worked in all-star service band directed by Sy Oliver at Camp Kilmer, New Jersey. After demobilisation he worked briefly with Rex Stewart's Band (early 1946), then solo work before returning to Hungary in 1948. Worked in Switzerland in 1949, then moved to Paris. During the 1950s played successful engagements in Europe, visited Britain for a vacation in 1959. Starting in 1962, played residency at La Calvados in Paris, also did concert dates in Switzerland during the 1970s. Continued to play regularly throughout the 1970s and 1980s, including engagements in the United States.

VALENTINE, 'Syd' Raymond
trumpet

Born: Indianapolis, Indiana, November 1908

Received trumpet tuition from Frank Clay, did local gigs, then toured with Fred Wisdom's Merrymakers, played in Paul Stewart's Wee Hour Serenaders and the Jigfield Follies before working in Horace Henderson's Collegians (c. 1929). Led own Patent Leather Kids (recorded for Gennett—October 1929), played in Sugar Cane Orchestra (early 1930), then with Bernie Young's Band (spring 1930). Worked briefly with Speed Webb, then long spell in the Hardy Brothers' Band; several leaves of absence, during one toured the R.K.O. circuit with Lucky Millinder (September 1931). With Elmer Calloway (c. 1933) and brief stay with Earl Hines. Gigged in New York during the mid-1930s, then toured with Irving Miller's 'Brownskin Models' (c. 1937). Gigged in Michigan during late 1930s before returning to Indianapolis in the early 1940s. Still plays occasionally.

VANCE, 'Dick' Richard Thomas
trumpet/arranger/vocals

Born: Mayfield, Kentucky, 28th November 1915

Raised in Cleveland, originally played violin, then switched to trumpet. Worked in J. Frank Terry's Band until 1934, then played in Buffalo and Detroit in big band led by Lil Armstrong (1934-5). Moved to New York, briefly with Willie Bryant and Kaiser Marshall before working with Fletcher Henderson from 1936 until 1938. Joined Chick Webb in 1939, remained after that leader's death to work with Ella Fitzgerald (including duties as staff arranger). With Charlie Barnet (early 1943), then joined Don Redman (June 1943). With Eddie Heywood from summer 1944 until early 1945, with Herman 'Humpy' Flintall (1945), Ben Webster (1946). Extensive studies at Juilliard Institute from 1944 until 1947. During the 1940s and 1950s also played in pit orchestras for many Broadway shows. Has been arranging regularly for over 30 years, scoring for Cab Calloway, Duke Ellington, Harry James, Glen Gray, Earl Hines, etc. During December 1950 worked with Fletcher Henderson's Sextet in New York (that leader's last engagement). Toured with Don Redman (autumn 1953), has led own band from 1954—during the 1950s co-led with Taft Jordan. Played long residencies at the Savoy Ballroom until its closure. Continued to play (and arrange) regularly during the 1960s, did overseas tour with own band (1969). Extensive free-lance work during the 1970s and 1980s, including playing for New York production of 'One Mo' Time'.

VAN EPS, George
guitar

Born: Plainfield, New Jersey, 7th August 1913

Three brothers became professional musicians: Bobby (piano), Freddy (trumpet), and John (tenor sax)—their father, Fred Van Eps, was a noted banjoist. George began gigging at 13, playing banjo in band led by his brother, Fred. Did first solo broadcast at the age of 14. Studied watch-making, but began touring with Harry Reser's Junior Artists, then worked with the Dutch Master Minstrels before joining Smith Ballew from 1929-31. Two-year spell with Freddy Martin, then with Benny Goodman in 1934 and 1935. Left in summer 1935 to work with Ray Noble's Orchestra, long spell of studio work in Hollywood, then again with Ray Noble from autumn 1940 until spring 1941. Spent two years in his father's sound laboratory, then moved to West Coast to recommence prolific studio work. Illness restricted activities during the early 1970s, is now semi-active, occasionally plays in public.

VENTURA, Charlie
(real name: Charles Venturo)
tenor/all saxes

Born: Philadelphia, Pennsylvania, 2nd December 1916

One of a large family, several of his brothers were sax players including Ernie and Ben. Began on 'C' melody at the age of 15, worked in family hat-making business during the 1930s, but did regular local gigs. With Gene Krupa from 1942 until 1946 (except for a spell with Teddy Powell 1943-4). Led own big band from August 1946 until 1947, then cut down to small group for two years, re-formed big band until early 1951. Led own Big Four (with Chubby Jackson, Buddy Rich, and Marty Napoleon) from summer of 1951, then toured Asia with Gene Krupa Trio from January until June 1952. Worked on and off with Gene Krupa Trio through the 1950s and 1960s, occasionally doubling on baritone and bass saxes, has also continued to lead own small groups in 1960s, long residencies in Las Vegas, Atlantic City, etc., etc. Moved to the East Coast in 1972, played regularly in New England area (1978). Continued to play regularly during the early 1980s, including dates with own band.

VENUTI, 'Joe' Giuseppe *Born: S. Philadelphia, Pennsylvania 16th September 1903*
violin *Died: Seattle, Washington, 14th August 1978*

Began playing violin during childhood. Attended Our Lady of Good Counsel School, then went to James Campbell Public School where he met Eddie Lang. Together they began working in Bert Estlow's Quintet in Atlantic City (1921), subsequently they played in the Hotel Knickerbocker Hotel Orchestra. Venuti played briefly with Red Nichols, then began directing the Book-Cadillac Hotel Orchestra for Jean Goldkette (late 1924). Moved to New York and took part in countless recording sessions with various leaders and waxed many sides in small groups with Eddie Lang—toured with Jean Goldkette, with Roger Wolfe Kahn (October 1925 until June 1926); played for many Broadway Shows. Worked in brief-lived Adrian Rollini Big Band (September 1927). Throughout the 1920s regularly co-led band with Ed Lang for seasons at the Silver Slipper, Atlantic City, also several New York residencies including Vanity Club (1928). Joined Paul Whiteman in May 1929, made remarkable recovery from injuries sustained in car crash (summer 1929), returned to Whiteman from October 1929 until May 1930. Briefly with Smith Ballew in autumn of 1930, then free-lance studio and session work in New York, again with Roger Wolfe Kahn in spring of 1932. To Europe (with guitarist Frank Victor) in 1934—during this visit recorded in London on violin and guitar. From 1935 regularly led own band, continued touring and residencies until the early 1940s. Call-up problems temporarily ended Venuti's career as bandleader (October 1943). He moved to California and early in 1944 became an M.G.M. studio musician. Led own band on the West Coast during the late 1940s, then recommenced widespread touring, occasionally working as a soloist. During the mid-1950s regular stint on station KNXT in Los Angeles. Visited Europe in spring 1953. Continued to work regularly throughout the 1960s, long engagements in Las Vegas, Los Angeles, Seattle, etc. Appeared with great success at 1968 Newport Jazz Festival and at London's 'Jazz Expo' (October 1969). Led in New York late in 1969. Was seriously ill in April 1970, but resumed regular playing later that year. Maintained full playing schedule during the 1970s, often working in Europe. In 1963 moved to Seattle, Washington, and thereafter played mainly in Seattle lounges with occasional forays to Los Angeles, Las Vegas, Washington, D.C., etc. Honored by Newport Hall of Fame at 1975 Newport Jazz Festival. Died of cancer.

Appeared in many films, featured in 'The Five Pennies'. Venuti's love of practical jokes was legendary, it extended to him giving different places (and different years) when asked about his origins. He was (according to his birth certificate) born at 1010 Christian Street, Philadelphia on 16th September 1903.

VIDACOVICH, 'Pinky' Irving J. *Born: Buras, Louisiana, 14th September 1904*
clarinet/saxes *Died: New Orleans, Louisiana, 25th July 1966*

Played with the Princeton Revellers before joining the New Orleans Owls in 1926. During the 1930s played regularly on radio station WWL in New Orleans including spell as musical director, also led own band for various residencies including Cedar Lane Club, St. Charles Hotel, etc. Played with band led by drummer Augie Schellang in 1937. Continued playing for WWL in the 1940s and 1950s, enjoyed considerable success on radio and records, acting the role of 'Cajun Pete'. He played occasionally with Sharkey Bonano in the early 1960s also played on recording sessions, then ceased regular playing and travelled as script-writer for popular trumpeter Al Hirt.

VINSON, 'Cleanhead' Eddie

alto sax/vocals

Born: Houston, Texas, 19th December 1917

First worked in Chester Boone's Band in late 1932, subsequently with Milt Larkin's Band during the 1930s, then with Floyd Ray's Orchestra (1940-1). To New York early in 1942, joined Cootie Williams' Big Band (his vocals with Cootie's band achieved great commercial success), brief Army service early in 1945, rejoined Cootie Williams from spring until September 1945, then formed own band. Late in the 1940s led own 16-piece band. Worked as a single during the early 1950s, rejoined Cootie Williams briefly in 1954. Reformed own band, played residencies in Chicago, then co-led with Arnett Cobb in Houston. Worked mainly in Kansas City, Missouri, during the early 1960s. Toured Europe with Jay McShann in 1969, then led own band in California, also with Johnny Otis. Starred at many international jazz festivals during the 1970s and 1980s.

VOYNOW, 'Dick' Richard F.

piano

Born: 1900
Died: Los Angeles, California, 15th September 1944

Replaced pianist Dud Mecum in The Wolverines during that band's initial booking at the Stockton Club, Hamilton, Ohio. Became business manager and nominal leader of The Wolverines, continued to lead the group after the rest of the original personnel had left. Regular touring until 1926, then spasmodic tours, on one occasion the band was fronted by Smith Ballew. From the late 1920s was employed as a recording manager for various companies including Brunswick-Decca. During the early 1940s worked on the West Coast as a recording executive. He died after a long illness.

WADE, 'Jimmy' James F.
trumpet/piano

Born: Jacksonville, Illinois. c. 1895
Died: Chicago, Illinois. February 1957

Led own band at Queen's Hall, Chicago (c. 1916), then spent several years as the director of band accompanying Lucille Hegamin, worked in Seattle, Washington, and New York with Lucille. Left c. 1922, moved to Chicago to join Doc Cooke, subsequently formed own band which played many residencies in Chicago, also appeared at the Savoy Ballroom in New York (1926) and Club Alabam, New York (1927), Eddie South fronted the band during the mid-1920s. During the late 1920s Wade occasionally worked for other leaders, but was mainly active with own band during the 1930s.

WALDER, Herman
alto sax

Born: Dallas, Texas, 2nd April 1905

Brother of clarinet-sax player Woodie Walder. Originally played trumpet with Jerry Westbrook's Band. After suffering an accident he switched to alto sax, worked with pianiste-vocaliste Laura Rucker, subsequently with Terrence Holder, George E. Lee, LaForest Dent, Thamon Hayes, Harlan Leonard, etc. Continued to work in Kansas City through the 1950s and 1960s, led own band for long residency at Mr. A's Bar. During the 1970s worked in Art Smith's Kansas City Jazz Band.

WALKER, 'T-Bone' Aaron Thibaud
guitar/vocals/piano

Born: Linden, near Texarkana, Texas, 22nd May 1909
Died: Los Angeles, California, 17th March 1975

Played in family group with his father (a bassist) and a cousin who played guitar and banjo. Worked as a solo act (dancing, singing, and playing) in Dallas before joining touring show headed by Ida Cox. Toured in 'B.B.' medicine show and made record debut (on Columbia) as 'Oak-cliff T-Bone'. During the early 1930s worked with a white touring band from Los Angeles, then two years with various shows including long spell with Ma Rainey. Moved to California in 1935, did a variety of day jobs before working full-time with Les Hite from 1940. During the early 1940s worked long solo residencies in Los Angeles (Capri Club, Trocadero, etc.), then began national touring. Continued to work as a single during the 1950s and 1960s including several tours of Europe.

WALKER, 'Jim Daddy' James
guitar

Born: Kansas City, Missouri. c. 1912
Died: Kansas City, Missouri, 10th May 1949

Attended Lincoln High School in Kansas City, played violin in school orchestra. Worked with George E. Lee, then with Jap Allen's Band (1930-1). From 1932 spent several years in Clarence Love's Band. From 1940 worked regularly in the Four Tons of Rhythm. Did last recording session three weeks before his death, accompanying vocalist Walter Brown.

WALLACE, Cedric
string bass

Born: Miami, Florida, 3rd August 1909

First professional work with the Honey Boys Orchestra. Moved to New York, worked with Reggie Johnson at the Saratoga Club (1932), also played with Jimmie Lunceford before working with Fats Waller from 1938 until 1942. Subsequently with Eugene Sedric, pianist Pat Flowers, and Garland Wilson before forming own band which played various residencies in the 1940s including one at Le Ruban Bleu, N.Y.C. in 1945. Continued to play occasional gigs during the 1970s.

WALLACE, Sippie
(née Beulah Thomas)
vocals/piano/organ

Born: Houston, Texas, 1st November 1898

Her niece, Hociel (vocals), died in 1952; Sippie's brother, Hersal (piano), died in 1926, another brother, George W. Thomas Jr., was also a professional musician and composer. Sippie's father was a church deacon, she began singing and playing organ in the local Baptist church. In the late 1910s the family lived in New Orleans. Sippie moved to Chicago

(c. 1923) and soon made her recording debut for Okeh. Did long theatre tours on T.O.B.A circuit throughout the 1920s, retired to Detroit during the 1930s, but continued singing and playing piano for church services. Recommenced recording in 1945, lived for many years in Detroit, then resumed touring in 1965. Visited Europe with American Folk Blues Tour in autumn 1966, and sang at various international festivals during the 1970s and early 1980s.

WALLER, 'Fats' Thomas Wright
piano/organ/vocals/composer

Born: New York City, 21st May 1904
Died: On board an express train near Union Station, Kansas City, Missouri, 15th December 1943

Two of Fat's sons, Thomas W. Waller (d. 1979) and Maurice Waller became professional pianists, another son, the late Ronald played sax. Fats's father was a church minister; mother played piano and organ. He began on piano at six, later attended the P.S. 89 School and played in school orchestra led by Edgar Sampson. Left school in spring of 1918, did various day jobs and also won talent contest at The Roosevelt Theatre, New York (playing 'Carolina Shout'). Received informal lessons from James P. Johnson (later Fats studied with Carl Bohn and Leopald Godowsky). Began recording career in 1922; played at many rent parties before becoming resident organist at the Lincoln Theatre, New York, also toured as accompanist to various variety performers: Brown and Williams, Art Jarrett, etc. Played as house pianist in New York at Leroy's, The Capitol, etc.; during the mid-1920s played residency in silent-movie house in Washington, D.C., and led own trio in Philadelphia. In New York did long spell of doubling at the Lincoln and Lafayette Theatres and began highly successfull collaboration with lyricist Andy Razaf (Fats having been regularly composing since his early teens). To Chicago in February 1927, was featured at the Vendome, Metropolitan, and Regal Theatres, then back to New York to face court charges relating to non-payment of alimony—during the late 1920s Fats was occasionally absent from the music scene. Worked with James P. Johnson in 'Keep Shufflin'' revue from February 1928—was also featured with James P. at a W. C. Handy concert at Carnegie Hall in April 1928. Fats left the show in June 1928, worked at Regal Theatre, Chicago, and Royal Grand in Philadelphia, returned to New York (c. September 1928) and left the music world temporarily. Throughout the 1920s and early 1930s Fats continued recording under his own name; during this period he also recorded with Fletcher Henderson, McKinney's, Jack Teagarden, Ted Lewis, etc. Featured at Connie's Inn in 1929, also scored songs for 'Hot Chocolates' show, later in the year featured at the Paramount, New York, the Regal, Chicago, etc. Broadcast on WABC radio series from 1930, worked with Otto Hardwick's Band and Elmer Snowden's Band at The Hot Feet Club in 1931-2. Led own band at Connie's Inn in autumn 1931. Visited France for a few weeks (with Spencer Williams) in August of 1932. In late 1932 began long residency on radio WLW in Cincinnati, also did regular tours; occasionally accompanied by Clarence Paige's Band, Eddie Johnson's Crackerjacks, etc. In 1934 commenced famous 'Fats Waller and his Rhythm' series of recordings, played residencies at Pod's and Jerry's, Adrian's Tap Room, etc., and had own C.B.S. radio series. During late 1934 and 1935 worked with Charlie Turner and his Arcadians, Fats fronted this unit and it temporarily became Fats Waller and his Orchestra. To West Coast in June 1935, appeared at Sebastian's Cotton Club accompanied by Les Hite and his Orchestra. Based mainly in New York during 1936 and 1937, also toured with own accompanying band. During 1938 began working with band led by pianist Don Donaldson. To Europe in July 1938, opened solo tour of Britain in Glasgow (August 1938), played briefly in Denmark, then returned to London and was featured on an early B.B.C. television programme. Back to U.S.A. in October 1938. Played residency at Yacht Club, New York, with own small band, then solo work in Britain from March until June 1939. Featured with own band at Famous Door, Apollo Theatre, New York, Milwaukee, Hotel Sherman, Chicago, etc., etc., during 1939 and 1940. Toured with own big band in 1941—disbanded in late 1942 and began working as a single—featured in concert at Carnegie Hall in January 1942. During early summer of 1943 played residency at the Tic-Toc Club, Boston—Fats' last big show, 'Early to Bed', opened in Boston in May 1943. Residency in New York in September, then did brief tour of service camps before moving to Hollywood for filming and residency at the Zanzibar Club, Los Angeles, until December 1943. Left to return to New York, whilst travelling with his manager Ed Kirkeby on board the Santa Fe Chief train he died of pneumonia.

Fats Waller made several short films and was also featured in 'Hooray for Love', 'King of Burlesque', 'Stormy Weather', etc. A partial listing of Fats Waller compositions serves to indicate his great writing skills: 'Ain't Misbehavin', 'Black and Blue', 'I'm Crazy 'Bout My Baby', 'I've Got a Feeling I'm Falling', 'Honeysuckle Rose'.

WALTON, Greely — *Born: Mobile, Alabama, 4th October 1904*
tenor sax/baritone sax/clarinet/flute

Violin at the age of 12. Attended school in St. Louis and Pittsburgh, then musical studies at University of Pittsburgh, switched to tenor sax. With Elmer Snowden (1926), Henri Saparo (1927-8), Benny Carter (1929), then with Luis Russell from 1930, remained to work under Louis Armstrong until 1937. With Vernon Andrade and his Renaissance Orchestra from 1938. Briefly with Horace Henderson from September 1941, then (on baritone sax) with Cootie Williams (1942-3), Cab Calloway (1943-5). Conductor for the Ink Spots Show (1945-7), then with Marcellino Guerra's Afro-Cuban Band in 1947 and 1948—during this period also doubled with Noble Sissle's Band at the Diamond Horseshoe. From 1948 worked for several years with Sy Oliver doing pilot radio and television shows, recordings, etc. Taught flute during the early 1950s, in 1955, after the death of his wife, he gave up playing. During the 1960s worked for a New York brokerage company.

WARE, Leonard — *Born: Richmond, Virginia, 28th December 1909*
guitar/composer

Originally an oboeist—studied at Tuskegee. Switched to guitar in the early 1930s and formed own highly successful trio which played many residencies in New York during the late 1930s and early 1940s. Recorded with other leaders including Sidney Bechet (1938), Herbie Fields (1944), Don Byas (1945), etc., etc. Left full-time music many years ago to work for the New York postal authorities.

WARE, 'Munn' Winfred Nettleton — *Born: Quincy, Massachusetts, 1909*
trombone — *Died: Daytona Beach, Florida, 9th August 1970*

During the late 1940s worked regularly in Bill Reinhardt's Band at Jazz Limited in Chicago; recorded with Sidney Bechet, Muggsy Spanier, Doc Evans, etc. Worked in New York in various Dixieland bands during the early 1950s then moved to Florida in 1952. Active free-lance work there, was also vice president of local musicians' union; died after suffering injuries in a car accident.

WARREN, Earle Ronald — *Born: Springfield, Ohio, 1st July 1914*
alto sax/clarinet/vocals

Brother of drummer Bob Warren, both their parents were amateur musicians. Earle began on piano, then switched to banjo-ukelele. At 12, together with his brother and sisters, did week-end gigs in Springfield. Started on 'C' melody sax at 13, spell on tenor sax, then specialised on alto. Played in high school band, then worked in local Elks' Band and with Frankie Greene before leading own band, Duke Warren and his Eight Counts of Syncopation until 1933. After leaving high school moved to Columbus, Ohio, led own band there from April until September (doubling trumpet), then joined Marion Sears' Band in Cleveland. Remained with Sears until spring 1935, also worked briefly with Ralph Sherman's Orchestra and Dale Stevens' Band, then co-led the 14-piece Kennerley-Warren Orchestra. In spring of 1937 subbed in Count Basie's Band whilst they were working in Cincinnati, joined Basie regularly in April 1937. Left Basie in May 1945, led own band, brief return to Basie in December 1945, then re-formed own band for residencies in Boston, Cincinnati, New York, etc. Rejoined Count Basie in late 1947, out again through illness in summer of 1948, rejoined in autumn 1948. Left Basie, then returned for 1949 and 1950. After working as manager for the successful Johnny Otis Band, he became musical director for various theatres. Acted as master of ceremonies for stage shows, continued in managerial work. Toured Europe with Buck Clayton in 1959 and 1961. Continued to play regularly during the 1960s, leading own band and playing in various big bands including a spell in Las Vegas with Ted Lewis in 1964. Brief return to Count Basie in spring 1967, toured Europe as a soloist in 1967. During 1969 did extensive touring with The Platters vocal group. Led own band during the 1970s, also worked as a guest soloist. Toured Europe with Dicky Wells and Claude Hopkins (1978). Made his home in Switzerland during the early 1980s, and continued to play many international festivals.

WARWICK, 'Bama' William Carl *Born: Brookside, Alabama, 27th October 1917*
trumpet

Moved to New Jersey in 1930. Was raised with Charlie Shavers. Gigged in New York, then worked with the Hardy Brothers before joining Frankie Fairfax in Philadelphia (c. 1936). Worked with Tiny Bradshaw, Lucky Millinder, Teddy Hill, Bunny Berigan, etc., before serving in U.S. Army during World War II, was musical director of an army band. After release worked for Woody Herman, Buddy Rich (1946 and again in 1947), and several commercial bands. During the early 1950s led own band in California, briefly with Lucky Millinder (1953), also co-led with tenorist Brew Moore (1954-5). With Dizzy Gillespie (1956-7), then free-lance studio work and a spell with drummer Louis Bellson's Band. During the 1960s led own band including service tours to Newfoundland (1963) and Greenland (1964). In 1966 was appointed musical director of the New York City Correctional Institution. Continued to play occasional engagements during the 1970s.

WASHINGTON, 'Al' Albert *Born: Chicago, Illinois, 6th October 1902*
tenor, alto sax/clarinet

Father worked on guitar in Omaha, Nebraska, before moving to Chicago. Al started on piano in 1912, switched to clarinet and sax in 1915, studied with O. K. Schnal and was later taught improvisation by Natty Dominique. Began working on soprano sax and clarinet with Al Simeon's Hot Six—took lessons from Omer Simeon. In 1924 worked with Detroit Shannon's Band at Cafe De Paris, Chicago; with Al Wynn's Paradise Night Owls (1925-6). In 1927 played in Louis Armstrong's Stompers on alto and tenor, then worked with Clarence Black at the Savoy Ballroom (1928). With Erskine Tate (on sax and oboe) and Boyd Atkins (1929-30). With pianist-organist Jerome Carrington at Regal Theatre, Chicago (early 1931), then toured with Louis Armstrong from March 1931 until March 1932. Remained in New York, worked with Fletcher Henderson at Savoy Ballroom, then joined bassist Charlie Turner's Arcadians, remained when Fats Waller fronted the band (1935-6). Moved back to Chicago, studied piano and theory at Roosevelt University, obtained a degree in music. Worked for various leaders: Floyd Campbell, Eddie King, Boyd Atkins, etc. Became a music teacher, and from 1955 was on the teaching staff of the Chicago Public Schools. Continued to play regular club jobs, working with: Big John Woodsit (1967), Russell Crider's Concert Band, Ben Branch's Martin Luther King Bread Baskets, Ged Hunter's Band (1969). Early in 1970 joined trombonist Harry Hulls' Big Band on lead alto. Brother-in-law of trombonist 'Kenneth' Stewart. Settled in Guadalajara, Mexico and continued to play engagements there during the late 1970s and early 1980s.

WASHINGTON, Booker T. *Born: Kansas City, Missouri, 9th April 1909*
trumpet

Father, Byrd Washington, was a musician, as was a brother, Melvin. First lessons from father at age of 13, did first local gigs in 1925. Worked with pianist Chauncey Downs' Rinky Tinks (1928), with Fred McGrew's Jazzers (1929), then worked with Benny Moten from 1929-33. With Harlan Leonard's Rockets from 1933-5, then long spell with sax-player La Forest Dent from 1936 until 1944. Gigged in and around Kansas City to the 1970s, during the late 1970s worked with drummer Art Smith's Band.

WASHINGTON, 'Buck' Ford Lee
piano/vocals/dancer/trumpet

Born: Louisville, Kentucky, 16th October 1903
Died: New York City, 31st January 1955

Long-time partner of John W. Sublett ('Buck and Bubbles'), both were orphans. They teamed up for local theatre work (c. 1917); throughout the 1920s, 1930s, and 1940s they enjoyed an international reputation as variety artistes. They toured Europe in 1931 and again in 1936. Buck made several recordings on piano: with Louis Armstrong (1930), Bessie Smith (1933), Coleman Hawkins (1934)—Billie Holiday said that Buck played piano on her first recording date (1933), also records with Bubbles and solo date. After the double act broke up in 1953 Buck worked for a while in the Jonah Jones group accompanying comedian Timmie Rogers. 'Buck and Bubbles' appeared in several films including: 'Cabin in the Sky', 'A Song is Born', etc.

WASHINGTON, 'Diamond' Leon
tenor sax/clarinet/arranger

Born: Jackson, Mississippi, 27th June 1909
Deceased

Moved with his parents to Chicago in 1912. First played clarinet (taught by Horace George), then tenor sax (lessons from Jerome Pasquall and Sandy Runyon). Worked with Zinky Cohn in Habor Springs, Michigan (summer 1926), gigged in Chicago, then in 1931 joined Bernie Young and his Creolians; toured with Young until 1933. With Carroll Dickerson in 1934-5, then with Louis Armstrong's Big Band (June-October 1935). Worked in Fats Waller's Big Band before returning to Chicago in 1936. Joined trumpeter Jimmy Cobb's Band at the Annex Cafe, then with Earl Hines from February 1937 until late 1938. With Red Saunders' Band from 1938 until 1963 (including 18 years' residency at Club De Lisa, Chicago); during this period did many free-lance recording sessions and arranged for many bands. Continued to play regularly in Chicago, combining this with his work as business agent for Local 10-208.

WASHINGTON, Freddie
piano

Born: Houston, Texas. c. 1900

Moved to the West Coast (c. 1918), joined Kid Ory in Oakland (1921) and recorded with Ory during the following year. Led own band in the 1920s and 1930s, also played with Ed Garland, Paul Howard, etc. Recorded with Zutty Singleton in 1943. Continued playing during the 1960s, regularly with trumpeter Eddie Smith's Band in 1963.

WASHINGTON, George
trombone/arranger

Born: Brunswick, Georgia, 18th October 1907

Raised in Jacksonville, Florida. Trombone from the age of 10, studied at the Edward Waters College in 1922. Worked locally with Eagle Eye Shields, then sailed up to Philadelphia in 1925. Played briefly with J. W. Pepper's Band, then did day work before moving to New York. Studied with Ernest Clarke and Walter Damrosch at the New York Conservatory. In 1925 worked in New York (and Florida) with Broadway Jones and his Band, then worked with Luckey Roberts. With Dave Alford (early 1927), Arthur Gibbs' Orchestra for a year from June 1927, then with Charlie Johnson and Vernon Andrade during the late 1920s. With Don Redman in 1931, Bennie Carter (1933), played with (and arranged for) the Mills Blue Rhythm Band on and off from summer 1932 until 1936, also staff arranger for impressario Irving Mills. With Fletcher Henderson early in 1937, then with Louis Armstrong Big Band from spring 1937 until 1943. Moved to West Coast, with Horace Henderson (summer 1945) and several stints with Benny Carter. Recorded with Count Basie (December 1947). Led own band in California and Las Vegas before working for many years in band led by drummer Johnny Otis. Worked with Joe Darensbourg in 1960, then free-lance session work and arranging.

Not to be confused with the New Orleans trombonist of the same name, who died many years ago.

WASHINGTON, 'Jack' Ronald
baritone/alto saxes

Born: Kansas City, 1912
Died: Oklahoma City, November 1964

Played soprano sax from the age of 13, joined Bennie Moten immediately after leaving school. Worked in Paul Banks' Band and Jesse Stone's Blues Serenaders before rejoining Moten (c. late 1927). Several years with Moten, then joined Count Basie in Kansas City. To New York with Basie in late 1936 and remained with the band until called up for service in the U.S. Army. Served in the 211th AGF Band at Fort Sill, Oklahoma, until demobilisation in late 1945. Rejoined Count Basie in spring 1946 and remained until 1949. Returned to Oklahoma City, left full-time music and worked as a redcap at the city airport. Continued to play local gigs, played on a New York recording session in the 1950s with ex-Basie colleagues.

WASHINGTON, 'Mack' William
drums

Born: Kansas City, Missouri, 1908
Died: Kansas City, Missouri, 1st October 1938

From 1926 worked for many years with Bennie Moten, with Count Basie at the Reno Club, Kansas City, in 1936 until replaced by Jo Jones, then worked with Buster Smith's Band.

WASHINGTON, Steve
banjo/vocals/occasionally piano and clarinet/arranger

Born: Philadelphia, Pennsylvania. c. 1900
Died: Boston, Massachusetts. c. January 1936

Worked as banjoist/vocalist with several bands in Pennsylvania including Humphries' Playboys (1931), Ben Smith's White Hut Orchestra (1932)—took part in recording sessions with Washboard Rhythm Kings/Boys. Worked as a solo cabaret artist for a while and recorded under own name in 1933 (accompanied by Benny Goodman, Joe Venuti, etc.). From 1934 until his death from pneumonia he was featured with the Sunset Royal Orchestra (led then by pianist Ace Harris).

WATERS, 'Benny' Benjamin
tenor/soprano/alto/clarinet/arranger

Born: Brighton, Maryland, 23rd January 1902

Taught music by his brother, who led own local band. Briefly on trumpet and E-flat clarinet, then sax from early teens. Joined Charlie Miller's Band in Philadelphia (c. 1918), played in that band for three years, then enrolled at Boston Conservatory—studied piano and theory there for several years. Gigged with various bandleaders in and around Boston including: pianist Tom Whaley, Skinny Johnson, etc.; played on local radio stations and did extensive teaching. In 1925 joined Charlie Johnson on alto, subsequently played tenor and arranged for Johnson until 1932 (also free-lance recordings with Clarence Williams and King Oliver). Gigged in New York (1933-4) and played residency at a dancing school. Several months with Fletcher Henderson from early 1935, rejoined Charlie Johnson (1936-7), then with Hot Lips Page Big Band at Small's, etc. (1938). With Claude Hopkins (1940-1), then rejoined Hot Lips Page, working with his sextet at Kelly's Stables, etc. (1941). With Jimmie Lunceford (on alto) from c. June 1942 until December 1942. In 1943 and 1944 led own small group for residency at Red Mill Cafe, New York, later led own group in California, then toured with Roy Milton. Gigged for a while in Philadelphia, then joined Jimmy Archey's Band (on soprano and clarinet) from summer of 1950 until November 1952. Left the band in Europe and began touring Switzerland, Germany, and France until 1954. Played residencies in Hamburg, then joined Jack Butler at La Cigale in Paris, worked regularly at that venue until early 1967; during this period also made solo appearances in Italy, Germany, and Belgium. Returned to La Cigale as leader 1968-early 1970. Then did extensive touring in Europe throughout the 1970s and early 1980s. During the early 1980s made brief return visits to the U.S.A. to play various engagements.

WATERS, Ethel
vocals

Born: Chester, Pennsylvania, 31st October 1896
Died: Los Angeles, 1st September 1977

Sang in church choirs as a child, during early teens worked as a maid, then won talent contest at local theatre. Played theatres in Philadelphia and Baltimore and gained the nickname 'Sweet Mama Stringbean' by reason of being tall and thin. Moved to New York in

1917 and was soon established as a top-of-the-bill act. In 1921-2 did widespread touring (accompanied by the Black Swan Troubadours directed by Fletcher Henderson). Made several big-selling records for Black Swan, Paramount, and Columbia. During the 1920s and 1930s was featured in many shows and revues including: 'Africana', 'Black Bottom Revue', 'Rhapsody in Black', 'The Blackbirds', 'As Thousands Cheer', 'Heat Wave', etc., etc. Visited Europe in 1930; recorded with Duke Ellington (1932), Benny Goodman (1933). From 1935 until 1939 headed own touring show—accompanied by Eddie Mallory (who was at that time her husband). In 1939 scored big success with her dramatic role in the play 'Mamba's Daughter'. During the 1940s worked mainly as a cabaret artiste, was also regularly featured as a film actress. Appeared in the Broadway play 'A Member of the Wedding' (1952-3), then resumed solo career. In 1961 starred in the 'Route 66' television episode 'Goodnight Sweet Blues' (with Coleman Hawkins, Roy Eldridge, Jo Jones, etc.), also featured on the Ed Sullivan Show in 1963. In spring of 1964 suffered a mild heart attack whilst appearing at the Pasadena Playhouse, but immediately resumed work. In later years continued to sing (appeared on Pearl Bailey television show, February 1971), also active in religious propagation.

Some of Ethel Waters' many film appearances include: 'On with the Show', 'The Gift of the Gab', 'Cabin in the Sky', 'Tales of Manhattan', 'Pinky', 'The Sound and the Fury', etc. Ethel Waters' autobiography, 'His Eye Is On The Sparrow', was first published in 1951.

WATSON, Leo
vocals/drums/trombone/tipple

Born: Kansas City, Missouri, 27th February 1898
Died: Los Angeles, California, 2nd May 1950

Worked originally as a solo vocalist. Moved to New York and joined Virgil Scroggins, Buddy Burton, Wilbur and Douglas Daniels in a musical novelty act touring with the Whitman Sisters' Show (1929). The group later became known as The Spirits of Rhythm (with Teddy Bunn in place of Burton). Leo's highly individual scat singing being one of the features of the group, he also recorded with the Washboard Rhythm Kings. From spring 1937 appeared with the John Kirby Band at the Onyx, occasionally playing drums and trombone. Featured with Artie Shaw's Band, then spent eight months with Gene Krupa from April 1938. Rejoined Spirits of Rhythm in January 1939 after illness on West Coast, moved back to New York, working briefly with Jimmy Mundy Big Band late in 1939. Again with Spirits of Rhythm for World's Fair Exhibition, New York (summer of 1940) before moving to the West Coast. Out of music temporarily in 1942, then with Teddy Bunn in Los Angeles (autumn 1943), together they took part in frequent re-formations of the Spirits of Rhythm. Then worked mainly as a solo cabaret artist; briefly in duo with Slim Gaillard early in 1946. Worked as vocalist-drummer with pianist Charley Raye (1948). In hospital during early 1949, recommenced working, then succumbed to pneumonia in May 1950.

WATTERS, 'Lu' Lucious
trumpet

Born: Santa Cruz, California, 19th December 1911

Worked as a ship's musician during vacations from high school and university. Worked with various bands in California during the 1930s, including long spell with Carol Lofner. Led own big band at Sweet's Ballroom in Oakland in the late 1930s prior to forming Yerba Buena Jazz Band (which featured Turk Murphy and Bob Scobey, etc.). Led Yerba Buena Band until December 1950, except for period of service in U.S. Navy during World War II. Service in Pacific and Orient, led own Navy Band, also sat in with Teddy Weatherford's Band in India. During the early 1950s Watters left full-time music and studied geology, he later led his own band again for a short while before retiring from music in the late 1950s. Attended Turk Murphy's 65th Birthday celebrations in San Francisco, December 1980.

WATTS, Grady
trumpet/composer

Born: Texarkana, Texas, 30th June 1908

Attended Allen Military Academy in Texas and University of Oklahoma. First professional work in Louisiana, then joined Frank Tracy-Nelson Brown Band (1929). With Austin Wylie

(1930), then became featured soloist with Casa Loma Band from 1931 until 1942. Worked in artist management from 1945 until 1952 then became an executive in chemical industry, formed own company in 1968.

WATTS, Joseph V. *Born: Jackson, Mississippi. 9th November 1905*
string bass/tuba *Died: Connecticut, 1979*

First lessons from George Comfort in 1919. First gigs in Atlanta, Georgia, working with Wayman Carver's Southern Ramblers (1925), also with Harold Finley, Harold Whittington and Neal Montgomery before moving to New York City. Worked often with James P. Johnson from 1934 until 1941, during this period also with Billy Fowler, Billy Butler, Adrian Rollini, Fess Williams, etc., also played club dates with Jelly Roll Morton, but did not record with Morton, did, however, record with Clarence Williams. After working with Fess Williams in 1937 left full-time music and became a restaurant owner in New London, Connecticut.

WAYLAND, 'Hank' Frederic Gregson *Born: Fall River, near Bedford, Massachusetts,*
string bass *21st January 1906*

Taught to read music by his father, later played in high school band. Moved to New York in 1926, played in various theatre and studio orchestras, then whilst working with Earl Carpenter's Band in New York was signed by Benny Goodman (early 1934), left later that year. Also did some studio work with Artie Shaw (1936), Bunny Berigan, Tommy Dorsey, Larry Clinton, etc. With Bob Chester Band 1941-2, then moved to West Coast early in 1943. Worked briefly in Eddie Miller's Big Band, then did extensive studio work, combining this with gigs for various leaders including Wingy Manone, Mike Riley, etc.

WEATHERFORD, Teddy *Born: Bluefield, West Virginia, 11th October 1903*
piano/arranger *Died: Calcutta, India, 25th April 1945*

Lived in New Orleans from 1915 until 1920; during this time learnt to play piano. Moved to Chicago, extensive gigging, then regular work with Jimmie Wade and Erskine Tate. Sailed to the Orient with Jack Carter's Orchestra in August 1926. Remained to work in the Far East, led own band in Singapore, Manila, Shanghai, etc. Brief return to U.S.A. in 1934 to recruit Buck Clayton's Big Band for residency at Candidrome, Shanghai. Except for visit to the Paris International Exposition (summer 1937) during which Hugues Panassié arranged recordings, he worked in Asia for the rest of his life; his band played for a long residency at the Grand Hotel, Calcutta, also appeared in Bombay, Ceylon, etc. Made a number of recordings whilst in India, some under his own name, others as featured accompanist for various popular artists including: American singer Bob Lee, violinist Zarata, and singer Paquita. Died of cholera in the Presidency General Hospital, Calcutta. (During 1937 also worked in Sweden.)

WEBB, 'Chick' William Henry *Born: Baltimore, Maryland, 10th February 1909*
drums *Died: Baltimore, Maryland, 16th June 1939*

Overcame physical deformity caused by tuberculosis of the spine. Bought first set of drums from his earnings as a newspaper boy. Joined local boys' band at the age of 11, later (together with John Trueheart) worked in the Jazzola Orchestra, playing mainly on pleasure steamers. Moved to New York (c. 1925), subsequently worked briefly in Edgar Dowell's Orchestra. In 1926 led own five-piece band at The Black Bottom Club, New York, for five-month residency. Later led own eight-piece at the Paddock Club before leading own Harlem Stompers at Savoy Ballroom from January 1927. Added three more musicians for stint at Rose Danceland (from December 1927). Worked mainly in New York during the late 1920s—several periods of inactivity—but during 1928 and 1929 played various venues including Strand Roof, Roseland, Cotton Club (July 1929), etc. During the early 1930s played the Roseland, Savoy Ballroom, and toured with the 'Hot Chocolates' revue. From late 1931 the band began playing long regular seasons at the Savoy Ballroom (later fronted by Bardu Ali). They continued to play theatre dates and tours and also did a season at the Casino de Paris, New York, in 1934 (in late 1932 the band did a series of theatre dates accompanying Louis Armstrong). By the mid-1930s Chick Webb's name was virtually synonymous with the Savoy Ballroom, in 1935 he introduced his new vocaliste, Ella Fitzgerald. The band also did regular far-ranging tours. During the summer of 1938 they broke several all-time attendance records at ballrooms and theatres, by then Chick's health had begun to fail. He left hospital in November 1938 and began a tour of Texas, he was stricken by pleurisy and again entered hospital until January 1939. He continued to appear regularly with the band until shortly before his death, playing his last engagement on a big riverboat sailing out of Washington. He died in the Johns Hopkins Hospital in Baltimore, shortly after undergoing a major urological operation. The personnel of the band remained together to work for a while under Ella Fitzgerald's leadership. In 1947 a memorial recreation centre, dedicated to the memory of Chick Webb, was opened in Baltimore. Showman Bardu Ali (from Wavesland, Mississippi) was for several years employed by Chick Webb to front the band and act as master of ceremonies.

WEBB, 'Speed' Lawrence Arthur *Born: Peru, Indiana, 18th July 1906*
leader/drums/vocals

Played violin and mellophone as a child, then switched to drums. Gained nickname by his skill as a baseball pitcher. In 1923 did gigs in small local hotel band with pianist Darrel Harris, then left Indiana to study embalming at the University of Illinois. Returned home in 1925 and became a founder-member of the Hoosier Melody Lads—which he subsequently led. During the summers of 1925 and 1926 played residencies at Forest Park, Toledo, Ohio, played at Valley Inn early in 1926 and recorded a session for Gennett in April 1926. Later that year moved to California, where the band played successful residencies in Los Angeles and Culver City, also took part in several films. Speed usually fronted the band, but occasionally played drums. In 1929 left California and formed a new band, using the nucleus of band led by saxist Leonard Gay. Continued leading this unit for touring and residencies until 1931. In late 1931 fronted new band The Hollywood Blue Devils. From 1932 until 1935 Speed Webb regularly fronted other bands for specific engagements; bands billed under his name included The Dixie Rhythm Kings, The Brown Buddies, and Jack Jackson's Pullman Porters. After leading in Cincinnati in the winter of 1937-8, Speed left music and completed his studies, gaining Master's degree in embalming (1942). Lived in South Bend, Indiana, for many years, running own mortician's business, also took an active interest in local politics and contributed regularly to the *Indiana Herald.*

Speed Webb's former sidemen include: Vic Dickenson, Roy Eldridge, Teddy Buckner, Henderson Chambers, Teddy Wilson, Art Tatum, Fitz Weston, etc., etc.

WEBSTER, 'Ben' Benjamin Francis *Born: Kansas City, Missouri, 27th March 1909*
tenor sax/occasionally piano/arranger *Died: Amsterdam, Holland, 20th September 1973*

First studied violin, then piano. Attended Wilberforce College. Played piano in a silent-movie house in Amarillo, Texas. First professional work with Bretho Nelson's Bànd (out of Enid, Oklahoma), then, still on piano, with Dutch Campbell's Band. Received early saxophone tuition from Budd Johnson. Joined family band led by W. H. Young (Lester's father) in Campbell Kirkie, New Mexico, toured with the band for three months and began specialising on sax. With Gene Coy's Band on alto and tenor (early 1930), then on tenor with Jap Allen's Band (summer 1930). With Blanche Calloway from April 1931, then joined Bennie Moten from winter 1931-2 until early 1933 (including visit to New York). In 1933 worked with Andy Kirk at Fairyland Park, Kansas City, moved to New York and joined Fletcher Henderson in July 1934. Later that year worked with Benny Carter, then joined Willie Bryant. Flew to Toronto to join Cab Calloway; with Cab from spring of 1936 until July 1937. Brief return to Kansas City, then rejoined Fletcher Henderson in Chicago (autumn 1937). Briefly with Stuff Smith and Roy Eldridge Band in 1938, then with Teddy Wilson's Big Band from April 1939 until January 1940. Joined Duke Ellington in Boston (January 1940); Ben had previously worked with Duke for two brief spells in 1935 and 1936. Left Duke in 1943. Led own band on 52nd Street, short stay in Sid Catlett's Band (early 1944), with Raymond Scott on C.B.S. and two months with John Kirby (June-July 1944). Brief spell with

Stuff Smith early in 1945, but from October 1944 mostly led own small groups for various residencies including: Spotlite and Three Deuces in New York and at Garrick Bar in Chicago (also guested with Henry Allen's Band at the Garrick). Rejoined Duke Ellington from November 1948 until September 1949, worked with Jay McShann in Kansas City, also toured with 'Jazz At The Philharmonic'. Returned to Kansas City, worked regularly with Bob Wilson's Band and free-lanced. Moved back to New York in late 1952, led own small groups, did studio work and free-lance recordings, then lived for several years in California, occasionally returning to New York during the late 1950s for residencies at Village Vanguard, etc. From 1962 worked mainly in New York, long bookings at The Shalimar, Half Note, etc. In December 1964 moved to Europe. Used Holland as a central base for solo tours in Europe, regular visits to Great Britain. Moved to Copenhagen in the late 1960s.

Ben appeared in films with Duke Ellington, he was also in Benny Carter's Band in 'Clash by Night' (1952) and in 1967 was the subject of a film made in Holland.

WEBSTER, Freddie — *Born: Cleveland, Ohio, 1916*
trumpet — *Died: Chicago, Illinois, 1st April 1947*

Attended Central High School in Cleveland. As a teenager led own band which included pianist Tadd Dameron, also worked in band led by saxist Marion Sears (brother of Al Sears). With Earl Hines, Erskine Tate (1938). Led own band before moving to New York. With Benny Carter, Ed Durham (1940), briefly with Louis Jordan (early 1941), then rejoined Earl Hines. With Lucky Millinder (autumn 1941 to spring 1942), then with Jimmie Lunceford until summer of 1943. Rejoined Benny Carter (autumn 1943), then worked with Sabby Lewis in New York (spring 1944). Again with Lucky Millinder, then brief spells with Cab Calloway and George Johnson (summer 1945). Played in John Kirby's Sextet for six months from c. August 1945. With Dizzy Gillespie (1946), worked briefly with 'Jazz At The Philharmonic' (early 1947). Collapsed and died in a hotel room whilst preparing to work with saxist Sonny Stitt in Chicago.

WEBSTER, Paul Francis — *Born: Kansas City, Missouri, 24th August 1909*
trumpet — *Died: New York City, 6th May 1966*

Tuition from his uncle, trumpeter Sam Ford. Attended Lincoln High School and gigged with band led by Clarence Lover (1925). Went to Fisk University and played with the Memphis band, The Boston Serenaders (1926), returned to Kansas City and worked as an embalmer before becoming a professional musician. Gigged with George E. Lee's Band and played with Bennie Moten regularly from summer of 1927 until summer of 1928—made brief returns to Moten's Band until the early 1930s. With Jap Allen (c. 1930), Jimmie Lunceford (1931), Tommy Douglas (c. 1931), and Eli Rice (1933-4). Joined Jimmie Lunceford in spring of 1935, left in 1944 and then began working for Cab Calloway; worked on and off with Cab in the late 1940s and early 1950s. With Charlie Barnet (1946-7), Sy Oliver (1947), briefly with Perez Prado, then Eddie Wilcox, Count Basie (in New York, spring 1950). Again with Charlie Barnet (1952-3), then took day job in the U.S. Immigration Service; later worked for New York subway, continued to play (and record) regularly in the early 1960s. Died of a respiratory ailment.

WEISS, 'Sammy' Samuel — *Born: New York City, 1st September 1910*
drums/vibes — *Died: Encino, California, 18th December 1977*

Began professional career in 1933, working with Al Lynn and Marty Beck at Jansen's Hoffbrau, New York. Played with Benny Goodman (1934), Tommy Dorsey (1935), Artie Shaw (1936), and Louis Prima (1937), during the 1930s and early 1940s also worked with Leo Reisman, Gene Kardos, Max Fischer, Paul Lavalle, and Paul Whiteman. Prolific free-lance recordings with: Adrian Rollini, Wingy Manone, Miff Mole, Louis Armstrong, Lil Armstrong, Johnny Guarnieri, Erskine Hawkins, Erskine Butterfield, Fred Rich, Mildred Bailey, Bob Howard, etc., etc. Moved to California in May 1945 and formed own highly successful orchestra, became a very successful bandleader, occasionally playing sessions with other leaders. Continued to lead throughout the 1960s, Hollywood Palladium, regular television programmes, etc., etc. His son, Maurice, doubled on trombone and drums.

WEISS, Sid *Born: Schenectady, N.Y., 30th April 1914*
string bass

Started on violin; played clarinet and tuba, then switched to string bass whilst at high school. At 17 worked in New York City with Joe Lefrance, then with Basil Rock Quartet in Rochester. In New York City again in 1934, subsequently worked for four months with Louis Prima, then year and a half with Wingy Manone. Briefly with Charlie Barnet, then gigged with society bands in Washington. With Artie Shaw's Band in 1936, again with Shaw from September 1937 until 1939 break-up. With Joe Marsala from November 1939, then Tommy Dorsey (March 1940 until November 1941). Worked mainly with Benny Goodman (1943-5), but also brief spells with Jerry Wald (summer 1942) and Abe Lyman (1943). In 1945 did overseas U.S.O. tour with Hal McIntyre. Mainly active as a studio musician from 1946, but also played occasionally with Eddie Condon, Joe Bushkin, and Benny Goodman (including appearance with Benny in the film 'Make Mine Music'). Prolific free-lance recordings. Moved to Los Angeles in August 1954. Worked for a tape recorder manufacturing company until 1958, did occasional sessions including spell with Paul Baron's Orchestra on the Johnny Carson television show. Continued to work in electronics until 1964, played club dates in Los Angeles, then free-lanced. Played for two weeks in Aspen, Colorado, with pianist Ralph Sutton, cornetist Ruby Braff, and Morey Feld, then in April 1968 was appointed business representative for recording department of Local 47, Musicians' Union.

WELLS, 'Dicky' William *Born: Centerville, Tennessee, 10th June 1907*
trombone/vocals/arranger/composer

Family moved to Louisville, Kentucky, in 1911. Studied music from the age of 10, played baritone horn in the Booker T. Washington Community Centre Band at 13. Trombone from the age of 16, played locally in Lucius Brown's Band, then to New York in drummer Lloyd W. Scott's Band (1926). Remained in New York with the band which was later led by Lloyd's brother Cecil Scott. Worked mainly with Cecil Scott until early 1930, then joined Elmer Snowden's Band (1930-1), appeared with Snowden in the film 'Smash Your Baggage'. Worked with Russell Wooding in 1932, also toured with Benny Carter (1932-3), brief spell with Charlie Johnson before joining Fletcher Henderson in 1933, also gigged with Chick Webb's Band at Lafayette Theatre (1933). Again with Benny Carter (early 1934), then joined Teddy Hill in September 1934 and remained with the band for trip to Europe (summer 1937). Joined Count Basie at The Famous Door in July 1938, regularly with Basie until early 1946. With J. C. Heard's Band in New York until joining Willie Bryant in June 1946, with Sy Oliver's Band (late 1946-7). Rejoined Count Basie from 1947 until 1950, then worked in Jimmy Rushing's Band before going to France in October 1952, toured Europe with Bill Coleman's Swing Stars. Returned to New York in February 1953, worked with Lucky Millinder (autumn 1953), briefly with Earl Hines in 1954, then free-lancing with various leaders, mainly in New York. Toured Europe in autumn 1959 and spring 1961 with Buck Clayton's All Stars. Joined Ray Charles' Big Band in November 1961 for 18 months. During summer of 1963 worked in Reuben Phillips' Band at The Apollo, New York. Toured Europe as a soloist in 1965. Continued to play regularly with various leaders, mainly in New York. After 1937 regularly led own recording bands, also appeared on many free-lance recordings. In late 1968 toured Europe with Buddy Tate's Band, played at New Orleans Jazz Fest in June 1969. Left full-time music, but continued to gig. 'The Night People' by Dicky Wells was first published in 1971. Was seriously injured in a mugging incident during 1976, but recovered and resumed playing. Toured Europe with Earle Warren and Claude Hopkins (1978). Continued to play during the early 1980s, often with Bobby Booker's Big Band.

WELLS, Henry James
trombone/vocals

Born: Dallas, Texas, 1906

Studied music at Fisk University and at Cincinnati Conservatory. In 1926 played in the Boston Serenaders (from Memphis), then worked with Jimmie Lunceford from 1929 until early 1935, during this period also worked briefly with Claude Hopkins and Cab Calloway. With Andy Kirk from 1936 until 1939, left to form own short-lived big band, worked briefly with Gene Krupa and Teddy Hill, then rejoined Andy Kirk in September 1940, regularly featured as vocalist. After service in U.S. Army during World War II, briefly with Andy Kirk, then worked in Rex Stewart's Band (spring 1946). With Sy Oliver's Band from late 1946 until 1948. In the 1960s worked in California.

WELLS, Johnny
drums

Born: Kentucky. c. 1905
Died: New York, 25th November 1965

Originally a vocalist/comedian/dancer, after working as an entertainer at the Apex Club, Chicago, he replaced Ollie Powers as drummer/vocalist with Jimmie Noone's Band. Worked with Bert Hall's Orchestra (c. 1927), then rejoined Jimmie Noone, worked mainly with Noone until the early 1930s. Moved to New York. Member of Joe Sullivan's Band in late 1939, also did free-lance recordings.

WELLS, Viola—known as 'Miss Rhapsody'
vocals

Born: Newark, New Jersey, 1902

First worked at Minis Theatre in Newark. Toured with travelling shows during the 1920s. Worked with Banjo Bernie's Band in the early 1930s prior to touring with Ida Cox's troupe. Led own group in Kansas City, ran own club and organised talent shows there c. 1937-38. Moved back to Newark. During the 1940s played many club dates in N.Y.C. including long residency at Kelly's Stables, also played dates at The Apollo and other theatres billed as Viola Underhill. Period of semi-retirement until the mid-1960s, recommenced recording. During the 1970s did widespread international touring with Clyde Bernhardt's Band.

WEST, 'Doc' Harold
drums

Born: Woolford, North Dakota, 12th August 1915
Died: Cleveland, Ohio, 4th May 1951

Played piano, cello, then drums. Joined Tiny Parham in 1932, also worked in Chicago with Erskine Tate and Roy Eldridge. In late 1938 deputised for Chick Webb (then ill with pleurisy) during band tour of Texas. With Hot Lips Page intermittently from September 1939 until 1941, during this time also did regular gigs at Minton's in New York, also deputised for Jo Jones in Count Basie's Band (early 1940). During the 1940s played on many small band recordings, also worked with Don Byas, Slam Stewart, Lester Young, Errol Garner, etc. Suffered a fatal heart attack whilst working in Roy Eldridge's Band.

WESTON, Fitz
piano

Born: Georgia. c. 1904
Died: New York City, 2nd January 1961

Doubled on several instruments early in his career. Played in travelling carnivals before joining Speed Webb in 1925. Left two years later to work in California with Red Spikes. Rejoined Webb in 1928, then worked in Los Angeles with Paul Howard. With Eddie White in Newark (1930-2), Eugene Kennedy's Band (1932-3), Sam Wooding (1933-4). Gigged with Louis Jordan before becoming accompanist to vocaliste Amanda Randolph (1935-8). Did trio work during the late 1930s, then led own band and played solo residencies. With Earl Bostic (1947-8), did regular U.S.O. tours and solo residencies during the 1950s.

WETHINGTON, Arthur Crawford
saxes/vocals

Born: Chicago, Illinois, 26th January 1908

Studied at Chicago College of Music. Worked with Lottie Hightower's Night Hawks in Chicago (c. 1925), then long spell with Carroll Dickerson, travelled to New York in band accompanying Louis Armstrong (1929). With the Mills Blue Rhythm Band from 1930 until 1936, then joined Edgar Hayes (1937). Left full-time playing, but continued to teach music. During the 1960s was a supervisor at a New York transit system power plant.

WETTLING, George Godfrey
drums

Born: Topeka, Kansas, 28th November 1907
Died: New York City, 6th June 1968

Lived in Chicago from the age of 14. Attended Calumet High School, was taught drums by Earl Wiley and Roy Knapp, inspired by Baby Dodds. Became professional musician in 1924, for the next 10 years worked for many leaders (mainly in Chicago) including: Elmo Mack, Floyd Town, Danny Altier, Seattle Harmony Kings, Louis Panico, Joe Kayser, Earl Maze, Art Jarrett, Jack Chapman, David Rose, Ralph Williams, Sol Wagner, etc. In 1935 worked briefly with Paul Mares, then joined band specially formed in America by English maestro Jack Hylton. Sat in with Wingy Manone in New York, continued touring with Hylton until the unit disbanded, then returned to Chicago and worked with Maurice Stein before joining Wingy Manone in Pittsburgh (1936). Settled in New York, joined Artie Shaw's first big band, left in March 1937 and joined Bunny Berigan until December 1937. With Red Norvo from January until December 1938, then joined Paul Whiteman, remained with Whiteman until March 1941—during this period worked briefly with Bobby Hackett and Muggsy Spanier and did free-lance recordings. Brief spells with Jimmy McPartland, Joe and Marty Marsala before joining band fronted by comedian Chico Marx (musical director: Ben Pollack). Worked with Benny Goodman (July 1943) and Abe Lyman (autumn 1943), regular appearances with Miff Mole's Band (1943-4). From 1943 until 1952 was a staff musician at the A.B.C. studios—during this period did many jazz gigs including long spells at Eddie Condon's Club, again with Paul Whiteman (August 1945). Briefly out of action in summer 1946 through broken arm. From 1953 led own small groups in New York, worked with Jimmy McPartland at The Metropole (1954), played many sessions with Eddie Condon during the 1950s, toured Great Britain with Condon in January 1957. Active as a free-lance musician, regular recording sessions and jazz festival appearances. With Muggsy Spanier occasionally in 1959 and 1960. Brief tour with Bud Freeman (autumn 1960); regular playing trips to Toronto during the 1960s, toured briefly with the Dukes of Dixieland. During the last years of his life led own trio at the Gaslight Club in New York, also worked in Clarence Hutchenrider's Trio. From the 1940s George devoted time to oil-painting; several exhibitions of his works were held in New York. He died of lung cancer in the Roosevelt Hospital, New York City, his burial took place in the Cedar Park Cemetery, Chicago.

WHALEY, Wade
clarinet

Born: New Orleans, Louisiana, 1895

Originally played string bass and guitar, then clarinet (taught by Lorenzo Tio Jr.). First work on clarinet with Armand Piron's Orchestra at the Temple Theatre, subsequently worked with the Crescent Band, Buddie Petit, Manuel Perez, Kid Ory, and John Robichaux. Formed own band in 1916, left to join Jelly Roll Morton in Los Angeles (1917), then returned to New Orleans and led own band in Bucktown. Moved back to the West Coast in November 1919 to join Kid Ory. Led own band, but worked regularly with Kid Ory from 1922. After Ory moved to Chicago (1925) Whaley formed own Black and Tan Jazz Hounds and achieved great success during the late 1920s. In the early 1930s played in pit orchestra at the Capitol Burlesque Hall in San Francisco, then from 1934 left full-time music to work in the shipyards at San Jose. Began working regularly on clarinet after appearing with the All-Star New Orleans Band in San Francisco (May 1943). In April 1944 (immediately after the death of Jimmie Noone) took part in broadcast with Kid Ory, this served to introduce him to a wider public and during the next few years continued to play regularly, taking part in several recording sessions.

WHEELER, E. B. De Priest
trombone

Born: Kansas City, Missouri, 1st March 1903

Played trumpet and mellophone in Knights of Pythias Band whilst attending Lincoln High

School in Kansas City, journeyed to St. Louis with the Knights of Pythias Band in 1917. Returned to Kansas City, worked in a local dance hall for a year, then in 1918 played in band resident at the Chauffeur's Club in St. Louis. With Dave Lewis' Jazz Boys in Kansas City, then toured with a circus band until 1922. Joined Wilson Robinson's Syncopators in St. Louis (1923) and toured the Pantages Circuit from Chicago to California with that band. The band settled in New York early in 1925 and were renamed The Cotton Club Orchestra, subsequently they worked under the leadership of violinist Andrew Preer until his death in 1927. Later on the group became known as The Missourians, and from 1930 worked as Cab Calloway's Band. Remained with Cab Calloway until January 1940 (including trip to Europe in 1934). Worked for the postal authorities for many years, but continued to play part-time with bands and orchestras.

WHETSOL, 'Artie' Arthur Parker
trumpet

Born: Punta Gorda, Florida, 1905
Died: New York City, 5th January 1940

Surname was originally Schiefe; Whetsol was his mother's maiden name. Raised in Washington, D.C. Boyhood friend of Duke Ellington, worked on many jobs with Duke Ellington from 1920, also did local work with Claude Hopkins and with the White Brothers' Orchestra. With Duke Ellington in New York for a short spell in late 1923, then returned to Washington to study medicine at Howard University. Rejoined Duke early in 1928 and remained with the band until forced to retire through illness in October 1937. He made several efforts to rejoin the band on a regular basis, but the advanced condition of his brain illness made this impossible.

WHITBY, 'Doc' Francis
reeds

Born: Oklahoma City, Oklahoma, 7th January 1911

Early efforts on violin then switched to tenor sax whilst in high school. Local gigs with pianist Wesley Manning then joined E. W. Perry's Orchestra (1928). Worked with Gene Coy's Happy Black Ace, and with Art Bronson's Bostonians before touring with King Oliver. Left Oliver in 1933. With Henry Walker's Orchestra and Buddy Conway's Band before briefly rejoining King Oliver (1934). Worked in Ohio then joined Erskine Tate in Chicago (1935), later that year worked briefly in Brazil with a Latin band, returned to Chicago and joined Jimmie Noone. Moved to New York (1936), toured with Eddie Mallory, then worked with Eddie Johnson's Crackerjacks (1937). Briefly with Erskine Hawkins, then worked with Dee 'Prince' Stewart in Kansas City. With Nat Towles (late 1938), Red Perkins, Lloyd Hunter (1939), Bob Dorsey, Horace Henderson (1940). Sailed to Hawaii with Andrew Blakeney (1941). Served in U.S. Army (1942-1944). Briefly with Erskine Hawkins then retired from full-time music and worked as an electrician.

WHITE, Amos M.
cornet

Born: Kingstree, South Carolina, 6th November 1889

Orphaned at the age of nine, entered Jenkins' Orphanage in Charleston, South Carolina. Began playing cornet, later toured with the orphanage band; studied at the Benedict College, South Carolina, then returned to the orphanage, did some teaching there, also more touring. From 1913 until 1918 worked with circus shows and minstrel bands. Served in the 816th Pioneer Infantry Band in France (1918-19), then settled in New Orleans, worked as a type-setter, but gigged with many leaders: Papa Celestin, Armand Piron, George Moret, and with The Excelsior. Led own band at The Spanish Fort before joining Fate Marable on the S.S. 'Capitol'. Worked on and off with Marable until 1924, worked with The Alabamians (under Ed Howard) in 1925. Then toured with Mamie Smith (1927), led Georgia Minstrels (1928), then with Harvey's Radio Minstrels (1928). Settled in Phoenix, Arizona, worked with Bradley's Dublin Orchestra (1929), then led own band and worked with Gregorio Goyer, W. Gills, Felipe Lopez, etc. Moved to Oakland, California, in 1934, ran own part-time band and did local gigs. Owned own print shop for many years, during the 1960s continued to play occasional dates with marching bands.

WHITE, 'Father' Harry Alexander
trombone/saxes/cornet/arranger/composer

Born: Bethlehem, Pennsylvania, 1st June 1898
Died: New York City, 14th August 1962

His brothers, Willie (trumpet-sax) and Eddie (piano), and his cousins, Gilbert (tenor sax/clarinet) and Morris (sax/piano), became professional musicians. Harry began his musical career as a drummer, played with various shows on the Keith Circuit from the age of 16. Settled in Washington, D.C. (c. 1919) and began specialising on trombone, did local gigs with Duke Ellington and Claude Hopkins, then with other members of the family formed the White Brothers' Orchestra. They did several seasons at the Roadside Inn, Philadelphia, from 1925, when not working with the orchestra Harry usually played in New York. Worked with June Clark's Revue Band and Elmer Snowden. Joined drummer George Howe's Band at The Nest Club, New York (1927) and thus became a member of Luis Russell's band, left Luis Russell in August 1928. Led own band in Newark during winters 1929-31, also led at The Nest Club. Played for several weeks in Duke Ellington's Cotton Club Orchestra until replaced by Juan Tizol (August 1929), then led own band at The Nest. With Cab Calloway in 1931, then became joint-director of the Mills Blue Rhythm Band (with Edgar Hayes). Rejoined Cab Calloway from June 1932 until early 1935 (except for trip to Europe in 1934). Whilst with Calloway he invented the word 'jitterbug' to describe a victim of delirium tremens. With Luis Russell (1935), Louis Armstrong's Orchestra (1935-6), then left full-time playing for a while, continued to arrange and compose. Worked on alto sax and trombone with Manzie Johnson's Band at the Palace (late 1938), then played and arranged for Hot Lips Page's Band (1938). With Edgar Hayes (late 1940), also arranged for Bud Freeman's Big Band (1940). Suffered a long layoff due to illness, but resumed part-time playing from 1947. Worked at a New York bank until shortly before his death, continued gigging and arranging through the 1950s including residency at Small's with Happy Caldwell in 1953.

WHITE, 'Fruit' Morris
guitar

Born: St. Louis, Missouri, 17th January 1911

Came from a musical family; his brother, Baxter, had his own musical act, The Pebbles, in the 1920s and 1930s. Began playing banjo during childhood, lived in Peoria, Illinois. Began doubling on guitar, moved back to St. Louis, joined Charlie Creath playing aboard the S.S. 'St. Paul' (1926). Worked with Dewey Jackson at the Chauffeur's Club, St. Louis (1927), then accompanied Ethel Waters in the touring show 'Africana'. In 1928, on the death of Charley Stamps, joined The Missourians, remained when the band became Cab Calloway's Orchestra, remained with Cab until 1940 (including trip to Europe in spring 1934). Briefly with Lionel Hampton (c. 1941), then service in U.S. Army including duty in South Pacific. In 1945 was given medical discharge, a persistent skin complaint forced him to retire from professional playing. Moved to St. Louis, ran own night club for a while, then organised own novelty business. Was at one time married to W. C. Handy's daughter, Elizabeth.

WHITE, 'Hy' Hyman
guitar

Born: Boston, Massachusetts, 17th December 1915

Played violin from the age of 11, changed to guitar at 17. Led own band and also worked with Rollie Rogers and Ted Rolfe before joining Woody Herman late in 1939, remained with Woody until joining Les Brown in 1944. Took part in many free-lance recordings during the 1940s and 1950s, mainly active as a studio musician and teacher during the 1960s. Lived in Riverdale, N.Y.

WHITE, 'Sonny' Ellerton Oswald
piano

Born: Panama, 11th November 1917
Died: New York City, 28th April 1971

Piano from the age of eight, became professional musician at the age of 18. Early work with Jesse Stone, then with Willie Bryant (1937) and Teddy Hill (1938). Regular accompanist for Billie Holiday (1939), later that year worked with Frankie Newton. Began long association with Benny Carter in February 1940, worked briefly with Artie Shaw in 1941, then regularly with Benny Carter until spending two years in U.S. Army (1943-5). Rejoined Benny Carter early in 1946, worked with Hot Lips Page in 1947, then from 1947 until 1954 played residency at Cinderella Club, New York, in band led by trumpeter Harvey Davis. In December 1954 joined Wilbur de Paris and worked regularly in that band until the early 1960s (including trip to Africa in 1957). From 1963 until 1967 worked mainly with Louis Metcalf at the Ali Baba, New York. With Eddie Barefield's Trio in late 1968. Joined Jonah Jones in April 1969.

WHITEMAN, Paul
leader/violin

Born: Denver, Colorado, 28th March 1890
Died: Doylestown, Pennsylvania, 29th December 1967

His father, Wilberforce J. Whiteman, was noted music teacher. Began playing violin at the age of seven, later studied viola. Played in the Denver Symphony Orchestra from 1912. Moved to San Francisco in 1915, worked in the World's Fair Orchestra and eventually joined the San Francisco Symphony Orchestra. Brief service in U.S. Navy during World War I. In 1919 was voted leader of the band at the Fairmont Hotel, San Francisco, later led in Los Angeles (December 1919) before moving to Atlantic City and New York in 1920 and gaining a national reputation. Toured Europe with his orchestra in 1923 and 1926; on 24th February 1924 'An Experiment in Modern Music' concert held at the Aeolian Hall in New York featured the orchestra. He continued to regularly lead large musical aggregations until the early 1940s. Though known as the 'King of Jazz' (following an extensive publicity campaign which culminated in the release of a Universal picture bearing that name) he is chiefly known to jazz fans as the employer of soloists such as Bix Beiderbecke, Bunny Berigan, Tommy and Jimmy Dorsey, Ed Lang, Andy Secrest, Frank Trumbauer, Jack and Charlie Teagarden, Joe Venuti, etc., etc. and vocalists Bing Crosby, Red McKenzie, Mildred Bailey, etc. Paul Whiteman re-formed his orchestra on several occasions during the 1940s and 1950s, but during this period was mainly occupied as a director of the American Broadcasting Company. In 1960 he led in Las Vegas and briefly led orchestra in 1962, but the last few years of his life were spent in virtual retirement, though he did occasionally make public appearances. Paul Jr. played drums with the orchestra in 1946. Featured in many films.

WHYTE, Zack
leader/banjo/arranger

Born: Richmond, Kentucky, 1898
Died: Kentucky, 10th March 1967

Studied at Wilberforce, Ohio, and worked in student band led by Horace Henderson (1922). Formed first band (c. 1923). During the late 1920s and 1930s led own highly successful 'Chocolate Beau Brummels' which at various times included: Floyd Brady, Herman Chittison, Vic Dickenson, Roy Eldridge, Quentin Jackson, Sy Oliver, Al Sears, etc.

WIGGS, Johnny
(real name: John Wigginton Hyman)
cornet

Born: New Orleans, Louisiana, 25th July 1899
Died: New Orleans, 9th October 1977

Originally played mandolin and violin; bought first cornet during childhood. Worked on violin in New York theatre orchestra, c. 1924. Returned to New Orleans, specialised on cornet. Worked with Norman Brownlee, Happy Schilling, Earl Crumb, Tony Parenti, Jimmy McGuire, Ellis Stratakos. Led own recording band (1927), also toured with vaudeville band, and worked briefly with Peck Kelley in Shreveport (1925). Left full-time music in the early 1930s and became a schoolteacher. Recommenced playing in the late 1940s, active member of the New Orleans Jazz Society. Taught music, also did many recording sessions and regular broadcasts. Ceased regular playing in 1960, but from 1965 onwards played occasional gigs; featured at New Orleans Jazz Fest (June 1969).

WILBORN, 'Dave' David Buckley
banjo/guitar/vocals

Born: Springfield, Ohio, 11th April 1904
Died: Detroit, Michigan, 25th April 1982

Began playing piano at the age of 12; his tutor's father played banjo and he became more interested in banjo than piano, abandoned piano studies at 14 and concentrated on banjo. In 1922 began playing with Cecil and Lloyd Scott's Band in and around Springfield. Sat in with McKinney's Synco Septette and was hired on the spot. Played with the band at Manitou Beach, Wisconsin, and Club Lido, Toledo, subsequently in Detroit the band became known as McKinney's Cotton Pickers. Regular member until 1934, then continued to work on and off with McKinney until 1937. In 1938 acted as master of ceremonies at the Melody Club, Detroit, then formed own sextet (switched to guitar), continued leading until 1950. Left full-time music, worked from 1950 until 1953 for the *Pittsburgh Courier* offices in Detroit. From September 1972 was featured vocalist with the New McKinney's Cotton Pickers. He collapsed and died whilst singing with that band at the Royalty House, in Warren, Detroit.

WILCOX, 'Eddie' Edwin Felix
piano/arranger

Born: Method, near Raleigh, North Carolina, 27th December 1907
Died: New York City, 29th September 1968

Played piano in local bands whilst at high school. Gained degree in music at Fisk University (1927), there first met Jimmie Lunceford, began gigging with his campus band. During summer of 1927 worked with drummer Beaty Connel in Belmar, New Jersey, during following summer did a season at Asbury Park. Joined Lunceford full-time in June 1929. Worked with the band (and did many arrangements) until Lunceford's death in 1947. Co-led the band with tenorist Joe Thomas for a while, then from January 1949 became sole leader. Continued leading during the early 1950s, then concentrated on solo and trio work. Played for almost 10 years at the Cafe Riviera, New York, then did residencies at the Garden Cafe, Banjo Inn, Broken Drum, Pink Poodle, etc. Did occasional gigs with jazz groups in New York, also, with Teddy McRae, ran the Raecox Record Co. During the summer of 1968 worked in Canada with band led by 'Big Chief' Russell Moore.

WILCOX, 'Spiegle' Newell
trombone

Born: Sherburne, New York, 2nd May 1903

Was originally taught valve-trombone by his father, played in Cortland school band. Changed to slide-trombone whilst at Manlius Military Academy (1918). Quit Manlius in 1920 joined Al Deisseroth Orchestra in Syracuse. Worked with Tige Jewett (1922) and Bob Causer's Big Four (1922-23), remained with this group when they became Paul Whiteman's Collegians (1924). Worked with Lakeside Park Band in Auburn, New York (1925), then played briefly in California Ramblers before joining Jean Goldkette (October 1925). Brief spell with Henry Thies Band then returned to Goldkette until June 1927. Went into family business, but also led own successful band in Syracuse area for many years. Took part in April 1975 Carnegie Hall tribute to Bix Beiderbecke, and thereafter played at many festivals both in the U.S.A. and in Europe.

WILEY, Lee
vocals/composer

Born: Fort Gibson, Oklahoma, 9th October 1915
Died: New York, 11th December 1975

Studied in Tulsa, Oklahoma, later moved to New York, sang in the Paramount Show (c. 1930), joined Leo Reisman at the Central Park Casino (c. 1931). Began regular radio work with Reisman and continued with radio series after leaving Reisman in 1933, later did radio shows with Paul Whiteman, Willard Robison, etc. Recorded with Johnny Green, The Casa Loma Band, and Victor Young—co-composed several numbers with Young including: 'Got the South in My Soul', 'Anytime, Anyday, Anywhere', and 'Eerie Moan'. During the late 1930s and early 1940s did a series of recordings (with all-star accompaniment) featuring compositions by George Gershwin, Cole Porter, Rodgers and Hart, and Harold Arlen. In June 1943 married Jess Stacy, their marriage lasted for five years, during the mid-1940s, Lee sang with Stacy's short-lived big band. Subsequently worked as a solo artiste, made occasional television and radio appearances. One of her early compositions, 'Anytime, Anyday, Anywhere', became a hit single through the Joe Morris-Laurie Tate recording, in 1963 a semi-biographical film of Lee's life was given world-wide television showings. Last public engagement was at Newport Festival, 1972.

WILLIAMS, 'Bearcat' John Overton — *Born: Memphis, Tennessee, 13th April 1905*
saxes/clarinet

High School in Kansas City, Missouri, gigged with local bands, then joined Paul Banks in 1922. Led own band from 1923 until 1928 (during this time he married Mary Lou Burleigh—they subsequently divorced in the early 1940s). In 1928 joined Terrence Holder's Band in Oklahoma City, a year later became founder-member of Andy Kirk's Band. Remained with Kirk until early 1939, left music temporarily until 1942 when he joined Cootie Williams' Big Band on alto and baritone. Ceased full-time playing many years ago.

Not to be confused with the alto sax player of the same name who worked and recorded with Cecil and Lloyd Scott—that musician, who died in 1932, was from Kentucky.

WILLIAMS, Clarence — *Born: Plaquemine Delta, Louisiana, 8th October 1898*
piano/vocals/arranger/composer/leader — *Died: Queens, New York, 6th November 1965*

Son of bass-player Dennis Williams. Clarence was married to Eva Taylor from 1921 until the time of his death; their daughter, Irene, did professional work as a singer. Family moved to New Orleans in 1906. At the age of 12 Clarence ran away with Billy Kersand's Minstrel Show, working as a master of ceremonies and singer. Returned to New Orleans and began concentrating on playing the piano, some tuition from Mrs. Ophelia Gould Smith. By 1913 had begun composing. Toured vaudeville circuits as a dancer, also did extensive touring in duo with Armand Piron, they toured briefly with W. C. Handy (c. 1917). Formed publishing company with Piron, when this broke up Williams moved to Chicago where he opened his own music store near to the Vendome Theatre. Later opened other shops in Chicago before moving to New York where he organised his own highly successful publishing company. Shared credit with Spencer Williams (no relation) on many successful tunes. During the 1920s and 1930s organised countless recording sessions, he played piano on many of these sessions, but sometimes acted solely as director. Was 'race-record' judge for Okeh recording company from 1923-8, occasionally led own bands at various venues, usually in and around New York, also appeared regularly on radio programmes, sometimes in company with Eva Taylor, sometimes as solo vocalist, pianist, and jug-player. Concentrated on composing from late 1930s, sold publishing catalogue to Decca in 1943 for a reputed $50,000. Ran own bargain store in New York for many years. Lost his sight after being knocked down by a taxi in 1956, but continued to work until shortly before his death. A prolific composer, his works include: 'Baby Won't You Please Come Home?', 'Royal Garden Blues', 'West Indies Blues', etc.

WILLIAMS, 'Cootie' Charles Melvin — *Born: Mobile, Alabama, 24th July 1910*
trumpet

Raised by an aunt after his mother (a pianiste) had died when Cootie was eight years old. Played in school band on trombone, tuba, and drums. Taught himself to play trumpet, then lessons from Charles Lipskin, began to do local gigs with Holman's Jazz Band and Johnny Pope's Band. At 14 did one summer tour with Young Family Band (with Lester and Lee). Moved to Pensacola, Florida (in company of Edmond Hall) and joined band led by Eagle Eye Shields, subsequently joined Alonzo Ross De Luxe Syncopators in 1926. Except for brief absence, worked with Alonzo Ross all through 1927; with the band to New York in spring of 1928, left after two weeks in New York—18th March to 1st April 1928. Depped for Jabbo Smith on James P. Johnson recordings in June 1928, worked briefly with Arthur 'Happy' Ford and with Chick Webb at the Savoy Ballroom. Briefly with Fletcher Henderson early in 1929, then joined Duke Ellington. Remained with Duke until November 1940, then joined Benny Goodman until October 1941 (Cootie had originally appeared with Benny Goodman at Carnegie Hall Concert in January 1938). Formed own big band, long residencies at Savoy Ballroom during 1940s, cut down to small band in 1948. After the Savoy closed, Cootie toured as a single; later formed own quartet. Toured Europe with own small band early in 1959. Returned to Benny Goodman briefly from late July 1962, then rejoined Duke Ellington in autumn of 1962, except for short breaks until Duke's death (1974), worked with Mercer Ellington's Band (1975). Continued to play during the late 1970s, including engagements in Europe.

WILLIAMS, Courtney
trumpet/arranger

Born: Asbury Park, New Jersey, 29th March 1916

Began on violin at 8, switched to trumpet at 15. Played local gigs in the early 1930s. With drummer Henry Miller in New York (1935) prior to working with Charlie Skeete. Toured with bassist Al Henderson's Band (1936). During the late 1930s worked with Tommy Stevenson, Fats Waller, Hot Lips Page, Leon Gross, etc., also did free-lance recording dates. During the 1940s worked with Louis Jordan, Snub Mosley, Benny Carter, Claude Hopkins, Cecil Scott, Noble Sissle, Lee Norman, Herman Flintall, Chick Morrison, etc. Gave up full-time playing in 1947 to work for N.Y. City civil service, but continued to write arrangements for various recording bands.

WILLIAMS, 'Eddie' Edward
saxes/clarinet

Born: New York. c. 1910

Worked with Napoleon Zias and his Savoy Ramblers and Claude Hopkins during early 1930s, later led own band at the Savoy Ballroom. With Lucky Millinder (1937), Don Redman (1939). Recordings with Jelly Roll Morton (1940), then with Lucky Millinder, Ella Fitzgerald (1941). Briefly with Henry Allen and Chris Columbus Band in 1942. With De Paris Brothers on and off during 1943 and 1944, during this period also with Don Redman, Cliff Jackson Trio, James P. Johnson Band, and spell on the West Coast with Garvin Bushell Band (late 1944). In U.S. Army 1945-6 including service as a musician in Europe. After demobilisation worked with Emmett Hobson Band (1946-8), then led own small band for several years. With altoist Porter Kilbert (1955-6), continued to lead own band occasionally, also worked regularly with Happy Caldwell in the 1960s.

WILLIAMS, Elmer A.
tenor sax/clarinet

Born: Red Bank, New Jersey, 1905
Died: Red Bank, New Jersey, June 1962

Nickname was 'Tone'. With Claude Hopkins (1926-7), then joined Chick Webb, worked mainly with Chick Webb until 1934 (briefly with McKinney's Cotton Pickers in summer of 1931). Regularly with Fletcher Henderson from 1936 until 1939. Joined Horace Henderson in June 1939. With Ella Fitzgerald in 1941, subsequently with Lucky Millinder (1944-5), Claude Hopkins (1946), etc. Toured with Herbert 'Kat' Cowens in summer of 1950, later in the 1950s worked in Milan, Italy, with tenorist Freddy Mitchell's Band. In later life he suffered from diabetes; eventually he had both legs amputated, but continued to play gigs in a wheelchair.

WILLIAMS, 'Fess' Stanley R.
clarinet/saxes

Born: Danville, Kentucky, 10th April 1894
Died: New York, 17th December 1975

Brother Rudolph was also a sax/clarinet player. Fess' sons, Rudy and Phil, both played saxophone, his daughter, Estella, was a vocaliste and pianiste. He was the uncle of bassist Charles Mingus. He originally played violin; at 15 went to Tuskegee to study with Major N. Clark-Smith, doubled on various instruments, but specialised on clarinet. Moved to Cincinnati in 1914, did local gigs on sax with Frank Port's Quartet. Led own band 1919-23, then joined Ollie Powers in Chicago. Formed own band to accompany Dave and Tressie's variety act and moved with them to New York in 1924. Led own trio in Albany, then own band at Rosemont Ballroom. From 1926 to January 1928 led own Royal Flush Orchestra at the Savoy Ballroom, New York City. Moved to Chicago to front Dave Peyton's Band in 1928 (own orchestra continued to work in New York—directed by Hank Duncan and Howard Johnson). Fess returned to New York in the spring of 1929 and continued leading bands throughout the 1930s—some touring and long residencies at Savoy, Rosemont, etc. Retired from full-time music to work in real estate, but continued to lead his own small vocal and instrumental group during the 1940s, with residencies in Newark, Staten Island, Pennsylvania, etc. During the 1960s he managed the Goldenairs vocal group, but occasionally played gigs and concerts. Williams was an executive at Local 802, New York City, until 1964.

Not related to the guitarist Rudolph 'Bull' Williams.

WILLIAMS, 'Fiddler' Claude *Born: Muskogee, Oklahoma, 22nd February 1908*
violin/guitar

First professional work with Terrence Holder's Band in Tulsa, Oklahoma (1927), remained with that band when it came under Andy Kirk's leadership (1929). With Alphonso Trent (1932), George E. Lee (1933), Chick Stevens (1934-35). With Count Basie on guitar (1936-early 1937), then worked with the Four Shades of Rhythm in Chicago, Cleveland and Flint, Michigan during the late 1930s and 1940s. Worked with Austin Powell in New York City during the early 1950s, then worked with Roy Milton in Los Angeles (1952). Moved to Kansas City in 1953, and led his own band for long residencies there. During the 1970s Williams toured regularly with Jay McShann's Trio (McShann working on piano, Williams both on violin and guitar, and Paul Gunther on drums), also did solo tour of Denmark (1976). Featured soloist at many jazz festivals during the late 1970s and early 1980s.

WILLIAMS, 'Franc' Francis *Born: McConnells Mills, Pennsylvania, 20th September 1910*
trumpet *Died: Houston, Pennsylvania, 2nd October 1983*

Played trumpet in high school band. During the 1930s toured with Frank Terry's Chicago Nightingales for almost four years. Played gigs in Albany, then moved to N.Y.C. and joined Fats Waller, tour with Waller (1940). During the early 1940s worked with Claude Hopkins, Edgar Hayes, Ella Fitzgerald, Sabby Lewis, and Machito's Orchestra. With Duke Ellington from late 1945 until fall of 1949 and again in late 1951. Played in various Latin bands from 1952-57, then two years of theatre orchestra work. With Earl Coleman (1959-62) then played Broadway shows for three years. During the 1970s worked regularly in Clyde Bernhardt's Band, including overseas tours. Played solo dates in London during summer of 1978. Regularly with Panama Francis & his Savoy Sultans during the late 1970s, also worked with Harlem Blues and Jazz Band. Was the father of actor Greg Morris.

WILLIAMS, Joe *Born: Cordele, Georgia, 12th December 1918*
(real name: Joseph Goreed)
vocals

Raised in Chicago, worked as solo act during the late 1930s and 1940s, but was often featured with various bands including Jimmie Noone, Coleman Hawkins, Lionel Hampton, Andy Kirk, etc. Worked briefly with Count Basie in 1950, then worked regularly with Basie from December 1954 until January 1961. Since then has followed solo career, undertaking international tours throughout the 1960s and 1970s, during that period also played reunion dates with Count Basie, and continued to record. Was featured at New York Jazz Fest (1981).

WILLIAMS, Johnny *Born: Memphis, Tennessee, 13th March 1908*
string bass/tuba

Studied violin for three years at the Popolardors School of Music in Memphis, then switched to tuba whilst completing four years at Booker T. Washington School, Memphis. Played in local Royal Circle marching band, then did first paid work at the Palace Theatre, Memphis. Went to Atlanta, Georgia, intending to enter college, but joined Graham Jackson Orchestra shortly after enrollment (1930). Decided to become a professional musician, switched to string bass and received tuition from William Graham. Worked with Jean Calloway, Belton Society Syncopators (from Florida) and Baron Guy Orchestra in New York. Played with Billy Kyle at Memphis Club, Philadelphia, then worked with Tiny Bradshaw's Band in Baltimore. To New York in late 1936 to join Lucky Millinder. Played for a while in Claude Hopkins' Band, then with Benny Carter from late 1938. With Benny Carter and Frankie Newton in 1939, then joined Coleman Hawkins' Big Band in February 1940. With Louis Armstrong for two years from May 1940, with Teddy Wilson (1942-3), Ed Hall (late 1944-7). With Tab Smith for three years, then in Johnny Hodges' small group in 1954. Ceased touring in 1956, free-lanced in New York throughout the 1960s (sometimes on electric bass). Often played in Buddy Tate's Band, toured Europe with Buddy in late 1968.

Active musically in 1970s, including international touring with Clyde Bernhardt's Band. Worked with Harlem Blues and Jazz Band regularly during the early 1980s, also toured Europe with pianist Bob Greene (1982).

WILLIAMS, Mary Lou
(née Mary Elfrieda Scruggs)
piano/arranger/composer

Born: Atlanta, Georgia, 8th May 1910
Died: Durham, North Carolina, 28th May 1981

Moved to Pittsburgh with her mother and sister at the age of four. Soon after began playing piano; gigged around East Liberty from an early age. Studied at Lincoln High School, then toured T.O.B.A. circuit accompanying show headed by Buzzin' Harris and Arletta. Worked as Mary Lou Burleigh (taking her step-father's surname). Left to resume studies at Westinghouse Junior High School in Pittsburgh, then rejoined Buzzin' Harris (played in saxist John Williams' Syncopators). The show eventually folded in Cincinnati and the band then began touring the Keith Circuit (as The Synco Jazzers) accompanying Seymour and Jeanette. After Seymour's death (November 1926) the band briefly toured with Jeanette, then Mary Lou travelled to Memphis with John Williams (by then her husband). Played with John Williams' Band at the Pink Rose Ballroom, Memphis (1927), when Williams left to join Terrence Holder, Mary Lou became leader of the group (Jimmie Lunceford joining the band on alto sax). During the following year moved to Oklahoma City where John Williams was playing with T. Holder's Band. Mary Lou worked for a while driving a hearse in Tulsa, then moved back to Philadelphia before rejoining her husband in Kansas City, by then Andy Kirk had been voted leader of T. Holder's Band. Mary Lou began arranging for the band (first score: 'Messa Stomp') and appeared on the band's recordings, travelled with them to New York and occasionally sat in with the band for feature numbers, but did not join the band as full-time member until 1931 residency at the Pearl Theatre, Philadelphia. Briefly shared piano duties with Marion Jackson (male), then became solo pianiste for the Clouds of Joy and also its principal arranger. Remained with Andy Kirk until May 1942—except for spell in hospital (spring 1938—temporarily replaced by Kansas City pianiste Countess Margaret Johnson). During the 1930s Mary Lou also arranged for Benny Goodman, Louis Armstrong's Big Band, Earl Hines, Tommy Dorsey, Glen Gray, Gus Arnheim, etc. Divorced from John Williams, subsequently married Harold Baker and with him led small band in Cleveland and New York (1942). After Baker joined Duke Ellington, Mary Lou led own sextet for a while, then travelled with Duke Ellington as staff arranger. In November 1944 started residency at Cafe Society (Downtown) New York, and for next four years played for long spells at both Cafe Society Clubs. During this period did extensive composing and premiered her extended work 'The Zodiac Suite'. Worked briefly with Benny Goodman in summer of 1948, then residencies in California before spell at Village Vanguard until November 1949. During the early 1950s worked mostly in New York including leading own trio at Bop City, then moved to Europe in December 1952. Lived and played in England and France before moving back to the U.S.A. in December 1954. Left full-time music for almost three years and devoted considerable time to religious studies and the organisation of the Bel Canto charity organisation. In August 1957 commenced residency at the Composer Club in New York, and from then on resumed regular public appearances. In the late 1950s and through the 1960s was featured at many jazz festivals and continued composing. Many residencies in New York during the 1960s including The Embers, Joe Wells', The Hickory House, The Cookery (1970-1). Toured Europe in 1969. Continued to play regularly during the 1970s, including tours of Europe and South America. Taught at Duke University, Durham, North Carolina during the 1970s.

WILLIAMS, Midge
vocals

Born: California. c. 1908
Deceased

First public appearances with family vocal quartet in California (c. 1925), professional from 1927. During the early 1930s did extensive touring in the Orient (including Japan—where she recorded 'Dinah' and 'Lazybones' in Japanese). In 1933 played residency at the Candidrome in Shanghai, then engagements at the Imperial Hotel, Tokyo, before moving back to the U.S.A. in 1934. Radio series in Los Angeles (1934-6), toured with Fats Waller for a while, also featured on Rudy Vallee's N.B.C. radio series. From early 1938 until 1941 sang with Louis Armstrong's Big Band, then worked as a solo vocaliste.

WILLIAMS, Nelson
trumpet/vocals

Born: Birmingham, Alabama, 26th September 1917
Died: Voorburg, Holland, November 1973

Began playing piano at the age of 13, then switched to trumpet. Played briefly with Cow Cow Davenport during the early 1930s, then toured with the Trianon Crackerjacks and Brown Skin Models (1936). Moved back to Birmingham and became musical director for the Dixie Rhythm Girls. Gigged in Philadelphia, then joined Tiny Bradshaw Band (1939). During World War II served in U.S. Army and played for three years in the Pacific area with an army band. After demobilisation, played in big band led by Billy Eckstine, then worked with John Kirby and Billy Kyle's Quartet (late 1948). With Duke Ellington from autumn 1949, left in 1951 and moved to Paris in October 1951. Throughout the 1950s and 1960s worked regularly in Europe, leading own band and working as a soloist except for brief return to Duke Ellington in spring of 1956. Was given the nickname 'Cadillac' whilst working with Duke Ellington, played concerts with Duke in Europe (November 1969).

WILLIAMS, Rudy
alto sax/clarinet

Born: Newark, New Jersey, 1909
Died: September 1954

Began playing sax at the age of 12. From 1937 until June 1943 was featured with Al Cooper's Savoy Sultans, then worked with Hot Lips Page (June 1943), Luis Russell (September 1943), Chris Columbus' Band (December 1943). Formed own band in February 1944, briefly with Henry Jerome Band, then from August 1944 with Dud Bascomb's Band. Short spell with John Kirby Sextet from June 1945, then from September of that year led own band at Minton's, New York. Toured Far East with U.S.O. Show from December 1945 until July 1946. In 1947 worked with the Jazz-in-Bebop Orchestra, formed own band during following year. Led in New York (1948) and in Boston (1949-50). Reformed own band for further residencies at Hi-Hat Club, Boston (spring 1951), then worked in California with Illinois Jacquet and with tenorist Gene Ammons. From late 1951 until spring 1952 did four months' tour of service bases in Far East in band which started the tour with bassist Oscar Pettiford as leader. Returned to U.S.A. and again worked with own band and free-lanced. Lost life in an underwater swimming accident.

WILLIAMS, 'Sandy' Alexander Balos
trombone

Born: Summerville, South Carolina, 24th October 1906

During early childhood moved with his family to Washington, D.C. After both parents died he was sent to St. Joseph's Industrial School in Delaware, played in school band, first on brass bass, then trombone. After two years he returned to Washington, received tuition from James Miller Sr., also some lessons from Juan Tizol. Did local gigs with various bands including Oliver Blackwell and Claude Hopkins, then resident job in pit orchestra at the Lincoln Theatre, Washington. Later joined the Miller Brothers' Orchestra (sons of his teacher) at the Howard Theatre, also did a season in Atlantic City with Claude Hopkins (1927), continued playing with Hopkins at the Smile-a-While Inn, Asbury Park, New Jersey (summer 1927). Moved into New York during 1927, only stayed for a brief time due to union problems, then moved back to Washington. Played in band led by drummer Tommy Myles, then left to tour with Horace Henderson's Band (1929), with that band on and off for almost three years, excluding brief spells with Claude Hopkins, Fletcher Henderson, and Cliff Jackson. Joined Fletcher Henderson from 1932 until summer of 1933, then long stay with Chick Webb from 1933, remained with the band and worked under the leadership of Ella Fitzgerald until spring of 1940. With Benny Carter's Big Band in spring of 1940, then from August 1940 until January 1941 with Coleman Hawkins' Band. From early 1941 worked on and off for almost two years with Fletcher Henderson, brief spells for other leaders including: Lucky Millinder, Cootie Williams, Sidney Bechet, Wild Bill Davison, Mezz Mezzrow, and Pete Brown. During the summer of 1943 played for 10 weeks with Duke Ellington (deputising for Lawrence Brown, who had temporarily moved back to the

West Coast), later that year worked with Don Redman and Hot Lips Page. Short spell away from full-time music, then several months with Roy Eldridge Big Band from summer of 1944, subsequently rejoined Claude Hopkins for a year commencing November 1944. Worked with Rex Stewart Band in New York during spring of 1946, then with Art Hodes through to summer of 1947. Rejoined Rex Stewart for tour of Europe (autumn 1947), returned to the U.S.A. in March 1948. Left full-time music to undergo extensive treatment for his health. Gigged at Ryan's with various leaders in 1949 and 1950, then suffered a complete breakdown in health. After his recovery he became the elevator operator at an apartment block, and from that time onwards remained steadfastly teetotal. In the late 1950s, after years of musical inactivity, he began appearing occasionally at the Central Plaza. During the 1960s continued to practise regularly, but dental problems precluded long engagements.

WILLIAMS, 'Skippy' Elbert
tenor sax/clarinet

Born: Tuscaloosa, Alabama, 27th July 1916

Brother of baritone saxist Ernest 'Pinky' Williams (born: 1914). Raised in Cleveland, began on soprano sax at the age of 13. Played local gigs, then formed own band. Played with Chester Clark and J. Frank Terry before moving to Chicago for long stint in bassist Eddie Cole's Band (1936-9). Briefly with Count Basie early in 1939, then with Edgar Hayes until joining Earl Bostic in New York (summer 1939). With Lucky Millinder (1940-1), during World War II did touring with U.S.O. shows. With Duke Ellington in 1942 and 1943. Worked with Jimmy Mundy, Bob Chester, Tommy Reynolds, Claude Hopkins, Cab Calloway, etc., then formed own band, led own group in New York, in Florida and on tour. Continued to lead own band in the 1960s and 1970s, combining this with duties as an airport worker. Played occasional dates with Duke Ellington until February 1965. His son James is a drummer.

WILLIAMS, Spencer
composer/piano/vocals

Born: New Orleans, Louisiana, 14th October. c. 1889
Died: Flushing, New York, 14th July 1965

Raised in Birmingham, Alabama. Worked as a pianist at Sans Souci Amusement Park, Chicago (c. 1907), then spent nine years working as a Pullman porter before settling in New York (c. 1916) to concentrate on composing. Collaborated with Fats Waller on 'Squeeze Me' and shared credit with Clarence Williams (no relation) on many successful tunes. Some of his biggest successes include: 'I Ain't Got Nobody', 'Basin Street Blues' (theme), "Royal Garden Blues', 'Tishomingo Blues', 'I Found a New Baby', 'Everybody Loves My Baby', etc., etc. During the early 1920s appeared in the 'Put and Take' show. Worked in Europe (1925-8), returned to U.S.A. After being acquitted of the murder of Hal Bakay (Baquet) in late 1931, he moved to Europe in 1932. Lived near London for many years before living in Stockholm throughout the 1950s.

WILSON, 'Buster' Albert W.
piano

Born: Atlanta, Georgia, 1897
Died: Los Angeles, California, 23rd October 1949

Family moved to California when 'Buster' was six. Worked with Dink Johnson's Five Hounds of Jazz in Los Angeles (1921), then organised co-operative band with Charlie Lawrence, this band was later called The Sunnyland Jazz Orchestra. Worked for many years in Paul Howard's Orchestra, then with Lionel Hampton's first big band (1935). Did solo work and played with various bands in Los Angeles during late 1930s. With Kid Ory from 1944 until early 1948 (except for spell of absence through pneumonia—late 1946). He occasionally sat in with Ory's band until shortly before his death.

WILSON, 'Dick' Richard
tenor sax

Born: Mount Vernon, Illinois, 11th November 1911
Died: New York, 24th November 1941

Both parents were musicians, his father played guitar and violin, his mother piano and guitar. The family moved to Seattle, Washington (c. 1916). Dick started on piano and vocals, then after leaving high school in Los Angeles, returned to Seattle and began taking alto sax lessons from Joe Darensbourg. Switched to tenor and joined Don Anderson's Band in Portland, Oregon (c. 1929), returned home the following year and played briefly in Joe Darensbourg's Band. Then joined Gene Coy's Band on the West Coast, took sax lessons from Franz Roth in Denver, Colorado. Played in Zack Whyte's Band, then joined Andy Kirk in Kansas City (early 1936). Except for a spell in hospital (summer 1939), he remained with Kirk until shortly before his death. He died of tuberculosis.

WILSON, Garland Lorenzo
piano

Born: Martinsburg, West Virginia, 13th June 1909
Died: Paris, France, 31st May 1954

Piano at 13, later studied at Howard University, Washington, D.C. Moved to New York (c. 1930), worked as solo pianist and accompanist for various singers, then became regular accompanist for Nina Mae McKinney, came to Europe with her in December 1932. Played long solo residencies in Paris and London from 1933 (also recorded with British bandleader Jack Payne and trumpeter Nat Gonella). Returned to the U.S.A. in October 1939, began long residency at the Reuben Bleu, later worked at Cerutti's and the Bon Soir. Returned to Europe in January 1951 and worked mainly in Paris until his death; accompanied vocaliste Mae Barnes in London, later played solo residencies in summer of 1953. Was taken ill whilst working at the Boeuf sur le Toit in Paris and died that same night.

WILSON, Gerald Stanley
trumpet/composer/arranger

Born: Shelby, Mississippi, 4th September 1918

Both parents were musical, mother a pianiste, father played clarinet and trombone. Began on piano during early childhood, school in Memphis prior to studying at Cass Technical College in Detroit, met up with Sam Donahue and trombonist Bobby Byrne, took trumpet lessons from Byrne's father. Played at Plantation Club in Detroit then went on tour with Chic Carter's Band prior to joining Jimmie Lunceford from late 1939 until April 1942. Moved to Los Angeles to do film sound-track work, also worked with Les Hite, pianist Phil Moore, and Benny Carter. Service in U.S. Navy 1943-44. Left Navy in September 1944, worked with Lee Young's Quartet in Hollywood, then led own small band at Rainbow Rendezvous prior to debuting own big band in November 1944. During the past 30-odd years has regularly led own big bands, has also occasionally played with other leaders including Count Basie and Dizzy Gillespie in the late 1940s. During the 1960s and 1970s was also active as successful conductor-arranger for various recordings stars, also composed several important symphonic works during the 1970s. In recent years has also been active in jazz education and broadcasting. Continued occasionally to lead own big band during the 1980s.

WILSON, 'Juice' Robert Edward
violin/multi-instrumentalist

Born: St. Louis, Missouri, 21st January 1904

Orphaned at three; raised in Chicago by an uncle. Played drums in Chicago Militia Boys' Band, started on violin in 1912. With Jimmy Wade's Band from 1916, joined Freddie Keppard at the Entertainers, Chicago, in 1918, left during the following summer to work for a season on the Great Lakes steamers. Quit Chicago in December 1919 to play a residency in Toledo, Ohio, in a band that included Jimmy Harrison, this unit moved on to Columbus, Ohio, then disbanded in Erie, Pennsylvania, there 'Juice' joined a band led by saxist Hershal Brassfield. Moved to Buffalo in 1921, briefly with Charles Swayne, then long stay in band led by drummer Eugene Primus (also played in the Buffalo Junior Symphony Orchestra). After working for a month in Atlantic City moved to New York in September 1928 and joined Lloyd W. Scott's Symphonic Syncopators at the Savoy Ballroom. Toured with Luckey Roberts from January-April 1929, then sailed to Europe with Noble Sissle in May 1929. Left in summer of 1930 to join Ed Swayzee's Band in Holland, then began touring Europe with Leon Abbey, worked in Berlin with Utica Jubilee Singers (autumn 1931), later joined the Louis Douglas Revue before working with pianist Tom Chase, then led own band in Spain until 1936 (also played in Harry Flemming's Band in Spain). Toured

North Africa with 'Little Mike' McKendrick's International Band, then from December 1937 began residencies in Malta. Played at the Cairo Bar for many years, featured on violin, piano, clarinet, trumpet, and saxes. Remained in Malta until 1954, then played residencies in the Mediterranean area (Italy, Gibraltar, Tangier, etc.). In the mid-1960s returned to the U.S.A. (via Paris).

WILSON, Quinn B.
string bass/tuba/arranger

Born: Chicago, Illinois, 26th December 1908
Died: Evanston, Illinois, 14th June 1978

Started on violin at the age of 10, later studied arranging and composing with Major N. Clark Smith in the *Chicago Defender*'s Boys' Band. First professional work with Monroe Richardson's Orchestra (1925), then with Art Simms (1926), after Simms' death worked with Oscar 'Bernie' Young (1927). Played with Tiny Parham before joining Walter Barnes (1928), then long spell with Erskine Tate (late 1928 to early 1931), also worked with Dave Peyton at the Regal Theatre, Chicago. (Did many free-lance recording sessions with Jelly Roll Morton, Richard M. Jones, etc.) With Jerome Carrington (early 1931), then Earl Hines from March 1931 until September 1939, arranged and composed whilst with Hines. With Walter Fuller until 1942. During the 1940s and 1950s free-lanced with many bands in Chicago (sometimes on electric bass), played for 11 years in rhythm-and-blues band led by William 'Lefty' Bates, made many records accompanying vocalists. In 1960 joined clarinettist Bill Reinhardt's house band at Jazz Ltd. and remained there throughout the 1960s playing string bass and tuba.

WILSON, 'Shadow' Rossiere
drums

Born: Yonkers, New York, 25th September 1919
Died: New York City, 11th July 1959

Worked in Philadelphia with Frankie Fairfax, Jimmy Gorham, and Bill Doggett before joining Lucky Millinder in 1939, later that year playing in short-lived Jimmy Mundy Big Band. Active with many bands during the 1940's including: Tiny Bradshaw, Benny Carter, Lionel Hampton, Earl Hines, Fats Waller, Georgie Auld, Louis Jordan, Count Basie, Woody Herman, etc., etc. During the 1950s with Illinois Jacquet, Errol Garner, Ella Fitzgerald, Thelonius Monk, etc.

WILSON, 'Teddy' Theodore Shaw
piano/arranger

Born: Austin, Texas, 24th November 1912

His brother, Augustus 'Gus' Wilson, was a trombonist and arranger. Family moved to Tuskegee (c. 1918) where both parents took up teaching appointments. Teddy studied piano and violin at Tuskegee for four years, also played E-flat clarinet and oboe in school band. Then spent a year at Talladega College, Alabama, where he majored in music. First professional work in Detroit (1929), then with Speed Webb (late 1929 to c. early 1931). Worked with Milton Senior in Toledo, Ohio, then settled in Chicago. Worked with Erskine Tate and Françis' Louisianians, then briefly with Clarence Moore's Band at the Grand Terrace Ballroom (early 1932), also with Eddie Mallory's Band at the Granada Cafe and Villa Venice, Chicago. Played in Louis Armstrong's Big Band (January-March 1933), then with Jimmie Noone at the Lido, Chicago. To New York in October 1933 to join Benny Carter's Orchestra. With Willie Bryant (1934 to early 1935), then worked as accompanist for The Charioteers and played at The Famous Door, New York. Also made many records with Billie Holiday. Began guesting with Benny Goodman, and officially joined Benny's Trio in April 1936. Featured with Benny Goodman until April 1939, left to form own big band which made its official debut at The Famous Door in May 1939, continued to lead own big band until conclusion of Golden Gate Ballroom residency in April 1940. From June 1940 until November 1944 led own highly successful sextet then rejoined Benny Goodman. From 1946 began long association with C.B.S. radio, also taught at Juilliard and Metropolitan Music Schools, studio work for WNEW from 1949-52, then toured Scandinavia (late 1952) before playing briefly in Britain (early 1953). In 1954-5 again on C.B.S. staff, then began doing regular tours with own trio. Throughout the 1950s and 1960s has frequently worked with Benny Goodman for reunions, record dates, and concert tours. Continued touring with own trio in late 1950s and 1960s including concerts at Brussels' World Fair during summer of 1958. Appeared with Benny Goodman Sextet in Russia (May 1962), also frequent solo tours of Europe, including visits to Britain in 1967 and 1969. Regular touring throughout the 1970s and early 1980s, including Europe, South America, Japan, Australia, etc.

WINFIELD, **George** *Born: Norfolk, Virginia, 24th November 1904*
trumpet

Father played violin, brother Emeile the clarinet and saxophone. Played in local Excelsior Band and with Lil Jones' Band before moving to Chicago in October 1923. Gigged with various bands then worked with Tommy Fox in Milwaukee (1924). Toured with Wendell Talbert (1925-27), brief spells in New York with Bill Benford, Wayman Carver, Henry Saparo, etc., again toured with Wen Talbert in late 1920s. With Billy Fowler, and Eubie Blake (1931). Joined Blackbirds' Show and worked with them in England (1934). With Eddie South in New York then joined Jesse Stone (late 1937). With Noble Sissle from 1938 until 1943. Mostly with bassist Lee Norman, 1946-50. Worked in South America with Tom Whaley's Band (1950). Gigged with various bands in New York until retiring from music in 1957.

'You Don't Know Me, But . . .', George Winfield's story, as told to Peter Carr, first published 1978.

WOOD, **'Bootie' Mitchell W.** *Born: Dayton, Ohio, 27th December 1919*
trombone

Toured with Chic Carter's Band in the late 1930s. During the early 1940s worked with Jimmy Raschel, Tiny Bradshaw and Lionel Hampton, prior to serving in U.S. Naval Band in World War II, after release rejoined Hampton until 1947. During the late 1940s and early 1950s worked with Arnett Cobb, and with Erskine Hawkins. Briefly with Count Basie in 1951, then temporarily left full-time music. Worked as a postman in Dayton, but also led own local group. Worked with Duke Ellington from 1959 until 1963, toured Europe with Earl Hines in 1968. Musically active throughout the 1970s.

WOODING, **'Sam' Samuel David** *Born: Philadelphia, Pennsylvania, 17th June 1895*
piano/arranger

During early teens spent long spells in Atlantic City where his father did summer-season as a waiter. Began gigging in Atlantic City (c. 1912), then moved to New York at 19 as accompanist for Madison Reid. Served in U.S. Army during World War I and played tenor horn in service band. After demobilisation in 1919 he began leading his own Society Syncopators at Scott's Hotel, Atlantic City, led in Detroit before taking own band into The Nest Club, New York, Barron Wilkins', etc. Toured briefly in a 'Plantation Days' show, then returned to New York for residency at the Club Alabam. Sailed to Europe in May 1925, leading orchestra accompanying 'Chocolate Kiddies' revue, played in Berlin and Hamburg, then toured Scandinavia, Russia, Turkey, Roumania, Hungary, Great Britain, Italy, etc. (In 1926 Sam left the revue company and led own orchestra.) The orchestra sailed from France in the spring of 1927 and worked in South America before returning to the U.S.A. in summer 1927. Played residencies in New York, Boston, Buffalo, etc., then (with personnel changes) sailed again to Europe in June 1928. After extensive touring in Germany, Scandinavia, France, Italy, and Spain the band broke up in Belgium in November 1931. Sam returned to the U.S.A. and re-formed own band for touring and various residencies including: Arcadia, New York, Pelham Heath (1932), Liberty Theatre, etc. He continued leading until 1935, disbanding after residency at the Pleasure Beach Park, Connecticut. Left full-time music to study at Pennsylvania University—gained a B.Sc. degree and Master's degree in music. From 1937 until 1941 led own Southland Spiritual Choir, touring U.S.A. and Canada, then full-time teaching (including spell at Wilmington High School). From the mid-1940s led own vocal group which appeared at Carnegie Hall in 1949. Extensive teaching in the early 1950s, also ran own Ding Dong record label, then formed duo with vocaliste Rae Harrison, they toured the world together during the 1960s, playing residencies in Germany, Israel, Turkey, Greece (1965), etc. Returned to the U.S.A. in 1966, then toured Japan in 1967. In 1968 made his home in Germany, visited Britain later that year, returned to the U.S.A. in summer of 1969. Visited Europe during the 1970s.

WRIGHT, Lammar *Born: Texarkana, Texas, 20th June 1907*
trumpet *Died: New York, 13th April 1973*

His two sons, Lamar and Elmon, were both professional trumpet players. Received musical tuition whilst attending Lincoln High School in Kansas City. Joined Bennie Moten at The Panama Club, Kansas City, and remained with Moten until 1927, then joined The Missourians. To New York with The Missourians and subsequently played with Cab Calloway, remained with Cab until January 1940. During the 1940s made several brief returns to Cab Calloway's Band, also worked with Don Redman (1943), Claude Hopkins (1944-6), Cootie Williams' Big Band, Lucky Millinder (1946), Sy Oliver (1947), etc. Occasionally led own band and did extensive free-lance recording work. By the 1950s was recognised as one of the leading trumpet teachers in New York, ran own tuition studio, but continued to do regular session work and played regularly in George Shearing's Big Band in 1959. Continued teaching throughout the 1960s; extensive free-lance work which included playing for the 1967 film 'The Night They Raided Minsky's'.

WRIGHTSMAN, 'Stan' Stanley *Born: Gotebo, Oklahoma, 15th June 1910*
piano *Died: Palm Springs, California, 17th December 1975*

First gigs were in band led by multi-instrumentalist father. The family had moved to Springfield, Missouri in 1914. Left home at 16 to work in a quintet playing residency in Gulfport, Mississippi, later played with territory bands around Oklahoma before becoming staff musician on radio station WKY in 1928. To West Coast with Henry Halstead in 1933, played in various California bands before moving to Chicago to join Ben Pollack in 1936. Was taken ill and returned to California to recuperate. In the late 1930s and 1940s did much film studio work, recording background music, occasionally appearing on screen. During the 1940s made many free-lance recordings, also worked with Wingy Manone, and Sonny Dunham (1940), and Eddie Miller (1943). Active free-lance for rest of career, played with Bob Crosby, Matty Matlock, Nappy Lamare, etc., and did television and radio work.

WYNN, Albert L. *Born: New Orleans, Louisiana, 29th July 1907*
trombone *Died: Chicago, Illinois, May 1973*

During childhood moved with his family to Chicago. Took up trombone whilst at school in Chicago—played left-handed for the first few years. Played in the Bluebirds' Kids' Band during the early 1920s; toured T.O.B.A. circuit with Ma Rainey and worked for a while on the S.S. 'St. Paul' with Charlie Creath's Jazz-o-Maniacs (1927). Led own band in Chicago (1926-8), then in France and Germany until the summer of 1929 when he joined Sam Wooding in Spain, worked for about 18 months with Wooding, left the band and remained in Europe until September 1932 (working for a time with vocalist Harry Flemming). Returned to New York, worked briefly in Bechet-Ladnier Feetwarmers, then returned to Chicago. Worked with Carroll Dickerson, Jesse Stone (August 1934), toured with Reuben Reeves (late 1934), then with Jesse Stone's Cyclones, Jimmie Noone, Richard M. Jones, briefly with Earl Hines, then with Fletcher Henderson from May 1937 until 1939. Played in Jimmie Noone's Big Band in late 1939; with Fletcher Butler's Band (1941). During the 1940s mainly free-lanced in Chicago, owned a record shop and was part-owner of The Ebony Lounge for a while. Continued playing regularly throughout the 1950s—from 1956 to 1960 with Franz Jackson's Original Jazz All Stars and from 1960 with the Gold Coast Jazz Band, with Little Brother Montgomery (1964). Ill health limited musical activities during later years.

YANCEY, 'Jimmy' James Edwards
piano

Born: Chicago, Illinois. c. 1894
Died: Chicago, Illinois, 17th September 1951

Husband of vocaliste Estella 'Mama' Yancey, his brother, Alonzo, was also a pianist. Father was a guitarist and singer. Jimmy began singing and dancing with a vaudeville company at the age of six. During adolescence toured with various troupes including: Bert Earle's, Jeannette Adler's, and Cozy Smith's. Long tour on Orpheum Circuit, then worked solely as a dancer; toured Europe in the years before World War I. Settled in Chicago in 1915, then as a self-taught pianist began playing regularly at rent parties. Played at various clubs including Moonlight Inn, The Beartrap Inn, etc. From 1925 ceased to earn his living from music and became a groundsman at Comiskey Park—home of the Chicago White Sox baseball team—he held that position for almost 25 years. With the pre-war revival of interest in boogie-woogie Yancey became a musical celebrity. Gigged in Chicago throughout the 1940s including solo spell at The Beehive (1948); often worked as accompanist for his wife—they appeared together at Carnegie Hall, New York, during the Kid Ory Concert Tour (April 1948). During the last year of his life his activities were severely curtailed by diabetes. Mama Yancey continued to sing at various festivals into the 1980s, including appearance at Carnegie Hall (1981).

YODER, 'Walt' Walter E.
string-bass

Born: Hutchinson, Kansas, 21st April 1914
Died: California, 2nd December 1978

Began playing piano at the age of ten, switched to bass during teens. Was one of the founder-members of Woody Herman's Band in 1936, prior to that had worked with Joe Haymes, Tommy and Jimmy Dorsey, and with Isham Jones. Left Herman in 1942, settled in California. Worked regularly with Ben Pollack in the late 1940s and early 1950s, also worked with Bob Crosby, Russ Morgan, Gordon Jenkins, etc. Free-lance from home in Studio City during 1970s.

YOUNG, David A.
tenor sax

Born: Nashville, Tennessee, 14th January 1912

Moved to Chicago during infancy, studied music with Major N. Clark-Smith. Worked in Burns Campbell Orchestra (1932), Jack Ellis Wildcats (1932-3), Frankie Jaxon (1933), Kenneth Anderson (1934), Jimmy Bell (1934), Carroll Dickerson (1936), Roy Eldridge (1936-38), Fletcher Henderson (1939), Horace Henderson (1939-40). During the early 1940s worked with: Walter Fuller, Roy Eldridge, Lucky Millinder, William (King Kolax) Little, then joined U.S. Navy—played in Lonnie Simmons Navy Band 1944-45. After demobilisation had own band in Chicago prior to leaving full-time music to work for the *Chicago Defender* newspaper.

YOUNG, 'Lee' Leonidas Raymond
drums/vocals

Born: New Orleans, Louisiana, 7th March 1917

Brother of Lester Young; their father, W. H. Young, was a bandleader and multi-instrumentalist. The family settled in Minneapolis from 1920, Lee began on soprano sax and was soon working with the family band's sax trio (with Lester and their sister Irma). Did various tours including T.O.B.A. circuit, then moved with parents to Los Angeles. Played in junior high school band in 1930 and also worked as a singer at the local Apex Club. In 1934 sang with pianist Walter Johnson, then gigged on drums with Mutt Carey's Jeffersonians. With Buck Clayton's 14 Gentlemen of Harlem in 1936, then eight months in Eddie Barefield's Big Band (1936-7). Briefly with Fats Waller, Eddie Mallory, and Les Hite, then from 1938-40 regular studio work for M.G.M., Paramount, etc., played on soundtracks of many films. Toured as vocalist-drummer with Lionel Hampton from September 1940 until January 1941, returned to Los Angeles and formed own small band. In May 1941 Lester became co-leader and the band played residencies in Los Angeles and New York before disbanding in August 1942. Led own small band for a while, then reverted to studio work, long spells at Columbia, M.G.M., etc., and recording sessions with Benny Goodman, Nellie Lutcher, Big Sis Andrews, etc., etc. With Nat 'King' Cole Trio from June 1953 until spring of 1962 (including overseas tours and appearance in the film 'St. Louis Blues')—had previously worked with Nat Cole in the 1930s. From 1962 worked in Los Angeles, formed own record comany and enjoyed great success as an a. and r. man for Vee-Jay Records. Began working as an executive for Motown Records in 1979.

YOUNG, 'Prez' Lester Willis
tenor sax/clarinet

Born: Woodville, Mississippi, 27th August 1909
Died: New York City, 15th March 1959

Brother of Lee Young, their father, W. H. Young, who had studied at Tuskegee Institute, tutored Lester, Lee, and their sister Irma. Several other relatives were musicians including the New Orleans trombonist-bassist Austin 'Boots' Young and saxist Isaiah 'Sports' Young. The family moved into New Orleans during Lester's infancy, he was taught trumpet, alto sax, violin, and drums by his father. By the time the family had settled in Minneapolis (1920), Lester was already playing drums in the family touring band, working through Minnesota, Kansas, New Mexico, Nebraska, and the Dakotas. Lester was unwilling to tour the South, and left the band in Phoenix, Arizona, he moved on to Salina, Kansas, and whilst at the Wiggly Cafe there, he met up with bandleader Art Bronson, who bought him a tenor sax. From January 1928 until January 1929 he did regular tours with Art Bronson's Bostonians, covering the Dakotas, Nebraska, Colorado, etc. He left Bronson to return to the family band, then rejoined Art Bronson from June-November 1930. Bronson disbanded in Wichita, and Lester moved on to Minnesota. Worked at the Nest Club, Minneapolis, then played in Eugene Schuck's Cotton Club Orchestra in Minnesota (summer 1931). Returned to Minneapolis and played under various leaders (Frank Hines, Eddie Barefield, etc.) at the Nest Club, also gigged with pianist Paul Cephas at the South Side Club. Lester occasionally doubled alto and baritone during the early 1930s. (In 1968 Benny Carter told this writer that he first heard Lester Young in Minneapolis (c. 1931), Lester was then playing alto sax.) Early in 1932, whilst working at the Nest Club with Frank Hines, he was signed as a member of the Original Blue Devils, after playing a residency in Oklahoma City (spring 1932) the band did extensive touring. Lester and several other members of the Blue Devils finally quit the band in the autumn of 1933 and moved to Kansas City to join Bennie Moten. Lester played briefly with Clarence Love's Band and with the Bennie Moten-George E. Lee Band, also worked (together with his brother-in-law, trombonist Otto 'Pete' Jones) in King Oliver's Band. In early 1934 left Kansas City with band organised by Count Basie, whilst playing in Little Rock, Arkansas, was offered a permanent job with Fletcher Henderson's Band. Joined Henderson in Detroit (31st March 1934), playing in the place vacated by Coleman Hawkins. Travelled to New York with Henderson, but left the band in mid-July 1934. Worked with Andy Kirk in Kansas City, then played residency with Boyd Atkins in Minneapolis (late 1934). Subsequently worked with Rook Ganz in Minneapolis, then moved back to Kansas City, gigged at various clubs including The Sunset and The Subway. During 1936 unsuccessfully auditioned for Earl Hines' Big Band. In 1936 joined Count Basie at the Reno Club, Kansas City. Left Kansas City with Basie, and made recording debut in October 1936. Remained with Basie until December 1940—during this period Lester did many recording sessions with Billie Holiday, who gave him the nickname 'Prez'—a contraction of 'The President'—earlier in his career Lester had been known as 'Red' Young. From 27th February until 18th March 1941 led own band at Kelly's Stables in New York, moved to California in May 1941 and formed band co-led with his brother Lee which made its debut at Billy Berg's Club, Los Angeles. After regular work on the West Coast the band temporarily teamed up with Slim Gaillard and Slam Stewart, then reverted to its former billing Lee and Lester Young's Band. The band moved to New York in August 1942 for a residency at Cafe Society (Downtown), played various venues before disbanding early in 1943. In the spring of 1943 Lester worked with Al Sears' Big Band at the Renaissance Casino in New York, subsequently did a U.S.O. tour with Al Sears. Worked with Count Basie at the Apollo Theatre, New York (October 1943), with Dizzy Gillespie at The Onyx Club, New York, then rejoined Basie from December 1943 until September 1944—he was inducted into the U.S. Army at Fort MacArthur early in October 1944. Whilst doing combat training at Camp McClellan, Alabama, he underwent surgery, soon after his return to duty he was court-martialled and sentenced to a year's detention. He was taken ill at Camp Gordon, Georgia, in June of

1945 and was subsequently released from the service. He moved back to California and did first regular playing at an October 1945 recording session. In 1946 he began his long association with Norman Granz's 'Jazz At The Philharmonic' shows, throughout the late 1940s and 1950s continued to lead own small groups (featured with own group at Carnegie Hall 21st February 1951). Did several overseas tours with 'J.A.T.P.' including one visit to London in March 1953, also did overseas tour with 'Birdland 1956' show. Guested with Count Basie at Newport Jazz Festival (July 1957). Lester, who neither drank nor smoked until his early twenties, had long spells of poor health for the last 14 years of his life, undergoing hospital treatment in 1947, 1955, 1957, and 1958. During his last years he worked mainly as a soloist. He began his last series of engagements at the Blue Note Club in Paris (January-March 1959). Within 24 hours of his return to the U.S.A. he died in his room at the Alvin Hotel, New York. His burial took place at the Evergreen Cemetery, Queens, New York.

Lester Young was prominently featured in the film 'Jammin' the Blues'.

YOUNG, 'Snookie' Eugene Edward *Born: Dayton, Ohio, 3rd February 1919*
trumpet

Brother of trumpeter Granville 'Catfish' Young (d. 1981). First instrument a zither, later switched to trumpet and played in family touring band. Worked in Eddie Heywood Sr. Band and with pianist Graham Jackson's Band in Atlanta, Georgia, then returned to Dayton to finish high school. Played in Wilberforce Collegians, then worked in Clarence 'Chic' Carter's Band from 1937 until 1939. In December 1939 joined Jimmie Lunceford (replacing Eddie Thompkins), worked with Count Basie and Lionel Hampton. Moved to California, worked with Les Hite, then spell with Benny Carter (early 1943). Rejoined Count Basie in June 1943, worked in Gerald Wilson's Big Band and with Lionel Hampton before returning to Count Basie from March 1945 until 1947. Returned to Dayton, and for almost 10 years led own band in and around Ohio. With Count Basie again from October 1957 until June 1962, left to concentrate on free-lance work in New York, worked with bassist Charles Mingus (late 1962). On N.B.C. television studio staff for several years, also worked with Benny Goodman (August 1964) and with Gerald Wilson Big Band and Thad Jones-Mel Lewis Band (1966). Continued with session work, worked with Charlie Barnet (late 1967), briefly in Kenny Clarke-Boland Big Band in 1968, toured Europe with Thad Jones-Mel Lewis Band in autumn of 1969. Worked at N.B.C. studios throughout 1970s, was featured at Nice Festival 1981. Continued to work regularly during early 1980s including dates with Gerald Wilson Orchestra (1983).

Played solo trumpet on several film soundtracks including 'Blues In The Night'.

YOUNG, 'Trummy' James Osborne *Born: Savannah, Georgia, 12th January 1912*
trombone/vocals/composer *Died: San Jose, California, 10th September 1984*

An uncle played trombone in Jim Europe's Band. Began playing trumpet in school band, brief spell on drums. Moved to Washington, D.C., concentrated on trombone, after leaving school did day work in a local hotel, gigged in Frank Betters' Band. First professional work with Booker Coleman's Hot Chocolates (1928), subsequently worked in the Hardy Brothers' Orchestra and with Elmer Calloway, then joined band led by drummer Tommy Myles (who nicknamed him Trummie, in later years this became Trummy). Moved to Chicago in late 1933 to join Earl Hines at the Grand Terrace, remained with Earl until August 1937 (during this period Trummy occasionally worked with other bands during the summer lay-offs, brief stints with Albert Ammons and with Roy Eldridge). Joined Jimmie Lunceford from September 1937 until March 1943, worked with Charlie Barnet before forming own band (November 1943). During 1944 worked with Boyd Raeburn, Tiny Grimes, Roy Eldridge, Claude Hopkins, and Paul Baron's C.B.S. Orchestra. With altoist Johnny Bothwell (January 1945), then with Benny Goodman (February-August 1945), again led own band, worked with Tiny Grimes (May 1946). Did regular tours with 'Jazz At The Philharmonic' in 1946 and 1947, briefly with Claude Hopkins in 1947. Left J.A.T.P. in California and went from there to Hawaii in band led by Cee Pee Johnson (October 1947). Remained in Honolulu, worked regularly with the Art Norkus Trio, also led own small band.

Left Honolulu in summer of 1952 to join Louis Armstrong's All Stars, worked with Louis from September 1952 until 1st January 1964. Returned to Hawaii (via Los Angeles) and remained there throughout the 1960s, gigging with various leaders and leading own group. Returned to California for Lunceford reunion recording (1970), also played in Colorado, and with Earl Hines at Disneyland (September 1971) Overcame serious illness in 1975, resumed leading own band in Hawaii. Made several tours of Europe during the late 1970s and 1980s.

Compositions include: 'Tain't What You Do . . .', 'Travellin' Light', 'A Lover is Blue', etc. Appeared with Louis Armstrong in 'The Glenn Miller Story' and 'The Five Pennies', etc.

YSAGUIRRE, 'Bob' Robert
string bass/tuba

Born: Belize, British Honduras, 22nd February 1897
Died: New York City, 27th March 1982

Began playing tuba at the age of 18, originally taught by Henry Buller. Served as a musician in British Honduras Territorial Band (4th Co. W.W.I.) from 1917 until 1919. Moved to the U.S.A., first professional work with cornetist Amos White in New Orleans at the Spanish Fort Pavilion (1922). Left New Orleans as a member of Armand J. Piron's Orchestra, with Piron until 1925, then joined Elmer Snowden's Band. Left in 1926, spent three years in Alex Jackson's Plantation Orchestra, briefly with Fletcher Henderson and Horace Henderson, then nine years with Don Redman Orchestra (1931-40). From that time until the late 1960s continued to gig in the New York area, but main occupation was painting and decorating.

YUKL, 'Joe' Joseph
trombone

Born: New York City, 5th March 1909
Died: Los Angeles, California, March 1981

Originally taught violin by his father. Began concentrating on trombone whilst at Maryland University, played with Maryland Collegians (1926), following year played in Ottawa, Canada, with this band. Stayed in New York at Tommy Dorsey's suggestion, gigged with Roger Wolfe Kahn and Red Nichols whilst awaiting union card, then studio work with Fred Rich's C.B.S. Orchestra. Inactive in 1929 through complications following an appendectomy, returned to Baltimore. After a year recommenced playing, joined Billy Lustig, then gigged mainly in Baltimore for two years. In 1933 joined Joe Haymes in New York, after a few months joined the Dorsey Brothers' Orchestra, remained with Jimmy Dorsey until January 1937. Settled in California, with Frank Trumbauer (1938), Ben Pollack, Ted Fio Rito (1939). From that time until the late 1960s continued to work mainly in Hollywood studio bands. Prolific free-lance recordings, also soundtracked countless films. Had acting role in 'Rhythm Inn' and coached actor James Stewart for his part in 'The Glenn Miller Story'.

Z

ZACK, George J.
piano/vocals

Born: Chicago, Illinois, 20th July 1908

During early teens played trumpet in *Chicago News* Boys' Band, then studied piano at Chicago Conservatory of Music. In 1924 left Chicago to work in Memphis and Indianapolis with band led by trombonist Mush Oliver, subsequently did extensive touring with Jimmy Joy's Orchestra. Returned to Chicago and played for a long spell with Eddie Neibauer's Orchestra—also worked in Chicago and Kansas City with Henry Halsted. Long residencies featuring his solo piano work and Louis Armstrong style vocals. Briefly with Muggsy Spanier in 1939, remained in New York during the early 1940s, then inactive through illness. Moved back to Chicago in 1945, played at Club Silhouette, Bee Hive, etc., and worked as accompanist for various vocalistes. Moved to Tucson, Arizona, and continued working there during the 1950s and 1960s, in the late 1950s worked briefly with Ray Bauduc and Nappy Lamare and with Bob Scobey. Made regular return trips to Chicago. During the 1970s worked in Tucson with Al Sanders and the Old Pueblo Jazz Band.

ZARDIS, Chester
string bass/tuba

Born: New Orleans, Louisiana, 27th May 1900

Known as 'Little Bear'. In 1915 spent a while in the local waifs' home, during following year bought his first string bass, took lessons from Billy Marrero and Dave Perkins. Played in local Merit Band (c. 1919), then professional work for a year with Buddie Petit's Band. Left the band in the early 1920s, returned to New Orleans; during the 1920s worked with Jack Carey, Chris Kelly, Kid Rena, and Armand Piron. During the early 1930s with Sydney Desvigne on riverboats, etc. (doubling tuba), then with James 'Kid' Clayton and Evan Thomas before joining Walter Pichon for work on the riverboats and residency at the Ole Plantation, Memphis (late 1934 to early 1935). Whilst with Duke Dejan's Dixie Rhythm Band (1936-7) briefly subbed in Count Basie's Band at the Apollo Theatre, New York. In 1937-8 led own Goldiggers' Band, then worked with Walter Pichon on S.S. 'Capitol' (1939), rejoined Kid Clayton in 1940. Recorded with Bunk Johnson in 1942 and with George Lewis in 1943 before serving in U.S. Army during World War II. After demobilisation settled in Denver, Colorado, played in Floyd Hunt's quartet, then long spell with George Morrison's Band; moved to Philadelphia and worked with Henry Lowe. In 1951 returned to New Orleans, free-lanced for a while, then in 1954 left full-time music and farmed in New Iberia. He returned to New Orleans in 1965 and began playing regularly, from 1966 was featured regularly at Preservation Hall; toured Japan with George 'Kid Sheik' Colar's Band in 1967, during that year also visited Europe with the Preservation Hall Band. During the late 1960s took part in several recording sessions, did occasional tours with various leaders, but worked mainly in New Orleans. Overcame ill health (late 1979), and resumed regular playing in the 1980s, including leading own band, toured Europe with Kid Thomas in 1983.

ZARCHY, 'Zeke' Rubin
trumpet

Born: New York City, 12th June 1915

During the Swing Era played lead trumpet with many famous bands including Joe Haymes, Benny Goodman, Artie Shaw, Bob Crosby, Tommy Dorsey, Red Norvo, Teddy Powell, then moved to California and played mainly in studio bands through to the 1970s. During the early 1980s often played in the Great Pacific Jazz Band.

ZURKE, 'Bob' Robert Albert
(real name: Boguslaw Albert Zukowski)
piano/composer

Born: Detroit, Michigan, 17th January 1912
Died: Los Angeles, California, 16th February 1944

Piano from the age of three, lessons from Professor Lewis; played for Paderewski in Detroit, 1922. During the mid-1920s appeared regularly at the Coliseum, Detroit, and at the Martha Washington Theatre in Hamtramck. Became professional in early teens, worked with Oliver Naylor's Orchestra at Palais D'Or and Orient Restaurant in Philadelphia, also with Thelma Terry, Hank Biagini, Seymour Simons, Frank Sidney, Don Zell, etc., before joining Bob Crosby in December 1936. Remained with Bob Crosby until May 1939 (except for brief absence through breaking leg, September-October 1937). Organised own big band, which lasted from summer of 1939 through to spring 1941, then Zurke began working as a solo pianist. Worked in Chicago (late 1940-early 1941), in Detroit (March 1941), St. Paul (May 1941) before moving to California in summer of 1941. Resident at The Hangover Club, Los Angeles from summer 1942 until time of his death. He collapsed at the club and was taken to the Los Angeles General Hospital where he died 24 hours later.

A month before he died Zurke recorded the music for a cartoon film, 'Jungle Jive'.

BIBLIOGRAPHY

Great Britain: Footnote, Melody Maker, Jazz Express, Jazz Journal, Jazz Monthly, Storyville, Eureka, Hot News, Jazz Forum, Jazz Magazine, Jazz Music, Jazzology, Jazz Tempo, Musical News and Dance Band, Pickup, Rhythm, Swing Music, Tune Times.

France: Bulletin du Hot Club de France, Jazz, Jazz Hot, Jazz Magazine.

Canada: Coda.

Eire: Hot Notes.

Australia: Jazz Notes, Jazz Quarterly.

Switzerland: Jazz Statistics.

U.S.A.: Cadence, downbeat, American Jazz Review, Basin Street, Clef, H.R.S. Rag, IAJRC Journal, International Musician, Jazz, The Jazzfinder, Jazz Information, Jazz Music, Jazz New England, Jazz Quarterly, Jazz Record, Jazz Register, Jazz Report (Bob Koester), Jazz Report (Paul Affeldt), Jazz Review, Jazz Session, Jazz To-day, Jersey Jazz, Metronome, Mississippi Rag, Music and Rhythm, The Needle, Orchestra World, Playback, Record Research, Second Line, Sounds and Fury, Swing, Tempo, The Record Changer.

New York Age, Amsterdam News, New York Clipper, New York World, Chicago Defender, Pittsburgh Courier, Baltimore Afro-American.

PHOTOGRAPH ACKNOWLEDGEMENTS

TERESA CHILTON: Pete Brown, Tony Parenti, Elmer Snowden, Rex Stewart, Dicky Wells
JOHN CHILTON: Earl Hines, Joe Turner
TERRY CRYER: Harold Baker and Jimmy Rushing
ERIC JELLY: Lawrence Brown
DAVID REDFERN: Benny Morton, Victoria Spivey
MEACAL PHOTOS: Snub Mosley
J SIMPSON: Alton Purnell, Russell Procope
BOB SKEETS: Johnny St. Cyr
RUDY POWELL: Floyd Casey and Ed Allen
HERBERT MATTER: Louis Armstrong in Zurich
KLAUS GURETSKI: Wallace Bishop
JEAN-PIERRE LELOIS: Sam Price
ERNST J STEINER: Louis Bacon and Johnny Russell
CHRISTIAN BAUR: Joe Turner (piano)
MAX JONES (courtesy of): Charlie Barnet, Emmett Berry, Andrew Blakeney/Joe Darensbourg/Kid Ory, Peter Bocage, Sharkey Bonano, Georg Brunis, Teddy Buckner, Joe Bushkin, June Clark, W C Handy, Woody Herman/Mary Lou Williams/Sidney Bechet, Bunk Johnson's Band, Jimmy McPartland, Lucky Millinder, Miff Mole, Herb Morand, Jelly Roll Morton, Vido Musso, Original Dixieland Jazz Band, Alphonse Picou, Louis Prima, Jack Purvis, Ike Quebec, Luis Russell, Pee Wee Russell, Stuff Smith and his Onyx Club Band, The Spirits of Rhythm, Charlie Spivak, Art Tatum, Cootie Williams, Spencer Williams, Lester Young and Benny Goodman, Bob Zurke's Big Band
***STORYVILLE* Magazine (courtesy of):** Clarence Williams, Sam Wooding
COVER PHOTOGRAPHS (clockwise beginning top left): Bix Beiderbecke, Duke Ellington, Count Basie, Louis Armstrong, Harry Carney and Johnny Hodges with Duke Ellington, Ma Rainey (**courtesy of Max Jones**)